Encyclopedia of
NEW HAMPSHIRE
INDIANS

Encyclopedia of
NEW HAMPSHIRE
INDIANS

TRIBES, NATIONS, TREATIES
OF THE NORTHEASTERN WOODLANDS

SOMERSET PUBLISHERS, INC.

P.O. BOX 160

ST. CLAIR SHORES, MI 48080

46798805

Copyright© 2000 by Somerset Publishers, Inc.

Printed in the United States of America

ISBN 0-403-09776-2

iv

FOREWORD

After almost five centuries of contact the original Americans and those who later came to call themselves Americans remain strangers. Much was written about the original occupants, collectively called Indians, but the writing often had the impersonal character of a naturalist's description of strange fauna. Or an another extreme, the writing projected the image of rude people waiting to be led out of darkness into the light. The Indians, for their part, having first offered hospitality only to find themselves misused, chose a course of passive non communication. There the matter rested through generations of sterile if not hostile coexistence. Neither learned from the other.

This condition is now changing. An obvious explanation is the change in social climate which rejects racist interpretations of historical process and fosters clinical studies of human developments. Apart from the theoretical concepts emerging in this later time, the effect of which is to provide a base for understanding, a major factor in bridging the long estrangement is the massive accumulation of information about native America. Every major university in the Western Hemisphere has involved itself at one time or another in projects to recover data from the archaeological past or from living Indian communities. Public works projects devoted to the damming of streams or the construction of highways uncovered ancient settlements. Trained students recorded languages, migrations, creation stories, folk history, social systems. Museums and laboratories, some in foreign lands, were filled with material objects and their accompanying field notes. Unfortunately at first, much of the accumulation was shelved and catalogued and made accessible only to erudite specialists.

While the archivists filled their bins, the Indians in recent years have been reconnoitering on their society. Indians in unprecedented numbers are pursuing college courses, even through graduate school. Indians are going into medicine and law. They are taking control of schools and school boards. Indian theatrical groups have come into existence. Indian poets, novelists, and playwrights are publishing. An Indian press association services local Indian publications across the country. Indian political leaders are reaching a constituency beyond tribal boundaries. Here are collective experiences finding voice and finding an audience as well.

It is not remarkable, all this considered, that the literature devoted to specific tribes, to historic periods, to official policy, and to critical evaluations of Indian-white relations has flourished in recent years. Scholarly monographs still appear in learned journals, but as much of the material previously available only in technical publications, obscured further by the idiom of the technician, now finds its way its books and articles for the general reader. While Folsom Man has not yet become a household word, much of the serious Indian history now being written makes acknowledgments of an Indian past extending beyond the coming of Europeans. Some glimmering of understanding appears in print suggesting not only time depth of New World occupation, but something of the nature of that occupation, of the relation of man and his environment, of what was valued and made holy.

It is against this background that the effort to create a state ENCYCLOPEDIA OF INDIANS is to be viewed. Here will be brought together the findings of many delivers in the past and may students who have looked critically at the impact of outlanders of native society. What can be hoped for from an enterprise of this magnitude is a further lessening estrangement and, on the positive side, an appreciation of the variety of adaptations achieved by the Indian in in his migrations. No continents than to place them securely n their proper course among the adventuring races of mankind.

CONTENTS

INDIANS OF NEW HAMPSHIRE AND THE EASTERN WOODLANDS -- A HISTORY

Today, the relatively few Native Americans still living in New Hampshire, the Northeastern Woodlands region of the United States, and in southeastern Canada, belie their former importance in shaping national experience and anthropological development in each country.

Most systematic research of New Hampshire and Northeastern Woodlands Indians began with first European explorations in the sixteenth century. However, ancestors of historic tribes inhabited the region from about 10,500 BC. Studies of prehistoric and historic natives became more extensive during the seventeenth, eighteenth, and nineteenth centuries. Yet even into the present, archaeologists have often disagreed on how Northeastern Woodlands Indians evolved from prehistoric times to the present.

The earliest Indians in New Hampshire probably entered the area at the close of the last ice-age, as mentioned. The big game animals were generally extinct by about 8000 BC, but for the relative newcomers, the bushy tundra and central spine of mixed conifer and hardwood forests, such as in the rugged Green Mountains, was home for moose, deer, bear, otter, beaver, mink, rabbit, bobcat, and a variety of gamebirds, including turkey. The rivers were full of fish, turtles, and shellfish. With its northerly climate not well-suited to farming, the first people in New Hampshire were quite naturally hunters and gatherers of plant foods including seeds and nuts. The natives, like their food sources, were concentrated along stream valleys, such as that of the Hudson River, southward from Lake Champlain, in Vermont, and into present New York State.

Not a great amount of archeological evidence exists for early inhabitants of New Hampshire. What is known of them is discussed in more detail below.

Early in the nation's pre-history, two great Indian linguistic families dominated the eastern region of the United States, the Algonquians and the Iroquoians. The realm of the Algonquians stretched from the Atlantic Ocean to the Great Lakes and beyond, and from the Carolinas to

Hudson Bay. Within this area was a small section where the Iroquois probably warred in New Hampshire against their Algonquian neighbors. The Indians formerly living in the immediate vicinity of Maine and New Hampshire are known generally by the name of Abnaki (men of the East, or Dawn People).

Within the confines of the State were such tribes as the Coosucs, who lived at the junction of the Connecticut and Ammonoosuc rivers and northward; the Piscataquas, near Dover; the Sokokis, known as Pequawkets on the upper Saco River and as Ossipees around the lake by that name; and the Merrimack River tribes, more often known as the Pennacook Confederacy. Members of this Confederacy in New Hampshire were the Nashuas residing along the river by that name, the Souhegans or Natacooks on the Souhegan River, the Amoskeags at Manchester, the Pennacooks proper at Concord, and the Winnipesaukees in central New Hampshire. Sometimes included are the Coosucs to the north, the Squamscots at Exeter, the Winnecowets at Hampton, the Piscataquas at Portsmouth, and the Newichawanocks near Rochester.

The Amarascoggins had a village on the Androscoggin River at Lewiston, Maine, and presumably roamed the eastern reaches of New Hampshire's north country. The Saint Francis Indians in Canada claimed portions of this area, and ranged in the vicinity. It was to this tribe that most of the New Hampshire Indians ultimately withdrew. For example, little is heard about the Pennacooks as a separate tribe after Queen Anne's War.

Moorehead, eminent chronicler of the 'Red Paint People' of Maine, made a survey of the Merrimack Valley in 1931 and reported evidences of this mysterious people in the New Hampshire lake country. The 'Red Paint People' represented a pre-Algonquian culture, and there is considerable probability that the Winnipesaukee district was the western outpost of their habitat.

Starr King, in the classic volume, *The White Hills*, deplored the absence of Indian names in the White Mountains, but aboriginal names still cling in the southern part of the State, in such villages as Penacook, Suncook, and Contoocook; in lakes as Baboosic, Massabesic, and Sunapee; and in streams as Soucook and Piscataquog. Within the mountain region are associated such legends as that of Chocorua, Passaconaway, Wannalancet, and the Great Carbuncle; in the folklore of other New Hampshire regions, the Indians have also left their trace.

Indian relics have been found in some quantities in New Hampshire. At least eight communities: Nashua, Manchester, Concord, Franklin,

The Weirs, Hooksett, Suncook and Laconia, were built on the sites of Indian villages. One of the most interesting of these primitive villages was at The Weirs on Lake Winnipesaukee, where a large weir or fish-trap in the shape of a "w" was built of stone and interwoven with saplings. It was thought that the Indians remained here until 1700. Another fishing village was at the division of the Merrimack into the Pemigewasset and Winnipesaukee rivers. At this point, the shad went to Lake Winnipesaukee and the salmon swam up the cooler waters of the Pemigewasset. At Franklin, many relics have been found and collected.

The remains of an Indian 'fort' at Little Bay in Sanbornton existed until well into the nineteenth century; it has been thought that this structure was built as a defense against the Mohawks sometime prior to 1675. Near Ossipee Lake, a large Indian burial mound was discovered, where skeletons were uncovered in sitting posture, grouped in circles. Skeletal remains have also been found at Brookline, Hudson, Dover, Sutton, Franklin, Keene, and Claremont.

Numerous artifacts have been discovered, including axes, knives, adzes, pestles, engraved stones, spearheads, arrowheads, gouges, and chisels. Occasionally pipes and pottery fragments have been dug up. The lake region and the Merrimack Valley have been the most prolific sources or relics. More important collections were established at the home of Mary A. Proctor of Franklin, the Manchester Institute of Arts and Sciences, the Manchester Historic Association, the Peabody Museum at Salem, and the Peabody Museum at Harvard University.

In general, the New Hampshire aborigines conformed to the general pattern of the eastern woodland Indians. Living in wigwams rudely constructed of bark and skins, they ranged the forest hunting and fishing, while their women cultivated the nearby fields. Hunting was carried on by means of the bow, spear, and *culheag* or log trap. Fish were taken at weirs, in nets, or by the spear aided by the flare of a pine knot. In agriculture, the Indians had made enough progress to be of invaluable aid to the white man when he came.

Maize or Indian corn was the chief crop. Early settlers found it most helpful to practice the Indian injunction to plant "when the leaves of the white oak are as big as the ear of a mouse." "Girdling," or cutting a ring deep enough in a tree to kill the foliage, thus letting in the light, was another device learned from the primitive farmers, and was much appreciated by the pioneers.

Maize was the staple, but Indian agriculture also included beans, squashes, and pumpkins. Tobacco seems to have been raised in New England as far north as the Kennebec Valley. Corn, when pounded in a mortar, was known as hominy; mixed with beans, it was called succotash. Mortars were manufactured of wood or stone; a glacial pothole, when small enough, was sometime used – an example of such an outdoor mortar is at Willow Hill in Franklin.

The religion of these primitives was animism, or belief in spirits representing nature in its various phases. The name *Manitou* was given to a spirit which might be good or evil, greater or lesser. Like many other tribes, the New Hampshire Indians had their story of the deluge. Josselyn, in his *Account of Two Voyages to New England*, reported the following version: "Ask whither they go when they dye, they will tell you pointing with their finger to Heaven beyond the white mountains, and do hint at 'Noah's Floud,' as may be conceived by a story they have received from Father to Son, time out of mind, that a great while ago their Countrey was drowned, and all the People and other Creatures in it, only one, *Powaw,* and his *Webb,* foreseeing the Floud fled to the white mountains carrying a hare along with them and so escaped; after a while the *Powaw* sent the hare away, who not returning emboldend them and thereby they descended, and lived many years after, and had many children, from whom the Countrie was filled again with Indians."

Several Indian sachems left their impression upon New Hampshire history and legend. The greatest leader was Passaconaway, head of the Pennacook Confederacy when the first Europeans came. His attitude was uniformly friendly to the newcomers, and he pursued a moderate policy in the face of white aggressions.

Passaconaway gained considerable reputation as a medicine man or *powwow*, as he was termed in the seventeenth century in this particular region. According to one chronicler, he could "... make the water burne, the rocks move, the trees dance, metamorphise himself into a flaming man. He will do more; for in winter, when there are no green leaves to be got, he will burne an old one to ashes, and putting those into water, produce a new green leaf, which you shall not only see, but substantially handle and carrie away; and make of a dead snake's skin a living snake, both to be seen, felt, and heard. This I write but upon the report of the Indians who confidently affirm stranger things."

As an old man, Passaconaway delivered a valedictory speech urging his followers to maintain peace with their new neighbors. This speech has been variously reported. One rather fanciful version is given by

Potter: "The oak will soon break before the whirlwind ... I commune with the Great Spirit. He whispers me now, 'Tell your people, Peace, Peace, is the only hope of your race. I have given fire and thunder to the pale faces for weapons. I have made them plentier than the leaves of the forest, and still shall they increase! These meadows they shall turn with the plow, these forests shall fall by the axe, The pale faces shall live upon your hunting grounds, and make their villages upon your fishing places!' The Great Spirit says this, and it must be so! We are few and powerless before them! We must bend before the storm! The wind blows hard! The old oak trembles! Its branches are gone! Its sap is frozen! It bends! It falls! Peace, Peace, with the white man – is the command of the Great Spirit – and the wish – the last wish – of Passaconaway."

Upon his death Passaconaway passed from history into legend, which relates that he was received into heaven after he had been transported to the summit of Mount Washington in a sledge drawn by wolves. It is probable that this Elijah story was invented originally for another Indian and another mountain, and then transferred to Passaconaway. His name has been preserved in New Hampshire by a village and a mountain.

Passaconaway was succeeded by his son Wonalancet, who strove to keep the peace even during King Philip's War. Unable to restrain his followers, he retired from leadership in 1685. A New Hampshire range and village perpetuate his name. His nephew, Kancamagus, after some provocation, led the assault on Dover in 1689; in spite of this, a mountain bears his name. Another opponent similarly honored is Paugus, the foe of Lovewell in the celebrated fight near Fryeburg, who can claim a peak in the Sandwich Range, thanks to the efforts of Lucy Larcom, poet and friend of Whittier.

The most celebrated of New Hampshire's Indian legends also has the least historical basis. From the top of the beautiful mountain that keeps his memory green, Chocorua is supposed to have launched his ineffective curse against the white men. This legend has been told in several forms, and is the subject of a celebrated painting, *The Death of Chocorua*, by Thomas Cole.

Elsewhere in the Northeast, and having a bearing on New Hampshire's development, are scattered all along the Maine coast and through southern New England, great shell-heaps, said to have been accumulated from one thousand to five thousand years ago. Allowing a century for a certain number of inches of mold and dirt deposits upon the mounds, archeologists have been able in some degree to estimate their great age. They were made, it is supposed, by the Indians who in summer migrated to the coast and reaped harvests from the sea. The heaps are so large that it must have required centuries of clam-feasts for their accumulation. They are valuable because of the many interesting relics found buried in them.

However, these are not the earliest archeological remains. Throughout the central and eastern part of the Northeastern Woodlands, along the coast and in stream valleys, since the time of the first settlers, white inhabitants have been discovering the graves of a prehistoric people who had either become extinct or had evolved a new civilization by the time the shell-heaps began to take form. While these graves occur most thickly in Maine, the area in which they are found extends throughout New England and into Canada.

Because the shell-heaps contain remains of mollusks now found only in southern waters, and the surface of the land along the shore seems to have suffered some change, we know that these early people existed in a time when geologic evolution was still going on, and the climate of New England was much warmer than it is now. That this people antedated those who made the shell-heaps is ascertained by the difference in the quality and workmanship of the weapons found in the shell-heaps and in the graves.

Very little actually is known about these earliest inhabitants. They are called the 'Red Paint People' because each of the discovered graves contains a quantity (varying from less than two quarts to a bushel) of a brilliant red ocher (powdered hematite). Sometimes, though rarely, this pigment is shaded to yellow or brown, the yellow coloration often found in the graves having been created by iron corrosion. The fact of 'ocher burial' is not particularly distinctive, however, because it is a characteristic of certain early peoples the world over. Paleolithic graves in France and Australia show evidences of ocher; later races in New England occasionally painted their bodies with it, and sometimes it is found in their graves.

The now extinct Beothuks of Newfoundland had a particular predilection for red ocher, not only smearing their bodies with it but also their huts, their canoes, and all their possessions; and for this they were called Red Indians by early explorers. The Beothuks were a comparatively modern race, however, and there are no evidences of Paleolithic man in this section of the New World. Maine's Red Paint People, apparently very early in the development of Neolithic culture, may be regarded then as a cultural unit.

Many of their stone artifacts are unlike those of the Indians who later occupied the same territory; certain of their implements, indeed, were made of different materials from any used by later Stone Age people. The similarity of their culture, as manifested by the stone implements, to that of the Eskimo has led some writers to suggest that they were not red Indians at all; others, influenced by their common use of ocher, see in them early relatives to the Beothuks of Newfoundland.

At any rate, they were a somewhat widely scattered and highly developed people. Although not farmers like later Indians who occupied the same territory, they had developed a high degree of craftsmanship. They used fire-making tools superior to those of the later Indians; their implements imply skill in woodworking, and they made boats, possibly log dugouts, in which they seem to have traveled considerable distances.

Since the time of the earliest white settlements, red ocher graves have been found. Early New Englanders regarded them with extreme suspicion; to find one was considered an evil omen. Hardy adventurers, however, unearthing the paint, put it to good advantage when they saw that it gave a satisfactory finish to their furniture and other woodwork. At first the ocher deposits, always accompanied by strange stone weapons, were not imagined to be associated with burials.

Only more recently have bone dust and even tiny fragments of undecayed human bone been discovered in them. A startling find was turned up in early decades of the twentieth century when city employees of Waterville, Maine, while excavating a public road, uncovered two skeletons preserved in red ocher; when the air struck them, they visibly turned to dust; only a few fragments are now preserved in Portland's Museum of Natural History.

In the late nineteenth century, Dr. Augustus C. Hamlin, of Bangor, requested a group of archeologists at Harvard University's Peabody Museum in to investigate the Maine Red Paint cemeteries. The first extensive exploration was carried on by the Peabody Museum, and later work was done by expeditions from Phillips Academy of Andover, Massachusetts. Some of the best collections of Red Paint artifacts are at the Peabody Museum and at Phillips Andover Academy, the largest at the latter. The findings in more than thirty Red Paint cemeteries have been recorded; the best early reference is C. C. Willoughby's *An-*

tiquities of the New England Indians (Peabody Museum Publications, 1935).

Of course, many other cemeteries were found, of which there were no record, the relics having been dug out and lost or scattered. All the early recorded cemeteries in the northeastern area were near water navigable by small boats. All but two were on stream banks or near the coast; the two exceptions, although on high ground, lie beside what may once have been the course of a stream now deflected in another direction. Early recorded cemeteries are as follows: on Penobscot waters, one each in Howland, Eddington, Hampden, Milford, and Swanville; two each in Bucksport, Bradley, Old Town, and Passadumkeag; five in Orland. On the Kennebec, one each at Kineo, Oakland, Waterville, and Winslow. Three have been found on the Georges River in the townships of Warren and Union; and two in Ellsworth on the Union River. One was discovered at Pemaquid Pond in Bristol, one in Bluehill on Bluehill Bay, and one at Sullivan Falls on Frenchman's Bay.

These are among the oldest archeological remains of North America, and are therefore of great importance. Most of the graves contain knives and spear-points, but not arrowheads, apparently the bow and arrow were not yet known to these people. Red Paint or, more properly, pre-Algonquian, implements consist mainly of adze blades, pear-shaped sinkers, fire-making sets, clipped-flint knives, long slender lance-heads and projectile points, sharpening stones, a few slate pendants in the form of a whale's tail, and several perforated slate ceremonials commonly called 'bannerstones.' These types are found to a rather less extent throughout New England and portions of the adjacent territory.

Instruments are found in varying numbers and of uneven workmanship, though of a fairly consistent high-grade quality. Some of them are covered with what seem to be inscriptions or designs, which obviously were meant to tell some story. In at least one case, inscriptions were made on a thin tablet intended for no other use.

But notwithstanding the discoveries made, no one has yet been able to say where these people came from, how long they were here, or whence and why they departed. Of them we really know very little; what they looked like, how they lived, even how they talked. The sources of certain types of minerals and rocks that they used have never been discovered. Their uses of certain specialized artifacts are unknown. No one has ever found the sites of any of their villages. theory that would account for their disappearance may be that they inhabited regions of the coast now sunk below the sea, and that they themselves or their villages were borne away in a tidal wave. Certain geological discoveries in regard to the sinking of the Maine coastal level seem to bear out this hypothesis.

Furthermore, some archeologists believe that many of the cemeteries are not on their original sites, having apparently been hastily moved *en masse,* as if it were that the sacred objects contained in the graves had to be carried to higher ground to escape the ravages of floods. This explanation does not, however, account for the disappearance of those pre-Algonquian people who lived further inland in states other than Maine. The supposition that they were an early branch of the Beothuks of Newfoundland, who they seem to resemble in many ways, is not proved. Some scientists continue to believe that the Red Paint People were driven into the North, and are now represented there by the Eskimos, many of whose ceremonial instruments closely resemble artifacts which have been unearthed in Maine.

There are collections of Red Paint artifacts in the Maine State Museum at Augusta, the Bangor Historical Society exhibit at the Bangor Public Library, the Maine Historical Society at Portland, Dr. J. Howard Wilson's Museum at Castine, the Knox County Historical Society at Thomaston, and the Robert Abbe Memorial Museum at Bar Harbor. Many other extensive and interesting collections are in the possession of individual persons or families throughout the State.

PALEO INDIANS

Initial penetration and settlement of New Hampshire and the rest of the Northeastern Woodlands region began about 10,500 BC - 6000 BC. Paleo Indians at that time were hunters, and their environment encompassed the tundra or park-tundra that adjoined the southern edge of the Wisconsin ice sheet, and the forests of the rugged mountains. When ice began to withdraw from the terminal moraine, the tundra and spruce woodlands followed it northward. In 6000 BC, after the last of the Canadian ice disappeared, flora and fauna zones stabilized.

Some writers speculate that there were actually two stages of Paleo Indians: Early and Late. Excavation sites, tools, and implements from each stage have been studied to determine subsistence patterns and climatic changes for the region in which they were used.

Early Paleo - 10,500 - 8000 BC

Scattered evidence for Early Paleo Indians was discovered in several sites in Vermont, New York, Massachusetts, and Ohio. Tool forms, especially fluted points, exhibited consistency through most areas. Bi-face knives, bi-face preforms, end scrapers, side scrapers, flake knives, and other uni-faces were also used. Very few known sites have produced tools of the "rough stone" category, such as hammer stones, anvil stones, pitted stones, or abraders.

The uniformity of fluted point tools is assumed to have resulted from a highly conservative way of life, adapted to a specific subsistence pattern. Most sites are located on hills or rises where good drainage was important. Rare are rock shelters or caves, and where they have been found, they were used mostly for protection from the wind, cold, or snow and rain.

Late Paleo - 8000-6000 BC

Point tools of Late Paleo Indians were discovered at excavation sites in Michigan, the Great Lakes, Upper Ohio Valley, Wisconsin, and the Canadian side of Lake Huron. Some speculation continues about items found at these sites, since they are determined to have been used for both prairie and lake cultures.

ARCHAIC INDIANS - to 3000 BC

Sometime between 6000 BC and 3000 BC, Paleo Indian cultures disappeared, and Archaic groups came into existence. While the Paleo Indian culture has usually been equated with big game hunting in the late glacial period, Archaic groups represented a more diverse culture of hunters, fishers, and gatherers that had adapted to post-glacial climate conditions.

The big game animals of the tundra and spruce woodlands were extinct by 8000 BC Archaic peoples depended primarily on deer, bear, elk or wapiti, smaller mammals, birds, turtles, fish, and shellfish for their subsistence. Also nuts, seeds, and other plant foods of area forests were gathered. Sites of Archaic Indians are more numerous and larger than those of the preceding era, and they reflect a larger and denser population as well as a more abundant subsistence base.

All of these changes reflect territorial and cultural diversity. Although it is assumed that Midwestern Archaic cultures evolved from Late Paleo-Indians, it is unlikely that any Asian migrations were represented. A few archeologists believe that Archaic cultures arose independently of Paleo Indians, but even those holding this view generally agree that there was probably some interaction between the two groups.

Eastern Archaic Indians have been divided into three sub- periods, which include Early Archaic (8000-6000 BC), Middle Archaic (6000-4000 BC), and Late Archaic (4000-1500 BC)

On the southern border of the Northeast culture area, the environment supported a number of small but widely distributed groups. For example, the Modoc Rockshelter in southern Illinois contains 28 feet of stratified deposits and remains that were radiocarbon dated to about 8000 BC. Deposits from another site, the Koster, located on the Illinois River, have been dated as far back as 5100 BC.

In New England, New York, and adjoining areas of this region, however, there are few Early or Middle Archaic remains. Some discoveries have been noted in Staten Island that date between 5310 and 7410 BC But since they occurred together on one level, there is speculation about a mixture of components. Other sites have included Harry's Farm on the Delaware River in New Jersey, and areas in Pennsylvania and New Hampshire.

Despite new data on artifact assemblages and radiocarbon dates, most information on Early and Middle Archaic cultures comes from the southern and coastal parts of the Northeast.

Following 3000 BC, several Late Archaic phases have been defined in New England, New York, and other sections of the Northeast. Occupancy has been determined by the size and number of sites and by the amount of refuse.

Some scientists speculate that an "explosion" in population and/or stability of occupation took place. It is possible that these changes occurred in response to further environmental changes, although the Northeast had evolved to an essentially modern environment at least one or two thousand years earlier.

CULTURAL DEVELOPMENTS: 3000 - 300 BC

More than a century of excavations revealed important artifacts to support theories about technology and subsistence patterns of Northeast Indians from the late Archaic and Early Woodland periods (and in some areas, transitional periods between these eras). Cultural patterns were probably determined by environmental differences as well as by communication and exchange networks, which followed a number of natural features including drainage patterns and ecological zones.

One important factor in determining cultural patterns in the Midwest was the mixed prairie-hardwood forest of western Indiana, Illinois, and areas southward and westward. Extensive grasslands and stands of oak and hickory trees provided the setting for deer and elk, beaver, bear, raccoon, fox, squirrel, and other mammals. Birds, especially wild turkeys, passenger pigeons, and migratory birds, and fish and shellfish were also important. Considerable evidence supports the notion that this environment may have been present prior to 3000 BC

Helton Culture. The Koster site in southern Illinois and several sites in Indiana have produced distinctive stone and bone components in the mixed prairie-hardwood zone. From findings at the Koster site, occupation is estimated between 5000 and 3000 BC, but it is probably closer to the end of the era. Preliminary data indicate that the Helton people from this time hunted, fished, and collected. Refuse gives evidence of subsistence and settlement patterns, but specific patterns have not yet been precisely defined.

Other evidence of the Helton culture is provided by the suggestion of wattle-and-daub houses with thatched roofs, racks for smoking or drying fish, and large roasting pits. Tools and implements were numerous and specific in their purpose.

Titterington Culture. The Titterington culture developed after the Helton culture. A variety of tools and implements used by this group were seemingly unrelated to those of the earlier culture.

Riverton Culture. Following this was the Riverton culture in the Wabash and other interior river valleys; artifacts from this complex reflect an apparent blending of midwestern and southern tradition with a lithic tradition derived from the east.

New England Coastal Area

During Late Archaic times, the coastal regions of northern New England, the Maritime Provinces of Canada, Newfoundland, and Labrador were regarded as a distinct culture area. The most important resources were connected with the sea, and the exploitation of these resources gave the Late Archaic culture of the coastal area its distinctive flavor.

Subsistence in the Maritime area included birds, fish, and mammals, with local variations such as swordfish harpooning in the southern region. Summers were spent on or near the coast, where sea mammals were available, and where Atlantic salmon, nesting birds, and plant foods could also be taken. At the first snow, a retreat was made from the coast to favorite hunting grounds, especially to crossing places of the caribou. During the remainder of the winter, beaver or other mammals provided red meat until spring, when a return to the coast was undertaken.

Weapons, implements, and tools implied hide- and bone- working industries. Woodworking tools were also made. Art, magic, and religion items were found in cemeteries in Maine and the Atlantic Provinces. Charms and amulets made from the feet and bills of diving birds, and claws and teeth of seals, bears, caribou, fox, and beaver were used for good luck in hunting. Burial ceremonies were elaborate.

By 1800 BC in Newfoundland, and by 100 BC south of the Saint Lawrence River, these people were replaced by groups of interior hunters who moved along the coast and began utilizing additional resources, especially shellfish. The newcomers may have originated in the Canadian Shield and slowly spread into the open pine and spruce forest of Maine and Atlantic Provinces. Evidence suggests that the Shield Archaic tradition can be traced forward to present-day Algonquian-speaking groups of the Northeast, including the Maliseet, and Maine's Micmac and Abenaki, in an essentially unbroken sequence.

Movement to the coast of Algonquian speakers is speculated to have occurred after Maritime Archaic people vacated the area (or, alternatively, may have been partly responsible for their demise). Continuity between earlier and later inhabitants has long been recognized, although research has not yet demonstrated any "direct" relationship between Maritime Archaic and later Algonquians.

Saint Lawrence Mixed Forest Area

Flora and fauna of the Northeast are highly homogenous south of the Great Lakes-Saint Lawrence formation. Along with a mixed prairie hardwood area, the oak, hickory, chestnut and deer-turkey environment was that of Late Archaic peoples on both Atlantic coastal and interior riverine drainages. Artifact types and varieties and adaptive patterns are similar in both major physiographic areas. Some likenesses may be the result of convergence, but others clearly show persistent contact between coastal and interior areas via rivers whose headwaters nearly meet in the Appalachian Mountains.

Atlantic Coastal Area

On the Atlantic coast, important mammals included the Virginia deer, black bear, raccoon, woodchuck, opossum, eastern and New England cottontail rabbit, otter, red and gray foxes, gray squirrel, and wolf. Also important were wild turkey, grouse, passenger pigeon, and migrating waterfowl of the eastern flyway during the fall and spring. Resident populations of sea birds and fish added variety to the diet.

Resources of this area set it apart from surrounding areas of the North, Northwest, and to a lesser extent, the West and South. Throughout the Late Archaic period, environmental differences are roughly parallel to differences in culture complexes. An increasing body of data indicates that a moderate population was already living on the northern fringes of the coastal plain during Middle or possibly Early Archaic times.

Some speculation exists as to whether a year-round coastal adaptation was present or whether coastal and inland areas represented seasonal camps of the same people. Data from "upriver" sites show a predominance of winter sites away from the coast, with summer sites surrounding the tidal marshes, ponds, and bays of the Atlantic coastal plain stretching from New Hampshire to North Carolina. People of this tradition were probably grouped in small, mobile bands. Each group likely moved seasonally within its own territory, regardless of whether coastal/inland movement was undertaken annually.

Nonperishable remains from the Late Archaic period in Middle Atlantic and southern New England states suggest a lack of elaborate technology. Many tools and implements were made from quartz and were known by various names. Art and ornamentation were virtually unknown on the coast during this period, although such crafts could have been made from easily disintegrated substances such as wood, bark, or skins. Little evidence suggests magical or religious beliefs, except for one discovery (Robbins, 1960) of a mortuary complex at the Wapanucket site in east Massachusetts.

Several local or regional cultures from the Late Archaic period in the Northeast interior had tools and implements that were similar to those of coastal complexes. Sites in Kentucky, Tennessee, New York, and Pennsylvania yielded implements and tools that are morphologically similar to eastern varieties and are probably related. Other elements show affinities with Mississippi Valley cultures.

The Riverton culture revolved around at least three seasonal camps. In the spring, riverbanks provided shellfish, turtles, and migratory birds. In fall, acorns, hickory nuts, and other vegetables were gathered. In winter, hunting camps provided deer and other mammals. Technology included sewing and weaving, and possibly hide-and-skin working. Woodworking was done, and smoking pipes, flutes, and box turtle rattles were fashioned.

The origin of this culture is unclear; it cannot be definitely traced to any earlier Archaic occupation. Similarly, there is little evidence to suggest a relationship between these people to succeeding Early Woodland peoples.

Great Lakes - Lake Forest Area

The Great Lakes drainage system, with its beech, maple, hemlock and maple-basswood forests (along with some oak, walnut, butternut, and pine,) provides evidence for the Great Lakes-Lake Forest Archaic. Two principal factors, the drainage system that was also a communication or exchange network, and the forest system, distinguish this culture from others (although some scientists believe that neither the Great Lakes Archaic or Lake Forest Archaic is entirely accurate, since the tradition is coterminous with neither).

Mammals, fish, and tools and implements found in this region show differences between northern and southern culture areas. One example is the method of fishing and the species of fish found in the Great Lakes area. While hook-and-line fishing was used throughout the Northeast in early historic times, harpoons and leisters (spears armed with three or more barbed prongs) were restricted to the Great Lakes and more northern areas, while simple spears were used in the south. Evidence also indicates that a distinctive set of resources was attached to an equally distinctive culture type, or cultural tradition, in the Great Lakes-Lake Forest zone from about 3000 to 1000 BC This culture was internally homogeneous yet distinct from surrounding cultural traditions. Tools and implements across a wide area suggest an actual movement of people into the Lake Forest area slightly prior to 3000 BC

In around 3000 BC, two indigenous industrial developments took place. In the east, a ground stone industry produced axes, adzes, gouges, knives, and spears, combined with the chipped stone complex common to most of the Lake Forest area. In the western region, the copper-producing area of the Upper Great Lakes known as the "Old Copper Culture" produced objects such as spear points. Many of the copper forms appear to be functional equivalents of ground-stone artifacts.

Although there is little evidence of settlement patterns or social organization among the Lake Forest Archaic people, discoveries suggest a well-defined territory that constituted the local unit, and temporary shelters for small, mobile bands. Seasonal movements were likely determined by a variety of subsistence resources, including mammals, birds, fish, and plant foods, as they became available. There are no common objects of personal adornment, decoration, or recreation in the Lake Forest Archaic, although these became increasingly more common after about 1500-1000 BC

Lake Forest Archaic cultural history is not completely understood (and perhaps will never be) due to the destruction of sites. Eastern portions of the Lake Forest provide data to support two phases of development: the Vosburgh, dated about 2500 BC, and the Vergennes, which was dated earlier. In the west, changes reflect minor alterations in tools, but in this area there is a somewhat greater suggestion of local or regional evolution of implement styles toward the Early Woodland forms.

TRANSITIONAL CULTURES

Late Archaic transitional cultures centered on the coast of the Middle Atlantic States and radiated along the coast and major river systems (the Susquehanna River being one of the major systems). Sites for this culture are all located along major rivers and their tributaries.

Later Susquehanna peoples added shellfish to their diet, while red meat still comprised a major portion of their food (as it had during the earlier Late Archaic period). Artifact forms changed somewhat, yet there seem to be no profound changes in the way of life between the two periods. The rapid spread of Susquehanna artifacts, however, clearly implies some adaptive advantages. There is also evidence of a more sedentary existence via discovery of heavy and not easily transportable soapstone bowls.

Although the cultural history of the Susquehanna tradition is complex and not yet completely understood, there is a strong indication that it arrived in the Northeast via the coastal plain during about 2000 BC. It flourished until after 1000 BC, while adopting or inventing the use of ceramic vessels. This marked the transition from Archaic to Woodland cultures.

LATE ARCHAIC-EARLY WOODLAND CULTURES

Recent studies by pre-historians have attempted to distinguish Archaic cultures from Early Woodland cultures, with perplexing results. It seems the only clear criterion has been the presence of ceramics in the latter. However, even this is not a clear indicator, since many Early Woodland sites are cremation burials and contain no ceramics as part of its mortuary offerings. Distinctions between Early and Middle Woodland cultures have been more numerous, yet no less confusing.

Two indigenous cultures seem to be part of the Early Woodland. (Additionally, there is a somewhat different development in northern New England and the Maritime area of eastern Canada.) The two evolved cultures appear to have had separate origins. Yet they held certain elements in common: an elaborate ritual system with lavish burial practices, and the making of thick, plain ceramics. Some scientists have called these cultures "transitional," since they represent people who produced the first ceramics in this area.

The first of the Late Archaic-Early Woodland cultures is speculated to be indigenous to the Lake Forest area, and presumes a lineal descendant of the Lake Forest Archaic. Living sites are very rare, but burial sites were found in the Lake Forest and Prairie Peninsula zones. The sites may represent a religious "overlay" on existing cultures. Artifacts from this time represent a positive link between this and the presumably later Meadow Wood culture of the Early Woodland in New York, Quebec, and Ontario.

The second of these cultures (and probably the one most clearly demonstrative of continuity during the second and early first millennia BC) is the so-called Old Copper culture in the western Great Lakes. Most sites of this complex are cemeteries, and offer little information about the life style of these Late Archaic-Early Woodland people.

Artifacts from sites in New York State, Montreal, Ontario, southern Quebec, and Upper Great Lakes indicate that the economic pursuits of these cultures was not vastly different from the Archaic. It is doubtful if there was any change from the small bands that characterized the Late Archaic peoples in the same area, and evidence is lacking for year-round habitation.

While developments from an Archaic base were discovered in the Lake Forest area, influences from the south were found in other parts of the Midwest. A limited amount of plant cultivation may have begun, especially in connection with the Adena culture, although this culture is known primarily as a mortuary complex.

Daily life in the Midwest during the Early Woodland period reveals some changes in subsistence and settlement. Yet none suggests that there was wholesale migration of new peoples to the area. Instead, new traits became incorporated from north and south into existing cultures in the river valleys of the Midwest. The result was a somewhat more stable and productive hunting and gathering subsistence base.

More or less permanent villages were comprised of circular houses with out-sloping walls and conical roofs, suggesting settled villages. However, the hunting-collecting base, as well as Adena material from rockshelters and other camping sites, suggests considerable movement.

Artifacts from this time period include spear or dart points, flat-bottomed ceramics of several varieties, chert end and side scrapers, drills, cigar-shaped or blocked-end-tube smoking pipes, and a number of ornamental and ceremonial items.

In a number of additional sections of the Northeast, other local developments took place. These sections included cultures in New York, southern Ontario, and southern Quebec, which developed from the earlier Meadow Wood phase. The Atlantic coast also had vaguely related assemblages. These cultures shared many technological elements with the Adena, and also with one another and with their local Archaic predecessors.

The invention or introduction of ceramics is evident in several places, including the Lake Forest area, the Middle Atlantic coast, and the Midwest, although here there were no drastic changes from earlier Archaic subsistence and settlement patterns. In some midwest river valleys, cultivation may have become increasingly important and set the stage for religious belief that centered around treatment of the dead. This may have persisted in the Northeast for as long as two millennia.

Northeast Mortuary Ceremonies

Since the time of first Late Archaic occupation in the Northeast, special treatment was accorded to the dead. A "basic case of religious belief" persisted through several millennia and culminated in the Hopewell religion.

Burial cults were evident in several regions of the Northeast, in Maine, New England and Long Island, the Great Lakes area, northern New York, Michigan, and Ontario. Each was distinctive, but all seemed to express a similar underlying set of beliefs that could be related to a burial cult that began before 3000 BC

Excluding a late Paleo-Indian site in Wisconsin and early burial mounds on the Labrador coast that dated before 5000 BC, burial ceremonies did not become important in the Northeast until the third millennium BC. The first unquestionably dated "red paint" cemeteries (so called because red ocher was often sprinkled at the burial site) were between 2000 and 1200 BC

The Maritime Archaic tradition has the strongest expression of these ceremonies. The ritual included flexed or bundle burials often located on high east-facing hills or bluffs; the site was covered with red ocher and contained tools, ornaments, weapons, charms, amulets, and medicine bundles. Because graves of newborn infants were also filled with such artifacts, it is speculated that these articles were not personal possessions, but rather intended for use in the afterworld.

In Later Maritime Archaic burials, ground slate spears and bayonets were exclusively made as funeral offerings. Objects were often deliberately broken, probably done to release the spirit of the artifact.

South of the Maritime area (and at least partly contemporaneous with this complex), indigenous groups from New England, Long Island, and the Middle Atlantic coast practiced their own version of the Northeast burial cult. Elements of the Susquehanna tradition figure prominently in ceremonies. The presence of red ocher, ritually broken artifacts, and choice of east-facing burials all seem to show a northern origin for basic elements of mortuary ceremonies. Cremation was an additional feature that may have begun in New England or along the Mid- Atlantic coast, and persisted until well into the Christian era.

In the Great Lakes area, similar rituals surrounded death and burial. However, cremation was the most common form. Bones and artifacts were burned either in place or in separate crematory basins; the residue was then collected and placed in a deep grave with red ocher and, occasionally, also with unburned offerings. Graves were on an east-facing slope or hill. Grave offerings included weapons, gorgets, copper tools, and ornaments.

In the west and south, other developments were taking place. Early Woodland ceremonies in southern Ohio was of the Adena complex. Theories have abounded concerning the origins of this group, from lost tribes or Mesoamerican migrants to much less exotic explanations. Numerous specific "traits" of the Adena have been widely studied, yet the most accepted explanation is that the Adena were closely related to, and probably derived from, the ancient Northeastern burial cult.

The means by which the Adena ceremonies were subsequently dispersed remains controversial. One suggestion is that the Adena people migrated from Middle West to the Atlantic coast. Others suggest diffusion or trade as the most reasonable explanation. Carbon-14 dating favors the former theory, while evidence of coastal Mid-Western interaction throughout the Archaic period favors the latter. Whatever theory best fits, the recurrence and elaborate elements of mortuary rituals demonstrate the only real unifying factor among otherwise varied aspects of Northeast cultures.

WOODLAND CULTURE 300 BC - AD 1000

Around 300 BC, quantitative changes were taking place in the prehistoric Northeast. The stability of Late Archaic and Early Woodland periods moved into the dynamic phase of the Middle Woodland, which made a relatively smooth transition into the Late Woodland period. In the several centuries before AD 1000, a new level of energy efficiency began to be achieved. Small climatic changes in the Northeast shifted environmental and cultural patterns. These changes were small, yet they eventually necessitated a change in the entire culture.

Climatic changes during the period of 300 BC to AD 300, called the Hopewell episode (or Sub-Atlantic episode), may have been mild to more severe, although the variation may have meant greater rainfall or a different distribution rather than temperature variation. The sea level changed dramatically along the Atlantic coast, and many coastal Middle Woodland sites eventually became submerged, which could account for the difficulty in defining cultural components during this period.

Following the Hopewell episode was the Scandic episode, which lasted from AD 300-400 to AD 800-900. In the Northeast, there seemed to be a generally colder period, and this may have placed stress on earlier Woodland adaptive patterns.

After the Scandic episode was the period from AD 800 to about AD 1300, called the Neo-Atlantic episode. The period was agriculturally favorable and helped with development of the first efficient agricultural systems in the Northeast. Following the Neo-Atlantic was the Pacific, lasting from AD 1300 to AD 1450. A return to Neo-Atlantic conditions came at AD 1450, and another cooling period occurred between AD 1550 and AD 1880.

Middle Woodland Culture

The Hopewell culture covers a wide geographical area that ranges from western New York to Kansas City and from the Gulf of Mexico to Lake Huron. The characteristics that define this time period include mound burials and earthworks, distinctively marked ceramic vessels, platform pipes (often carved), cut animal jaws and teeth, pan pipes, and other artifacts.

Grave offerings in the Hopewell period led early investigators to group this culture with Adena as Mound Builders, whom they believed were genetically different from, and culturally superior to, the Native Americans who lived during the time of European contact. Recent work demonstrates that Hopewell, like Adena, was part of a local developmental sequence in the area in which it was found; all seem to be the work of prehistoric American Indians.

In spite of widespread similarities in the style of artifacts, each region of Hopewell is distinctive; it appears to be wiser to interpret the culture in terms of local sequences than as part of a broad cultural horizon. One major aspect of Hopewell in the Northeast is the evidence of widespread exchange networks. Long distance trade was carried to its peak during the Middle Woodland Period, evidenced by conch shells from the Gulf coast discovered in Michigan and Wisconsin. Also, shark's teeth were found in Illinois, and an effigy alligator pipe dated to the period was found in western Michigan. The distribution of these and other goods strengthens the notion that some exchange network, whether social or religious or both, existed at the time.

Before 1950, most archaeologists viewed Ohio as the source of Hopewell developments in other areas; more and larger sites, with better quality grave goods, were found here than in any other area. After 1950, however, it became clear that many things that had been called Hopewellian outside of Ohio were different than were those in Ohio. Ceramics and burial mounds in the Great Lakes-Riverine area and other complexes differed from those in the Ohio region. A number of archaeological writers created elaborate divisions and distinctions to explain the complex differences. Adding to the confusion were developmental trends in different regions.

Presently, several patterns seem to have emerged from the study of the Middle Woodland period in the Northeast. First, in the Middle Woodland (and to a lesser degree, in the Late Woodland era), there seems to be a division between southern and northern cultures in adaptive strategies, economic base, social organization, and material culture.

Second, climatic trends seem to have affected the Middle Woodland culture throughout this time period. Thus, a cause and effect relationship is indicated, and both cultural and environmental factors need to be considered. In the northern section, for example, agricultural innovations were implemented at a later time than in southern regions.

Third, within a single time frame, elements of cultural developments interacted at different times. Next, the Middle Woodland cultural climax spread to the north from the south along the same channels as did earlier agriculture and ceramics. However, in spite of a lag in origin, northern and southern cultures reached their peak of development at approximately the same time.

The change from Middle Woodland to Late Woodland was primarily an artistic emphasis, and this was also a trend that moved from south to north. The subsequent Middle Mississippian influence was weaker and more varied in northern cultures than in southern, due to the northern economic base being essentially the same for Middle and Late Woodland periods, while establishment of an efficient agricultural system in southern areas had tremendous social and demographic impact.

It is clear that the cultural history of the Northeast remains to be completely understood. Radiocarbon dating provides some clues; however, interpretations continue to differ, and the mystery remains for future scientists to unravel.

LATE PREHISTORY CULTURE PATTERNS

During late prehistory, native groups from three distinct cultural areas in the Northeast lived and maintained their separate cultural traditions. They included the Coastal, St. Lawrence, and Great Lakes Indians.

Coastal Region

It was primarily river drainage systems that determined the economic shift from generalized hunting and gathering, toward more specialized exploitation of natural resources. This shift seems to have taken place earlier in the southern than in the northern region of the Northeast.

On the East Coast, drainage basins of rivers and streams that flow into the Atlantic and into the southern part of the Gulf of Saint Lawrence were occupied by Eastern Algonquian tribes. Extremely south were Iroquoian groups of the upper drainages of the Neuse, Tar, Roanoke, and Chowan rivers.

Given the ecological differences between Newfoundland at the one extreme and coastal North Carolina at the other, the cultural pattern of the Coastal region has three separate patterns. At the southern extreme lived Virginia and Carolina Algonquians; their pattern was one of well-developed farming. Villages were small, and had anywhere from several to a few dozen houses. Although this group had essentially permanent dwellings, depletion of soil and other resources required relocation within intervals of 5 to 20 years.

Their houses were elongated bark-or-mat covered, and barrel-roofed with straight or rounded ends. Population density was higher than in northern drainages, and strong cultural influences were affected from the greater Southeast. On the same rivers, but upstream, lived various Iroquoian and Siouan tribes who combined hunting, farming, and fishing.

In the middle drainage systems, from the Delaware to the Merrimack, farming was also important. However, it was of greater importance to those along the lower coastal portions of the drainages, where fishing and shellfish gathering supplemented agricultural pursuits. Upstream and downstream groups were closely related, but hunting and gathering were more important to the latter. Within each drainage, regular interactions took place between upstream and downstream communities, and it is likely that economic exchange also took place.

In both areas, houses were large enough to accommodate extended family groups, although none were as large as the communal dwellings of the Iroquoians. Nonetheless, studies have shown that dwellings were larger in areas where Iroquois influence was greater. Villages were sometimes palisaded, and settlements were permanent for a decade or more in areas where agriculture was possible. Settlements in the interior uplands were less so. The Algonquians of the middle drainages were influenced by Iroquoians of the interior.

In the area of the Eastern Abenaki to the Beothuk of Newfoundland, on the other hand, farming was of little importance. Settlements were less permanent toward the northeast, and houses were smaller in the northern drainages. The settlements were probably abandoned during the season when shellfish collecting or interior hunting were done, which differed from farther south where some of the young and old probably stayed behind to protect crops during the summer.

The economic importance of shellfish decreased northward. In northern drainages, hunting and fishing were more important than they were in the south. There is some evidence for division of local tribes into upstream and downstream groups, and it is likely that this was for economic reasons. On some rivers, it seems that there was a tendency for some groups to specialize in exploitation of marine resources, while others exploited resources of interior forests and streams.

Although conflicts apparently sometimes arose between local Eastern Algonquian communities, there seems to have been some general feeling of common culture between them. Frequent trade and intermarriage likely diffused the groups somewhat.

Since about 6000 BC, prehistoric cultures of the coastal plain have differed from those of upland oak-chestnut-hickory forests. Archaeological sequences suggest that the coastal area was characterized by a steady development without any notable discontinuities, and implies that prehistoric traditions that led to historic cultures extend back several thousand years. Archaeology does not support origin myths that say that most tribes were relatively recent arrivals from distant and nonspecific regions. Rather, it seems generally that many parallel sequences were part of a broader pattern of development, and each diverged somewhat from the mainstream in response to local conditions.

The late prehistory of East Coast cultures appears to be a smooth outgrowth from earlier periods. Each local sequence reflects a long-term stability, and there are a number of in- place developments, each of which was contained within a natural drainage unit. Innovations moved from south to north through the area as local cultures adapted to conditions. Stronger waves of change moved northward over time as such economic activities as ceramic manufacture, agriculture, and shellfish gathering were extended.

HISTORIC NORTHEAST INDIANS

It is difficult to determine when the first meetings between Europeans and Native Americans took place. Limited definitive information, along with distortions by European ideas and interpretations, raise questions about the accuracy of information obtained from this time period. Generalizations abound, and differences between northern and southern groups were often not addressed. However, it is clear that European contact greatly affected changes in aboriginal cultures.

The earliest recorded European contacts seem to have been of brief duration and were largely insignificant to natives in the areas of contact. However, by the fifteenth and sixteenth centuries, economic interests motivated further exploration by Europeans. Increasingly, dependence on importation of expensive goods from Asia by an overland route to Venice forced Europe to consider finding a shorter route. Nautical knowledge was increasing, especially in Portugal, and merchants were willing to give financial support to transoceanic explorations.

In the late 1400s, Spain and other western European nations began to move forward with maritime adventures across the Atlantic. In 1497, five years after Christopher Columbus discovered the Bahamas, John Cabot took possession of Newfoundland in the name of the English crown. Although he probably made no real contact with local natives, he did discover their fishing nets and other tools.

Portuguese interests focused on the southern route to India, but also included a concern with the North Atlantic. In 1500 and again in 1501, Gaspar Corte-Real explored coastal Newfoundland. Upon return from his second voyage, he kidnapped 57 Indians. With their capture and enslavement, a new aspect of commerce was introduced. More frequently, a few Indians were kidnapped in order to be used as interpreters in later contacts, or to be displayed in European cities, or to become slaves.

In the early years of the sixteenth century, many European fishermen began entering the Newfoundland region. Their activities centered mainly around the coast, and by about 1530, fisheries had expanded along the entire coastline from Labrador to south Nova Scotia. By 1550, about 30 French ships were sailing into Newfoundland. Reports in 1578 listed 50 English, 150 French, and 100 Spanish fishing boats in the general area.

Most early fishermen salted their catches at sea and sailed for home. After the middle of the sixteenth century, it was decided that "dry-fishing" was more economical. Camps were established on the shores, particularly along the eastern coast of Newfoundland and in Labrador. Although no specific exploration was done in the interior, contacts with the natives were likely frequent.

Limited data from the period reveal that the Indians were apparently at ease with Europeans, as they sometimes worked as fishermen for European captains, and they freely boarded the ships in nearby harbors. Such relationships provided the basis for satisfactory trade.

However, this was not the case everywhere. Clearing the lands around harbors on Newfoundland resulted in forest fires that lasted for weeks. Native food sources were often wasted. Kidnappings and other experiences caused some Indians to move further and further into the interior, which was the case of the Beothuk. Relationships with the Europeans continued to deteriorate. An extremely unfavorable stereotype was developed by the Europeans, and it was clear that the Beothuk were considered by them to be merely a nuisance and of no economic value.

In North America, it was not fishing but development of the fur trade that became historically and economically important. The potential of adding profits by trading furs with the Indians was seen by fishermen before 1519. There was strong incentive for Europeans to explore the coasts before returning home, and Maine Indians had already become acquainted with Europeans' desire for furs by 1524. Jacques Cartier was offered furs by Chaleur Bay Indians in 1534, and Indians from the Saint Lawrence came up the coast to trade with Europeans and hunt for seals as early as 1540.

The coastline between Nova Scotia and Florida appeared on European maps as a result of Spanish and French explorations. Spanish slave hunters were conducting raid along the coast of South Carolina after 1520, and on one trip they captured some 150 Indians to ship to the West Indies. News of these excursions spread far and wide to coastal tribes.

Giovanni de Verrazano's voyage in 1524 is the earliest known continuous voyage along the eastern coast of North America. According to his writings, he found the natives to be friendly and as curious as was he himself. However, when he met Indians in Maine, it was clear that they had had previous unpleasant contact with Europeans. They were less friendly, and there was no hospitality between the groups after they were done exchanging goods.

In the latter decades of the century, the fur trade changed from a subsidiary activity of many fishermen to a major occupation. Rivalry increased between the French and English in North America for the fur trade, and many early traders stereotyped the Indians they met as a result of manipulations and distortions about the native society.

Colonization Efforts

By the first quarter of the sixteenth century, slave raids had made the local Indians in New England suspicious about Europeans, and the growing prospect that these cruel strangers intended to become neighbors may have caused even further hostility.

Some early attempts at colonization met with failure. In 1585, 100 English colonists and two Indian guides came to Roanoke Island on the coast of North Carolina with the idea of colonizing. Of their initial contact with the natives, no information is recorded. However, trouble began when a silver cup was found missing. The English burned the Indians' corn and destroyed the village. They killed the Indian chief and left for home. In 1587, another group of English attempted colonization, but the natives had not forgotten the earlier destruction. When supplies arrived for the colonists at the settlement, there was no one left to receive them. Although some have speculated that the colonists joined the Croatoans, the tribe of their loyal Indian guide and interpreter, no definite explanation has been given.

During the sixteenth century, all attempts at colonization were dismal failures. However, northern areas remained favored for trading, as hunting and fishing were more profitable here than further south and on the coast.

English interests brought about an increasing desire by the French to realize their own claims in the New World. In 1604, a group of French colonists settled on the Saint Croix River in Maine. From there, Samuel

Champlain explored the New England coast south to Cape Cod in search of a better location for the French colony. The influence of the French was strong, and some of the Indians along the coast began to sport European clothing or speak some French and Basque words.

In 1607, when the French colonists temporarily gave up their coastal enterprise and left for home, some 120 English settlers and two Indian guides arrived on the Kennebec River to begin another colony. It was also doomed to fail. The first Indians they met spoke some French, and conflicts ensued. After a severe winter in which a fire also burned most of the English supplies and lodgings, the colonists returned to England in 1608. Coastal Maine remained a source of conflict between English and French throughout the seventeenth century.

On the Chesapeake Bay in Virginia, a group of 144 English colonists arrived in 1607. The next year, another 190 joined the group. The colony survived despite quarrels, starvation, and hostility with the Indians, mostly because of the dealings of Captain John Smith. His success began the start of a new phase in relationships between Indians and whites along the central East Coast.

Increasing numbers of Europeans arrived, and the Indians were introduced to a range of new cultural aspects. The newcomers differed from fur traders primarily in their interests: they were less interested in the furs of the Indians than they were in their land.

Henry Hudson explored the New England coast in 1609 while searching for a passage to China. He found a cheaper way to obtain furs than trading with the Indians: He and his crew drove the Indians from their homes and took their goods. He then sailed up the river that bears his name. One month earlier, Champlain had defeated a group of Mohawks on Lake Champlain, north of the Hudson River.

Amsterdam merchants had heard about Hudson's bartering with the Indians and, by 1610, Dutch ships were also entering the Hudson River to engage in fur trade. They operated as far as Narragansett Bay, where they maintained a trading post long after the English had tried, without success, to take the local fur trade away from them.

In 1624, the first colonists arrived to settle the town of New Amsterdam on Manhattan Island; trading posts were established on the Connecticut and Delaware rivers. But the beaver population was soon depleted, and furs here became more difficult to obtain. The Dutch began to treat the coastal Indians with scorn, while attempting to establish friendly relationships with Indians of the interior. They desired to divert some of the trade from the French in the Saint Lawrence valley to the Hudson.

Although the fur trade brought many outsiders into the lands of the Native Americans, no proper settlement was established until 1620, when the Pilgrims arrived in Massachusetts. After landing on Cape Cod, they soon settled in former Pawtuxet territory (the tribe was earlier decimated by an epidemic of European origin). All of this activity began an era of grave importance to North American Indians. It was the onset of major cultural and environmental changes, and forced the natives to face a number of new challenges.

Native Americans after Contact

It is difficult to establish an accurate history of the Indians after European contact. The natives did not have any significant writings, and their accounts of contacts with whites were scanty at best. The full nature of events after contact with European traders and colonists is essentially one-sided, and only the main points can be understood.

The first reaction of the Indians to contact with whites was probably curiosity; some may have believed that the newcomers were supernatural. However, after only a short time, they became suspicious and hostile. As the whites began the widespread depletion of their food sources, their economy was severely disrupted. Even more destructive were the diseases that the Europeans unknowingly introduced, such as measles, smallpox, and typhus, for which the Native Americans had no immunity.

As epidemics began to ravage many coastal communities, the populations of the natives dwindled severely. A particularly devastating epidemic in 1617 decimated thousands of Indians between the Penobscot River and Cape Cod. In 1622, and again in 1631, whole communities south of the Merrimack River were exterminated. In 1633, 700 Narragansetts of Rhode Island died from smallpox. On the Connecticut River in 1634, four Dutch traders spent the winter among the natives. After an epidemic broke out, the population of some 1,000 Indians dwindled to 50 survivors. Hudson River Indians reported in 1640 that their numbers had dropped to less than one-tenth of their original population due to disease. Wampanoag, Abenaki, and Micmac natives reported similar losses. In addition, syphilis was determined as the cause of death in skeletons found along the Potomac River, and it is speculated that the promiscuous behavior of some of the fishermen and traders spread such venereal diseases through native lands.

Liquor was another cause of the decline of native populations. Early Basques and other fishermen apparently used it freely in their fur-trading negotiations with Indians. By the time the first French settlers had arrived in some regions, many Indians were already addicted to alcohol. Drunkenness reached incredible proportions among some groups. By the early decades of the seventeenth century, the Montagnais were highly addicted, and at some point, brandy became the only item of trade with which the French could compete with English and Dutch, who could sell it for less.

All of these elements had serious repercussions in the life of the Indians. Fear affected the attitude of the natives toward the Europeans. Especially with regard to disease, some tribes believed that European diseases required special European curing rituals. For the Micmac, religious rituals became altered; they believed that baptism from French missionaries could affect a cure from virulent European diseases.

The most profound changes were experienced in the fur trade and in intertribal relationships. The ancient trails and waterworks of the Native Americans were traveled by white newcomers, and some Indians provided information regarding access to remote areas along the coast. Archaeological discoveries have revealed that pottery, shell beads, and copper was used for trade, as well as more profitable goods. Some tribes began to produce specialized trading items, such as the Nanticoke who made beaded items, and the Iroquois who fashioned pipes.

Of all the Indians involved in this new enterprise, only the Beothuk of Newfoundland refused to trade with the Europeans. In horticultural areas, groups were often passively resistant to the changes. However, the lure of new commodities proved to be irresistible. To obtain more of the white man's goods, the Indians needed to devote more and more time to hunting and trapping fur-bearing animals. In general, the fur trade upset and unbalanced the entire annual cycle of traditional aboriginal activities.

In Maine, where agriculture was less abundant, hunting and trapping increased to the point that interest in agricultural cultivation decreased even further. In some areas, particularly in Nova Scotia and coastal Quebec, adjusting to the fur-trade economy took its toll in the decrease of seashore activities; reliance on traders to bring European foods sometimes resulted in famine.

Another important change was in the hunting itself. Because it took more time and effort to trap sufficient numbers of small fur-bearing animals, larger mammals were not hunted as often, and their food and skins were less utilized. In addition, because any specific fur-trapping area was frequented more often than previously, the size of Indians' bands changed; larger bands became less common. Territoriality among native groups increased and became more defined.

Initially, many regional Indians welcomed the selection of specific bays as trading centers. But rivalry for access to trade areas sometimes resulted in intertribal warfare. An example is the friction that developed between Iroquois Indians and the Montagnais along Quebec's East Coast. It did not take long for more remote groups to realize that they were being cheated by coastal natives, and intertribal conflicts grew. In the course of these wars, political alliances were strengthened; by conquest or incorporation, local units merged into tribes, and tribes entered into confederacies.

Economic dependence, less reliance on making one's own tools and ceramics, and a weakening interest in other traditional activities frequently resulted in a decline of material culture traits. Poverty and malnutrition were often experienced after the loss of the fur trade.

Seventeenth Century Indian Wars

While powerful inland tribes in the Southeast and in interior New York did not become involved in warfare with the English until the eighteenth century, coastal tribes with whom the Europeans were in direct contact in the seventeenth century eventually became involved in full-scale warfare.

Early conflicts between New England natives and Plymouth leaders were resolved by means of a treaty of friendship. By the terms of this agreement, both sides were to keep peace, and offenses of one side to the other were punished. This peace lasted for more than one half century, although some Plymouth colonists' and Pilgrims' assaults on Indian groups raise questions.

New England's first great Indian war did not take place until 1637 against the Pequot tribe. Although one can only assume the motives of the participants, both the established colony of Massachusetts and the newer colony of Connecticut sought to profit from destruction of the powerful tribe. The occasion of the first major conflict was the murder of an Englishman, Captain John Stone, by Western Niantics allied with the Pequots. Retaliation was averted for a time by a treaty signed on November 1, 1634. In 1636, another ship captain, John Oldham, was killed on Block Island by a group of Narragansetts.

Orders were given to John Endecott and an expedition of 90 volunteers to kill the native men, capture the women and children, and take the island. The expedition was then to go to Pequot country to demand the murderers of Captain Stone and others, and collect 1,000 fathoms of wampum for damages. If the Pequots refused, force was to be used.

The expedition failed miserably. The tactic destroyed what little peace still existed between the English and the Pequots, and put in grave peril the Saybrook fort at the mouth of the Connecticut River. Indian raids on outlying settlements increased. The Pequots sought to heal their breach with their former enemy, the Narragansetts, to fight the English. Roger Williams was able to interrupt the council that was to meet for this purpose, and the English offered to aid the Narragansetts in their efforts against the Pequots. The Narragansetts agreed to the alliance with the English. However, this agreement also brought about the later destruction of the Narragansetts.

On May 1, 1637, the General Court of the colony of Connecticut declared war on the Pequots. Both Connecticut and Massachusetts sent expeditions against the tribe, and both seemed to anticipate advantages that would be gained by being the first to destroy them. Captain John Mason of Connecticut, with 90 Englishmen and hundreds of Indian allies, torched one of the Pequot villages on the Mystic River and slaughtered all the inhabitants, a total of 300 to 700. The Narraganset allies of the English were appalled by their ruthlessness, and by their murder and enslavement of Pequot survivors.

This conflict is closely related to the creation of a league uniting the Puritan colonies of Massachusetts, Connecticut, New Haven, and Plymouth under Articles of Confederation in 1643. However, Roger Williams' Providence Plantations colony was excluded from the league. Seeing a threat to his colony and to the Narragansetts, he sought protection against the English. Intertribal wars and retaliations, agreements and breaking of agreements became part of the chaos that developed between tribes, sachems, chiefs, and their English allies. The Narragansetts soon became pawns in the conflicts, and the confederated colonies declared war on the Narragansetts.

While numerous causes have been alleged in justification of the declaration, the principal reason seems to be the Narragansetts' desire to maintain control of their own affairs in making war and making agreements. Although the tribe sought to avoid violence against the English and to meet reasonable demands, they were strongly opposed to the destruction of their position as an autonomous nation. However, a treaty was agreed upon on August 28, 1645 that made all the sachems acknowledge guilt for various misdeeds. They were to pay 2,000 fathoms of wampum and an annual tribute for each Pequot living among them, cede the whole Pequot country to the English colonies, and give hostages to the English as a pledge of good behavior.

Relations between the Narragansetts and the colonists continued to be marked by conflicts, rumors of conspiracies, and occasional punitive expeditions.

Further conflicts included King Philip's War, a bloody battle in 1675 between the Plymouth colonists and the Wampanoag Indians based on the issue of land. King William's War (1689-1697) and Queen Anne's War (1702-1711) were part of an international struggle between Great Britain and France, and the Indians played a secondary role to the two nations.

In Virginia, conflicts between the Indians and the colonists were similar to those in New England. Suspicion, violence against the natives, and broken trade agreements escalated until war was inevitable. Destruction wrought retaliation, and further attacks were carried out by both factions. Bacon's Rebellion in 1675-1676 was a terrible battle fought over the Indians' fear of losing control and the English desire to dominate trade and land ownership.

In analyzing the process by which wars developed between Indians and whites in New England, there appears to be no single explanation. It is possible that war was inevitable considering the expansiveness and aggression of white settlement, and the decline of population of the Indians due to epidemics and other problems introduced by Europeans. Another cause might be the passions and misunderstandings that were created by particular individuals at particular times. Still another may be the questionable legal status of the colonists and Indians in their relationships to one another regarding trade and land ownership.

A more ethnocentric reason might be the hatred the Puritans bore toward the native culture that contradicted with their system of beliefs, and by other European whites who did not and would not accept the natives as equals. Whatever the final analysis, the wars of the seventeenth century changed the life of the Northeast Indians irrevocably.

SAINT LAWRENCE LOWLANDS PATTERNS

In the area that runs from Schoharie Creek west of Schenectady to the Genesee at Rochester lived the Iroquois Indians. The Adirondacks and Lake Ontario were the northern border of this region, and the headwaters of the Delaware, Susquehanna, and Allegheny flanked to the south. The Iroquois comprised the Five Nations of New York (Mohawk, Oneida, Onondaga, Cayuga, and Seneca) and after 1772, the Six Nations that included the Tuscarora. Their way of life was not unique, but was shared by other local groups, especially the Hurons.

Iroquoia, the territory south of Ontario that was the early Longhouse of the Five Nations, lay just north of Lake Ontario and Lake Erie and southeast of Lake Huron. The Trent waterway connected Iroquoia via the Thousand Islands with Huronia. Southeast of Lake Ontario was the Mohawk River, whose broad valley cut through the uplifted plateau and the higher Adirondack Mountains to the north, and this was the only water route through the Appalachian chain. These were the communication routes of the Iroquois and neighboring tribes, and they were the natives' corridors for trade, war, and peace. This was also the area that, for Europeans, became the avenue of exploration and expansion.

Deciduous birch-beech-maple-elm trees and coniferous pine and hemlock grew in the forests of this region, along with fir and spruce to the north. In the Appalachian area, oak, chestnut, and yellow poplar reached toward eastern Iroquoia via valleys tributary to the Hudson. However, the sugar maple, American elm, and white pine were the trees most important to Iroquois technology.

Elm bark was important for shelter, containers, and vessels. Deer, bear, and small mammals were hunted in the forests about one day's travel from Iroquois settlements. Turkey, partridge, and a large number of migratory game birds also provided food for the group. Freshwater fish in lakes and streams were caught, and turtles, especially the snapper, were trapped.

Of all the Eastern Woodland Indians, the Iroquois were the best known as horticulturists. Slash-and-burn agriculture was practiced by women, and fishing and hunting were done by men. After a harvest, hunting parties would abandon villages, leaving the old natives, pregnant women, and children to tend the crops. Bows and arrows, knives, traps, and later, guns were used to obtain meat and skins.

Among the Iroquois, food taboos were almost nonexistent. Diet consisted of most things that walked, crawled, swam, or flew. However, although they were in theory conservationists, in practice they often contributed to the decline of species, especially in the eighteenth century when beaver and deer populations dwindled.

Maple was harvested, although this industry was later taken over by Europeans of New York and New France. Salt was not exploited until after European contact, when some tribes became heavy users. Berries were picked and dried for winter use, and nuts from a variety of trees were gathered.

"Indian tobacco" was grown for ceremonial and social smoking. Maize, beans, and squash, the "three sisters" of Iroquois ceremonial, were cultivated. Settlements had up to 1,500 people. Iroquois women grew and harvested the crops, and their work operated on a principle of mutual cooperation. Rituals, songs, and drama were part of the growing cycle; Green Corn and harvest festivals were celebrated.

Iroquois life moved in an ecological cycle. Hunting and gathering were keyed to a lunar calendar and divided into four seasons, each marked with special ceremonies and rituals. Although it is believed that the Indians were earlier primarily hunters and gatherers, crop-growing later became more important, with far less dependency on meat and gathered foodstuffs.

Material Culture

The technology of the Iroquois showed a great capacity to use available materials. One example is the grotesque wooden masks that were worn by members of the Society of Faces, known commonly as false faces. (These masks are now exhibited in many major ethnographical museums throughout the world and in contemporary shows of American Indian art.) After the introduction of steel tools, the art evolved considerably, but all are related to a specific type of woodworking.

Many items from the nineteenth century were embroidered with moose or deer hair and porcupine quill. The Iroquois knew how to bend and shape wood for house frames, pack frames, toboggans, snowshoes, basket rims, handles, and lacrosse sticks. Their understanding about the principle of gravity was apparent in their deadfalls and corn pounders. Their war clubs and pump drills showed an understanding of centrifugal force, and they moved and erected timbers by way of levers. Blow and dart guns utilized the principle of the piston.

Structures were highlighted by the longhouse. A typical dwelling had from three to five fires, each shared by two nuclear families of five or six members. Houses averaged about 25 feet in width, and length was determined by the number of families to be sheltered. The longhouse was the most conspicuous feature of Iroquois settlements. It was synonymous with residential units, the household or maternal lineage, and was their symbol of identity. The Iroquois called their confederacy "The People of the Longhouse."

Settlements typically had from 30 to 150 longhouses surrounded by a palisade, and were situated on high land accessible to drinking water and near a navigable waterway.

The Iroquois were travelers, and they covered vast distances over forested trails quickly. In contrast, the Hurons were primarily traders and canoeists.

Museums do not have many exhibits of Iroquois and Huron clothing. However, both seemed to favor black-dyed buckskin. The Iroquois wore twined cornhusk slippers in summer. Decoration included face painting. In general, black was used for war or mourning. Northern Iroquoians, especially Mohawks, were tattooed with geometric designs, double-curl motif, and clan crests, which were pierced with bone awl and rubbed with charcoal on the chest, shoulders, and face.

Social Organization

One of the primary patterns of social structure of the Iroquois was based on the division of labor between the sexes. Although towns were built and governed by men, men owed their offices to female succession, and the village and its environs were the domain of women. Men were active in the council and in the forest where they hunted, warred, and maintained peace and trade.

Each tribe was divided into villages and longhouse families. These were divided into two moieties; each moiety comprised two or more clans. Clans were segmented into one or more maternal families or lineage. Each maternal family traced its home to some longhouse of which it once formed the household. Lineages were the building blocks of the entire social system.

The "fireside" or nuclear family was the simplest unit of Iroquois society; within it were the husband and wife and their children. From the fireside family stemmed the siblings of the wife's mother, the wife's siblings, the wife's children and her daughter's children, and descendants of the preceding women in the female line. The senior woman was the matriarch and presided over the household. A lineage of persons traced from a common mother. Some call this the "maternal" family, and it was the primary unit of Iroquois government. In time, it might occupy several longhouses in several villages, and give rise to segments of a clan.

A clan was composed of two or more maternal families that behaved as if the members of each generation were siblings, or as if they constituted a single maternal family. One or more clans constituted a moiety, and acted together as if they were siblings. Usually two moieties existed in any Iroquoian community. Political structure extended the basic pattern of social structure.

Warfare

Although the message of peace was inherent in the longhouse society, Iroquois men revered war above all else. After introduction of the fur trade, this became a powerful force that threatened the very structure of Iroquoian society. Much energy was expended in training, preparation, and travel for war, and heavy losses of manpower were only partly compensated by the adoption of captives. The native population of Iroquois towns steadily dropped during the seventeenth century, and from the middle of that century, there were more outlanders than natives in Iroquoia.

Early Iroquoian Contact with Europeans

By AD 1500, Iroquoian-speaking peoples of the Northeast had evolved a cultural pattern with most elements that had characterized them in the historic period. Their subsistence was based primarily on horticulture and fishing. Extended families lived in longhouses. Clan segments joined together in villages with 1,000 or more inhabitants. Neighboring villages were linked together to form tribes.

The age of the Iroquois confederacy is uncertain, but it appears that the five tribes that formed the Five Nations were joined together in the sixteenth century. There is no evidence that membership in the confederacy at this time involved more than an agreement among tribes to avoid blood feuds and cease raiding one another.

Iroquoian-speaking peoples lived in tribal cluster areas, each of which had several thousand people located in one or more nearby villages. Clusters were separated from one another by extensive tracts of hunting and fishing territory spread out over a large area that centered on Lake Ontario. Between this and the shores of Georgian Bay lived four Huron tribes and the Petun. West of Lake Ontario and in the Niagara Peninsula were various Neutral tribes. The Erie, Wenro, and possibly other groups lived southeast of Lake Erie.

Beyond the Niagara River, the five tribes of the Iroquois stretched across upper New York State as far as the Mohawk River valley. Along the Susquehanna River were one or more Iroquoian tribes, and the Saint Lawrence lowlands were occupied by more groups that became known as the Saint Lawrence Iroquoians.

The late prehistoric period was one of local self-sufficiency. Intertribal warfare was common, and long-distance trade was limited in volume and restricted to luxury items such as native copper and marine shells. A notable exception was the Hurons living in Simcoe County, Ontario, who appear to have traded tobacco, fishing nets, and other items for skins and dried fish and meat produced by hunting tribes to the north. Some evidence points to a similar trade between Iroquoian tribes in the upper Saint Lawrence Valley and Algonquians and Montagnais north of them.

When the northern Iroquoians first encountered Europeans in the first half of the sixteenth century, their history and cultural development became inseparably linked with the newcomers. The first recorded contact between Europeans and Iroquoians was in the Baie de Gaspe on July 16, 1534. French explorer Jacques Cartier was sailing north when inclement weather forced him to take shelter in this bay. The French met some 300 men, women, and children who had come down the Saint Lawrence River from Quebec City to fish for mackerel.

The Native Americans welcomed the French with songs and dances. They desired some small articles the French had brought, including combs, knives, and other items. In fact, the French later described the natives as being great thieves. However, the French showed themselves to be greater thieves, for they kidnapped two sons of the fishing party's leader, Donnacona, and took them back to France in hopes that they might serve as guides and interpreters on future voyages.

Cartier returned to Canada the next year, directed by Donnacona's sons, and sailed up the Saint Lawrence to visit Iroquoian villages in Quebec and on Montreal Island. While spending the winter in Quebec, Cartier heard accounts of a wealthy kingdom called Saguenay where native copper existed. Wishing for King Francis I to hear these stories firsthand, he kidnapped Donnacona and took him and nine others back to France. None of the Indians ever saw their homeland again.

Donnacona's interview with Francis I eventually led to two short-lived colonies becoming established a few miles upriver from Quebec City, in 1541-1542 and 1542-1543. Both were abandoned, in part because of the hostility of Saint Lawrence Iroquoians toward the French due to kidnappings and intrusion into their territory. For many years, the opposition of the tribe ruled out further attempts by Europeans to travel upriver from Tadoussac, which became the main trading center.

The fur trade had a great impact on Iroquoian-speakers of the Northeast. By 1534, European fishermen were earning extra money by trading furs with Indians in the Gulf of Saint Lawrence. By the middle of the century, Basque whale hunters had penetrated up the Saint Lawrence to Tadoussac. By the latter decades, the demand for beaver pelts had increased significantly.

Around 1580, the expanding fur trade on the Saint Lawrence gave ship owners the impetus to again hazard up the Saint Lawrence. The main center of trade was still the port of Tadoussac.

In the early part of the seventeenth century, the Montagnais and Algonquians attempted to break the power of the Iroquoian Mohawks who had overrun the area. The growing fur trade in Tadoussac probably gave both northern Algonquians and remaining Saint Lawrence Iroquoians a great advantage over Iroquois tribes living further to the south.

The Mohawks seem to have begun raids on the Saint Lawrence Valley in order to plunder trade goods from Saint Lawrence Iroquoians and Algonquians. It is possible that they attempted to drive the groups from the valley so that they might gain control of the nearest center of trade goods in Tadoussac. In fact, it has been speculated that the need to obtain European goods and resist northern tribes might have been influential in the formation of the Iroquois confederacy.

Failure to gain access to trading ports drove the Mohawks to remain dependent on warfare for obtaining a supply of iron tools. When Champlain discovered them in 1609, this was the situation that existed.

SEVENTEENTH CENTURY INDIANS

Tribal life became very complex and difficult after the Europeans established trade in the Saint Lawrence-Lowlands region. In the early part of the seventeenth century, the Montagnais at Tadoussac were middlemen in any trade between the French and the Indians living further inland. Tribal etiquette made it an offense for one group to travel across the territory of another without permission; to protect their trading interests, the Montagnais would not allow tribes living in the interior to visit Tadoussac, nor would they permit Frenchmen to travel up the Saguenay River.

In about 1603, in order to fight the Iroquois who threatened their trade monopoly, the Montagnais enlisted the aid of Algonquians who lived west of them. As allies, Algonquians were allowed to come to Tadoussac and trade with the French. It was during this period that many peoples living north of the Saint Lawrence became allied against the Iroquois, and this played an important role in the historical development of the time.

The Hurons also began to obtain some European trade goods about 1580, but only in very small quantities. Algonquians probably increased their trade with the Hurons for corn. For the Hurons, the impact of receiving trade goods was significant; most of what they obtained was not utilitarian, but luxury items. They increased their numbers by allowing the Arendaronon and the Tahontaenrat to join the Huron confederacy and move into Simcoe County. The four Huron tribes continued to live in close proximity to the only supply of trade goods they could obtain.

The Hurons also began to supply trade goods in limited supply and at high prices to the Iroquoians living in southwest Ontario. A growing demand for trade goods from the south led the Hurons to have contact with other tribes, especially the Susquehannocks.

Possession of trade goods provided the impetus for Seneca and other neighboring Iroquois tribes to attack the Hurons. It was at this time that an important transformation took place. The largely ritual warfare of prehistoric times gave way to economic warfare.

The Hurons sought to establish their own trading relationship with the French. This action opposed the self- interests of the Algonquians who, like the Montagnais, wished to preserve their role as middlemen. As Iroquois raiders began increasing attacks on Algonquians in order to steal trade goods, Algonquians were forced to look for military allies. Soon they enlisted their Huron trading partners to become allied with them, and together they began to fight the Mohawks in the Saint Lawrence Valley.

French traders realized that a coalition of northern tribes would greatly increase the volume of furs from the interior. They sought to develop new trading posts upriver from Tadoussac, and make the Saint Lawrence River a main artery of trade. In 1608, Samuel de Champlain built a fortified trading post at Quebec, and the following summer, the French sought to intervene in the struggle to control the Saint Lawrence. They joined the Montagnais and Algonquians in an expedition against the Iroquois.

The French and their allies made the Mohawks' attacks on the Saint Lawrence Valley dangerous. The Mohawks were forced to abandon their quest for a time, but they soon found another source of obtaining goods by establishing a trade exchange with the Dutch who had begun to develop trading relationships in the Hudson valley and along the Saint Lawrence.

The Dutch, however, had their trading agenda. They sought to establish good relations with Algonquians and Montagnais in hopes of diverting rich furs away from French trading centers to their own. Since the Dutch also controlled sources of wampum in the vicinity of Long Island, they could offer the Indians this as well as European goods.

The Mohawks were aware that they had less to offer the Dutch than did their northern rivals, and their fear of again being prevented from trading with Europeans drove them to seize control of the area around the Dutch trading post, then called Fort Orange. Although the struggle lasted four years, the Mohawks were finally victors and gained control of the route to Fort Orange.

The Dutch had no choice but to comply with the Mohawks, and since the Mohawks would not allow the Algonquians, Montagnais, or any other northern group to trade with the Dutch except with themselves as middlemen, Dutch trading ambitions became severely crippled.

French-Huron Alliance

The first contact between Hurons and French was through Arendaronon warriors who accompanied the expedition by Champlain against the Mohawks in 1609. Two years later, Huron council chiefs sent an expensive present to Champlain and expressed their desire to have a trade alliance that was independent of their alliance with the Algonquians. The Algonquians naturally protested this threat to their role as middlemen, and Champlain was prevented from further visits with the Huron for several years.

In 1615, Champlain offered to assist the Hurons and Algonquians in raiding central tribes of the enemy Iroquois confederacy. Although the raid was a failure, it opened the door for Champlain to meet Huron headmen and create an alliance with them. The Algonquians were too few in number and too dependent on the Huron for corn and military assistance to prevent this trade alliance.

From 1615 to 1629, the Hurons traded with the French, and also traded with the Nipissings and Ottawas to obtain additional furs for the French. Hurons also traded with Algonquians in Ottawa Valley to obtain corn that was traded for furs, as the expanding fur trade required that Hurons have corn to exchange. The wealth from trade activities did not cripple the social system of the Hurons, but instead continued to strengthen it.

Because the lands of the Huron were remote from areas of European settlement, the number of Europeans who visited their region was small. Jesuit missionaries began their work in the area sometime after 1629, and their attempts at conversion of the Indians had enormous impact. One proof of this was in 1627, when a Huron trader allowed his son Amantacha to travel to France, where he remained for two years and learned to speak, write, and read French. After his return to Huron country, he became important as an intermediary between the Huron people and French.

Jesuits gained more strength in Huron country after 1634. Their goal was to convert whole communities rather than individuals, and ultimately to convert the entire confederacy. Although they did not succeed in their quest, they were eventually successful in upsetting the balance of the Huron social culture. After 1640, about 100 Hurons per year were converted. However, it is important to remember that the primary reason was not religious belief, but the fact that Christians were better treated than non-Christians in trading with the French, and they were paid a higher price for their furs.

The Jesuits created new factions within the Huron culture. The group was now separated into Hurons for and against one another, the French, and Christianity. The growing division within the Hurons came at a very disastrous time because the confederacy was fighting for its very survival.

Epidemics

Epidemics plagued all the Saint Lawrence tribes. A number of severe outbreaks left many groups in this region with declining populations. In 1634-1635, a number of Mohawks died from smallpox. Between 1635 and 1640, epidemics reduced the population of the Hurons from 20,000 to 10,000. In 1646-1647, another smallpox epidemic swept through the Iroquois country and killed over 1,000.

Not only were the deaths from epidemics horrific and devastating, but they also changed the structure of Indian society. Some of the tribes' great leaders died, and many of the groups suffered severely from a weakening or lack of effective leadership.

Iroquois Wars

Throughout the first half of the seventeenth century, all of the Iroquois tribes in the Northeast grew increasingly more dependent on European trade goods. This was especially true for the Mohawks and the Susquehannocks, as they lived closest to European trading posts. By the 1630s, Hurons were also greatly dependent on trade goods.

By 1640, beaver populations were dwindling. In that year, Iroquois furs were also being diverted by New England traders that had gained the Mohawk market by offering to sell them guns. The Iroquois became increasingly more militant, and began to steal skins from parties traveling with trade goods. Conquering whole villages of other Indians, they would plunder them before burning them to the ground.

It is speculated that by this time, Iroquois men were split into two factions. While half of the men were waging wars, the other half was hunting beaver for trade. Although the Iroquois were highly effective warriors, they did not cultivate any entrepreneurial skills in order to compete with other tribes for resources. They did not form alliances as middlemen, nor did they cultivate any trading relationships with tribes to obtain trade goods.

Only the Mohawks sought to secure French neutrality in trading. By 1642, western tribes of the Iroquois confederacy were attacking Huron villages to obtain furs. Many tribes of the Huron confederacy were attacked in a methodical matter, beginning with more remote communities on the eastern border and moving inward. Village by village, the Hurons were forced to disperse.

By 1650, Iroquois warriors had dispersed many of the tribes they had sought to destroy, and they now moved more westward and into Erie country. The Erie had gained strength by adopting many of the Huron who had been dispersed, and also by adopted many Neutral refugees. The Erie region inhibited the Iroquois from raiding and hunting in the Ohio Valley where beaver was plentiful.

In 1651-1652, the Mohawks attempted to attack the Susquehannocks, hoping to disperse them as they had the Huron. However, they failed because the Erie and Susquehannocks had become powerful and strong in number. In 1653, the Seneca led the Iroquois confederacy into the first general peace between themselves and the French. This peace lasted until 1658. However, their war with the Erie continued until 1657.

After 1650, the Mohawks became extremely aggressive in dealing with other tribes of the Iroquois, and the western tribes sought an alliance with the French. The conflict led to hostilities resuming between the Iroquois and the French.

In 1663, the power of the Susquehannocks was broken. But this did not come as a result of victory by the Iroquois, but by an attack by European backwoodsmen from Maryland and Virginia. The defeat of the Susquehannocks was the last of the Iroquoian groups that had surrounded the Five Nations Iroquois. The Iroquois victory did not, however, bring them the peace or prosperity they sought. The French were now able to trade not only in the north, but also to extend their trade routes into the lower Great Lakes and Illinois country.

Although the Iroquois launched a full-scale war with the Illinois in 1680, the attack not only brought them into conflict with their Indian enemies but also with Frenchmen who were competing with them for furs. The Iroquois were forced to enter into a new era, one in which they would have more direct involvement with European powers now establishing them selves in North America.

Rising mortality rates among Iroquois males due to war brought about social changes as well. Women had begun to play a greater role in village management and political activities than ever before. In a generally sense, women's political importance rose dramatically during this period.

GREAT LAKES-RIVERINE REGION PATTERNS

The societies that were established in the upper Great Lakes and in the valleys of Ohio and upper Mississippi were mostly Algonquian, along with some Siouan-speaking Winnebagos. Native Americans in this region were organized into two primary types of social and political organization.

The first type included the Shawnee, Illinois and Miami tribes, Sauk, Menominee, and Potawatomi; the Winnebagos reflected strong post-European Algonquian influence. All shared a maize agriculture economic base, and all tribes did seasonal hunting and gathering. Settlement patterns alternated between semi-permanent riverine villages in the summer months, and large camps during the winter. In spring and fall, camps would disperse.

Each tribe had a system of patrilineal clans that emphasized rituals and extended into political organization. Outsiders were integrated into the society. Each group was organized as tribes, and had a dual political structure that consisted of organizations for peace and war, and different officials associated with each.

The second type included the Ottawa and Chippewa who lived along the northern fringe of the region. Their settlement patterns were not primarily agricultural, but instead included fishing sites in the summer and dispersal the remainder of the year. Settlements were generally small. Patrilineal clans were present but weak. Political organization was of the band type, with some sporadic tendencies toward integration.

For the Potawatomi tribe, most members fell into Type 1, but some northern groups fell into Type 2. Several features suggest that this tribe was unique in that it shifted from the second type to the first at a relatively late date, probably during early historical time.

Although there were a vast number of differences between societies, each group within the two types shared significant features.

Type 1 Systems

Groups in this society were organized into patrilineal clans. Clan names were most often derived from animals or mythical beings, such as Wolf, Bear, Elk, Fox, Deer, Thunder, Water-Spirit, or Panther. Bird and fish eponyms were less common and more likely to be specific to a particular tribe. Plant eponyms were very rare.

At one time, clan and lineage relationships were equivalent, but after post-contact, the functions of lineages became somewhat eroded. However, lineage still determined political office and ceremonial leadership. Although members could punish infringements of some rights, lineages had no functions connected with land-holding and ownership of non-ritual property. There is some evidence that lineage determined residence, but this appears to have been strongest in the Menominee and Winnebago.

Clan systems of the group may be divided into several defined types. The first included the Sauk, Fox, Kickapoo, and Potawatomi. They had primarily group and cult names, and contact with the supernatural was achieved through the vision quest. Each clan was founded through a vision in which the clan ancestor was blessed by a spirit in the form of the eponym. The vision included instructions for ceremonies, and the person who received the vision was directed to assemble such ceremonies. Ritual societies consisted of persons blessed by the same spirit, and sometimes assumed certain clan traits such as inheritance of membership. Each clan owned a stock of personal names, which was given to each member shortly after birth, and reverted back to the clan stock at its holder's death. These names carried with them a degree of power derived from the vision in which the clan was founded. Clan names also were used for horses and dogs.

The Winnebago system had some differences, especially in the concept of descent from the eponym and a much stronger association of specific political functions with particular clans.

The Shawnee apparently restructured their clans during the nineteenth century, and many features of their earlier structure are uncertain. Instead of name stocks owned by clans, they obtained personal names from the dreams of name-givers that were called upon shortly after a birth. Positions in warfare, government, and ritual that were given to individuals or clans were based on qualities considered appropriate for the action required. Shawnee clans were not cult groups, and major ritual units comprised divisions or communities, each presenting annual ceremonies in which positions were given according to clan affiliation.

Among the Illinois and Menominee, only scanty information is known. It appears that Miami clans controlled names through a system similar to the Shawnees, and that they had a similar role in the organization of ritual and ritual aspects of warfare.

The Menominee clan system broke down before pre-contact, and thus little of it is known. However, it appears that they contrasted strongly with preceding tribes in that an elaborate origin legend described the formation of the clan system, and each clan owned a few eponymous names. However, these were primary titles given to certain adults. Ordinary names were derived from dreams of shamans or parents, and these were given without reference to clan affiliation. Individuals could obtain supernatural power through their eponyms or with their aid on an individual basis. There appears to have been some association between clans and political organization.

Type 2 Systems

The political organization of Type 2 tribes appears to have been loose and informal, although the use of ritual strongly parallels similar functions as Type 1.

Formal offices were usually held by men. There are occasional references to female chiefs; however, it is unclear whether these women actually held the office or whether they dominated their communities through ability. Potawatomi women were apparently an exception, as women were among those who signed several treaties with the United States. One Shawnee report states that a widow of a divisional chief would take over his functions until his successor was appointed.

Political Organization

For all tribes in the Great-Lakes Riverine region, political organization seems to have become more decentralized after contact. From large villages, many groups divided into smaller units. In general, a major division separated the institutions centering on peace from those centering on war.

Peace organizations were headed by a tribal chief and lesser chiefs of similar type who may have been clan heads. These officials had assistants who were called criers, ceremonial runners, and speakers. Peace organization chiefs were expected to show behavior appropriate to their role and avoid any display of anger or aggression. Participation in warfare was generally forbidden.

On the other hand, war organizations were based on hierarchy. The office appears to have been achieved through consistently successful leadership of war parties. War organizations were also headed by a chief and by lesser chiefs, as well as by a group of warriors who sometimes also carried out police functions and could enforce tribal regulations.

A third organization, called the tribal council, probably included both war and peace officials. All aspects of political organization were highly ritualized. War organizations enforced regulations on specific occasions, and the men who were charged with this duty were chosen by the war chief. Tribal councils were convened by the presiding chief, although these were classed with peace organizations, war officials were apparently present and discussions included issues such as war.

As was true in many other areas of North America, the political and social organization of local natives of the Great Lakes-Riverine region changed considerably and irrevocably after European contact.

White Exploration of Great Lakes Region

The first record of white exploration on Lake Huron was by Samuel de Champlain in 1615, while he was traveling in the Nipissing-Huron area. In his reports, he made many scattered comments about Indians to the west and north of Georgian Bay. From his accounts as well as those in the *Jesuit Relations,* generalizations have been drawn about the Indians of the Great Lakes during the early decades of the seventeenth century.

Ottawa and Chippewa tribes dwelled here. Many European reports also mentioned a system of exchange between the Nipissings and Hurons in which they traded fish and furs for corn. Intertribal bands and relationships were not determined by cultural or linguistic affinity. An Algonquian band would go to war against another group of Indians for a variety of reasons, but would fight against other Algonquians as easily as Iroquoian or Siouan groups.

Semi-nomadic hunting and fishing tribes of Algonquians dominated the Upper Great Lakes early in the century. Siouan groups (Dakota and Assiniboin) controlled the western edge of Lake Superior; other Siouans (Winnebago) lived along the western side of Lake Michigan. After 1650, scattered Iroquoian bands came to the Michigan side of the present Michigan-Ontario border.

Until the Huron-Iroquois war of the late 1640s, European contact had little impact on the area. However, Upper Great Lakes groups were familiar with French trade goods after their introduction by the Huron in exchange for furs. The Hurons were important middlemen in the French fur trade during the 1630s and 1640s, and although tribes from the area participated in the trade, no real evidence shows their culture or material possessions being affected significantly by their participation.

Native Americans after Contact

By the middle of the seventeenth century, the Neutral and then the Iroquois had begun attacks on indigenous tribes of southern Michigan in order to seize furs and expand their hunting grounds. Sauk, Fox, Mascouten, Miami, Kickapoo, and some Potawatomi retreated west into the prairie and wild-rice areas of Illinois and Wisconsin, where they encountered Menominee and various Siouan groups.

The contacts between tribes led to major cultural changes and created economic and political conflicts that led all the groups to become involved in the fur trade. Before this process was complete, Hurons and other Ontario Iroquoian groups (Petun and Neutral) experienced great difficulty with the French. In a major Indian war between 1648 and 1650, Iroquoian warriors burned five Huron villages, and many other villages were abandoned. The blow scattered the Hurons, and survivors were absorbed by the Petun, Neutral, and other groups. Huron and Petun who sought refuge in the Upper Great Lakes region came to be called the Wyandots.

After dispersal of the Hurons and through the 1690s, further economic and social upheaval took place as the French founded missions, forts, and trading posts. By the late 1660s, small French groups had penetrated from Quebec to Hudson Bay, West Lake Superior, and Green Bay. Key Jesuit missions had become established before 1670 in Western Lake Superior, Sault Saint Marie, and Green Bay. An important mission was built in 1671 at present Saint Ignace, Michigan, by Jesuit Father Jacques Marquette.

Before 1649, the Ottawas played a subsidiary role, while Hurons were the key middlemen in trade with the French. After the Huron-Petun dispersion, the Ottawa assumed a dominant role in trade exchange. For the next century, Ottawa and Wyandot villages were established side by side, especially in Chaquamegon Bay, Mackinac, and Detroit. The Wyandot became part of an uneasy arrangement with the Algonquian Ottawa, who were hunters and fishermen as well as agriculturists.

47

European Alliances

The European presence on the Native Americans became overwhelming. Beaver areas determined trade routes and tribal locations, and this led to the French establishing Jesuit missions. The missions became social and economic centers, encouraged by French traders and missionaries. Before long, military posts and mission centers attracted other bands. Such tribes as Nipissing, Fox, Sauk, Potawatomi, and Chippewa began to gather, along with the Ottawa and Wyandot, and considerable interaction took place. Native settlement patterns became altered, to the advantage of the economic and religious interests of the French.

As the distinct cultural and geographic identity of the Indians weakened, the French economic, religious, political, and military influences became stronger, and soon French interests were a major determining factor of the natives' activities. The Indians were aware of these changes, and sought the most advantageous alliances with Europeans to meet their own needs. In return, Europeans sought to ensure support of the tribes by giving gifts of trade goods and supplies.

Several important French centers were established in the late 1600s to discourage English encroachments, including Fort de Buade at Saint Ignace, Michigan; Fort Saint Joseph at Port Huron, Michigan; and Fort Saint Joseph at Niles, Michigan. North of Lake Superior, the French also built Fort La Tourette and Fort de Francais, both constructed to threaten British interests on Hudson Bay.

Warfare activities of Upper Great Lakes tribes also became greatly influenced by French interests. Smaller groups who, just a few decades earlier, were involved in local hunting, fishing, and warfare were now forming large groups from many tribes to travel in a large war party and pursue the goals of French powers.

In 1697, the French government ordered the closing of posts in the Upper Great Lakes region. By this time, the Mackinac center had become a key site for houses of worship and trading activities, for obtaining brandy, and for tribes and bands to meet. The Jesuits were blaming the army and traders of degrading the Indians, and said that many Indian women were experiencing major problems with the French. The Jesuits recommended closing the posts, and Fort de Buade at the Straits of Mackinac was abandoned in the late 1690s.

Cadillac convinced the French government to build a post at Detroit to prevent English penetration and to aid the Indians and French to establish a settlement. Fort Ponchartrain was built in 1701, and many Great Lakes Indians came to settle. Villages included those of Chippewa, Huron, Fox, Potawatomi, Sauk, and Miami. Mississauga, Shawnee, and other tribes sometimes came to trade. Detroit soon became a major center for both Indians and French.

After the Treaty of Utrecht in 1713, which ended Queen Anne's War, the French attitude changed. The treaty made the Iroquois English subjects, and the French logically feared that this would weaken their trade interests, since the treaty permitted both English and French to trade with western Indians. Also, the Indians were aware that English trade goods were less expensive and of better quality than those of the French.

A string of military and trading posts was established in the Upper Great Lakes region by the French, in response to the treaty. They included Michilimackinac in 1715, Fort Saint Joseph at Niles in 1715, and Fort Beauharnois in Minnesota in 1728.

French interests were not always harmonious. Intertribal disputes began being resolved by French and Indian allies, sometimes with fatal consequences on both sides. Many expeditions were sent out, and many of them failed. But they created even more hostility between Indians who were allies of the French and those who were not.

The French increased gifts and supplies to Indian allies in the 1740s in response to a series of minor revolts. The prestige and success awarded to Great Lakes Indians was closely related to French aims during the era. By the mid-1750s, Indian tribal and band names were used with less frequency as settlement patterns shifted and cultural differences between Indian groups decreased. Many village warriors of different groups now had muskets, iron hatchets, tobacco, knives, clothing, and other goods provided by the French. Cultural differences became subordinate to political and economic considerations.

The French and Indian War in 1756-1760 created a major change in Indian life. The event, a further extension of hostilities in Europe, forced Indians into yet another alliance with whites. Although most of the fighting took place in the eastern region of the country, many Upper Great Lakes warriors aided the French in expeditions at Pennsylvania and New York. After the English won the war, they seized control of the Saint Lawrence valley, and terminated all French military activity in North America. Algonquian tribes of the Upper Great Lakes were forced to make major adjustments as the primary political and economic policies affecting them were now British, enforced by British military operations.

British Regime, 1760-1796

Most of the major hostilities of the French and Indian War ended in September 1760 after Montreal and the French colony of Canada were surrendered to British forces. All French military posts in the Upper Great Lakes region transferred to British control. Although the end of the conflict did not produce immediate dramatic changes in the existing relationships between the French and Indians, due in part because the French civilian population remained, a new political system was implemented in which the British philosophy, objectives, and methods of administration would alter the life of the Indians in further ways.

The British victors were interested in pursuit of the fur trade. However, they also sought to expand colonization and settlement in North America, and to develop new resources and products such as mining interests, and agricultural and forest products. Their interest in native religions was limited.

At the time of Great Britain's victory, the Great Lakes region Indians had become more centralized near major forts and trading posts. The native groups had become increasingly more dependent on European trade goods for their existence, and had largely abandoned their former traditional tools and methods in response to more efficient and durable goods by the Europeans. The Indians' ability to provide for themselves had also decreased with the scarcity of important game animals and less emphasis on hunting, fishing, and agriculture for subsistence in favor of those activities that would be useful for trade. It was now essential for the Indians to participate in the fur trade, as this was the only way to ensure continued access to European staple supplies and trade goods.

Native culture changes accelerated and diversified ever more rapidly during the several decades after 1760 due to increased adaptation of European objectives. The Indians soon felt the effects of British policy changes. Trade goods and provisions were not freely dispensed to the natives as a means of securing alliance and cooperation, as they had been during French control. Instead, these goods and provisions were distributed only in exchange for commodities valued by the British, especially furs. Fraudulent trade practices, a fear of losing their lands, and the denial of guns and ammunition resulted in an Indian rebellion against the British in 1763, led by Ottawa Chief Pontiac. Fort Michilimackinac and other western posts were taken.

In response, the British imposed changes in Indian policies that were supposedly designed to benefit the natives, including one that reserved all lands west of the Alleghenies for the Indians, and one that prohibited

Indian land purchases except by royal agents. European traders were required to have licenses to conduct trade, and trade could only be done at major military posts, regulated by the officer in charge. Although this initially seemed to allow more freedom than had the French monopoly, since anyone could obtain a license, in reality it increased the number of traders, and fur-trade interests led to more competition in a now rapidly diminishing resource, with the result that fur-trade practices became more fraudulent. Although proposed new land policies had some positive results early in the era, after 1776 colonial land interests and the American Revolution caused a loss of any benefits.

Indian support and alliances were again promoted during the American Revolution. Native Americans were called upon by the British to assist in putting down the colonial rebellion, and most Upper Great Lakes groups, excluding the Sauk and Fox, aligned themselves with the British because they believed they were less a threat to their lands than the expansion-oriented American colonists. On the opposing side were the American revolutionaries, along with French and Spanish allies. Ironically, the Indians had again become allies with the losing side in a major conflict of European powers.

Although the primary battles of the American Revolution were fought in the East, major effects were experienced in the Great Lakes area as well. British forts were strengthened by Indian warriors, and the Indians left their homes to participate; trade became more difficult because a license and a pass were needed to enter the Great Lakes area; restrictions on ship passage into the area also slowed trade. The decrease in trade activity put severe hardship on the Indians.

After the Americans won the war, and especially after 1783, land policies presented more critical problems for the Indians. Western lands were viewed by Americans as conquered and, thus, available for development and settlement. Although the Indians were allotted reservations, and American settler encroachment was forbidden, much of their former lands were ceded to the American government to compensate for their part in the revolutionary conflict. The ceded land was eventually sold to American settlers, and the lands reserved for Indians were ultimately claimed by Americans. Indian rebellions were begun, and put down by American forces.

Although the British lost title to most of the Upper Great Lakes at the close of the American Revolution, they remained for a time at western posts and continued to control the fur trade and their Indian allies until 1796, when the posts were turned over to the Americans. Trading establishments such as the North West Company and the Mackinaw Company, established in the 1780s, introduced new trade patterns for the Indians.

Specific Indian bands and tribes during the period were relatively stable. Most of the Ottawas, Chippewas, and Hurons were in southeastern Michigan and adjacent Ohio. Smaller bands of Chippewa were living in Mackinac, Chaquamegon, Sault Saint Marie, Saginaw, and along the western shore of Lake Superior. A group of Ottawas also had a settlement at L'Arbre Croche on the northeast shore of Lake Michigan below Mackinac. The Potawatomi were located in southwestern Michigan near Fort Saint Joseph, and the Sauk and Fox were living in Wisconsin, although they had now moved farther north and west along the Mississippi.

American Regime, 1796-1800s

After the establishment of the American Fur Company in 1808, which was centered in Mackinac, the fur trade reached its peak. Subagents were scattered through the area, and this lessened the need for Indians to gather at central points. They now delivered their furs to settlements such as Grand Haven, Milwaukee, and Green Bay, where they would receive trade goods in return. Until the decline of the trade in the 1830s and 1840s, their annual cycle changed to one of trapping in the winter, delivering furs in the spring, and gearing up for the next winter's trapping activities.

Half-breeds, called Metis, became a strong force in fur trade and Indian life. In the villages around the Upper Great Lakes and west of Lake Superior, their numbers ranged in the thousands, and many had settlements of their own. Most Metis were French and Indian, although a considerable number were of Scotch or Irish ancestry. The Metis commonly held a higher position in the fur trade than did the Indians, as they were socially and culturally more European than Indian.

European conflicts continued to plague the American frontier. In the War of 1812, the Indians again were forced to choose between two foreign nations. Most sided with the British, assuming that if the Americans won the war, the country would soon be teeming with American settlers. Indians aided in successful attacks at Fort Mackinac and Detroit. Shawnees, led by Chief Tecumseh, were the most notable.

However, after this war ended, problems for the Indians intensified enormously. Once again, they had backed the side of the loser. In a series of treaties from 1814 to 1825, primarily controlled or encouraged by

Michigan territorial governor Lewis Cass, they were reminded of their error of participating with the wrong side during the war.

The Indian Removal Act of 1830 resulted in some of the Upper Great Lakes tribes joining other tribes and finding new homes west of the Mississippi. Potawatomis from southwest Michigan, along with Ottawas and Wyandots from Southeast Michigan, were removed to Kansas and Indian Territory. Some fled to Canada.

Periodically, pressure was put upon the government to remove large bands of Ottawa and Chippewa. Some Winnebagos were removed from Wisconsin to Minnesota. A comment from the *Minnesota Pioneer* dated December 29, 1853, states the position of most citizens who sought Indian lands and allegedly wished to protect the natives: "It is a fact, well established by experience, that the Indian and the white man cannot 'dwell together in unity,' and in nothing has the philanthropic justice of our Government been more apparent than in the removal of Indians from land to which the Indian title has been extinguished, before they become contaminated by intercourse with the whites on the ceded lands."

From the 1790s to 1870, a number of treaties were created by the United States Government to deal with the Indian problem. Many tribes sold their lands in Wisconsin, Michigan, and Minnesota. They were assigned reservations that slowly but surely diminished in area by later treaties. Americans were eager for the copper, lead, iron, and timberlands of the region, and in some cases, land surveys were already in progress at the time the treaties were ratified.

The federal government made some token efforts in the treaties that were meant to "civilize" the Indians; occasionally a blacksmith, carpenter, or farmer was placed at a reservation. The government also provided funding for Protestant and Catholic missions for reservation schools. The American Fur Company usually favored Protestants, and the Indians were frequently forced to take sides with beliefs and powers that they did not understand in order to conduct trade.

During most of the nineteenth century, superintendents and agencies handled Indian issues. Superintendents were responsible for specific geographic areas, while agents had responsibility for individual tribes or reservations. In Michigan, the superintendent operated in Detroit, while agents functioned in Mackinac Island, Traverse Bay, Sault Saint Marie, L'Anse, and Saginaw Bay. As white settlements increased, the influence of agencies decreased. After the Treaty of 1836, most Indian title to land in northwestern Michigan was ceded to the government.

By the middle of the nineteenth century, most tribes of the Upper Great Lakes region had experienced a common fate. Most were shifted from place to place, and many tribes were removed to areas in which they were ill equipped to adapt, such as the forest-dwelling Winnebagos who were moved to the Dakota plains. Multi-cultural activities were common, such as the Green Bay Agency, where Ottawas, Menominees, Chippewas, Winnebagos, and Potawatomis lived; all were Algonquian speakers except for the Siouan-speaking Winnebago.

Indians of different linguistic and cultural backgrounds changed their lifestyles to adapt to a new way of life. They were now far removed from their former hunting-trapping-gathering traditions, and were exposed to the problems of inadequate living conditions and influences by religious and social foreigners. Some of the agents attempted to end the old traditions, such as the traditional hatred the Chippewa and Sioux had for one another. Most efforts were unsuccessful.

By the late nineteenth century, most tribes had sold their best lands, and many were removed far from their traditional homes. Others were placed on small reserves.

Some of the Great Lakes Indians received a more favorable fate. In the 1830s and 1840s, many Ottawas and some Ojibwa left the Midwest and were settled on Manitoulin Island, Parry Island, and other parts of Ontario under British control. Because land pressures were not as intense in Ontario and Manitoba, many of the natives were able to maintain their traditional practices for a longer time than did those in the United States, where lumbering, mining, farming, and manufacturing continued to develop on lands that once belonged to the Indians.

History of Ohio Valley Region

The Ohio Valley was inhabited by a number of little-known tribes who were apparently sedentary. After the so-called Beaver Wars in 1680, this area became hunting lands. As the fur trade changed, the region underwent further alterations and was repopulated by groups whose original homes had been beyond its borders.

European contact affected some Ohio groups earlier than others. The Susquehannocks traded with the Dutch and the Swedes on Delaware Bay, and the southern area Shawnee appeared to have had early commerce with Spaniards. It may be assumed that epidemics introduced by Europeans spread along routes of native communications far beyond actual contact areas. Epidemics may have played a part in depopulating the region.

The dispersal of early Ohio Valley natives is generally attributed to the Iroquois, although there is some evidence that the Susquehannock also had a hand before their defeat in 1675. European exploration of the Ohio section came at a relatively late date, and its geographical location contributed to this. A mountain barrier of the east delayed entry by the coastal colonies, and the Great Lakes and Ottawa River further north provided easier access from Canada to the interior of the country and to the Mississippi. It was by this route that French explorers first reached the mouth of the Ohio.

Information about the people living in the Ohio Valley began with the Erie. They were mentioned in 1635 as one of a number of groups who spoke Iroquoian languages. According to reports by Jesuits in 1647-1648, they were forced to retire far inland to escape their enemies further to the west. (These enemies were apparently not the Iroquois, since they did not defeat and disperse the Erie until 1654.)

The French learned about the Ohio River in about 1670. Two years earlier, La Salle was in Montreal and learned from some visiting Iroquois that the river was a three-day journey from Seneca. The following year, La Salle visited the Seneca and was told that descending the river would be dangerous because both the Touguenha and Antastoez (Susquehannock) dwelled there.

In 1673, Louis Jolliet and Jacques Marquette descended the Mississippi and passed the mouth of the Ohio, where the Shawnee lived in great numbers. From Indian informants it was learned that the people of the Ohio spoke languages of the Algonquian and Iroquoian families. (Other languages may also have been spoken.)

To the west, Iroquois Indians had begun attacks on the Illinois beginning in 1680. They were slowed by distance and by the beginning of French-supported opposition. To the south, after dispersal of the Shawnee, raids and retaliations had begun with the Cherokee. All of this warring activity was called the Beaver Wars, and it provided the basis for official English and French official claims to the area.

The English claimed that the Iroquois had submitted their lands to the British crown in 1701, after their conquest of the Ohio country, and by the Treaty of Utrecht in 1713 were acknowledged as being under British dominion. At the same time, the French claimed the country on the grounds that La Salle had taken possession of it when inhabited by the Shawnee.

The Iroquois wanted possession of the Ohio Valley region not for habitation, but for hunting. After gaining possession through raids, they did not attempt to resettle the area. The French as well as other Indians challenged the Iroquois' right to these lands because they had been obtained through forcible possession.

In 1681, La Salle met a party of 40 Algonquians from the Hudson-Delaware area near the southern end of Lake Michigan. In 1686, a Miami war party was seen near Rochester, New York. Indians came into the area from two major directions: from the north, where the French were establishing posts along the lakes; and from the east, where the British had settled or acquired coastal colonies. It was this that set the stage for the later Anglo-French struggle of the fur trade.

The first of the new settlers from the north were the Wyandot (Huron) and Miami. Illinois, Ottawa, and others operated as French auxiliaries in the colonial wars. Kickapoo and Potawatomi tribes also came at a later date. From the east came Iroquois, especially Seneca, Delaware, and Shawnee tribes, along with some other small bands. Southern warriors included Cherokee, Catawba, and others who were British auxiliaries in the Upper Ohio region in 1757-2758.

The Wyandot and Ottawa were the first two groups settled at Detroit, aided by the French who operated a post there in 1701. Under French protection, the Wyandot hunted toward the Ohio.

In 1732, when the French encouraged the Shawnee to the upper Ohio, the Wyandot rejected any settlement in fear that this would upset their hunting rights. Trouble with the Ottawa led to Wyandot chiefs seeking to move elsewhere. Some located at Sandusky Bay under the influence of English traders and English- affiliated Indians. The Wyandot also had a small village or post on the Tuscarawas River.

In 1747, England and France were at war. The Wyandot broke with the French under Chief Orontony, who burned the village at Sandusky Bay and withdrew to Ohio country. About 100 warriors settled near Coshocton, Ohio at Conchake. Orontony and 30 others fled to the Beaver River. It is assumed that the Wyandot abandoned the Beaver River area in 1750 after Orontony's death. Those at Conchake returned to Sandusky Bay at the outbreak of the French and Indian War.

The first contact between the Miami and the French was in Wisconsin before 1670, but in 1680, a part of the tribe was at the south end of Lake Michigan. In the next 20 years, war and hunting parties of this group ranged into New York, Pennsylvania, and Maryland.

Fox refugees were marginal in the Ohio area. In 1712, two bands joined the Iroquois after being defeated by the Wyandot and Ottawa. Others joined the Seneca after problems with the French in 1730. Most settled on the border of Seneca country in New York; one group moved further down the Allegheny River.

Reentry into Ohio country from the east was made under Iroquois supervision, and involved groups interested not only in hunting but also in residence. Although these groups were classified as hunters and were unqualified to sit on council or negotiate with their neighbors, the Iroquois desired to settle dependent groups around their borders and create a buffer zone. They extended permission to the Ohio, where refugee Fox, Shawnee, and Delaware were allowed to settle on and near the Allegheny River.

For the Seneca, possession of Ohio country had specific advantages. They had the readiest access to the new hunting territory, and they also had the greatest opportunity to increase their numbers by adopting refugees and captives. However, they were badly situated for trade, since the Susquehannock banned them from any trade on Delaware and Chesapeake bays.

In 1690, the defeat of the Susquehannock allowed the Seneca to build a town called Conestoga in the Susquehannock Valley for trade with the south. A French post at Niagara in 1720, and later establishment of English trading activities to the Ohio further reduced the importance of this town.

Iroquoian settlements in Ohio were primarily family-sized settlements. Iroquoian families were also scattered among other populations.

In 1692, refugee Shawnee arrived in Maryland. One band received permission from the Iroquois to settle on the upper Delaware; the move became the start of a long and respected relationship between the Delaware and the Shawnee. Another group received Iroquois permission to live on the lower Susquehanna in 1701.

However, the Iroquois kept a close watch over their former enemies, and after a small disturbance in 1728, they ordered the groups to leave the area and go back to Ohio. By 1731, the Shawnee had established three towns on the Kiskimintas River, and later settlements were established on the lower Allegheny and upper Ohio rivers.

In 1734, a Shawnee division from the south killed a Seneca chief. The French sought out the Shawnee in order to offset the work of English traders, but the French were unsuccessful until 1745, when Martin Chartier's half-breed son Peter persuaded the tribe to plunder traders of Pennsylvania and decamp down the Ohio. Instead of remaining on the Wabash where the French had allowed them to settle, they divided and part followed Chartier to Alabama, while the remainder settled at the mouth of the Scioto River. Along with other Shawnee on the Ohio, this group enlisted Iroquois aid in 1748 for renewed friendship with Pennsylvania. A French minister in charge of the colonies at the time wrote that these Shawnees had formed a kind of republic that was dominated by Iroquois of the Five Nations.

British colony traders who were active in the Ohio country, along with resident Indians, were finding it difficult to negotiate with the Iroquois Council at Onondaga. Without permission, they began direct negotiations with one another. The trading post at Logstown became the site for treaties between Pennsylvania and Virginia officials with the Indians. The colonies and a Seneca spokesman designated Shingas (a Delaware) as the ruler of these people. The trade republic was added to by Wyandot and Miami that had defected from the French in 1747. However, it was disrupted by French occupation of the Forks of the Ohio in 1754. Logstown was torched and pro-British followers retired to eastern Pennsylvania and then to Iroquois country in New York.

The Shawnee defected to the French, and a new village was built for them at Logstown. Ohio Iroquois who accepted French occupation lost their status after the British were victorious in 1758; some who remained formed detached, roving bands that were later identified as Mingo. The Iroquoian League retained considerable prestige and influence. However, the British had no further need to support claims to the Ohio country, and the Iroquois were not in any position to repeat warlike activities of the previous century.

Delaware migration to the Ohio country was sporadic and piecemeal. By 1737, the Delaware had sold all their land in Pennsylvania and were primarily living on lands assigned to them by the Iroquois. Some Delaware later settled as far upriver as present Warren. Others moved down the river to and below the Forks of the Ohio; by 1751, their farthest boundary was a town on the Scioto a few miles above its mouth. These Delaware became part of the Logstown trading complex. Lacking any unified tribal organization, they accommodated themselves to the French military occupation of 1753-1759 in a variety of ways that ranged from retirement to attacks on English settlements.

The war and subsequent British occupation accelerated the western movement of the Indians. Scattered Delaware groups contributed in the 1760s to a resurgence of the "Delaware nation" under leadership of King Netawatwees. Although he did not succeed in uniting all the Delaware, his influence survived his death in 1776.

Shawnee bands around the Scioto River were less successful. The fugitive band in Alabama returned from the south and moved to Illinois. They may have rejoined those living on the Scioto River after the French defeat in 1760. A group was involved in hostilities with Virginia in 1774.

American Revolution

At the onset of the American Revolution, the Delaware underwent a difficult time; along with their western neighbors, the Miami, they shifted their settlements westward; some small parties broke away and crossed the Mississippi.

The second dispersal of Indians from the Ohio Valley was final. Pontiac's War in 1783-1784 was a somewhat planned but partly spontaneous uprising. It involved most British groups of the area but failed in its attempt to end British occupation and halt English settlement. At the first Treaty of Fort Stanwix in 1768, the Iroquois surrendered claims to lands south of the Ohio to the Kittanning. The eastern section of this area was the first part of the Ohio Valley that the Indians lost to white settlement.

After the American Revolution, the new nation handled the claims of the Indians of Ohio in two treaties. The first was with the Iroquois at Fort Stanwix in 1784, and the second was with the western tribes at Fort McIntosh in 1785. The Iroquois surrendered to the United States all their claims to lands west of New York and Pennsylvania. In separate negotiations, they released to Pennsylvania all land claims within that state. The settlement at Fort McIntosh was repudiated by the Indians, but eventually the Delaware and Wyandot also released their holdings. The Treaty of Greenville in 1795 was a further loss of Indian lands that included almost all of the Ohio Valley in the present state of Ohio. Other tribal cessions, both individual and collective, followed, and by 1818, the Indians had released almost all of Ohio and most of Indiana south of the Wabash.

The government sought to expedite white settlement and began to move the tribes to reservation lands beyond the Mississippi River. However, the final cessions of Ohio Valley lands were delayed until 1840, at which time the Miami surrendered their tract around Kokomo, Indiana. In 1842, the Wyandot released their land at Upper Sandusky in Ohio.

History of Illinois Region

The Illinois region was early occupied by a group of 12 related villages or tribes that were later referred to as the Illinois Confederacy. Included were the Kaskaskia, Maroa, Cahoka, Tamaroa, Peoria, Tapouaro, Coiracoentanon, Moingwea, Chinkoa, Espeminkia, Michigamea, and Chepoussa. This confederacy was never as politically organized as the Iroquois Confederacy.

In about 1673, when Europeans first extended into the Illinois region, the Illinois occupied a roughly triangle section; the base extended from the Chicago River westward into western Iowa, the eastern boundary extended southward through eastern Illinois along the Mississippi-Wabash watershed, and the apex was located in northeastern Arkansas. The French referred to this area as the "Illinois country." Until 1717, it was under the authority of New France, and afterward the portion south of a line eastward from the mouth of the Illinois River became part of Louisiana.

During the late prehistoric period, the Miami lived immediately to the east of the Illinois; this group included the Wea and Piankashaw, who later were regarded as distinct groups. The Shawnee were further to the east. The Sauk, Kickapoo, Fox, and Mascouten lived on the lower Michigan peninsula, and to the north of them were the Potawatomi. All groups were linguistically related to the Illinois. However, traditional mistrust and inherent differences discouraged any close or lasting alliances. All took up residence in Illinois country at different times throughout the historic period.

North and northwest of the Illinois was the land of the hostile Chiwere Sioux and their linguistic kin, the Winnebago. South of the Ohio River and southwest were unfriendly Dhegiha Sioux. Beyond the western limits and the Mississippi River lived the Pawnee and Arikara, Caddoan-speakers who were traditional enemies of the Illinois.

During the mid-seventeenth century, a westward thrust by the Neutral and then the Iroquois exerted strong pressure on tribes to the east and northeast of the Illinois. By mid-century, the Miami and their related tribes had moved westward and settled in northwest Illinois and adjacent sections of Iowa and Wisconsin from which the Chiwere Sioux had earlier withdrawn. Tribes in Lower Michigan had withdrawn around the head of Lake Michigan into northern Illinois and southeastern Wisconsin. From the Straits of Mackinac, the Potawatomi had moved westward to

Washington Island and the Door County peninsula of Wisconsin. For reasons still unknown, the Dhegiha Sioux abandoned the lower Ohio River during this same time.

History of Upper Great Lakes Region

The Iroquois first attacked the Illinois about 1655. Periodic raids as far as the Chicago River and upper Illinois were to plague the Illinois throughout the next half-century. When the Illinois were not directly threatened by the Iroquois, their warriors often waged battles against the Quapaw, Osage, and northern Sioux.

About 1667, the Illinois became firmly associated with the French. When a mission was established at Saint Esprit and the nearby trading post near La Pointe, small groups of Illinois became frequent visitors to the post and mission. They also visited the French trading center at the Miami-Mascouten village about 1670.

In 1673, Louis Jolliet and Father Jacques Marquette visited three villages of Peoria and Tapouaro on the Iowa River. A rumor that the two visitors intended to set up a trading post and mission on the Illinois River resulted in bands and villages of Illinois coming to the Kaskaskia village the following year. The mission of the Immaculate Conception of the Blessed Virgin was established among the Kaskaskia. By 1680, La Salle found some 11 tribes of Illinois living in lodges at Grand Kaskaskia Village.

The threat of an Iroquois war party in September 1680 caused most of the Illinois to abandon the Grand Kaskaskia village and move to the Mississippi. After destroying the village, the Iroquois pursued, and the Tapouraro, Maroa, and Espeminkia tribes who had chosen to remain at the mouth of the Illinois were attacked and suffered heavy losses.

The Illinois reassembled on the Ohio River after Henri Tonti constructed Fort Saint Louis at the top of Starved Rock in 1682. Shawnee, Miami, Wea, and Piankashaw were also present, as were some 18 Eastern Algonquian warriors and their families. A new village was established across the river, and some 4,000 warriors represented a population of about 18,000 people. However, the community was plagued by intertribal distrust and jealousies, and the Miami elected to abandon the area in 1688. The Shawnee left the following year.

The Kaskaskia village site was abandoned in 1691, and a new village called Pimiteoui was established lower on the Illinois River. Tonti relocated the fort and trading post close to the area. The mission was also moved. The community had 260-300 lodges and a population of over

61

3,500 in six groups that included the Peoria, Coiracoentanon, Kaskaskia, Monngwena, Maroa, and Tapouaro.

As Kaskaskia Indians became more Christianized, their relationship with the Peoria became strained. Two events led to the community's eventual demise; England's restriction of trade to the Illinois River, and Pierre Le Moyne d'Iberville's arrival at the mouth of the Mississippi. The Kaskaskia left the village in 1700 after hearing about d'Iberville's plan to relocate the upper Mississippi. They traveled as far as the Des Peres River across the Mississippi from where the Tamaroa settled. The two tribes joined together the next year and, in 1703, they moved the village to the mouth of the Kaskaskia River. In 1714, an epidemic reduced the community by about one-fourth.

The Mission of the Immaculate Conception, under direction of Father Gabriel Marest, went with the Kaskaskia to the Kaskaskia River, and missionary influence continued until the Jesuits were banned from the Mississippi in 1763.

Other tribes in Illinois country also relocated: The Tamaroa moved to the eastern side of the Mississippi River and established a village near the present village of Cahokia. The Cahokia tribes also moved near the Tamaroa. In 1700, the two villages had about 90 lodges. The Moing-wena remained with the Peoria.

To the south, Chepoussa and Michigamea were forced to withdraw up the Mississippi due to hostility with the Quapaw. By 1693, they had settled on both sides of that river near the mouth of the Kaskaskia. Many of the smaller tribes were generally absorbed into larger ones, resulting in a loss of a clear individual identity for some groups.

In the next six decades, three Illinois populations existed. Michigamea and Kaskaskias on and near the Kaskaskia River totaled some 250 warriors; Cahokias and Peorias at Cahokia had 200; Peorias on the Illinois River totaled 50; altogether there were more than 2,500 individuals.

Soon after 1710, the arrival and development of a French agricultural-based society in Illinois country created a situation in which previous trade-mission-garrison relationships waned. Contentions now arose over land ownership and social discrimination. In a move to alleviate tensions in 1719, the commandant at Kaskaskia requested that the Indians remove from the French settlement. All the existing tribes moved away from the settlement, but in close proximity to their former communities.

Despite some harsh treatment from the French, the Illinois remained constant in their loyalty and continued to deal with them after English possession of Canada. They harassed the British during their 10-year occupation of Fort de Chartres. They also supported the colonies in the American Revolution, and during subsequent confrontations with British.

Due to their loyalty, the Illinois were attacked by the Fox and other pro-British followers to the north, and occasionally by the Shawnee and Chickasaw from the south. The Cahokia suffered heavy losses when their village was destroyed in 1752, and survivors settled near the Michigamea.

Peorias were forced to withdraw from the Illinois River valley on several occasions, the last in 1769. After the Peoria killed Ottawa chief Pontiac, a combined force of Ottawa, Potawatomi, Chippewa, Fox, Winnebago, and others attacked and forced the Peoria to withdraw. Abandoning their traditional homeland, they settled on the western side of the Mississippi.

In the last three decades of the century, Illinois tribes were confined to the waters of the Kaskaskia and Big Muddy rivers. Struggles with Piankashaw, Kickapoo, Potawatomi, and Shawnee ensued, with heavy losses for all tribes. The Kaskaskias ceded their land south of a line drawn eastward from the mouth of the Illinois River, with two small tracts reserved on the Big Muddy. The remnants of the Illinois in the state established their last village in their traditional homeland on one of the tracts.

In 1832, the Peoria (including the Tamaroa, Michigamea, and Cahokia) ceded their land north of the line, and the Kaskaskia ceded their two remaining tracts. The last of the Illinois thus withdrew permanently from the Illinois county.

Miami, Wea, and Piankashaw. The Miami tribes included the Atchat chakangouen, Kilatika, Mengakonkia, and Pepikokia, and sometimes also included the Wea and Piankashaw, although both these groups maintained political independence until the nineteenth century.

After they withdrew from the Wabash-Saint Joseph region in mid-seventeenth century, the main body of the Miami settled in central and southwest Wisconsin. Some went to northwestern Illinois. The Wea and Piankashaw settled in western Wisconsin, and some went into northern Iowa.

In 1679, Green Bay traders aided a group of Atchatchakangouen, Mascouten, and Wea to settle on the Saint Joseph River to prevent La Salle from gaining access to the Illinois on the Illinois River. After attacks from Iroquois, they accepted La Salle's invitation in 1682 to make peace with the Illinois and move near Fort La Salle on the Illinois River.

The combined population of villages near the Iroquois River and Fort Saint Louis was about 7,500.

However, the Miami found it difficult to overcome their traditional distrust of the Illinois, and in 1688 they abandoned the area. Some settled on the Mississippi, and some returned to the Saint Joseph River. A few years later, they moved down to the Wabash. The Wea occupied the area of Chicago until 1698, when French trade was restricted. In about 1717, they moved to the Wabash River, where they established the village of Ouiatonon. A French post was also established nearby.

Shortly after 1700, the Miami of the Maramek and Miami in Wisconsin moved to the eastern side of the Wabash between the Wea and Piankashaw. In time, their range extended eastward into Ohio. The Miami established a firm attachment to the British, along with Wea and Piankashaw.

In about 1800, small bands of Miami, Wea, and Piankashaw moved to the western side of the Mississippi. Treaties beginning in 1803 ceded their land to the government. In 1828, the last of the Piankashaw left Illinois. The Wea left Indiana in 1832. The Miami made a last Indiana land cession in 1840.

Sauk and Fox Tribes. After moving from Michigan, the Sauk (Sac) settled on the lower Fox River of Wisconsin, and the Fox (Masquaki) removed to the upper Fox River southeast to the Chicago River.

Loyalty of the Sauk vacillated between the British and the French. Fox warriors defended the French until their tribe was almost destroyed in 1712 at Fort Ponchartrain. The incident began the "Fox War," a retaliatory effort in which Fox were joined by Mascouten and Kickapoo. In 1730, some 300 Fox left the area and moved to New York to join a band that had settled with the Seneca some 20 years previously. They were intercepted in central Illinois and suffered heavy losses. They eventually returned to the Fox River.

In 1733, the French determined to settle the problem with the Fox by destroying them. The Fox sought sanctuary with the Sauk, but eventually both groups were forced to abandon the fort and remove to the banks of the Mississippi. In 1743, the French persuaded some Sauk to return to the Fox River.

The Sauk and Fox continued to vacillate during the French and British conflict. At the conclusion of the war, they promised loyalty to the British, but continued a close contact with French traders who had moved across the Mississippi into Spanish territory. At the outbreak of the American Revolution, the two tribes were again split in their loyalty.

After an American attack on Rock River villages, the tribes turned against the Americans and supported the British through the War of 1812. (A negotiation in 1804 by Governor William H. Harrison of Indiana Territory had already relinquished claims of Sauk and Fox to all land lying east of the Mississippi.) Although the main body of both tribes denounced the treaty, it was ratified by each near the close of the War of 1812.

By 1829, most Sauk and Fox had moved to the western side of the Mississippi. Black Hawk eventually accepted the treaty of 1804 and moved into Iowa, but he refused to abandon the ancestral burial ground on the Rock River and continued to visit annually. He visited the site in 1832, in defiance of an agreement made in 1831, and General Henry Atkinson defined this as an invasion of the United States. A subsequent military campaign resulted in a defeat of Black Hawk and his followers at Bad Axe Creek, and the Sauk and Fox left Illinois.

Kickapoo and Mascouten. The Kickapoo and Mascouten moved from Michigan with the Sauk and Fox. In 1679, a band of Mascouten joined in the effort to cut off La Salle's approach to the Illinois country. After the failure of the effort, they later reoccupied their old village on the Fox River. Internal conflicts resulted in some Mascouten joining the Miami, while others joined the Fox. The main body joined with the Kickapoo.

In 1702, a band of Mascouten moved to the mouth of the Ohio, but the following year, smallpox decimated this community. Survivors settled on both sides of the Wabash, and were joined by other groups. Eventually they lost their individual identity and were absorbed by their neighbors, especially the Kickapoo.

The Kickapoo were the most conservative tribe in the Illinois region, and thus they maintained a general anti-European position throughout the early historical period. They became attached to Nicolas Perrot, an Indian agent and trader, in 1685. They were a small tribe, and some joined with the Wea during the early 1700s, and some with the Fox. By 1717 they had been reduced by about one-third. Internal conflicts within the group were strong until they turned against the Americans who were moving into the Wabash valley. Some of their villages were destroyed. They joined with Tecumseh and in 1811 suffered in the defeat of Tippecanoe, and the following year some of their towns were destroyed on the Sangamon and one at Peoria.

After 1800, small bands began moving to the west of the Mississippi, with an acceleration of emigration after destruction of the Prairie towns. In 1819, two groups in separate treaties ceded their lands in Illinois and

Indiana, providing they could still hunt and live on the land. In 1832, the government ordered their removal to Kansas.

Potawatomi, Ottawa, and Chippewa. Potawatomi tribes moved into the Green Bay area from the Straits of Mackinac about 1641. They became allies of the French until 1699, when restricted trade caused relationships to deteriorate. Several bands moved to the Saint Joseph River and sought contact with the British, but they were unable to establish a relationship with the Iroquois. In 1712, they resumed friendly contact with the French at Fort Ponchartrain.

After the Peoria were driven from the Illinois valley by the Three Fires Group, the Potawatomi occupied the whole of the upper Illinois River valley. They remained loyal to the French through the French and Indian War. After the conflict ended, they continued to trade with the French. However, conflict with American colonies caused them to support the British, which continued through the War of 1812. Although some Potawatomi leaders retained a friendship with American settlers, especially Shabonee, the majority continued an anti-American movement.

The economy of the Potawatomi, based on fur-trading, lasted into the first quarter of the nineteenth century. The increasing density of white settlers denied them access to beaver ponds, and buffalo and wapiti had diminished in number. Small bands were forced to move west of the Mississippi. Land cessions began in 1816, with others in the 1820s and 1830s. After each cession, populations were displaced and groups moved west of the Mississippi. By 1834, there were few Potawatomi left in Illinois and Indiana.

Shawnee and Delaware. The Shawnee spoke Algonquian, and were often victims of Iroquois attacks. Groups on the upper Ohio River sought security with the French, and began to appear in large numbers in Illinois in 1683.

When relationships with the Illinois became strained, and after the Miami withdrew from the Fort Saint Louis community in 1688, the Shawnee also withdrew the following year. Joining neighbors on the Cumberland River in Tennessee, they became attached to the British. They began more frequent attacks against the Illinois.

After 1759, the Shawnee returned to the Scioto River. The Delaware also moved down the Ohio and settled among the Shawnee on the Scioto and westward into Indiana. A large body settled in Missouri in 1787, and Illinois became a thoroughfare between the Scioto and the Mississippi. Shawnee again occupied the Shawnee- town site, and Delaware settled nearby, along the western bank of the Wabash and on Saline Creek.

Although the Delaware established a relationship with the Kaskaskia who were their neighbors, the Shawnee did not attempt to establish villages in the area. They encroached on Illinois hunting grounds on the eastern side of the Muddy River, and strong resistance from Kaskaskia resulted in a final confrontation in 1802, when Shawnee warriors took a heavy toll on a Kaskaskia village. The Shawnee continued to pass through southern Illinois until the nineteenth century was underway, but they did not claim the region.

Winnebago. The Winnebago's traditional lands were in the Lake Winnebago-Green Bay region. However, reduced by warfare and disease, they became dependent on their newer neighbors, the Potawatomi, Sauk, and Fox. They were allies of the French, and enemies of the Illinois. Their intent to destroy the Illinois resulted in the expulsion of the Peoria from the Illinois River valley.

Before 1770, the Winnebago began moving onto the headwaters of the Rock River. After the Middle Rock valley was abandoned by the Kickapoo, they moved into the region and had direct contact with the Sauk and Fox on the Mississippi River.

Some Winnebago were actively involved against the Americans during the War of 1812. Most of the tribe declared themselves at peace with the government in 1816. In 1829, the group ceded the region in Illinois that the government had designated as Winnebago land, but they were granted fishing and living rights. When Black Hawk defied the government in 1832, the Winnebago Prophet was still living at Prophetstown 40 miles up from the mouth of the Rock River. The Prophet aided his nephew Black Hawk, and then joined him in the retreat up the Rock River. Later in the same year, the Winnebago ceded their remaining lands in Illinois and left the area. The Menominee intermarried with many of their native neighbors in later historic times, and many small groups attached themselves to Potawatomi, Fox, Miami, Sauk, and Winnebago, often only temporarily. However, these relationships account for the fact that Menominee families still live in northern Illinois, especially on the Fox and Rock rivers, and also in mixed villages identified as Menominee that are located in the area.

CONTEMPORARY NORTHEAST INDIANS

Of the many tribes of Indians that inhabited Maine at the time of the white man's coming in the early seventeenth century, only two remain: the Penobscots and the Passamaquoddies. They are all that is left of the Abnaki or Wabenaki, 'people of the dawn,' a once powerful nation of more than twenty tribes inhabiting parts of Canada, Maine, Vermont, New Hampshire, and northern Massachusetts. The Passamaquoddies and the Indians of the Saint John River are descendants of the ancient Etchimins, a seafaring people who were originally a branch of the Abnaki. However much they differ in customs and in dialect, both of these tribes derive their language and principal characteristics from a common Algonquian stock. They are the least disintegrated racially of all the present-day descendants of New England's aborigines; many families among them have a heritage unmixed with white or African blood. But their tribal distinctions have long since become blurred by interassociation with the remnants of other vanishing tribes, and by the effacing of many of their traditions under the stress of modern industrial life. Also, they have adopted some manners and costumes entirely foreign to their former heritage.

The Penobscots live mainly on a reservation at Indian or Panawamske Island in Old Town; The Passamaquoddies or Pestumokadyik (people who spear pollock) have reservations at Pleasant Point near Eastport, and at Peter Dana Point near Princeton. There are probably less than one thousand Indians of fairly unadulterated stock in Maine today, the majority of whom live at Old Town; but that is a considerably larger number than was estimated to be living in the State almost two hundred years ago.

The Indians of Maine have always been a peaceful and friendly people, living chiefly by agricultural activities. It was they who kept the early settlers of Massachusetts alive by sending presents of food to the settlements. They were ultimately aroused to violent action only by the prolonged aggression of the settlers and by being forced to take sides in the English-French struggles. And when they did rise up, whole tribes were remorselessly exterminated. It is a significant fact that the custom of taking scalps was not known among them until instituted by English officers. Today they live harmoniously among themselves and with their white neighbors, and in general maintain high standards of conduct.

The Indian villages are primarily autonomous in government, each electing its own officer. The tribes may send representatives to the State legislature, although the people are not citizens. Most of them are deeply religious, the majority being members of the Roman Catholic Church. They have convents and schools, the latter supported in part by the State. Each summer the Old Town Indians present an historical pageant. They commonly dress in conventional clothes. Many speak English, own their homes, drive automobiles, and indeed are indistinguishable from their white neighbors. They are, however, taught to speak their native language at an early age, and much is being done among them to preserve their native traditions and arts.

For most of them, each family has an inherited income from funds held in trust for them. In 1786, a treaty confirmed to the Indians certain lands as well as financial gifts. These lands were sold at various times to Massachusetts and to Maine for considerable sums, to be held for the Indians and their descendants. In 1818, Massachusetts agreed to pay the Penobscots the following: one six-pounder cannon, one swivel, fifty good knives, two hundred yards of calico, two drums, four rifles, one box of pipes, three hundred yards of ribbon; and in October of each year, "as long as the Penobscots shall remain a nation," to give them five hundred bushels of corn, fifteen barrels of wheat, seven barrels of clear pork, one hogshead of molasses, one hundred yards of double-width broadcloth (red one year and blue the next), fifty good blankets, one hundred pounds of gunpowder, six boxes of chocolate, one hundred and fifty pounds of tobacco, and fifty dollars in silver, or their equivalents.

Since for many years, certain families did not draw upon the sums due them, among the Indians today there must be persons of considerable wealth. The average Indian takes up his income in trade at the agency store. The Penobscot tribe now receives further compensation from the corporations using the Indian shore on the river above Old Town. The tribe owns all of the one hundred and forty-six islands above Old Town, with a total area of forty-five hundred acres. The Indians work as river-drivers and as guides to hunting and fishing parties, and they make baskets that they sell tourists.

The Penobscots are sometimes erroneously called Tarantines, a name for an earlier tribe or group of tribes. The Puritans called the Abnaki 'Tarrateens.' Among the Penobscots today live descendants of Baron de Castin, who married the daughter of Chief Madockowando 'of the Tarrateens,' but the latter was an Etchimin and not a Penobscot. It may be that the Pentagoets of Castine, the remnants of the so-called Tarantines of de Castin, have moved to Old Town and joined with the Penobscots. There was once a clan or totem system among the tribes, but it is now largely obliterated. The Bear Clan, one of the largest groups, still has representatives among both Pasamaquoddies and Penobscots, who say the clan originated with a lost child who was brought up by a mother bear. Joseph Polis, the Penobscot Indian who served as Thoreau's guide in the Maine woods, used a drawing of a bear on his canoe as a personal emblem. Old Governor Neptune, the Penobscot descendant of a long line of chiefs and governors, used the sign of the snake, signifying mental prowess.

The office of chief or governor (president, sachem, or sagamore) was formerly held for life, but in 1862 it became annually elective. Even so, the same man often held the position through life, and from him it might pass to his son – as in the Attean family. Dissension at the elections gave rise to the 'Old Party' and 'New Party,' which now take turns in electing officers each year. One of the most famous governors was Joseph Orono, for whom the town of Orono was named – a blue-eyed Indian believed to be a natural son of the Baron de Castin. He is said to have saved Maine for the Union by rallying his men to the aid of the whites in the wars with the Mohawks. He died in 1801, at the reputed age of one hundred and thirteen. Another Indian equally revered was the saintly Aspinquid, one of John Eliot's converts who did much toward spreading Christianity and peace among the New England tribes.

It was the Abnaki, indeed, who of the North American Indians first embraced Christianity. In the past, Saint Aspinquid's grave-marker could be found, high on Mount Agamenticus; it bore this inscription:

> Present Useful: Absent wanted.
> Lived Desired: Died Lamented.

The Indians no longer practice many of the old crafts of making fish-nets, spears, bows and arrows, wampum, carved pipes, and pottery. Such things as canoes, snowshoes, and moccasins, formerly produced by them, are now more efficiently turned out in large factories. But the Penob-scots still excel in basket-making. The Passamaquoddies also make baskets, but are more expert as fishermen and hunters. Baskets are usually made from the flexible wood of the brown ash, although basswood and sweetgrass are also used. With Penobscot women, sewing is a fine art; but weaving seems always to have been unknown to them. Lovely designs are made by threading dyed quills upon cloth or leather. Some striking examples of Indian carving and painting are occasionally seen.

Before their movements were restricted by white settlers, the Indians used to wander with the seasons, according to the location of food supplies. In the spring they went to the rivers for alewives, shad, and salmon; on the banks they planted corn, squash, beans, and other vegetables. In June they went to the sea for porpoise and seal in order to get oil and skins, and for the eggs and nestlings of sea birds; they dried clams and lobsters, and stored them for winter use. In September they returned to the river valleys to harvest their crops, and in October they went into the big woods to hunt.

Before Christmas they held their annual thanksgiving feast for not less than two weeks. Our national Thanksgiving Day is a direct imitation of the Indian celebration, even including the foods we cook and serve: turkey, cranberries, Indian pudding. When snow came they went into the deep woods hunting for moose and setting traps. Before the ice broke up in March or April, they had made their spring catch of otter and beaver. When the ice broke and the river was clear, they were ready for the catching of muskrat; they could start out in their canoes to fish and go to the lower valleys for the planting. Throughout Maine, the scene has actually changed but little since the time of the Indians' supremacy.

Maine, in recent years, has seen the Penobscot and Passamaquoddy Indian tribes successfully challenge the doctrine of "federal recognition." United States Bureau of Indian Affairs (BIA) advice was made available to some Indian groups, largely in the west, south, and, southwest, but not to others, including all New England tribes. In 1972 the tribes asked the United States Department of Justice to file suit on their tribe's behalf against the state of Maine for taking land illegally in 1794, in violation of a 1790 statute. When the government refused to do so on the grounds that the Penobscot and Passamaquoddy tribes were "recognized" or eligible for federal protection, the tribes filed suit against the Federal Government challenging this administrative decision.

In a landmark decision, *Passamaquoddy versus Morton,* the federal district court ruled in January 1975 that the tribes should receive federal protection and ordered the government to file suit for them. This decision, which was upheld on appeal, is generally accepted as the first step to making Indians who are not federally recognized, to be eligible not only for Federal protection but also for Bureau of Indian Affairs services.

The two tribes continued their demands that the state return land taken in violation of the Non–Intercourse Act of 1790. The federal government agreed to rile the suit if the claim was not settled out of court, and the Departments of Justice and the Interior have said that the Indians have a valid legal claim to five million acres of forest land in northern Maine. Because of the suit, not only land transactions but also many other state projects such as federally–funded public works programs were stalled for several months. In the spring of 1977, President

Carter appointed a special federal mediator to help both sides reach an agreement to be approved by Congress.

The issue of federal recognition and the problem of inadequate state and federal services to Indians began in the early 1970s. Following a study of the plight of the Maine Indians, a major recommendation was the extension of federal protection and Bureau of Indian Affairs services to the Maine Indians. Among other recommendations made to the federal, state, and local governments, those for the creation of a state office for off–reservation Indians and an Indian police department were subsequently implemented.

The Indians have exacerbated long–standing mistrust, animosity, and misunderstanding between Indian and non–Indian residents of the state. Both deep–seated racism and a lack of knowledge and appreciation for Indian culture have been reported.

Public education through publications, public forums and other meetings, and more material on Indian history and culture in public school and university curricula are needed to promote understanding between Indians and non–Indians. Equally important is the speedy conclusion of the negotiations on the Indian land claims.

The long–neglected social, economic, educational, health, and housing problems of Indians both on and off reservations also must be addressed. In recent years, extremely high unemployment rates on some reservations, inadequate housing, and serious health needs existed. These problems recently were documented again at a hearing held in Boston, Massachusetts, which was sponsored by the Northeastern Regional Office of the United States Commission on Civil Rights.

As a result of *Posamaqudddy v. Morton,* Bureau of Indian Affairs and Indian Health Service programs are now available to many Maine Indians. However, the budgets of these agencies are limited, and the bulk of their services continue to go to Indians on reservations in the Southwest and West. Other federal departments, and particularly the state government, have been urged to increase aid to Maine Indians.

At least half the state's Indians live off–reservation. Most of these Indians are members of the Micmac and Malism tribes, which are not eligible for help from the Bureau of Indian Affairs or the Indian Health Services, because their reservations are located in Canada, across "the white man's border." Despite the establishment of a unit within the main Department of Indian Affairs to serve off–reservation Indians, these Native Americans remain among the poorest of citizens.

Of New Hampshire's, Maine's and Vermont's Indians, in fact of all the large and populous groups that once inhabited the Northeast, few remain today. Although a number of small tribes became decimated by epidemics, wars, and by dispersal, others became absorbed into larger groups and lost their individual identity. For some tribes, the only evidence of their former existence remains in the place names of locations where they once dwelled.

Some Indians of the Northeast have lived in relative isolation and poverty since their removal to federal or state reservation lands. In many cases, allotted lands have slowly but surely diminished in size. However, some groups have sought to reestablish tribal rights and gain economic independence. A number of large Northeast tribes, along with the tribes who were adopted by them, have recently fought for additional lands and resources.

The Micmacs, with a population of 482 residents, now live in northern Maine. The group has established tribal and intertribal councils and political groups, and has revived traditional arts, organizations, and language. In 1991, they gained recognition of their tribal status and together with 28 other bands in Canada formed part of the Micmac Nation. In 1982, the Aroostook Micmac Council was incorporated, and established its headquarters in Presque Isle.

Another Coastal tribe that has somewhat overcome adversity is the Delaware, who now live in scattered communities of Ontario and Oklahoma. Although many were formerly unskilled laborers, increasing numbers have sought to become professionals. In recent years, scheduled events have gathered together leaders from scattered communities, and increased efforts to renew contacts between all Delawares have been aided by such organizations as the Delaware Nation Grand Council of North America, incorporated in Ohio in 1992.

The Huron-Wyandots of the Saint Lawrence region have also gained political and economic strength by making scholarships available, providing daily meals for elder residents, creating a health center, and purchasing land in Park City, Kansas for the purpose of building a gambling casino. They have begun efforts to preserve and maintain their heritage, including establishing a library of archives.

Mohawk communities and lifestyles underwent major changes in the twentieth century. Former farming, dairy cattle raising, and sport fishing activities have been replaced primarily by iron-working activities, which is considered a source of pride and self-esteem by many Mohawks.

However, political differences between traditionalists and more acculturated members have continued to plague some Mohawk communities.

Seneca-Cayuga Indians maintain reservation lands in Oklahoma. Their population of 2,460 continues to practice tribal rituals, and many are involved in ranching. Many members of the Tuscarora tribe who live in Lewiston, New York are employed in industrial plants and in structural steel work.

Of the large population of Shawnees who formerly lived in the Great Lakes area, three bands currently reside in Oklahoma: the Absentee Shawnee, the Eastern Shawnee, and the Loyal Shawnee. Each group derives income from a number of industries including farming, livestock, small businesses, and other mainstream American activities. Most members also maintain their tribal culture, including seasonal dances.

The Sauk and Fox tribes today are federally recognized as the "Sac and Fox of the Mississippi in Iowa." They are known as the Mesquaki Nation (Red Earth People) and live near their tribal-owned settlement on the Iowa River. Many grow corn and soybeans, and others work in surrounding communities. In the 1980s, the group established the Economic Development Zone and opened a bingo facility. These economic opportunities have not weakened Mesquaki kinship ties or their sense of family. Religious ceremonies and powwows continue to dominate their cultural life.

A number of other reservations have also established health centers, funding for homes, scholarships, and cultural centers. Many former laborers now hold skilled positions, especially in iron working. Many of today's steel bridges and skyscrapers were built by a variety of Indians. In addition, educational dropout rates have been reduced significantly in some groups.

Although it is true that a few tribes from the Northeast have maintained their traditional hostilities towards other groups and non-natives, many have instead focused their energies on reestablishing tribal customs and maintaining cultural identity. Educational opportunities, self-sufficiency, and employment advances continue to help some Native Americans gain a sense of pride. Celebrations and rituals, once such a large part of Indian societies, were abandoned but are again being practiced.

INDIANS OF NEW HAMPSHIRE AND THE NORTHEAST
A to Z

ABNAKI

The Abnaki (sometimes called Abenaki) are a group of coastal Algonquian tribes that lived in the area that is now Maine, New Hampshire, Vermont, eastern Quebec, and the Canadian Maritime Provinces. The Missiassik Tribe of Abnaki lived in the Missiquoi River valley in Franklin County, Vermont. Their village, of the same name, was on Lake Champlain at the mouth of the Missiquoi.

"Abnaki," (more correctly, Wabanaki) from *wabun* ("light") and *dik* ("land"), means "people from the eastland or land of sunrise, or "dawn people." The Puritans called these people Tarratines. The name Abnaki is also applied more narrowly to a tribe that formerly lived along the Kennebec River in Maine and now reside in Quebec on Odanak Reserve near the Saint Francis River, at Becancour near Trois Rivieres, and further north in Cacouna.The Western Abnaki, treated elsewhere occupied most what is now Vermont.

The Abnaki group includes the Penobscot of Penobscot Bay and the Penobscot River; the Passamaquoddy of Passamaquoddy Bay; the Malecite of Saint John's River; the Micmac of the coast of New Brunswick, Nova Scotia, Prince Edward Island, Cape Breton, and Newfoundland; and the Abnaki tribe proper. The Malecite and Passamaquoddy together were sometimes called the Etchemin. The Pennacook of New Hampshire are sometimes classed with the Abnaki group on linguistic grounds, although in culture they may have been somewhat closer to more southerly Algonquian–speaking tribes. In historic times the Penobscot, Passamaquoddy, Malecite, and Micmac joined into a political unit termed the Wabanaki Confederacy.

Language and culture. Some linguists consider Eastern Abnaki (Penobscot) and Western Abnaki (Saint Francis) to be two distinct languages, with a complex history resulting from the absorption of speakers of other dialects. Nevertheless, recent findings indicate that all the Abnaki tribes had one and the same language. The Micmac, however, have a more diversified dialect. All the Abnaki spoke related Algonquian languages.

In precontact and early colonial times, Abnaki political organization did not go beyond the level of the hunting band. Each band respected the hunting territories of every other band. These small bands generally hunted and trapped moose, elk, beaver, otter, muskrat, and other animals during the winter months upstream along the watercourses.

In the summer they fished for alewives, shad, and salmon, and gathered shellfish along the lower courses of the streams and along the seacoast. They also harvested wild plants and perhaps such products as maple sugar. At the time of European contact, the Malecite and some other groups were growing maize (corn), fertilizing the fields by placing one or two surplus fish near the roots of the plants.

Tobacco may also have been grown or received in trade from tribes to the south. The office of chief has always been regarded with deep respect and honor among the Abnaki. The British and the French tried to belittle the place of the chief, or at times they tried to manipulate the chief into persuading his people to sign over land to the foreigners, but the Indians, for the most part, maintained their strong sense of respect for the position of the chief.

Religious beliefs focused on numerous supernatural beings, for example, the god of the forest, the god of thunder and lightning, and so on. One of the most prominent gods was Glooskap (abbreviated from *Gelowasid–skidup*, meaning "good man") who was believed to have created man by shooting at ash trees with his bow and arrow: the Indians came out of the bark of the trees. The Abnaki believed that Glooskap was capable of doing extraordinary good things for them and bad things to the evil spirits.

They believed that he was an example for them of how they were to live, much as Christians believe in Jesus Christ. Animal tricksters, in the form of badgers, rabbits, raccoons, wolverines, and lynxes, were also prominent in Abnaki mythology. Although the Abnaki legends have come to be regarded as fairy tales, each one had a meaning and a message about life.

With the Europeans, beginning in the sixteenth century, came the fur trade, a development that increased the importance of beaver trapping in the Abnaki economics and led to social changes.

Family hunting and trapping territories became more formalized. Boundaries were marked by natural landmarks such as rivers, brooks, trees, and hills, and in some cases, perhaps, by blazing marks upon trees. Territories were inherited through the male line. Larger and more permanent settlements developed along the major rivers, with both summer residences and established villages. Houses were conical and were covered with birch bark or woven mats. Each was occupied by several families. Some of the villages were enclosed in palisades, and each contained a large, oblong council house, Iron received in trade began to displace stone, bone, wood, bark, and antler in arrowheads, tomahawks, axes, knives, kettles, and other implements.

Guns began to displace bows and arrows. Imported beads replaced shelf ornaments, and European clothing replaced native furs. Birch bark canoes, however, remained the major mode of transportation. The structure of the family bands, each named after a land or sea animal, also became more formalized, and the chief became, in addition to being a leader in the hunt and in war, the commercial representative of the band in the fur trade. Christian rites and beliefs were adopted, sometimes subordinating aboriginal ones, but not eliminating them entirely. Polygyny and shamanism, opposed by the missionaries, gradually declined.

Finally, pressure from Iroquois (particularly Mohawk) attacks and European incursions led to the formation of the Abnaki Confederacy, which was similar to the League of the Iroquois. Within the Abnaki group the delegates of each tribe had equal influence in the councils. According to some observers, however, the Penobscot were considered the leading members and were referred to *as* "older brothers" by the others. By the mid–eighteenth century, the Abnaki made peace with the Mohawks and established an alliance with them and with neighboring Algonquian tribes led by the Ottawa. The alliance lasted some 100 years.

History. The Abnaki tribes may have encountered Norse visitors as early as AD 1000, but continuous contact with whites (French and British fishermen at first) did not begin until the sixteenth century. In 1604 Samuel de Champlain visited several Abnaki bands, and friendly relations were established with the French. French missions were successful in making converts to Christianity among these groups.

English settlement of their area began about this time, but ill–treatment of the Abnaki, including kidnapping and enslavement, gained their enmity. Much land was signed over to Englishmen, the Indians probably believing that they were agreeing to share their lands, not to sell them. As a result, the French succeeded in attracting Abnaki support in their dispute with the English over territory, and they provided weapons for the Abnaki to use against the English.

The Abnaki proper and some others gradually withdrew from Maine to Canada and, after King Philip's War (1675 – 76). Many of the survivors fled their homelands, settling eventually at Saint Francis in Quebec. The withdrawal was essentially completed after the outbreak of the French and Indian War in 1755. From there they continued to fight New England settlers until 1759, when an English force attacked and burned Saint Francis and killed some 200 men, women, and children.

The end of French power in North America generally ended the hostilities between the Abnaki and the British. The Penobscot, Passamaquoddy, and Malecite had remained in their traditional lands, and in 1749 the Penobscot made peace with the English and accepted fixed bounds. Many of the Penobscot and Passamaquoddy now live on reservations in Maine. The Mjcmacs concluded a peace with the English in 1760, but disputes lasted until 1779.

Population.   The Abnaki, including the Penobscot and Passamaquoddy, may have numbered about 3,000 in 1600. Contact with Europeans soon brought a decline in population through the introduction of new diseases (among them smallpox, tuberculosis, and syphilis) and alcohol, through the depletion of food resources and the replacement of the balanced native diet with imported European foods, through intertribal conflict fostered by the fur trade, through war with the English, and in general through the social disorganization wrought by all these factors.

About 800 Abnaki lived in Quebec (at Odanak, Becancour, and Cacouna) in a recent count. In the Maritime Provinces there were about 5,000 Abnaki, including 2,000 Malecite and 3,000 Micmac, in New Brunswick; 5,000 Micmac in Nova Scotia; 1,000 Micmac in Prince Edward Island; and 400 Micmac in Newfoundland, More than 1,000 Passamaquoddy and 800 Penobscot Indians were enrolled as tribal members in Maine in recent times. They were legally wards of the state and were untaxed.

ADARIO

Adario (Tionontati, ? - August 1, 1701) was a chief whose sabotage of a peace effort between the French and the Iroquois Confederacy led to a massive Iroquois attack on settlements in New France, now Canada.

In 1688, the French enlisted Adario's support against his hereditary enemies, the Iroquois. Early in his mission against the Iroquois, Adario stopped at Cataracuoy, now Kingston, Ontario, Canada, where the French Commandant told him to halt his expedition because an Iroquois embassy soon was expected in Montreal to negotiate a peace. However, Adario, fearing that his people would be abandoned to the Iroquois for the sake of French self-interest, ambushed the Iroquois delegation.

Adario told the Iroquois that the French had commissioned him to kill the party. When the Iroquois stated their mission, Adario feigned surprise and outrage at the alleged French treachery. He released all but one of the Iroquois, the one remaining to replace one of his own men who had been killed in the ambush, and urged them to take revenge on the French.

Adario took his single captive to the French at Michilimackinac, who had not yet heard of the plans for peace with the Iroquois, and who therefore put the prisoner to death. To be certain that the confederacy learned of his act, Adario released a long-held Iroquois prisoner from his own village and bade him tell the confederacy that Adario had been unable to save the man.

The Iroquois, believing Adario's representations, were enraged. On August 25, 1689, some 1,200 Iroquois attacked Montreal, where they killed hundreds of French and burned their houses. They also raided other settlements on the Saint Lawrence River. The French were saved from extinction only by their strong forts.

Adario was later converted to Christianity and became a friend of the French. In 1701, while part of a delegation concluding a peace treaty at Montreal, Adario became ill and died. The French buried him with military honors.

AGAWAM

Agawam means "fish-curing place," and the name occurs frequently in Massachusetts and throughout southern New England, and on Long Island. "Agawam" designated at least three Indian villages or tribes in Massachusetts.

The most important of these sites was at Ipswich, Essex County Massachusetts. The Agawam Chief sold the site in 1638. Its jurisdiction included the land on Newbury River, and the tribe was a member of the Pennacook confederacy. It was almost extinct in 1658, but as late as 1726 there were still three families living near Wigwam Hill.

The second tribe or band of that name had its chief town on Long Hill, near present Springfield, in Hampden County. Springfield was sold in

1635 and the Indian town was in existence in 1675. This tribe was commonly classed with the Pocomtuc.

The third was near present Wareham, in Plymouth County, the site of which was sold in 1655. It was probably subject to the Wampanoag, but was joined in the plot against the English in 1621.

The larger tribes of the Pennacook and Pocomtuc also lived in the valleys of the Merrimac River in New Hampshire, and the Connecticut River in Vermont, New Hampshire, Massachusetts, and northern Connecticut and in neighboring areas. Their descendants, along with the Agawam, now live with the Saint Francis Obnaki in Quebec, Canada. They spoke Algonquian languages.

EUSTANCE AHATSISTARI

Eustance Ahatsistari (Huron, ? - August, 1642) was a chief who distinguished himself in warfare against the Iroquois Confederacy, the traditional enemy of the Huron.

In 1641, Ahatsistari and 50 Huron warriors defeated about 300 Iroquois. Earlier, under his leadership, the Hurons had routed a large party of Iroquois in war canoes on Lake Ontario. In August 1642, while leading a small party of Huron and French up Lake Saint Peter, Ahatsistari and his group were ambushed by a band of Mohawk Indians. He was killed several days after the ambush.

ALGONKIN

"Algonkin" deserves being differentiated from "Algonquian," "Algonquian Family," and "Algonquin." The true meaning or significance of the term "Algonkin" remains uncertain, but Hodge in 1907 thought it might have come from the Micmac *algooomeaking,* or *algoomaking,* "at the place of spearing fish or eels (from the bow of a canoe)."

Algonkin, as a designation, originally applied only to the Weskarini Band. They were most easterly division of the Chippewa group of the Algonquian linguistic stock. The Weskarini held the north side of Ottawa River below Allumette Island and on Gatineau River, The Lieure River, the Petite-Nation River, and the Rouge River. To the south of the Weskarini were another of the Chippewa group, the Ononchataronon, that occupied the land between the Saint Lawrence and Ottawa Rivers, and near Montreal.

Since *Algonkin* first referred to only the Weskarini, but later to the Ottawa River Valley group, and *Algonquin* later meant the same group plus more related bands to the east, neither term should be blurred in meaning to also designate the "Algonquian Family," which refers to the widespread group that speaks the same language in eastern and central Canada, along the north Atlantic seaboard, and in the western Great Lakes region of the United States.

Again, this same source for *Algonkin* was later applied to *Algonquin*, which contained more bands and sub-bands of the area. However, in 1927, Day believed *Algonquin* was derived from the Maliseet *elakomkwik* "they are our relatives (or allies)." Samuel de Champlain was the first to record the word and wrote it *Algonquian*. In 1632, *Algonquian* appeared in the Jesuit Relations for the first time. Regardless of its origin, early writers quickly used the term to denote the varied Algonquian-speaking Indians in eastern Canada, and are therefore the dastardly culprits responsible for centuries of head-scratching.

Territory. However convoluted the trail may be, the original Algonkin band that bore the name was the source for the term that later was applied by the French to the group of closely related bands in the Ottawa Valley and adjacent eastern areas in the first half of the seventeenth century.

Another of the related groups, The Kitchesipirini, lived west of the Weskarini,on Morrison's Island in the Petawawa River, and are often called Algonkins of the Island. Directly south of them was the Keinouche Band. Further south, along the Madawaska River, also a tributary of the Ottawa River, was the Matouweskerini Band. Westernmost of the group were the Otaguottouemins, along the Ottawa River itself

Original Algonquin subdivisions were the: Abitibi, around Lake Abitibi; Barriere, near Kakabong and Barriere Lakes; Dumoine, on Dumoine Lake and River, in Ontario; Kipawa, on Kipawa River, Maganasibi River, and the north bank of Ottawa River opposite Mattawa; Lac des Quinze, Lac des Quinze and to the north and east; Maniwaki or River Desert, from the upper course of the Riviere Lievre to Black River; Sagaiguninini, southwest of Ottawa River; Timiskiming, on and near Lake Timiskaming.

Known Algonkin-related villages were at: Egan, Maniwaki township, Ottawa County, Quebec; Hartwell, in Ottawa County, Quebec; at Isle aux Tourtes, mission from Algonkin and Nipissing, which was probably first located on Ottawa River, but was soon moved.

Language. They all spoke mutually-intelligible dialects of the Algonquian language family. The Algonquin language is classified as belonging to the "middle tier" of Algonquian, along with Ojibwa, Ottawa, and Salteaux. The Middle Tier is defined as a single language, with

81

contiguous dialects that were mutually understandable. Although the relationship between Algonquin and Ojibwa is obvious, it is perhaps not as close as has been assumed on the basis of data from the Lake of Two Mountains mission, which held both Algonquins and Nipissings. By 1850 Algonquin had disappeared, and the combined groups in fact spoke Nipissing.

History. The French encountered the Algonkin-related bands when France began to settle Canada in the early 1600s. The first historical mention of the tribe was in 1603 at Tadoussac, as participants with the Montagnais and Etchemins in a victory celebration after defeating the Iroquois after a war that had gone on since about 1570. They also appear to have been trading for some tiome with the French, and had aligned with the Montaganais against the Iroquois.

It is likely that earlier they held part of the Saint Lawrence valley, and had been at peace with the Iroquoians of that area. The Algonkins soon became attached to the French, and in the French and Iroquois Wars, many bands of Algonkin-related Indians were forced from their homelands. Some joined the Ottawa, but others quickly spread east and north until the fighting died down. Since then, despite all, they have remained in the same area although they have of course endured great hardship during steady, forced changes to their culture by intruding Europeans.

The Algonkin (Weskarini), as did their related nearby bands, lived in thick forests of pine and hardwoods, and quite naturally they fished, hunted, trapped, and did a small amount of farming. They had particular interest and involvement in Trois Rivieres. After the French-aided conflicts with the Iroquois, peace returned in the 1620s, and some Algonkins mixed with the Montagnais and settled there to do limited farming. The Algonkin and related bands became embittered when the French established direct trade with the Hurons, a more powerful group, and they did all they could to harass Huron traders and to pit them against the French. The effort backfired, however, as this required the French traders to live with the Huron, encouraging them to travel through Algonkin territory.

Throughout history the Algonkin and their allied bands were buffeted by the Huron, Iroquois, Mohawk and others. They had many decades-long wars with them over trading rights with the French, control of hunting territory and the like. The Algonkin and kin would ally with one or another of the invaders in order to fend off yet another. They tried to place the French and Dutch at odds to maintain the middleman role in trade throughout the area. The 1600s were wild, tumultuous years for them. In the early 1640s the Weskarinis had to flee to the Kichespirinis to escape the better-armed Mohawk, the biggest enemy of the moment.

In 1634 they made yet another peace treaty with the Mohawk. Oumasasikweie, a headman of the Kichesipirini, and Tessouat, the principal headman of the band, hoped the treaty would permit them to travel through Mohawk country for trade with the Dutch. However, when Oumasasikweie tried it, the Mohawks killed him and all his party, obviously not particularly anxious to let the fur-rich Algonquins start trading with the Dutch.

Here we go again. This started a new war between the tribes. The growing need of the Mohawks for furs turned it into a fight for survival. The Iroquois obtained the most guns, which made them the victors.

It was not long before the Kichespirinis had to weather the resulting series of crises by taking refuge in French settlements along the Saint Lawrence River. The French made peace with the Iroquois and abandoned the non-christian Algonkins and their local brethren. Some moved to the Jesuit Mission at Sillery after it came to being in 1637, but the easterly bands centered in the Trois Rivieres area.

The so-called "peace" of 1645 allowed the aggressive Iroquois to hunt the edges of Algonkin territory, and they stripped it of 2,000 deer that first winter. In 1646 the peace was shattered when the Mohawks treacherously killed Simon Piskaret, the most respected of Algonkin-related warriors, who were considered better fighters than the Mohawks. However, They could not seem to coordinate their battle efforts, despite an attempted alliance with the Attikamegues, the Montagnais, the Micmac, and the Nipissing.

The Algonkins and their associated bands were forced out of Ottawa Valley between 1650 and 1675, and little is known of them during that period. Some went to the Lake Saint John region and stayed there at least 60 years. The Kichespirinis and their 400 warriors commanded enough respect to allow them to remain on Morrison's Island. The French had to retreat from the Hurons in 1650, and Tessouat added to the indignity of their flight by having the Superior of the Jesuit Mission suspended by his armpits for refusing to offer the customary gifts for being allowed to cross their territory.

Almost all of those that joined the mission at Sillery died during epidemics by 1676. The French encouraged others to remain at Trois Rivieres, and there they stayed until the final few families were exiled to Oklahoma Indian Territory in 1830. New missions took in more of the ousted Indians in the late 1600s and early 1700s

83

Whatever hunting territory they had south of the Saint Lawrence River was taken by the Abnaki during the latter part of the 1600s. Some eastern Abnaki from the Androscoggin River actually asked permission to settle. Thereafter relations between the two groups were good, and they agreed upon the Saint Lawrence River as a dividing line.

After 1701, when the Iroquois and French made peace, trade began between Albany and the northern Indians. The Algonkin-related bands remained loyal to the French during the frequent conflicts with the British. They began to prosper somewhat by trading furs, and relied little on farming. About 1750 some of the bands became members of the confederacy of French mission Indians, called the Seven Nations of Canada. In the last half of the 1700s, the Two Mountain Algonquins and others became involved with the big fur-trading companies. A group that settled on Golden Lake in 1807 eventually had a reserve established there in 1870.

Gradually, during the first half of the nineteenth century, many Algonquin and Nipissing familes moved from Lake of Two Mountains to River Desert, and had their own reservation established at Maniwaki in 1874. Other bands still on the Gatineau and Ottawa rivers in the 1800s were the Atibibi, Grand Lake Victoria, Kipawa, Mattawa, Lake Dumoine, Quinze Lake, and Temiskaming. Lesser bands continued to live at Lac Simon and Lac Barriere. Today's descendants still regard the region of Mazinaw Lake, Otter Lake, Baptiste Lake, and Bonnechere and Mattawa Rivers as their territory south of the Ottawa River. Unfortunately, it was sold long ago by the Iroquois, Missigaus, and Ojibwas. During the twentieth century many non-reservation Algonkin-related Indians continued to live on the Lievre and the Ottawa Rivers.

Culture. The Algonkin culture was a combination of the bordering subarctic and northeastern cultures. The Huron were on their southeast, and the Montagnais on the east. The Cree were most likely to their north and the Ottawa were on their west and southwest. The Ottawa were their most important neighbors, and with whom they eventually merged.

Knowledge of their culture is quite limited. The bands of the seventeenth century were probably patrilineally extended, and appear to have lived together in a single village in the summer, taking advantage of good local fishing. They must have dispersed in hunting parties during winter. They lived too far north to have a good growing season, so corn did not play a large part in their lives.

They did some planting of crops that could ripen quickly, however, including some maize, beans, and squash. Europeans introduced peas about 1600, and the Indians made good use of the crop from then on. They also fished with nets through the ice during winter, and enjoyed eating dogs, a practice abhored by the Montagnais. They tended their guests but did not eat with them, and smoked tobacco silently before anything of importance was discussed.

They apparently borrowed from the Hurons the turtle-shell-rattling ceremony to cure illness. They built longhouses, but this was not peculiar to the Algonkin-related bands. They also borrowed the craft of splint basketry from the Abnaki or the Iroquois. Important individual's graves were covered with painted, ridge-roofed structures about seven feet long and four feet wide. At one end was placed a figure representing the dead person.

Regardless of where their customs came from before contact with Europeans, it is evident that twentieth century members have many of the same traits and characterisitics of neighboring forest peoples. Some shared myths and legends include: a supreme being, owner of all; a trickster-transformer culture hero; The Windigo; the *Pa kahk;* a diembodied starveling, the *pakwacininiwak,* a race of powerful little men; shamanism and the shaking tent; the dream vision quest; scrying and scapulimancy. They had the typical world-view of a hunting-fishing people.

Major material items were the birchbark canoe; snowshoes; the toboggan; rectangular bark huntin camp structures, birchbark containers, porcupine quillwork insome of the southern band areas; moosehide tumplines; basswood bags, mats, and temporary tumplines; deer and moosehide clothing; cradleboards and blanket hammocks; moccasins of beavertail and deernose types; bows, preferably made of hop hornbeam. Maple sugar was made by some of the bands, and they all had an extensive knowledge of plants and their properties.

Population. There may have been about 6,000 Algonkin-related Indians before contact with whites. In a recent count, in Quebec there were some 200 at Barriere Lake, 250 at Grand Lake Victoria, 300 at Lac Simon, 950 at River Desert, 5 at Argonaut, 15 at Hunters Point, 100 at Kipawa, 300 at Long Point, 425 at Timiskaming, and about 75 at Wolfe Lake, for a total of about 2600.

In Ontario in recent times there were about 500 at Golden Lake, and an unknown number in the Ottawa Valley that were unaffiliated with any reserve. The total population appears to be stable, having shown a small increase during the 1900s. (See ALGONQUIAN, ALGONQUIAN FAMILY, and ALGONQUIN)

ALGONQUIAN

"Algonquian" refers to the group of languages that, at the time of the first white exploration and settlement of North America, was spoken along the Atlantic Coast from Labrador to the Carolinas and westward in what are now Canada and the northern United States as far as the Great Plains. Two languages of northern California, Wiyot and Yurok, are closely related to Algonquian, making it an extremely widespread language family.

The exact relationships between the Algonquian family and several other groups of North American Indian languages are still under study, but the Algonquian languages have been shown to resemble languages spoken around the Gulf of Mexico, a relationship that may date back 5,000 to 6,000 years.

Number and name. Although the distinction between a language and a dialect is often difficult to make, at present it is generally believed that Algonquian comprises nearly 30 distinct languages and numerous dialects (see table). The name of the language family derives from the name "Algonquin," which first appears in the records in 1603 as "Algounequin," a tribe encountered by the French explorer Samuel de Champlain in Canada. The name probably comes from the Malecite word meaning, "they are our relatives or allies."

General characteristics. Despite their differences, the Algonquian languages share certain basic features. (Arapaho, Blackfeet, and Cheyenne, of the western Algonquian area, exhibit the most differences, but these arise as generally superficial historical changes.) The languages are polysynthetic or incorporating, that is, their word forms are long and morphologically complex containing numerous bound morphemes (units of meaning that cannot appear alone as words) which would be translated by several separate words in English. Single words may constitute whole sentences in themselves. The languages are also inflective, for example, the words change in form to mark such distinctions as tense, person, number, case, and gender. Algonquian nouns are classified into two genders: animate and inanimate.

Among the former are all persons, animals, spirits, and large trees, and certain other objects, including tobacco, maize (corn), raspberry, and nettle. Nouns are inflected for number (singular and plural), with different endings for the two genders. Suffixes and, much less frequently, prefixes tire employed; inner stems are also modified, as by reduplication (repetition of part or all of the root form). Case is weakly developed.

86

In Algonquian, as in classical Greek and Latin, syntactical and morphological features correspond closely to each other, with most grammatical categories and functions having unique morphemes associated with them. As in Latin, and in contrast to English, word order is of secondary importance: the arrangement of words is less a matter of primary grammatical relations than of rhetorical style. .

Historical changes. By studying various Algonquian languages, linguists have reconstructed the proto–Algonquian language, the ancestor of the modern Algonquian language family. Furthermore, by re–constructing words for flora and fauna, one scholar has proposed that the proto–Algonquian people may have lived in the, eastern upper Great Lakes region about 1200 to 900 BC. The Algonquian peoples were, of course, greatly affected by white occupation, and dislocations, particularly in the path of the most intensive white settlement, occurred.

The western Algonquian–speaking peoples generally moved westward and southward into the Great Plains region. Delaware, once spoken in New Jersey, New York, Pennsylvania, and Delaware, now survives among small groups in Ontario and Oklahoma. Kickapoo, once spoken in Michigan, Illinois, Indiana, and Kansas, now is heard in Mexico and Oklahoma. Some languages, such as Abnaki, absorbed speakers of other dialects. Other languages, particularly along the Atlantic Coast, where white impact was early and strong, have disappeared.

The data on these languages are often quite Limited: for example, in the case of Beotbuk, which was spoken in Newfoundland but disappeared in the early nineteenth century, the information is so limited that it can only be said that the language probably belongs to the Algonquian family. It is not known whether any languages disappeared for which no record remains today.

Written versions. Written descriptions of Algonquian languages date back to the sixteenth century, when travelers and then Christian missionaries began to record the Native American languages. The first French notation of an Algonquian dialect, close to Micmac, was made by the explorer Jacques Cartier in July 1534. The first missionaries among the Algonquians, French priests who arrived in Port Royal in 1611, began immediately to learn the language of the Micmac of that area, Throughout the seventeenth and eighteenth centuries, French Jesuits, Recollets, and Suipicians studied the northern Algonquian languages in what is now eastern Canada and the northeastern United States, producing word lists, or dictionaries and grammars.

87

A notable example is an extensive 1691 Abnaki dictionary. Their primary goal, of course, was not to produce linguistic documents but to learn the languages in order to convert the Indians to Christianity. The languages were transcribed into the Latin alphabet, although some special symbols were introduced to overcome that alphabet's inadequacy for expressing the sounds of the Algonquian languages.

Protestant missionaries studied Algonquian languages in New England. John Eliot, while serving as pastor in Roxbury, Massachusetts, learned Natick, or Massachusett (now extinct), and began to preach his sermons in that language. He translated the Bible (1663) and other religious literature into Natick and published a grammatical study of the language (1666). He used an English-based writing system, with some Special inventions for sounds not found in English. In Providence, Rhode Island, Roger Williams learned the Narragansett language and published a phrase book in 1643.

About 1840 James Evans, also a missionary, developed a syllabary for Plains Cree. This was later adapted for other Algonquian languages and is still in use today. It consists of geometric symbols and is not based on the Latin alphabet.

Effect on English. One of the results of contact between Indian and white cultures was the adoption of Algonquian words into American English. In addition to words commonly associated with Indian life, such as "moccasin," "manitou," "papoose," "squaw," "pemmican," "powwow," "sachem," "sagamore," "tomahawk," "totem," "wampum," and "wigwam," many terms for native foods, plants, and animals have been adopted. Among these words are "caribou," "chipmunk," "hickory," "hominy," "moose," "opossum," "pecan," "persimmon," "pone," "porgy," "raccoon," "skunk," "squash," "succotash," "terrapin," and "woodchuck." The term "caucus" is probably of Algonquian origin, from a word meaning elder, adviser, or counselor, and the famous Tammany Society of New York politics took its name from Tamanend,'s seventeenth-century Delaware chief.

Like other American Indian languages, many of the existing Algonquian languages are in danger of becoming extinct within a generation, particularly those languages now spoken by only a few elderly people.

ALGONQUIAN FAMILY

"Algonquian Family" is the term adapted from the name of the Algonquin tribe. This linguistic stock formerly occupied a more extended area than any other in North America. The terrirtory of the people who used this linguistic system reached from the east shore of Newfoundland (the Rocky Mountains and from Churchill River to Pimlico Sound.) The east parts of this territory were separated by an area occupied by Iroquoian tribe on the east. Algonquian tribes skirted the Atlantic coast from Newfoundland to Neuse River on the south, they touched on the territories of eastern Siouan, southern Iroquoian, and Muskhogean families; on the west, they bordered on the Siouan area; on the northwest, on the Kituna and Athapascan.

In Labrador, they came into contact with the Eskimo; in Newfoundland, they surrounded three sides of the Beothuk. The Cheyenne and Arapaho moved from the main body and drifted out into the Plains. Although there is a general agreement as to the peoples that should be included in this family, information in regard to the numerous dialects is too limited to justify an attempt to give a strict linguistic classification. The data is, in fact, so meager in many instances that it leaves it doubtful whether certain bodies were confederacies, tribes, bands, or clans, especially bodies that have become extinct or can not be identified.

Early writers have frequently designated settlements or bands of the same tribe as distinct tribes. As in the case of all Native Americans, travelers observing part of a tribe settled at one place and part at another have frequently taken them for different peoples, and have signified single villages, settlements, or bands with the title "tribe" or "nation," named from the locality or the chief. It is generally impossible to discriminate between tribes and villages throughout the greater part of New England and along the Atlantic coast, for the Indians there seem to have been grouped into small communities, each taking its name from the principal village of the group or from a neighboring stream or other natural feature.

In many instances, it is impossible to determine whether these groups were insubordinate to some real tribal authority or of equal rank and interdependent, although still allied. Since true tribal organization is found among the better known branches and can be traced in several instances in the eastern division, it is presumed that it was general. A geographic classification of the Algonquian tribes follows: Western division, comprising three groups dwelling along the east slope of the Rocky Mountains: Blackfoot confederacy, composed of the, Siksika, Kainah, and Piegan; Arapaho and Cheyenne.

The Northern division, the most extensive, stretches from the extreme northwest of the Algonquian area to the extreme east, chiefly North of the Saint Lawrence and the Great Lakes, including several groups that, because of insufficient knowledge of their linguistic relations, can only partially be outlined: Chippewa group, embracing the Cree, Ottawa, Chippewa, and Missisauga; Algonkin group, comprising the Nipissing, Temiscaming, Abittibi, and Algonkin.

The Northeastern division embraces the tribes inhabiting East Quebec, the Maritime Provinces, and East Maine: the Montagnais group, composed of the Nascapee, Montagnais, Mistassin, Bersiamite, and Papinachois; Abnaki group, comprising the tribes of the Micmac, Malecite, Passamaquoddy, Arosagkintacook, Sokoki, Penobscot, And the Norridgewock.

The Central division, includes groups that resided in Wisconsin, Illinois, Indiana, Michigan, and Ohio: Menominee; the Sauk group, including the Sauk, Fox, Kickapoo, Mascouten, and Potawatomi. The Illinois branch of the Miami group is comprised of the Peoria, Kaskaskia, Cahokia, Tamaroa, and Michigamea; Miami branch, composed of the Miami, Piankashaw, and Wea.

The eastern division embraces all the Algonquian tribes that lived along the Atlantic coast south of the Abnaki and including several confederacies and groups as the Pennacook, Massachuset, Wampanoag, Narraganset, Nipmuc, Montauk, Mohegan, Mahican, Wappinger, Delawares, Shawnee, Nanticoke, Conoy, Powhatan, and Pamlico.

As the early settlements of the French, Dutch, and English were all within the territory of the eastern members of the family, they were the first aborigines north of the gulf of Mexico to feel the blighting effect of contact with a more advanced race. As a rule, the relations of the French with the Algonquian tribes were friendly, the Foxes being the only tribe against whom they waged war. The English settlements were often engaged in border wars with their Algonquian neighbors, who continually pressed farther toward the interior by the advancing white immigration and, for a time, kept up a futile struggle for the possession of their territory.

The eastern tribes, from Maine to Carolina, were defeated and tribal organization broken up. Some withdrew to Canada, others crossed the mountains into the Ohio valley, while a few bands located on reservations by the whites, only to dwindle and ultimately become extinct. Of many of the smaller tribes of New England, Virginia, and other eastern states, there are no living representatives.

Even the languages of some are known only by a few words mentioned by early historians, while some tribes are known only by name.

The Abnaki and others who fled to Canada settled along the Saint Lawrence under the protection of the French, whose active allies they became in all subsequent wars with the English down to the fall of the French power in Canada.

Those who crossed the Allegheny Mountains into the Ohio valley, together with the Wyandot and the native Algonquian tribes of that region, formed themselves into a loose confederacy, allied first with the French, and afterward with the English, against advancing settlements, and with the declared purpose of preserving the Ohio River as the Indian boundary. Wayne's victory in 1794 put an end to the struggle, and at the treaty of Greenville in 1795, the Indians acknowledged their defeat and made the first cession of land west of the Ohio.

Tecumseh and his brother, Ellskwatawa, instigated by British intriguers, again aroused the western tribes against the United States a few years later, but the disastrous defeat at Tippecanoe in 1811 and the death of their leader broke the spirit of The Indians. In 1815 those who had taken part against the United States during the War of 1812 made peace with the Government. Then began the series of treaties by which, within thirty years, most of the Indians of this region ceded their lands and removed west of the Mississippi.

This factor contributed greatly to the decline of the Algonquian ascendancy, and was the power of the Iroquoian confederacy which, by the beginning of the seventeenth century, had developed a power destined to make them the scourge of the other Indian populations from the Atlantic to the Mississippi and from Ottawa River in Canada to the Tennessee.

After destroying the Huron and the Erie, they turned their power chiefly against the Algonquian tribes, and before long, Ohio and Indiana were nearly deserted, with only a few villages of Miami remaining here and there in the northern portion. The Algonquian tribes fled before them to the region of the upper lakes and the batiks of the Mississippi, and only when the French had guaranteed them protection against their deadly foes did they venture to turn back toward the east.

The central Algonquians are tall, averaging about 173 centimeters; they have the typical Native American nose, heavy and prominent, somewhat hooked in men, flatter in women; their cheek bones are heavy; the head among the tribes of the Great Lakes is very large and almost brachycephalic, but showing considerable variation; the face is very large.

91

The Atlantic coast Algonquians can hardly be determined from living individuals, as no full–bloods survive, but skulls found in old burial grounds show that they were tall, their faces not quite so broad, the heads much more elongated and remarkably high, resembling present Inuit, and suggesting the possibility that along the New England coast, there may have been some mixture with that type.

The Cheyenne and Arapaho are even taller than the central Algonquians; their faces are larger, their heads more elongated. It is worth noting that in the region in which the mound builders' remains are found, rounded heads prevailed, and in 1905 the population of the region were also more round–headed, perhaps suggesting fusion of blood.

Religion. Religious beliefs of the eastern Algonquian tribes were similar in their leading features, Their myths are, numerous. Their deities, or *mantis,* including objects animate and inanimate, were many, but the chief culture hero *huh,* to whom the creation and control of the world were ascribed, was substantially the same in character, although known by various names among different tribes. As Manibozho, or Mount Chabo, among the Chippewa and other lake tribes, he was usually identified as a fabulous great rabbit, bearing some relation to the sun.

This identification with the great rabbit appeared to have prevailed among other tribes, being found as far south as Maryland. Brinton believes this mythological animal to have been merely a symbol of light, adopted because of the similarity between the Algonquian words for rabbit and light.

Among the Siksika. this chief beneficent deity was known as Napiw. among the Abnaki as Ketchiniwesk, among the New England tribes as Kichtan, Woonand, Can tantowit, and so forth. It was he who created the world by magic power, peopled it with game and the other animals, taught his favorite people the arts of the chase, and gave them corn and beans. However, this deity was distinguished more for his magical powers and his ability to overcome opposition by trickery, deception, and falsehood than to benevolent qualities.

The objects of nature were deities as well: the sun, moon, fire, trees, lakes, and various animals. Respect was also paid to the four cardinal points. There was a general belief in a soul shade, or immortal spiritual nature not only in man but in animals and all other things, and in a spiritual abode to which the soul went after the death of the body, in which the occupations and enjoyments were supposed to be similar to those of this life.

Priests, or conjurers, called medicine men by the whites, played an important part in social, political, and religious systems. They were supposed to possess, influence with spirits of other agencies, which they could bring to their aid in prying into the future, inflicting or curing disease, and so forth.

Descent. Among the tribes from south New England to Carolina, including especially the Mohegan, Delawares, the people of the Powhatan confederacy, and the Chippewa, descent was reckoned in the female line; among the Potawatomi, Abnaki, Blackfeet, and probably most the northern tribes, in the male line. Within recent times, descent has been paternal the, Menominee, Sauk and Fox, Illinois, Kickapoo, and Shawnee.

Although it has been stated that descent was anciently maternal, there is not satisfactory proof of this. The Cree, Arapaho, and Cheyenne are without clans or gentes. The gentes or clans were usually governed by a chief, who in some cases was installed by the heads of the clans or genies. The, tribe also had its chief, usually selected from a particular clan or gens, though the manner of choosing a chief and the authority vested in him varied somewhat in the different tribes. There was the peace chief, whose authority was not absolute, and who had no part in the declaration of war or in carrying it on, the leader in the campaign being one who had acquired a right to the position by noted deeds and skill.

In some tribes the title of chief was hereditary, and the distinction between a peace chief and a war chief was not observed. The chief's powers among some tribes, as the Miami, were greater than in others. The government was directed in weighty matters by a council, consisting of the chiefs of the clans or gentes of the tribe. It was by their authority that tribal war was undertaken, peace concluded, territory sold, and so forth.

Food. The Algonquian tribes were mainly sedentary and agricultural, probably the only exceptions being those of the cold regions of Canada and the Siksika of the Plains. The Chippewa did not formerly cultivate the soil. Maize was the staple native food product, but the tribes of the region of the Great Lakes, particularly the Menominee, made extensive use of wild rice. The Powhatan tribes raised enough maize to supply not only their own wants, but those of the Virginia colonists for some years after the founding of Jamestown, and the New England colonists were more than once relieved from hunger by corn raised by the natives.

In 1792, Wayne's army found a continuous plantation along the entire length of the Maumee from Fort Wayne to Lake Erie. Although depending chiefly on hunting and fishing for subsistence, the New England tribes cultivated large quantities of maize, beans, pumpkins, and tobacco. It is said that they understood the advantage of fertilizing, using fish, shells, and ashes for this purpose. The tools they used in preparing the ground and in cultivation were usually wooden spades or hoes, the latter being made by fastening a shell, shoulder blade of an animal, or a tortoise shell to a stick handle.

It was from the Algonquian tribes that the whites learned to make hominy, succotash, maple sugar, johnnycake, and so forth. Gookin, in 1674, thus describes the method of preparing food among the Indians of Massachusetts: "Their food is generally boiled maize, or Indian corn, mixed with kidney beans, or sometimes without. Also, they frequently boil in this pottage fish and flesh of all sorts, either new taken or dried, as shad, eels, alewives, or a kind of herring, or any other sort of fish. But they dry mostly those sorts before mentioned. These they cut in pieces, bones and all, and boil them in the aforesaid pottage.

"I have wondered many times that they were not in danger of being choked with fish bones; but they are so dexterous in separating the bones from the fish in their eating thereof that they are in no hazard. Also, they boil in this frumenty all sorts of flesh they take in hunting, as venison, beaver, bear's flesh, moose, otters, raccoons, and so forth, cutting this flesh in small pieces and boiling it as aforesaid. Also, they mix with the said pottage several sorts of roots, as Jerusalem artichokes, and groundnuts, and other roots, and pompions, and squashes, and also several sorts of nuts or masts, as oak acorns, chestnuts, and walnuts; these husked and dried and powdered, they thicken their pottage therewith.

"Also, sometimes, they beat their maize into meal and sift it through a basket made for that purpose. With this meal they make bread, baking it in the ashes, covering the dough with leaves. Sometimes they make of their meal a small sort of cakes and boil them. They make also a certain sort of meal of parched maize. This meal they call *nokake*."

Their pots were made of clay, somewhat egg–shaped; their dishes, spoons, and ladles of wood; their water pails of birch bark, doubled up so as to make them four–cornered, with a handle. They also had baskets of various sizes in which they placed their provisions; these were made of rushes, stalks, cornhusks, grass, and bark, often ornamented with colored figures of animals. Mats woven of bark and rushes, dressed deerskins, feather garments, and utensils of wood, stone, and horn are mentioned by explorers.

Fish were taken with hooks, spears, and nets, in canoes and along the shore, on the sea and in the ponds and rivers. They captured without much trouble all the smaller kinds of fish, and, in their canoes, often dragged sturgeon with nets stoutly made of Canada hemp. Canoes used for fishing were of two kinds: one of birch bark, very light, but liable to overset; the other made from the trunk of a large tree.

Clothing. Clothes were composed chiefly of the skins of animals, tanned until soft and pliable, and sometimes ornamented with paint and beads made from shells. Occasionally they decked themselves with mantles made of feathers overlapping each other as on the back of the fowl. The dress of the women consisted usually of two articles, a leather shirt, or undergarment, ornamented with fringe, and a skirt of the same material fastened round the waist with a belt and reaching nearly to the feet; moccasins were of soft dressed leather, often embroidered with wampum.

The men usually covered the lower part of the body with a breechcloth, and often wore a skin mantle thrown over one shoulder. The women dressed their hair in a thick, heavy plait that fell down the neck, and sometimes ornamented their heads with bands decorated with wampum or with a small cap. Higginson, in *New England's Plantation*, 1629, says: "Their hair is usually cut before, leaving one lock longer than the rest."

The men went bareheaded, with their hair fantastically trimmed, each according to his fancy. One would shave it on one side and leave it long on the other; another left an unshaved strip, two or three inches wide, running from the forehead to the nape of the neck.

Housing. The typical Algonquian lodge of the woods and lakes was oval, and the conical lodge, made of sheets of birch–bark, also occurred. The Mohegan, and to some extent the Virginia Indians, constructed long communal houses which accommodated a number of families. The dwellings in the north were sometimes built of logs, while those in the south and parts of the west were constructed of saplings fixed in the ground, bent over at the top, and covered with movable matting, thus forming a long round–roofed house. The Delawares and some other eastern tribes, preferring to live separately, built smaller dwellings.

The manner of construction among the Delawares is thus described by Zeisberger: "They peel trees, abounding with sap, such as lime trees, and so forth, then cutting the bark into pieces of two or three yards in length, they lay heavy stones upon them, that they may become flat and even drying. The frame of the hut is made by driving poles into the ground and strengthening them by cross beams. This framework is covered, both within and without, with the above- mentioned pieces of bark, fastened very tight with bast or twigs of hickory, which are remarkably tough. The roof runs up to a ridge, and is covered in the same manner. These huts have one opening in the roof to let out the smoke and one in the side for an entrance.

"The door is made of a large piece of bark without either bolt or lock, a stick leaning against the outside being a sign that nobody is at home. The light enters by small openings furnished with sliding shutters." The covering was sometimes rushes or long reed grass. The houses of the Illinois are described by Hennepin as being "made like long arbors" and covered with double mats of flat flags.

Those of the Chippewa and the Plains tribes were circular or conical, a framework covered with bark among the former, a frame of movable poles covered with dressed skins among the latter. The villages, especially along the Atlantic coast, were frequently surrounded with stockades of tall, stout stakes firmly set in the ground. A number of the western Algonquian towns are described by early explorers as fortified or as surrounded with stockades of tall, stout stakes firmly set in the ground.

In no other tribes north of Mexico was picture writing developed to the advanced stage that it reached among the Delawares and the Chippewa. The figures were scratched or painted on pieces of bark or on stabs of wood. Some of the tribes, especially the Ottawa, were great traders, acting as chief middlemen between the more distant Indians and the early French settlements. Some of the interior tribes of Illinois and Wisconsin made but little use of the canoe, traveling almost always afoot; while others who lived along the upper lakes and the Atlantic coast were expert canoeists.

The canoes of the upper lakes were of birch-bark, strengthened on the inside with ribs or knees, The more solid and substantial boat of Virginia and the western rivers was the dugout, made from the trunk of a large tree. The manufacture of pottery, though the product was small, except in one or two tribes, was widespread. Judging by the number of vessels found in the graves of the regions occupied by the Shawnee, this tribe carried on the manufacture to a greater extent than any other.

Mortuary Customs. The usual method of burial was in graves, with each clan or gens having its own cemetery. The mortuary ceremonies among the eastern and central tribes were substantially as described by Zeisberger. "Immediately after death the corpse was arrayed in the deceased's best clothing and decked with the chief ornaments worn in life, sometimes having the face and shirt painted red, then laid on a mat or skin in the middle of the hut; weapons and other personal effects were placed about it.

"After sunset, and also before daybreak, the female relations and friends assembled around the body to mourn over it. The grave was dug generally by old women; inside it was lined with bark, and when the corpse was placed in it, four sticks were laid across. A covering of bark was placed over these and the grave was then filled with earth."

An earlier custom was to place in the grave the personal effects or those indicative of the character and occupation of the deceased, as well as food, cooking utensils, and so forth. Usually the body was placed horizontally, although among some of the western tribes, as the Foxes, sometimes buried the dead in a sitting posture. It was the custom of probably most of the tribes to light fires on the grave for four nights after burial. The Illinois, Chippewa, and some of the extreme western tribes frequently practiced tree or scaffold burial.

The bodies of the chiefs of the Powhatan confederacy were stripped of the flesh and skeletons were placed on scaffolds in a chart house. The Ottawa usually placed the body to short time on a scaffold near the grave prior to burial. The Shawnee, and possibly one or more of the southern Illinois tribes, were accustomed to burying their dead in box–shaped sepulchers made of undressed stone slabs. The Nanticoke and some of the western tribes, after temporary burial in the ground or exposure on scaffolds, removed the flesh and reburied the skeletons.

The eastern Algonquian tribes probably equaled the Iroquois in bravery, intelligence, and physical powers, but lacked their constant solidity of character and capability of organization, and do not appear to have appreciated the power and influence they might have wielded in combination. The alliances between tribes were generally temporary and without real cohesion. There seems to have been in their character something that rendered them incapable of combining in large bodies, even against a common enemy.

Some of their great chieftains, Philip, Pontiac, and Tecumseh, attempted at different periods to unite the kindred tribes in an effort to resist the advance of the white race; but each in turn found that a single

97

great defeat disheartened his followers and rendered all his efforts fruitless, and the former two fell by the hands of deserters from their own ranks.

The Virginia tribes, under the able guidance of Powhatan and Opechancanough, formed an exception to the general rule. They presented a united front to the whites, and resisted for years every step of their advance until the Indians were practically exterminated. From the close of the Revolution to the treaty of Greenville (1795), the tribes of the Ohio valley also made a desperate stand against the Americans, but in this they had the encouragement, if not the more active support, of the British in Canada as well as of other Indians. In individual character, many of the Algonquian chiefs rank high, and Tecumseh stands out prominently as one of the noblest figures in Indian history.

ALGONQUIN

"Algonquin" refers to a number of related Canadian Indian bands that are collectively called the Algonquin. This term should not be confused with Algonquian, which refers to the widespread language family in eastern and central Canada, and along the north Atlantic seaboard and in the western Great Lakes region in the United States. The name Algonquian, however, comes from the tribal group, the Algonquin, that are one component member of the language group.

At the time of first white contact, the Algonquin lived in the Ottawa Valley in Quebec and Ontario. Between the seventeenth and nineteenth century, the Algonquin were dispersed by other Indian groups as well as white settlers and suffered great losses because of disease and other effects of white contact. Living in a densely wooded mixed coniferous and deciduous forest region, their culture reflected their environment: the Algonquin fished, hunted, trapped, and practiced marginal horticulture.

NAME, SUBDIVISIONS AND LANGUAGE

Tribal name. The meaning of the word *Algonquin* is not entirely clear. The most recent suggestion is that it is derived from the Malecite word *eleknokwik, which* means "they are our relatives (or allies)." An earlier suggestion attributed the word to the Micmac *algootneakirig* "at the place of spearing fish and eels (from the bow of a canoe)." Samuel de Champlain was the first to record the word and wrote it *Algounequin.* In 1632, Algonquian appeared in T*he Jesuit Relations* for the first time.

The names that the Algonquin give themselves and the names that other Indian groups have for them, however, are very different. The Algonquin call themselves *omamiwininiwak* and *anisinabeg*. The Huron called them *Aquanaques*; the Iroquois called them *Adirondacks*; and the Western Abnaki call them *Wesogenak*. *The Handbook of American Indians North of Mexico,* edited by F. W. Hodge (1912), spells the name *Algonkin,* gives other variants in spelling, and provides reference as to first appearance of these forms.

Cultural Boundaries and Subdivisions. The Algonquin occupy a marginal position between the Subarctic and Northeastern culture areas. Harold Driver places them in the Eastern Subarctic culture area. A. L. Kroeber puts them, along with the Ojibwa and the Ottawa to the west, in the Northern Great Lakes culture area. He separates them from groups immediately to the north, his Eastern Subarctic, and from Iroquoian–speaking groups immediately to the south, his Lower Great Lakes culture area. Occupying the southern boundary of Driver's Eastern Subarctic, the Algonquin borrowed many traits from their Iroquoian–speaking neighbors. This made the Algonquin divergent in many ways from their Eastern Subarctic neighbors to the north.

Specifically, the Algonquin were bordered on the southeast by the Huron, and on the east by the Montagnais and the Tete de Boule, and, although the seventeenth–century boundaries are not distinct, by the Cree on the north, and on the west and southwest by the Ottawa, with whom the Algonquin merged culturally and linguistically.

The historical Algonquin of the seventeenth century consisted of the following related bands: the Wescafini on the Rouge, the Petite–Nation, the Matouwescarini in the Madawaska Valley in Ontario; the Keinoche between Pembroke and Renfrew, Ontario, in the Muskrat Lake region; the Kichesipirini on Morrison Island, Quebec, a small island in the Ottawa River off Allumette Island; the Otaguottouemins in the upper valley north of the Kichesipirini; and the Onontchataronon on the South Nation River in eastern Ontario.

The territory occupied by the Algonquin in the seventeenth century was from roughly the Saint Maurice River in Quebec to the area in Ontario drained by the Ottawa River and its tributaries. The Abitibi, Timiskaming, and Nipissing, formerly speaking related dialects, assimilated with the Algonquin culturally and linguistically in the following centuries.

Language. As previously stated, the Algonquin are members of the widespread Algonquian language family. They speak dialects of a language shared with the Ojibwa, the Saulteaux, and the Ottawa. Neighboring bands along this chain from Ojibwa to Algonquin speak mutually intelligible dialects, although culturally the groups are given different "tribal" designations.

TRIBAL HISTORY

Sixteenth and seventeenth centuries. The earliest European accounts of the Algonquin, which date from 1603, found them at Tadoussac. Here, with other Algonquian groups, they were celebrating a victory feast over the Lower Saint Lawrence Iroquoians whom they had ousted from the region. The struggle between the Lower Saint Lawrence Iroquoians and the Algonquin, along with their allies, other Algonquian-speaking groups in the east, had been going on for at least 30 years.

Before 1570, however, Algonquians and the Lower Saint Lawrence Iroquoians appear to have lived together on friendly terms. This 30–years war was likely precipitated because the Iroquoians wanted to carry out trade directly with the French and not through the Algonquian groups which at that time were acting as middlemen.

Champlain came up the Ottawa River into Algonquin territory in 1613 and identified the seventeenth–century bands given above. He found the Kichesipirini on Morrison Island living in constant fear of Iroquois (Mohawk) attacks. The Algonquin were allies of the Huron, and both were traditional enemies of the Iroquois. The enmity between the Iroquois and the Huron was felt in Algonquin territory because the Algonquin provided the Huron with European goods for which they received in exchange corn, *hemp* nets, and wampum.

Because the Iroquois occupied the Saint Lawrence River above the Ottawa, the Algonquin, with their strategically advantageous position on the Ottawa River, provided not only the closest but also the safest route to Lake Huron for the French. The Huron–Algonquin alliance was extremely beneficial to the Algonquin, and they attempted, however unsuccessfully, to keep the French from trading with the Huron.

The presence of armed Frenchmen traveling through Algonquin country to trade with the Huron, however, led to a brief period of peace in the 1620s, as the Iroquois, which had been spurred on by the Dutch who had subsidized them to hijack their fleets on the Ottawa River, now hesitated to attack the Algonquin. This lull in fighting led to another direction in the quest for furs. To better their position, the Algonquin, with their access to furs from more northern groups, attempted to assume trade links with the Dutch at Fort Orange.

The Mohawk, nevertheless, would not permit this competition, and in the 1630s and early 1640s the Mohawk and the Algonquin were again at war. At this time the superior Mohawk control of arms led to the ousting of the southernmost Algonquin from the Ottawa Valley. These Algonquin were forced to find asylum with the more inaccessible Algonquin bands to the north and west.

Peace proposals were begun in 1645 by the French on behalf of the several Algonquian–speaking groups and the Iroquois, but the Algonquin found themselves ultimately at a disadvantage, as the Iroquois were now permitted to hunt at the southern edge of Algonquin territory. The following year the Mohawk invaded Algonquin territories. Raids weakened the Algonquin, and the assistance sought from neighboring Algonquin groups brought little success.

Between 1650 and 1675, the Algonquin temporarily left the Ottawa Valley. Some went to the Lake Saint John region of Quebec; others went to the mission at Sillery, above Quebec, and still others went to Trois Rivieres and to the mission at Montreal. Around the end of the seventeenth century, the Algonquin at Trois Rivieres amicably gave up their hunting grounds to the south of the Saint Lawrence to the Abnaki, another Algonquian group.

Eighteenth and nineteenth centuries. The Great Peace seated between the French, their Algonquian allies, and the Iroquois was established in 1701. From this time on, the Algonquin carried on extensive trade with Albany. In 1704 a mission for the Algonquin was established by the French at Saint–Anne–du–bout–de–file, and in 1721 one for the Christian Iroquois, the Nipissing, and the Algonquin at Lake of Two Mountains, the present Oka Reserve near Montreal. The Two Mountains Algonquin were not cultivators at this time but were living from the profit from furs, which they continued to obtain in winter by hunting and trapping on family hunting rounds on the Upper Ottawa River. The nineteenth century brought considerable movement of Algonquin groups once more.

As early as 1807, some Lake of Two Mountains Algonquin and Tirniskaming had dispersed northward to Golden Lake, Ontario, and a reserve was established for them in 1870. In 1830 Algonquin from Trois Rivi6res moved to Lake of Two Mountains. Other Lake of Two Mountain Algonquin settled at Miniwaki, where a reserve was established in 1854. Many of the remaining Algonquin left Lake of Two Mountains after 1868. Other Algonquin reserves established in Quebec were at Argonaut, Barrierre Lake, Grand Lake Victoria, Kipewa, Lake

101

Simon, Long Point Timiskaming, and Wolfe Lake. Many Algonquin lived off reserve on the River du Lifavre and the Ottawa.

Tribal culture. The way of life of the Algonquin at the time of first French contact is difficult to determine. The first writers usually failed to specify which Algonquian group they were discussing under the heading Algonquin. Moreover, since the writers had religious and economic motives in mind, the description of aboriginal traits was irrelevant in such contact situations.

The descriptions made by twentieth–century writers, too, are not necessarily representative of the early Algonquin. During the nineteenth century, the Algonquin had borrowed much from tribes farther north, who were more thoroughly Subarctic in character.

In terms of the seventeenth century, Bruce Trigger and Gordon Day, Canadian anthropologists, suggest that the Algonquin bands likely were patrilineal clans. A patrilineal clan consisted of a number of families related to one another through males who married women from outside the clan. Each of these clans may have formed a village at favored fishing spots during the warmer months. In winter they dispersed or sent out hunting parties to obtain deer, beaver, moose, and in some districts caribou as well. A 1761 description of these family hunting grounds coincides closely to what F. G. Speck's informants still remembered in 1913.

Family tracts were delimited by such natural boundaries as lakes and rivers. Trespass on another's hunting ground was avoided. Fear of revenge through witchcraft was the most widespread sanction against trespass violation. If, however, a family were badly in need of food, permission was often given to the man to hunt in the territory of another. Game, moreover, was consistently preserved: pregnant female animals or those with young were not killed; attempts were made to permit the game to replenish itself in a given tract if it was in danger of extinction.

Speck refers to this as "farming" the game. Seventeenth–century Algonquin who lived in close proximity to the Saint Lawrence Iroquois grew some crops where the soil was suitable. The dense wooded areas were cleared by burning the trees and under growth, and here corn, beans, squash, and, after French contact, peas were planted. These crops, however, provided only a minimal amount of their food requirements. The Algonquin also shared a number of traits from contact with the Huron. Among these was the hemp net. With the hemp net the Algonquin fished through holes in the ice in winter.

Moreover, the Algonquin ate dogs on special occasions. They entertained guests in the Huron manner, for example,, hosts served their guests but did not themselves eat the food they had prepared. At council, tobacco was smoked before any discussion began. The graves of prominent persons were covered with painted wooden structures called grave houses. The largest of these were seven feet long and four feet wide. At one end a wooden figure was attached, representing the deceased.

Descriptions by twentieth–century writers show that the Algonquin shared many traits identified with Algonquian–speaking peoples to the north. For example, in terms of cosmology and religion, the Algonquin believed in a Supreme Being who was owner of everything. In addition, their mythology tells of a trickster–transformer culture hero called Wiskedjak who spent his life going about wherever there were Indians. He teased and played tricks, but because he was so humorous the Algonquin liked to have him around. Moreover, he had the power to make everything in nature respond to him. Another supernatural being was the Windigo, a man–eating creature who roamed through the woods, devouring all humans in sight.

Not to be forgotten was Paguk, a skeleton who made great rattling and squeaking noises. His presence was an omen that some friend would become lost. Finally, there were the Pugwudgjnwug, a race of powerful little men.

All men, if they were to be successful hunters, must have a guardian spirit. These were obtained through the dream–vision quest. The shaman, or religious practitioner, was simply a man who had more power than the ordinary hunter. This power, too, was obtained from one or more guardian spirits. Using the shaking tent, the shaman or conjurer, through clairvoyance, could determine such causes of illness as sorcery and taboo violation. He could core those illnesses resulting from sorcery.

Practically all hunters knew some form of divination: some knew scapulamancy. This one ritual was performed to discover where game was to be found or to identify the species of game. A charred shoulder blade or scapula is read like a map to direct the hunter where to hunt, or like a drawing to see what kind of animal he might bag. In addition, a number of omens were recognized: a white animal was a sign of bad luck, while a dwarfed animal foretold misfortune.

Items of material culture made by the Algonquin, were also common to much of the Subarctic: birchbark canoe, snowshoe, toboggan, rectangular bark hunting camp, birchbark container, clothing of deer and moosehide, and cradle board, to name a few.

CONTEMPORARY SITUATION

The survivors of the Algonquin, all of whom have considerable white intermixture, either live on the reservations as mentioned above, or have intermarried with whites and live largely off reserve, or have intermarried with other tribal groupings and live on reserves which are not considered Algonquin. These include: the Iroquois at Oka and Gibson; the Cree at Manowan, Weymontachie, Obedjiwan, and Abitibi; the Montagnais at Lake Saint John; and the Ojibwa (Ottawa) on Georgian Bay and Lake Ontario.

Depending upon location and resources available, the present–day Algonquin work as truck gardeners, hunters, guides, and trappers. Many Algonquin women have married white trappers, lumbermen, and pioneer farmers, both in the past and at present. Their descendants have assimilated with the whites that originally displaced and dispersed the Algonquin from their traditional hunting territories.

Population. It is possible that at the time of first white contact the Algonquin may have numbered between 3,000 and 4,000 persons. On January 1, 1970, the Algonquin bands in Quebec had the following populations: Argonaut 2; Barriere Lake 214; Grand Lake Victoria 192; Kipawa III; Lake Simon 371; Long Point 269; River Desert 946; Timiskaming 384; and Wolfe Lake 58. In Ontario the Gold Lake band had a population of 475.

In addition there were approximately 2,500 persons of Algonquin descent distributed through the Ottawa Valley but unaffiliated with any band. The population of the Algonquin has shown a slight increase since 1900.

ANNAWAN

Annawan (Wampanoag, ? - August 12, 1676) was a sachem who served as chief counselor and captain under King Philip (Metacom). He had earlier served under Philip's father, Massassoit, in wars against other New England Indian nations. Even among his enemies, Annawan was recognized as a great and valiant soldier.

When Philip was killed in an attack on his swamp fortress, Annawan rallied the surviving warriors. They escaped and continued to attack settlers of Swansea and Plymouth, constantly moving their camp to avoid detection.

Later that year, a captive Indian led a small party under Captain Benjamin Church to Annawan's retreat, (now known as Annawan's Rock), a hill set in a swamp near the Reheboth River. There they surprised and captured Annawan and his chief counselors. The main party of warriors was deceived into surrendering when Church told them that his army had surrounded them. Annawan, correctly believing his party to be the last to resist the English, gave Church a deerskin bundle containing Philip's wampum belts, symbols of his office and other effects.

Although Church pleaded for Annawan's life, his confession that he had tortured and killed several English captives led the Plymouth authorities to behead him while Church was away.

ASPENQUID

Aspenquid (Abnaki; mid-seventeenth century), was one of the first American Indians to be converted to Christianity by French missionaries. He was born in Agamenticus, Maine, in the late sixteen-hundreds. He travelled widely throughout northern New England and eastern Canada, preaching to the Indian tribes. His fame as a preacher and orator spread among both Indians and whites. He is believed that he was buried on the slopes of Mount Agamenticus. For many years after his death, sometime after 1682 in Maine, an Aspenquid Day was observed in Halifax, Nova Scotia.

ASPINET

Aspinet (Wampanoag, ? - 1623?) was a sagamore (tribute chief over two or more subtribes) and chief of the Nauset tribe on Cape Cod at present Eastham, Massachusetts. Although a small group of Nauset warriors ambushed an initial scouting party sent out from the Mayflower, Aspinet always gave the appearance of being a firm friend of the Plymouth colonists. In 1621 he assisted in returning young John Billington to the Plymouth settlement after the boy was found lost in the woods. During the winter of 1622, Aspinet's people gave beans and corn to the starving colonists. Although Miles Standish's intemperate outbursts often might have provoked Aspinet to act against the colonists, he seemed to prefer peace.

Aspinet died about 1623 in a hiding place in the swamps after being driven there from threat of attack by the colonists. In spite of the friendship he displayed toward the English, Aspinet appears to have been one of the leaders of a conspiracy of other Wampanoag sagamores and Mas-

sachuset and Narraganset Indians to destroy Plymouth. The plot was
discovered by Massassoit, principal chief of the Wampanoag.

ASSACOMBUIT

Assacombuit (Abnaki; ? -1727), also known as Charlevoix, was a chief
who supported the activities of the French in North America until his
death. On November 30, 1696, during King William's War (1689-97), he
assisted Pierre le Moyne d'Iberville in the destruction of Fort Saint Johns,
Newfoundland. The fort was later retaken by the British. Assacombuit
and other Abnaki chiefs joined the French in attacking outlying New
England settlements during Queen Anne's War (1702-13). On August 10,
1703, as part of a general Abnaki assault on Maine settlers, he helped
lead the attack on the fort at Casco, Maine, and between 1704 and 1705
helped the British from Newfoundland. As Partial reward for his service
to the French, Assacombuit travelled through France (1706-07) and was
knighted by Louis XIV for his activities in New England. Returning to
North America, he participated in an assault on Haverhill, Massachusetts,
in 1708.

ATTIGNAWANTAN

One of the largest tribes of the Huron confederacy, The Attignawantan
at one time comprised about half the Huron population, and formerly
lived on Nottawasaga Bay, Ontario, Canada. In 1638 they were settled in
14 towns and villages. Collectively, the Huron called themselves *Quen-
dot* (Wendat). The Attignawantan (Bear) among the Huron, had tribal
names that were also names perhaps taken from main area clans.

The Jesuit missions of Saint Joseph and La Conception were established among them. The Jesuits wrote that the Attignawanton and Petun
Huron spoke the same language, and had similar customs, even extending to female hairstyles. Vague tribal oral tradition says that the Attignawantan formed the nucleus of the Huron Confederation in about A.D.
1400.

The Arendaronon were indicated as the first of the Huron confederacy
to establish trade with the French in about 1609, control of this trade was
effectively seized by the Attignawantan, who apparently dominated the
confederacy in many ways. Late in the 1630s the Jesuits described the
Huron Confederacy as consisting of the Attignawantan, Attigneenongnahac, Arendaronon, Tahonaenrat, and Ataronchronon.

By the late 1640s, the Jesuits had made many conversions to Christianity among the tribe, which was also the most hostile among the Huron to their long-standing enemy, the Iroquois.

Their diet was about 85 percent vegetables, mostly corn, 15 percent fish, and five percent meat. They were quite healthy and showed no nutritional deficiencies, records indicate.

Eventually, the Iroquois pushed many of the Huron, now generally referred to as Wyandotte, west to Ohio and Michigan. In 1843 the United States moved them by force to Kansas. They were pushed further west and settled in southeastern Oklahoma in 1857.

They moved deeper into the Indian Nation to avoid the opposing factions of the United States Civil War. Their reservation was broken up by allotment in the 1890s. Those arriving too late to receive lands returned to Kansas, Ohio, Michigan, or Quebec.

In 1937 they officially formed the Wyandotte Tribe. They were singled out for extinction as a tribe in 1956, but after twenty years' struggle, regained federal recognition. A recent count showed over 3600 tribal members in Oklahoma. In the 1990s they owned 192 acres in common, plus individually held allotments.

AXION

The Axion were a division of the New Jersey Delawares formerly living on the east bank of Delaware River, between Rancocas Creek and the present Trenton. In 1648 they were one of the largest tribes on the river, being estimated at 200 warriors. Brinton thinks the name may be a corruption of Assiscunk, the name of a creek above Burlington. They disappeared as a distinct band before 1700.

BLACK BEAVER

Black Beaver (Delaware, 1806 - May 8, 1880), also known as Se-ket-Tu Ma-Qua, distinguished himself as an intelligent and trustworthy guide for United States explorers crossing the continent, and also as a remarkable Indian scout and faithful friend of the United States Army and early pioneers. He was born at the present site of Belleville, Illinois, probably during his family's move west to a new home.

In February 1824, when the Delawares were being relocated on White River in Arkansas, white men stole almost all their horses, worsening the Indians' already desperate situation. William Anderson, the head chief, Black Beaver, Natacoming and other Delawares sent this letter to General William Clark requesting aid, "Last summer a number of our people died just for the want of something to live on ... We have got in a country where we do not find all as stated to us when we was asked to swap lands with you ... Father. We did not think that big man would tell us things that was not true ... Father, you know it is hard to go hungry, if you do not know it we poor Indians know it ... We are obliged to call on you once more for assistance in the name of God ..."

Black Beaver again came to the attention of the United States government in 1834 when he served Colonel Richard Irving Dodge as interpreter at a conference with the Comanche, Kiowa and Wichita tribes on the Upper Red River. Black Beaver's skills as a translator earned the admiration of military and scientific explorers who were embarking upon transcontinental expeditions. Black Beaver was among thirty-two Indians hired for the Dragoon expedition of 1834, commanded by General Henry Leavenworth, and from that time on Black Beaver was in constant demand as a guide and interpreter.

He served on many expeditions, helping to push the frontier American settlement steadily westward from the Plains to the Rocky Mountains. Black Beaver also served as a Captain in 1846 during the war with Mexico, commanding a company of Delaware and Shawnee Indians.

In April of 1849, Captain Randolph B. Marcy was ordered to escort five hundred emigrants to California from Fort Smith, Arkansas, and to find the best route. At Shawneetown he was fortunate to meet Black Beaver and enlist him for the journey. Describing Black Beaver's qualifications, the impressed Marcy wrote, "He has traveled a great deal among the western and northern tribes of Indians, is well acquainted with their character and habits, and converses fluently with the Comanche and most of the other prairie tribes. He has spent five years in Oregon and California, two years among the Crow and Black Feet Indians. (He) Has trapped beaver in the Gila, the Columbia, the Rio Grande, and the Pecos; has crossed the Rocky Mountains at many different points, and indeed is one of those men that are seldom met with except in the mountains."

"He had for ten years been in the employ of the American Fur Company, and during this time had visited nearly every point of interest within the limits of our unsettled territory. He had set his traps and spread his blanket upon the headwaters of the Missouri and Columbia; and his wanderings had led him south of the Colorado and Gila, and thence to the shores of the Pacific in Southern California. His life is that of a veritable cosmopolite, filled with scenes of intense and startling interest, bold and reckless adventure."

Black Beaver had been to California before, along with Jesse Chisholm and other guides, and their experience and counsel was regarded by all with great respect. Most of Captain Marcy's success and reputation as a pathfinder in the Southwest was due to Black Beaver.

On October 7,1849, a lieutenant from Captain Marcy's party left camp to examine a ravine about two miles ahead. Lieutenant Montgomery Pike Harrison, the grandson of President William Henry Harrison and an older brother of President Benjamin Harrison, never returned. Captain Marcy sent Black Beaver and Lieutenant Joseph Updegraff to search for him.

They followed his tracks to a place about a mile and a half past the ravine, where it appeared that Harrison had met a party of Indians and gone on with them. His body was found further up the trail near a small branch of the Colorado River, by Lieutenant Delos B. Sacket. According to Marcy, Black Beaver studied the tracks and grass and reconstructed the crime: "The murder was committed by two men. They had two mules and one horse with them. They came down upon their victim at a full gallop, but finding that he was not disposed to fly, but ... walked his horse towards them, they also pulled up to a walk ... They rode a short distance together, then dismounted, and seating themselves on the grass, smoked together. Here they got possession of his rifle to examine it."

After they had taken his only weapon, they overpowered him, tied him up on his horse and led him into some timber where one of the Indians shot him in the head. They stripped and scalped the lieutenant, then threw his body into the ravine where it was found later by the search party. When the identity of the Kiowa murderers was discovered, Black Beaver's reconstruction was found to be correct.

Black Beaver worked two seasons as a guide for Captain Marcy, who wrote in his book, The Prairie Traveler, that he always found Black Beaver "perfectly reliable, brave, and competent. His reputation as a resolute, determined, and fearless warrior, did not admit of question, yet I have never seen a man who wore his laurels with less vanity."

Marcy also recorded Black Beaver's description of his marital relationship: "One time he catch 'um wife. I pay that woman, his modder, one hoss-one saddle-one bridle-two plug tobacco, and plenty goods. I take him home to my house-got plenty meat-plenty corn--plenty everything. One time me go to take walk, maybe so three, maybe so two hours. When I come home, that woman he say, 'Black Beaver, what for you go away long time?' I say, 'I not go nowhere; I just take one littel walk.' Then that woman he get heap mad, and say, 'No, Black Beaver, you go to see nodder woman.' I say, 'Maybe not.' Then that woman cry long time, and all e'time now he mad. You never see 'Merican woman that a-way?"

In his Journal of Army Life, Doctor Rodney Glisan described a small band of Delaware Indians, under the leadership of Black Beaver, occupying the deserted army camp near the Canadian River in the spring of 1851. "They make the most trustworthy and useful guides of any Indians in the country-from the fact of their exact knowledge of all parts of the West ... having traded, hunted and trapped among nearly every tribe of wild Indians in the United States."

In 1853-1854, Lieutenant A.W. Whipple mentioned Black Beaver in his journal several times. Black Beaver was also noted in Baldwin Milhausen's Diary of a Journey from the Mississippi to the Coasts of the Pacific during this same time period. Whipple was exploring for a railway from Fort Smith to Los Angeles and tried to engage Black Beaver as a guide several times by messenger. When Whipple's expedition reached Fort Arbuckle, Whipple and several men visited Black Beaver's log house where, "under a simple corridor, on a rough wooden settle, an Indian sat cross-legged smoking his pipe, and awaiting his visitors in perfect tranquility. He was a meager-looking man of middle size, and his long black hair framed in a face that was clever, but which bore a melancholy expression of sickness and sorrow, though more than forty winters could not have passed over it."

Black Beaver was approximately 47 years of age at that time. He spoke fluent English, French, and Spanish, and about eight separate Indian languages.

For three days Whipple attempted to persuade Black Beaver to join his expedition and though more tempting offers were made to him, Black Beaver sadly declined, saying, "Seven times I have seen the Pacific Ocean at various points; I have accompanied the Americans in three wars, and I have brought home more scalps from my hunting expeditions than one of you could lift. I should like to see the salt water for the eighth time. But I am sick, you offer me more money than has ever been offered to me before, but I am sick. But if I die, I should like to be buried by my own people."

It seemed to Whipple that each time Black Beaver was almost persuaded, Black Beaver's wife, who was sitting nearby playing with their only son and a black bear cub, spoke to him in her native tongue and Black Beaver declined Whipple's offer.

110

Baldwin Millhausen, in his Diary, explained that the abandoned post had been given to the Delaware chief "named Si-ki- yo-ma-ker (the Black Beaver), who had done the United States good service in the Mexican war as a hunter and guide. The position was quite in accordance with his wishes; others of his race settled near him, and they now live very happily under the protection of the astute and experienced 'Black Beaver.' The fort itself is such as one might expect to find in these wild regions, consisting of a number of log-houses built in a right angle at the edge of the forest, about a mile from the Canadian, which formerly served as barracks for soldiers; and there is also a separate court surrounded by a high palisade, that is intended as a place of refuge for cattle in case of attack. Several Delaware families have now taken possession of the abandoned barracks, and are continuing the cultivation of the rice fields laid out by the former garrison..."

The Delaware and Caddo Indians lived with the Wichitas on the North side of the Washita on Sugar Tree Creek. Matthew Leeper, the new agent in Indian Territory, included Black Beaver in his first report on September 26, 1860: "The best improvement found on the reserve is a private enterprise of Black Beaver, a Delaware Indian located here. He has a pretty good double log house, with two shed rooms in rear, a porch in front and two fireplaces, and a field of forty-one and a half acres enclosed with a good stake-and-rider fence, thirty-six and a half of which have been cultivated."

On April 16, 1861 at the beginning of the Civil War, Fort Washita was abandoned and the troops there joined with Colonel William H. Emory's forces at Fort Cobb. They captured the advance guard of the Confederate Texas troops and Emory marched to Fort Leavenworth. Meanwhile, Black Beaver led the command into the Cherokee Outlet, near where the Chisholm Trail later crossed Kansas' southern border.

Israel Yore recorded, "General Emory, then in command of the United States troops in that section of the country, learning that the rebels were marching directly upon him, urged Black Beaver to act as a guide, to enable him with the combined commands of Forts Smith, Cobb, and Arbuckle, to elude the enemy, and, by seeking the open prairies, to reach Fort Leavenworth, Kansas. Emory, states that, 'of all the Indians upon whom the Government had lavished its bounty, Black Beaver was the only one that would consent to guide the column.' To do so he abandoned his property, which appears to have been seized and destroyed by the enemy. The command reached Leavenworth in safety, and several

111

officers certify to the great value of his services and his unflinching patriotism."

According to historian George Rainey in The Cherokee Strip, when Black Beaver led the Federal troops from the Indian Territory forts to Fort Leavenworth, Kansas, they arrived at "Fort Leavenworth in fine condition without the loss of a man, horse or wagon, although two men deserted on the journey."

Years later, Black Beaver filed a claim with the United States Government to be reimbursed for his property, including 600 head of cattle, 300 hogs, horses, mules, wagons, harness, farming implements, tools, 4,500 bushels of corn, household equipment and a four-room hewed log house with a passageway through the center. The committee on Indians Affairs granted him $5,000, less than one-fourth of his claim.

In *The Trampling Herd*, Paul I. Wellman wrote, "Led by the celebrated old Delaware Black Beaver ... Emory ... marched his 750 soldiers and 150 non-combatants north across the best fords of the Canadian, Cimarron, Chiaskia, Ninnescah to the Arkansas River to the site of the present Wichita from where he dispatched his first message to military headquarters announcing the finish of his march ..."

In July 1867, Black Beaver was summoned to Lawrence, Kansas by Superintendent James Wortham, who employed him as interpreter for the Indian relocation to the Leased Lands west of the Chickasaw Nation. For his services as guide in preparation for and during the removal of the tribes from Kansas to the Leased Lands, Black Beaver was promised one thousand dollars a year.

F.A. Rector left the following record, "... while en route the cholera made its appearance among the Indians, causing the immediate stampede of every white Man accompanying the expedition (sic) except C.F. Garrett and the deponent -- That had it not been for the presence of Black Beaver, it would have been impossible, (in his opinion), to have kept the Indians together and affected their removal to the Leased Lands at that time ... after their arrival ... Black Beaver was left in charge of them for several months without an Agent, or Government official of any kind."

In the fall of 1867, many prominent Indians and army officers, Indian agents and newspaper correspondents attended the Medicine Lodge Peace Council, which was called in an attempt to end a three-year war started by the Chivington massacre in Colorado. Black Beaver, then 61 years old, was in attendance.

Black Beaver was a delegate to the International Indian Council held at Okmulgee on August 1, 1870, where an inquiry was made into the

Kiowas who had been raiding in Texas. Black Beaver criticized the mild speeches from the Five Civilized Tribes and proposed to speak plainly and brutally to the wild Indians. He prepared a speech in English with the aid of Cyrus Bede, representing the Indian superintendent, delivered it in English and it was translated for the different tribes.

A new teacher among the Caddoes on the False Washita River, Thomas C. Battey wrote in his diary that on February 18, 1872, he first saw the farm of Captain Black Beaver. "In conversation with him at one time," wrote Battey, "he told me of having visited, on two different occasions, among the mountains of Arizona, the remnant of a white race, who lived in a walled town, or rather a town built on a kind of peninsula, being nearly surrounded by a canon, or impassable ravine, so that there was but one way of approach and that by a narrow neck of land, across which they had built a wall, which effectually excluded the wild tribes by which they were surrounded ... He described them as living entirely at peace, being kind and hospitable to strangers whom they admit to their town. The second time he visited them, they recognized him and his party while at a distance, and a deputation carrying fruits were sent out to offer them the hospitalities of their town ..

"Captain Black Beaver has a large farm under cultivation, and lives in a very comfortable manner, having good, substantial frontier buildings. He commenced life as a wild Indian trapper, until, becoming familiar with almost all the unexplored regions of the west, and being a remarkably truthful and reliable man, he was much sought after as a guide, and accompanied several expeditions in that capacity. His life has been one of bold adventure, fraught with many interesting incidents, which, if properly written out, would form an interesting and entertaining volume."

Stanley Pumphrey, in his *Indian Civilization, A Lecture*, saw Black Beaver as a true Christian when he saw him at the Wichita Agency. "The Quakers are your friends," said Black Beaver of the Delawares in 1872. "Their fathers and ours bound themselves to be friends forever. Their treaty was never broken. The Indians have never taken any Quaker's blood, and the Quakers have always been true friends to the Indians. Our Grandfather at Washington knew this, and for this reason has sent them among us. He knew that they would do right by his red grand-children."

Still trying to get the Kiowas to "make one road and travel in it", the International Council was held at Anadarko in August, 1872, and featured speeches by Captain James Vann of the Cherokee Nation, John Jumper of the Seminoles, and Captain Black Beaver who said, "I am mighty glad that all we red people meet here together this pleasant morning. That shows for our brethren our good part that we feel for one another. I wish it had been sooner that we meet together. Now I am an old man, I know all these people, my red brethren. I have traveled all over this country but I have never been over the waters ... all this western country I know it, and it knows me. I have been in it. The reason I do that, I want to know how many nations of my red brethren are in this country. I know them all. I have had pretty hard troubles, sometimes I see hard times, but I would not give up ... Sometimes I have to eat mule for a month. I did not want to, but I have to, to save my life ... I traveled five years for that suffering I got. When I come home I was not satisfied and traveled south."

"I find here lots of Indians, just my color; Wichitas, Ionies, Pen-e-tethcas, also some others of my brethren. Then my brethren just like the wild ones (here pointing to Cheyennes and Arapahoes). Then they make treaty with the United States. The first one they break up before I got in; second treaty I was in. Then I see Pen-e-teth-cas, Caddoes, &c., and they say here is my war hatchet; no more war."

"We planted an ear of corn in the ground, and promised to go to raising corn. At that time Indians had mighty good chiefs; they are all dead now, but the young chiefs are all here to carry out the same provisions; 'Keep the war hatchet buried ...' We all want peace among ourselves and with the United States. We want our country; we love it all here together. Well, now after we make friends, all of us, no more bad, then we are no more afraid to go anywhere; go all over the United States; meet white man, he asks what tribe you belong to; we tell him; he say that is mighty good Indian. We like that. I hope we are all united together, all chiefs, that's what we want - peace. That much I talk to my brothers." Black Beaver then encouraged the attending wild Indians to help the Kiowas get out of trouble and persuade them to make peace with the government.

In October 1872, Black Beaver was part of a delegation of plains Indians that Special Indian Commissioner Captain Henry E. Alvord took to Washington and New York. The tribes represented were Delaware, Kiowa, Comanche, Apache, Arapaho, Caddo, Wichita, Waco, Tawoccaro, and Kichai. The New York Herald reported on October 31, 1872 that "The Red Men were on a tour to learn Fraternity and Christian Virtues." Black Beaver was introduced as a former guide to Audubon.

Israel G. Yore, Black Beaver's old friend, spent the winter of 1873-1874 at his home and during this time convinced Black Beaver to dictate his memoirs, which he then recorded. For several years, Black

Beaver acted as an interpreter for various Baptist missionaries and preachers and, in September of 1876, he and several other Indians were baptized in Sugar Creek. In later life, he became a Baptist minister. He also attended the Grand Council held at Okmulgee in May 1878, still in demand as an interpreter.

On June 2, 1880, Indian Agent P.B. Hunt of the Kiowa, Comanche & Wichita Agency in Anadarko, Indian Territory, wrote to the commissioner of Indian affairs in Washington, "On the 8th day of May, Black Beaver, a Delaware, and the most prominent of all the Indians belonging to the old Wichita Agency, died suddenly of heart disease, in the 72nd (74th) year of his age.

"He was many years ago a noted guide and acted in that capacity for Fremont, Auderbon (sic) and Marcy; had acquired a fair knowledge of English & delighted in speaking it, when occasion offered; was a good friend of the white men, had professed religion, had consented to two of his daughters marrying white men, & set his red brethern (sic) a good example by his tiring industry & earnest desire to follow the white man's road to the end."

His burial took place the day following his death, and more than 150 persons showed the esteem in which he was held, by following the remains to their last earthly resting-place. The coffin was borne by Agency employees and other white residents, and the burial services were conducted by the Delawares led by their Seminole preacher."

He was buried a short distance southwest of his farm. His daughter Lucy married an Osborne who died tragically. In 1871, she married H. Pat Pruner. Black Beaver's four grandchildren were John R. Osborne, Charles Beaver Pruner, Margaret Osborne McLane, and Mattie Pruner Sturm, who married Jesse Sturm, son of J.J. Sturm.

Black Beaver's skills as a scout and interpreter earned the Delaware Indian a reputation as one of the best guides in the United States. His friend Israel Yore called him one of God's noblemen, honest and truthful.

BLACKSNAKE

Blacksnake (Seneca, 1760 - December 26, 1859), also known as Thaona Wyuthe (variant spellings: Thaowanyuths, Tenwaneus, or Twyneash), a name meaning the "Chain Breaker," and Dadgayadoh, "The Boys Betting", was an important Seneca chief during the turbulent period following the American Revolution. Born about 1760 at Cattaraugus, New York, about a mile north of Cold Spring, he was a nephew of Cornplanter, the great Seneca chief of the later 1700s and the early

1800s, and of the prophet Handsome Lake. As a young man Blacksnake took part in many major tribal meetings, largely due to his oratorical skills. He received the Wolf Clan name Thaonawyuthe when he became a war chief.

During the American Revolution Blacksnake served on the British side, as did most of the Iroquois. He figured prominently in many battles, including those at Oriskany and in the Wyoming Valley. He is said to have taken part in the Wyoming massacre of 1778.

After the war Blacksnake and other Indian leaders met with officials of the newly formed United States government in an attempt to establish firm boundaries and obtain better treatment for the Indians of the frontier. Washington and other white leaders were sympathetic, but the tide of settlers continued to flow westward. While there were no more full-scale battles between whites and Indians in Iroquois country, there were many local incidents of violence.

The Indians were aware that their traditions and heritage were threatened by the advancing white civilization. In 1799 Blacksnake's uncle, Handsome Lake, had a series of visions that led him to found a new religion that was, in essence, a return to the old tribal culture. The religion also had elements of a social reform movement. Blacksnake was so impressed that he became an early disciple of Gaiwlio, the "Good Word." Like many other people, he believed that indulgence in drink and other aspects of the white man's culture had to be eliminated from Indian life. He remained a believer even when he disagreed with Handsome Lake's often-dictatorial methods of dealing with political problems.

In the War of 1812, Blacksnake fought on the side of the United States. He took part in the Battle of Lake George in 1813. After the war, when he became the principal leader of the Seneca people, he was popularly known as Governor Blacksnake. From his home on the Allegheny River he continued efforts to secure justice for the Iroquois from both the state and federal governments. He also took a leading role in preaching the religion of Handsome Lake following the latter's death in 1815.

Although Blacksnake remained a staunch traditionalist and leader of the so-called "pagan party," his became a strong voice in favor of improved education for tribal youths, the use of modern agriculture, and other changes in Indian life, but in a way that would not mean the end of the traditional life style. His oral version of the Code of Handsome Lake found acceptance among many of the Senecas. He is remembered today as having kept the Seneca people together in the critical period following the death of Handsome Lake. At that time the religion, once so effective as a force binding the people into a single group, could have collapsed, thus destroying their unity and vitality.

Blacksnake died at Cold Spring, New York on December 26, 1859, at the age of 99 years.

JOSEPH BRANT

Joseph Brant (Iroquois, 1742 - November 24, 1807), also known as Thayendanegea, from the Iroquois thayendane-ke, "He Places Two Bets," was an important Mohawk chief who was born while his parents were on a hunting trip along the Ohio River in 1742. His father was Tehowaghwengaraghkwin, a Mohawk Wolf Clan chief, and his mother a full or half-blooded Indian. Because his mother was apparently not a Mohawk, Brant never became a sachem even though his father bore that title. He did, however, become a Mohawk chief.

When his father died, grant's mother remarried. Her second husband, Nicklaus Brant, gave Joseph his English name. Young Joseph grew up at Canajoharie Castle, the family home in the Mohawk Valley. His older sister, Molly, married Sir William Johnson, an English trader who later became the British Superintendent of Indian Affairs.

After his marriage to Molly, Johnson adopted the boy and assumed the responsibility for his education. When he was 13, Brant accompanied Johnson in the campaign of 1755, an episode in the French and Indian War of 1754-63. During the campaign he was present at the Battle of Lake George. In 1759, he took part in the Niagara campaign, becoming known for his outstanding bravery.

Brant was educated for a year at Eliazer Wheelock's Indian Charity School in Lebanon, Connecticut, the forerunner of Dartmouth College. At the Charity School he became a Christian convert, learned to read and write English, and began translating the Bible into the Mohawk language. That project occupied him intermittently for the rest of his life.

In 1763, shortly after leaving school, Brant fought with the British in the war against the Ottawa Indian Chief Pontiac. He married the daughter of an Oneida chief in 1765. By the1770s he was recognized as a prominent leader in the Iroquois League.

As the American Revolution began, Brant became secretary to Guy Johnson, appointed to the post of British Superintendent of Indian Affairs following the death of his uncle, William. Accompanying Guy Johnson to England in 1775, Brant was presented at court and had his portrait painted by the British artist George Romney. He came home more devoted than ever to the British cause; ironically, his influence contributed to the disunity of the Iroquois League during and after the American Revolution. After lengthy debate, the Six Nations of the league divided; the Seneca, Cayuga, Onondaga, and Mohawk factions joined Brant while the Oneida and Tuscarora sided with the Americans.

Brant became a British colonel and participated in devastating raids throughout the Mohawk Valley. A commander of Indian forces at the Battle of Oriskany on August 6, 1777, he displayed desperate courage. Afterward the Six Nations Indians, fighting with the British, harried the Mohawk Valley, southern New York, and northern Pennsylvania, attacking sometimes alone, sometimes with British sympathizers in the colonies.

Brant is believed to have directed the Cherry Valley massacre of 1778 as well as many others. Brant's defenders have claimed that he tried to protect women, children, prisoners, and wounded. If so, he was not always successful. He is known to have taken part in the massacre at Minisink in July 1779.

After the Revolution, he used his influence to establish peace on the Mohawk frontier and to protect his people from American reprisals. He also tried without success to resolve the Iroquois land claims against the new American government. In 1786, while still a British officer on half-pay, Brant returned to England for a visit. The British rewarded him for his efforts in the war with a land grant at Anaquaqua, along the Grand River in Ontario, Canada. He retired to that area with his Mohawk followers. Other Indians from the League joined the group and the area became the Six Nations Reserve.

Brant built the first Episcopal Church in Upper Canada at Brantford, a town that was named for him. He devoted his remaining years to missionary work and translations of sacred texts. He had helped establish "the Old Mohawk Church;" his translations into Mohawk included the Book of Common Prayer and Saint Mark's Gospel. In July 1793, at the request of George Washington, he helped bring peace between the Miami Indians and the United States.

Brant became a strong believer in evangelical Christianity. His first wife died, leaving him two children; he married her half-sister, who was childless. His third wife gave him seven children. He died on his own Ontario estate and was buried near the church he had built.

The American Revolution helped bring about a split in the Iroquois League that was never healed. Brant nonetheless followed the course in which he believed, and his loyalty to the British never waned. A complex man of many talents, he was a scholar, translator, man of religion, highly respected leader of the people, and a courageous, ferocious war-rior. In 1886 the Canadian government donated 13 bronze cannons for a statue to be erected in Brant's memory.

BUCKONGAHELAS

Buckongahelas (Delaware, eighteenth century), was a war chief during the Indian uprisings of the 1790s who won the admiration of his enemies for his candor and humanitarian principles. Born in the mid-eighteenth century, probably in western Ohio, Buckongahelas became Chief of the Delaware on the White and Miami rivers.

Although he eventually fought for the British in the American Revolu-tion, he distrusted the white man and evacuated as many of his people as would follow him to the upper Miami River in April 1781, where he hoped they would find sanctuary. Almost all of the Christian Delaware at Gnadenhutten and Salem, Ohio, declined his invitation as he passed through, and nearly 100 of these peaceful Indians were massacred 11 months later by the Pennsylvania militia.

In the 1790s Buckongahelas was prominent among the leaders of the Indian uprising against the United States. The Delaware, Shawnee, Mi-ami, and other tribes destroyed the force of General Arthur Saint Clair on November 4, 1791, north of Hamilton, Ohio, but were conclusively de-feated themselves on August 20, 1794, by General Anthony Wayne at the Battle of Fallen Timbers. The retreating Indians were denied entrance to Fort Miami, Ohio, a sanctuary promised by the British who incited the uprising.

This treachery ended Buckongahelas' alliance with England. He pledged allegiance to the United States in the Treaty of Greenville on August 3, 1795, but by December 1802 he found it necessary to confront President Thomas Jefferson in Washington, D.C., with what he believed were illegal land appropriations by the government. Later, probably un-der pressure from General William H. Harrison, he ratified the cessions in treaties signed in Indiana at Fort Wayne on June 7, 1803, and in Vin-cennes on August 18, 1804.

Buckongahelas died in 1804 or 1805, probably in Buckongahgelas' Town on the White River near present-day Muncie, Indiana. He never retracted his words to the Delaware at Gnadenhutten before their massa-cre: "I admit that there are good white men, but they bear no proportion to the bad, for the bad rule."

CANARSEE

The Algonquian-speaking Canarsee were formerly a leading tribe of present-day Long Island, New York, living in what is now Kings County, centered near Flatlands. According to Ruttenber they were connected or subject to the Montauk. This is doubtful, however, as those Indians on the western end of the island, at the time of the Dutch settlement, appear to have been paying tribute to the Iroquois.

Canarsee, their main village, was most likely near Flatlands; in addition to which they had others at Maspeth and Hempstead. The site of present-day Brooklyn was originally theirs. After the Dutch appeared, they became independent of the Mohawk, and were nearly exterminated in an attack by them. During the war of the Long Island tribes against the Dutch, the Canarsee suffered greatly.

Their supposed last survivor died in 1800. Any possible survivors may have descendants now living in small communities in the area, including the Poosepatuck and Shinnecock Reservations and the Montauk Indian Village.

CANONCHET

Canonchet (Narraganset, ? - 1676) was a seventeenth century chief, son of Miantonomo, and a leader in the war of King Philip (Metacom), chief of the Wampanoag, against the English in 1675-76. The Narraganset at first refrained from an active part in the war, but probably provided refuge to the Wampanoag and perhaps a few warriors for Philip's forces. In October 1675, Canonchet signed a treaty with the English in which he agreed to surrender refugee Wampanoag. Apparently, Canonchet never intended to deliver the refugees for he is reported to have said: "Not a Wampanoag will I ever give up. No, not the paring of a Wampanoag's nail!"

On December 16, 1675, a force of more than 1,000 men from the New England Confederation attacked the swamp fort of the Narraganset. The Indians suffered heavy losses, but Canonchet escaped and actively fought in the war against the whites. He led several raids against the English settlements, and in March 1676 he defeated English troops under Captain Michael Peirse.

In April 1676, while on a mission to obtain seed corn for planting, Canonchet, surprised by an English force, was captured. When he was sentenced to death, Canonchet stated, "I like it well; for I shall die before my heart is soft, or I have spoken anything unworthy of myself."

120

At Stonington, Connecticut, Canonchet was shot, beheaded, and his body burned by representatives of the English allies: the Pequot, the Mohegan, and the Niantic. His head was sent to Hartford as a trophy. Canonchet's death was a serious blow to Philip's movement, and because it left the Narraganset with no other leader as capable as Canonchet, it probably shortened the course of the war.

CAYUGA

The Cayuga (*Kwenio-gwe*, "The place where the locusts are taken out"), was a tribe of the Iroquois Confederation, formerly living on the shores of Cayuga Lake, New York. Their local council had four clan phratries. This became the pattern of the confederation of the Five Nations of the Iroquois, in which the Cayuga had 10 delegates. There were some 1,500 Cayugas in 1660. When the American Revolution began, most of the tribe went to Canada, never to return.

The remainder were scattered among other confederacy tribes, and soon sold their lands to New York. Some Cayuga went to Ohio, joining other Iroquois in the "Seneca of the Sanduskey". Their descendants are now in Oklahoma. Other Cayuga joined the Oneida reservation in Wisconsin, while about 200 went with the Iroquois of New York, their descendants living on the Allegany, Cattaraugus, Tonawanda, Onondaga, Oneida, and Saint Regis reservations in that state. The Majority, however, some 700 or 800 in 1900, were relocated to the Grand River Reservation in Ontario, Canada, and are now represented on the Six Nations, Caughnawaga, and Tyendinaga (Bay of Quintes) reserves in Canada.

They had three villages in 1670: Kiohero, Goiogouen, and Onondare. Up to the early to mid-1800s, their main village was Gayagaanha. Lesser villages, according to Morgan, were Ganogeh, Gewauga, and Neodakheat. Others were Chonodote, Gandaseteiagon, Kawauka, Kente, Nuquiage, Ondachoe, Owego, Onugareclury, Sant Joseph, Sannio, Skannayutenate, and Swahyaawanh. Their clans were Iroquoian. The Canadian Iroquois recently numbered about 20,500, while the United States Iroquois numbered some 22,000.

CALEB CHEESHATEAUMUCK

Caleb Cheeshateaumuck (Wampanoag, ? - 1666), was the first American Indian to receive a degree from Harvard College (1665). The son of chief, he was born in the area of Martha's Vineyard, Massachusetts.

CHOCORUA

Chocorua (Abnaki; eighteenth century) is presumed to be the last survivor of a small Abnaki tribe in New Hampshire that was driven to extinction about 1766 when English farmers and their cattle encroached on Indian hunting grounds. Chocorua, seeking safety on what is now Mount Chocorua, was shot or pushed over a cliff by a settler, and before he died he cursed the English and their cattle. His existence may be merely legend, fabricated to explain the name of the mountain and the difficulty English settlers had in raising cattle in the region.

CHOPTANK

The Choptank were apparently an Algonquian-speaking tribe consisting of three subtribes, the Ababco, Hutsawap, and Tequassimo, formerly living on the Choptank River in Maryland. Choptank was also a village name, and Abaco was one of their chiefs. They lived along the Choptank River in Dorchester County on the Eastern shore. The Choptank were among the signers of the Treaty of 1659, and were lone signers of a similar treaty in 1705. Such treaties failed to protect the Indians from the encroachment of white settlers.

The Indians typically complained of the destruction of fences around their cornfields by the English and their livestock, while the English claimed the Indians were killing their hogs. Increasing white pressure by whites and the Five Nation Iroquois led the Choptank and other scattered groups in Southern Maryland to consolidate on reservations in the 1680s. Choptank lands were greatly reduced by a series of more or less forced land sales.

Scarcity of deer in the area made a greater reliance on fowling and fishing. They greatly relied on crops, planted by women on patches cleared by the men, and included corn, beans, and pumpkins. The men hunted deer, bear, squirrel, turkeys, partridges and other game and fowl with bows and arrows, whose wood or reed shafts bore glued-on tips of stone, antler, or bone, and were fletched with turkey feathers. Guns soon replaced bows and arrow, as did metal trade tomahawks for wooden clubs. Trapping increased with the developing beaver pelt trade. Along the coast, fishing and shellfishing was also important.

Corn meal was baked into bread, and whole corn was boiled into hominy. Meat was spit-roasted, or stewed with oysters. Food was served in wooden bowls, with shells for spoons. Women made baskets of yucca fiber or reeds. Their boats were dugouts or bark canoes. Skin clothing was worn by adults, while children often went naked in fair weather.

European clothing was adopted early, especially by Indians of high status.

The Choptanks, closely associated with the Nanticokes, had several chiefs, perhaps representing villages, but central authority was weakly developed. There is evidence of Choptank independence, but they are variously mentioned as if part of the Nanticokes or Assateagues, reflecting temporary shifts in location between 1684 and 1694.

Seventeenth population estimates say of the Choptank, "tis almost impossible to have the exact number of men or towns". A few members of mixed Native American and Black blood remained along the Choptank River as late as 1837. Their remnants lost their tribal status and became known as "free Negroes". Close association with blacks is reflected in a 1740's word list that identified several words as Mandingo, a West African Language. This black element may account for early reports about the dark complexion of most of the tribes of southern Maryland.

COCKENOE

Cockenoe (Montauk, 1630-1700), taught John Eliot, the Puritans' "Apostle to the Indians," the language of the Massachusetts Indians and assisted Eliot in translating the Bible into Algonquian. Captured in the Pequot War of 1637, Cockenoe soon was helping Eliot preach to local Indians in their native tongue. Eliot's Bible, the first complete Bible printed in the colonies, probably would not have come into existence were it not for Cockenoe's translation. Cockenoe later served as interpreter for the civil authorities in New York and New England.

CONESTOGA

The name "Conestoga" comes from the word *Kanastoge*, "at the place of the immersed pole." The Conestoga were an important Iroquoian tribal group that formerly lived on Susquehanna River and its branches. When first met by Captain John Smith, in 1608, and until their conquest by the Iroquois Confederation in 1675, they were allied with the Algonquian tribes of the east shore of Chesapeake Bay and at war with those on the west shore. They were described as warlike, with a physique far superior to that of neighboring tribes. By conquest, they claimed the lands on both sides of Chesapeake Bay, from the Choptank and Patuxent Rivers north to the territory of the Iroquois.

In 1675, after their defeat, they established themselves on the east bank of the Potomac, in Maryland, immediately north of Piscataway Creek, below which the Doag (Nanticoke) were then living. They formed a close alliance with the Dutch, Swedes, and the English of Maryland. The Iroquois had carried on relentless war against them, with varying success, which finally reduced them from about 3,000 in 1608 to about 550 in 1648, while their allies brought the aggregate to about 1,250.

Champlain says that in 1615 they had more than 20 villages, of which only three were then at war with the Iroquois, and that their town of Carantouan alone could muster more than 800 warriors. The Iroquois of the north drove the Conestoga down on the tribes to the south and west, which were allies of the English, a movement involving the Conestoga in a war with Maryland and Virginia in 1675. Finding themselves surrounded by enemies on all sides, a portion of them abandoned their country and took refuge with the Occaneechi on Roanoke River, while the rest remained in Pennsylvania.

A quarrel occurred soon with the Occaneechi, who joined the whites against the fugitive Conestoga, who were compelled to return to Susquehanna River and submit to the Iroquois. According to Colden they were all finally removed to Oneida country, where they remained until they lost their language.

They were later allowed to return to Conestoga, their ancient town. Here they wasted rapidly, until, at the close of the year 1763, the remnant, numbering only 20, were massacred by a party of rioters inflamed by the accounts of the Indian war then raging along the Pennsylvania frontier.

Around 1675 their stockade, where they were defeated by the Maryland forces, was on the eastern side of Susquehanna River, three miles below Columbia, Pennsylvania. Herman's map of 1676 located it at nearly the same point on the river, but on the western bank, The Swedes and Dutch called them Minqua, from the Delaware name applied to all tribes of Iroquoian stock. The Powhatan tribes called them Susquehannock, a name signifying "roily river," which was adopted by the English of Virginia and Maryland. The names of their villages are Attock, Carantouan, Cepowig, Oscalui, Quadroque, Sasquesahanough, Testhigh, and Utchowig. The Meherrin on the river of that name in southeast Virginia, were officially reported to be a band of the Conestoga driven south by the Virginians during Bacon's Rebellion in 1675-76. (See SUSQUE-HANNA and SUSQUAHANNOCK.)

CONOY

An Algonquian tribe, the Conoy (Piscataway) were related to the Delawares, from whose ancestral line they apparently sprang, but their closest relations were the Nanticoke. The Conoy were probably united with them in late prehistoric times. The two formed a single tribe, while their language is supposed to have been allied to that spoken by the Powhatan in Virginia. Heckewelder believed them to be identical with the Kanawha, who gave the name to the chief river of West Virginia. Along with the Nanticoke Indians, they lived on the eastern and western shores of Chesapeake Bay and the Potomac River in Maryland, and in southern Delaware.

Thirteen generations would carry back the date of their first "emperor" to the beginning of the sixteenth century. Lord Baltimore's colonists in 1634 established a mission among them, and the Emperor Chitomachen, otherwise known as Tayac, said to be ruler over a dominion extending 130 miles east and west, was converted, with his family. They were, however, so harassed by the Conestoga that a few years later they abandoned their country and moved farther up the Potomac.

Rapidly decreasing, they were in 1673 assigned a tract on that stream, which may have been near the site of Washington, District of Columbia. The Conestoga, when driven from their own country by the Iroquois in 1675, again invaded the territory of the Conoy and forced that tribe up the Potomac and into Pennsylvania. This was gradual, unless it took place at a much later period, for Baron Graffenried, while searching for a reported silver mine in 1711, found them on the Maryland side of the Potomac about 50 miles above Washington, and made a treaty of friendship with them. He calls them "Canawest".

About then the Iroquois assigned them lands at Conejoholo on the Susquehanna, near present Bainbridge, Pennsylvania in the vicinity of the Nanticoke and Conestoga. Here they first began to be known as Conoy. Some of them were living with these tribes at Conestoga in 1742.

They gradually made their way up the Susquehanna River, stopping at Harrisburg, Shamokin, Catawissa, and Wyoming, and in 1765 were living in south New York, at Oswego, Chugnut, and Chenang, on the east branch of the Susquehanna. At that time they numbered only about 150, and, with their associates, the Nanticoke and Mahican, were dependent on the Iroquois. They moved west with the Mahican and Delawares, and soon became known only as a part of those tribes. In 1793 they attended a council near Detroit and used the turkey as their signature.

The customs and beliefs of the Conoy may best be given by the following quotation from White's *Relatio Itineris*, 1635, although the author's interpretations of customs often go far astray, "The natives are very tall and well proportioned; their skin is naturally rather dark, and they make it uglier by staining it, generally with red paint mixed with oil, to keep off the mosquitoes, thinking more of their own comfort than of appearances.

"They disfigure their countenances with other colors, too, painting them in various and truly hideous and frightful ways, either a dark blue above the nose and red below, or the reverse. And as they live almost to extreme old age without having beards, they counterfeit them with paint, by drawing lines of various colors from the extremities of the lips to the ears.

"They generally have black hair, which they carry round in a knot to the left ear, and fasten with a band, adding some ornament which is in estimation among them. Some of them wear on their foreheads the figure of a fish made of copper. They adorn their necks with glass beads strung on a thread like necklaces, though these beads are getting to be less valued among them and less useful for trade. They are clothed for the most part in deerskins or some similar kind of covering, which hangs down behind like a cloak. They wear aprons round the middle, and leave the rest of the body naked. The young boys and girls go about with nothing on them.

"The soles of their feet are as hard a horn, and they tread on thorns and briers without being hurt. Their arms are bows, and arrows three feet long, tipped with stags horn, or a white flint sharpened at the end. They shoot these with such skill that they can stand off and hit a sparrow in the middle; and, in order to become expert by practice, they throw a spear up in the air and then send an arrow from the bow string and drive it into the spear before it falls. But since they do not string the bow very tight, they can not hit a mark at a great distance. They live by means of these weapons, and go out every day through the fields and woods to hunt squirrels, partridges, turkeys, and wild animals. For there is an abundance of all these, though we ourselves do not yet venture to procure food by hunting, for fear of ambushes.

"They live in houses built in an oblong, oval shape. Light is admitted into these through the roof, by a window a foot and a half long; this also serves to carry off the smoke, for they kindle the fire in the middle of the floor, and sleep around the fire. Their kings, however, and chief men have private apartments, as it were, of their own and beds, made by driving four posts into the ground, and arranging poles above they horizontally.

According to the same authority, they acknowledged one god of heaven, yet paid him no outward worship, but strove in every way to appease a certain imaginary spirit, which they called Ochre, that he might not hurt them. They also worshiped corn and fire. The missionary probably here alludes to the use of corn and fire in certain religious ceremonies. The Conoy villages were Catawissa, Conedogwinit, Conejoholo, Conoytown, Kittamaquindi, Onuatuc, Opamemt, Peixtan.

Their descendants now live in the Nanticoke Community in Sussex County, Delaware and numbered about 400 in a recent count.

CORNPLANTER

Cornplanter (Seneca, 1732 - February 18, 1836), also known as John O'Bail, (his Indian name was Gayentwahga), was a chief who fought against the Americans during the United States War of Independence, but who later concluded treaties that ceded substantial tracts of Indian land to the United States. Born at Conewaugus, New York, Cornplanter was of mixed parentage. He derived his exalted position among the Seneca from his mother, a descendant of the tribe's ruling family.

Cornplanter's father was a white trader of either English or Dutch ancestry named John O'Bail or O'Beal who lived in Albany, New York. Little is known of his early life, although it is generally believed that he was present at the defeat of General Edward Braddock near Fort Duquesne, present-day Pittsburgh, Pennsylvania, in 1775. Also as a young man he visited his father in Albany.

Although he was reluctant to join the other tribes of the Iroquois League on the British side during the American Revolution, Cornplanter finally went along with the tribes in the confederacy that pledged allegiance to the crown. He was one of the two Iroquois war chiefs named by the British.

Throughout the hostilities, Cornplanter participated in raiding parties that terrorized white settlements throughout New York and Pennsylvania. When General John Sullivan invaded Seneca country in 1779, Cornplanter fought valiantly, but his hated rival, another Seneca chief named Red Jacket, fled upon catching sight of Sullivan's troops at Lake Canandaigua. Sullivan defeated the Seneca, inflicting heavy losses, burning the villages, and destroying the crops.

Nevertheless, the Seneca, as well as the other Iroquois tribes, never felt that they had been conquered by the Americans. Therefore, when Cornplanter participated in the treaties of 1784, 1789, 1797, and 1802, all of which ceded substantial Indian land in western New York to the United States, his stature among the Seneca went into eclipse. Meanwhile, Red Jacket seized upon the tribe's sense of humiliation at this time to promote his own power and popularity. He protested the land cessions to which Cornplanter signed his name. In fact, Cornplanter became so despised that for a time his life was in danger by members of his own tribe. Cornplanter, however, an eloquent orator, continued to work to assure that the United States Government would live up to the provisions of the treaties. In 1790 he sent a message to President George Washington in Philadelphia, laying before him the grievances of the Seneca.

The white inhabitants of New York and Pennsylvania began to look upon Cornplanter in a different light. Far from the terrifying enemy he had been during the Revolution, Cornplanter was later considered to be a "good Indian." On March 16, 1796, therefore, the State of Pennsylvania granted the Seneca chief a 640-acre tract of land "for his many valuable services to the whites." By 1816 Cornplanter owned 1,300 acres along the banks of the Allegheny River, and he received a pension of $250 annually from the United States Government.

About 1820 Cornplanter experienced a series of visions which he claimed were confrontations with the Great Spirit. Instructed by the Great Spirit to sever all ties with white people, Cornplanter suddenly renounced Christianity and burned all the mementos (flag, medals, belt, hat, sword, etc.) of his warrior days. Moreover, his favorite son, Henry O'Bail, who had been carefully educated, became a drunkard, adding to the trials of Cornplanter's later years. He was still an impressive figure at the time of his death in 1836. A monument was erected in his honor by the State of Pennsylvania, at the site where he was buried on his land near the Allegheny.

COWESET

The Coweset Indians of Massachusetts were a small tribe of band that was subject to the Narragansett. However, they threw off that connection by 1660. Many of the descendants of the Coweset and Narraganset, along with those of the Massachusett, Nauset, Nipmuc, Wampanoag, and Natick, now live in the Nipmuc Community, near Worcester, Massachusetts; On Martha's Vineyar (Gay Head); and on Cape Cod (Mashpee). They all spoke Algonquian languages.

DEKANAWIDA

Dekanawida (Huron, sixteenth century), was a prophet, statesman, and lawgiver who determined to unite the entire human race into a confederation based upon the principles of equity and righteousness, and succeeded in laying the moral and political foundation for the Iroquois Confederacy.

A mystical-being during his lifetime, Dekanawida has been shrouded in mystery. No doubt a real person, he ranks as a demigod in Iroquois legend. In fact, stories about him often confuse Christian theology with Iroquois tradition.

Dekanawida, says tradition, was born near present-day Kingston, Ontario, the son of a virgin. After his birth, however, the mother and grandmother attempted to murder Dekanawida, fearing that the child had an evil destiny. The grandmother learned in a dream that the child would indirectly cause the destruction of the Huron people. The Iroquois Confederacy that Dekanawida helped establish did in fact destroy the Huron Confederacy. Mother and grandmother tried three times to kill the newborn infant, pushing him through a hole in the ice of a frozen stream; but in each instance the baby was found alive and unharmed in its mother's arms when she awoke the following morning.

Dekanawida grew up an outcast, shunned by the Huron. No doubt his alienation from the tribe contributed greatly to his inability to speak without stammering. Nonetheless, he was convinced that he had a divine mission, a conviction reinforced by his vision of all mankind united, living in peace and brotherhood.

Three sets of double principles formed the constitutional framework for his unification of all tribes throughout the world: 1. Equity and justice, and righteousness in conduct, thought, and speech. 2. Physical strength and civil authority, plus inner spiritual power. 3. Sanity of mind and physical health, and peace among individuals and groups. Dekanawida, sure of his destiny, set out from the land of the Huron to go to Iroquois territory. There he won converts to what would come to be called "The Great Peace."

The exact circumstances are buried deep in mystery and obscure legend, but in some way Dekanawida joined forces with Hiawatha, who had been trying to unite the Iroquois. Although well intentioned, Hiawatha had lacked specific principles to construct a lasting confederation. Dekanawida converted Hiawatha to his code for the unification of all people under the three sets of double principles, and the two embarked upon winning over the main stumbling block to the Iroquois Confederation, the Onondaga chief Wathatotarho. Dekanawida was the prophet; Hiawatha was the spokesman. Together they converted Wathatotarho and aligned the five Iroquois nations, (Onondaga, Mohawk, Cayuga, Seneca, and Oneida) into a powerful league that would last for more than two centuries.

The league was ruled by a council of 50 peace chiefs, known as sachems, which were chosen from specific clans. Since he was not an Iroquois by birth, Dekanawida became a chief on the basis of merit, and he forbade the appointment of a successor to his office.

Believing that this great triumph was merely the beginning of the realization of his divine mission, Dekanawida left the Iroquois to take his message to the world. As legend has it, he paddled out on Lake Ontario in a canoe made from brilliant white stone, and disappeared into the sunset.

DEKANISORA

Dekanisora (Onondaga, ? - 1730), was an Iroquois chief and an a noted orator who tried to maintain peace with both the French and the English. Dekanisora (Teganessorens) is first mentioned as a leader of an Iroquois peace embassy to Montreal in 1682. In 1688 he was one of the deputies captured and then released by Adario, in his successful effort to reopen hostilities between the French and the Iroquois.

In 1694 Dekanisora arranged a truce with the French at Quebec, but insisted that English allies be included in the peace negotiations. At Albany, Dekanisora found the English opposed to any reconciliation between the Iroquois and the French. He reaffirmed his loyalty to the English but asserted the Iroquois right to act independently. Nevertheless, the Iroquois could not come to terms with the French, and general peace failed. In 1701, however, Dekanisora represented the Indians in a lasting peace treaty with the French.

In 1726 Dekanisora was again an ambassador to Albany, where he helped to execute an agreement that placed Iroquois hunting grounds under the protection of the king of England. He died about 1780 at an advanced age.

Because of his reputation as a speaker among the Iroquois, Dekanisora took part in most of their negotiations with the French and English. He was described by his contemporary Cadwallader Colden as having "a great fluency in speaking and a graceful elocution that would have pleased in any part of the world. "He may have been a Christian convert.

Dekanisora helped to preserve, so far as was possible, the independence of the Five Nations from both European powers.

FREDERICK J. DOCKSTADER

Frederick J. Dockstader (Oneida-Navajo, February 3, 1919 -), a distinguished anthropologist, author, and expert on Indian arts, was born at Los Angeles, California, and spent much of his early life on the Navajo and Hopi reservations in Arizona. After an early teaching career, Dockstader became a staff ethnologist at the Cranbrook Institute of Sciences (1950), and later became the curator of anthropology at Dartmouth College (1952). He joined the staff of the Museum of the American Indian, Heye Foundation, in New York City as assistant director (1955) and became director in 1960.

Dockstader, a practicing silversmith, was named the commissioner of the Indian Arts and Crafts Board of the United States Department of the Interior in 1955. His publications include Great North American Indians (1977), Indian Art in America (1961), Indian Art in Middle America (1964), Indian Art in South America (1967), and Pre-Columbian Art and Later Indian Tribal Arts (1968).

ERIE

Now extinct, the Erie were a populous, sedentary Iroquoian tribe. In the seventeenth century, their territory extended south from Lake Erie to the Ohio River, east to the lands of the Conestoga along the Allegheny River, and the Seneca along the Genesee River, and north to those of the Neutral of Lake Erie.

Historically, little is known of the Erie and their political and social organization, but it was similar to that of the Huron. The Jesuits gave a few glimpses of their lives, while describing their last wars with the Iroquois Confederation. The Erie had many towns and villages, and were organized into several divisions; they cultivated the soil, and spoke a language resembling that of the Huron.

It is not known which four of the five Huron dialects, usually called "Wendat" (Wyandot) by theirselves, was actually spoken. From the same sources comes a rough estimate of the population of the Erie at the period of final war. At the taking of the Erie town of Rique in 1654, it is claimed that the defenders numbered between 3,000 and 4,000. But since it is not likely that all warriors of the tribe were present, 14,500 would probably be a conservative estimate of the population of the Erieat the time.

The years 1655-56 were the last for the Erie. Thirty ambassadors of the Cat Nation were sent to Sonontouan, the Seneca capital, to renew the existing peace. Through an accident, one of the men of the Cat Nation killed a Seneca. The incensed Seneca massacred all except five of the ambassadors, which led to the final war between the Erie and the confederated tribes of the Iroquois, especially the Seneca, Cayuga, Oneida, and Onondaga.

The Erie were brave and warlike, employing only bows and poisoned arrows. Following the rupture of relations between the Erie and the Iroquois in 1653, the Erie burned a Seneca town, pursued an Iroquois war party returning from the Great Lakes, and slaughtered 80 men, while Erie scouts had come to the very gates of one of the Iroquois palisaded towns and captured Annenraes (Annencraos), "one of the greatest captains." All this, of course, roused the Iroquois, who raised 1,800 men to punish the Erie.

After stubborn resistance, the Erie were overrun and the Onondaga "entered the fort and so many women and children were killed that blood was knee-deep in certain places." This was at the town of Rique, which was defended by between 3,000 to 4,000 Indians, and was assailed by the 1,800 Iroquois. This devastating war lasted until about the close of 1656, when Erie power was broken and its members were destroyed, dispersed, or captured. Six hundred surrendered at one time and were led to the Iroquois country to be adopted as one of the constituent people of the Iroquois tribes. The defeat at Rique forced the Iroquois to remain in enemy territory for two months, caring for the wounded and burying the dead.

FIVE NATIONS IROQUOIS

When Europeans first encountered Indians in what is now upstate New York, they met the Five Nations Iroquois. This confederacy was to play an important role in the struggles among Europeans and Americans for control of the northeastern woodlands.

The Iroquois got their name from their Algonquin Indian enemies; Iroquois is thought to mean "real adders." The five tribes called themselves the *Ongwanonhsioni,* meaning "longhouse builders," or *Hodinonhsioni,* "people of the longhouse," in reference to their confederacy. The five tribes of the confederacy were the Seneca, Cayuga, Onondaga, Oneida, and Mohawk. These names were applied to the tribes by themselves, as well as by other Indians, the French, the Dutch, the English, and the Americans, over several hundred years. Each tribe had a name for itself, meaning the "people of" a particular town or place. The Seneca were Onondewagano, the Cayuga were Gayokwehono, the Onondaga were Onontaga, the Oneida were Oneyotdehaga, and the Mohawk were Kany-engehaga. The Iroquois are believed to have descended from hunters and gatherers who lived for thousands of years in upstate New York. The actual date of the formation of the League of the Iroquois is not known. Most estimates fall between AD 1400 and 1600. The Iroquois generally stated that the league was formed before European contact. In Iroquois oral tradition, two men, Deganawida and Hiawatha (not Long-fellow's Hiawatha), founded the league.

At the time of European contact, the Seneca, Cayuga, Onondaga, Oneida, and Mohawk, in that order, lived from west to east in the region between the Genesee River and Schoharie Creek.Their hunters, traders, and warriors ranged from the Mississippi River to New England.

The Five Nations spoke Northern Iroquoian languages. Each tribe's speech was sufficiently distinct to call it a separate language, but there was also enough mutual intelligibility between them that they could be called dialects of a single language. The Iroquois made pictographs, but did not develop a written alphabet.

The Iroquois believed that the world had many supernatural spirits whose goodwill was needed for a bountiful life. Therefore, everyday activities were closely interwoven with religious beliefs. The core belief for the Iroquoian-speaking confederacy was an elaborate funeral rite known as the Condolence. Through time, this rite became the vehicle for political meetings, and it brought together leaders from various Iroquois tribes and villages. Although some of the leaders were identified as peace chiefs or sachems, the real political power of the confederacy resided with the war chiefs.

The group held seasonal festivals and ceremonies to give thanks to their spiritual leaders. The Iroquois year began in the spring, and a festival was held to express gratitude to "The Creator" and "The Maple" for the sweet syrup made from sap. Spawning fish and roosting pigeons were caught. During this season, clearings were made in the forests to replace old fields and also to build new palisaded villages.

Villages had to be moved every ten to twenty years, as firewood supplies and fields became exhausted. By May, "The Three Sisters" of maize, beans, and squash were planted, and a festival was held to give thanks for these foods, their main sustenance. Elm bark for longhouses, canoes, and containers, was then gathered. Wild strawberries appeared in the woods, and a festival was held in thanks for these first fruits. In

133

summer, most men departed to trade or go into battle. Women gathered wild plants for food and medicine, worked in the fields, and harvested and stored the crops. Festivals were held to honor "The Corn Mother" and to celebrate the harvest.

In the fall, deer were hunted, nuts were gathered, and fish were caught in preparation for winter. Councils were held during this time, as snow confined them to their villages for the most part. Winter was a time for socializing, storytelling, and the manufacture and repair of tools and clothing. Raw products, including stone, clay, plant fibers, and animal products were made into knives, axes, drills, bows, arrows, clubs, jars, bowls, mortars, mats, baskets, fishhooks, needles, snowshoes, lacrosse sticks, dolls, and much more. The New Year came after winter solstice, and Midwinter, another important festival, was held to strengthen "The Creator" after his winter struggle with his evil twin.

Iroquois children were free of responsibilities, and all played together until the age of eight or nine, when the boys and girls were separated and began to acquire adult skills through observation and mimicry. After marriage, the husband usually went to live in his wife's longhouse. Their children belonged to the mother's clan. Each longhouse held several families, which belonged to a single matriclan, tracing descent through the women.

Villages contained at least three of twelve different clans. The clans had ceremonial duties towards each other in various games and rituals. The clans were the basis of political organization at all levels. Clan chiefs and other elders determined village policy. The clan matrons selected the fifty hereditary sachems representing the tribes at the confederacy's councils, Other leaders, such as war chiefs, were selected on the basis of merit.

Contact with white culture brought many changes. The Iroquois adopted western technology, but their rich cultural traditions survived, as shown in their art forms, including pottery, basketry, bead and porcupine quill decoration, silversmithing, and carving. They are best known for false masks used at healing ceremonies.

After European contact, the Iroquois fell into competition with surrounding Indian groups for hunting territory in order to obtain furs for trading for French, Dutch and, later, English goods, such as cloth, beads, guns, metal axes, knives, and kettles. Between 1638 and 1675, the Iroquois defeated the Wenro, Huron, Petun, Neutral, Erie, and Susquehannock confederacies. Many of the defeated Indians moved among the victorious Iroquois.

Throughout most of the seventeenth and eighteenth centuries, the Iroquois maintained their position between the British and the French by a combination of warfare and skillful diplomacy. French Jesuits began missionary activities among the Iroquois after 1653. Their missions were soon closed, but were resumed in 1668. Relations with the French became strained and the missions were abandoned in the early 1680s. The Iroquois raided the French, who attacked the Seneca in 1687, the Mohawk in 1693, and the Onondaga and Oneida in 1696.

Smallpox and warfare reduced the Iroquois population during the seventeenth century, though some of their loss was made up by the adoption of other Indians. In 1660, the Iroquois tribes were believed to have had less than 2,200 warriors.

Starting in the latter part of the seventeenth century, a number of Iroquois left their traditional homeland. During the 1660s, some Cayuga settled along the Saint Lawrence River in Canada, and by the mid-eighteenth century, they had established large settlements at Saint Regis and Caughnawaga.

Cayugas, Onondagas, and Oneidas also moved to the Saint Lawrence area and, in the 1750s, a number were living at Oswegatchie (now Ogdensburg, New York).

The Five Nations Iroquois added the Tuscarora to their confederacy in the 1700s, and the name was changed to the Six Nations Confederacy. In 1753, the Cayuga adopted the Tutelo and Saponi, who established a village south of Cayuga Lake. After the British defeated the French at Montreal in 1760, the Iroquois could no longer control the balance of power. When the American Revolution broke out, the Iroquois attempted to remain neutral. Eventually most of them were drawn in on the side of the British, though some Oneida sided with the Americans. In 1779, an American army destroyed the homeland of the Iroquois, who fled to western New York and Canada.

The American Revolution destroyed the power of the league. The Americans made treaties with the Iroquois, forcing them to sell their remaining lands in New York, except for a few reservations. Many Iroquois moved to reserves in Canada and some went west. Two councils were formed, one in Canada, and one in the United States. After the last treaty was signed in 1842, land continued to be sold or leased to whites.

The change to reservation life was a difficult one. Drinking and fighting became serious problems. However, the teachings of Handsome Lake, a Seneca, reconciled traditional religious beliefs with white material culture and helped the Iroquois adapt to their new lives. Constitutional governments replaced the hereditary chiefs on the Allegany and Cattaraugus reservations in 1848, and in 1924, the Canadians forced an elected council on the Grand River Reserve. By the late 1980s, the Iroquois population on reservations in Canada and in the United States was estimated at about 30,000 people.

Today the Iroquois live both on and off the reservations. Except for garden plots, farming in general has decreased in importance, as individuals seek wage labor. For example, Mohawks from the Saint Regis and Caughnanwaga Reserves have achieved prominence as high steelworkers. On reservations, many old practices and beliefs are maintained by traditional members of the community, though most Iroquois are Christians. Ceremonies for traditional foods, healing rituals, and the Midwinter Festival are still held. The League of the Iroquois continues in existence, and clan mothers wield their influence in selecting chiefs. The Iroquois genius for survival has kept their cultural heritage alive through the present.

The underlying myth of the present-day Six Nations Confederacy was the journey of a cultural hero named Deganawidah, who brought forth a plan of peace and harmony to the five warring tribes. From this reformation came a confederacy calling for establishment of a hereditary council of fifty sachems from the five tribes, appointed by clan matrons, and a ceremonial and political protocol that is rooted in kinship structure and traditional world view of the people.

The Code of Handsome Lake, by which the hereditary councils still function, is a formalized belief system set forth in 1799 by Seneca sachem, Handsome Lake, after he had a series of visions that called upon the Iroquois to return to their former ways. The code provides an ideological and political link to all the reservation communities.

Although today there is less than a full complement of sachems in the Canadian and New York reservation confederacies, chiefs and titles are often "borrowed." Neither confederacy is officially recognized by its respective state, provincial or federal government, but both have considerable political influence. The New York confederacy seeks to extend authority over all Iroquois communities and replace remaining elective systems with hereditary councils.

The New York confederacy today is strengthened and sustained by its nativistic beliefs, assertions and expressions of sovereignty, and a small corp of leaders who are both skilled politicians and information managers. Activities are focused on state and federal governments. Recently, the confederation intervened in the Seneca lease issue and land claims, though not without opposition from other Iroquois. In 1989, after years of negotiations and demands, the State of New York returned 12 wampum belts to the Onondaga, who now hold them in their traditional role as wampum keepers of the confederacy.

New legislative efforts have resulted in introduction of an Indian burial protection bills, and passage of a measure exempting Indians from the oath of allegiance to New York. Over the last several years, the confederacy has sought to control land claims and to prevent gambling casinos from operating on reservations. (See also IROQUOIAN FAMILY, IRO-QUOIS, and IROQUOIS CONFEDERACY)

HACKENSACK

The Hackensack consisted of a number of Munsee Delaware-speaking groups which inhabited the coastal lowlands of northeastern New Jersey to the east of the Watchung Hills from the Hackensack-Passaic River drainage south to the lower reaches of the Raritan River. The Hackensack, who were no longer identifiable as a tribe by the mid-1700s, are today known almost exclusively through the surviving documentation of the successive Dutch (1609-1664), English (1664-1782), and American (1782- present) regimes. Archaeology has failed to establish a connection between any known site and a historically known Hackensack settlement.

The first documentary record of aboriginal occupation in Hackensack territory occurred in a 1616 Dutch reference to a group located along the west bank of the Hudson River opposite Manhattan Island. Identified as the Machkentiwomi, this group may have had people "dwelling over against the Manhattans," who were decimated by epidemic disease and dispersed by the Wappinger sometime before 1628.

A number of "aboriginal proprietors" later identified as Hackensack sachems, or leaders, participated in a series of land sales to the authorities of the Dutch colony of New Netherland in 1630.

Among the native signers were a number of "Virginians." The terms "Virginian" and "Southern Indian" referred to native people from groups that inhabited lands to the south of the Delaware River and the southern boundary of New Netherland. The presence of Virginians, along with the dispersion of the earlier native population of the Hackensack Valley, clearly point out the enormous changes that were occurring among native groups during the opening years of European intrusion. This also indicates that the group later known as the Hackensack was made up of a number of different peoples from several regions.

137

The 1630 land sales conveyed the Bayonne Peninsula and Staten Island to the Dutch. The Dutch soon established trading posts and plantations on these lands, which were located close to the centers of Hackensack settlement. The major Hackensack communities of the period were Ahasimus, on the Bayonne Peninsula, Hespatingh, in the city of the same name, and the Hackensack Castle, situated in the highlands to the northwest of Hackensack.

The Dutch settlements became a source of friction between the Hackensack and the Dutch soon after their establishment in the early 1630s. Sharp trade deals, defective trade goods, and liquor defrauded many of the Indians. The fatal shooting of a Dutchman by a "Hackingsack" man at Pavonia, now New Jersey City, in 1642, marked the first time the Hackensack were mentioned by name in the Dutch records. This and other incidents led the Dutch to consider retaliation against the lower Hudson River Native groups. The Dutch got their opportunity when a large Mahican war party attacked the Wiechquaeskeck of the east bank of the lower Hudson River during February 1643. The Wiechquaeskeck claimed and received refuge from the Mahican under the walls of Fort Amsterdam in lower Manhattan and at Pavonia across the river in Hackensack territory. Both camps were simultaneously subjected to Dutch surprise attacks during the night of February 25-26, 1643. The lower Hudson River groups were outraged by this massacre.

Many Hackensack reportedly perished, along with some 120 Wiechquaeskeck people at Pavonia. The lower Hudson River groups immediately burned the outlying Dutch settlements throughout the region and drove their inhabitants to the shelter of Fort Amsterdam.

The conflict was ruinous for both sides, dependent as they were upon each other. New Netherland was a trading colony, and the native people of the area provided the furs that were the raw material of the commerce. The Dutch, on their part, supplied the metal tools, cloth, muskets, and other trade goods that had become an indispensable part of aboriginal life. The Hackensack sachem, Oratam, accordingly agitated for peace, and succeeded in arranging a truce with the Dutch on April 22, 1643 on behalf of "the savages living at Ackinkes hacky...and...Tappaen, Rechgawawanc, Kichtawanc, and Sinsinck."

Oratam continued to play a major role in negotiations between the remaining native rebels and the Dutch. Two years later, on August 30, 1645, Oratam signed the general peace treaty that ended the conflict, known thereafter as "The Governor Kieft War," after the Director of the Colony of New Netherland. The Wiechquaeskeck and their allies did not participate in this treaty. Finally, following pressure from the powerful Susquehannock group, and under Hackensack sponsor, the last remaining hostile groups pledged to keep the peace with the Dutch on July 19, 1649.

The Hackensack were again split into pro and antiwar factions during the brief "Peach War" of 1655-1656. A report dated November 10, 1655 noted that the Hackensack and Tappan groups did the most damage to the Dutch; Oratam's speaker, Pennekeck, served as a key intermediary between the warring groups, and assisted in ransoming a large number of white captives during the conflict.

These wars resulted in extensive changes in native life. Large numbers of native people living near the center of the Dutch settlement immigrated to more hospitable regions. The Hackensack accepted a substantial number of Western Long Island, Staten Island, and Wiechquaeskeck immigrants. The nature of the Hackensack settlement also changed at this time. The natives of the region found that their large fortified towns were easy targets for Dutch armies.

Population losses caused by wars and epidemics made such large settlements even more vulnerable. The Hackensack and their neighbors accordingly chose to settle in small hamlets scattered throughout their territories. These were more difficult to surprise, easier to escape from, and gave the impression of a sizable native presence in their territories.

Oratam and the Hackensack served as intermediaries between the hostile Esopus groups of the mid-Hudson valley and the Dutch during the "Esopus Wars" of 1659-1664. Favoring the Esopus pro-peace faction, Oratam secured asylum for their sachems, ransomed white captives, and gave the Dutch information of Esopus activities. Other Hackensack sided with the hostile Esopus, and supported their operations. Dutch military successes and Hackensack diplomacy brought the contending parties to the conference table, and a treaty was signed by the Esopus and the Dutch on May 15, 1664.

The Hackensack swiftly allied with the English following the capture of New Netherland by the forces of the Duke of York on September 6, 1664. The English quickly embarked on a series of land purchases that increasingly crowded the Hackensack out of their traditional territories along the lower reaches of the Hackensack and Passaic rivers. Relations with the English remained peaceable, however, and the Hackensack submitted to English jurisdiction.

The Hackensack responded to English territorial demands by selling small parcels and demanding the right to remain in their small settlements. Relentless English pressure gradually drove them northward to the headwaters of the northeastern New Jersey River drainage by the turn of the eighteenth century. The records indicate that the Hackensack increasingly became involved with the Tappan, their northern neighbors. Sachems like Mindawassa and Jan Claes came to represent both groups, and the Hackensack and Tappan effectively merged by 1700.

The Hackensack and Tappan were last mentioned by name on April 19, 1693. The people that made up these groups did not, however, disappear along with their name. They remained in small communities scattered throughout the upland portions of the Passaic watershed during the first half of the eighteenth century. Their leaders, Memshe, Memerescum, Taphow and others, signed documents as sachems, "of all the nations on Romopuck, Sadie, Pasqueek, Narashunk, Hackensack rivers and Tappan."

The northern New Jersey Indians became increasingly connected with their Minisink neighbors to the west along the upper Delaware River Valley. Most of them either joined the Minisink or moved further south to settlements at the "Forks of the Delaware" at Easton, Pennsylvania. Both groups finally sided against the English during their last war with the French over control of North America, known as the Seven Years', or French and Indian War (1755-1762).

Not all of the native people of the region chose to oppose English dominion, however, and most of the remaining groups still in New Jersey signed a treaty with the English at Crosswicks on January 8-9, 1756. A number of otherwise unidentified "Indians in the County of Bergen," the heart of traditional Hackensack territory, claimed English protection under the provisions of the Crosswicks Treaty on March 16, 1756.

They and other natives living north of the Raritan River were confined to an area between the Hudson River and the western limits of the Passaic and Raritan valleys for the duration of the conflict. The "Bergen County Indians" and their neighbors were unable to wait the conflict out, however.

On October 23, 1758, the Minisink sold their last claims to land in northern New Jersey from the Raritan River north to the New York-New Jersey line. They and their allies then moved into the western Susquehanna and Allegheny River valleys of Pennsylvaniaby June 15, 1759. It was reported that "the Indians in the northern parts of the Province (of New Jersey) have entirely exited it and are going to Sesquehannah." The descendants of the Hackensack were among those westward immigrants, and today they reside in the surviving Munsee communities in Wisconsin, Oklahoma, and Ontario, Canada.

HALF KING

Half King (Huron, late eighteenth century), was a Wyandotte chief in the area of Sandusky, Ohio, who joined the British during the War of Independence to fight against American encroachment on Indian territory west of the Allegheny Mountains. During the Revolution he commanded Ottawa, Chippewa, Shawnee, and other tribes of warriors in addition to his Huron followers. He won particular recognition for the firm discipline he required of this composite force. To assure the good behavior of his warriors, Half King took special pains to prevent their access to alcohol. The result was that Half King's Indian army behaved well in combat and avoided the temptation to spill white blood indiscriminately.

The primary beneficiaries of Half King's efforts were the Moravians of Lichtenau, an evangelical Protestant sect that settled in Ohio. At times during 1777 as many as 200 warriors camped immediately outside of Lichtenau, and since it was largely anti-settler sentiment that motivated many of the Indians to fight on the British side, the Moravians could easily have been massacred. Half King kept the mixed assemblage of warriors from making the Moravians the victims of their wrath.

Nevertheless, Half King did insist upon the removal of Christianized Indians from the Sandusky area. This was done not so much out of hostility to Christianity as from concern that such Indians were not safe among their unconverted brethren. He continued to protect the Moravians and their converts after the Revolution, even when the Protestants abandoned his domain and went to Detroit.

On March 6, 1782, two Indian families were killed by settlers' militia. The northern Ohio area tribes, even those supporting the colonies, arose to seek revenge. On June 4, about two miles from his village, Half King met the militia under Colonel William Crawford. With the aid of Butler's Rangers (British reinforcements), and warriors sent from the Delaware and Shawnee tribes, Half King overwhelmed the colonial militia and caught and executed Crawford. After the Revolution, Half King signed the Treaty of Fort McIntosh on January 2, 1785.

HANDSOME LAKE

Handsome Lake (Seneca, 1735 - August 10, 1815), also known as Ganiod'yo, was a chief and a religious elder who developed an ethical code which became the basis of a new religion for the Iroquois people, known as the Handsome Lake religion, or the Longhouse religion.

Handsome Lake, was born at Ganawaugus, New York, at the end of the era of power and prosperity for the Seneca nation. During his youth and early manhood, he watched his society and his culture disintegrate while he fought as a warrior against the British in Pontiac's Conspiracy, then against the Cherokee and Choctaw, and during the Revolution against the Americans. At the council with the British at Oswego, New York, in the early summer of 1777, Handsome Lake supported the position of his brother, Cornplanter, that the Iroquois should remain neutral in what was a civil war among white people. However, the warriors voted to go to war and Handsome Lake fought with his people.

He took an active part in the drawn-out negotiations between the Iroquois and the Americans following the war. After several disastrous treaties, the Seneca sold all their lands, with the exception of a few reservations, at the Treaty of Big Tree in 1797.

After a period of prolonged whiskey drinking, Handsome Lake became seriously ill in 1799 and was near death. He recovered and declared that he had been visited by three spirits, and that had revealed to him the will of the Creator. More visions followed, and from 1800 Handsome Lake became an itinerant preacher of the religion that he called Gaiwiio ("good message").

His message was predominated by three apocalyptic themes: the imminence of world destruction, the definition of sin, and the prescription for salvation following the practices he recommended). He condemned the drinking of whiskey and the practice of witchcraft and magic, and he urged his people to confess their sins and abandon their evil ways. His message was a combination of traditional Iroquois beliefs and Christian ethics. It provided the Iroquois with a faith that revitalized their civilization at a time when it was threatened with extinction.

In 1801 Handsome Lake accused Red Jacket of witchcraft. The confrontation was precipitated by an argument over land. Red Jacket favored selling to the State of New York a strip of land along the Niagara River, which was a favorite fishing place of the Seneca. Handsome Lake was a leader of the opposition, and his "slanders" against Red Jacket for a time cost him his position of sachem.

Beginning in the fall of 1801 and increasingly in the years thereafter, Handsome Lake emphasized a social message: temperance in daily life, peace, land retention, domestic morality, and acculturation. In the winter of 1801-02, he led a delegation of Seneca to Washington and met with

President Thomas Jefferson. Although his political power waned in later years, Handsome Lake always remained a triumphantly successful evangelist. He died on a visit to Onondaga, New York, and was buried there in the center of the council house.

HAVERSTRAW

The Haverstraw tribe was also known as the Remahenonck and Rechgawawanck. They were a small group speaking Munsee-Delaware, that lived on a stretch of shoreline along the western banks of the Haverstraw Bay reach of the Hudson River, in southeastern New York. Closely hemmed in by the steep walls of the northernmost escarpment of the Palisades Highlands, the Haverstraw settlements were bounded on the south by the territories of the Tappan group, and by the slopes of the Hudson Highlands to the west and north. The village of Haverstraw today occupies the central portion of the traditional Haverstraw country.

The Haverstraw were named after a prominent sachem, or peace leader, as were many Delaware groups. A manuscript dated March 6, 1660 documented the fact that their chief was named "Rumanchenanck, alias Haverstroo." This practice has long contributed to the misidentification of the Rechgawawanck as the Manhattan Indians of central Manhattan Island and the adjacent southwest Bronx. The Reverend Robert Bolton, a prominent early nineteenth century student of local native ethno-history in Westchester County, New York, first made this connection.

He noted that a sachem named Rechgewac signed over a number of tracts of land in Manhattan and the Bronx to Dutch purchasers. He further noted that several place names on Manhattan, most notably Rechewas Point and Rechewanes, seemed to suggest a relationship with Rechgewac. It only took a small leap to name the otherwise unlocated Rechgawawanck of the colonial literature after this sachem.

The problem with this interpretation is the fact that many place names based upon the Delaware words *lekau*, "sand" and *lechauwaak*, "fork, branch" occur widely throughout this region by virtue of the extensive presence of sand and complex river systems. Further, the Rechgawawanck were repeatedly mentioned in company with the Tappan and Hackensack, neighbors of the Haverstraw.

The Hudson River was a formidable boundary, and the other ethno-historic data does not support extensive connections between the downriver groups fronting its shorelines. Finally, the only known Rechgawawanck sachem was listed as Sesekemu, which was another spelling for Sessikout, an influential Haverstraw paramount sachem.

143

The Haverstraw first appeared in Dutch documentation of their New Netherland colony in 1642, when some chiefs from "Ackinghsack and Rechawanck" reported that the murderer of a Dutchman in the Hackensack area had fled into the interior. A number of them were later victims of a Dutch massacre of fugitives from the Mahican raid on Manhattan and at Pavonia, now Jersey City, New Jersey, on the night of February 25-26, 1643. They were among the groups represented by the Hackensack sachem, Oratam, in subsequent peace negotiations with the Dutch. Oratam concluded the peace on April 22, 1643 on behalf of his own people and for "the savages of Tappaen, Rechgawawanc, Kichtawanc, and Sintsinck."

The latter two groups lived along the eastern banks of the Tappan Zee and Haverstraw Bay reaches of the Hudson River, opposite the Tappan and Haverstraw groups. The sachems Sesekemu (Sessikout) and Willem of "Tappaens and Rechgawawanch" signed the final peace treaty of August 30, 1645 that ended the Governor Kieft War (1640-1645) on behalf of their people. These friendly relations were reaffirmed on July 19, 1649 by the group, then identified as the Remahenonck.

The Haverstraw were first mentioned by that name on the 1656 Adriaen van der Donck map of New Netherland. Documents related to the events of the Esopus Wars (1659-1664) indicated close relations between Haverstraw neighbors. On July 10, 1657, a Haverstraw chief named Keghtackcean sold out his land holdings to the Dutch. He then moved north among the Esopus of the lower Wallkill River Valley. On March 15, 1664, it was revealed that Sessikout was the brother of an Esopus sachem. An earlier document, dated March 6, 1660, noted that Corruspin, often mistaken for the chief sachem of the Haverstraw, was actually the brother of Sessikout. Both citations clearly demonstrate the principle of matrilineal descent commonly found among native peoples of the mid-Atlantic Coast. This kinship held that leadership was inherited not by a person's son, but by brothers and sisters, and then by sisters' children.

Many Haverstraw chose to support the Esopus and their allies in the struggle against the Dutch. Confused by Haverstraw intentions, and lacking direct evidence of their participation in the war, the Dutch attempted to obtain confirmation of war or peace from their sachems on April 21, 1664. The Dutch were put off at that time, but "Ses-Segh-Hout, chief of the Rewechnongh or Haverstraw" placed his mark upon the May 16, 1664 treaty that ended the Esopus War.

The English takeover of New Netherlands on September 6, 1664 did not immediately affect the Haverstraw. Corruspin signed the April 13, 1671 deed to lands along the Palisades in Hackensack territory as "Croppun, sachima of Haverstroo." This land conveyance did not, however, concern any part of the traditional Haverstraw homeland. It did serve to emphasize the connections between the Haverstraw and the Hackensack.

English interest finally focused directly upon the Haverstraw territory during the following decade, and two land cessions, dated July 13, 1683 and September 10, 1684, completely sold off their homeland. A number of Haverstraw families moved north to the Esopus, though most moved among their Tappan- Hackensack neighbors in the upper Ramapo and Pequannock River drainages in northern New Jersey.

Known during the following century as part of the River Indians, descendants of the Haverstraw may today reside on two reservations in Ontario, Canada; on the Stockbridge-Munsee Indian Reservation in Wisconsin; and on the former Cherokee, Wichita, and Caddo Reservations in Oklahoma.

HENDRICK

Hendrick (Mohawk, 1700 - September 8, 1755), also known as Tee Yee Neen Ho Ga Row (Christianized Hendrick), was an influential chief and one of the "Four Indian Kings."

HIACOOMES

Hiacoomes (Wampanoag, 1610 - 1690), was allegedly the first Indian in North America to be converted to Christianity and the first to be ordained a Christian clergyman. Information about his life is largely unsubstantiated, but apparently he lived on Martha's Vineyard, Massachusetts, near Thomas Mayhew, Junior, who settled there in 1642. Hiacoomes was Mayhew's first convert in 1643. He began preaching in 1646, and was ordained in August 1670. For some years before his death, he was unable to preach.

HIAWATHA

Hiawatha (Mohawk or Onondaga, 1525 - 1590), also known as Teharonhiawagon, was an apostle of peace and brotherhood, who according to tradition, devoted his life to ending the bloodshed among the Mohawk, Oneida, Cayuga, Seneca, and Onondaga, and to uniting these five tribes into the League of the Iroquois (the Confederation of Five Nations).

Possessing exceptional oratorical powers, Hiawatha was a medicine man and magician among the Onondaga, and like them, he probably practiced cannibalism. Distressed at the constant warfare and never-ending feuds among the five tribes, though, Hiawatha emerged as a reform leader, advocating the unification of the tribes and the cessation of blood revenge. His bitter opponent, the Onondaga chief Wathatotarho, did all he could to prevent the reformers from achieving their objectives, including having one of Hiawatha's daughters murdered. Unable to overcome Wathatotarho's opposition, Hiawatha left the Onondaga to preach his message of peace and brotherhood to the Mohawk, Oneida, and Cayuga, all of whom agreed to unite and abandon bloodshed among fellow Iroquois on the condition that Wathatotarho and the Onondaga did likewise.

Apparently defeated in his reform efforts once again, Hiawatha was about to abandon hope when he fell under the influence of a mystical peacemaker and prophet named Dekanawida. He converted Hiawatha from cannibalism and convinced him that the obstinate and evil Wathatotarho could be won over to what would later be called The Great Peace. Together, Hiawatha and Dekanawida persuaded the Onondaga chief to join the league. During the negotiations Wathatotarho won certain concessions, but the League of the Iroquois became a reality, cannibalism was outlawed (except in times of war), and blood revenge was ended among the five tribes.

Hiawatha now turned missionary, carrying Dekanawida's confederation ideas and moral principles to other tribes. He roamed far from his home territory, traveling as far away as Lake Superior and the Mississippi River. Although he had some success in winning converts to the Great Peace, no other tribes joined the confederation until the white man had advanced so far that various tribes were forced to seek sanctuary on the lands of the Five Nations. The remnants of the conquered Tuscarora, for example, became the sixth nation in the league about the year 1715.

Meanwhile, the Iroquois were committed to warring against tribes who rejected their overtures of peace, with the ironic result being that the whites came to know the Confederation of Five Nations only as cruel and bloodthirsty warriors, the antithesis of the pacifist principles to which Hiawatha had devoted his life. The apostle and missionary himself probably spent his last days as an elder statesman among the Mohawk. The confederation he had helped to forge, however, lasted until the American Revolution, inspiring the colonists in their dream of creating a stable federal union.

In the second quarter of the nineteenth century, Henry R. Schoolcraft, an early United States ethnologist, collected some of the Iroquois legends and published them in such a way that Hiawatha became identified as the greatest of the Iroquoian gods, Teharonhiawagon ("The Master of Life"), which Schoolcraft apparently assumed was just another way of spelling Hiawatha. He went on to identify this same god with the chief deity of the Chippewa (Ojibwa) Indians, who lived farther west in the Great Lakes region.

The ethnologist referred to the Chippewa deity Manabozho as Hiawatha in a series of Chippewa myths that he published. The error was compounded by Henry Wadsworth Longfellow. Fascinated by Schoolcraft's Chippewa legends, Longfellow based his famous poem, written in 1855, on them, and the name Hiawatha became identified with a fictionalized Chippewa god and hero.

HOPOCAN

Hopocan (Delaware, ? - 1794), also known as Chief Captain Pipe, known by his own people as Konieschguanokee, was a hereditary sachem and a tribal war chief who fought with the British during the American Revolution, but later became a signer of the first peace agreement on September 17, 1778. Hopocan fought with the French during the French and Indian War and participated in Pontiac's Conspiracy (1763-64) to throw the English from their outposts west of the Appalachians. In the attempt to overtake Fort Pitt, however, Hopocan was captured and never took arms against the British again.

Following the failure of Pontiac's Conspiracy, Hopocan moved to the upper Muskingum River in Ohio. He had been a prominent member of councils held at Turtle Village and at Fort Pitt, and he enjoyed a reputation for possessing wisdom and superb oratory. When the colonists declared their independence from the British, the Delaware chief accepted a position on the side of the crown fighting against the Americans and their Indian allies. Hopocan foresaw, however, what might happen to him and his tribe when the conflicting whites patched up their differences. Therefore, he made a point of informing the British commander at Detroit that the Delaware would not act cruelly.

His people had no interest in the struggle for independence and sought only to maintain their own well being. Nevertheless, Hopocan did violate this pledge once during the Revolution. In retaliation for a party of whites killing a group of Indians, Hopocan had United States Colonel William Crawford tortured after Crawford was captured during a rout of

147

his regiment in May 1782. Well before the war was over, though, Hopocan signed a treaty with the United States. On September 17, 1778, at Fort Pitt, the Delaware chief endorsed the first treaty between the new government and an Indian nation. Later, he signed additional treaties, including those at Fort McIntosh, Ohio, (January 21, 1785), and at Fort Harmar, Ohio (January 9, 1787). During the early 1780s Hopocan moved to what was called Captain Pipe's Village near the Upper Sandusky River in Ohio.

HURON

During the first half of the seventeenth century, French soldiers, explorers, and missionaries observed and described a confederation of several tribes living in a small region of southern Ontario between Lake Simcoe and Georgian Bay, which they referred to as the Hurons. These people were sedentary farmers, living in semi-permanent stockaded towns, and spoke a language belonging to the Iroquois language family. They were similar in culture and language to the Five Nation Iroquois of New York State, with whom they probably shared a biological ancestry. They had even closer affinities with other Iroquoian peoples in the Great Lakes area: the Saint Lawrence Iroquois, the Neutrals of southwestern Ontario, and the Petun of the Blue Mountain region, just west of the Huron.

NAME

Huron is a French word that was applied to people in all the tribes of the Huron Confederacy. The word itself means a "a wild boar," and may refer to the hairstyle of Huron men at the time; it was also used more generally as a name for rough or rustic people. The name used by the Hurons themselves to refer to the whole confederacy was *Wendar*. This is often interpreted to mean "people living on an island," and could refer to the fact that the Huron territory in the seventeenth century was almost surrounded by water. It has also been translated as "people who speak a common language."

This receives some support from the fact that the Hurons referred to neighboring Iroquoian groups, such as the Neutrals, as Attiwandaronk, "people who speak a slightly different language," and this was the same name by which these neighbors referred to the Hurons themselves.

HISTORY

Huron culture can be traced archaeologically to approximately AD 1200, at which time the Hurons can be recognized as occupying several "tribal" areas, each comprising a few villages, in a triangle bounded by Hamilton, Kingston, and Penetanguishene. These local groups appear to have been relatively independent. At approximately AD 1500, European trade goods were introduced to the Hurons from the Saint Lawrence Iroquois, who werein contact with Portuguese, Basque, and Breton people exploiting the Gulf of Saint Lawrence.

This led to competition among the Hurons for access to this trade, resulting in new patterns of intertribal alliances, warfare, and migrations. At approximately 1550, probably because of a depletion of furs in the southern regions as well as hostilities, there was a gradual movement away from Lake Ontario towards the upper Trent River Valley and "historic" Huronia. Following the intensification of hostilities between the Hurons and the New York Iroquois at the end of the sixteenth century, the Hurons all moved into Huronia, forming the Huron Confederacy.

Hurons were first met by the French at Quebec in the opening years of the seventeenth century, after which an alliance was forged between the French and the Hurons involving trade agreements, and commitments of military aid against their respective enemies. The most intensive contact between the Hurons and the French resulted from the establishment of Jesuit missions in Huronia in the 1630s and 1640s. During this time, the Huron continued to trade with French commercial interests at Quebec. As a result of competition for the fur trade, the Hurons were attacked and dispersed by the New York Iroquois in 1649, and many Hurons became captives of the Iroquois. Others fled to neighboring tribes such as the Neutrals, only again to be attacked by the Iroquois. One group fled westward with the Petun, and spent the next 150 years in a series of movements throughout the western Great Lakes. In 1815 they settled in Ohio and Michigan, only to move a few years later to Oklahoma. A small group of Hurons made it to Quebec in 1656, and were later known as the Hurons of Lorette. An average estimate for the total population of Huronia, around 1630, is between 25,000 and 30,000. Within the ensuing 20 years, warfare and disease had reduced the population to 10,000 or less.

CULTURAL BOUNDARIES AND SUBDIVISIONS

: By the early seventeenth century, when first coming into contact with the Europeans, all the Hurons lived in a small region referred to now as historic Huronia, extending from the town of Orillia on Lake Simcoe to the Penetang Peninsula on Georgian Bay. This is a region of rolling sandy terrain which, at that time, would have been covered with areas of maple-beech forest and open country.

There were uninhabited areas adjacent to Huronia, such as the valley of the Trent River system, which the Hurons controlled and used as hunting territories. The Huron country was divided into five areas, each occupied by a tribal nation, whose names were Attignawantan (Bear), Arendahrenon (Rock), Attigneenongnahac (Cord), Tohontaenrat (Deer, or One White Lodge), and Ataronchronon (People of the Fens). They all shared a common language and essentially the same culture. The number of towns and villages comprisin each nation ranged from one to fourteen.

TERRITORY

In the seventeenth century the Hurons were crowded into a territory measuring approximately 35 miles by 15 miles, in a band from Orillia to the Penetang Peninsula. It is clear from archaeological evidence that prior to AD 1600 the Hurons inhabited a much broader region than this. Pre-contact Huron village sites were known not only from historic Huronia, but all over an area bounded on the west by the Niagara escarpment, on the south by Lake Ontario, and on the east and north by the Canadian Shield. Villages appear to be concentrated in the region from Toronto northward to Huronia, along the shore of Lake Ontario, and in the valley of the Trent River system.

LANGUAGE

The Huron nations spoke a common Iroquois Family language. The Petun, just to the west, spoke the same language, while the Neutral to the southwest apparently spoke a language that was somewhat different. Huron is more distantly related to the languages of the League Iroquois, suggesting that the two groups have been linguistically separated for some time, perhaps more than 2,000 years. The Iroquois language family also includes Cherokee, and the family as a whole is related to the Siouan family.

CULTURE: SUBSISTENCE AND ECONOMY

Huron subsistence was based upon farming, hunting, fishing, and gathering of wild plants. Plants cultivated by the Huron included maize, beans, squash, pumpkins, sunflowers, and tobacco. While men cleared the fields of trees and brush, women took on the task of planting, tending and harvesting the crops. After harvesting, corn was dried and pounded into a meal and stored for use during the winter, when it served as a staple food.

During the fall and early winter, Huron men hunted mostly whitetail deer, beaver, and bear. Other animals that were eaten included rabbits, ground hogs, squirrels, raccoons, skunks, turtles, and birds. Hunting techniques made use of traps, snares, spears, and bows and arrows. In at least some villages, substantial numbers of domestic dogs were raised for food.

Fish formed an important part of the Huron diet, and were used in soups as well as eaten fresh, dried or smoked. Fishing was a communal activity, carried out primarily in Spring and Fall. Fish were caught in lakes and streams, by nets, weirs and lines. In wintertime, some ice fishing was done with nets or lines.

Wild plant foods used by the Huron included several kinds of berries, nuts, plums, cherries, grapes, apples, beans and peas, and a few roots. Many of the fruits were dried for winter use. An important aspect of Huron economy was trade, particularly in the historic period. During their involvement in the fur trade, the Hurons traded corn and other items to the more northerly Algonquians for animal skins and fish. The animal skins, particularly beaver, were taken to Quebec, where they were traded to the French for European goods.

SETTLEMENT AND EARLY VILLAGE LIFE

The focal point of Huron life was the semi-permanent village. Most villages were enclosed and might occupy over 20 acres. These villages were relocated every 10 to 30 years, when soil and firewood had been exhausted. Huron houses were of the longhouse type, and accommodated several related families, being approximately 25 feet wide and anywhere from 30 to 200 feet long. Houses were constructed of poles that were bent over and tied together to form a roof, and covered with bark. Down the center of the house was a common passageway that contained cooking fires shared by individual families, who occupied compartments down each side of the house. On the average, a longhouse might accommodate about 10 families, or roughly 50 to 70 people.

A small village might contain just a few such houses, while the larger ones might contain as many as 100. One large Huron village on the early seventeenth century was reported to have 200 longhouses. The Huron population spent the winter in the villages, living on preserved and fresh game, and crops and other foods stored during the summer and fall. During this season, much time was spent at games, ceremonies, and

151

feasts. In spring, many people left the village for varying periods, the men spending the summer in fishing and hunting, warfare, and trading. The women grew crops, and many of them built houses and lived in the cornfields during the growing season. During the fall, people gathered at favorite fishing places, after which men were busy hunting. The population finally reassembled in the village during December.

TECHNOLOGY

Prior to the introduction of European materials in the sixteenth century, Hurons had what could be termed a neolithic level of technology. Metallurgy was virtually unknown; most tools, weapons and utensils were made from wood, bone, antler, shell, stone, or pottery. Native copper was sometimes used for implements such as awls, or for beads. Household utensils included pottery vessels for cooking and storage, wooden bowls, spoons and forks, and other containers of wood and bark. Women's tools included flint knives, flint scrapers and bone fishers for preparing animal hides, and bone awls and needles for piercing and sewing leather.

Hunting implements included arrows tipped with flint, bone or antler, harpoons with barbed bone or antler points, and spears tipped with stone. Axes and adzes of ground or polished stone were used for felling trees, and dressing poles for houses and palisades. Principal war weapons were bows and arrows, and wooden clubs. Also used were shields of leather or bark, and armor made of wooden slats laced together. Following contact with the French, native technology was quickly replaced by the use of European copper kettles, iron axes, knives and awls.

SOCIAL AND POLITICAL ORGANIZATION

The basic economic and social unit of Huron life was the family, which had the responsibility for providing for its members. A household accommodated a number of families related through the female line, thus approximating a matrilineal extended family. The families sharing a house customarily cooperated in many ventures, and were expected to share and to help each other when necessary. The village seems to have enjoyed a high degree of autonomy, but was tied to other villages by common concerns and activities.

Village affairs were governed by a council of older men. Among these councilors were chiefs of two kinds: those concerned with the government of the village, including such things as feasts, games and funerals; and those concerned with war. Becoming chief was largely hereditary, so

152

that when a chief died, the successor was selected from among his sisters' sons. Certain of the chiefs were recognized as being preeminent by virtue of their personal qualities of wealth, and their influence was corresponding greater than that of the other chiefs. Above the village level, tribal affairs were governed by a council composed of the most respected chiefs from all the villages in that tribe.

Of this council, one member was recognized as being the principal chief of the nation. This chief and his council had the responsibility for making treaties with other nations, declaring war, and giving permission for foreigners to cross the tribal territory. The entire confederacy of the Huron was likewise governed by a council, which probably consisted of a combination of the various tribal councils.

Religion. The Huron believed that every object, as well as people and animals, possessed souls or spirits. Some of these spirits had the ability to affect human affairs, and were propitiated by offerings. Among the most important spirits were those of the sky, and of certain geographical entities such as lakes, islands, large rocks, etc. Some people, such as shamans, were believed to have a familiar spirit who was acquired in a vision or dream, and whose aid they could enlist. The most important function of shamans was curing the sick. This was accomplished by extracting an offending object from the patient's body, breaking a sorcerer's spell, or interpreting and fulfilling the patient's dreams. Other shaman functions included controlling weather, and bringing good luck in hunting, fishing, or warfare.

The Hurons regarded dreams as the means whereby the soul made its thoughts and desires known; to let such desires go unfulfilled could bring sickness and death. Thus, if a man dreamed that he would die if he were not presented with certain gifts, the required items would be found and given to him. Charms were objects found and collected by Huron men which were believed to bring luck in hunting, war, and other activities. They were held in awe, and feasts might be given to maintain their power.

Life Cycles: For the first two or three years of its life, a Huron baby was breast-fed and fed meat previously chewed by its mother. During this time, the infant spent the day in a cradle-board, was wrapped in fur, or roamed the floor of the house. At night it slept between its parents. The period between infancy and adulthood was spent in games that anticipated adult activities. Boys spent their time shooting bows and arrows or playing games of physical skill, while girls engaged in play imitating the grinding of corn or other household activities.

Relations between the youth of different sexes seem to have been generally uninhibited, and girls apparently competed for the greatest number of lovers. When a girl became pregnant, her lovers would all claim that the child was theirs, and she would choose from among them the one she liked best for a husband. When a young man and woman decided to marry, the man asked for the permission of the woman's parents. If he was an acceptable suitor to both the woman and her parents, a wedding feast was held for the couple's friends and relatives, at which their marriage was announced. A man's own children were not his heirs, but rather the heirs of his wife's brother.

Similarly, his own heirs were his sister's children; to them he would pass on his titles and possessions, and they, in turn, supported him in his old age. The elderly were respected, and their opinions were sought on matters of importance.

Death was approached calmly by the Hurons. If a man was dying of natural causes, he might give a farewell feast for his friends and, as his death approached, he was shown the clothes and finery in which he would be buried. Immediately following death, the body was wrapped in a robe, and covered in furs and bark. The death was announced through the village, and feasts were held. Three days after the death, the body was carried to the cemetery just outside the village, where it was placed in a tomb made of bark. Sometimes bodies were buried in the ground, and a small hut of bark was erected over the grave.

Every 10 years, several Huron villages cooperated in holding a Feast of the Dead, at which the bodies of those who had died since the last feast were removed from their graves and reburied in a common pit, amid a great deal of feasting and exchanging of presents.

Conclusion. The available information on the Hurons depicts a relatively large aboriginal group being profoundly affected and disrupted by the complex events surrounding the arrival of Europeans in the eastern part of North America. Traditional Huron patterns of settlement, subsistence, and politics were greatly modified by the effects of the European presence. Huron involvement in European politics in North America helped to weld them into a confederacy, allied with the crown of France.

It also led to, a scant 50 years later, their destruction as a social and cultural entity at the hands of the League of the Iroquois. Most Hurons today are called Wyandotte, although the name Huron is still used by members of the tribe living in Quebec. Some contemporary Hurons still live on the Saint Lawrence River. The Wyandotte Tribe of Oklahoma was established in 1937 after the Oklahoma Indian Welfare Act of 1936.

The constitution provides for a tribal government composed of a chief, a Tribal Council that meets each month, and elected representatives. During the Eisenhower administration in 1956, the Wyandotte were one of the tribes singled out to lose its tribal identity. After a twenty-year struggle, in 1978 the tribe successfully regained federal recognition. In Oklahoma, a recent count showed 3,617 members. Significant social, educational, and cultural advances have been made, including tribal government scholarships, daily meals for elders, a health center, new homes for tribal members, a preschool facility, and a tribal center and meeting hall. Funding has been granted for establishment of the Wyandotte museum and Cultural Center, and money has been made available for locating, purchasing, and cataloguing material culture.

Oral interviews with elders have helped to renew the Wyandotte heritage and language, and a library and archives have recently received funding. The tribal historical committee has published a book that provides a brief history of the tribe, and a series of paperbacks is forthcoming. The tribe today remains diverse; its members are employed in nursing, teaching, ranching, art, farming, labor, clerking, and secretarial positions. The group in Oklahoma, as well as elsewhere, maintains pride in its Indian identity and cultural heritage.

IROQUOIAN FAMILY

The Iroquoian Family is a linguistic stock of the following tribes and tribal groups: the Hurons were composed of the Attignaouantan (Bear people), the Attigneenongnahac (Cord people), the Arendahronon (Rock people), the Tohontaenrat *Atahontaenrat* or *Tohontaenrat*, White-eared or Deer people), the Wenrohronon, the Ataronchronon, and the Atonthrataronon (Otter people, an Algonquian tribe); the Tionontati or Tobacco people or nation; the Confederation of the Attiwendaronk or Neutrals, composed of the Neutrals proper, the Aondironon, the Ongniarahronon, and the Atiragenratka, *Atiraguenrek*; the Conkhandeenrhonon; the Iroquois Confederation composed of the Mohawk, the Oneida, the Onondaga, the Cayuga, and the Seneca, with the Tuscarora after 1726.

In later times, the incorporated remnants of a number of alien tribes, such as the Tutelo, the Saponi, the Nanticoke, the Conoy, and the Muskwaki or Foxes; the Conestoga or Susquehanna of at least three tribes, of which one was the Akhrakouaehronon or Atrakouaehronon; the Erie or Cat Nation of at least two allied peoples; the Tuscarora Confederation composed of several leagued tribes, the names of which are now unknown; the Nottaway; the Meherrin; and the Cherokee composed of at least three divisions, the Elati, the Middle Cherokee, and the Ataii, and the Onnontioga consisting of the Iroquois-Catholic seceders on the Saint Lawrence.

Each tribe was an independent political unit, except those which formed leagues in which the constituent tribes, while enjoying local self-government, acted jointly in common affairs. For this reason, there were no general names for themselves common to all tribes. In 1534, Jacques Cartier met people of the Iroquoian stock on the shore of Gaspe Basin; the following year, he again encountered their home on the site of the city of Quebec, Canada. Both banks of the Saint Lawrence River above Quebec, as far as present Montreal, were occupied by people of this family.

He visited the villages of Hagonchenda, Hochelaga, Hochelayi, Stadacona, and Tutonaguy. This was the first known habitat of an Iroquoian people. Champlain found these territories entirely deserted 70 years later, and Lescarbot found people roving over this area speaking an entirely different language from that recorded by Cartier.

He believed that this change of languages was due to "a destruction of people," because, he wrote, "some years ago the Iroquois assembled themselves to the number of 8,000 men and destroyed all their enemies, whom they surprised in their enclosures." The new language that he recorded was Algonquian, spoken by bands that passed over this region on warlike forays.

The early occupants of the Saint Lawrence were probably the Arendahronon and Tohontaenrat, tribes of the Hurons. Their lands bordered on those of the Iroquois, whose territory extended westward to that of the Neutrals, neighbors of the Tionontati and western Huron tribes to the north, and the Erie to the south and west. The Conestoga occupied the middle and lower basin of the Susquehanna, south of the Iroquois. The northern Iroquoian area, which Algonquian tribes surrounded on nearly every side, therefore embraced nearly the entire valley of the Saint Lawrence, the basins of Lake Ontario and Lake Erie, the southeastern shores of Lake Huron and Georgian Bay, all of the present New York State, except the lower Hudson Valley, all of central Pennsylvania, and the shores of Chesapeake Bay in Maryland as far as the Choptank and Patuxent rivers. In the south, the Cherokee area, surrounded by Algonquian tribes in the north, Siouan in the east, and Muskhogean and Uchean tribes in the south and west, embraced the valleys of the Tennessee and upper

Savannah rivers and the mountainous parts of Virginia, the Carolinas, and Alabama.

Separated from the Cherokee by the territory of the eastern Siouan tribes was the area occupied by the Tuscarora in the eastern part of North Carolina and by the Meherrin and Nottoway north of them in southeastern Virginia. The northern Iroquoian tribes, especially those of the Five Nations, were second to no other Indian people north of Mexico in political organization, statesmanship, and military prowess. Their leaders were astute diplomats, as the wily French and English statesmen with whom they dealt soon discovered. In war, they practiced ferocious cruelty toward their prisoners, burning even their unadopted women and infant prisoners.

However, far from being a race of rude and savage warriors, they were a kindly and affectionate people, full of keen sympathy for kin and friends in distress, kind and deferential to their women, exceedingly fond of their children, anxiously striving for peace and goodwill among men, and profoundly imbued with a just reverence for the constitution of their commonwealth and for its founders. Their wars were waged primarily to secure and perpetuate their political life and independence. The fundamental principles of their confederation, persistently maintained for centuries by force of arms and by compacts with other peoples, were based primarily on blood relationships, and they shaped and directed their foreign and internal policy on consonance with these principles.

The underlying motive for the institution of the Iroquois League was to secure universal peace and welfare among men by recognition and enforcement of the forms of civil government. This was to be done through direction and regulation of personal and public conduct and thought, in accordance with beneficent customs and council degrees; by stopping bloodshed in the blood feud through tender of a prescribed price for killing a co-tribesman; by abstaining from eating human flesh; and, lastly, by maintenance and necessary exercise of power, not only military, but also magic power, which were believed to be embodied in the forms of their ceremonial activities.

The tender for a homicide, or the murder or killing by accident of a co-tribesman, was twenty strings of wampum, ten for the dead person, and ten for the forfeited life of the homicide. The religious activities of these tribes expressed themselves in the worship of all environing elements and bodies and many creatures of a teeming fancy, which, directly or remotely affected their welfare. They were regarded as man-beings or anthropomorphic personages endowed with life, volition, and peculiar individual "orenda," or magic power. In the practice of this religion, ethics or morals did not have a primary consideration, but only a secondary one, if any.

The status and personal relations of the personages of their pantheon were fixed and regulated by rules and customs similar to those in vogue in the social and political organization of the people, and there was therefore, among at least the principal gods, a kinship system patterned on that of the people themselves. The mental superiority of the Hurons over their Algonquian neighbors was frequently mentioned by the early French missionaries.

A remainder of the Tionontati, with a few refugee Hurons among them, fled to the region of the upper lakes (along with certain Ottawa tribes) to escape the Iroquois invasion in 1649, and maintained among their fellow refugees a predominating influence. This was largely because, like other Iroquoian tribes, they had been highly organized socially and politically, and were therefore trained in definite parliamentary customs and procedures.

Although they were a small tribe, the Hurons claimed and exercised the right of lighting the council fire at all general gatherings, showing the esteem in which they were held by their neighbors. The Cherokee were the first tribe to adopt a constitutional form of government, embodied in a code of laws written in their own language, in an alphabet based on the Roman characters adapted by one of them. Although in weighing these facts, the vast influence of their commingling with white settlers must be considered. The social organization of the Iroquoian tribes was, in some respects, similar to that of other Indians, but much more complex and cohesive, and there was a notable difference in regard to the important position accorded the women. Among the Cherokee, the Iroquois, the Hurons, and probably among the other tribes, the women performed important and essential functions in their government.

Every chief was chosen, and retained his position, and every important measure was enacted by the consent and cooperation of the childbearing women, and the candidate for the position of chief was nominated by the matrons of this group. His selection by them from among their sons had to be confirmed by the tribal and federal councils, respectively, and finally, he was installed by federal officers. Lands and houses belonged solely to the women. All the Iroquoian tribes were sedentary and agricultural, depending on the chase for only a small part of their subsistence.

The northern tribes were especially noted for their skill in fortification and house building. Their so-called castles were solid log structures, with platforms running around the top on the inside, from which stones and other missiles could be hurled down upon attackers. The population of tribes composing the Iroquoian family is detailed in the entry for the Iroquois Confederacy, and the descriptions of the various Iroquoian tribes. (See FIVE NATIONS IROQUOIS, IROQUOIS, and IROQUOIS CONFEDERACY)

IROQUOIS

The Iroquois Tribes are known in history (among other names) as the Five Nations, comprising the Cayuga, Mohawk, Oneida, Onondaga, and Seneca. Among the Iroquoian tribes, kinship was traced through the blood of the woman only. Kinship meant membership in a family, and this in turn, constituted citizenship in the tribe, conferring certain social, political, and religious privileges, duties, and rights which were denied to persons of alien blood; however, by a legal fiction embodied in the right of adoption, the blood of the alien could be figuratively changed into one of the strains of the Iroquoian blood, and thus citizenship could be conferred on a person of alien lineage. In an Iroquoian tribe, the legislative, judicial, and executive functions were usually exercised by one and the same class of persons, commonly called chiefs in English, who were organized into councils.

There were three grades of chiefs. Becoming Chief was hereditary in certain of the simplest political units in the government of the tribe. A chief was nominated by unit matrons, and the nomination was confirmed by the tribal and federal councils. The functions of the three grades of chiefs were defined in the rules of procedure. When the five Iroquoian tribes were organized into a confederation, its government was only a development of that of the separate tribes, just as the government of each of the constituent tribes was a development of that of the several clans of which it was composed. The government of the clan was a development of the several brood families of which it was composed, and the brood family, strictly speaking, was composed of the progeny of a woman and her female descendants, counting through the female line only.

Therefore the clan could be described as a permanent body of kindred, socially and organized politically, who traced actual and theoretical descent through the female line only. The simpler units surrendered part of their autonomy to the next higher units, and as such, the whole was closely interdependent and cohesive. The establishment of the higher unit created new rights, privileges, and duties. This was the principle of organization of the confederation of the five Iroquoian tribes.

159

The date of the formation of this confederation (probably not the first, but the last of a series of attempts to unite the several tribes in a federal union) was not earlier than about the year 1570, which was some 30 years earlier to that of the Huron tribes. The Delawares gave them the name of Mingwe. The northern and western Algonquians called them Nadowa "adders." The Powhatan called them Massawomekes. The English knew them as the Confederation of the Five Nations, and after the admission of the Tuscarora in 1722, as the Six Nations. Moreover, the names Maqua, Mohawk, Seneca, and Tsonnontowan, by which their leading tribes were called, were also applied to them collectively.

The League of the Iroquois, when first known to Europeans, was composed of the five tribes, and occupied the territory extending from the eastern watershed of Lake Champlain to the western watershed of Genesee River, and from the Adirondacks southward to the territory of the Conestoga. The date of the formation of the league is not certain, but there was evidence that it took place about 1570, occasioned by wars with Algonquian and Huron tribes. The confederated Iroquois immediately began to make their united power felt. After the coming of the Dutch, from whom they procured firearms, they were able to extend their conquests over all the neighboring tribes until their dominion was acknowledged from the Ottawa River to the Tennessee and from the Kennebec to the Illinois River, and Lake Michigan. Their westward advance was checked by the Chippewa. The Cherokee and the Catawba proved an effectual barrier in the South, while in the North, they were hampered by the operations of the French in Canada.

Champlain, on one of his early expeditions, joined a party of Canadian Indians against the Iroquois. This made them bitter enemies of the French, whom they afterward opposed at every step, to the close of the French regime in Canada in 1763, while they were firm allies of the English. The French made several attempts through missionaries to win over the Iroquois, and were so successful that a considerable number of individuals from the different tribes, most of them Mohawk and Onondaga, withdrew from the several tribes and formed Catholic settlements at Caughnawaga, Saint Regis, and Oka, on the Saint Lawrence.

The tribes of the league repeatedly tried, but without success, to induce them to return, and finally, in 1684, declared them to be traitors. In later wars, Catholic Iroquois took part with the French against their former brethren. Upon the outbreak of the Revolutionary War, the League of the Iroquois decided not to take part in the conflict, but to allow each tribe to decide for itself what action to take.

All the tribes, with the exception of the Oneida and about half of the Tuscarora, joined the English. After the revolution of the Mohawk and Cayuga, (with other Iroquoian tribes that were in the English interest), they were finally settled by the Canadian government on a reservation on Grand River, Ontario, where they continued to reside, although a few individuals emigrated to Gibson, Bay of Quinte, Caughnawaga, and Saint Thomas, Ontario.

A large number of the Iroquois population within the United States resided on reservations in New York with the exception of the Oneida, many of whom settled near Green Bay, Wisconsin. The so-called Seneca of Oklahoma were composed of the remnants of many tribes, among which may be mentioned the Conestoga and Hurons, and of emigrants from all the tribes of the Iroquoian Confederation. It was very probable that the nucleus of these Seneca was the remnant of the ancient Erie.

The Catholic Iroquois of Caughnawaga, Saint Regis, and Oka, although having no connection with the confederation, supplied many recruits to the fur trade, and a large number of them joined northwestern tribes of the United States and Canada.

The number of the Iroquois villages varied greatly at different periods and from decade to decade. In 1657 there were about 24, but after the conquest of the Erie, the entire country from the Genesee to the western watershed of Lake Erie came into possession of the Iroquoian tribes, which afterward settled colonies on the upper waters of the Allegheny and Susquehanna, and on the northern shore of Lake Ontario, so that by 1750, their villages may have numbered about 50.

The population of the Iroquois also varied much at different periods. Their constant wars greatly weakened them. In 1689, it was estimated that they had 2,250 warriors; that numbers, which was reduced by war, disease, and defections to Canada, dropped to 1,230 by 1698.

Their losses were largely made up by their system of wholesale adoption, which was carried on to such an extent that at one time their adopted aliens were reported to equal or exceed the number of native Iroquois. Due to the defection of the Catholic Iroquois and the omission of the Tuscarora from the estimates, it is impossible to get a statement of the full strength of the Iroquois until much later. Around the middle of the seventeenth century, the Five Nations were supposed to have reached their highest point, and in 1677 and 1685, they were estimated at about 12,850, but in the next nine years, they lost more than half by war and by desertions to Canada.

The most accurate estimates for the eighteenth century gave the Six Nations and their colonies between 10,000 and 12,000 members. In 1774, they were estimated at 10,000 to 12,500. In 1904, they numbered about 16,100, including more than 3,000 mixed-bloods, as follows: In Ontario, Iroquois and Algonkin at Watha (Gibson), 139 (about one-half Iroquois); Mohawk of the Bay of Quinte, 1,271; Oneida of the Thames, 770; Six Nations on the Grand Reservation, 4,195 (including about 150 Delawares). In Quebec: Iroquois of Caughnawaga, 2,074; of Saint Regis, 1,426; of Lake of Two Mountains, 393. The total in Canada was about 10,418.

The Iroquois of New York in 1904 were distributed as follows: Onondaga and Seneca on the Allegany Reservation, 1,041; Cayuga, Onondaga, and Seneca on the Cattaraugus Reservation, 1,456; Oneida on the Oneida Reservation, 150; Oneida and Onondaga on the Onondaga Reservation, 513; Saint Regis Reservation, 1,208; Cayuga and Seneca on the Tonawanda Reservation, 512; Onondaga and Tuscarora on the Tuscarora Reservation, 410. Total, 5,290. In 1905, there were also 366 Indians classed as Seneca under the Seneca School in Oklahoma. The Algonquian and other Indians included with the Iroquois were probably outnumbered by the Caughnawaga and others in the Canadian Northwest, who were not separately enumerated.

The following villages were Iroquois, but the particular tribes to which they belonged were either unknown or were collective: Adjouquay, Allaquippa, Anpuaqun, Aquatsagana, Aratumquat, Awegen, Blackleg's Village, Buckaloon, Cahunghage, Canowdowsa, Caughnawaga, Chartierstown, Chemegaide, Chenango, Chinklacamoose, Chugnut, Churamuk Codocoraren, Cokanuck, Conaquanosshan, Conejoholo, Conemaugh, Conihunta, Connosomothdian, Conoytown (mixed Conoy and Iroquois), Coreorgonel (mixed), Cowawago, Cussewago, Ganadoga, Ganagarahhare, Ganasarage, Ganeraske, Ganneious, Gannentaha, Glasswanoge, Goshgoshunk (mixed), Grand River Indians, Hickorytown (mixed), Janundat, Jedakne, Johnstown, Jonondes, Juniata, Juraken (2), Kahendohon, Kanaghsaws, Kannawalohatta, Kanesadageh, Karaken, Karhationni, Karhawenradon, Kayehkwarageh, Kaygen, Kente, Kickenapawling, Kiskiminetas, Kittaning, Kuskuski (mixed), Lawunkhannek, Logstown, Loyalhannon (?), Mahusquechikoken, Mahican, Mahoning, Manckatawangum, Matchasaung, Middletown, Mingo Town, Mohanet, Nescopeck, Newtown (4 settlements), Newtychaning, Octageron, Ohrekionni, Onaweron, Onkwelyede, Opolopong, Oquaga, Osewingo, Oskawaserenhon, Ostonwackin, Oswegatchie, Otiahanague, Otskwirakeron,

Ousagwentera, Owego, Paille Coupee, Pluggy's Town, Punxatawney, Quinaouatoua, Runonvea, Saint Regis, Sawcunk, Schoharie, Schohorage, Sconassi, Scoutash's Town, Seneca Town, Sevege, Sevickly's Old Town, Shamokin, Shannopin, Shenango, Sheshequin, Sheoquage, Sittawingo, Skannayutenate, Skehandowa, Solocka, Swahadowri, Taiaiagon, Tewanondadon, Tioga, Tohoguses Cabins, Tonihata, Tullihas, Tuscarora, Tuskokogie, Tutelo, Unadilia, Venango, Wakatomica, Wakerhon, Wauteghe, Yoghroonwago, Youcham. Catholic missions among the Iroquois were: Caughnawaga, Indian Point, La Montagne, La Prairie, Oka, Oswegatchie, Saint Regis, and Sault au Recollet. For the other Iroquois settlements, see under the several tribal names.

Disregarding the extraordinary estimates of some early writers, it is evident that the modern Iroquois, instead of decreasing in population, have increased, and number more at present than at any former period. (See FIVE NATIONS IROQUOIS, IROQUOIS FAMILY, and IROQUOIS CONFEDERACY)

JAMES THE PRINTER

James The Printer (Nipmuc, 1643 - 1728), also known as Wowanus, aided the Reverend John Eliot to translate and print the Saint James English Bible into the Indian language. The first edition was completed in 1663.

A member of Eliot's second "praying band," the Hassanamisco, James attended Cambridge Charity School and then, beginning in 1659, was apprenticed for 16 years to the printer Samuel Green. He left Green in 1675 to join King Philip's forces and fight the English.

He was later given amnesty and returned to present-day Grafton, Massachusetts, to teach both Indians and colonials to read and write English. It is assumed that his brother, Tukapewillen, died on Deer Island while imprisoned by the English during King Philip's war. James' name appears as the printer of a psalter published in 1709.

EMILY PAULINE JOHNSON

Emily Pauline Johnson (Mohawk, March 10, 1861 - March 7, 1913), also known as Tekahionwake or "Double Wampum," was a critically acclaimed poet. Born near Brantford, Ontario, Canada, she was the daughter of a Mohawk Chief, Henry Martin Johnson, and an English woman, Emily S. Howells.

Her love of the written word started early on and by the age of 12, she had read most of the classics, such as the work of Shakespeare, Longfellow, Byron and others. It was around that time that she began writing poetry.

While still a teenager, she sent a poem to a local newspaper whose editor advised her to send it to publications with a larger audience. Soon she began having her work published in such periodicals as Harper's Weekly, Smart Set, and The Atheneum.

In 1892, she attended a program sponsored by the Young Liberals Club of Toronto devoted to the presentation of Canadian literature. Attending in full Mohawk regalia, she read a poem entitled, "A Cry From an Indian Wife," about the Northwest Rebellion from the Native point of view: "O! coward self, I hesitate no more; Go forth, and win the glories of the war. Go forth, nor bend to greed of white men's hands, By right, by birth, we Indians own these lands.

She made an impression on her audience and her performance was written about in the newspaper on the following day. She then began to give solo readings of her work, one included the famous *My Paddle Sings.* In 1889, she had her first book published, entitled *Songs of the Great Dominion*, and soon began to travel throughout Canada and to London to give her readings.

She continued to meet with critical acclaim and in 1895 wrote *White Wampum.* She toured extensively for the next fifteen years, adding the United States to her itinerary, and in 1903 she published her third book, *Canadian Born*, which was quite successful.

When she stopped touring, she settled in Vancouver, British Columbia. Her next book was a collection, called *Legends of Vancouver*, published in 1911. It was described by one critic as "an imaginative treatment of Indian folklore...the beginning of a new literature." During 1913, a short time before her death, she published *The Shaganappi* and *Flint and Feathers.* She died of cancer on March 7 of that year. In 1961, the Canadian government honored her with the issue of a 5-cent postage stamp celebrating the hundredth anniversary of her birth. It was the first time both a Canadian author and an Indian had been honored in that manner.

LAPPAWINZO

Lappawinzo (Delaware, eighteenth century), was one of several to sign the notorious Walking Purchase Treaty in Philadelphia in 1737. He refused to leave his land after signing the treaty, claiming fraud, but was finally forced out by pressure from the Six Nations, and remained bitter lifelong over the English deceit. Lappawinzo was one of several noted Delaware chiefs, including Nutimus and Sassoonon, who lived in the

Forks region west of Philadelphia, probably between the Lehigh and Delaware rivers.

Lappawinzo's home may have been the village of Hockendocqua. The chief signed the Walking Purchase on August 25, in Philadelphia, but was outraged by the English use of trained runners to pace out boundaries far in excess of the Delawares' intent and refused to make way for the English settlers.

It is said that when Edward Marshall, one of the runners, stopped by Hockendocqua to ask Lappawinzo for an Indian to accompany him, the chief said "they had got all the best land, and they might go to the Devil for the bad, and he would send no Indian with them." In July 1742, Pennsylvanians James Logan and Governor George Thomas persuaded the chiefs of the Six Nations, overlords of the Delawares, to rebuke their rebellious subjects for not adhering to the treaty.

The chiefs sent their famous orator Canasatego to tongue-lash Lappawinzo and the other chiefs, and after their conference on July 12, 1742, the Delawares departed for land set aside for them by the Six Nations chiefs on the Susquehanna River at Shamokin and Wyoming. Bitter to the, Lappawinzo was overheard to remark in reminiscence about the English runner's "walk: "No sit down to smoke, no shoot a squirrel, but fun, fun, fun, (sic) all day long."

JOHN LOGAN

John Logan (Cayuga, 1725 - 1780) was a leader of the Iroquois tribes living along the Ohio and Scioto Rivers during the middle of the eighteenth century. He led a retaliatory attack upon white settlers after whites had massacred members of his family. Logan was born in Shamokin, Pennsylvania. Although his father was white, in all probability Logan took his English name from his friend James Logan, secretary and later acting governor of Pennsylvania.

The Cayuga leader lived near Reedsville, Pennsylvania, for many years, acquiring a reputation for being a staunch friend of the white settlers. He hunted and sold skins to support himself and his family. Around 1770, Logan moved to the banks of the Ohio River, and by 1774 he was living at Old Chillicothe. During that year, a group of white settlers attacked and killed a large number of Indians at the mouth of Yellow Creek in Ohio.

Among the natives murdered were several of Logan's relatives, including his sister. In retaliation, the formerly friendly Cayuga chief led bands of warriors in raids upon nearby white settlements. During the several months that Logan was on the warpath, many frontier families were butchered. Finally, Governor Dunmore established a treaty meeting to make peace with Logan and put a halt to the killing.

Logan's speech at the time he laid down the tomahawk was so eloquent that Thomas Jefferson was moved to compare it with the orations of Demosthenes and Cicero. Sadly, Logan had begun to drink about the time he first settled along the Ohio and, after peace was reestablished with the whites, he became a notable drunkard.

The remainder of his life was undistinguished, six years after he had taken up the tomahawk, John Logan was killed by his nephew during a quarrel that took place on a return trip from a visit to Detroit. A monument has been erected at Auburn, New York, to honor his memory.

MADOKAWANDO

Madokawando (Penobscot; ca. 1631 - 1698), was also sometimes called Madackawando, was the adopted son of the Kennebec chief Assaminasqua, who, like many Indians then and later, was able to maintain peaceful relations with the colonists until their encroachmnets upon Indian lands became intolerable.

In 1676 he attended a meeting at Taconnet, Maine, with four other chiefs, with Abraham Shurte and with Sylvanus Davis who represented the traders in the Maine area, and who sought assurances of peace among the tribes and with the colonists. Although nothing tangible resulted from these negotiations, Madokawando did sign a peace treaty on November 6, 1696.

Some time in 1685, the French Baron de Saint Castin, interested in the Maine fur trade, befriended Madokawando, married his daughter, and soon became almost a titulary head of the tribe. During King William's War (1689-97), Madokawando joined the English, killing 77 people at York (1691). He then participated in the raids that left Maine uninhabitable to white settlers
. By 1693 Madokawando, and his son-in-law, realized that the French could not win, and that Boston was the best market for selling furs. Over the protests of the French missionary priests and the younger warriors, Madokawando proclaimed peace with the English. He died in Maine.

MAHICANS

The Mahicans were an Algonquian tribe that occupied both banks of the upper Hudson River in New York, extending north almost to Lake Champlain. To the Dutch they were known as River Indians, while the

French grouped them and the closely connected Munsee and Delaware under the same name of Loups ("wolves"). The same tribes were called the *Akochakenen* ("stammerers)" by the Iroquois. On the western bank they joined the Musee at Catskill Creek, and on the east bank they joined the Wappinger near Poughkeepsie. They extended east into Massachusetts and held the upper part of Housatonic Valley. Mahiucan bands hunted in the southwestern part of Vermont and made temporary settlements there on several occasions. Winooskeek, one such village, was probably located at the Winooski River mouth.

Their council fire was at Schodac, on an island near Albany, and it is probable that they had 40 villages within their territory. Their name, in a variety of forms, has been applied to all the Indians from the Hudson River to Narragansett Bay, but in practical use has been limited to two bodies, one on the lower Connecticut River, in Connecticut, known dialectically as Mohegan, and the other on the Hudson River, known as Mahican. They were engaged in a war with the Mohawk, their nearest neighbors on the west, when the Dutch appeared on the scene, which lasted until 1673. In 1664 the inroads of the Mohawk compelled them to remove their council fire from Schodac to Westenhuck, the modern Stockbridge, Massachusetts.

As the settlements crowded upon them, the Mahican sold their territory piecemeal, and about 1730 a large body emigrated to the Susquehanna River and settled near Wyoming, Pennsylvania, in the vicinity of the Delaware and Munsee, with whom they afterward moved to the Ohio region, finally losing their identity. A previous emigration had formed the main body of the mixed tribe of the Scaticook.

As early as 1721 a band of Mahican found their way to Indiana, where they had a village on Kankakee River. In 1736 those living in the Housatonic Valley were gathered into a mission at Stockbridge, Massachusetts, where they maintained a separate existence under the name of Stockbridge Indians. These are the only Mahican who have preserved their identity.

In 1756 a large body of Mahican and Wappinger removed from the Hudson to the east beach of the Susquehanna, settling, with the Nanticoke and others, under Iroquois protection at Chenango, Chugnut, and Oswego, in Broome and Tioga Counties, New York. They probably later found their way to their relatives in the west. A few Mahican remained about their ancient homes on the Hudson for some years after the revolution, but finally disappeared unnoticed. If any remain they are included among the Stockbridge.

167

According to Ruttenber, the Mahican confederacy comprised at least five divisions or subtribes, the Mahican proper, Wiskagjoc, Mechken-towoon, Wawyachtonoc, and Westenbuck (Stockbridges). It is impossible to estimate their population, as the different bands were always confounded, or included with neighboring tribes, of whom they afterward became an integral part.

According to Ruttenber's account, the government of the Mahican was a democracy, but his statement that the office of the sachem was hereditary by the lineage of the wife of the sachem, which appears to be correct, does not indicate a real democracy. His statement with regard to the duties of the sachem and other officers is as follows: "The sachem was assisted by counselors, and also by one hero, one owl, and one runner; the rest of the nation were called young men or warriors. The sachem, or more properly king, remained concerned for their welfare. He had charge of the 'mnoti,' or bag of peace, which contained the belts and strings used to establish peace and friendship with different nations, and if they concluded to take up the hatchet, the matter was put in the hands of the heroes for execution.

When peace was proposed, the heroes put the negotiations in the hands of the sachem and counselors. The office of owl was also one of merit. He required a strong memory and needed to be a good speaker. His business was to sit beside his sachem and proclaim his orders to the people in a loud voice. He was also to get up every morning at daylight to arouse the people and order them to their daily duties. The business of runner was to carry messages and to convene councils."

The Mahicans were generally well built. As fighting men they were perfidious, accomplishing their designs by treachery, using stratagem to deceive their enemies and making their most hazardous attacks under cover of darkness. The women ornamented themselves more than the men. "All were around the waist a girdle made of the fin of the whale or of sewant." The men originally wore a breechloth made of skins, but after the Dutch came, those who could obtain it wore "between their legs a lap of duffels cloth half an ell broad and nine quarters long," which they girded around their waist and drew up in a fold "with a flap of each end hanging down in front and rear." In addition to this they had mantles of feathers and at a later period decked them selves with "plaid duffels cloth," in the form of a sash, which was worn over the right shoulder, drawn in a knot around the body with the ends extending down below the knees.

When the young men wished to look especially attractive they wore "a band about their heads, manufactured and braided with scarlet deer hair, interwoven with soft, shining red hair." According to Van der Donck, the women wore a cloth around their bodies, fastened by a girdle which extended below the knees, but next to the body under this coat they used a dressed deerskin coat, girt around the waist. The lower body of this skirt was ornamented with strips tastefully decorated with wampum, which was frequently worth from 100 to 300 guilders (40 to 120 dollars).

"They bound their hair behind in a club, about a hand long, in the form of a beaver's tail, over which they drew a square wampum-ornamented cap, and when they desired to be fine they drew around the forehead a band, also ornamented with wampum, which was fastened behind in a knot. Around their neck they hung various ornaments. They also wore bracelets, curiously wrought and interwoven with wampum," said Van der Donk.

Polygamy was practiced to some extent, though mostly by chiefs. Maidens were allowed to signify their desire to enter matrimonial life, upon which a marriage would be formally arranged. Widows and widowers were left to their own inclinations.

In addition to the usual manifestations of grief at the death of a relative or friend, they cut off their hair and burned it on the grave. The dead, according to Ruttenber, were usually buried in a sitting posture. It was usual to place by the side of the body a pot, kettle, platter, spoon, and provisions. Wood was then placed around the body, and the hole was covered with earth and stones, outside of which pickets were directed so that the tomb resembled a little house.

Their houses were of the communal support and differed usually only in length. They were formed by long, slender, hickory saplings, set in the ground in two rows of straight lines. The poles were then bent toward each other in the form of an arch and secured together, giving the appearance of a garden arbor. The sides and roof were then latched with split poles, and over this bark was lapped fastened with wythes to the lathing. The smoke hole was left in the roof, and a single doorway was provided. These houses rarely exceeded 20 feet in length, but they were sometimes 180 feet long.

Their so-called "castles" were strong, firm structures and were situated usually on a steep, high, flat-topped hill near a stream. The top of the hill was enclosed with a strong stockade, having large logs for a foundation, on both sides of which oak posts forming a palisade were set in the ground, the upper ends being crossed and joined together. Inside the walls of such enclosures were often 20 or 30 houses. Besides their strongholds they had villages and towns which were enclosed or stockaded and which usually had woodland on one side and corn land on the other.

Their religious beliefs were essentially the same as those of the New England Indians. Barton gives the Mahican three clans, Muchquauh (Bear), Mechchaooh (Wolf), and Toonpaooh (Turtle). According to Morgan they had originally the same clans as the Delawares and Munsee, the Wolf, Turtle, and Turkey, but these ultimately developed into phraties, subdivided into clans as follows: The Tooksetuk (Wolf) phratry into the Nehjao (Wolf), Makwa (Bear), Ndeyao (Dog), and Wapakwe (Opossum) clans; the Tonebao (Turtle) phratry into the Gakpomute (Little Turtle), (Mud Turtle), Tonebao (Greater Turtle), and Wesawmaun (Yellow Eel) clans; the Turkey phratry into the Naahmao (Turkey), Ganko (Crane) and (Chicken) clans.

The villages of the Mahican, so far as their names have been recorded, were Aepjin, Kaunaumeek (Stockbridge), Maringoman's Castle, Monemius, Potic, Scaticook (three villages in Dutchess and Rensselaer Counties, New York, and Litchfield County, Connecticut), Schodac, Wiatiac, Wiltmeet, Winooskeek, and Wyantenuc. (See MOHEGANS)

MALECITE

The meaning of the tribal name is uncertain since the Malecite so closely resembled the Micmac in their customs that early writers seldom distinguished the two tribes clearly. Their dialect, however, was quite different, and they raised considerable crops of maize, so that they were rather less dependent on fishing and hunting than their neighbors, who seem not to have practiced agriculture before the seventeenth century. Politically, the Malecite were completely independent, and indeed on one occasion, actively hostile to the Micmac. The boundary between the two tribes was roughly the height of land separating the waters that flow into the St. John River from those that enter the Gulf of St. Lawrence. The territory of the Malecite, however, stretched beyond the drainage basin of St. John River to the shore of the St. Lawrence opposite Tadoussac, and included part of the state of Maine.

They joined with several Algonquian tribes to the south to form a loose confederacy generally known as the Abnaki (Eastern) Confederacy, which supported the French against the English colonists of New England and the league of the Iroquois. Driven across the border into Canada, they shared the same fate as the Micmac, being confined to a few

170

reserves in New Brunswick and Quebec. Today they number about 800, approximately the same as in pre-European times, but all the present population bears a strong infusion of white blood.
 (See also ABNAKI)

MASSACHUSETTS

The Massachusetts (*Massa-adchu-es-et*, "at or about the great hill") tribe was a confederacy that occupied the territory around Massachusetts Bay, including the present site of Boston. In their heyday the tribe had thirty villages, and since warfare was chronic, especially with the Mohican and the Narragansett, each village was fortified with palisades of heavy logs.

Their homes were the dome-shaped structures called wigwams, each with a smokehole cut into the ceiling. Poles or saplings, birch bark, bulrushes, cattails, cedar bark, and grass mats went into the house. Men ordinarily prepared the poles and the framework, and women then fastened the mats or other coverings over it.

To make the homes sturdier, women frequently made ropes of woven fibers long enough to extend across a wigwam and finally be fastened down to stakes on either side. Since a wigwam was big enough for two or three families, a walled village often had a population of eight or nine hundred. The Confederacy spoke Algonquian, one of the largest linguistic stocks in native North America. From well beyond Hudson's Bay on the west, to Newfoundland on the east, the tribes were all solidly Algonquian. The Algonquians moved down through New England and Virginia, crossed to include all states north of Tennessee, and traveled down the eastern side of the Mississippi Valley.

There was one additional though small pocket of Algonquian: in the prairie states, both the Cheyenne and the Arapaho spoke Algonquian. These Algonquian villagers were corn-growers and hunters. In winter, men strapped on snowshoes and went on the "long hunt" to add fresh deer, bear, and turkey to the smoked fish, dried clams, and jerky already on hand. But when planting time arrived, the Algonquians left their villages for favorite fishing streams and planted their crops nearby. The men used the slash-and-burn process to prepare the fields, and even planted some of the corn. Then the women took over with hoes of shell or bone, hoping that their mysterious power of producing children would be magically transferred to make the earth yield abundantly.

Like most hunters, Algonquians counted descent in the male line, but the fields generally went to the women. They planted pumpkin, eight varieties of squash, corn in a variety of colors, and between the rows, sixty varieties of beans. When berries ripened, and nuts began to fall, they were added to the larder. Spring was the time to tap the sugar maples and use the syrup, or even make candy by pouring boiled syrup in the packed snow. It was the Algonquian who taught the settlers about succotash, hominy, cornpone, planked shad, clambakes, and New England's specialty, beans cooked for twenty-four hours in a warm place without a fire.

Male clothing consisted of skin leggings, breechcloths or skin trousers and shirts, especially in winter, plus soft-soled moccasins. Female clothing included wrap-around skirts and poncho-type blouses; some one-piece dresses, occasionally soft-soled moccasins, robes woven in rabbit skin, and feather cloaks. Household items included birch bark, elm bark, and wooden dishes and vessels; bed frames and cornhusk mattresses; pottery; mats of reed and cedar bark and cornhusks; bone and shell utensils; woven bags; quill and later bead decorations on many household containers; hairbrushes of stiff grass or of porcupine quills; and baskets of rush coils, splint plaiting, or sweetgrass.

Transportation included birch-bark canoes, which a man or woman could create in two weeks. They were quite light and could be carried by one person over several miles of portage, and were easily repaired. The Native Americans also used snowshoes, which the settlers also called snow racquets. Except for his scalp lock, a warrior pulled out hair with mussel-shell tweezers.

For war and ceremonies, the Brave's face was painted, and he often wore a crown of upright feathers, a turkey-feather cloak, necklaces of bone or shell, and sometimes a string of wampum. War weapons included bows and arrows; wooden shields and some slat armor; war clubs, knives, and tomahawks (which meant a ball-headed club with a triangle of bone or shell in its knob). Algonquian tribes who were constantly at war used quick commando raids, and took scalps and tortured prisoners, as did their enemies.

The Algonquians invented wampum, calling it *wampompeag*. The settlers shortened it because it was easier to say, and no ceremonial was complete without a wampum record.

A man, wise in years, learned the wampum belts by heart, and saw to it that his successor would do exactly as well. Making and drilling wampum, which was white beads from clamshells and purple ones from mussels or quahogs, took great skill and was usually done by women experts. Once settlers brought in steel awls, the women could work faster, and the

English and Dutch soon accepted wampum in trade either loose, on strings, or woven into belts. However, by 1640, the Dutch already had an ordinance against wampum, which white counterfeiters were turning out. To the settlers, both English and Dutch, wampum was money used in trade, whether used by Indians or themselves.

To the Algonquians, however, wampum always had a sacred quality. One use of wampum was to pay the medicine man (shaman) for his services. Indian medicine was closely allied to religion, and most internal diseases were attributed to supernatural causes. Rattles and sleight-of-hand tricks characterized the Massachusetts medicine men or "Pow-wows," as the settlers called them. Nor did they resort only to the sweat bath, profuse sweating in a confined space followed by a plunge into cold water. There was an incredible amount to be learned about folk medicine, but there was too wide a gap between the "Puritan Saints" and the "Savage Hounds" to accomplish much.

John Josselyn, in his *New England's Rarities*, had Indian cures for scurvy and fevers, among a dozen others, and Cotton Mather, in *The Angel of Bethesda*, the earliest medical treatise to be written in this country, claimed that "our Indians cure consumption with a Mullein-Tea." Even in 1920, thirty drugs used by New England Indians were still official in the United States pharmacopoeia. By the time the Puritans were well settled, the Massachusetts tribes were already on the verge of extinction, hit by the same plagues that struck the Algonquians on the northeast coast from Narragansett Bay to the Kennebec River, and inland for twenty or thirty miles.

The Indian had no immunity to the white man's diseases, but if this one disease was an attack of bubonic plague, neither had the white man. Almost all of the seventeenth century writers say the plague killed nineteen of every twenty Indians. Thomas Morton, in his *New English Canaan* (1637), vividly described the results of the plague: "For in a place where many inhabited, there hath been but one left alive, to tell what became of the rest, the living being (as it seemed) not able to bury the dead, and they were left for crowes, kites, and vermin to prey upon. And the bones and skulls upon the several places of their habitations, made such a spectacle after my coming into those partes, that as I travailed into that Forrest, near the Massachusetts, it seemed to me a new found Golgotha."

Once again, in 1622, the Massachusetts led a conspiracy to exterminate the whites nearby, and once more "a great sickness fell upon them." This time the illness may have been smallpox, but from all accounts by people who saw the results, it was "not unlike the plague, if not the same." Since

173

the Puritans, early on, had classified the Massachusetts' beliefs as devil-ish, there has only been a vague picture of their real beliefs. Some of them included the Great Spirit, or Manitou, the thunder-beings; a huge bird armored in wampum, the sun and the moon as Manitous.

An age-old theory of the hunting people was that a slain animal did not die, but sent its spirit back to its own village in human form to see if man had enough gratitude to return the bones of water animals to water, and to hang up the skulls of land animals with a prayer for forgiveness and an offering of tobacco. Finally, John Eliot (pastor and Cambridge graduate) conceived the idea that the heathen beliefs of the natives could not be expected to yield to Christian doctrines, nor could they be converted, until they heard these in their own tongue.

Cotton Mather was horrified "to think of raising these hideous creatures into our holy religion." Could Eliot "see anything angelical to encourage his labors? All was diabolical among them." Just the same, Eliot took a Natick Indian into his home so he could learn the language. He trans-lated the Bible (the first edition in the New World), and by 1675, he had 1,150 "praying Indians" in fourteen villages. Unfortunately, 1675 was the year when King Philip of Mount Hope and Cononclet of the Narra-gansett led their warriors against the whites. Most of Eliot's converts joined the Indians.

Those who did not were deported by the whites, which feared them. Population figures for the Massachusetts were probably 2,500 or 3,000 in their heyday. If any are left, they probably have been thoroughly mixed with whites. Between the plague and the aftermath of King Philip's War, when most of them were sold into slavery, the Massachusetts seem to have become extinct as a separate tribe.

MASSAPEQUA

Massapequa ("Great Pond", from *massa*, "great", and *peàg* or *pequa*, "pond", the term frequently occurring in dialectic forms in New England and on Long Island). The Massapequa were an Algonquian tribe for-merly of the South coast of Long Island, New York, near Seaford and Babylon, extending from Fort Neck to Islip. Massapequa, their chief village, was most likely at Fort Neck. According to Flint, "Under con-stant fear of attack from their more warlike neighbors, the Indians at each end of the island had built at Fort Neck and Fort Pond, or Konkhongauk, a place of refuge capable of holding 500 men". This stronghold was de-stroyed in 1653 by a Captain Underhill, in the only great Indian battle fought on Long Island. Squaw Island was a refuge for women and children during the conflict.

The remains of the quadrangular building, with 90-foot sides, were evident until the late 1800s. The Massapequa sachem Tackapousha exasperated the white settlers in his vicinity, being forced to pay tribute to him repeatedly. He was one of the most turbulent of Long Island Indians. The Massapequa were a farming and fishing people who inhabited several settlements on necks of land surrounded by low marshy hummocks and protected from the ocean by the barrier island of Long Beach. They further resided in smaller settlements in the interior to the south of the Ronkinkoma Moraine, a highland ridge that ran lengthwise along Long Island from Great Peconic Bay on the east, to the westernmost tip of present Brooklyn. Their settlements generally consisted of one or more longhouses or roundhouses covered with a combination of grass mats and sheets of bark.

The Massapequa also constructed large fortified villages surrounded by palisades of closely spaced timbers during times of war. Their principal fort was located at Fort Neck near Rockville Center, Long Island. The Massapequa took their life from the sea. Their villages bordered the calm shallow lagoons and rich beds between the main island and the barrier beaches. They netted, speared, trapped, and gathered large quantities of fish and shellfish from those waters. Across the barrier islands they cast nets and spears into the surf to harvest the open ocean.

They traveled throughout their territories in lithe dugout canoes. Small groups paddled into the interior during the colder months to live in hunting and trapping camps, stalking deer and bear. These increased in importance during the early years of Dutch colonization in the early seventeenth century. The fur trade brought metal tools, firearms, cloth, and alcohol in exchange for animal skins. The Indians of New Netherland quickly became dependent upon these trade items, and the pace of hunting, trapping, and processing furs was stepped up accordingly. The Massapequas were first mentioned in the Dutch records of January 15, 1639. On that date, "Mechoswodt, chief Sachem of Marossepinck" put the entire Massapequa territory under Dutch protection. The document further stipulated that the Massapequa would only sell their lands to the Dutch, and that they would retain the rights to dwell, plant, fish, and hunt at their accustomed places. This manuscript confirmed the special relationship between the Massapequa and Dutch.

Part of the price for this special relationship was Massapequa military service whenever the Dutch requested it. The Dutch called in that debt in

1641, when they asked that the Massapequa send war parties against the Raritan of central New Jersey. The Raritan had retaliated against a Dutch attack upon their settlements in Staten Island, New York in 1640 by burning Dutch plantations there during the summer of 1641. The Massapequa, accordingly, sent their warriors to the Raritan country, and they returned with many scalps.

The Massapequa were horrified by the unprovoked massacre of the refugee lower Hudson River Delawaran groups by the Dutch, near Fort Amsterdam on the night of February 25-26, 1643. They did not, however, make immediate moves against the Dutch as did most of their Native allies and relations. Most of the Massapequa moved, along with many other Long Island Native groups, to the remote village of Rechqua Akie, near modern Far Rockaway, to await events and avoid Dutch attack.

On March 5, 1643 a one-eyed sachem, later identified as Mechoswodt, received a party of Dutch diplomats headed by David de Vries at Rechqua Akie. These negotiations led to the signing of a peace agreement between them on March 25, 1643. On November 13, 1643, the natives of "Masepeage, Merriack, or Rockaway" sold what was apparently the western half of their territories around Hempstead, Long Island. The deed was signed by "the Sagamore or Maespeage" and a number of other persons. The Governor Kieft War increased in intensity during the winter of 1643-1644. A number of Dutch attacks against native settlements caused the deaths of hundred of Native people on the mainland and on Long Island. Those desiring neutrality were forced to renegotiate with the Dutch.

The Matinecock sachem, Gauwaroe, accordingly entered into a new peace agreement with the Dutch on behalf of his people and for the "villages" of Marospinc and Siketeuhacky (Setauket) on April 15, 1644. Gauwaroe further promised that his people would not support the still hostile Rockaway, Jamaica Bay, and Marechkawieck groups. A final peace treaty signed on May 24, 1645, ended the war for all of the Long Island groups. Tackapousha, the successor of Mechoswoldt, renewed his people's friendship with the Dutch during the opening days of the Peach War on November 7, 1655.

Two years later, on July 4, 1657, "Takaposha, sachem of Mersapeage" confirmed the November 13, 1643 sale of Hempstead. Witnessed by the Montauk sachem, Wantaugh, the sale was reconfirmed by Tackapousha and his followers on May 11, 1658. These reaffirmations did not succeed in determining the precise boundaries of the sale, and the English of

Hempstead repeatedly claimed that the 1643 deed sold all of the Massapequa lands, while the Massapequa claimed they had only the western half of their domain.

This dispute continued until March 24, 1685, when Tackapousha and his followers conveyed all of their lands to the English, reserving the right to remain at their main settlement at Cow Neck. On March 6, 1660, during the Esopus Wars, "Tapousah, chief of Marsepingh and Rechkawyck (Rockaway)" renewed the peace with the Dutch and pledged warriors to join their forces in the Esopus country in the mid-Hudson River Valley. Many men were sent, and Massapequa forces numbered some forty-six men by October 1663. These warriors served as scouts and were effective soldiers against the Esopus villages.

Somewhat illtreated by the race-proud Dutch, the Massapequa contingent repeatedly complained that they were not given a fair share of the booty. On May 15, 1664, Siejpekenouw, the brother of Tackapousha and leader of the warriors, signed the peace treaty ending the Esopus Wars on behalf of the Massapequa and their Long Island allies. The threat of the Massapequa involved in the King Philip's War, that had engulfed the adjacent English colonies of New England, renewed European interest in them during 1675-1676.

The English, who had conquered New Netherland in 1664, were gratified to hear on October 21, 1675 that "Tackerparis of Marsepeake and Marricoke" had moved closer to the English settlements some three to four years earlier. Living near the English and under direct surveillance, the English authorities were able to discount rumors spread by the Hempstead settlers that the Rockaway and "Masha-Peage" were contemplating an attack against them. The close connection between the Massapequa and the Rockaway sachems was identified as Tackapousha's son. A year earlier, Tackapousha reaffirmed a friendship with the English on behalf of the "Rockaway, Mashepeage, Maricock, Vinchechauge, and Sequetalke."

Two years later, on April 2, 1678, he renewed their alliance for all these groups. Most of the Massapequa moved east among the Unchechauge near Patchogue, Long Island, following the final sale of their traditional homeland on March 24, 1685. They were joined by a large number of western Long Island Native people. This community became known as the Poosepatuck group during the early 1700s.

The group gathered around the nucleus of the Unchechauge Reservation first established in 1666. These people lived by whaling, fishing, shellfishing, peddling their baskets and other handicrafts, and by selling herbal cures to their white neighbors. A large number of Poosepatuck left the reservation in 1775 to join the Native missionary, Samson Occum, in Connecticut. Only three old women spoke the old language when Thomas Jefferson visited the community in 1791.

Ten families were recorded as residents on the reservation toward the end of the nineteenth century, and their last sachem, Elizabeth Joe, died at Poosepatuck in 1832. The Poosepatuck reservation continues to exist today as a state reservation. Its inhabitants, many of them intermarried with blacks and other Native groups, still live on ancestral land.

MASSASOIT

Massasoit (Wampanoag, 1600 - 1661), was also known as Woosamequin), the chief of the Wampanoag in southeastern New England at the time of the Pilgrims' landing, opted for the friendship of the whites at the price of enormous tracts of tribal lands. Massasoit, born near present-day Bristol, Rhode Island, felt threatened by the Narraganset Indians who lived across the bay from the Wampanoag, and was quick to appreciate the advantages of the alliance with Plymouth colonists. There were other reasons for Massasoit's desire to fulfill the Pilgrims' image of "the good Indian." From his first visit in 1621, Massasoit was treated as royalty by the struggling colonists.

Introduced to the Europeans by Samoset, who led the chief and 60 Wampanoag warriors from their Rhode Island villages to the whites' crude cabins, Massasoit made his mark on a treaty of alliance between the Wampanoag and King James I of England. In December 1621, Massasoit made another journey to Plymouth, this time to help the Pilgrims celebrate a day of thanksgiving for their having survived the first year in the wilderness. Two years later, in 1623, a group of settlers traveled to the Wampanoag village upon hearing that Massasoit was dying.

To the Indians' amazement, the Puritans nursed the sachem back to health, thereby creating an even closer relationship between Massasoit, his people, and the colonists. The close bond between Massasoit and the whites, though, veiled the growing animosity on the part of the Wampanoag and the increasing anxiety on the part of the Pilgrims. The 40-year period between Massasoit's first meeting with the settlers in 1621 and his death in 1661 saw the steady expansion of white towns into what had been Wampaneag territory. Massasoit ceded major portions of the tribe's other manufactured goods. The guns and factory goods, of course, entranced Massasoit's personal power and prestige vis-a-vis the neighboring Narraganset Indians, but he sold his tribe's birthright in exchange.

The Europeans even seized lands that had not been granted to them, and then jailed Indians who dared to trespass on what the settlers considered to be private property. Massasoit seldom supported the rights of his people when those rights came into conflict with the colonists' expansionist desires. His aping of white ways even went so far as his request that the General Court in Plymouth provide English names to his two older boys, Wamsutta and Metacom.

They became Alexander and Philip, but following Massasoit's death in 1661, the policy of friendship at any price came to an end; the Wampanoag sachem called Philip launched a war of revenge in 1675, a war to regain all that his father had given away so cheaply.

MATINECOC

The Matinecoc, a Delaware-Munsee speaking group, were an Algonquin tribe that formerly lived on the northwest coast of Long Island, New York, from present Newton, Queens County, to Smithtown, Suffolk County. There were Matenecoc villages at Flushing, Glen Cove, Cold Spring, Huntington, and Cow Harbor, but even before whites intruded, they had been greatly reduced. This was most likely from wars with the Iroquois, to whom they paid tribute. After the war of 1643, most Matinecoc survivors moved to their settlement at Nissequaque, on the Nesaquake River, near present Smithtown, Suffolk County, Long Island New York.

Records indicate that by 1650 there were only about 50 families of this once important tribe. Ruttenberger includes the Matinecoc as having melded with his Montauk group, which is about equivalent to Metoac; but the interrelationship of the tribes in the western part of Long Island was not definitely determined. In 1628, Isaak de Rasieres reported that on Long Island "many savages dwell, who support themselves by planting maize (corn) and making sewan," or wampum, a form of shell money.

He further reported that "the tribes are held in subjection by, and are tributary to, the Pyquans," also known as the Pequot, an Algonquian-speaking group that lived in eastern coastal Connecticut. The Pequot were scattered by the English in 1637, and many of their survivors settled among the natives of Long Island.   On January 15, 1639, Mechoswodt "Chief Sachem of Marossepinck, Sintsinck (otherwise called Schout's Bay) and its dependencies" conveyed the entire western half of Long Island to the Dutch of New Netherland. This was not an outright land sale, however.

Mechoswodt, "with his people and friends" reserved the right "to remain upon the land, plant corn, fish, hunt, and make a living." He further placed himself and his followers under Dutch protection. This document was clearly meant to seat an alliance between the western Long Island groups and the Dutch by granting the latter rights to unclaimed lands in the area.

On May 13, 1640, the sachem Penhawitz notified the Dutch that a number of English settlers were squatting on unpurchased lands of Schout's Bay. By August 9, 1640, Natives at Martin Gerritsen's Bay tore down the coat of arms of the State General of the Netherlands and replaced it with a fool's head. This open act of defiance of Dutch authority resulted in a Dutch resolution to attack and subdue the perpetrators. War with the Raritan of central New Jersey diverted Dutch attention, however. A number of Matinecock probably joined the war parties that attacked the Raritan, due to their alliance with the Dutch throughout 1641. Many Matinecock and their relations were killed in the Dutch massacre of the refugee villages near the walls of Fort Amsterdam on the night of February 25-26, 1643. Mechoswodt and Penhawitz signed a peace agreement with the Dutch on March 25, 1643.

A substantial number of western Long Island Indians refused to honor this treaty, and their warriors harassed the Dutch and English settlements repeatedly during 1643. The Dutch attacked the village of Matsepe, and a smaller settlement during the winter of 1643-1644. Over one hundred and twenty men and an unknown number of women and children were killed in both assaults. These actions brought the Matinecock and their allies to the conference table. On April 15, 1644 "Gauwarowe, sachem of Matinecock, Marospinc and Siketeuhacky" signed a peace agreement with the Dutch.

He further agreed not to support the still hostile "Indians of Reckonhacky, the bays and Marechkaqieck." On May 24, 1645, the sachems of the eastern Long Island Montauk and Shinnecock groups signed a final peace agreement with the Dutch that ended their participation in the Governor Kieft War. They acted on both their own behalf and for the villages of "Onheywichkingh, Sichteyhacky, and Reckoouhacky", the latter of which was reported as being under Native eastern Long Island protection. This document also noted that the "Matinnekoncx" were living at Nisinckquehacky during the conflict. Disputes between the

180

English settlers at Hempstead and their Matinecock and Massapequa neighbors became more frequent toward the end of the war.

English cattle and hogs overran and destroyed unfenced Native gardens and fields. The lucrative liquor trade demoralized and defrauded the Native people. They responded by shooting marauding animals, and alternately calling for prohibition of the liquor trade and increasing consumption of alcohol. On August 23, 1647 the Hempstead settlers accused the Massapequa sachem, Tackapousha, of plotting an attack against the Europeans. These repeated accusations were denied by the Western Long Island groups.

The Hempstead settlers felt that the January 15, 1639 deed entitled them to the Matinecock land, an assumption the Matinecock strenuously contested. War scares were only part of the Hempstead strategy to dispossess the Matinecock from their lands.

The Dutch speculator, Cornelis van Tienhoven, wrote in his land promotion pamphlet of March 4, 1650 that the "Martinne houck" had their plantations along the smallest of three streams that flowed into Martin Gerritsen's Bay. He further wrote that "this tribe is not strong, and consists of about 30 families.

They were formerly in and about this bay, great numbers of Indian Plantations, which now lie waste and vacant." This grim testimony gave witness to the toll of a half-century of epidemic diseases and wars with the Dutch and their own traditional native enemies. The outbreak of the Peach War (1655-1657) cast suspicion on all of the Native groups of New Netherland.

On September 30, 1656, a delegation of Massapequa men reported that "the savages of Matinecogh of the tribe called Sicketawagh" had stolen some clothing from them and that they were further sympathetic to the Wappinger, a group at war with the Dutch. This complaint was accomplished by an expression of Tackapousha's anger at this act, his assurance that he would control the Matinecock, and a reaffirmation of his support of the Dutch in the war. Several Matinecock were included among the 26 warriors furnished by Tackapousha to serve with the Dutch against the Esopus of the mid-Hudson River Valley in 1659.

This contingent, which swelled to include 46 Long Island warriors by 1663, gave crucial support to the Dutch during the Esopus War (1659-1664). On September 6, 1664, New Netherland passed into English hands. This event signaled an increased tempo of Hempstead demands for the eviction of the Matinecock. On March 14, 1667, the Matinecock refused to sell their lands to the Hempstead settlers. They did, however, permit the seven families already living on their lands to remain.

On June 8, 1669, the Governor of New York advised the Hempstead men to prove that the Matinecock were party to the 1639 conveyance. Evidently unable to show that the Matinecock were subjects to the Massapequa, the Hempstead settlers nevertheless continued to litigate for the Matinecock lands. Finally, on May 17, 1676, the Matinecock sold "three parcels of land one mile square each about Muskitoe Cove" to the Hempstead men for 600 guilders of wampum.

A final sale of all of the disputed lands on western Long Island on March 24, 1685 completely cleared the English title to the Matinecock territory. The majority of the Matinecock moved east to the Poosepatuck Reservation near Patchogue, Suffolk County.

A portion of the group chose to remain in their homeland. These settled in small hamlets along the north shore near the sites of their earlier villages. Many of their number became expert harpooners on the ships of the burgeoning whaling fleets that sprang up in many north shore ports during the latter years of the seventeenth century.

Other Matinecock worked on the English plantations, sold medicinal herbs, acted as midwives and surgeons, and sold homemade handicrafts. Many Matinecock served among the 150 Long Island Indians who fought for the English against the French in the Queen Anne's War (1702-1713). On September 12, 1711, it was reported that they were "being of great use for managing batteus (long boats) and canoes and all other hard labour."

The Long Island people also provided warriors for the English during the Seven Years War (1755-1762), and the Americans during the American Revolution (1775-1783). The Matinecock have continued to live in their ancestral territory. A number of families claiming Matinecock heritage today live near Glen Cove in Nassau County, New York. Other descendants of the Matinecock groups may be found in the modern Poosepatuck, Shinnecock, and Montauk reservation communities in Suffolk County, New York.

METOAC

Metoac, according to Gerard, is from "*metau-hok*", "the periwinkle, from the columella of which beads were made". It is also a collective term embracing the Indians of Long Island, New York, who seem to have been divided into the following tribes, subtribes, or bands: Canarsee, Corchaug, Manhasset, Massepequa, Matinecoc, Merric, Montauk,

182

Nesquake, Patchoag, Rockaway, Secatoag, Setauket, and Shinnecock. There were some minor bands or villages that received special designations.

They were all closely connected linguistically and politically, and were probably derived from the same ethnic system. Ruttenber classes them as branches of the Mahican.

The Montauk, who formed the leading tribe in the eastern part of the island, are often confounded with Metoac, and in some instances the Canarsee of the western portion have also been confounded with them. The eastern tribes were at one time subject to the Pequot and afterward to the Naraganset, while the Iroquois claimed dominion over the western tribes.

They were numerous at the first settlement of the island, but rapidly wasted away from epidemics and wars with other Indians and with the Dutch, disposing of their land piece by piece to the Whites. About 1778 a large part of the survivors joined the Brotherton Indians in Oneida County, New York.

The rest, represented chiefly by the Montauk and Shinnecock, dwindled to perhaps a dozen individuals of mixed blood. The Indians of Long Island were a seafaring people, mile in temperament, diligent in the pursuits determined by their environment, skilled in the management of the canoe, seine, and spear, and dexterous in the making of Seawan or Wampum, according to Flint. The Chieftancies were hereditary by lineal descent, including females when there was no male representative. Metoac villages were Canarsee, Cotsjewaminck, Cutchogue (Corchaug), Merric, Mirrachtauhacky, Mochgonnekonck, Montauk, Nachaquatuck, Nesaquake, Ouheywichkingh, Patchoag, Rechquaakie, Setauket, Sitchteyhacky, Wawapex (Matinecock).

Descendants of the Metoac now live on the small Poosepatuck and Shinnecock Reservations in the area, or in the Montauk Indian Village.

MOGG

Mogg (Abnaki; ?-August 23, 1724) was a chief sachem of Norridgewock, killed when a combined English and French force attacked the French mission of Father Sebastian Rale. The English, who had burned the mission twice before (1705, 1722), also wanted to gain title to Indian lands. Mogg refused to retreat from the surprise attack led by Captain Moulton and was killed in his wigwam. John G. Whittier describes the attack in *Mogg Megone.*

MOHAWK

"Mohawk" is cognate with the Narraganset *Mohowauuck*, "they eat (animate) things," hence "man–eaters." The most easterly tribe of Iroquois confederacy, the Mohawk called themselves Kanyengehaga, "people of the place of the flint."

In the federal council and in other intertribal assemblies, the Mohawks sat with the tribal clans, which was formally called the "Three Elder Brothers," and of which the other members were the Seneca and the Onondaga. Like the Oneida, the Mohawk have only three clans, namely the Bear, the Wolf, and the Turtle. The tribe is represented in the federal council by nine chiefs of the rank of "roianer" being three from every clan.

These chiefships were known by specific names that were conferred with the office. These official titles are Tekarihoken, Haienhwatha, and Satekarihwate, of the first group; Orenrehkowa, Deionhehkon, and Sharenhowanen, of the second group; and Dehennakarine, Rastawenserontha, and Shoskoharowanen, of the third group.

The first two groups or clans formed an intratribal clan, while the last, or Bear clan group, was the other clan. The people at times assembled by clans, and each occupied a side of the council fire opposite that occupied by the second phratry. The second title in the foregoing list has been Anglicized into the Hiawatha.

From *The Jesuit Relation for 1660* it is learned that the Mohawk, during a period of sixty years, had been many times both at the top and the bottom of the ladder of success, their being "insolent and warlike." They had attacked Abnaki at the East, the Conestoga at the South, the Hurons at the West and North, and the Algonquian tribes at the North. At the close of the sixteenth century the Algonquian had so reduced them that there appeared to be none left, but that the remainder increased so rapidly that in a few years they had in turn overthrown the Algonquian.

This success did not last long. The Conestoga waged war against them so vigorously for ten years that for the second time the Mohawk were overthrown so completely that they appeared to be extinct. About 1614 the Dutch arrived in their country, and being attracted by beaver skins they furnished the Mohawk with firearms in order that the pelts might be obtained in greater abundance.

From then on the Mohawk and their confederates became formidable adversaries and were victorious almost everywhere, so that by 1660 the conquests of the Iroquois confederacy, though they were not numerous, extended over nearly 1500 miles of territory. The Mohawk at that time numbered not more than 500 warriors and lived in four or five wretched villages.

The accounts of Mohawk migration previous to the historical period are largely conjectural. Some writers do not clearly differentiate between the Mohawk and Huron tribes at the north and west, and from their own confederates as a whole. Besides fragmentary and untrustworthy traditions, little is definitely known regarding the migratory movements of the Mohawk.

In 1603 Champlain, while at Tadousac, heard of the Mohawk and their country. On July 30, 1609, he encountered, on the lake to which he gave his own name, a party of nearly 200 Iroquois warriors under three chiefs. In a skirmish he shot two of the chiefs dead and wounded the third and defeated this party, which was most probably largely Mohawk. Dismayed by the firearms of the Frenchmen, whom they had now met for the first time, the Indians fled. The Iroquois of this party wore arrow–proof armor and had both stone and iron hatchets, the latter having been obtained in trade.

The fact that in Captain Hendricksen's report to the States General, August 18, 1616, he says that he had "bought from the inhabitants, the Minquaes (Conestoga), three persons being people belonging to this company," who were "employed by the service of the Mohawks and the Mahicans," giving, he says, for them in exchange "kettles, beads, and merchandise." This shows how extensively the inland trade was between the Dutch and the Mohawk. The latter were at war with the Mohegan and other New England tribes with only intermittent periods of peace. In 1623 a Mohegan fort stood opposite Castle Island in the Hudson and was "built against their enemies, the Maquaes, a powerful people."

In 1626 the Dutch commander of Fort Orange (Albany) and six of his men joined the Mohegan in an expedition to invade the Mohawk country. They were met about three miles from the fort by a party of Mohawk armed only with bows and arrows and were defeated. The Dutch commander and three of his men were killed and one, probably the commander, was cooked and eaten by the Mohawk. This intermittent warfare continued until the Mohegan were finally forced to withdraw from the upper waters of the Hudson.

They did not, however, relinquish their territorial rights to their native adversaries, so in 1630 they began to sell their land to the Dutch. The deed to the Manor of Rensselaerwyck, which extended west of the river two days' journey and was mainly on the east side of the river, was dated 1630. In 1637 Killian Van Rensslaer bought more land on the East.

Subsequently the Mohegan became the friends and allies of the Mohawk, their former adversaries.

In 1641 Ahatsistari, a noted Huron chief with only fifty companions attacked and defeated 300 Iroquois, largely Mohawk, taking some prisoners. In the preceding summer he had attacked, on lake Ontario, a number of large canoes manned by Iroquois, probably chiefly Mohawk, and defeated them after sinking several canoes and killing a number of their crew. In 1642, eleven Huron canoes were attacked on the Ottawa River by Mohawk and Oneida warriors, about forty miles above Montreal. In the same year the Mohawk captured Father Isaac Jogues, two French companions, and some Huron allies. They took the Frenchmen to their villages, where they underwent cruel tortures.

Jogues, by the aid of the Dutch, escaped in the following year, but in 1646 he went to the Mohawk in an attempt to convert them and to confirm the peace which had been made with them. On May 16, 1646, Father Jogues went to the Mohawk as an envoy and returned to Three Rivers in July in good health. In September he again started for the Mohawk country to establish a mission there, but owing to the presence of an epidemic among the Mohawk and to the failure of their crops, they accused Father Jogues of "having concealed certain charms in a small coffer which they had left with his host as a pledge of his return," which they believed was the cause of their afflictions.

So upon his arrival in their village for the third time, he and his companion, a young Frenchman, were seized, stripped, and threatened with death. Father Jogues had been adopted by the Wolf clan of the Mohawk. Therefore, his clan was that of the Turtle, which with the Wolf, formed a clan or brotherhood, and tried to save the lives of the Frenchmen. However, the Bear clan which formed a clan by itself, and being only cousins to the others, one of which Father Jogues was a member, had decided to kill him because he was a sorcerer.

On October 17, 1646, the unfortunates were told that they would be killed, but not burned, the next day. On the evening of the eighteenth Father Jogues was invited to a supper in the Bear lodge. Having accepted the invitation he went there, and while entering the lodge a man concealed behind the door struck him down with an axe. He was beheaded, his head elevated on the palisade, and his body thrown into the river. The next morning Jogues' companion suffered a similar fate.

Father Jogues left an account of a Mohawk sacrifice to the god Aireskoi ("the Master or God of War"). While speaking of the cruelties exercised by the Mohawk toward their prisoners, and specifically toward three women, he said, "One of them (a thing not hitherto done) was burned all over her body and afterwards thrown into a huge pyre," and that "at every burn which they caused by applying lighted torches to her body an old man in a loud voice exclaimed 'Daimon, Aireskoi, we offer thee this victim, whom we burn for thee, that thou mayest be filled with her flesh and render us ever anew victorious over our enemies.' Her body was cut up, sent to the various villages, and devoured."

Megapolensis (1644), a contemporary of Father Jogues, says that when the Mohawk were unfortunate in war they would kill, cut up, and roast a bear and then make an offering of it to this war god with the accompanying prayer: "Oh, great and mighty Aireskuoni, we know that we have offended against thee inasmuch as we have not killed and eaten our captive enemies; forgive us this. We promise that we will kill and eat all the captives we shall hereafter take, as certainly as we have killed and now eat this bear." He adds, "Finally they roast their prisoners dead before a slow fire for some days and then eat them. The common people eat the arms, buttocks and trunk, but the chiefs eat the head and the heart."

The *Jesuit Relation for 1646* says that, properly speaking, the French had at that time peace with only the Mohawk, who were their neighbors, and who gave them the most trouble. The Mohegan (Mahingans or Mahinganak) who had had firm alliances with Algonquian allies of the French, were already conquered by the Mohawk, with whom they had formed a defensive and offensive alliance. During this year some Sokoki (Assoksekik) murdered some Algonquian, whereupon the latter determined, under a misapprehension, to massacre some Mohawk, who were then among them and the French. Fortunately, two wounded persons escaped, said that the murderers spoke a language quite different them that of the Iroquois tongue.

Suspicion was at once removed from the Mohawk who then hunted freely in the immediate vicinity of the Algonquian north of the Saint Lawrence. Thereafter these hitherto and implacable enemies frequently met on the best of terms. At this time the Mohawk refused Sokoki ambassadors a new contact to wage war on the Algonquian.

The Dutch introduced the Mohawk to firearms. They were among the first of their region to procure them, and this marked an important era in their history. It enabled them and related Iroquois tribes to subjugate the Delawares and the Munsee.

This began a career of conquest that carried their war parties to the Mississippi River and to the shores of the Hudson Bay. The Mohawk villages were in the valley of the Mohawk River, New York, from the vicinity of Schenectady nearly to Utica, and their territory extended north to the Saint Lawrence and south to the watershed of Schoharie Creek and the eastern branch of the Susquehanna. On the east their territories adjoined those of the Mahican who held the Hudson River.

From their position on the eastern frontier of the Iroquois confederation, the Mohawk were among the most prominent of the Iroquoian tribes in early Indian wars and in official negotiations with the Colonies. Their name was frequently used by the tribes of New England and by the whites as a synonym for the confederation. Owing to their position they also suffered much more than their confederates in some of the Indian and French wars. Their seven villages of 1644 were reduced to five by 1677.

At the beginning of the revolution the Mohawk took the side of the British and at its conclusion the larger portion of them under Brant and Johnson were moved to Canada, where they have since resided on lands granted to them by the British government. In 1777 the Oneida expelled the remainder of the tribe and burned their villages.

In 1650 the Mohawk had an estimated population of 5,000, which was probably more than the actual number, for ten years later they were estimated at only 2,500. They then underwent a rapid decline caused by their wars with the Mahican, Conestoga, other tribes, the French, and also by removal of a large part of the tribe to Caughnawaga and other mission villages.

Later estimates of their population have been 1,500 in 1677 (an alleged decrease of 3,500 in twenty–seven years), 400 in 1736 (an alleged decrease of 1,100 in thirty–six years), 500 in 1741, 800 in 1765, 500 in 1778, 1,500 in 1783, and about 1,200 in 1851. These estimates are evidently a little better than vague guesses. In 1884 they were on three reservations in Ontario, 956 at the Bay of Quinte near the eastern end of Lake Ontario, the settlement at Gibson, and the reserve of the Six Nations on Grand River. Besides these were a few individuals scattered among different Iroquois tribes in the United States. In 1906 the Bay of Quinte settlement contained 1,320. There were 140 (including Algonquian) at Watha, the former Gibson band which was removed earlier from Oka, and the Six Nations included an indeterminate number.

In a recent count, about 5600 Mohawk lived on the American side of the United States–Canadian border, which splits the Akwesasne Mohawk Community. The American Mohawk live on about 14,600 acres south of the Saint Lawrence River. On the Canadian side, over 7,600 Mohawk live on approximately 7,400 acres along the northern side of the Saint Lawrence River, and on Cornwall Island.

The Mohawk participated in the following treaties with the United States: Fort Stanwix, New York, October 22, 1784, being a treaty of peace between the United States and the Six Nations and defining their boundaries, supplemented by the Treaty of Fort Harmar, Ohio, January 9, 1789, Konondaigua (Canandaigua), New York, November 11, 1794, establishing peace relations with the Six Nations and agreeing to certain reservations and boundaries, Albany, New York, March 29, 1797, by which the United States sanctioned the cession by the Mohawk to New York of all their lands herein.

The following were Mohawk villages: Canajoharie, Canastigaone, Canienga, Caugh–hnawaga, Chuchtononeda, Kanagaro, Kowogoc–on-nughariegugharie, Nowadaga, Ohnowalagantles, Ohsarakas, Onekagoncka, Onoalagona, Osguage, Osquake, Saratoga, Schaunactada (Schenectady), Schoharie, Teatontaloga, and Tewanondadon.

MOHEGANS

Popularly memorialized in James Fenimore Cooper's novel, *The Mohegans* (also known as Mahicans, from *maingan*, "wolf") were decimated by a plague in 1616-17. This tribe, of Algonquian stock, had originally ranged from New York into the upper portions of the Housatonic Valley in Massachusetts. In 1664, their council moved its fire from Albany to Stockbridge, Massachusetts. From Stockbridge, some of the Mohegans migrated to the Susquehanna River, but the remnants of these people were gathered into a mission at Stockbridge, with a forlorn hope for perpetuation.

In winter, the men wore a costume later adopted by white hunters: leggings, dressed buckskin shirts, breechcloths and moccasins, and sometimes fur caps. In summer, the breechcloths and moccasins formed a complete costume. Women wore leggings and long gowns. Garments were decorated with fringes and sometimes painted with simple designs. Both sexes painted their faces. Tattooing was confined to the cheeks, upon which totemic figures were permanently placed by the insertion of black pigment beneath the surface of the skin.

The men plucked their beards, and hair was dressed in various styles according to the sex, age, and station of the individual. The primary weapon was the wooden bow strung with moose sinew, and wooden arrows tipped with stone or bone and carried in quivers of skin. In warfare the usual offensive weapon was the tomahawk, with bark shields serving to some extent for defense. Communities were built on hunting and agriculture.

Members of the tribes or communities were the recognized proprietors of certain hunting, fishing, and agricultural lands, held as a rule in common. The winter villages were usually situated in warm, thickly wooded valleys near a lake or river. The early spring was spent on the fishing grounds, and when the planting season arrived, the tribe moved to its summer fields. Each family had its garden of corn, beans, pumpkins, squash, artichokes, and tobacco, cultivated with hoes of stone, wood, or clamshells, and fertilized by herring and shad.

Wild berries, roots, and nuts furnished other sources of food, supplemented by fish and by the meat of the larger mammals preserved by cutting in strips and smokedrying. The Indians divided themselves very strictly into three social classes: those of royal blood, including the sachems, shamans, elders of the council, and subordinate chiefs; commoners or freemen with rights to the tribal lands; and "outsiders" of alien blood, usually captives, with no tribal rights.

Descent was through the female line, and the office of head chief or sachem was hereditary. If tribes were large and important they might be governed by several under-chiefs, and each tribe had a council of elders of noble blood. The shamans possessed great influence. They were partly seers and partly physicians. When, as occasionally happened, the offices of sachem and shaman were combined, the person vested with this dual authority held tremendous power. Polygamy was fairly common, and divorce was frequent, the right being exercised as freely by women as by men. Justice was a simple matter. If any tribesman was wronged, all related to him were bound to see that proper restitution was made. Murder was avenged or suitably punished by the kinsmen of the victim.

Their descendants may now be among Indians now living on the Western Pequot Reservations, and the Schaghticoke Reservation, and in the Mohegan Community in Connecticut, and the Narraganset Community in Rhode Island. A recent count showed about 1000 on the tribal roll. (See also MAHICANS)

MONTAUK

The meaning of *Montauk* is uncertain, and has been used in different senses, sometimes limited to the particular band or tribe known by this name, but in a broader sense including most of the tribes of Long Island, excepting those about the west end. It is occasionally used incorrectly as equivalent to Metoac. The Indians of Long Island were closely related to the Indians of Massachusetts and Connecticut. The dialect of the Montauk was more nearly related to the Natick of Massachusetts than was the Narraganset. The Montauk, in the limited sense, formerly occupied Easthampton Township, Suffolk County, at the eastern end of Long Island, and controlled all the other tribes of the island, except those near the western end. That these so-called tribes were but parts of one group, or tribe, or the loosely connected elements of what had been an organized body, seems apparent.

Ruttenber, speaking of the Montauk in the limited sense, says: "This chieftaincy was acknowledged by both the Indians and the Europeans as the ruling family of the island". They were indeed the head of the tribe of Montauk, the other divisions named being simply clans or groups, as in the case of other tribes. Wyandance, their sachem, was also the grand sachem of Paumanacke, or Sewanhackey, as the island was called.

Nearly all land deeds were confirmed by him. His younger brothers, Nowedonah and Poygratasuck (Poggatacut), were respectively sachems of the Shinnecock and the Manhasset." The Rockaway and Cannarsee at the West End were probably not included. It is doubtful whether he is correct in including the west-end Indians in the confederacy.

The principal Montauk village, which probably bore the name of the tribe, was about Fort Pond, near Montauk Point. The Pequot made them and their subordinates tributary, and on the destruction of that tribe in 1637, the Narraganset began a series of attacks which finally, about 1659, forced the Montauk, who had lost the greater part of their number by pestilence, to retire for protection by the whites at Easthampton.

Since 1641 they had been tributary to New England. When first known they were numerous, and even after the pestilence of 1658-59, were estimated at about 500. Then began a rapid decline, and a century later only 162 remained, most of whom joined the Brotherton Indians of New York about 1788. In 1829 only about 30 were left on Long Island, and 40 years later these had dwindled to half a dozen individuals, who, with a few Shinnecock, were the last representatives of the Long Island tribes. They preserved a form of tribal organization into the nineteenth century and retained their hereditary chiefs until the death of the last "king," David Pharaoh, about 1875.

Only a few mixed-blood Montauk now remain. Montauk descendants may be found among the approximate 400 Indians now living in small communities in the area, including the Poosepatuck and Shinnecock Reservations, and the Montauk Indian Village.

MORAVIANS

Mahicans, Munsees, and Delawares who followed the teachings of the Moravian Brethren, were gathered by them into villages apart from their tribes. The majority of "Moravian Indians" were Munsee. In 1740 the Moravian missionaries began their work at the Mahican village of Shekomeko in New York. Meeting with many obstacles there, they moved with their converts in 1746 to Pennsylvania, where they built the new mission village of Friedenshuetten on the Susquehanna. Here they were more successful and largely recruited from the Munsee and Delawares, almost all of the former tribe not absorbed by the Delawares finally joining them.

They made another settlement at Wyalusing, but on the advance of the white population, removed to Beaver River in west Pennsylvania, where they built the village of Friedensstadt. They remained here about a year, and in 1773 removed to Muskingum River in Ohio, in the neighborhood of the others of their tribes, and occupied the three villages of Gnadenhuetten, Salem, and Schoenbrunn. In 1781, during the border troubles of the American Revolution, the Hurons moved them to the region of the Sandusky and Scioto, in north Ohio, either to prevent their giving information to the colonists or to protect them from the hostility of the frontiersmen.

The next spring, a party of approximately 140 were allowed to return to their abandoned villages to gather corn, where they were treacherously attacked by a party of border ruffians. Most were massacred, and their villages burned. The remaining Moravians moved to Canada in 1791, under the leadership of Zeisberger, and built the village of Fairfield on the Thames River. The village was burned by the Americans in the War of 1812, so the Indians rebuilt on the opposite side of the river, in Orford Township, Kent County, Ontario, Canada. The tribe numbered 275 in 1884, but had increased to 348 in 1906. There were, until recently, a few in Franklin County, Kansas.

MOXUS

Moxus (Abnaki; early eighteenth century), also known as *Agamagus*, was a chief whose relations with the English during the French and Indian Wars around 1700 fluctuated between war and peace. He directed the capture of Fort Charles at Pemaquid, Maine, from the English in 1689, and signed treaties with them in 1699 and 1702. He then besieged the English fort at Casco, Maine, in 1703 (Probably incited by French missionaries), and later signed more treaties with the English at Casco in 1713, and at Georgetown, Arowsike Island, in 1717.

NAMASKET

The Namasket, from *namaus* "fish", *aki* "land", *et* "at," was a tribe or band that formerly lived in a village of the same name near present Middleboro, Massachusetts. They were subordinate to the Wampanoag. The village was populous when first known, but the Indians rapidly decreased as white setlements advanced.

In 1794 there were still about 40 members of the tribe. One family, named Mitchell still lived near Middleboro in the early 1900s, and claimed descent from the famous Indian King Philip.

NARRAGANSET

The Narraganset were first mentioned by Giovanni da Verranzano in 1524. The name and tribal identity have persisted to the present with no alternate nomenclature, but with various spellings. The name may mean "people of the place crossing over." This Algonquian-speaking tribe, along with the Mohegan, Pequot, and Niantic long lived in the region. The Narraganset occupied the land surrounding Narrangansett Bay on the southern shore of Rhode Island and westward through the present town of Charleston, Rhode Island, off their southern coasts. The aboriginal culture of the Narraganset people, including their tributaries and near neighbors, was a combination of hunting, fishing, gathering and farming. Living close to the ocean and saltwater inlets, the Indians had readily available sources of fish and shellfish. Freshwater fish from the many ponds and rivers was also abundant.

Ocean fishing and shellfish gathering were activities of the spring, summer, and early autumn. At these times, families camped near the salt water. In early and midsummer, family groups settled further inland and cultivated garden plots of maize, beans, squash and tobacco. Wild plant foods were also gathered, such as berries, ferns and mushrooms. In late autumn and throughout the winter the family groups lived inland and hunted deer, bear and small animals.

Their housing was the wigwam; a bowl shaped structure of pole supports covered with bark siding and further covered with woven reed

193

mats. These were single nuclear family homes built in villages of at least 10 such houses of related families. There were at least 20 such villages between Providence and Westerly, Rhode Island. Clothing was made mostly of animal skins. Women wore a wraparound skirt topped by a sleeveless jacket with removable sleeves. Men wore a tunic of deerskin, loincloth and leggings. Both wore soft-soled moccasins and winter robes of woven strips of rabbit skin or bearskin. Garments were decorated with dyed porcupine quills embroidered in geometric designs. Also, wampum beads were used for decoration as well as for symbolism of states of friendship or war. There were well-established foot-trails, some of which have become modern roads.

On water the dugout canoe was used, and some were reputed to hold 60 people, able to transverse the Long Island Sound and go as far as present Martha's Vineyard and Nantuckett Islands. Their religion was largely shamanistic. The shaman or "medicine man" cured the sick by super-natural means. It also included seasonal ceremonies related to planting and harvest. An important divinity was Cautantowit, a creator of man-kind, and Chepi, who was involved with the spirits of the dead. There was also a belief in "spirits" in natural things. Strange and inexplicable things were given the term "manitoo" and thus, in a way, deified.

The raven was believed to have brought maize from the south. The earth was the mother of all things and the winds of the four directions shared in deification through their separate beneficences. The dead were buried with their heads toward the west or southwest. At first slow to accept Christianity, by the mid-eighteenth century the tribe had built a Protestant Church on their reservation and all of its ministers have been Narragansett.

Social life centered about the extended family. Most authorities con-tend that family relationship and inheritance was passed down through the female line for non-sachem families. Polygamy was practiced. Women performed most of the farm work and shellfish gathering, while men made dugout canoes, hunted, fished in the ocean, fought other tribes, and raised tobacco. Genealogies and recorded history reveal that the sa-chem position was inherited through the male line and that chief-based families were linked through marriage with such families of neighboring tribes. Concerning political organization, three early accounts mention dual sachems, with the two of them being related in the male line and about a generation apart, but not father and son.

These were the great sachems with tributary sachems of lower degree, who knew the bounds and landmarks of their territories and composed a council that advised the great sachems, but were not expected to join them in wars. The sachems had the responsibility of providing for orphans and dependent people. The strength of the Narragansetts was continuously being lost through sales of land to European colonists, some of whom were honest, some fraudulent. For the Narragansett tribe, the King Philip's War, (1675-1676) was a major disaster. The officially neutral Narragansetts sheltered neighboring Wampanoags as well as their own women, children and elderly in their territory.

This shelter was discovered by the colonial forces and destroyed by fire. The loss of life was speculated to be in the hundreds along with supplies of stored food. Narragansett power was broken and they were subjected to the will of the colonists. Some were taken into homes of Rhode Island colonists as indentured servants. Some, captured by other colonies, were sent to the West Indies to be sold as slaves. To save the remaining Indians from ongoing land loss through sales, some by the Indian sachems themselves, in 1709 the Rhode Island colonial legislature limited a reservation of 64 square miles for Indian occupancy only. However, sales continued.

By 1740 a school for Indian children had been built on it. In 1792 the new Rhode Island Assembly drew up a constitution for the Narragansetts. It specified regular elections of a president and 4 councilmen instead of following the old government of an hereditary sachem and his chosen advisors. In 1850 the tribe accepted a detailed constitution from the Assembly and agreed to keep a ledger and minutes of their monthly meetings. It reveals their means for providing for their elderly poor, their maintenance of the reservation schoolhouse, and their mediation of land inheritance and boundary problems within the reservation. In 1880 the tribal council voted to end the tribe as an organization, and to sell what was left of the reservation to the State of Rhode Island.

There are different opinions as to their reasons for doing so. As a result, they no longer existed as an entity in State politics. However, they never ceased to exist as a group through the institutions of their tribal organization with elected officers, regular meetings, their own church and Indian ministers, and their annual August Meeting or Powwow, on old reservation grounds. In the 1970's, the Narragansetts were encouraged to reclaim their reservation lands, and, in 1975, with the aid of non-Indian lawyers, filed a suit to reclaim some of the land that they had sold in 1880. They won their case in 1979 in an Act of Congress that returned over 1,800 acres to them. The land was to be managed by a nine-person council, five Indians chosen by the tribe, and four non-Indians. Several hundred acres were donated to the Narragansett by Irving and Arlene Crandall in 1991. In 1833, the population was about 250.

There could have been many more uncounted. In 1880, 324 were agreed upon to receive payment for a share in the sale of the reservation. In the 1970s, the tribal membership was around 300. A recent count shows membership of some 2,400 individuals.

NASHUA

The Nashua tribe formerly lived on the upper Nashua River, and are said by some to have been connected with the Massachusetts, but classed by Potter with the Pennacook. They had a village called Nashua near the present Leominister, but their principal village seems to have been Weshacum, a few miles farther south. The Nashua tract extended for several miles in every direction around Lancaster. At the outbreak of King Philip's War in 1675, they joined the hostile Indians and, numbering several-hundred, attempted to escape death in two groups to the east and west.

Both parties were pursued and a large number were killed or captured, the prisoners being afterward sold into slavery. A few who escaped eastward joined the Pennacook, while about 200 others crossed the Hudson to join the Mahican or the Munsee, causing the Nashua to cease existing as a separate tribe. A few remained near their old homes as late as 1701.

NAUMKEAG

The Naumkeag ("fishing place," from *namaas* "fish," *ki* "place," *–ag* "at") Tribe or band probably belonged to the Pennacook confederacy, which formerly occupied the site of Salem Massachusetts.

It appears, however, that the natives had abandoned the locality before the English reached it, as there is no record that the latter found any Indians on the spot. It has been noticed in regard to native burials in this locality that the bodies were usually placed in a sitting posture.

NAUSET

An Algonquian tribe formerly living on Cape Cod east of Bass River, The Nauset formed a part of, or were under control of, the Wampanoag. A writer noted: "The Indians in the county of Barnstable were a distinct people, but they were subject in some respects to the chief sachem of the

Wampanoags." They probably came in contact with the whites at an early date, as the Cape was frequently visited by navigators. From this tribe, Hunt, in 1614, carried off seven natives and sold them into slavery with 20 Indians of Patuxet.

Champlain had an encounter with the Nauset immediately before returning to Europe. They seem to have escaped the great pestilence that prevailed along the New England coast in 1617. Although disposed to attack the colonists at their first meeting, the two groups eventually became friends, and with few exceptions, remained faithful to their friendship through King Philip's War, in some instances even lending each other assistance.

Most of them had been Christianized before this war broke out. The estimated population in 1621 was 500, but this is probably below their real strength at that time. About 1710, by which time they were all organized into churches, they lost a great many by fever. In 1764 they had decreased to 106, living mainly at Potanumaquut, but in 1802, only four were said to remain. Their principal village, Nauset, was near the present Eastham. Although their location indicates that fish furnished their chief sustenance, the Nauset were evidently farmers, as supplies of corn and beans were obtained from them by the famishing Plymouth colonists in 1622.

TOM NEPANET

Tom Nepanet (Nipmuc, late seventeenth century), one of the Christian Indians unjustly imprisoned on Deer Island in Boston Harbor during King Philip's War, nevertheless risked his life to help the English recover prisoners taken by Nipmuc warriors allied with Philip. Beginning in April, 1676, he acted as liaison between the Massachusetts colonists and the Nipmuc chiefs, carrying letters which at length won freedom for the Rowlandson family and others.

In May 1676, he helped Captain Henchman successfully ambush a party of Nipmuc near Lancaster, Massachusetts.

NETAWATWEES

Netawatwees (Delaware, 1678 - October 31, 1776), also known as Newcomer, whose name means skilled advisor, was a Delaware chief of the Turtle subtribe, appearing in colonial records as Netawatwees, Netahutquemaled, Netodwehement, Natautwhalemund, etc. Probably born in the Delaware River Valley around 1678, Netawatwees in his youth was forced to move west with other members of the tribe due to white pressures. In July of 1758, he was living in a Delaware Indian settlement at the mouth of Beaver Creek, a tributary of the Ohio below Pittsburgh, where the records identify him as "ye great man of the Unamie nation." (The Unamie was a tribal division of the Delawares along with the Munsie and Unalachtigo).

Netawatwees moved to Ohio with other migrant Delawares during the French and Indian War and established a village at present Cuyahoga Falls. From there he moved to the Tuscarawas, a tributary of the Muskingum, where he became a chieftain at the Delaware town called Gekelmukpechink, "still water". This town, which became known as Newcomer's Town, was on the north bank of the Tuscarawas on the eastern outskirts of present Newcomerstown, Oxford Township, Tuscarawas County.

The Great Council met here until the Delaware population was consolidated at nearby Coshocton. In the fall of 1764, Colonel Henry Bouquet led a campaign against the Delawares, Shawnee, Mingoes, and Mahican in Ohio, who were considered hostile to the British. Because Netawatwees refused to discuss peace terms, Bouquet deposed him.

After peace was negotiated and Bouquet departed, Netawatwees resumed his chieftancy, his Delaware followers remaining loyal. Although Netawatwees was never converted to Christianity, the Moravian missionaries made a strong impression on him. Infirm in his old age, he was succeeded by White Eyes in 1776. His dying words implored the Delawares to give up teachings of the Moravian pastors. He was survived by his grandson, Captain John Killbuck, Junior.

NEUTRAL

The Neutral consisted of a group of tribes joined into a loose confederacy with a common policy towards their neighbors. Each tribe was composed of a number of largely autonomous villages who shared a common tribal history and were probably tied to each other through intermarriage. Their economy revolved around slash-and-burn farming, operated by women, of which the principal crop was corn. The men hunted, fished, and carried on warfare. Their language was a dialect of Iroquoian and their culture in almost all respects was similar to the other Iroquoian groups in the eastern Great Lakes area. The term Neutral was first used by the French explorer Samuel de Champlain when he heard about the group on his visit to the Petun country in 1616.

His reason for calling them that was their neutrality in the wars between the Huron-Petun alliance and the five New York Iroquois tribes.

The Huron name for the Neutral was Atiouandaronk, Attiwanfron, or Attiuindaron. The meaning of the name, according to Jerome Lalemant, was "people of a slightly different language." Their own collective, or confederacy name is not known. As among the Huron, it is probable that the tribal names were of greater importance than the confederacy name. The number of tribes belonging to the Neutral Confederacy is not known.

The known: Aondironnon (Ahondihronnon); the Onguiarahronon (Ongmarahronon, Niagagarega); and until 1638, the Wento (Ahouenro-chrhonon, Oeanohoronons, Oenroronon, Oneronon), and others. Judging from seventeenth century maps and tribal lists, the following may also have been Neutral tribes: Antouaronon, Kakouagogo (Rakouagega, Ohreokouaehronon), and perhaps the Atiraguenrek (Attiragenrega). The latter name is thought by some to be a variant of Attiouandaronk, the collective term. In the first half of the seventeenth century, the Neutral occupied a territory which arched around the west end of Lake Ontario from the present town of Milton, Ontario, through the Niagara Peninsula into New York State as far as Oak Orchard Creek.

No villages existed west of the Grand River in Ontario and south of Buffalo Creek in New York. Of the various Neutral tribes, the Aondi-rononnon occupied the northern frontier in Ontario; the Antouaronon were in the lower Grand River Valley; the Onguiarahronon were on the lands adjacent to the Niagara River; the Kakouagoga were at the site of the present city of Buffalo. The Wenro were in an area thirty miles east of the Niagara near Oak Orchard Swamp. The main concentration of Neutral villages appears to have been between the cities of Hamilton and Brantford, Ontario. This was the area occupied by the Atiraguenrek.

Language. No specimens of the Neutral language have survived. The Jesuits considered it to be similar to Huron, in other words, a dialect of Iroquoian. The linguistic similarities between the various Iroquoian speakers led the Jesuits to speculate that at one time the Huron, Neutral, and Iroquois had been one group. On their visit to the Neutral in 1640, Fathers Chaumonot and Brebeuf were able to adjust their Huron diction-ary and syntax to the Neutral dialect in only twenty-five days. The Wenro dialect may have been more similar to Seneca than to Huron.

Tribal culture. The area occupied by the Neutral is in the northern limits of the deciduous Carolinian forest zone in Ontario. As such, it has a milder climate and longer growing season than any other part of eastern Canada, a fact noted by all the seventeenth century visitors. Of particular importance were the extensive stretches of oak and chestnut forest throughout the area because they attracted large concentrations of deer.

Extensive areas of well-drained sandy soil, preferred by all the Iroquoian groups for their crops, were common, as were excellent fishing sites at the mouths of the many creeks flowing into Lakes Ontario and Erie.

In the opinion of seventeenth century visitors, the Neutral shared almost all aspects of their culture with their cultural relatives, the Huron, Petun, and other Iroquoian groups. Judging from the distribution of archaeological sites containing French trade material, the various Neutral tribes were composed of spatially separated village clusters much like the five Iroquois tribes, but unlike the Huron and Petun. Most of the villages were fortified with a palisade.

On the average, their villages seem to have been smaller than those of the Huron, although some were up to eight acres in size, housing perhaps 2,000 people. Similar to other Iroquoian groups, the Neutral formed nuclear families gathered together into closely co-operating matrilineal extended families, each of which occupied a longhouse. The length of the longhouses varied in size of the extended family, but could be well over 100 feet. In width, these homes were about 25 feet, reflecting limitations in the bent saplings and bark, bonded together, that were used as construction materials.

Similar to the Huron, it is likely that the various extended families were put into matrilineal groups according to known descent along the female line. It is also likely that the Neutral had a clan system similar to the other Iroquoian groups, which would have acted as a socio-political force giving internal cohesion to the confederacy. The main staple was corn, followed by beans and squash. Hunting and fishing were well developed, although hunting seems to have been more important than among the Huron. All the early writers mention the high densities of deer, elk, and beaver in the area. Other important animals were the moose, turkey, raccoon, and black squirrel, with the latter two being hunted for their pelts. Neutral farming technology was typical of mild latitude slash-and-burn horticulture.

As a consequence, soils became exhausted over time, sometimes contributing to village relocation. Tobacco was a major crop grown for domestic use as well as export to the Huron. Politically, the Neutral were organized into largely autonomous villages whose affairs were regulated by a village council composed of the male heads of the extended families and presided over by a chief elected from one of the prominent clan segments. The powers of the chiefs were informal.

Most acted as chairmen of the councils and spokesmen for the village. None had coercive powers. The most influential chiefs were those who had proven ability as leaders in war, were liberal with gifts, and were persuasive orators. Politics at the tribal and confederacy level is not clear.

Father Daillon reported the existence of a tribal or confederacy chief that had more power than his equivalent among the Huron. The function of such a chief would have been to call meetings of the tribal or confederacy councils that were made up of representatives from the various villages. Such meetings were to discuss common problems of trade and war. It is likely that the unusual powers described by Daillon for the Neutral chief were the reflection of personal qualities rather than powers that came with his office. Like their Iroquoian neighbors, the Neutral believed in a spirit world.

All animate and inanimate things had spirits that exercised a considerable influence on human affairs. Dream interpretation was important. This required the presence of a shaman, who was an influential member of the community. Similar to the Huron, the Neutral had a winter festival called *ononharoia*, or "the upsetting of the brain."

In describing this festival, Brebeuf and Chaumonot stated that its function was to drive out demons that possessed individuals. Judging from their description, two of the prime functions of *ononharoia* were to vent pent-up emotions and to redistribute wealth. During the festival, articles were seized from non- participants and not returned. The Neutral also practiced resurrection of the dead. This seems to have been an organized attempt to pass the virtues of a great man who had just died onto a deserving individual. After the ceremony, the individual so honored proceeded to act, and was treated like, the person whose spirit he had just acquired.

The Jesuits reported only four aspects of culture in which the Neutral differed from their neighbors. The first of these was their lack of dress. Although the women were covered from their waist to their knees, most of the men wore nothing. What clothes they had were highly decorated. The second way in which the Neutral differed was their fondness for tattooing and painting their entire bodies. Thirdly, the Jesuits reported somewhat different burial customs. The Neutral and Huron practiced ossuary burial, a large communal grave that was prepared during the feast-of-the-dead shortly before a village was moved. The difference between the groups concerns the disposal of the bodies before they were interred in the ossuary.

While the Hurons would place their deceased into temporary graves or on scaffolds outside the village, the Neutral would keep them in their

201

houses until the corpses were in an advanced state of decomposition. The remaining flesh would then be removed for mourners until the feast-of-the-dead. Fourthly, the Jesuits reported that although the torture of male prisoners was common among all groups, the Neutral also tortured and burned to death female prisoners. Finally, the Jesuits were under the impression that the physique of the Neutrals appeared to be "taller, stronger, and better proportioned," than the Huron. Daillon reported that on his visit he "met no humpback, one-eyed, or deformed persons."

Foreign Relations. At the time of European contact, the Neutral were at peace with their Iroquoian neighbors. The Huron-Petun and five Iroquois tribes, protagonists in an ancient war, considered the Neutral villages to be a sanctuary in which they were secure from attack. The reasons for their neutrality are not known. It is probable that it was in the interests of both warring groups to preserve friendly relations with the Neutral. The Neutral population was greater than the Huron and larger than the combined Iroquois tribes. Neither side could afford to wage war against a Neutral-Huron or Neutral-Iroquois alliance.

The Jesuits stated that because the main route traveled by the Huron and Seneca war parties lay through Neutral territory, it was in the interest of these tribes that they stay at peace with the Neutral. The Neutral on their part were engaged in a protracted conflict with the Assistaeronnon "fire people" or Mascouten, a group of semi-sedentary Algonquian tribes in the Michigan peninsula. In this conflict, they were aided by the Ottawa. For this reason, it was also in the interest of the Neutral to keep at peace with the Huron and five Iroquois tribes. The Neutral had strong trading ties with the Ottawa, Petun, and Huron. Algonquian products filtered south to the Neutral, while exotic skins, tobacco, and perhaps chert were traded in return. The extent of Neutral trade with their other Iroquoian neighbors is not known. It is probable that they traded with the Erie, Seneca, and Susquehannock.

History. The prehistoric origins of the Neutral have been traced to archaeological cultures in Southwestern Ontario. Their first contact with Europeans was with Champlain, who was visiting the Petun in 1616. Although the Neutral invited Champlain to visit them, the Petun and Ottawa dissuaded him, saying that the Neutral would kill him in revenge for a Neutral they had killed earlier. As knowledge of the Neutral grew, some Frenchmen began to contact them directly. Best known of these men were the interpreters and traders, Brule and Grenole. It was Brule who kindled the interest of the Recollet Order in sending a missionary to

the Neutral. As a result, Father Joseph de la Roche Daillon set out from
the Huron in October 1626 to spend part of the winter with the Neutral.
The object of his trip was not only to spread the Gospel, but also to conclude a trade agreement with the Neutral. The Neutral showed some
interest in his proposals, but were apparently unskilled in the use of canoes, and unfamiliar with the route to the Saint Lawrence River.

When the Huron heard of Daillon's proposals, they did everything to
turn the Neutral against the priest. Over the years, the Huron had assumed a position as middlemen in a lucrative trade between the French
and a number of inland tribes, including the Neutral. This trade would
have evaporated if the Neutral had developed direct trade contacts with
the French.

As a result of Huron innuendoes, Daillon was driven from the Neutral
villages and considered hisself lucky to escape with his life. Little was
known about the Neutral until 1638, when some 600 desperately ill and
starving refugee Wenro tribal members arrived at the village of Ossossane in Huronia. Earlier they had sent an embassy to the Huron requesting that they be permitted to settle there.

The original cause for the Wenro migration is not known. For some
reason they had incurred the displeasure of the other Neutral tribes, who
terminated their alliance with them. This placed the Wenro open to attack from their eastern neighbors, the Seneca. Unable to mount an adequate defense, and suffering from epidemic diseases, the Wenro decided
to leave their territory and join the Huron. A small number of Wenro
settled among the Neutral.

A possible reason for Seneca animosity towards the Wenro may have
been the latter's attempts to trade directly with the Dutch and English, a
prerogative that the Seneca and their Iroquois allies probably tried to
keep for themselves. Evidence of Wenro occupation has been determined archaeologically in Huronia at the site of Ossossane and neighboring villages. In 1639 the Neutral were hit by a severe famine.

Some fled to the Petun, while others sold their children for corn. During that year and the previous two, smallpox and other contagious diseases had gripped the Neutral as well as the Petun and Huron.

In November 1640, the Jesuits opened their mission for the Neutral
under Fathers Brebeuf and Chaumonot. The Neutral had somewhat of a
preconceived notion of fear concerning the priests because some Huron
had claimed the latter were sorcerers who were causing the epidemics.
The Jesuits, in turn, tried to allay these fears by pretending to be traders.
Once the Jesuits had been tentatively accepted, they sought permission to

spend the winter in the country. The confederacy council finally rendered the decision to let them remain until their chief, Souharissen, had returned from war. Only he, they claimed, could make the final decision.

The Jesuits then dropped their pretense as traders and began missionary activities. When the Huron saw that the Jesuits were permitted to remain among the Neutral, their fear of a French-Neutral trade alliance was heightened. Consequently, they began an active campaign to either have the Jesuits thrown out of the country, or have them killed. Their principal accusation was that the Jesuits wanted to kill as many Neutral as possible through their sorcery and diseases in order to gain their souls. The Huron also accused the Jesuits, principally Brebeuf, of seeking an alliance with the Seneca against the Neutral.

The result of these accusations was that the Neutral council asked the Jesuits to leave. Brebeuf and Chaumonot, however, refused and found shelter among some individuals who were better disposed toward them. Finally, in March 1642, when it seemed as if the two priests were in serious danger, the decision was made by the Order to remove them from the Neutral, thus ending the Neutral mission and direct French contact. During the next few years, the Jesuits attempted to carry on the mission by sending Huron converts to the Neutral. The success of these men appears to have been limited.

In spite of the fact that 100 Neutral came to Huronia in 1643 requesting the Jesuits to return, the mission was not reopened. During the 1640s, the Iroquois tribes were carrying their war more successfully into Huronia. In 1647, they succeeded in dispersing the Arendaronon, a Huron tribe on the eastern frontier of Huronia. That same year, the victorious Seneca turned on the Neutral and managed to destroy the main village of the Aondironnon territory.

Since the Aondironnon had not prevented the deaths, they had compromised their neutrality. To the surprise of the Huron and the Jesuits, the Neutral Confederacy made no effort to avenge the destruction of the Aondironnon. Instead, the Neutral tried to have their captives among the Seneca restored peacefully. The Seneca attack may have been the first phase in a deliberate plan to disperse the Neutral in order to gain access to their beaver hunting grounds.

As Seneca power declined, the Neutral probably felt that they were in a poor position to engage the Iroquois tribes militarily. In 1649, the Iroquois, largely led by the Seneca and Onondaga, managed to destroy and disperse the Huron. By the spring of 1650, the Petun were also forced to abandon their country. Many Huron and Petun fled to the Neutral, who were now seeking arms and other help from the French.

The Iroquois, however, moved swiftly against the Neutral, and in the autumn of 1650, they destroyed one of the principal Neutral villages with a force of 1,500 men. The Neutral, led by a Huron contingent, retaliated and killed 200 Iroquois. The news of this defeat caused the Seneca to move the population of their main village temporarily to the Cayuga. At about this time the Neutral concluded an alliance with the Susquehannock, with whom they had had a long-standing trading alliance. The Iroquois were quick to avenge their losses. In the early winter of 1651, they returned with an army of 600 to 1200 men and destroyed the main Neutral village, Teotondiation.

As a result of this loss the Neutral, along with the Petun and Huron refugees, began to disperse. Some were captured, and others joined the Seneca, where they were still reported as maintaining an identity as late as 1673. Others may have fled to the Erie and the Susquehannock.

In July 1653, a group of 800 Neutral were reported wintering in eastern Michigan on the peninsula between Saginaw Bay and Lower Lake Huron. Their aim was to join with the refugee Petun camped on the south shore of the Straits of Mackinac, as well as with some Algonquian bands from the Sault Saint Marie area. It is possible that this group merged with the Petun to become the historic Wyandotte.

Population. Estimates of the total Neutral population have varied greatly. Champlain, who had never come in contact with the Neutral, considered them to be a powerful group with 40 villages, capable of fielding 4,000 warriors, while others reported 5,000 to 6,000 warriors. Father Daillon, after his 1626 visit to the Neutral, wrote that they had 28 principal villages. Probably the most accurate estimate of population was made by Fathers Brebeuf and Chaumonot after their five months sojourn among the Neutral. It was their opinion that there were about 40 villages containing 12,000 people and 4,000 warriors. The Fathers added that the original population had been greatly reduced by three years of famine, epidemics, and war.

The ten villages in which the Fathers stayed the longest had 500 fires and 3,000 people. The figures given by Brebeuf and Chaumonot represent a post epidemic population, which, of course, did not include the Wenro, most of which had left the area by 1638. Death rates among the neighboring Huron during the same period were estimated at 60 percent. A similar death rate among the Neutral would place their pre-epidemic population in the neighborhood of 30,000 people, excluding the Wenro.

A second approach to the problem is the relationship between 500 fires and 300 people. Since there were two nuclear families to a fire in an Iroquoian longhouse, these figures imply a post- epidemic family size of three people. In view of what is known about Iroquoian family structure, this figure should be doubled, implying a loss of life of at least 50 percent as a result of the epidemics.

A final pre-epidemic estimate of 33,000, including the Wenro, does not seem unreasonable. This estimate lends support to Father Le Jeune's statement, written in 1634, that the Neutral were "much more populous than the Huron," and that their numbers were roughly around 30,000; later estimates reduced the number to 18,000 or 21,000. Since the Neutral ceased to exist as a tribal entity in 1651, post-dispersal population estimates are not available.

Conclusions. From the little that is known about the Neutral, it appears that in the early part of the seventeenth century they were the largest of the native confederacies in the Great Lakes area. For some time, they managed to remain at peace with the other warring Iroquoian groups, but fought extensive campaigns against the Algonquian Mascouten in the Michigan area.

As competition for trading rights and beaver hunting areas increased during the 1630s and 1640s, the Neutral Confederacy began to disintegrate. In 1638, the Wenro were abandoned by the Neutral and defeated by the Seneca, followed by the Aondironnon in 1647. In spite of these setbacks, and with either an inability or unwillingness to perceive the consequences of their policy, the Neutral still tried to remain outside the Huron-Iroquois conflict.

By 1649, when the Huron were destroyed, the balance of power shifted dramatically in favor of the Iroquois. Too late, the Neutral entered the war joined by Petun and Huron refugees. In two years, the Neutral were defeated and dispersed to such an extent that there is no further mention of them after 1653. Twenty years after their defeat, the old Neutral territory was known as a beaver hunting ground of the Iroquois.

Like many northeastern native groups, the Neutral got caught in events not of their making and rivalries they thought had nothing to do with them. Like the Huron, the Neutral failed to appreciate the changing motives and methods of Iroquois warfare until it was too late.

NIANTIC

The Niantic were an Algonquian tribe formerly living on the coast of Connecticut, from Niantic Bay to the Connecticut River. According to

De Forest, they once formed one tribe with the Niantic of Rhode Island, which was cut in two by the Pequot invasion. Their main village, also called Niantic, was near the present town of that name. Another important village was Wekapaug, on the great pond near present Charlestown. They were subject to the Pequot, and had no political connection with the eastern Niantic. They were nearly destroyed in the war of 1637, with its survivors placed under Mohegan rule.

They became so closely connected with the Narragansett, they formed practically one tribe with them. By refusing to join in King Phillip's war in 1675, they preserved their territory and tribal organization. At the close of the war, the Narragansett, who had submitted to the English, were placed with the Niantic under Ninigret, and the whole body thereafter took the name of Narragansett.

They numbered about 100 in 1638, and about 85 in 1761. Many traceable Niantic members joined the Brotherton Indians in New York about 1788, with none now existing under their own name. According to Kendall, they had a village near Danbury, Connecticut in 1809, but were probably a remnant of the western Connecticut tribes, not Niantic. According to Speck, many mixed-Niantic-Mohegan lived into the early 1900s, descendants of a pure Niantic woman from the mouth of the Niantic River. Their voices were reportedly more high-pitched than their neighbors.

Today's Niantics, or their mixed-blood descendants, may live on the Eastern and Western Pequot Reservations, and the Schaghticoke Reservation, and in the Mohegan Community in Connecticut, and the Narraganset Community in Rhode Island.

DANIEL NINHAM

Daniel Ninham (Wappinger, 1710 - August 1778), was a chief of the Mahican in Westenhuck, New York who supported the colonial settlers in both the French and Indian War, and the American Revolution, and who pressed Wappinger territorial claims all the way to England. He became principal chief of his tribe in 1740.

During the hostilities of 1740-48 Nimham supported the British forces against the French. He enlisted his warriors under Sir William Johnson in 1755 to fight for the colonial settlers during the French and Indian War, and participated in the construction of Fort William Henry and the Battle of Lake George in September, 1755. About 1762 Nimham and a group of Connecticut Mahican chiefs travelled to England to press the recovery of certain tribal lands from the colonies. Having been well received, they returned to North America and entered into court proceedings to regain their territory. Unfortunately the American Revolution began shortly, and the court claims were never settled.

Once more Nimham joined the colonial settlers, and in August 1778 was killed in battle at Kingsbridge, New York. The state of New York regarded Nimham as a loyal and steadfast citizen, and entered his name in the memorial lists of those who served in the Revolution.

NINIGRET

Ninigret (Niantic, 1600 - 1678), also known as Nenekunat, Ninicraft, Janemo and Ayanemo, was a sachem of the Narraganset Tribe. He lived in Wequapaug, Rhode Island, and found himself continually having to walk a tight wire of diplomacy, because of the always-tenuous relationship between whites and Indians. He tried to remain neutral during the Pequot-Narragansett War in 1632, but the Boston authorities were offended by his independent stance and it caused a rift in their relations. In 1637, Uncas felt that he was siding with the Pequot, claiming that he was harboring some of their warriors and Ninigret had to appear before the colonial court to defend himself against these charges.

He was also involved in a treaty situation where he was forced to abide by, as well as to pay a large annual amount of "good white wampum." Then in May of 1645, he was brought into court again on another charge, plus his failure to pay the sum of wampum from the first agreement. He was one of a whole group of Narragansett chiefs that was fined 2,000 fathoms of the wampum, which amounted to a string of handmade shell beads almost two and a half miles in length.

It was an amount that was beyond the means of the tribe to pay and was a constant source of contention between them and the whites. Until this amount was settled, the Natives were not allowed to leave Boston. When Ninigret finally left Boston for a short time in 1652, he visited the city of Manhattan, spending the winter with the Dutch. Uncas once again leveled accusations at him, telling the colonists that he was conspiring against the English, and during the next year, he was summoned to Boston.

None of the charges could be confirmed, and the situation deepened Ninigret's anger at the whites. He was also involved in intertribal problems, attacking the Long Islands Indians, which resulted in the death of his nephew. He intended to declare all out war, but the English got wind of it and gathered some 300 men led by Major Willard. Ninigret tried hard, abandoning his village, and hiding in a nearby swamp, but eventually he was again forced to swallow his pride and agree to a peace treaty in which it was required of him to pay more wampum. Both the Niantic and Narragansett Tribes continued to do battle with the Long Island Indians and Uncas continued to accuse Ninigret and others of various infractions, when it would suit his purpose.

After a colonist's home was set on fire by an unknown tribal member, Ninigret, along with other chiefs were ordered to deliver the perpetrators to Boston for punishment, otherwise they would have to pay more wampum fines. In addition, Ninigret was presented with a bill for his outstanding fines from before, and was issued a threat that if it were not paid, his people would be sold into slavery in the Barbados Islands. It is doubtful that the British were ever paid their wampum, as authorities later accepted a mortgage on Niantic land. After a time, Ninigret backed off from the fray and began to live out the rest of his years quietly, avoiding too much involvement in King Philip's War of 1675-1676. He died at his Wequapaug home. He had his admirers, including Roger Williams, who described him as "proud and fierce".

NIPMUC

The Nipmuc (from *nipamaug* "freshwater fishing place") are one of the inland tribes of central Massachusetts that originally lived chiefly in the south part of Worcester County, extending into Connecticut and Rhode Island. Their chief seats were on the headwaters of the Blackstone and Quinebaug rivers, and around the ponds of Brookfield. Hassanamesit seems to have been their principal village in 1674, but their villages had no apparent political connection, and the different parts of their territory were subject to their more powerful neighbors, the Massachusetts, Wampanoag, Narragansett, and Mohegan, and even the Mohawk.

The Nashua, dwelling farther north, were sometimes classed with the Nipmuc, but were rather a distinct body. The New England missionaries had seven villages of Christian Indians among them in 1674; but at the outbreak of King Philip's War in the next year, almost all of them joined the hostile tribes.

At its close, they fled to Canada or westward to the Mahican and other tribes on the Hudson. During the early twentieth century, social activities and public education were begun, and the Council of New England Indians was founded, with a Nipmuc chapter formed later. In the 1970s, the Massachusetts Commission on Indian Affairs was created, and this reaffirmed stewardship by the state. The tribe petitioned for federal acknowledgment in the 1980s. Although the Nipmuc has no land, two parcels are held privately for their use, the Chaubunagungamaug Reservation in Thompson, Connecticut, and the Hassanamesit in Webster, Massachusetts.

The group today has organized the Nipmuc Tribal Acknowledgment Project in Worcester, which is funded by grants and private support. Economic and social development programs have been planned, and the project will also aid in publishing information on Nipmuc history and culture. A government was created in 1991, and its organization is being formed and initiated.

Distinct social groups continue to be maintained, and a number of powwows, festivals, and ceremonial events are held. Crafts, language, and traditional philosophy are maintained through the Algonquian School in Providence, Rhode Island.

NORWOOTUC

The Norwootuc Indians were and Algonquian tribe or band whose possesions extended from the "great falls" at South Hadley to Mount Sugar Loaf, in the Connecticut Valley, Massachusetts. They were attacked by the Mohegan about 1656, and were at war with the Montauk and Narraganset.

They were probably part of the Indians that took part in King Philip's War in 1675, and afterward fled the country, as "Norwootuck plantations" were mentioned in 1678 as if they were a new settlement. The Norwootuc were probably the "Nowonthwog or the Eastward Indians," that in 1700 combined with the Mohawks against English colonists.

JOSEPH ONASAKENRAT

Joseph Onasakenrat (Mohawk, September 4, 1845 - February 8, 1881), also known as White Feather, was a chief noted for translations of religious works into his native language. Born on his father's farm, near Oka, Canada. At fourteen years of age, he was sent to Montreal College to be educated for the priesthood, remainin about four years. He was afterward converted to Protestantism and became an evangelical preacher.

On June 15, 1877, the Catholic Church of Oka was burned, and Chief Joseph was tried for the offense, but was not convicted. Among his translations into the Mohawk dialect are the Gospels (1880) and a volume of hymns. He died suddenly, February 8, 1881, at Caughnawaga. At the time of his death, he was engaged in translating the remainder of the Bible, having reached the Epistles to the Hebrews.

ONEIDA

Oneida is an Anglicized compressed form of the common Iroquois term *tiionen'iote,* "there it is - rock has - set up (continuative)," i.e. "a rock that something set up and is still standing", referring to a large boulder near the site of one of their ancient villages. A tribe of the Five Nations Iroquois Confederacy, the Oneida formerly occupied the country south of Oneida Lake, Oneida County, New York, and including the upper waters of the Susquehanna. According to authentic tradition, the Oneida was the second tribe to accept the proposition of Dekanawida and Hiawatha to form a defensive and offensive league of all the tribes of men for the promotion of mutual welfare and security. In the federal council and in other federal assemblies, they had the right to representation by nine federal chieftains of the highest rank.

Like the Mohawk, the Oneida had only three clans: The Turtle, the Wolf, and the Bear, each clan being represented by three of the nine federal representatives of this tribe. Insofar as eldership, a member of a clan phratry can give precedence in roll-call and the right to discuss first in order all matters coming before its side of the council fire. The Oneida were the dominant tribe within the tribal phratry, called the Four (originally two) Brothers and "Offspring," to which they belonged. In tribal assemblies, the Turtle and the Wolf constituted a clan phratry, and the Bear another. The Oneida were usually conservative in dealing with others.

In 1635 they, with the Onondaga, Cayuga, and Mohawk, sought to become parties to the peace concluded in the preceding year between the Seneca and the Hurons. At this period they were called sedentary and quite populous, but only from Indian reports.

The *Jesuit Relation* for 1646 said that with the exception of the Mohawk, there was no treaty, properly speaking, then in existence between the Iroquois tribes inclusive of the Oneida and the French. From the same book, it was learned that "Onnicoute" (*Oneniote*), the principal Oneida village of that time, having lost the greater portion of its men in a war with the "upper Algonquin," was compelled to request the Mohawk to lend aid in repeopling the village by granting thereto a colony of men, and that it was for this reason that the Mohawk ceremonially and publicly call the Oneida their daughters or sons.

This story was probably due to a misconception of the fictitious political kinships and relationships established between the several tribes at the time of the institution and organization of the League. The Cayuga and the Tuscarora were likewise called "Offspring," but not for the same rea-

211

son. The *Jesuit Relation* for 1648) first definitely located the Oneida. From the Relation for 1641, it is gathered that the Jesuit fathers had learned that the Oneida had a peculiar form of government in which the rulership alternated between the two sexes.

This statement was likewise apparently due to a misconception of the fact that among Iroquois tribes, the titles to the chieftanships belonged to the women of certain clans in the tribe and not to the men, although men were chosen by the women to exercise the rights and privileges and to perform the duties pertaining to these chieftanships.

There were, and still are, a number of women filling federal chieftanships bearing the name of the highest class. These women chieftains had approximately the same rights, privileges, and immunities as the men chiefs, but exercised them fully only in emergencies. They also maintained the institutions of society and government among women. The *Jesuit Relation* for 1667 declared that the Oneida were then the least tractable of the Iroquois tribes. It was at this period that Father Bruyas was stationed at the mission of Saint Francois Xavier among the Oneida. This same source relates that the Mohegan and the Conestoga menaced the Oneida. While on this mission, Father Bruyas suffered malnutrition a part of the year and was compelled to live on dried frogs.

By the end of 1669, he had baptized 30 people. In 1660, the Oneida with the Mohawk were the least populous of the Iroquois tribes. *The Jesuit Relation* for 1669-70 speaks of the Oneida being present at a "feast of the dead" held at the Mohawk village of Caughnawaga, showing that in a modified form at least, the decennial ceremony of the so-called "Dead Feast" was practiced among the Iroquois when first known.

On January 30, 1671, the Oneida prolonged the torture of a captive Conestoga woman through two days and two nights. Some records say that a town that was defended by four lines of palisades closely fastened together, and attacked by Champlain with his Huron and Algonquian allies in 1615 was an Oneida village, Other authorities place it elsewhere, on Onondaga territory.

In fact, the wars of the Oneida were those of the League, although like the other tribes, they seem to have put forth most energy against their greatest enemies, the Catawba and Muskhogean tribes, as well as the Susquehanna River Indians, and the Conestoga. After the conquest of the tribes on the Susquehanna and its tributaries, and those on the Potomac, chiefly by the warriors of the Oneida, the Cayuga, and the Seneca, and those tribes which had submitted to Iroquois rule, a question arose as to the propriety of the Mohawk receiving bounty while not having aided in the struggle.

For a time the Mohawk received no enrichment from this source, until the Iroquois tribes became divided and the Mohawk sold the lands in the Wyoming Valley region of Pennsylvania to the Susquehanna Land Company of Connecticut. In 1728, the great federal council of the league at Onondaga sent Shikellamy, an Oneida chief, as a superintendent, to the forks of the Susquehanna to watching over the affairs and the interests of the Six Nations of Iroquois in Pennsylvania. At first, Shikellamy supervised only the Shawnee and the Delawares, who thereafter had to consult him in all matters concerning the proprietary government. He performed his duty so well that in 1745, Shikellamy was made full superintendent over all the dependent tribes on the Susquehanna, with his residence at Shamokin. He showed great astuteness, seeking at all times to promote the interests of his people.

Such was the influence that the Oneida exercised on the Susquehanna. In 1687 the Oneida were included in the warrant of the King of Great Britain to Governor Dongan of New York authorizing him to protect the Five Nations as subjects of Great Britain.

In 1696, Count Frontenac burned the Oneida castle, destroyed all their corn, and made prisoners of 30 men, women, and children. In 1645-46, the Oneida were at war with the Nipissing, and one band of 17 warriors from "Ononiiote" defeated an Algonquin party under Teswshat, their one-eyed chief, killing his son and taking two women prisoners. The Iroquois party later was defeated by 30 Hurons, and the two women were recaptured.

In the *Jesuit Relation for 1666-68*, Father Bruyas wrote that the Oneida were reputed to be the most cruel of all the Iroquois tribes, that they always made war on the Algonquin and the Hurons, and that two-thirds of their villages were composed of the people of these two tribes who had become Iroquois in temper and inclination. This missionary added that the nature of the Oneida was then altogether barbarous, cruel, sly, cunning, and prone to bloodshed and carnage. In 1655, a party of 60 Oneida warriors was sent against the Amikwa, or Beaver Indians.

This war was still in progress in 1661, for in that year, two bands, one of 24 and the other of 30 warriors, were encountered on their way to fight the Amikwa. Chauchetiere, in a letter in *Jesuit Relations, Thwaites ed., 1900* (LXI, 185), said "war is blazing in the country of the Outaouaks," and that the Iroquois, especially the Oneida, continued their hatred of the

Outagami (Foxes) and the Illinois, and so had slain and captured many Illinois.

In 1681, they killed or captured about 1,000 of these unfortunate people. In 1711, about half of the Tuscarora tribe then dwelling in North Carolina, seems to have conspired with several alien neighboring tribes and bands to destroy the Carolina settlers.

The colonists, however, recollecting the ancient feud between the Southern and the Northern Indians, allied themselves with the Catawba and some Muskhogean tribes. The Tuscarora, sustaining several severe defeats, were finally driven from their homes and hunting grounds. This act of the Southern Indians made the hatred of the Iroquois against the Catawba more bitter and merciless. The Oneida were at times friendly to the French and to the Jesuit missionaries, while the other Iroquois were their determined enemies.

A great part of the Oneida and the Tuscarora, through the influence of Reverend Samuel Kirkland, remained neutral in the American Revolution, while the majority of the confederation of the Iroquois were divided and did not act as a unit in this manner.

Early in that struggle, the hostile Iroquois tribes attacked the Oneida and burned one of their villages, forcing them to take refuge near the Americans in the vicinity of Schenectady, where they remained until the close of the war. Shortly after, the main body of the tribe returned to their former homes. Later, many imigrated to Canada and settled on Grand River and Thames River, Ontario. Another small band, called Oriskas, formed a new settlement at Ganowarohare, a few miles from the main body in Oneida County, New York.

At different earlier periods, the Oneida adopted and gave lands to the Tuscarora, the Stockbridges, and the Brothertons. The Tuscarora moved afterward to land granted by the Seneca in western New York. In 1846, having sold most of their lands in New York, the greater part of the Oneida, together with their last two adopted tribes, moved to a tract on Green Bay, Wisconsin.

Among those living in New York when moved were two parties known respectively as the First Christian and the Second Christian or Orchard party. The Oneida entered into treaties with the United States at Fort Stanwix, New York on October 22, 1784; at Fort Harmar on January 9, 1789; at Canandaigua, New York on November 11, 1794; Oneida, New York on December 2, 1794; at Buffalo Creek, New York on January 15, 1838; and at Washington, D.C. on February 3, 1838.

They also held no fewer than 30 treaties with the State of New York between the years 1788 and 1842. Oneida towns, so far as known, were: Awegen, Brothertown, Cahunghage, Canowdowsa, Cowassalon, Chittenango, Ganadoga, Hostayuntwa, Oneida, Opolopong, Oriska, Ossewingo, Ostogeron, Schoherage, Sevege, Solocka, Stockbridge, Tegasoke, Teseroken, Teiosweken, and Tkanetota. In 1792, about 630 Oneida were left in New York. About this time, they began selling their lands and looking for homes farther west, free from encroachment from whites. Most other Oneida, who were loyal to the British, had moved to Canada.

The Oneida purchased land in the early 1800s from the Memominees in Wisconsin. Most of this land was later lost through legal battles, treaties, and fraud. In more recent times, about 2,000 tribally owned acres remained, along with nearly 500 acres of allotted lands. About 3,000 Oneida were living in the Wisconsin area, and another 2,000 were living either in New York or along the Thames River in Ontario, Canada.

Today, there are three separate Oneida communities, each with its own political system. They include the Wisconsin, the Ontario, and the New York Oneidas. The Wisconsin community is located in the Green Bay area. Many members of the Wisconsin tribe belong to the Episcopal and Methodist churches. Some also practice the Longhouse Religion of Handsome Lake.

Few members still speak the native language. However, the tribal school holds language classes. Arts and crafts have continued, including beadwork, silverwork, and carving. The Tribe holds an annual powwow. In a recent count, the community had 11,000 tribal members. The New York tribe lives near Oneida, New York.

A traditional system functions, although there has been much conflict between factions within the tribe. There were recently 700 tribal members, and many Christian denominations have followers among them. Many individuals also practice the Longhouse Religion. The Ontario Oneidas are ruled by an elective system consisting of 12 members and one chief. Conflicts have arisen between those who practice traditional religious beliefs and those who belong to other religions.

About 3,000 tribal members were counted recently in Ontario, Canada. Through the twentieth century, each of the tribes retained its identity. The two tribes located in the United States have facilities for gambling. All three tribes have filed a land claim against New York State asking for the return of, or payment for, land taken from them in the eighteenth and nineteenth centuries. Although they have won twice in the United States

Supreme Court, resolution of the case has been ongoing for more than twenty years. (See FIVE NATIONS IROQUOIS, and IROQUOIS CONFEDERACY)

ONONDAGA

An important tribe of the Five Nations Iroquois Confederation, The Onondaga formerly lived on the mountain, lake, and creek bearing their name, in the present Onondaga County, New York, and extending northward to Lake Ontario and southward perhaps to the Susquehanna River. In Iroquois councils they are known as *Hodisennageta*, "they (are) the name bearers." their principal village, also the capital of the confederation, was called Onondaga, later Onondaga Castle; it was situated from before 1654 to 1681 on Indian hill, in the present town of Pompey.

In 1677, it contained 140 cabins. It was removed to Butternut Creek, where the fort was burned in 1696. In 1720 it was again removed to Onondaga Creek, and their later reserve was in that valley, a few miles south of the lake. The Onondaga of Grand River Reservation, Canada, have 9 clans, namely: Wolf, Tortoise, Bear, Deer, Eel, Beaver, Ball, Plover, and Pigeonhawk.

The Wolf, Bear, Plover, Ball, and Pigeonhawk clans have each only one federal chiefship; the Beaver, Tortoise, and Eel clans have each two federal chiefships, while the Deer clan has three. The reason for this marked difference in the quotas of chiefships for the several clans is not definitely known, but it may be due to the adoption of groups of persons who already possessed chieftanship titles.

In federal ceremonial and social assemblies, the Onondaga by right of membership therein, take their places with the tribal phratry of the "Three Brothers," of which the Mohawk and the Seneca are the other two members. In federal councils, those in which sit the federal representatives of all the five (latterly six) Iroquois tribes, the Onondaga tribe itself constitutes a tribal clan. The Mohawk and the Seneca together form a second; and the Oneida and the Cayuga originally, and later the Tuscarora, form a third tribal clan.

The federal council is organized on the basis of these three tribal clans. The functions of the Onondaga phratry are in many respects similar to those of a judge holding court with a jury. The question before the council is discussed respectively by the Mohawk and Seneca tribes on the one side, and then by the Oneida, the Cayuga, and, later, the Tuscarora tribes on the other, within their own phratries.

When these two clans have independently reached the same or a differing opinion, it is then submitted to the Onondaga phratry for confirmation or rejection.

Confirmation of a common opinion or of one of the two differing opinions makes it the decree of the council. In refusing to confirm an opinion, the Onondaga must show that it is in conflict with established custom or with public policy; when two differing opinions are rejected, the Onondaga may suggest to the two clans a course by which they may be able to reach a common opinion; but the Onondaga may confirm one of two differing opinions submitted to it. Each chieftain has the right to discuss and argue the question before the council either for or against its adoption by the council, in a speech or speeches addressed to the entire body of councilors and to the public.

Champlain related that in 1622, the Montagnais, the Etchemin, and the Hurons had for a long time sought peace between themselves and the Iroquois, but that up to that time there was always some serious obstacle to the consummation of an agreement on account of the fixed distrust which each side had for the other. Many times they asked Champlain himself to help make a firm and durable peace.

They informed him that they understood by making a treaty that the interview of the ambassadors must be amicable, the one side accepting the words of faith of the other not to harm or prevent them from hunting throughout the country, and they on their side agreeing to act in like manner toward their enemies, in this case the Iroquois, and that they had no other agreements or compacts precedent to the making of a firm peace.

They importuned Champlain many times to give them his advice in this matter, which they promised faithfully to follow. They assured him that they were then exhausted and weary of the wars which they had waged against each other for more than fifty years, and that, on account of their burning desire for revenge for the murder of their kin and friends, their ancestors had never before thought of peace. In this last statement is probably found approximately the epoch of that historic feud mentioned in the *Jesuit Relation* for 1660 and by Nicholas Perrot, which made the Iroquois tribes, on the one hand, and the Algonquin on the Ottawa and Saint Lawrence Rivers, on the other, inveterate enemies, although this may have been but a renewal and widening of a still earlier quarrel.

In 1535, Cartier learned from the Iroquoian tribes on the Saint Lawrence River that they were continually tormented by enemies to the southward, called Toudamani (probably identical with Tsonnontouan, or

Seneca, a name then meaning 'Upper Iroquois'), who continually waged war on them. In September 1655, the Onondaga sent a delegation of 18 persons to Quebec to confer with Governor de Lauson and with the Algonkin and Hurons. The Onondaga spokesman used 24 wampum belts in his address; the first 8 were presents to the Hurons and the Algonquin, whose leading chiefs were there.

Each present had their name. The Onondaga professed to speak for the "four upper Iroquois Nations," namely, the Seneca, Cayuga, Oneida, and Onondaga, thus leaving only the Mohawk, the "lower Iroquois," from this peace conference, but the Onondaga speaker promised to persuade the Mohawk to change their minds and to make peace. The Onondaga asked for priests to live among them and for French soldiers to aid them in their war against the Erie. In May 1657, 10 years after the dispersion of the Hurons from their motherland, the Onondaga sought, by the giving of numerous presents and by covert threats of war, to persuade the Hurons who had fled to the vicinity of Quebec, to return to their country and to form with them a single people.

The Mohawk and the Seneca also were engaged in this business. Finally, the Hurons were forced to submit to the persistent demands of the Iroquois tribes. In 1686, the Onondaga were at war against the Cherermons. They were divided into two bands, one of 50 and another of 250, 50 of the latter being from other tribes. But in 1688, the Onondaga were considerably under French influence and were regarded as chief among the Iroquois tribes. In 1682, at Albany, the Onondaga, with the Mohawk, the Oneida, the Cayuga, and the Seneca, entered into a treaty of peace with the commissioners from the colony of Maryland, who contracted not only for the white settlers, but also for the Piscataway Indians.

With the exception of a part of the Seneca, the Onondaga were the last of the five tribes originally forming the League of the Iroquois to accept fully the principles of the universal peace proposed by Dekanawida and Hiawatha. Early in 1647, a band of Onondaga approaching the Huron country was defeated by a troop of Huron warriors, the Onondaga chief being killed and a number were taken prisoners. Among the latter was Annenraes, a man of character and authority among the Onondaga. In the following spring, he learned that some of the Hurons who had been bitterly disappointed because his life had been spared intended to kill him.

To some of his Huron friends, he related what he had heard, and that he intended to escape. His resolution, and the reason for making it, was reported to the leading Huron chiefs of the council, and they concluded to aid him, trusting that he would render service in return. Giving presents and provisions, they sent him off secretly at night.

Crossing Lake Ontario, he unexpectedly encountered 300 Onondaga making canoes to cross the lake for the purpose of avenging his death (believing he had been killed by the Hurons), and awaiting the arrival of 800 Seneca and Cayuga reinforcements. His countrymen regarded Annenraes as one risen from the dead. He persuaded the 300 Onondaga to give up all thought of war, whereupon the band, without waiting for the expected reinforcements, returned to Onondaga.

A tribal council resolved to send an embassy with presents to the Hurons to negotiate peace. The chief of this embassy was by birth a Huron named Soiones, so naturalized in the country of his adoption that it was said of him that "no Iroquois had done more massacres in these countries, nor blows more wicked than he." He was accompanied by three other Hurons, which had not long been captives at Onondaga. The embassy arrived at Saint Ignace July 9, 1647, and found the Hurons divided as to the expediency of agreeing to the Onondaga proposals; the Bear Tribe of the Hurons justly feared duplicity, though the enemy bore presents.

However, the Rock Tribe and many villages desired peace, hoping for the return of their kin, captured by the Onondaga. After many councils and conferences, an embassy was sent to Onondaga to better to fathom this matter. For presents, the Hurons took valuable furs, while the Iroquois Onondaga used belts of wampum. The Huron embassy was well received at Onondaga, where a month was spent in holding councils. Finally the Onondaga resolved to send back a second embassy, headed by Skanawati (Scandaouati), a federal chieftain, 60 years of age, who was to be accompanied by two other Onondaga and by 15 Huron captives. One of the Huron embassy remained as a hostage.

This embassy was 30 days on the way, although it was in fact only 10 days' journey. Jean Baptiste, the returning Huron delegate, brought back seven wampum belts of the largest kind, each composed of 3,000 or 4,000 beads. By these belts the Onondaga sought to confirm the peace, assuring the Hurons that they could hope for the deliverance of at least 100 more of their captive kin. The Onondaga desired this peace not only because the life of Annenraes had been spared, but also because they were jealous lest the Mohawk, who had become insolent from their victories and were overbearing even to their allies, might become more so if the Hurons failed to unite all their forces against them, and further because of fear of the power of the Conestoga.

In this Onondaga project of peace, the Cayuga and Oneida showed favorable interest, but the Seneca would not listen to it. The Mohawk were still more averse to it as they were jealous of what had been done by the Onondaga. Hence these last two tribes sent forces to attack the village of Saint Ignace at the end of the winter of 1647-48. Early in January 1648 the Hurons sent another embassy to Onondaga. They sent six men, accompanied by one of the three Onondaga ambassadors then in their country, the other two, including Skanawati, the head of the Onondaga embassy, remaining as hostages.

Unfortunately the new Huron embassy was captured and killed by a force of 100 Mohawk and Seneca who had come to the borders of the Huron country. The Onondaga accompanying this embassy was spared, and two Hurons escaped. Early in April, when the distressing news reached the ears of Skanawati, the proud Onondaga ambassador remaining with the Hurons as a hostage, he suddenly disappeared. The Hurons believed that he had stolen away, but, a few days after his disappearance, his corpse was found in the forest lying on a bed of fir branches, where he had taken his own life by cutting his throat.

His companion, who was notified in order to exonerate the Hurons, said that the cause of his despair was the shame he felt at the contempt shown for the sacredness of his person by the Seneca and the Mohawk in going to the Huron country and massacring the Huron people, while his life was pledged for the keeping of the faith of his people. Of such men was the great federal council of the Iroquois composed.

The Onondaga had good reason for fearing the Conestoga, for the *Jesuit Relation* for 1647-48 states that in a single village there were 1,300 men capable war, indicating for this village alone a population of more than 4,500.

At this time the Conestoga chiefs, through two messengers, informed the Hurons that if they felt too weak to defend themselves, they should send the Conestoga word by an embassy. The Hurons eagerly seized this opportunity by sending on this mission four Christian Indians and four "infidels," headed by one Charles Ondaaiondiont. They arrived at Conestoga early in June 1647.

The Huron deputies informed their Conestoga friends that they had come from a land of souls, where war and the fear of their enemies had spread desolation everywhere, where the fields were covered with blood and the lodges were filled with corpses, and they themselves had only life enough left to enable them to come to ask their friends to save their country, which was drawing rapidly toward its end. This spirited but laconic address moved the Conestoga to send an embassy into the Iroquois country to urge upon the Iroquois the advantage of making a lasting peace with their Huron adversaries.

Jean Baptiste, a Huron ambassador mentioned before, being at Onondaga at the end of summer, learned that this embassy of the Conestoga had reached the Iroquois country, as he even saw some of the Conestoga presents. It was the purpose of the Conestoga to bring about firm peace with the Hurons and the Onondaga, the Oneida and the Cayuga, and, if possible, the Seneca, and to renew the war against the Mohawk, should they then refuse to become parties to it.

The Conestoga did not fear the Mohawk. The *Jesuit Relation* for 1660 states that about the year 1600, the Mohawk had been greatly humbled by the Algonquin, and that after they had regained somewhat their former standing, the Conestoga, in a war lasting 10 years, had nearly exterminated the Mohawk, who since, however, had partially recovered from the defeat. Many of the Onondaga joined the Catholic Iroquois colonies on the Saint Lawrence River, and in 1751 about half the tribe was said to be living in Canada.

On the breaking out of the American Revolution in 1775, nearly all the Onondaga, together with the majority of the other Iroquois tribes, joined the British, and at the close of the war, the British government granted them a tract on Grand River, Ontario, where a portion of them still reside. The rest are still in New York, the greater number being on the Onondaga Reservation, and the others with the Seneca and Tuscarora on their several reservations.

The Onondaga made or joined in treaties with the state of New York at Fort Schuyler (formerly Fort Stanwix), September 12, 1788; Onondaga, November 18, 1793; Cayuga Ferry, July 28, 1795; Albany, February 25, 1817, February 11, 1822, and February 28, 1829.

They also joined in treaties between the Six Nations and the United States at Fort Stanwix, New York, October 22, 1784; Fort Harmar, Ohio, January 9, 1789; Canandaigua, New York, November 11, 1794, and Buffalo Creek, New York, January 15, 1838.

The Jesuits estimated the Onondaga at about 1,500 persons, while Greenhalgh in 1677 placed them at 1,750, probably their greatest strength. Later authorities give the numbers as 1,250 (1721), 1,000 (1736), 1,300 (1765), and 1,150 (1778), but these figures do not include those on the Saint Lawrence. In 1851 Morgan estimated their total number at about 900, including 400 on Grand River. In 1906 those in New

York numbered 553, the rest of the tribe being with the Six Nations in Canada.

Today, most of the Onondaga live on reservation lands of 6,100 acres south of Syracuse, New York. The New York tribe, in a recent count had some 1,600 members. The Six Nations Reserves in Ontario had about 500 members. In the 1960s and 1970s, the Onondaga led a unity movement and assumed political leadership among the Iroquois tribes, especially those allied with the Confederacy. In the next two decades, political activism resulted in return of many wampum belts that had been held by the New York State Museum. In the early 1970s, a school boycott called attention to education concerns of the tribe, and negotiations with the State Education Department began.

The reservation continues to operate a grade school. The tribe also fought against the state taking their land to widen Interstate 81, and then Governor Rockefeller met with tribal members to settle the dispute. The tribe then began plans to file land claims against the state. The Onondagas are governed by a Council of hereditary chiefs selected by clan mothers; both religious and secular affairs are handled by the council. All chiefs must be followers of teachings of Handsome Lake, and this links them to Longhouses on the other Iroquois reservations. Chiefs also represent the tribe at Confederacy councils, and continue to affirm traditional Iroquois ideology and culture.

A number of renowned artists and athletes are Onondagas, and the community is a well-known training ground for world-class lacrosse players. Some tribal members hold jobs in nearby Syracuse as tradespeople, construction workers (especially high steel), railroad workers, and service workers, and others are professionals in administration and teaching. However, unemployment remains high.

ORATAMIN

Oratamin (Hackensack, seventeenth century), also known as Oratam, Oratan, Oraton, or Oritany (Oratamy), was a chief (1667) in what is now New Jersey, who exercised prominent roles in treaty relations between the Dutch and neighboring Indian tribes, especially the Esopus. A period of border warfare between the Dutch and 10 or 11 area tribes was caused by the slaughter of 80 to 120 Indians at Pavonia and Corlaer's Hook, on February 25, 1643.

Oratamin represented the Hackensack, Tappan, Manhattan, Kitchawank, and Sitsink in a treaty of conciliation signed April 22, 1643. Although new hostilities led by younger warriors erupted immediately, a new treaty drawn at Fort Amsterdam, New Netherland, August 30, 1645, through Oratamin's efforts led to a general peace among all the Indians. Through 1660 Oratamin participated in and often initiated discussions that established the principle of negotiation to settle all intertribal and tribal-settler disputes, and that brought about peace treaties between the Dutch and the Wappinger on May 18, 1660, and finally Esopus on July 15, 1660, who had been the constant enemy of the settlers and a disgrace to the surrounding Indian nations.

The treaties of 1660 did not survive. Within months the Wappinger aided the Esopus in hostility against the Dutch. Wishing to contain the war, Oratamin served as in intermediary and "intelligence officer" for Peter Stuyvescant, governor of New Netherlands. Oratamin, with the Nyack chief Matteno, were called upon to establish negotiations between the two sides.

By November 1663, after the Wappinger and Esopus were informed that the British would not assist them, an armistice was called. With the return of Dutch captives held by the Indians, three Esopus chiefs presented themselves at Fort Amsterdam and formalized a peace treaty on May 16, 1664, which was ratified by most of the surrounding Indian nations and for which Oratamin and Matteno offered themselves as security.

ORONO

Orono (Penobscot; ca. 1688 - Feb. 5, 1802), was a Penobscot chief who supported the colonies during the American Revolution. Born about 1688 but perhaps as late as 1698 on the Penobscot River, Maine. His mother was half French and half Penobscot, and his father was French, perhaps Baron de Castine. Orono had all the physical characteristics of a European and none of a Penobscot Indian. At a very young age he converted to Christianity and became a devout Roman Catholic. For most of his life he was a subordinate chief, and served under Tomasus (Tomer) who was followed by Osson. Orono finally became chief about 1770 or 1774.

During the French and Indian War (1754-63) Tomasus, Osson, and Orono desired peace and supported a position of coexistence with both the English and the French. But like many chiefs of that time, they were forced by English attacks and land encroachments to join with the French against the English, and participated in the series of raids that left Maine uninhabitable to whites. Although Orono's actual activities from 1754-1774 were consistent with tribal policy, his convictions remained on the side of cooperation. Having earlier rejected the French cause, he refused to allow the British to arouse his people against the Massachusetts colony. On July 21, 1775, as chief, he and three others of his tribe met with the Provincial Congress at Watertown, Massachusetts and drew up a treaty of friendship end aid that resulted in his tribe providing great assistance to Massachusetts during the Revolution.

After the war the commonwealth of Massachusetts regarded Orono as a loyal friend and held him and his tribe in high esteem. Between 1785 and 1796 Orono entered into a number of amicable treaty negotiations that released parcels of land to Massachusetts, and that detemined tribal territorial boundaries. Orono died at Oldtown, Maine and was buried at Stillwater. The town of Orono, Maine is named for him.

P. P. OSUNKHIRHINE

Pierre Paul Osunkhirhine (Abnaki; nineteenth century) translated religious works into the Penobscot dialect of the Abnaki language. After attending Moore's Charity School in Hanover, New Hampshire, Osunkhirhine returned to his home near Pierreville, Quebec to work as a Protestant missionary. From 1830 to 1844 he published a great volume of religious works translated into his native tongue.

ELY SAMUEL PARKER

Ely Samuel Parker (Seneca; 1828 - August 31, 1895), also known as Hasanoanda, "The Reader," and Donehogawa, "He Holds the Door Open," was a sachem of the Seneca Tribe who was the military secretary to General Ulysses S. Grant during the Civil War. Born at Indian Falls at Pembroke near New York, he attended a mission school and various local academies.

Although he studied law, Parker was not allowed to become a member of the bar because as an Indian, he was not considered to be a citizen. However, it was only a small setback for Parker, who traveled to Washington, D.C. as his tribe's representative in order to prosecute land claims on their behalf.

While there, he impressed a number of prominent people, and was even invited to dine with President Polk. In 1951, Parker and ethnologist Lewis H. Morgan published the first scientific study of a North American Indian tribe entitled, League of the Iroquois. A year later he was named a Seneca chief.

PASSACONAWAY

Passaconaway (Pennacook; mid-seventeenth century), also known as Papisecoewa, was a powerful New Hampshire chief who at first opposed English settlement but later accepted it as inevitable. His principal village seems to have been near present-day Concord, New Hampshire on the Merrimac River. In 1642, after the English kidnapped his son Wannalancet, Passaconaway treated with the colonists, apparently in Boston, but formal submission of his lands and people to the Massachusetts Bay Colony seems not to have come until 1644. The chief was a famous sorcerer and was very old at the time of his death, almost certainly before King Philip's War (1675).

PASSAMAQUODDY

The Passamaquoddy, along with the Penobscot, is one of the only remaining tribes of the many that inhabited Maine at the time of coming of the white man in the early seventeenth century. They are all that is left of the Abnaki or Wabanaki, "people of the dawn," a once powerful nation of more than twenty tribes inhabiting parts of Canada, Maine, New Hampshire, and northern Massachusetts.

The Passamaquoddy and the Indians of the Saint John River are descendants of the ancient Etchimins, a seafaring people who were originally a branch of the Abnaki. However much they differ in customs and in dialect, both of these tribes derive their language and principal characteristics from a common Algonquian stock. They are the least disintegrated racially of all the present-day descendants of New England's natives; many families among them have a heritage unmixed with white or African blood.

But their tribal distinctions have long since become blurred by inter-association with the remnants of other vanishing tribes, and by the effacing of many of their traditions under the stress of modern industrial life.

The Passamaquoddy or *Pestumokadyik* (people who spear pollock) have always been a peaceful and friendly people, living chiefly by agricultural activities. It was they who kept the early settlers of Massachusetts alive by sending presents of food to the settlements. They were ultimately aroused to violent action only by the prolonged aggression of the settlers and by being forced to take sides in the English-French struggles. And when they did rise up, whole tribes were remorselessly exterminated. It is a significant fact that the custom of taking scalps was not known among them until instituted by English officers.

Before their movements were restricted by white settlers, the Indians wandered with the seasons, according to the location of food. In the spring they went to the rivers for alewives, shad, and salmon. On the banks they planted corn, squash, beans and other vegetables. In June they went to the sea to catch porpoise and seal, to get oil and skins, and for the eggs and nestlings of sea birds. They dried clams and lobsters, and stored them for winter use. In September they returned to the river valleys to harvest their crops, and in October they went into the big woods to hunt.

Before Christmas they held their annual thanksgiving feast for not less than two weeks. Our National Thanksgiving Day is a direct imitation of the Indian festival, even to the kinds of food served: turkey, cranberries, and Indian pudding. When snow came, they went into the deep woods hunting for moose and setting traps. Before the ice broke and the river was clear, they were ready for the catching of muskrat; they could start out in their canoes to fish and to go to the lower valleys for the planting.

Throughout Maine, the scene has changed little since the time of the Indians' supremacy. Today, in the great woods or by the lonely shore, one can see them in the mind's eye, a people historically great neither in numbers nor in deeds, but industrious, loyal and generous.

Today they live harmoniously among themselves and with their white neighbors, and in general maintain high standards of conduct. The Indian villages are autonomous in government, each electing its own officers. The tribes may send representatives to the State legislature, although the people are not citizens. Most of them are deeply religious, the majority being communicants of the Roman Catholic Church.

They have their own convents and schools, the latter supported largely by the State. Each summer the Old Town Indians present an historical pageant. They commonly dress in conventional costume and speak English, own homes and radios, drive automobiles, and indeed are indistinguishable from their white neighbors. They are, however, taught to speak their native language at an early age, and much is being done among them to preserve their native traditions and arts.

For most of them, no great effort is required to make a living, since each family has an inherited income from funds held in trust for them. In 1786, a treaty confirmed to the Indians certain lands as well as liberal gifts. These lands were sold at various times to Massachusetts and to Maine for considerable sums, to be held for the Indians and their descendants. The average Indian takes up his income in trade at the agency store. The Indians work as river drivers and as guides to hunting and fishing parties, or they make baskets, which they sell to tourists.

There was once a clan or totem system among the tribes, but it is now largely obliterated. The Bear Clan, one of the largest groups, still has its representatives among the Passamaquoddy, who say the clan originated with a lost child who was brought up by a mother bear.

The office of chief or governor (president, sachem, or sagamore) was formerly held for life, but in 1862 it became annually elective. Even so, the same man often held the position through life, and from him it might pass to his son, as in the Attean family. Dissension at the elections gave rise to the Old Party and New Party, which now take turns in electing officers each year.

The Indians no longer practice the old crafts of making fishnets, spears, bows and arrows, wampum, carved pipes, and pottery; and such things as canoes, snowshoes, and moccasins, formerly produced by them, are now more efficiently turned out in large factories. The Passamaquoddy make baskets, and are more expert as fishermen and hunters. Baskets are usually made from the flexible wood of the brown ash, although basswood and sweetgrass are also used. Lovely designs are made by threading dyed quills upon cloth or leather. Some striking examples of Indian carving and painting are also seen.

Two reservations are located in the easternmost county of Maine. Pleasant Point Reservation is in Sipayik village near Eastport, and Motahkokmikuk is in Indian Township on the Schoodic Lakes chain. The latter was founded in 1852 by a conservative faction after a political quarrel with more progressive Sipayik members. It consists of two neighborhoods that are separated by a seven-mile paved road: Peter Dana Point at Big Lake, and the Strip near the town of Princeton. The tribe today has about 2,500 members, and about fifty percent live off the reservations.

Each reservation today elects a government consisting of a governor, lieutenant governor, and a six-member council. The sixteen–member Joint Tribal Council makes decisions concerning the tribe as a whole. A tribal representative is still chosen alternately from the two reservations.

The tribe has purchased about 134,000 acres of trust land. They operate a high-stakes bingo operation, own two radio stations, operate small businesses, and operate a cable television station. They also own a patent on a scrubber designed to control coal emissions that cause acid rain.

The tribal government has provided new offices, a health center, primary school, and new homes, and has become the largest and best-paying employer. New housing and free health care have drawn many Native Americans back to the reservation, and employment opportunities have lowered the unemployment rate from eighty percent to thirty percent. Many members are enrolled in the university.

The language is still spoken by many adults, and the tribe had its language codified in the 1970s to teach the native tongue. History, crafts, and arts are taught, and celebrations are held. The Wapohnaki Museum at Sipayik also provides information about the tribe's culture and traditions.

PENNACOOK

Southern and central New Hampshire was the main area occupied by the Pennacook. They extended into northeastern Massachusetts, eastern Vermont, and southern Maine. The Pennacook were among the Western Abnaki Algonquian-speaking groups whose ancestors lived along the upper Merrimack River, especially in the neighborhood of present Concord, New Hampshire, and between the Merrimack and Connecticut Rivers. Other near-relatives were the Penobscot, Passamaquoddy, and the Malecite. "Western Abenaki" was still spoken in recent times in Odanak. *Pennacook* was derived from the Massachusetts Algonquian words for "crooked river" or "the place where the river bends." *Abenaki* (sometimes *Abnaki*) means "eastern" or "dawn" people. The Pennacook name is from Abnaki *penakuk*, "at the bottom of the hill," or simply "down hill," according to Gerard. They have also been called Owaragees by the Iroquois, Nechegansett, and Merrimac, from the river.

Their New Hampshire villages included: Amoskeag, at Amoskeag Falls on the Merrimac River; Coosuc division along the Connecticut River between the Upper and Lower Ammonoosuc Rivers; Pennacook, the division on both sides of the Merrimac River below and above Concord, with the main village at present Concord; Piscataqua, on Piscataqua River near Dover; Souhegan division on the Souhegan River near Amherst in Hillsborough County; Squamscot, near Exeter, on the Exeter River; Winnecowet, in Rockingham County; Winnipesaukee, at Lake Winnipesaukee.

The Pennacook lived in a northern environment of mixed forest suitable for light farming. Deer, moose, bear, small mammals, fish from fresh water rivers and lakes, migratory birds, salt water fish, and shellfish contributed most of the diet in season. Although the area is rather north for agriculture, maize and probably beans were raised. Fish caught were sturgeon, shad, and alewives; turtles and clams were harvested. Wild plant foods were grapes, berries, and maple syrup and sugar.

Any one family or village-group occupied more than one residence. In deep winter, groups lived together far inland where hunting was best. In spring and summer, they camped near saltwater shores where shellfishing was most easily done; in summer, they lived along river valleys where planted food seeds could grow best. They are therefore best described as riverine people. Fifty to 300 persons formed a village, often pallisaded.

Transportation was by dugout canoes and backpacking. Varied traps, nets, hooks, spears, and weirs were used to gather seafoods, and for animals later used for food or clothing. More permanent villages were located at Pawtucket Falls and Wamesit Falls and present Concord, New Hampshire. Implements were made of stone, bone, turtle shell, grasses, and reeds. They took the form of stone projectile points, gorgets, and "banner stones" which probably helped project darts and spears before the advent of the bow in about A.D. 1100. Pottery with incised decoration and clay pipes was made.

Art took the form of geometrical incision of pottery, animal forms on pipes, and mostly geometric or symbolic designs on woven baskets and mats. Houses were bark-covered, either conical one-family homes, or rectangular, tunnel-shaped, multifamily buildings, all built on pole frames. The political life of a village has been described as "despotic" or "paternal."

These descriptions can be interpreted to mean that the chief of a village behaved in a paternalistic way, was autocratic on occasion, but could not hold individuals, including "minor chiefs," to fight with and for him, and anyone could expatriate himself at will. The position of chief was hereditary and seems to have been at least partly in the male line. However, the intermarriage between ruling families within an area makes it difficult to determine rules of chiefdom inheritance. Social life was focused in the extended family. There were rather rigid sex dichotomies as to work. Polygamy was accepted, and divorce could be initiated by either sex.

Lineage was matrilineal except, possibly, in chieftan families. Next to the chief in communal importance was the medicine man, or shaman. He (sometimes she), was primarily a healer using herbs as supernatural means to effect cures. There was also an undescribed water cure. The shamans were also influential in secular affairs, advising the chiefs, and sometimes becoming chiefs themselves.

This position may have been due to their status in the genealogy of chieftan families. An example is Chief Passaconaway, reputed to make trees dance, boulders march, snow burn, flowers grow through ice, and trees to grow leaves in midwinter. The religion also included veneration of the sun, moon, and a few star constellations. The changes of the seasons were considered to have supernatural power. Humans and animals were believed to have immortal souls that went to the far southwest.

Two interesting archaeological finds revealed something of religious practices. One was the skeleton of a man buried in a sitting position facing east; his skull had been fractured. Near him, the skeleton of a woman was found. Another find was a dugout canoe found at the bottom of a lake. The canoe had been filled with stones, thus purposefully sunk. Besides obviously religious rituals, the Indians played Lacrosse, gambled, and did mimetic dances, some of which had religious significance. Concerning intertribal ritual, the Algonquian-speaking Indians seem to have had a mostly peaceful relationship among them selves, but at the beginning of recorded history, the Mohawks were encroaching into their territory.

In 1670, the Mohawks invaded the Pennacook area and defeated and killed most of the local groups that resisted them. In 1614, Captain John Smith was the first European to record a visit to the Merrimack River. A few years after his exploration, trading with the Indians began.

The Indians exchanged food, furs, and baskets, mostly for English manufactured goods. Between 1614 and 1620, the mysterious two-year pestilence that ravaged coastal New England, from southern Maine to Narragansett Bay, caused disastrous decimation of Indian population and affected the Indians of the Merrimack River as well. English domination over the Indians of the Pennacook area started in the late 1620s. Chief Passaconaway, first mentioned in 1623, deeded a large tract of land to an individual Englishman. Chief Passaconaway's compliance with, and submissiveness to, the English was practically absolute.

For example, he sent to Boston for punishment, probably hanging, one of his tribe who had killed an English trader. Also, after an outrage to his son and daughter-in-law, he apologized and gave the English all his guns. In 1644, he was the first chief of the area to submit to a redivision of his lands. In 1660, upon abdication, he warned the Indians not to fight the English because of reprisals too great to withstand. Conversion began in or shortly before 1653, when John Eliot obtained an act from the General Court to reserve an undocumented tract of land for exclusive Indian use.

Within this tract, the village Wamesit was overseen by Daniel Gookin and taught Christianity by John Eliot. In 1675, King Philips' War began in southern New England and from then on, the English performed acts of arrogance and wanton destruction against the Indians of the Merrimack River area.

After the English victory over the southern New England tribes, and the killing of King Philip in 1676, the fighting continued in the northern part of Massachusetts Colony. By then the Indians had lost population and reserve food. During this time, sachem Wanalancet not only maintained neutrality, but also signed a treaty not to harm any English. To ensure this, he and most of his tribe retreated north into the forest.

Through a ruse, 200 Indians of the Neutral area were taken to Boston, where some were hanged and some were "sold into slavery in foreign parts," mostly the West Indies and Bermuda.

Eventually, in 1677, a group of Indians from the Pennacook area went to the Saint Francis Mission on the Saint Lawrence River in Quebec, where some identity has been maintained through their language. Throughout the eighteenth century, Pennacooks and other Western Abenakis were confusedly drawn into other colonial wars and the American Revolution.

Mooney assumed that in 1600 there were about 2,000 Pennacook. In a count of 1676 they reportedly had about 1,250. Tribal remnants were counted among the 280 Saint Francis Indians in 1924.

In the twentieth century, some tribal members have returned to ancestral lands to hunt, fish, and guide non-Indian sportsmen. Industry around Concord also attracted some back. In a recent census, there were some 360 Indian residents in New Hampshire with no listed tribal identity.

PENOBSCOT

The Penobscot Indians are the only remaining tribe, except for the Passamaquoddy, that still exists in Maine. They are all that is left of the Abnaki or Wabenaki, "people of the dawn", a once powerful nation of more than twenty tribes inhabiting parts of Canada, Maine, New Hampshire, and northern Massachusetts. However much they differ in customs and in dialect, both of these tribes derive their language and principal characteristics from a common Algonquian stock. They are the least disintegrated racially of all the present-day descendants of New England's aborigines; many families among them have a heritage unmixed with white or African blood. But their tribal distinctions have long since become blurred by inter-association with the remnants of other vanishing tribes, and by the loss of many of their traditions under the stress of modern industrial life.

Before their movements were restricted by white settlers, the Indians used to wander with the seasons according to the location of food supplies. In the spring they went to the rivers for ale-wives, shad and salmon; on the banks they planted corn, squash, beans, and other vegetables. In June they went to the sea for porpoise and seal in order to get oil and skins, and for the eggs and nestlings of sea birds; they dried clams and lobsters, and stored them for winter use. In September they returned to the river valleys to harvest, and in October, they went into the big woods to hunt. Before Christmas they held their annual thanksgiving feast for not less than two weeks. (Our National Thanksgiving Day is a direct imitation of the Indian festival, even to the kinds of food served: turkey, cranberries, Indian pudding.)

When snow came, they went deep into the woods hunting for moose and setting traps. Before the ice broke up in March or April, they had made their spring catch of otter or beaver. After the ice broke and the river was clear, they were ready for the catching of muskrat; they could start out in their canoes to fish and to go to the lower valleys for the planting.

The Penobscot have always been a peaceful and friendly people, living chiefly by agricultural activities. It was they, along with the Passamaquoddy, who kept the early settlers of Massachusetts alive by providing food for them during the harsh winters. They were ultimately aroused to violent action only by the prolonged aggression of the settlers and by being forced to take sides in the English-French struggles. And when they did rise up, whole tribes were systematically exterminated. It is a significant fact that the custom of taking scalps was not known among them until instituted by English officers. Today they live harmoniously among themselves and with their white neighbors, and in general maintain high standards of conduct.

The Penobscot have sometimes been erroneously called Tarantins, a name for an earlier tribe or group of tribes. The Puritans called the Abnaki Tarrateens. Among the Penobscot today live descendants of Baron de Castin, who married the daughter of Chief Madockowando of the Tarantines, but the latter was an Etchimin and not a Penobscot. It may be that the Pentagoets of Castine, the remnants of the so-called Tarantines of de Castine, moved to Old Town and joined with the Penobscots. There was once a clan or totem among the tribes, but it is now largely obliterated. The Bear Clan, one of the largest groups, still has its representatives among the Penobscot, who say the clan originated with a lost child who was brought up by a mother bear.

232

Joseph Polis, the Penobscot Indian who served as David Henry Thoreau's guide in the Maine woods, used a drawing of a bear on his canoe as a personal emblem. Old Governor Nepture, the Penobscot descendant of a long line of chiefs and governors, used the sign of the snake, signifying mental prowess.

The Penobscot Indian Nation today lives mainly on the Indian Island Reservation at Old Town in Maine. Population of the group in 1991 was 1,984, and about twenty–five percent live on the reservation.

The Penobscot have a democratic government. Officers including a governor, lieutenant governor, and a tribal representative to the Maine Legislature are elected biennially. An elected Tribal Council of twelve members serve four-year terms, and a police force, tribal court, and primary school are maintained.

One of the tribe's most famous governors was Joseph Orono, for whom the town of Orono was named; a blue- eyed Indian believed to be a natural son of the Baron de Castin. He is said to have saved Maine for the Union by rallying his men to the aid of the whites in the wars with the Mohawks. He died in 1801, at the reputed age of one hundred and thirteen. Another Indian equally revered was the saintly Aspinquid, one of John Eliot's converts, who did much toward spreading Christianity and peace among the New England tribes. It was the Abnaki, indeed, who, of the North American Indians, first embraced Christianity. In the past, Saint Aspinquid's grave-maker could be found, high on Mount Agamenticus; it bore this inscription: Present Useful: Absent Wanted: Lived Desired: Died Lamented.

Most of the Penobscot are deeply religious, the majority being communicants of the Roman Catholic Church. They have their own convents and schools; the latter supported largely by the State. Each summer the Old Town Indians present an historical pageant. They commonly dress in conventional costume and speak English, own their homes and radios, drive automobiles, and indeed are indistinguishable from their white neighbors.

In 1786, a treaty confirmed to the Indians certain lands as well as liberal gifts. These lands were sold at various times to Massachusetts and Maine for considerable sums, to be held for the Indians and their descendants. In 1818, Massachusetts agreed to pay the Penobscots the following: one six-pounded cannon, one swivel, fifty good knives, two hundred yards of calico, two drums, four rifles, one box of pipes, three hundred yards of ribbon; and in October of each year, as long as the Penobscots shall remain a nation, five hundred bushels of corn, fifteen barrels of wheat, seven barrels of clear pork, one hogshead of molasses, one hundred yards of double-width broadcloth (red one year and blue the next), fifty good blankets, one hundred pounds of gunpowder, six boxes of chocolate, one hundred fifty pounds of tobacco, and fifty dollars in silver or their equivalents.

The Penobscot tribe receives further compensation from corporations which make use of the Indian shore on the river above Old Town; the tribe owns about two hundred islands in the Penobscot River between Old Town and Medway and up the east and west branches of the river to Chesunkook and Mattagamon lakes.

The Indians no longer practice the old crafts of making fishnets, spears, bows and arrows, wampum, carved pipes, and pottery; and such things as canoes, snowshoes, and moccasins, formerly produced by them, are now more efficiently turned out in large factories. The Penobscot still excel in basket-making. Baskets are usually made from the flexible wood of the brown ash, although basswood and sweetgrass are also used. With the Penobscot women, sewing is a fine art; but weaving seems always to have been unknown to them. Lovely designs are made by threading dyed quills upon cloth or leather. Some striking examples of Indian carving and painting are occasionally seen.

In the 1950s, a small ferry was replaced by a new bridge to connect Indian Island to the mainland. In 1954, they gained the right to vote in state elections. Because they feared what they considered to be a threat to their tribal sovereignty, they became organized as the Penobscot Nation and began researching their historical claims. In 1965, they joined with other Maine Indians and asserted themselves to gain improved state services, resulting in the founding of a new Department of Indian Affairs.

They joined the Passamaquoddy in a massive land claim in 1972, and in 1979 gained federal recognition. In addition to a funded health care system, they became eligible for large-scale funding for community projects, including tribal offices, a sewer system, and low income housing.

In 1980, a majority voted to settle their land claim against Maine, and the Penobscot Reservation was given the powers of a municipality. An award of 40.3 million dollars allowed them to acquire additional trust lands, upon which the tribe sets hunting and fishing regulations. Thus far, 55,278 acres of trust land and 69,485 acres of fee-simple lands have been purchased by the tribe. Log–ging operations, an audio-cassette manufacturing plant, and other economic activities have helped the unemployment rate to lower. However, poverty remains for some, and alcohol and drug abuse continues to be problems.

Although some of the traditional Penobscot traditions and culture have been lost, serious efforts have been made to preserve the language and teach the few remaining traditions. Recently, there has also been renewed interest in Native spiritualism.

PEQUOT
Before the arrival of Europeans, the old settled Algonquian tribes that occupied the Connecticut River Valley were harassed by fierce invaders from New York, that they called *Pequots* ("destroyers"). The settled tribes were the Podunk, Poquenock, Nipmuck, Niantic, Quinnipiac, Saukiog, Wangnuk, Hammonasset, Montowese, Menunktuck, Paugusset, Swianog, and Tunxis.

The invaders were Mohegans, who conquered and exacted tribute from the native tribes. In 1633 the Pequot-Mohegans sold land to the Dutch, who established a short-lived trading post, Fort Good Hope, at what is now Hartford. Hoping to balance this power combine, the Connecticut tribes sold land to English settlers from the Massachusetts Bay Colony.

The Dutch soon became exasperated with the Pequots and killed their sachem, Wopigwooit, who was succeeded by his son Sassacus. Sassacus intermittently warred against the Dutch to avenge his father's death. In addition, the Pequots were held responsible for the death of two English traders, and consequently the English, under John Endicott, led a punitive expedition against them, burning their villages. Sassacus retaliated by burning the English settlement at Saybrook, and attacking Wethersfield, killing eight settlers and taking two girls captive. This called for a full-scale war, launched by the English under Captain John Mason in 1637.

He was aided by the Sagamore Uncas, rival of Sassacus, for tribal leadership. Uncas withdrew from the Pequots with a number of followers, the Mohegans, and joined the English. The Narragansett Indians and some of the conquered tribes were also allies. In a surprise attack, the English stormed and burned the Pequot's palisaded stronghold near the Mystic River, killing 400 inhabitants and taking seven captives.

Another colony of Pequots, who were trapped in a swamp while fleeing the English, was taken captive and sold into slavery. Sassacus escaped, but was put to death by the Mohawks from whom he sought asylum. The power of the Pequots was decisively crushed, but the Mohegans, protected by the English, were able to harass the peaceful tribes until the death of their leader, Uncas, in 1683.

In the last half of the seventeenth century, two separate Pequot Indian tribes were granted land in Connecticut: the federally recognized Mashantucket or Western Pequot of Ledyard, and the state-recognized Paucatuck or Eastern Pequots. The latter occupy the Lantern Hill Reservation in North Stonington. For both groups, the twentieth century became a period of decline for many decades. For the Eastern Pequots, efforts were begun in the 1970s to gain federal recognition, and the issue remains to be settled. Today there are about 18 homes on the reservation of 226 acres. A principal conflict remains between the State of Connecticut and the tribe relating to land claims.

Factionalism within the tribe had made resolution of the issue a difficult task. However, efforts to provide leadership during the conflicts continue. The Mashantucket Pequots reorganized their tribal government in 1974, and a constitution was drafted. A chairman now heads the Mashantucket Pequot Tribal Council. In 1976, efforts were begun for filing suit over lands taken from the tribe.

After years of negotiation, the land claim was settled in 1983 and the group was provided federal recognition. Changes since federal recognition have been dramatic for the Mashantucket Pequots. The land base was increased from 214 acres in 1983 to 1,795 acres in 1991.

A number of economic development initiatives have been implemented, and employment has increased on the reservation. A high-stakes bingo operation was developed, and a gambling casino was opened in 1992. A recent census showed about 282 enrolled tribal members of the Mashantucket Pequot.

PHILIP

Philip (Wampanoag, 1638, - August 12, 1676), also known as Metacomet of Pokanoket, was one of the first Indians to comprehend the threat posed by European settlement in the New World, and he formed a short-lived confederacy in an abortive attempt to drive the English from the land. Second son of Massassoit, who had lived on peaceful terms with the whites from the founding of Plymouth colony in 1620 to his death in 1661, Philip was a marked contrast to his father in terms of both temperament and objectives. Massasoit had sold substantial amounts of Indian land in order to enhance his own power and prestige through an alliance with the English.

By the time Philip became sachem in 1662, the white settlements had penetrated deep into the wilderness of southeastern Massachusetts. Philip saw clearly that if white encroachements were not stopped quickly, tribal lands would be overwhelmed. From the day he donned the wampum mark of chieftainship at Mount Hope in Rhode Island until his death there in 1676, Philip plotted and nearly executed the extermination of every settler in New England. From 1662 to 1675, Philip kept the colonists wondering. Unlike his father, Philip could not be bribed into submission, a state of affairs that profoundly distressed the Puritan community.

They never knew whether Philip would soon again be on the warpath. Actually, Philip was a realist, and he knew that the Wampanoags by themselves were too few to destroy the enemy. He recognized that the road to salvation led to a confederation of all the regional tribes, despite past rivalries and hostilities. Therefore, he devoted himself to forging alliances based strictly upon race; it was to a confederation of Indians, regardless of tribe, against the invaders.

For thirteen years, he "traveled throughout the area, frying to enlist support, but when the inevitable war began, Philip still was not ready. He was able to ally the Nipmucks and the Narragansets, but the active opposition of other tribes against Philip's forces is probably what turned the tide in the Puritans' favor during "King Philip's War".

The shooting started shortly after three of Philip's warriors were hanged, following their conviction for the murder of an Indian informer named John Sassamon. Sassamon had told the settlers of Philip's plotting, but Philip claimed that the entire incident fell outside of Plymouth colony's jurisdiction. Several Wampaneags went on the warpath (June 20, 1675) in retaliation for the hangings, and Philip followed with strikes against outlying white settlements.

As the Puritans responded in panic, Philip divided his time between strengthening his confederation and scalping as many whites as possible. Hostilities quieted during the winter, but flared again in February 1676. Wampanoag, Nipmuck, and Narraganset warriors attacked 52 out of the 90 white settlements in New England, totally destroying twelve of them. Philip even led a strike inside the town of Plymouth itself. Just at the moment that victory seemed possible, however, Philip's confederation began to collapse. Combinations of pro-white natives and colonists began to track down the marauding bands, inflicting so many casualties that Philip's forces disintegrated.

With the losses, more braves allied to Philip went over to the colony, and the defections snowballed. Those loyal to the Wampanoag chief faced starvation as summer approached and they were deprived of their hunting and planting grounds. Realizing that defeat was inevitable but unwilling to surrender, Philip led a small band of his followers back to Mount Hope; he wished to die on the lands of his ancestors. The victim of constant betrayals during his lifetime, Philip was to be so victimized one more time. One of his warriors went to the colonists and offered to lead them to Philip's hideout.

On August 12, 1676, the combined native and English force killed Philip, quartered his body, and carried his head back to Plymouth. It remained on public display for 25 years, a reminder of the fate in store for any Indian who dared to resist the march of civilization.

POCOMTUC

Although the Pocomtuc Indians formerly lived primarily on the Deerfield and Connecticut Rivers in Franklin County, Massachusetts, their northernmost bands extended into the southern part of Vermont. Their principal village, of the same name, was near the present Deerfield Indians. They had a fort on Fort Hill in the same vicinity, which was destroyed by the Mohawks after a hard battle in 1666.

They were an important tribe, and seem to have ruled over the other Indians of the Connecticut Valley within the limits of Massachusetts, including those at Agawam, Nonetue, and Squawkeag. They combined with the Narragansett and Tunnis in attacks on Uncas, the Mohegan chief. All these tribes joined the hostile Indians under King Philip in 1675.

JOHN W. QUINNEY

John W. Quinney (Stockbridge, 1797 - July 21, 1855), was a highly educated leader and elected chief in 1852 of the Stockbridge, New York Iroquois, whose relations with the United States government displayed his brilliance as a negotiator and gained him the complete trust of his tribe.

In 1822 he assisted in the negotiations with the Menominee in purchasing land in the area of Green Bay Wisconsin, for the relocation of the tribe, and three years later was largely was responsible for the New York legislature paying the Stockbridge the market value of their New York lands, enabling them to move to Wisconsin. Under the Treaty of Butte des Morts (1827), the Menominee ceded the land around the southern end of Green Bay to the Stockbridge.

In 1828 Quinney approached the United States Congress to establish the tribe's legal rights to the land, but by 1830 the Winnebago Indians and Green Bay whites were urging the Menominee to disavow the treaty.

The matter was referred to the federal government. Although the tribe eventually lost this land, after protracted work within the Congress, Quinney secured $25,000 for improvements made and the grants to two townships on the eastern side of Lake Winnebago. By 1843 the United States demanded the relocation of the Stockbridge.

Quinney concluded a treaty in which assistance in finding an acceptable new home west of the Mississippi River, and in relocating the tribe was promised. United States citizenship previously granted to the tribe was revoked through his efforts, thereby maintaining tribal self-government under a constitution he framed in 1833, which protected tribal customs. The tribe found no land for relocation. Quinney returned to Washington with a uniquely bold proposal. A new treaty was signed, and in 1854 Congress passed a law giving the tribe title to 460 acres in Stockbridge, New York.

John Quinney died with the distinction not only of successfully having steered his tribe away from the horrors of Indian relocation, but also of having eventually won the encounter.

RED JACKET

Red Jacket (Seneca, 1758 - January 20, 1830), also known as Otetiani, assumed the name Sagoyewatha upon his election to the Seneca chieftainship. Although accused of cowardice in battle, he used his gift for oratory to remain Chief. Red Jacket, of course, was his English name, bestowed upon him as a result of the succession of red coats he wore while on the British side during the American Revolution. Red Jacket, along with some Seneca warriors, though, retreated precipitously at the approach of General Sullivan's troops in 1779.

He even attempted to conclude a separate peace with the Americans, but his plans were frustrated by the Mohawk Chief, Joseph Brant. For all these actions, Red Jacket was considered a coward by many of his own people. When many of the braver chiefs and warriors were killed, moreover, Red Jacket seized the opportunity to consolidate his power. In 1786, at an Indian council along the Detroit River, Red Jacket used his splendid oratory to protest the inevitable peacemaking with the United States. Most likely, the hostile position he assumed was political trickery aimed primarily at currying favor with those who had thought their chief cowardly in combat.

Red Jacket constantly sought to portray himself as a bitter enemy of the whites and protector of his people, but to a great extent his oratory was a facade, masking his naked ambition for all forms of self-aggrandizement.

For example, in 1787, 1788, and 1790, he publicly opposed land sales in order to maintain his popularity with the Seneca, but he secretly signed the property cessions in order to protect his prestige with the Americans. As he strengthened his leadership position, however, he seems to have become more sincere in his protestations against white influence upon the customs, religion, and language of his tribe.

He vehemently opposed missionaries living on Indian lands. Following the New York legislature's decree in 1821 forbidding white residence on Indian Territory, Red Jacket led a contingent of the tribe in ousting the local missionary. He also vainly attempted to preserve Indian jurisdiction over criminal acts committed on Indian property. In the Tommy Jemmy case (1821), Red Jacket stated that the Seneca council that had tried a squaw for witchcraft and the warrior who had executed her were outside the jursidiction of the United States.

During the 1820s, Red Jacket began to lose prestige as his drinking and general dissipation grew more observable. In 1827 his wife joined the church, and Red Jacket fulfilled his threat to leave her, an action which prompted his further denigration. Although he returned to his wife a few months later, he was deposed as chief by a council of 26 tribal leaders, only to be reinstated through a personal effort at reform and the help of the United States Office of Indian Affairs.

The reinstated chief quickly fell back into his old ways, however. By the time of his death in 1830, Red Jacket's anti-white and anti-Christian policies were long out of date, and he was surrounded by a largely Christianized tribe in which he was an alien presence. In fact, though his wishes were to the contrary, Red Jacket was given a Christian funeral and was buried in the cemetery of his reservation's Christian mission.

SASSACUS

Saccassus (Pequot; 1560 - 1637), perhaps the same as Massachusetts *Sassakusu*, "he is wild", was the noted and last important chief of the Pequot tribe. He was the son and successor of Wopigwooit, the first chief of the tribe contacted by whites. He was killed by the Dutch, about 1632, at or near the site of Hartford, Connecticut, then the principal Pequot settlement. Soon after becoming chief in October, 1634, Sassacus sent an emissary to the governor of the Massachusetts Bay colony to ask for a treaty of friendship, offering as an inducement, to surrender all rights of the Pequot to the lands they had conquered, provided the colonists would settle a plantation among his people. It was an offer that he must have known he could not carry out, and perhaps had no intention of trying to fulfill, as he bitterly hated whites. This proposal had the effect of turning Uncus, the Mohegan chief, against him. Pequot territory during Sassacus's leadership extended from Narragansett Bay to the Hudson River, and included the larger part of Long Island.

It is said that at the height of his prosperity no fewer than 26 sachems were subordinate to him. Because of his depredations especially on the neighboring tribes, the colonists decided in 1636 to make war on the Pequot. The name of Sassacus had inspired such terror among the surrounding tribes that the Indian allies of the whites could not believe the latter would dare to make a direct attack on the stronghold of this wily chief. The war was soon ended, and Sassacus, having suffered defeat and the loss of most of his people, fled with 20 or 30 of his warriors to the Mohawk country. He found no safety, and in late 1637 his scalp and those of his brother and five other Pequot chiefs were sent to the Governor of Massachusetts by the Mohawk. As Sassacus had taken much wampum on his flight, Mohawk desire for this treasure of strung beads may have led to the murders.

SCAROUADY (HALF KING)

Scarouady (Oneida; eighteenth century), also known as Half King, was chief of the Oneida Indians in western Pennsylvania. He allied himself and his tribe firmly with English colonists during the British-French imperial conflicts of the 1750s. Scarouady hated the French, and to escape their influence he moved from Logstown to Aughwick, Pennsylvania in 1754.

There he assumed command over the western Pennsylvania Oneida, succeeding Half-King Scruniyatha. A great orator, frequently the leading speaker at intertribal conferences, Scarouady summoned all his considerable talent in 1754 to urge the Indians of Fort Cumberland to accompany the British expedition under General Braddock on its ill-fated march against the alliance of French and Indians along the western frontier.

By 1756, however, the Oneida chief was making speeches advocating peace. One such speech occurred on July 1, 1756 before Sir William Johnson, British representative to the North American tribes, at a conference of the Six Nations.

SENECA

The tribal name *Seneca* means "place of the stone"; it is the Anglicized form of the Dutch enunciation of the Mohegan rendering of the Iroquoian ethnic appellative *Oneida*, with a different ethnic suffix, meaning "people of the standing or projecting rock or stone." They are a prominent and influential tribe of the Iroquois. When first known, they occupied the part of western New York between Seneca Lake and Geneva River, having their council fire at Tsonontowan, near Naples, in Ontario County.

After the political destruction of the Erie and Neutrals, about the middle of the seventeenth century, the Seneca and other Iroquois people migrate to Lake Erie and southward along the Allegheny River, into Pennsylvania.

They also accepted into their tribe some of the conquered Indians, becoming the largest tribe of the confederation and one of the most important. The Seneca are now chiefly settled on the Allegany, Cattaraugus, and Tonawanda reservations in New York.

A portion of them remained under British jurisdiction after the declaration of peace, and lived on the Grand River Reservation, Ontario. Various local bands have been known as Buffalo, Tonawanda, and Cornplanter Indians; and the Mingo, formerly in Ohio, have become officially known as Seneca from the large number of that tribe among them. No considerable number of the Seneca ever joined the Catholic Iroquois colonies. In the third quarter of the sixteenth century, the Senecas were the last, save one, of the Iroquois tribes to vote in favor of the abolition of murder and war, the suppression of cannibalism, and the establishment of the principles upon which the League of the Iroquois was founded.

However, a large division of the tribe did not initially adopt the course of the main body, but, on obtaining coveted privileges and prerogatives, the recalcitrant body was admitted as a constituent member in the structure of the League. The two chieftancies last added to the quota of the Seneca were admitted on condition of their exercising functions belonging to a sergeant-at-arms of a modern legislative body, as well as those belonging to a modern secretary of state for foreign affairs, in addition to their duties as federal chieftains.

Indeed, they became the warders of the famous "Great Black Doorway" of the League of the Iroquois, called *Ka'nho'hwadji'go'na* by the Onondaga. In historical times, the Seneca have been by far the most populous of the five tribes originally composing the League of the Iroquois.

The Seneca belong, in the federal organization, to the tribal clan known by the political name *hondonnus*, meaning, "they are clansmen of the fathers." The Mohawk are the other members, when the tribes are organized as a federal council; but when ceremonially organized, the Onondaga also belong to this phratry.

In the federal council, the Seneca are represented by eight federal chiefs, but two of these were added to the original six present at the first federal council, to give representation to that part of the tribe which had at first refused to join the League. Since the organization of the League of the Iroquois, approximately in the third quarter of the sixteenth century, the number of Seneca clans, which were organized into two phratries for the performance of both ceremonial and civil functions, have varied.

In a list of clan names made in 1838 by General Dearborn from information given him by Mister Cone, an interpreter of the Tonawanda band, the Heron clan is called the Swan clan with the native name given above. Of these clans, only five had an unequal representation in the federal council of the League: namely, the Sandpiper, three; the Turtle, two; the Hawk, one; the Wolf, one; and the Bear, one. One of the earliest known references to the ethnic name Seneca is that on the Original Carte Figurative, annexed to the Memorial presented to the States General of the Netherlands, August 18, 1616, on which it appears with the Dutch plural as *Sennecas*. This map is remarkable also for the first known mention of the ancient Erie, sometimes called Gahkwas or Kahkwah. The name did not originally belong to the Seneca, but to the Oneida.

In the early part of December 1634, Arent Van Curler (or Corlaer), the commissary or factor of the Manor of Rensselaerwyck (his uncle's estate), set out from Fort Orange, now Albany, New York, in the interest of the fur trade, to visit the Mohawk and the Sinnekens. Strictly speaking, the latter name designated the Oneida, but at this time it was a general name, usually comprising the Onondaga, the Cayuga, and the Seneca, in addition.

At that period, the Dutch and the French commonly divided the Five Iroquois tribes into two identical groups; to the first, the Dutch gave the name Maquas (Mohawk), and to the latter, Sinnekens (Seneca, the final-ens being the Dutch genitive plural), with the connotation of the four tribes mentioned above.

The French gave to the latter group the general name "les Iroquois Superieurs," i.e., the Upper Iroquois "les Hiroquois des pays plus hauts, nommes Sontouaheronnons," (literally, 'the Iroquois of the upper country, called Sontouaheronnons'), the latter being only another form of *les Tsonnontouans* (the Seneca); and to the first group the designations "les Iroquois inferieurs" (the Lower Iroquois), and "les Hiroquois d'en teas, nommes Agnechronnons" (the Mohawk; literally, 'the Iroquois from below, named Agnechronnons').

This geographical, rather than political division of the Iroquois tribes, first made by Champlain and the early Dutch at Fort Orange, prevailed until about the third quarter of the seventeenth century. Indeed, Governor Andros, two years after Greenhalgh's visit to the several tribes of the Iroquois in 1677, still wrote, "Ye Oneidas deemed ye first nation of sineques."

The journal of Van Curler records the interesting fact that during his visit to the tribes, he celebrated the New Year of 1635 at a place called Enneyattehage or Sinnekens. The first of these names was the Iroquois, and the second, the Mohegan name for the place, or, preferably, the Mohegan translation of the Iroquois name. The Dutch received their first knowledge of the Iroquois tribes through the Mohegan. At that date, this was the chief town of the Oneida.

Van Curler's journal identifies the name Sinnekens with this town, which is presumptive evidence that it is the Mohegan rendering of the Iroquois local name Onen'iute', 'it is a standing or projecting stone', employed as an ethnic appellative. The derivation of *Sinnekens* from Mohegan appears to be as follows: *a'sinni*, 'a stone, or rock', *-ika* or *-iga*, denotive of 'place of', or 'abundance of', and the final *-ens* supplied by the Dutch genitive plural ending, the whole Mohegan synthesis meaning 'place of the standing stone'; and with a suitable pronominal affix, like *oor wa-*, which was not recorded by the Dutch writers, the translation signifies, 'they are of the place of the standing store.'

This derivation is confirmed by the Delaware name, W'tassone, for the Oneida, which has a similar derivation. The initial "w" represents approximately an "o" sound, and is the affix of verbs and nouns denotive of the third person; it is evident that assone is only another form of *a'sinni*, 'stone', cited above. Therefore it appears that the Mohegan and Delaware names for the Oneida are cognate in derivation and identical in significance. Heckewelder erroneously translated *W'tassone* as "stone pipe makers". Previous to the defeat and dissipation of the Neutrals in 1651 and the Erie in 1656, the Seneca occupied the territory drained by the Genesee River, eastward to the lands of the Cayuga along the line of the watershed between Seneca and Cayuga lakes.

The political history of the Seneca is largely that of the League of the Iroquois, although owing to petty jealousies among the various tribes, the Seneca, like the others, sometimes acted independently in their dealings with aliens. However, their independent action appears never to have

244

been a serious and deliberate rupture of the bonds uniting them with the federal government of the League, thus vindicating the wisdom and foresight of its founders in permitting every tribe to retain and exercise a large measure of autonomy in the structure of that government. It was sometimes apparently imperative that one of the tribes should enter into a treaty or other compact with its enemies, while the others might still maintain a hostile attitude toward the aliens.

During 1622, the Montagnais, the Algonquin, and the Hurons sought to conclude peace with the Iroquois (Iroquois Mohawk Division?), because "they were weary and fatigued with the wars which they had had for more than 50 years." The armistice was concluded in 1624, but was broken by the continued guerrilla warfare of the Algonquin warriors; for this reason, the Seneca killed in the "village of the Yrocois" those in the embassy, a Frenchman, Pierre Magnan, and three Algonquin ambassadors. This resulted in the renewal of the war.

So in September 1627, the Iroquois, including the Seneca, declared war against the Indians and the French on the Saint Lawrence and its northern effluents by sending various parties of warriors against them. From the *Jesuit Relation* for 1635, it was learned that the Seneca, after defeating the Hurons in the spring of 1634, made peace with them. The Hurons in the following year sent an embassy to Sonontouan, the chief town of the Seneca, to ratify the peace, and while there, learned that the Onondaga, the Oneida, the Cayuga, and the Mohawk wished to become parties to the treaty.

In 1639, the war was renewed by the Hurons. In May they captured 12 prisoners from the Seneca, then regarded as a powerful people. The war continued with varying success. The *Jesuit Relation* for 1641 said that the Seneca were the most feared of the enemies of the Hurons, and that they were only one day's journey from Ongniaahra (Niagara), the most easterly town of the Neutrals.

The *Jesuit Relation* for 1643 said that the Seneca, including the Cayuga, the Oneida, and the Onondaga, equaled, if not exceeded, in number and power, the Hurons, who previously had had this advantage; and that the Mohawk at this time had three villages with 700 or 800 men of arms who possessed 300 arquebuses (matchlock guns fired from a support) that they had obtained from the Dutch and which they used with skill and boldness.

According to the *Jesuit Relation for 1648*, 300 Seneca attacked the village of the Aondironnons, and killed or captured as many of its inhabitants as possible, although these people were a dependency of the

Neutrals who were at peace with the Seneca at this time. This affront nearly precipitated war between the Iroquois and the Neutrals.

Seneca warriors composed the larger part of the Iroquois warriors who in 1648-49, assailed, destroyed, and dispersed the Huron tribes; it was likewise they who, in 1649, sacked the chief towns of the Tionontati, or Tobacco tribe; and the Seneca also took a leading part in the defeat and subjugation of the Neutrals in 1651, and of the Erie in 1656. From the *Journal des PP. Jesuites for 1651-52*, it was learned that in 1651, the Seneca, in waging war against the Neutrals, had been so soundly defeated that their women and children were compelled to flee from Sonontowan, their capital, to seek refuge among the neighboring Cayuga.

In 1652, the Seneca were plotting with the Mohawk to destroy and ruin the French settlements on the Saint Lawrence River. Two years later, the Seneca sent an embassy to the French for the purpose of making peace with them, a movement which was probably brought about by their rupture with the Erie. But the Mohawk, not desiring peace at that time with the French, perhaps on account of their desire to attack the Hurons on Orleans Island, murdered two of the three Seneca ambassadors, the other having remained as a hostage with the French.

This act almost resulted in war between the two hostile tribes. Foreign affairs, however, were in such condition as to prevent hostility. On September 19, 1655, Fathers Chaumonot and Dablon, after pressing invitations to do so, started from Quebec to visit and view the Seneca country, and to establish there a French habitation, and to teach the Seneca their religion. In 1657 the Seneca, in carrying out the policy of the League to adopt conquered tribes upon submission, and the expression of a desire to live under the form of government established by the League, had thus incorporated eleven different tribes. In 1652, Maryland bought from the Minqua, or Susquehanna Indians, i.e. the Conestoga, all their land claims on both sides of Chesapeake Bay up to the mouth of the Susquehanna River.

In 1663, 800 Seneca and Cayuga warriors from the Confederation of the Five Nations were defeated by the Minqua, aided by the Marylanders. The Iroquois did not terminate their hostilities until famine had so reduced the Conestoga that in 1675, when the Marylanders disagreed with them and withdrew their alliance, the Conestoga were completely subdued by the Five Nations. The Five Nations thereafter claimed a right to the Minqua lands up to the head of the Chesapeake Bay.

In 1744, the influence of the French was rapidly gaining ground among the Seneca; meanwhile, the astute and persuasive Colonel Johnson was gradually winning the Mohawk as close allies of the British, while the Onondaga, Cayuga, and Oneida, under strong pressure from Pennsylvania and Virginia, sought to be neutral.

In 1686, 200 Seneca warriors went west against the Miami. The Illinois, in the meantime, had been overcome by the Iroquois in a war lasting about five years. In 1687, the Marquis Denonville assembled a great horde of Indians from the region of the upper lakes and from the Saint Lawrence River: Hurons, Ottawa, Chippewa, Missisauga, Miami, Illinois, Montagnais, Amikwa, and others under Durantaye, DuLuth, and Tonti, to serve as an auxiliary force to about 1,200 French and colonial levies. They were used to attack and destroy the Seneca.

After reaching Irondequoit, the Seneca landing place on Lake Ontario. Denonville built a stockade there in which he left a garrison of 440 men. While advancing to attack the Seneca villages, he was ambushed by 600 to 800 Seneca, who charged and drove back the colonials and their Indian allies, and threw the veteran regiments into disorder. Only by the overwhelming numbers was the traitorous Denonville saved from disastrous defeat. In 1763, at Bloody Run and the Devil's Hole, situated on Niagara River about 4 miles below the falls, the Seneca ambushed a British supply train on the portage road from Fort Schlosser to Fort Niagara, with only three escaping from a force of nearly 100. At a short distance, the same Seneca ambushed a British force of two companies hastening to aid the supply train.

Only eight escaped massacre. These bloody and harsh measures were the direct result of the general unrest of the Six Nations and the western tribes, arising from the manner of the British, after the surrender of Canada by the French on September 8, 1760. They contrasted the sympathetic and bountiful paternalism of the French regime with the neglect that characterized British rule.

On July 29, 1761, Sir William Johnson wrote to General Amherst, "I see plainly that there appears to be an universal jealousy amongst every nation, on account of the hasty steps they look upon we are taking towards getting possession of this country, which measures, I am certain, will never subside whilst we encroach within the limits which you may recollect have been put under the protection of the King in the year 1726, and confirmed to them by him and his successors ever since and by the orders sent to the governors not to allow anyone of his subjects settling thereon ... but that it should remain their absolute property."

However, by the beginning of the American Revolution, so well had the British agents reconciled them to the rule of Great Britain that the

247

Seneca, together with a large majority of the people of the Six Nations, notwithstanding their pledges to the contrary, reluctantly espoused the cause of the British against the colonies. Consequently, they suffered retribution for their folly when General Sullivan, in 1779, after defeating their warriors, burned their villages and destroyed their crops. There is no historical evidence that the Seneca on the Ohio and the southern shore of Lake Erie in the eighteenth and nineteenth centuries were chiefly an outlying colony from the Iroquois tribe of that name living in New York.

In fact, in historical times their affiliations were never with the Iroquois, but rather with tribes usually hostile to them. This is explained by the presumption that they were rather some remnant of a subjugated tribe dependent on the Seneca and living on lands under the jurisdiction of their conquerors. It is a fair inference that they were largely subjugated Erie and Conestoga. Regarding the identity of these Indians, the following citation from Howe is pertinent: "The so-called Senecas of Sandusky owned and occupied 40,000 acres of choice land on the east side of Sandusky River, being mostly in this (Seneca) and partly in Sandusky County.

Thirty thousand acres of this land was granted to them on the 29th of September, 1817, at the treaty ... of Maumee Rapids ... The remaining 10,000 acres, lying south of the other, was granted by the treaty at Saint Mary's ... seventeenth of September, 1818." By the treaty concluded at Washington on February 28, 1831, these Seneca ceded their lands in Ohio to the United States and agreed to emigrate southwest of Missouri, on Neosho River. The same writer stated that in 1831 "their principal chiefs were Coonstick, Small Cloud Spicer, Seneca Steel, Hard Hickory, Tall Chief, and Good Hunter, the last two of whom were their principal orators.

The old chief Good Hunter told Henry C. Brish, their subagent, that this band (which numbered 390 in 1908) were in fact the remnant of Logan's tribe, and says Mister Brish in a communication: "I cannot to this day surmise why they were called Senecas.

"I never found a Seneca among them. They were Cayugas, who were Mingoes, among whom were a few Oneidas, Mohawks, Onondagas, Tuscarawas, and Wyandots." The majority of them were certainly not Cayuga, as Logan was Conestoga or Mingo on his maternal side. In 1677, the Seneca had but four villages, but a century later, the number had increased to about 30.

The following are the better known Seneca towns, which were not at all contemporary: Canadasaga, Canandaigua, Caneadea, Catherine's Town,

Cattaraugus, Chemung, New Chemung, Old Chemung, Chenango, Cheronderoga, Chinoshageh, Condawhaw, Connewango, Dayoitgao Deonundagae, Deyodeshot, Deyohnegano, Deyonongdadagana, Dyosyowan, Gaandowanang, Gadaho, Gahato, Ganos, Gaousge, Geneseo, Kannassarago, Newtown, Onnahee, Onondarka, Sheshequin, Sonojowauga, Tonawanda, Tsonontowanen, Yoroonwago.

The earliest estimates of the numbers of the Seneca, in 1660 and 1677, gave them about 5,000 members. Later estimates of the population: 3,500 (1721); 1,750 (1736); 5,000 (1765); 3,250 (1778); 2,000 (1783); 3,000 (1783), and 1,780 (1796). In 1825, those in New York were reported at 2,325. In 1850, according to Morgan, those in New York numbered 2,712, while about 210 more were on Grand River Reservation in Canada. In 1909, those in New York numbered 2,749 on the three reservations, which, with those on Grand River, Ontario, would have given them a total of 2,962.

Today, the Seneca live in four main political and community groups in the United States and Canada. They include the Seneca Nation of Indians, located on three reservations in Cattaraugus and Allegany counties in New York; the Tonawanda Band of Seneca near Akron, New York; the Six Nations Reserve near Brantford, Ontario; and the Seneca-Cayuga Tribe, located in northeastern Oklahoma.

During the twentieth century, the Seneca Nation of Indians and the Tonawanda Band of Senecas fought against government intrusions. Both tribal governments rejected the Indian Reorganization Act of 1934. After Congress unilaterally transferred criminal and civil jurisdiction over American Indian affairs to New York State, the two tribes contested, but lost their battles with the courts.

The Seneca Nation faced a major crisis when the federal government constructed the Kinzua Dam in the 1960s. The dam flooded more than 9,000 acres of the Cornplanter tract and Allegany Reservation, and traditional Seneca life was disrupted. More recently, the Seneca Nation has attempted to settle the problem of 3,000 ninety-nine year leases on their lands in and around Salamanca, New York.

In 1990, they received a $35 million settlement award from the federal government for its failure to protect Indian rights in the matter. In 1992, they received $25 million from New York State for further compensations. The leases have been renewed under new terms with the city of Salamanca. Both main groups have sought economic self-determination in their opposition to the states' taxing of reservation sales of petroleum and tobacco to non-Indians. Many Seneca have jobs in Rochester and

Buffalo, and the Seneca Nations have convenience stores in several locations. Bingo operations are held on the Allegany and Cattaraugus reservations.

Tribal government is also a major employer, and casino gambling has been proposed, although opposing factions within the tribe have not reached any agreement. Seneca arts and crafts have been stimulated by such projects as the WPA Indian Arts Project and the World's Fair of 1939. The Tonawanda Indian Community House, another WPA project, was built by Indian labor in the 1930s.

The community house was the first of its kind in New York, and still aids the tribe's social service, education, and health needs. Recent achievements of the Senecas include the Seneca Nation health department, created to deliver services to the Cattaraugus and Allegany reservations and the urban Seneca population; direct clinic services are a function of the department.

The Seneca maintain their matrilineal kinship system. Clan affiliation and traditional religion also continue to be important to the group. Today, there are 6,241 members of the Seneca Nation; 600 members of the Cornplanter Grant; 1,050 members of the Tonawanda Band; 539 Canadian Senecas, and 2,460 members of the Seneca-Cayuga. (See FIVE NATIONS IROQUOIS, and IROQUOIAN FAMILY)

SHIKELLAMY

Shikellamy (Oneida, ? - 1748), an Oneida chieftain, was the exponent of the colonial policy of the great federal Iroquois council at Onondaga, and was sent by it to the forks of the Susquehanna in 1728 to conserve the interests of the Six Nations and to keep watch over the Shawnee and Delaware Indians. A man of great dignity, he always showed marked kindness, especially to the missionaries. In the execution of his trust, Shikellamy conducted many important embassies between the government of Pennsylvania and the Iroquois council at Onondaga, and he also attended many if not most of the councils held at Philadelphia, Conestoga, and elsewhere.

His importance is evident in that the valley of the Susquehanna, after the Conestoga were subjugated in 1676 by the Iroquois, was assigned by the Five Nations of Iroquois as a hunting ground to the Shawnee, Delawares, Conoy, Nanticoke, Munsee, Tutelo, Saponi, and Conestoga tribes. When the Mohawk sold the Wyoming region in Pennsylvania to the Susquehanna Land Company, although his tribe had never aided in conquests in this valley, the council at Onondaga began to realize that this section, with its valuable land and many dependent tribes, was worthy of careful attention; hence these tribes were made to understand that in the future they must transact all business with the proprietary government solely through their deputy.

With his residence fixed at Shamokin (now Sunbury), Pennsylvania, Shikellamy was promoted in 1745 to full Vice-General over the tributary tribes in the Susquehanna valley, and intricate and important interests committed to him received the care of an astute statesman and diplomat. The effects of the liquor traffic on the Indians led to prohibitory decrees on the part of the government of Pennsylvania, and later, evidently through the influence of traders, when these prohibitive measures became lax, Shikellamy in 1731 delivered an ultimatum to the Pennsylvania government that unless the liquor trade was better regulated, friendly relations between the proprietary government and the Six Nations would cease.

As the difficulties arising from the sale of liquor had forced a large number of Shawnee to migrate from the Susquehanna to the Ohio River in 1730, and as French emissaries were taking advantage of this condition to alienate the Shawnee from the English interest, a governor decided in 1731 to send Shikellamy, "a trusty, good man, and a great lover of the English," to Onondaga to invite the Six Nations to Philadelphia. In 1736 Shikellamy's influence was enlisted to bring about a conference at which the entire confederation of the Six Nations would be represented, and in less than two months' time Conrad Weiser informed the Governor of Pennsylvania that more than a hundred chiefs of the Iroquois, with their retinues, were on their way to Philadelphia.

By this treaty of 1736 the Six Nations deeded all their Susquehanna lands south and east of the Blue Mountains. Some weeks later, when nearly all the leading Indians had departed, another deed was prepared and signed by the remaining Indians, which purported to include the lands ostensibly claimed by the Six Nations within the drainage of Delaware River south of the Blue Mountains, a treaty that, "established a precedent for an Iroquois claim to lands owned by the Delaware Indians," a claim that had never been advanced before. Weiser helped Shikellamy sow the seed that drenched Pennsylvania in blood from 1755 to 1764.

In a war with the Delaware, Weiser had many good reasons for regarding Shikellamy as the key to the secret policies of the council of the Iroquois at Onondaga. In 1745 Shikellamy was requested by Governor Thomas to visit the Six Nations and gain peace with the Catawba. The acquisition of firearms became a necessity to the Indian hunters and warriors. Shikellamy persuaded the colonial government to establish a forge at Shamokin.

This was granted on condition that the Indians would permit the Moravians to begin a mission at the place, which the missionaries regarded as the greatest stronghold of paganism. To this proposal Shikellamy readily consented, and in April 1747, a blacksmith shop and a mission house were erected there.

A year later, Zeisberger, who had become proficient in the Mohawk tongue, became an assistant missionary at Shamokin, and while there began the preparation of an Onondaga dictionary under the interested instruction of Shikellamy.

During 1748 Shikellamy received from Count Zinzendorf a silver knife, fork, and spoon, and an ivory drinking cup richly mounted in silver, accompanied with a message entreating him to hold fast to the gospel which he had heard from the count's own lips. This resulted in the conversion of Shilkellamy at Bethlehem shortly afterward. The Moravians did not baptize him, however, because he had been baptized many years before by a Jesuit priest in Canada.

On his way to Shamokin he fell ill at Tulpehocking. Zeisberger, who had returned to his post, ministered to the stricken chieftain until his death. The colonial government sent a message of condolence, and requested the eldest son of Shikellamy, John or Thachnechtoris (Tagheghdoarus) to serve as the Iroquois deputy governor until the council at Onondaga could make a permanent appointment.

SHINNECOCK

The Shinnecock were an Algonquian tribe or band on Long Island, New York, formerly occupying the southern coast from Shinnecock Bay to Montauk Point. Many of them joined the Brotherton Indians in New York. About 150 still remained on a reservation of 750 acres, three miles west of Southampton, having intermarried with blacks until their aboriginal character was almost obliterated. Nowedonah, brother of the noted Wyandanch, was once their chief, and upon his death, his sister, wife of Cockenoe, became his successor.

In December of 1876, 28 Shinnecock men died in an attempt to save a ship stranded off Easthampton, after which a number of members, especially the younger people, left the reservation and became scattered. They had a Presbyterian and an Adventist church. The men gained a livelihood by employment as farmhands, baymen, berry pickers, and so forth, and the women as laundresses.

A few families made and sold baskets and a sort of brush made of oak splints. There was almost no agriculture. In recent times, the population of the mixed-blood tribal members numbered approximately 200.

By the beginning of the twentieth century, almost all of the Shinnecock culture, including their Algonquian language, had disappeared. The remaining members honored their heritage by staging an annual Labor Day Powwow. Today, there are about 400 descendants of the tribe and those of other Long Island Tribes, including the Montauk, Corchaug, Shinnecock, Manhasset, Rockaway and Patchogue.

They live in small area communities, including the Shinnecock Indian Reservation, located on the south fork of eastern Long Island in the town of Southampton in New York, plus on the Poosepatuck Reservation and in the Montauk Indian Village. Many return regularly to participate in tribal events and family gatherings. The group maintains houses, a cemetery, powwow grounds, tribal programs, beaches, and offices on land surrounded by the Shinnecock Bay.

SIWANOY

From having lived on the seacoast, the tribal name Siwanoy may be a corruption of "*Siwanak*", "salt people", a dialectic form of "*Suwanak*", a name given by the Delawares to the English, according to Gerard. The Siwanoy were a principal tribe of the Mahican Wappinger confederacy, formerly living along the north shore of Long Island Sound, from New York to Norwalk, Connecticut, and inland as far as White Plains.

They were one of the seven tribes of the seacoast and had a number of villages, the principal one in the 1600s being Poningo. *Siwanoy* has traditionally been used to refer to a number of poorly known groups that speak Munsee-Delaware. Johan de Laet specifically located them in 1625 as dwelling "along the coast for 8 leagues (24 miles) to the neighborhood of Hellegate" at the confluence of the East and Harlem rivers by Bronx, Manhattan, and Queens Counties, New York City. Last mentioned as the Siwanoys in the 1656 van der Donck map, these groups thickly inhabited the coastline and adjacent interior from Bronx County, New York to Norwalk, Connecticut.

The first Dutch voyages of exploration between 1614 and 1616 discovered a substantial number of populous settlements located at the mouths of the many rivers that flowed into Long Island Sound. These were later known as Snakapins, on Clasons Point, Bronx County, Pon-

253

ingo, at Rye, New York, the settlements of Assamuck, Patomuck, Petuc-
quapoch, Sachus, Shippan, and Toquams between Greenwich and
Stamford, Connecticut, and the towns of Makentouh and Norwalk at
Norwalk, Connecticut. Two other groups, the Pachami and the Tankiteke
lived in an as yet undetermined area in the interior between Long Island
Sound and the Hudson River beyond the headwaters of the coastal rivers.

All of the above mentioned groups had intimate connections with the
Wiechquaesgeck, Kichtawanck, and other groups along the eastern banks
of the lower Hudson River. The Long Island Sound peoples were blessed
with a moderate climate and ample rainfall. Their settlements were
shielded by the mass of Long Island from the violent storms blowing in
from the Atlantic Ocean. Major towns were on lagoons and islands at the
mouths of estuaries. Each group controlled a river drainage, with settlements at the fall-line between fresh and salt water, and along the upper
reaches of the river valley.

Their settlement pattern followed the flow of the seasons. During
winter they lived in scattered hunting camps in the sheltered interior valleys. In springtime they gathered at the fall line to harvest runs of
salmon, herring, shad, and other anadromous fish that ascended the rivers
in the millions. As the weather moderated, they moved to large coastal
villages for rich saltwater fish and shellfish. The well-drained sandy soils
of the coast further supported fine crops of corn, beans, squash, melons,
tobacco, and other cultivated plants. Huge flocks of passenger pigeons,
ducks, geese, and other migratory birds darkened the late spring and early
autumn skies.

The peoples of the Long Island Sound coast lived in large villages
made up of two or more longhouses or roundhouses. Constructed of bent
timbers and covered with a combination of grass mats and sheets of bark,
each structure housed a matriclan consisting of a number of related
women, their children, and their husbands. These clustered together in
fortified settlements surrounded by log stockades in the interior swamps
and remote valleys during times of war. The fall-line fishing villages
also served as festival sites for the observance of the many major religious ceremonies. The Siwanoy were among the first Native groups in
New Netherland to experience direct and overwhelming European contact.

The Dutch took an early interest in their lands, and a number of land
sales were finalized during the 1630s. The Siwanoy fell victim to the
massive measles, plague, and smallpox epidemics that swept the coastal
villages during the first half of the seventeenth century. Uncounted thou-

sands of coastal Long Island people were killed by these diseases. Put under tribute by the powerful Pequot group of eastern Connecticut, they were compelled to give a sizable portion of their yearly produce to them.

The Siwanoy were further victimized by the unfair trading practices of the Dutch. Fascinated by alcohol, they were continually made drunk by Dutch traders and defrauded of their trade goods and possessions. Tensions were reaching the breaking point when the Dutch called upon the Long Island Sound people to join them in their war against the Raritan and their allies in central New Jersey in 1641.

Siwanoy war parties were soon at the gates of Fort Amsterdam on the southern tip of Manhattan Island with trophies from slain Raritan warriors. The tables were turned when a number of Siwanoy were counted among the lower Hudson River people killed by the Dutch in their surprise attack upon the refugee camps near Fort Amsterdam and at Pavonia, now Jersey City, New Jersey during the night of February 25, 1643. The Siwanoy did not immediately retaliate, but chose to await a more favorable opportunity to strike back. Their warriors finally fell upon the English and Huguenot settlements in their territories during the autumn of 1643.

Among their victims was Anne Hutchinson, the Puritan freethinker who squatted upon unpurchased Siwanoy land in Pelham, New York after she was banished from the Massachusetts Bay Colony. The Long Island Sound peoples were swiftly subjected to several Dutch assaults. A mixed force of Dutch and English under the command of John Underhill, who had participated in the 1637 destruction of the Pequot, located a large village of Wiechquaesgeck, Siwanoy, and Wappingers deep in the interior of Westchester County in today's Ward Pound Ridge Reservation during the winter of 1643-1644.

They destroyed the village and killed some five hundred Indians. This catastrophe effectively removed the Long Island Sound peoples from the struggle, and the Mahican chief Aepjen signed the treaty ending the conflict, known as the Governor Keift War, on their behalf on August 30, 1645. The Dutch increased the tempo of their land seizing along the north shore of Long Island Sound following the end of the war. Increased friction led the natives to join allies against the Dutch during the Peach War, 1655-1657. Participation in this desultory struggle did not, however, discourage Dutch efforts to possess the Long Island Sound coast, and most of it was in Dutch hands when the English conquered New Netherland on September 6, 1664.

The English corrected many of the abuses of the Dutch regime and permitted the natives to live at their old settlements along the shore during the warmer months. The land sales had forced those Native people who elected to remain in their homeland deep into the highland interior river valleys. Many clustered in small settlements under the sachem Katonah in the uplands above Bedford, New York around the modern villages of Cross River and Katonah. Those living further east congregated in settlements along the Byram and Rippowam rivers in Fairfield County, Connecticut. These became collectively known as the Stamford Indians.

The English attempted to intern both groups at the Hellgate during the King Phillip's War, 1675 to 1676. The natives convinced the English of their peaceful intentions, and were permitted to remain on their lands after surrendering their firearms until the war ended. A substantial number of Long Island Sound people moved northward among the Mahican groups of the upper Housatonic and northern Hudson River valleys following the death of Katonah and a number of influential Stamford Indian chiefs during the opening decades of the eighteenth century.

Most, however, remained in a number of tiny family hamlets scattered through the interior of Fairfield County. These people made their living by traveling widely through the region laboring on white-owned farms, curing the sick, dispensing herbs, and selling homemade baskets, brooms, and other handicrafts. In 1761, it was reported that Kockopotananh, "sachem of the Derby, Milford, and Stratford Indians" had sixty men under him when he died in 1731. Large numbers of his followers and other Long Island Sound people became involved in the first mission settlement on the upper Housatonic. Established by the Reverend John Sergeant in 1735, it became known as Stockbridge.

In time, Stockbridge became the major mission community in the region and attracted large numbers of upper Hudson River Delawareans, Mahicans, and several Connecticut groups. Other Long Island Sound people joined the Moravian mission villages at Shekomeko and Pleasant Plains, Dutchess County, New York, following their establishment in 1744. Most moved with the settlements to the Bethlehem, Pennsylvania area following their eviction by white authorities in 1746. At least sixty-one Native people were reported living in Fairfield County on January 1, 1774. Many of these joined with the Stockbridge on the Continental side against the English in the War of Independence.

These volunteers suffered dreadful losses during the conflict, and many families were forced to join their brethren at Schagiticoke, New York and in villages in Pennsylvania and Ohio. Most of the Stockbridge moved among the Oneida in New York following the end of the war. Their descendants today reside on the Stockbridge-Munsee Reservation in Wisconsin. A small number of their relatives refused to leave the valleys of their ancestors.

The state of Connecticut created a small reservation for them at Schagiticoke, near Kent, along the upper reaches of the Housatonic River. Many Native people moved to the reserve, but most also maintained dwellings off the reservation. The land remains today, but the people continue to live off the reservation.

SKENANDOA

Skenandoa (Oneida, 1704 - March 11, 1816), also known as Schenandoah, Shenondoa, Scanondo, and Skennondon, was a principal Oneida chief in New York, and a friend of white colonists. During the American Revolution he championed Iroquois confederacy neutrality but often gave assistance to the United States. He aided the Boston colonists at the outbreak of hostilities, helped prevent invasions from Canada, and the destruction of the German Flats, New York settlements, and provided scouts and spies to the colonists.

In May 1775, he led 11 other Oneida chiefs in officially declaring neutrality. In September 1776 he refused to participate in the Niagara council ending Iroquois neutrality, and was joined by a number of Tuscarora chiefs. The Oneida and Tuscarora were considered "dissenting bodies" by the other Iroquois nations, and toward the end of the Revolution Skenandoa had to take refuge at Schenectady from the British and pro-British Indians who, under General John Burgoyne, attacked the main Oneida village. In 1794 Skenandoa pledged continued neutrality during the Iroquois uprisings. He protested but permitted recruiting of Indian volunteers during the War of 1812.

To him the conflict was the confrontation between Tecumseh's teachings and Christianity. When first introduced to the Iroquois nations, alcohol was taken usually only during celebrations, but like many chiefs of his day Skenandoa became a chronic alcoholic. While in Albany in 1775 he became so drunk that his badge of chieftainship was stolen from him. He pledged never to drink again, and through the Reverend Samuel Kirkland, Missionary to the Oneida, became a devout Christian. After the Revolution the economic and social situation of the Indians declined rapidly. By 1812 Skenandoa resumed drinking. He died at Oneida Castle, New York.

257

SQUANDO

Squando (Abnaki; seventeenth century), was an Abnaki sachem of the Sokoki people of the Saco River region. Known as the sagamore of Saco. Squando was described by Increase Mather as a "strange, enthusiastical sagamore."

Squando claimed to have had visions in which God appeared and told him to observe the sabbath, to avoid liquor, to pray, and to listen to the word preached. All this Squando did for several years. A vision also told him that God had left the English people to be destroyed by the Indians.

It is said that about 1675 some drunken English sailors, either to achieve mischief or to test a report that Indian children could swim instinctively from birth, overturned a canoe containing Squando's wife and child. Although the mother managed to swim with the child to safety, the child died a few days later. Anger over this incident (and probably also over the increasing white encroachment on Indian lands and the kidnapping sale of Indians into slavery) led Squando to join in the war against the English in 1675.

Squando took part in the burning of the English settlement at Saco. He is reported to have released one young girl taken captive after her family was killed, an act that caused chronicler William Hubbard to describe Squando as "a strange mixture of mercy and cruelty." His abilities in war gained him the characterization of "diabolical miscreant," yet Hubbard also reports that the sachem opposed cruelty and murder against those opponents who were willing to yield to him.

In 1676 Squando was among the signers of a peace treaty with the English at Cochecho.

SQUAWKEAG

Squawkeag, as interpreted by Hewlitt, means "red earth or land." The Squawkeag tribe or band once occupied considerable territory on both banks of the Connecticut River, in Franklin County Massachusetts,

Their principal village, of the same name, was near present Northfield. Some of the group was still at that site as late as 1688. They may have associated with the Pennacook, and spoke an Algonquian language. Their descendants probably now live with the Saint Francis Abnaki in Quebec, Canada.

J. W. STEVENS

Jown W. Stevens (Passamaquoddy; August 11, 1933, -) became chief of the Passamaquoddy Indians of Indian Township, Maine, in 1955. Born in Washington County, Maine, Stevens served with the United States Marines during the Korean War. As tribal chief he has been active in the struggle of Indians against discrimination and poverty.

SUSQUEHANNOCK

Now extinct, The Susquehannock were a group of one of the least-known tribes of the northeast. They appeared along the Susquehanna watershed at the beginning of white colonization, fought bitterly with both the Delaware and the Five Nations, and then faded into obscurity. Although of Iroquoian stock, they reorganized no allegiance to the Massomacks, the Iroquois name for the confederacy. Several explanations are suggested for the derivation of their name, one being that it comes from the Algonquian *Sas-k-we-an-og,* meaning "The river that rubs upon the shore."

All the Susquehanna Iroquoian groups, however, were called the Carantouan by the Five Nations. The most important were the Susquehannock on the lower reaches of the river. Those along the upper river were known as the Andaste. They were first visited by a white man in 1616, when Etienne Brule, Champlain's interpreter, came down from Canada to enlist their aid in a French attack against the Five Nations stronghold in New York. It was this alliance of the Carantouan and Huron with the French that later led to the destruction of these tribes by the Iroquois. The early Swedes in Pennsylvania called the Susquehannock "Black Minquas."

This term probably came from the Lenape, who used the Algonquian mingee or mengwe ("treacherous") as a classification for all detached bands of Iroquois. Corrupted to "Mingo," the term was widely and loosely applied by Indian and white settlers alike from early Colonial days until long after the American Revolution. In some parts of the State, entire tribes or their remnants became known as Mingo, while further confusion in classification of tribal units resulted from amalgamation, adoption, and intermarriage. The Susquehannock were tall, aggressive, and keen of mind. They had dispersed the Raritan and Piscataway in the Chesapeake Bay area and were in control of that territory when Captain John Smith encountered them in 1608. Excavations of their early burials indicate that some used platforms on which to place their dead until the flesh disappeared.

Skeletal remains were then buried at a depth of three feet, with the skull surmounting the pile. The power of the Susquehannock in Maryland and Virginia was broken by conflict with the whites early in the seventeenth

259

century. In Pennsylvania, however, their war activities were centered chiefly against the Five Nations, for whom they had an undying hatred. The seat of their power in Pennsylvania was a stronghold near what is now Washington Borough.

In 1663 they repulsed an attack of Seneca and Cayuga warriors, and sent the defeated Iroquois back to their longhouse bearing messages of derision. By 1667, however, the Susquehannock had begun to feel the effects of continued warfare and sickness, and in 1670 they sent emissaries to the Five Nations in an attempt to make peace.

The enraged Iroquois refused to bury the tomahawk, and hostilities continued until most of the Susquehannock were captured or slain. The main body of the survivors fled to Maryland. Others found refuge along the Susquehanna's west branch, and those remaining were absorbed by tribes of the confederacy. Many years later a group of exiled Susquehannock returned to their former home in Lancaster County and became known as the Conestoga.

Crowded on all sides by white settlers and by tribes they once held in contempt, the Conestoga diminished until in 1763, only a few remained. In that year, a band of white rioters, known as the "Paxton Boys," inflamed by accounts of Indian depredations along the frontiers, broke into the Lancaster jail where the Conestoga had taken refuge, and murdered all of them. With this massacre, the last known group of Susquehannock passed out of existence. (See CONESTOGA)

TAMAQUE

Tamaque (Delaware, 1725 - 1770), also known as The Beaver, and King Beaver, was alternately friendly and hostile to eighteenth century English settlers along the frontier. Brother of Shingas, a merciless and treacherous enemy of colonial pioneers in western Pennsylvania, Tamaque, like his brother, became an important Delaware chieftain.

Moving to Fort Ohio following the British occupation of Fort Duquesne, he settled near the junction of the Tuscarawas and Big Sandy at a village called The Beaver's Town. There he carried on friendly relations with the English until 1755, but following British General Braddock's defeat at the hands of a combined French and Indian force, Tamaque switched his alliance from the English to the French. By 1758 the chief was expressing his desire to resume good relations with the English, and he attended a council at Fort Pitt in 1759 and another in 1760 to further this desire.

In 1762 Tamaque promised the colonial governor of Pennsylvania that the Delaware under his command would return all captured whites held as prisoners, but then he joined enthusiastically in Pontiac's conspiracy, leading several Indian raids against frontier settlements. When Pontiac's plans to drive the English out of the Great Lakes region met defeat, however, the fickle Tamaque again agreed to keep the peace. His years of war-making done, the Delaware chief permitted himself to be converted to Christianity by Moravian missionaries and spent his final years as a zealous advocate of his new faith.

TARHE (CRANE)

Tarhe (Wyandotte, 1742 – November 1818), also known as The Crane, born in Detroit, was a Wyandotte chief and head priest of the Porcupine branch, and was a strong opponent of Tecumseh. In 1774 he fought under the Shawnee chief Cornstalk at the battle of Point Pleasant in present West Virginia. He served under Blue Jacket at the Battle of Fallen Timbers, Ohio, August 2O, 1794, and, although seriously wounded, was the only chief to escape.

In 1795, resisting tribal opposition, he was a leader in the negotiations that resulted in the August 3, Treaty of Greenville, Ohio signed by 12 Indian tribes, opening the territory to white settlers. As a result of this treaty Tarhe became a United States pensioner. Tarhe was a leader in the opposition to Tecumseh's plans.

Although he too was aware of the continued encroachments by whites upon Indian lands, he refused to join Tecumseh. Acting for the United States government, Tarhe called a meeting of Northwest Indian chiefs loyal to the United States at Brownstown on the Detroit River to plead for their continued neutrality.

At the same time Tecumseh, in response to Tarhe's actions called a meeting of anti-United States chiefs at Amhertsburg, Ontario, Canada, across the Detroit River from Brownstown, Although Tecumseh soon invaded the Brownstown encampment and pressed many of the chiefs into joining him, Tarhe fled upon learning of the imminent attack and avoided facing Tecumseh.

During the War of 1812 Tarhe led his warriors in the service of General William H. Harrison in his campaign into Canada, and helped defeat Tecumseh at the October 5, 1813 Battle of the Thames River. After the War, Tarhe returned to central Ohio where he became well known to white settlers. His friendship was held highly by everyone, especially Harrison. Tarhe died at Cranetown near Upper Sandusky, Ohio.

TEEDYUSCUNG

Teedyuscung (Delaware, 1700 - 1763), was a leader in colonial Pennsylvania during the period of the land cessions and frontier wars that forced these Indians westward toward the Ohio country. He advocated resistance to white pressures and became a notable Delaware spokesman at numerous treaties and councils. Teedyuscung was born about 1700 in New Jersey, near present-day Trenton, and lived in the remnant Indian community until about 1830, when the family moved across the Delaware River and settled along the Lehigh Valley.

The Indians were ousted from there in 1737 by the so-called Walking Purchase. The purchase allegedly covering these lands actually had been made years before but it was not until 1737 that, according to the provisions of a later agreement, two well-supplied white men walked off its extent in a day-and-a-half. The Indians protested, charging that the intent had been to alienate far less land, and that the government of Pennsylvania was perpetrating a fraud. Resentment over the Walking Purchase was in large part responsible for Teedyuscung's and other Delaware Indian's demands at later treaties and eventually for the defection of Teedyuscung's band to the French side during the French and Indian War.

At first, however, Teedyuscung attempted to remain on the lands. However, white settlers began to enter the Forks of the Delaware, and the Iroquois, who claimed an authority of sorts over the Delaware, in 1742 ordered the Delaware of the Forks to vacate their lands, and in 1749 the Iroquois purported to sell these and other lands to the Penns. Many of the Indians now left for new homes on the Susquehanna. Teedyuscung remained, converting to the Moravian faith and living in the communal settlement of some 500 Christian Indians at Gnadenhutten, north of the Moravian headquarters at Bethlehem.

He remained there until 1754, when along with most of the others, under Iroquois insistence, he moved to Wyoming, on the Susquehanna (where Wilkes-Barre now stands). His political career dates from that move. Before 1754 and his death in 1763, Teedyuscung was active as a council speaker for the Delaware Indians of Wyoming. During the hostilities on Pennsylvania's frontier, he was a warrior and leader of the Wyoming Delaware.

The faction used the military crisis to extort concessions from the province of Pennsylvania, threatening (and occasionally carrying out) reprisal raids if redress was not offered for land grievances and if Penn-

262

sylvania did not cease to endorse, or even promote, the Iroquois claims to sovereignty over the Delaware.

At a series of council meetings with whites from 1756 to 1760, he articulated the Delaware position in eloquent speeches. These speeches were set down, in English translation, and published in the minutes of Indian treaties printed by Benjamin Franklin.

He thus came to be widely known as a persuasive Indian spokesman. Teedyuscung was given political support by the Quakers of the province who wanted to embarrass their opponents, the Proprietary party, by publicizing the Delaware charges of misconduct in Indian affairs.

This did not endear him to the government of Pennsylvania, or to Sir William Johnson, the Crown's Superintendent of Indian Affairs, and they did much to discredit him. He died at Wyoming, however, resisting an invasion by Connecticut settlers.

He was allegedly murdered. Teedyuscung's diplomacy was unable to prevent the rapid erosion of the Indian position in the east. Whether or not his specific charges were valid, he was a widely cited symbol of Indian resistance to white rapacity, because of the publicity given to his cause by the Quakers and the printing of the Indian treaties.

He, and other Indian spokesmen like him, was able to insist on a policy less destructive to Indians than that desired by many frontiersmen and land speculators.

TIONONTATI

In the second half of the seventeenth century the Wyandottes were often known to both the French and the English by variants of the name of their largest constituent group, the Tionontati (Petun). The English continued this usage into the mid-1700s. Examples from French sources are; Tionnontatehronnons, 1654; Tionnontate, 1672; Tionontates, 1682; Donondates; and Tynondady, 1757. Equivalent to this is the Onondaga name *tyonontate-ka*, according to Hewitt.

UNCAS

Uncas (Mohegan; ? - 1682), also known as Fox, (literally the circler), was chief of the Mohegan, played an important role in the Indian history of colonial southern New England. As a subchief under Pequot Chief Sachem Sassacus, Uncas rebelled and with a band of followers settled on the west bank of the Pequot (Thames) River about three miles south of the present Norwich, Connecticut.

This group known as Mohegan is mentioned as a tribe in early records beginning about 1636. Uncas and the Mohegan supported the English in the Pequot War (1636), King Philip's war (1675), and through the Revolutionary Period. Uncas was noted for his strategy and cunning in warfare; for being a faithful friend; and for being relentless toward his enemies.

Uncas, wiley strategist that he was, saw that it was to his advantage to support the English and adopt their ways as a means of survival for his people. For this stand he was condemned by many and lauded by others. Uncas was the older of two sons of Oweneco and Meeken-ump. His brother was named Waweequa. References to the early life of Uncas are lacking. As for tribal affiliations it appears that the Mohegan (Mohican Wolf People) migrated from the upper Hudson River valley in the early 1600s to the present Connecticut and parts of eastern New York and western Massachusetts.

Local tribes called them pequataug meaning destroyers or invaders hence the name Mohegan Pequot. The Moihican (Mohegan, Mahikan) were related to the northern or "Wolf" division of the Delawares or Lenni-Lenape. According to Delaware tradition, "Some of the Wolves went east," and the Connecticut Mohegan always maintained that, "Our people came from the northwest", indicating the area in eastern New York state and northwestern Massachusetts.

The group finally settled near present New London and Groton, Connecticut, and were generally known as Pequot. In 1626, Uncas married the daughter of Sassacus, Grand Sachem of the Pequot. Claiming to be a distant cousin of Sassacus this union made him more closely connected with the Royal Family, and he felt that he should be granted more authority within the band of followers withdrawing and settling on the west bank of the Pequot (Thames) River. This group, known as Mohegan, is mentioned in Colonial records beginning about 1636. Uncas and the Mohegan were friendly toward the Colonists, much to the displeasure of the Pequot and other local Indian leaders in the area. Uncas realized that having a small band of less than a hundred, they would soon be dominated by white men, as would be the other small tribes in the area, so it was to his advantage to adopt the ways of the colonists.

Trouble was brewing within the Pequot and English villages and following hostilities against the English, the Pequot became involved in a war with the colonists in 1637. Uncas assisted Roger Williams in securing the aid of Indian allies in joining an attack on the Pequot Fort at Mystic, which annihilated most within the fort. An estimated 700 men, women and children were believed to have been within the village and only a few escaped. English losses were light, with only some twenty wounded and two killed. Survivors sought refuge with other Indians. Sassacus fled to the Mohawk where he was slain.

With the death of Sassacus, the Pequot no longer had an existing power in Indian affairs. Uncas was in control of the remaining Indian tribes throughout Connecticut. There was more trouble ahead for Uncas and the Mohegan when word was received that Chief Miantonomoh and the Narragansett chiefs had existed for a long time and in 1643 the battle was on at the Great Plain in Mohegan territory outside present Norwich, Connecticut.

Mohegan scouts informed Uncas of the approaching Narragansett chief and his warriors. Estimates vary, but It seems likely that the Narragansett numbered around 500 and the Mohegan not more that 200. Uncas sent one of his men to ask Miantonomoh if he would agree to the two chiefs meeting man to man to settle their grievances. The offer was rejected. Miantonomoh said, "My men came to fight and fight they will."

Uncas had told the Mohegan men that if his offer was rejected that he would fall on his face as a signal for them to charge the enemy. Upon receiving the negative reply, Uncas fell on his face and the Mohegan put the Narragansett to flight, many losing their lives as they attempted to leap over the falls of the Yantic River. Miantonomoh was pursued by a Mohegan, Tantaquiesen (Tantaquidgeon) an aide to Uncas who was "the first to lay hands on the enemy chief.

"This enabled Chief Uncas to have the honor of capturing Miantonomoh. Traditionally "A Chief must take a Chief" thus Tantaquidgeon being of lesser rank could not have the honor. This has been referred to as the most purely Indian battle in the annals of New England."

Only bows and arrows and clubs were used and the English were not directly concerned. Miantonomoh was taken to the Fort of Uncas and a meeting was arranged with the Commissioners at Hartford, Connecticut, to discuss his fate. Uncas was told that he could use his judgment in disposing of his captive but it must be carried out beyond the boundaries of Hartford, in other words, in Mohegan territory.

Miantonomoh was slain by Uncas' brother, Waweequa. Angered by the capture and death of their chief at the hands of Uncas, the Narragansett besieged the Mohegan village at Fort Shantok in 1645. Food supplies were low and Uncas sent a scout to Saybrook, the nearest English settlement, to tell them of the plight of the Mohegan.

In response to Uncas' plea for aid, beef, beans, and corn were brought by boat up the Pequot (Thames) river and smuggled into the Fort under cover of darkness. At daybreak, the Mohegan hoisted a piece of beef on a pole outside the Fort. Seeing the beef and some Englishmen in the area, the Narragansett left the scene.

In 1765, Uncas and a few Mohegan men joined the English in the struggle known as King Philip's War, which lasted most of the year. None of the battles were fought on Connecticut soil but Connecticut tribes were involved, in some conflicts with Indians; others with the English.

This proved to have been the last open warfare between the Indian tribes of southern New England and the colonists. Through the years, Uncas and his sons, Oweneco and Attawanhood (Joshua) had deeded many acres of Mohegan land to their English friends for favors accorded them during times of warfare. Uncas and his remaining tribal members survived on surviving tribal grounds with more and more non-Indians taking up residence among them. Uncas finally retired to his wigwam at a place called Uncas Hill in Mohegan, Montville Township Connecticut.

There he died at a great age in 1682 or '83. At the top of Mohegan Hill, on Connecticut Route 32, is a marker erected by the State, which reads, "Mohegan: Seat of Uncas-Friend of the English." Here live 35 of the 200 descendants of the Mohegan on land that is individually owned. The reservation system was terminated in 1860 at the request of Mohegan leaders. Nearby, is a small Indian museum owned and operated by Chief Harold Tantaquidgeon X and his sister, Gladys Tantaquidgeon, tenth generation descendants of Chief Uncas. The museum is dedicated to the history and traditions of the Mohegan and other New England Indians.

WABAN

Waban (Nipmuc, ? - 1677), was a seventeenth century friend of Missionary John Eliot, and a leader of the Christian converts among the Indians. Waban was probably born at Musketaquid, which is now Concord, Massachusetts. He was living at Nonantum (now Newton) in 1646, when he welcomed John Eliot as a Chief Minister of Justice at the time. Eliot conducted his first service in the Algonquin language at Nonantum and returned there regularly to preach. Waban requested of Eliot land on which to build a town, and this Eliot obtained from the General Court of Massachusetts.

When the new town was established at Natick in 1651, Waban was its town clerk. At Eliot's recommendation, the government of the town followed the Biblical pattern of a hierarchy of one ruler of one hundred, two rulers of fifty, and ten rulers of ten. Waban was chosen as a ruler of fifty. He was later the Justice of the Peace, and in 1670 was said to be the chief ruler of this community of Christian Indians (which four years later numbered 29 families, or about 145 persons).

Shortly before the outbreak of King Philip's War in 1675, Waban learned of the impending Indian attack and warned the English. However, the whites suspected the Christian Indians of duplicity, and Waban was among many sent as prisoners to Deer Island later that year. He was among the sick who were returned in 1676.

He probably died about 1677. Waban encouraged many other Indians to accept Christianity. Daniel Gookin described him as "a person of great prudence and piety." Eliot stated that Waban's gift lay in "ruling, judging of cases, wherein he is patient, constant, and prudent, insomuch that he is respected among them, for they have chosen him a ruler of fifty, and he ruleth well according to his measure."

WAMESIT

The Wamesit was an important tribe of the Algonquian-speaking Pennacook confederacy, occupying the southern bank of the Merrimac River, below the mouth of the Concord River in Massachusetts. The village of the Wamesit, situated near present Lowell, Massachusetts, was the gathering-place of the confederacy during fishing season: hence the name. It was one of the "Praying Indian" towns before the outbreak of King Philip's War in 1675.

In that war, the Wamesit suffered severe losses, subsequently selling their territory and probably joining the other Pennacook at Saint Francis in Quebec, Canada, where their descendants now live.

WAMPANOAG

The Wampanoag are one of the tribes associated with the original group of Pilgrims who came to North America on the Mayflower. One tribal member was an Indian the Pilgrims would soon rank as "a special instrument sent of God; for their good beyond their expectation." This Indian was Squanto, Tisquantum being his Indian name, the last of the Patuxet. He had been carried off to slavery in Spain, been owned for a while by some local friars, and had finally escaped to England, where he had lived some years with a wealthy merchant in Cornhill, London, be-

267

fore he finally made his way back to America. He had arrived at Patuxet six months before the arrival of the Mayflower, and finding not one of his tribe alive, he went back to Sowams, Massasoit's village.

A man named Samoset brought Squanto back because his English was much better, and without Squanto and his native skill and knowledge of the country, the Pilgrims would have perished. Starvation haunted them, and they barely managed to pull through. Almost an hour after Squanto's appearance, Massasoit arrived with sixty warriors behind him. If he had come to fight, he could have swept Plymouth out of existence, but he came in peace, and with Samoset and Squanto as interpreters, Massasoit and Governor Carter of Plymouth signed the Treaty of Plymouth, a non-aggression pact.

Provisions stated that if the peace were broken by an Indian, he would be sent to Plymouth for punishment; if broken by a Pilgrim, he would be sent to Sowams for punishment. Indians coming to visit Plymouth were to leave their arms behind, and the Pilgrims were to do the same on their visits. If anyone "unjustly" attacked either party to the Treaty, the other was to come immediately to his assistance. The pact was to apply to all tribes under the dominion of the Wampanoag, and Massasoit undertook "to certisfie them of this."

This non-aggression pact was repeatedly renewed during the 40 years of Massasoit's life, but after his death the old alliance between Pilgrim and Indian began to give way to constant suspicion. Massasoit's sons, Wansutta, Alexander to the English, now sachem, and Metacom, Philip to the English, came to Plymouth to sign the old nonaggression pact, but it was not long before rumors from Boston reported that Alexander was plotting against the Pilgrims. When he failed to appear at the General Court to explain, Major Winslow and ten armed men seized Alexander at a hunting lodge, treating him as a felon, with a pistol at his back, instead of as a sovereign ally.

Questioned by Governor Prence, Alexander was released, desperately sick of fever, and died within two or three days at Plymouth. His warriors carried him on their shoulders to Sowams for burial among his people, but his brother Philip always believed he was poisoned. The fundamental cause of conflict lay in the opposed land systems of the whites and the Indians, and the irritation became acute when the Wampanoags began complaining that the Pilgrims were encroaching on their hunting grounds.

Other things annoyed the Indians. By 1643, no "stray" Indian was to be allowed in Plymouth. And if an Indian was guilty of theft, he was to make fourfold restitution; if he was unable to do so, he was to work it off at 12 pence a day or "be sold for his theft."

By 1656, Plymouth decreed that no boats, or sails or riggings, and no horse, mare, colt, or foal could be sold to an Indian. No colony would legally sell liquor or firearms to any Indian, but the Pilgrims were increasingly distressed by the alleged traffic, especially in firearms. Probably what most infuriated the Pilgrims was that, like his father Massasoit, Philip refused to let anyone try proselytizing his tribe. When John Eliot tried to convert Philip, the Indian snapped the missionary's jacket button and said, "I care no more for your gospel than that."

Things continued to go from bad to worse, and by 1675, war was inevitable, the beginning of one of the great Indian wars. By the most brilliant diplomatic skill, Philip had managed to break down age-old jealousies and had rallied practically every New England tribe to his side. In the spring of 1676, however, the tide began to turn against Philip. The Indians had no food, and diseased, hungry, and weak, they began to desert.

Philip had gone back to the land of his ancestors, to Mount Hope, and a traitor to his cause offered to show the Pilgrims his hiding place. Then a "Praying Indian" managed to shoot him, and his severed head was placed on a pike in the watchtower at Plymouth for more than 20 years. When the war ended, 900 Indians were dead, 800 white men killed, 25 white towns burned to the ground, and more than 1,350,000 dollars was the Colonies' war debt. As Indian captives, men, women, and children poured into Plymouth, all were sold into slavery, some to local planters, but most in the West Indies.

"To sell souls for money seemeth to me a dangerous merchandise," said John Eliot in protest, and Captain David Gookin, superintendent of the Praying Indians, gave his own opinions so vigorously that he began to be "afraid to go about the streets." In Massachusetts, where 200 Praying Indians deserted to Philip, there had been panic, and even on Cape Cod, drastic measures had to be taken. Indian women were seized as hostages, and no Indian was allowed to approach nearer to Plymouth than Sandwich, on pain of instant death.

In spite of all this, the Cape tribes technically under Philip, remained useful allies to the English, serving particularly as scouts. Today, the Wampanoag are divided into five regional, autonomous groups, including Gay Head on Martha's Vineyard, Mashpee on Cape Cod, Assonet from New Bedford to Rehoboth, Herring Pond from Wareham to Middleboro, and Nemasket in the Middleboro area. Tribal councils manage the political affairs of the bands, and represent them at state and federal levels.

They have continued to petition the federal government for federal recognition. There were 2,600 to 2,800 Wampanoag members in a recent count. The Gay Head group on Martha's Vineyard does not have a reservation, but the tribe owns lands in trust.

Tourism has become an economic development here, and many tribal members operate snack bars and shops of the island. In 1987, the Gay Head group won federal recognition, and a number of educational, social, and housing services have been provided. The group maintains many of their traditional celebrations. Population recently totaled 260 members. The Mashpee living in Mashpee filed a claim with the federal government in 1976 to recover the town of Mashpee. They claimed the state had violated the Federal Nonintercourse Act of 1799 by splitting up tribal territory among individual Indians and allowing non-Indians to buy the land without Congressional approval.

When the case came to trial in January 1977, a Federal jury ruled against the Wampanoags on the theory that they were not a tribe when the first of the Nonintercourse Acts passed, and that while they might have been after that date, they had not been one for more than a century. After that ruling, the tribe took their case to the United States Supreme Court, which refused to hear the case. The Wampanoag case was financed by the Native American Rights Fund.

Although the group has felt overwhelmed by land purchases by whites in the area, and a 1988 shooting of a tribal member by a policeman threatened to further deteriorate an already difficult relationship between whites and Indians, recently the two opposing groups have begun a dialogue to resolve the issue and other concerns that threaten the well-being of all community members.

The Mashpee Tribal Council, the political arm of the tribe, is primarily responsible for the continuing land suit as well as other issues. The group maintains traditional ceremonies, bringing together local members and those from around the country. Recently there were 1,060 members of the Mashpee group, with about 600 living in Mashpee.

WAPPINGER

The Wappinger were a Mahican Algonquian-speaking group that inhabited the eastern banks of the mid-Hudson River Valley of New York, above the Hudson Highlands. First identified as the Wappenox in 1626, they were described as active participants in the riverside fur trade with

Dutch peddlers. The "Wappenos" reportedly drove a number of lower Hudson River Delawarean-speaking groups from their homes sometime prior to 1628. Long-standing allies of the Dutch colony of New Netherland, Wappinger warriors participated in a number of raids against the Raritan during 1641 and 1642. The Dutch massacre of over 120 lower Hudson River refugees from a Mahican attack on the night of February 25-26, 1643 dramatically reversed Wappinger allegiance.

Their war parties attacked Dutch shipping on the Hudson River during the spring of 1643, effectively cutting communication between Fort Amsterdam at the mouth of the Hudson River and Fort Orange near Albany, New York. Some 25 Wappingers were killed in the Dutch assault upon the large Wiechqusesgeck village in the Pound Ridge area of Westchester County, New York, during the winter of 1643-44.

This disaster led the Wappinger to sue for peace along with the Kichtawanck, Wiechquaesgeck, Sintsing, and Nochpemm on April 6, 1644. The Mahican sachem Aepjen represented these groups in the final peace treaty ending the conflict, known as the Governor Kieft War (1640-1645), on August 30, 1645. The Wappinger next went to war against the Dutch during the Peach War (1655-1657). Still belligerent following the end of that conflict, the Wappinger managed to avoid direct involvement in the first years of the Esopus War (1659-1664).

Wappinger diplomats alternately served as intermediaries between the Dutch and Esopus and covert allies of the Esopus troupe. They participated in the July 15, 1660 treaty that ended the first phase of the fighting, and a number of Wappinger warriors fought with the Esopus when fighting broke out again during the summer of 1663. On July 8, 1663, nine Wappinger and thirty Minisink men were included among the 200 Esopus warriors. Other Wappinger families held a number of Dutch captives and sheltered the relatives of Esopus warriors.

On May 15, 1664, T'Sees-Sagh-Gauw, chief of the Wappinghs, signed the peace treaty ending the Esopus War. The Dutch colony of New Netherland fell to the English on September 6, 1664. On September 24, 1664 the "Wampings and Espachomy (Esopus)" submitted themselves to English protection. This protection was not immediately forthcoming, however, and the Wappinger were attacked by Mohawks in 1669.

On December 29, 1669, the Highland Indians often mentioned in the English records were identified as the "Wappingoes and Wickershick (Wiechquaesgeck)." Increasing number of Wiechquaegeck, Kichtawanck, and Siwanoy moved north among the Wappinger during the last decades of the seventeenth century.

Many Wappinger, disenchanted with the English and resentful of their continued demands for lands and labor, moved further north to the French settlements along the Saint Lawrence River below Montreal, Canada. The Wappinger and their neighbors came to be known collectively as River Indians during the late seventeenth century. Many of them extended hunting and trapping grounds far west into the Ohio River Valley during the 1680s. A large number of River Indian men served with the English against the French during the King William's War (1689 and 1697).

This war was an unqualified disaster for the River Indians; on April 19, 1698, it was reported that only 90 River Indian men out of 250 had survived. By 1700, many of these moved to the village of Schagticoke above Albany, New York. On July 20, 1702 it was noted that 110 River Indians were "at Skachcock and 87 below ye towne" in their traditional territories.

The Schagticoke village served as an outpost that protected the northern New York frontier from surprise attacks by the French and their Native allies. The River Indians became increasingly associated with their Mahican neighbors during the opening decades of the 1700s. The Wappingers greatly increased their settlement area at that time, and they came to inhabit small hamlets located in western Connecticut, the Hudson River drainage, and along the upper Delaware River valley between New York and Pennsylvania.

They followed a wide-ranging seasonal round of activities that carried them through this region at various times of the year. Many Wappinger were undoubtedly among the numerous River Indian parties reported as far west as the Mississippi River country during the early eighteenth century. Some 98 River Indians, including "19 lowermost River Indians and 21 highland Indians," joined the English in an expedition against French Canada on August 24, 1711, during the Queen Anne's War (1702-1713). An increasing number of River Indians moved to Canada following the war to escape the liquor trade that pauperized them and put them in debt to English traders.

In 1735, a large number of River Indians moved to the Stockbridge mission settlement on the upper Housatonic River in Connecticut. Others, including a large number of Wappinger, went to the Moravian missions at Shekomeko and Pleasant Plains in 1744. Most of these Wappinger then removed to the Moravian settlements at the Forks of the Delaware River near Easton, Pennsylvania, following their eviction from Dutchess County in 1746.

The pagan Wappinger continued to inhabit their substantial range in the region. Their main settlements were at Wikopy, in Dutchess County, New York; Pompton, in north Central New Jersey; and Cochecton, a large village on the upper Delaware River. On January 3, 1745, a party of 12 "Cashington Indians" came to Goshen, New York to enter into a "friendship" agreement with the New York government.

This was agreed to on January 17, 1746, and the mixed Wappinger, Esopus, Minisink, and Wappinger community at Cochecton both hunted and patrolled the western frontier of the province of New York for a decade. War between the English and the Delaware, Minisink, and the "Opings or Pomptowns" broke out in 1755 as part of the widening struggle called the Seven-Year's War (1735 and 1762).

Their sachem, Nimham, led the Wappinger warriors in a series of devastating raids upon the English settlements in eastern Pennsylvania and western New Jersey during the first years of the conflict.

He signed over Wappinger land claims in northern New Jersey and concluded a peace with the English on October 23, 1758. Most of his followers moved with the Minisink and their Mahican brothers to the Wyoming Valley in the upper Susquehanna drainage.

By August 26, 1761, it was reported that "the chief of the Mohickons Opies have settled with Six Nations, at a place called Chenango" above Binghamton, New York. Dissatisfied with living as exiles in Pennsylvania, and unwilling to move further west as English pressure increased, Nimham led his people back to their Dutchess County homeland during the early 1760s. In 1765, he litigated for the right to retain title to land in Dutchess and Columbia counties.

Though he failed to legally regain title to the Wappinger lands there, his people were permitted to live in small settlements scattered through the backcountry of both counties. These Wappinger became increasingly involved with the Stockbridge Indian community, which by then had moved to near Albany, New York. About 300 fighting men were listed among the River Indians on June 11, 1774.

These included the "Montocks and others of Long Island, Wappingers of Dutchess County, Esopus, Papagonck & Co. in Ulster County, and a few Skachticokes." The Wappinger and other River Indians elected to join the rebels during the American Revolution (1775-1781). A force of some 60 Wappinger warriors set out to join Washington's forces during the summer of 1778. This force was surprised by the British at Yonkers, New York, and nearly 40 of them were either killed or wounded on July 30, 1778, in the battle of Cortland's Ridge.

273

Nimham was killed during the struggle, and the survivors returned to their homes at Stockbridge for the remainder of the war. The Wappinger chose to remain at the Stockbridge settlement after the war. This mixed Wappinger, Mahican, and Housatonic community moved to the settlement of New Stockbridge among the Oneida in 1785. There they became involved with the Brotherton of southern New Jersey and New England, as well as with their Oneida hosts. This community, heavily influenced by its Christian missionaries and highly skilled in white customs, remained in New York until the 1820s.

White land sales resulted in the virtual extinction of Native title to lands in New York during the first decades of the nineteenth century. Speculators and settlers exerted pressure to induce the Stockbridge and their Oneida hosts to migrate westward. In 1821 the Stockbridge bought some land in Wisconsin from the Menominee and Winnebago. The New Stockbridge people began moving to the new reservation shortly thereafter, and the mission officially reopened there in 1835.

This reservation, known as the Stockbridge-Munsee Reservation, persists to the present day, and the modern descendants of the Wappinger reside there as relatively affluent middle class Christians. Well-educated, economically prosperous, and blessed with a growing population, the Stockbridge-Munsee community is among the most successful reservation groups in the country.

A recent count showed some 1500 Indians on the Stockbridge-Munsee Reservation, which sits in a rural, woodland area in Shawano County, In North Central Wisconsin, near the village of Bowler. Reservation boundaries hold two townships, Bartelme, and Red Springs, with a total of some 46,000 acres. About 16,00 acres of this land is held in trust for the tribe, which has resisted breaking the reservation into allotments.

WHITE EYES

White Eyes (Delaware, 1730 - November 1778), also known as Coquetakeghton "that which is put near the head" because of his light-colored eyes, the Delaware war captain Koquethagetchan, was called White Eyes, sometimes Grey Eyes. Possibly there was white ancestry in his background.

The date and place of his birth are unknown, but in 1762 he was living at a Delaware Indian town at the mouth of Beaver Creek, a tributary of the Ohio River, south of Pittsburgh, Pennsylvania. With other migrant Delawares, whose original homes were in the Delaware River area, he moved to the Muskingum valley in Tuscarawas County, Ohio prior to the American Revolution.

Colonel George Morgan, Indian agent for the Continental Congress, became a good friend of White Eyes, and persuaded him to use his influence to consolidate the Delawares at a new location at present Coshocton, Ohio. There a new council fire was kindled. Small but resolute, brave, and highly intelligent, White Eyes was selected in 1776 by the Delaware Great Council to replace the aging and infirm principal chief, Netawatwees. He appeared before the Congress in Philadelphia where he was officially thanked for promoting peace between the Delawares and the whites.

Congress gave him $300 and two fine horses with saddles and bridles. White Eyes agreed that in the event of war with the British, the Delawares would aid the Americans, and he proposed that the Delaware tribe should constitute a fourteenth state in the American union. These points were incorporated in a treaty at Pittsburgh, September 17, 1778, of which he, along with John Killbuck, Junior, and Captain Pipe, were signatories. He was commissioned a Lieutenant Colonel, and while serving as a guide for troops under command of General Lachlan McIntosh, was murdered in November 1778 by an unknown assailant.

Following his death, a pro-British faction seized control of the tribe and persuaded the majority of the Delaware warriors to war against the Americans. The hostility broke the treaty of 1778, and alienated Americans from the Delawares. George White Eyes and Joseph White Eyes were two of the chief's sons, but the names of his wife and other children are not known.

WYANDOTTE

The people who became known as Wyandottes to the English and Americans represent an emergent tribal society that developed out of the surviving remnants of three great Ontario Iroquoian confederacies, the Huron, Petun, and Neutrals. Wyandotte, the name that this group selected for themselves in the 1740s, is a corruption of the old self-name of the Huron Confederacy, Wendat. Earlier, these refugees had been known to the French as the Hurons of the West, or the Petun (Tobacco) Hurons, and to the English as the Dionondade.

Because those who finally settled in Ohio and Pennsylvania insisted on being identified as Wendat, a name the English authorities finally accepted, they produced one of the rare instances in Indian history where an Indian society reasserted its traditional identity after decades of being

275

called names derived by Europeans. After the defeat and dispersal of the Ontario Iroquoian confederacies by the New York Iroquois in 1651, some of the survivors fled to the Upper Great Lakes country with their traditional partner, the Ottawa.

There followed a complicated series of migrations into Wisconsin, Minnesota, Michigan, and Iowa, as these refugees sought to establish themselves in a productive new habitat where they might forge a new tribal organization. Driven by the Sioux from their Chequamegon Bay base in 1670, they moved next to Michillimackinac, where they lived until 1704, when they again resettled near Detroit under French auspices. It was from this Detroit village that dissident members of the Turtle clans, anti-French and anti-Catholic, began moving into long-vacant Ohio country along the richly fertile Sandusky River valley and plain.

During their years as refugees in the west (1650-1703) the Wyandottes worked to maintain their old position as a favored middleman in the fur trade with the French. However, they were too few to dominate their Algonquian neighbors and allies, mainly the Ottawa, Chippewa, and Potawatomi, or to overawe and conquer their enemies such as the Sioux, for their population did not exceed 1500 in the years 1651-1703. Hence they were constantly involved in political intrigue, playing one ally against another.

Eventually they developed a reputation for such untrustworthiness that their old allies threatened war with them. However, once settled in Ohio, they emerged as the symbolic leaders of the loose intertribal coalition composed of Michigan, Indiana, and Ohio tribes. Thus for many years, their villages near Detroit and Sandusky were used as the sites for important councils, as well as the depository for the valuable wampum belts which were the diplomatic records and documents of such negotiations. The Wyandottes, who were mainly Petun (Tionontate) and Huron (Wendat) in origin, spoke a northern language.

Their culture history after 1650 is one of near constant migration and readjustment to the unsettled conditions of the frontier in the Old Northwest Territory, and they also maintained several small villages in Ontario at modern Windsor and Amherstburg. Those who lived in British territory continued to be called Hurons of Lorette on the Saint Lawrence River, who were a different group of refugees. Before the diaspora of the 1650s, these Iroquoians had been the target of major French missionary effort, and this acculturative influence continued strong in the west, particularly so at Michillimackinac and Detroit. But it also produced the reaction of an anti-French factional split in the 1730s. The anti-French faction, mainly representing the Turtle clans led by Nicholas Orontony, broke away, settling in Ohio, and developed relationships with English colonists, while the Deer and Wolf clans remained attached to the French.

After Orontony led an abortive attempt to destroy the French fort at Detroit, most of the Wyandotte settled in Ohio, where they nurtured their influence, ultimately inviting the Delaware and Shawnee to join them there in an alliance with the English. After the British defeated the French in 1760, the Wyandotte became extremely reluctant supporters of Pontiac, and it was the Wyandotte who welcomed Sir William Johnson to Detroit after the Ottawa leader's defeat. But by that year, 1764, the Wyandotte control of the Ohio heartland had only a half century to run, for by moving eastward they occupied valuable ground squarely in the path of American expansion.

Therefore, after the Revolutionary War, in which the Wyandottes joined the English and the Great Lakes tribes in opposing the Americans, they came under heavy pressure to cede their lands. The Wyandottes had already participated in three treaties with Americans when they met with General Anthony Wayne, the victor of Fallen Timbers, at Fort Greenville in 1795.

In the treaty negotiations that year, their chief Tarhe (The Crane) stood out as the main speaker for all the tribes participating. Tarhe made it plain that the Wyandotte fully recognized that a new era had dawned, acknowledging American sovereignty over the Great Lakes- Ohio Valley area.

Through the 1830s, while the Wyandottes were ceding most of their lands to the Americans, their kinsmen, the Hurons of Anderdon, were similarly negotiating with British authorities. Although under very heavy pressure to sell their last reservation in Ohio and Michigan, and to move west of the Mississippi, the Wyandottes resisted until 1843. Finally selling their last lands, that year they boarded steamboats and traveled west to take possession of a 36-section tract where modern Kansas City, Kansas now stands. The 1842 treaty was supported by the Wyandotte Pagan faction and opposed by the Citizen party.

The former, consisting of most of the traditional Wyandotte, saw The West as a place to escape the problems of living amid dense American agricultural settlements in Ohio, while the Citizen faction was led by the well educated sons of British and American agents , and traders who had married into the tribe.

277

On their Ohio Reservation, the Wyandottes had governed themselves under a written constitution, with their own legislative, judicial, and police systems. This practice, Protestant missionary developed, continued in Kansas, but the community there was short lived, for once again they had selected as their home, lands coveted by American speculators and settlers. Most of the Wyandotte by that time had converted to the Methodist Episcopal Church; and in Kansas, during the disturbed years before the Civil War, they became embroiled in the anti-slavery controversy.

Since the Wyandotte tribe had assimilated as full citizens a number of freed Blacks and escaped slaves, they were opposed to slavery. In these same years, some Wyandottes were caught up by the Gold Rush and resettled in California, while several leaders worked at organizing Nebraska Territory. Indeed, one leader was elected the first provisional governor of that territory, but lost his position because of the anti-slavery stance. In 1855 the Wyandotte tribe, under a new treaty, was disbanded and its lands divided into individual holdings.

By 1857 several hundred had migrated to Oklahoma to settle on the Seneca Reservation there. Meanwhile, their lands in Kansas were entirely lost through sale or tax foreclosure. By 1872 most identifiable Wyandottes had moved to Oklahoma, where 220 of them lived that year. At that point, all were American citizens and farmers, and acculturation pressure continued strong, so much so that by the 1960s, only two elderly people could still use the language, while by then the traditional culture and social institutions had disappeared. During their years of migration, the Wyandottes were known by various names to their French, British, American, and Indian neighbors. The names mainly reflected the largest parts of this composite refugee population, such as Tionontati (Petun) and Huron (Wendat).

English colonial authorities came to know them, through New York Iroquois intermediaries, as Dionondades or Jenondades. After England took possession of French North America, they continued to call the community at Anderdon (Amherstburg), Ontario Hurons, but by then New York and Pennsylvania colonial authorities had adopted Wyandotte for those south of the Great Lakes. Sometimes parts of the whole tribe were known after the names of their most influential clans, particularly of the Deer phratry, or by the name of the Deer phratry chief, Sastaretsy.

The Central Algonquians of the Great Lakes area, on the other hand, called the Wyandotte Nadowe (Timber Rattlesnakes), as they did all the Northern Iroquoians. Today, the Wyandotte live on the Oklahoma reservation. In 1956, they were singled out for "extermination" as a tribal entity, but after 20 years of protest, they succeeded in regaining federal recognition in 1978. Many new developments have resulted from recognition, including scholarships, daily meals for elders, new homes, a health center, a tribal center and meeting hall, and a preschool facility.

They purchased 10 acres of land in Park City, Kansas to build a gambling hall, and have received a grant to fund the Wyandotte Museum and Cultural Center. Additional funds have aided in the location, purchase, and catalogue of the material culture. The Wyandotte tribe seeks to maintain its heritage and the remnants of its language. A library and archives are part of the potential new developments. In a recent count there were over 3,600 enrolled members of the tribe in Oklahoma.

TREATY COMMITMENTS
--a History of Broken Promises

The classic book, *A Century of Dishonor*, by Helen Jackson, was published in 1880. Subtitled "A Sketch of the United States Government's Dealings With Some of The Indian Tribes," it remains a compelling narrative of the incredibly unjust treatment of America's natives, focusing mainly on the hundred years ending in the late 1870s, the first century of the United States as a nation.

It is highly recommended in its entirety, and with apologies this brief outline of her work is included, using Helen Jackson's words as much as possible. This is the essence of her work, minus many vivid and fascinating details.

The question of whether the United States dealt honorably with the Indians turns on a much disputed and little understood point. Some sentimentalists say that the Indians were the real owners of the land, while some politicians hold that they had no right of ownership whatever. Between these views lay innumerable grades and confusions of opinion.

The Indians "right of occupancy" was recognized by all the great discovering Powers. Did the United States, on taking its place among the Nations, also recognize the Indian "right of occupancy"? On this point there is no doubt.

Stealing is everywhere held to be dishonorable, as is lying, in all its forms. Breaking of promises and betrayals of trust are scorned even among the most ignorant of people. However, when the acts of nations are discussed, there seems to be a less clear conception, a less uniform standard of right and wrong, honor and dishonor.

In charging a government or nation with dishonorable conduct, it should merely be shown that its moral standard ought not differ from the moral standard of an individual. What is cowardly, cruel, and base in a man, is cowardly, cruel, and base in a government or nation.

The right of refusing to submit to injustice, of resisting injustice by force if necessary, is part of the law of nature, and as such is recognized by the law of nations. From this arises the right to a just defense, which belongs to every nation and to every individual. Men pledge justice to each other by promises or contracts, while between nations, treaties are made. National contracts or treaties are even more solemn and sacred than private ones on account of the great interests involved.

It has been said by those defending the United States Government's repeated disregard of its treaties with the Indians, that no Congress can be held responsible for the acts of the Congress following it. In other words, each Congress may undo all that has been done by previous Congresses.

This is true of some legislative acts, but is clearly not true of treaties, according to the basic principals of international law. Further, the violation of any one article of a treaty is a violation of the whole treaty.

The robbery, the cruelty which were done under the cloak of this hundred years of treaty-making and treaty-breaking, are greater than can be told. Neither mountains nor deserts stopped them. It took two oceans to set their bounds.

In 1871, Congress, either ashamed of making treaties only to break them, or grudging the time, money and paper it wasted, decided that no Indian tribe would thereafter be considered a foreign nation with whom the United States might contract by treaty. They did add a proviso to the act that it should not be construed as invalidating any treaties already made.

This avowed sense of obligation was short-lived, as they unabashedly negotiated and broke treaty after treaty, calling them "conventions", or "agreements". The difference was in name only. From unquestioned tenets of international law, nations may be held to standards of justice and good faith, as are men.

A nation that steals and lies and breaks its promises, will be no more respected or unpunished than a man who steals and lies and breaks his promises. Certain natural punishment sooner or later comes from evildoing.

To prove all this it is only necessary to study the history of any one of the Indian tribes. The following entries are mere outline sketches of the history of a few of them, containing only the details necessary to show the repeated broken faith of the United States Government toward them. It would take many years and many volumes for a full history of the wrongs that the natives of America have suffered at the hands of military and civil authorities, and of the citizens of this country.

THE DELAWARES

When Hendrik Hudson anchored his ship, the Half Moon, off New York Island in 1609, great numbers of Delawares stood on the shore, ready for a visit with the gods. More than a hundred years later, the aged Moravian missionary Heckewelder recorded a Delaware Chief as saying, "I admit that there are good white men, but they bear no proportion to the bad. The bad must be the strongest, for they rule. They do what they please. They enslave those who are not of their color, although created by the same Great Spirit who created them. They would make slaves of us if they could; but as they cannot do it, they kill us. I know the Long-knives. They are not to be trusted".

The original name of the Delawares was Lenni Lenape, or "original people". Their lands stretched from the Hudson River to the Potomac. They were a noble-spirited, gentle people, under the control ot the arrogant and all-powerful Iroquois, who degradingly called the Delawares "women", who were forced to make war or give up land at the pleasure of their masters.

During William Penn's humane administration of Pennsylvania, the Delawares were his most devoted friends. They called him Elder Brother. In the French and Indian War of 1755, many fought with the French against the English, and in the beginning of the Revolutionary War the majority of the Delawares sided with the English. Most of the Indian massacres during this period were the result of either French or English influence. Neither nation was high-minded enough to scorn having native allies do the bloody work which either would not dare risk national reputation by doing themselves.

The United States' first treaty with the Delawares was made in 1778, at Fort Pitt. It was a treaty of friendship that permitted government troops a right of passage through "the Delaware Nation", upon paying for any supplies they might use. It also stated that the Delawares could send a representative to Congress. The provisions were never fully carried out, starting the pattern of future treaties. The Delawares agreed to send all the warriors they could spare to fight for the Americans.

At that time the rest of the Ohio tribes, most of the New York Tribes, and a large part of the Delawares were in arms on the British side. After the Revolutionary War, they were all forced to make peace as best they could with the Americans, and the next treaty, made at Fort McIntosh in 1785, reinstated the Delaware Chiefs and headmen who had made that old alliance with the Americans, thus having lost caste in their tribe for fighting on the side of the United States. The Wyandottes, Chippewas, and Ottawas joined the Delawares in the treaty.

The Indians lands comprised within lines partly indicated by the Cuyahoga, Big Miami, and Ohio Rivers and their Branches, and fronting on Lake Erie. The treaty included the provision that, "If any citizen of the United States, or any other person not an Indian, attempted to settle on

Delaware or Wyandotte lands, the Indians may punish him as they please". Michigan, Ohio, Indiana, and Pennsylvania are all largely made up of the lands which were given to the Indians by that treaty.

Five years later, by another treaty at Fort Harmar, the boundaries were changed somewhat, and more accurately defined. Hunting privileges for Indians on all lands reserved to the United States was promised, "So long as they behaved themselves peaceably". It was also promised that white men and Indians committing offenses would be punished in the same way.

The Indians had been dissatisfied since the first treaty was made, claiming that it had been made by only a few of them, and in 1786 they complained to Congress of white encroachment. Only the year before the United States expressly told these Indians that any white citizens attempting to settle on their lands could be punished as they pleased.

The very next year the President instructed a "careful examination of the real temper of the Indian tribes in the Northwest Ohio Territory. The treaties, which have been made, must not be departed from, unless a boundary beneficial to the United States can be obtained. You will not neglect any opportunity that may offer of extinguishing the Indians rights to the westward, as far as the Mississippi".

Even the wildest greedy dream at that time did not look beyond that river.

Not seen in any accounts of the Indian hostilities of the Northwestern frontier during this period is any reference to the repeated permissions given by the United States to the Indians, to defend their lands as they saw fit. Most Americans of that day were honestly unaware, and therefor incredulous, that the Indians had either the provocation or right to kill intruders on their lands.

Thus early in our history was the ingenious plan evolved of first maddening the Indians into war, and then falling upon them with exterminating punishment. Under all these conditions, it is no wonder that the frontier was a scene of perpetual devastation and bloodshed; and that year by year, there grew stronger in the minds of whites a terror and hatred of Indians; and in the minds of the Indians a stronger and stronger distrust and hatred of the whites.

The Delawares were friendly through the earlier part of these troubles. However, in 1792 they were mentioned among the hostile tribes to whom the Government sent this deceptive message,"That you believe the United States want to deprive you of your lands, and drive you out of the country, be assured that this is not so. Remember that no additional lands will be required of you or any other tribe, to those that have been ceded by former treaties".

In 1793 a great council was held, attended by the Delaware chiefs and those of twelve other tribes. The purpose was to settle the vexing boundary question. The United States commissioners would not agree to Indian contentions.

The Indians finally said, "Money to us is of no value, and to most of us unknown: and as no consideration whatever can induce us to sell the land on which we get sustenance for our women and children, we hope we may be allowed to point out a method by which your settlers may be easily removed, and peace thereby obtained. Divide this large sum of money which you have offered us among these people; give to each, also, a proportion of what you say you would give to us annually."

"...We desire you to consider, brothers, that our only demand is the peaceable possession of a small part of our once great country. Look back and review the lands from whence we have been driven to this spot. We can retreat no further, and we have therefore resolved to leave our bones in this small space to which we are confined."

General Anthony Wayne led what would have been a bloody surprise raid on a major Delaware settlement. The natives were able to flee in advance due to a deserter's warning. The General consoled himself that he didn't get to slaughter the large community, reporting that he had "gained possession of the grand emporium of the hostile Indians of the West without loss of blood."

He then burned and destroyed all the well tended villages and fields, finally catching up with the fleeing Indians and killed many in a sharp fight. After a winter of suffering and hunger, the Indians yielded to the inevitable, and in the summer of 1795 they once more had to make a treaty, and were told again the , "the heart of General Washington, the Great Chief of America, wishes for nothing so much as peace and brotherly love".

By this treaty nearly two-thirds of the present state of Ohio was ceded to the United States, except for, "all other Indian lands northward of the River Ohio, eastward of the Mississippi, and westward and southward of the Great Lakes and the waters uniting them in the year 1783," with the exception of four tracts of land, "to connect the settlements of the people of the United States".

The treaty again explicitly stated that the Indian tribes were to quietly enjoy their lands so long as they pleased, without molestation from the United States. The same old worthless pledge was included, that the Indians could drive off or otherwise punish whites attempting to settle on their land, "in such manner as they shall think fit". With promised (but never fully delivered) immediate payment of goods and annual allotments of more, peace was declared to be "perpetual".

In less than a year, the Delawares were forced into yet another treaty, ceding a tract of land between the Ohio and Wash Rivers, for which they were to receive a three hundred dollar annual pittance. In one more year there was yet another treaty, in which a still further cession of land was made for a "permanent" annuity of one thousand dollars. A General Harrison noted that the Indians were beginning to learn the value of land, but they must not have reached a true estimate of values, as the General said, "the tract now ceded contains at least two million acres, and embraces some of the finest lands in the western country".

The sale was unbelievably cheap at one thousand dollars, even with a black slave thrown in for the Turtle, the Delaware Chief.

Four years later, in 1809, by the Treaty of Fort Wayne, a few more dollars were promised, and a great deal of land taken. In 1817 a new treaty ceded nearly all the Indian land in Ohio, and parts of Indiana and Michigan. At least the Secretary of War had the honesty to admit that the only objection anyone could have to the amount of money paid, was that it, "was not an adequate one". The Indians had lost almost the last of their hunting grounds and would soon be driven to depend wholly upon farming.

In 1818 the Delawares had to cede all of their lands in Indians, and the United States promised to provide them "a country to reside in on the west side of the Mississippi," and to "guarantee to them peaceable possession" of it. The federal government showed a trace of compunction and pity in 1829, saying that since the Delaware were willing to move, that the country in the fork of the Kansas and Missouri Rivers, selected for their home, "shall be conveyed and forever secured by the United States to the said Delaware Nation, as their permanent residence".

The Secretary of War congratulated the country in 1834 on the fact that "the country north of the Ohio, east of the Mississippi, including the States of Ohio, Indians, Illinois, and Territory of Michigan as far as the Fox and Wisconsin rivers," had been practically, "cleared of the embarrassments of Indian relations," as there were not more than five thousand Indians left in the whole region.

For almost ten years after making this last treaty, there was little official mention of the Delawares, except for fiscal reports. In 1838 they were reported as cultivating one thousand five hundred acres in grain and vegetables, and raising great numbers of hogs, cattle, and horses. "They are a brave, enterprising people, at peace with all neighboring Indians". In ten more years it was noted that "almost every family is well supplied with farming stock. ...They dwell in good log cabins, and some have extremely neat houses, well furnished. In 1853 the Delawares are recorded as being "among the most remarkable of our colonized tribes".

The influx of white settlers into Kansas had become so great by 1854, that it became evident that the Indians reservations there could not be kept intact. The Delawares were coerced into ceding back a large portion of their lands to the United States. For this they were to receive ten thousand dollars and 250 dollar annuities for each of their five aging, poor chiefs. The next year their agent writes of the results of opening this large tract to white settlers: "The Indians have experienced enough to shake their confidence in the laws which govern the white race. The Government is bound in good faith to protect this people, yet white men have wasted their most valuable timber with an unsparing hand. The trust lands have been greatly injured in consequence of the settlements thereon." Yet nothing was done for the Indians.

The next treaty forced on the Delawares was in 1860, in which they were pressured to give the Leavenworth, Pawnee, and Western Railroad Company right of way and certain lands in their reserve. In 1862 two regiments of Delawares and Osages enlisted as soldiers in an expedition to the Indian Territory. Their Commanding Officer said of them, "The Indian soldiers have far exceed expectations. ...They bore the brunt of the fighting, and had they been properly sustained, would have ended the sway of the rebels in the Indian Territory".

Also during 1862 was a terrible condition in Kansas and the Indian Territory. The Indians were largely on the side of the Southern Rebels, because the Government had wholly failed to keep its treaty stipulations with the Delawares by withdrawing all protection for them, leaving them at the mercy of the rebels. However, the Delawares in 1862 enlisted one hundred and seventy men in the Union Army, out of a population of only two hundred males between the ages of eighteen and forty-five. This was probably the greatest ratio of volunteers in the United States.

Already, however, the "interests" of the white settlers in Kansas were beginning to be clearly in opposition to the interests of the Indians. The Commissioner said in 1863, "I can see nothing in the future for them but destruction. I think it is for the interest of the Indians that they be removed to some other locality as soon as possible."

Reluctantly, The Delawares petitioned to send a delegation of chiefs to the Rocky Mountains, to look for a new home. They were not allowed to, and ordered to the Indian Territory. During 1864, the greater part of their personal property being in livestock, The Delawares lost twenty thousand dollars worth to white thieves. The community was understandably depressed, what with most of the men away at war, old men, women, and children working the farms, and having twenty thousand dollars in stock stolen in one year.

Most of those in the Army were mustered out in 1865. They returned home after having distinguished themselves and were immediately prohibited by the Government from carrying revolvers. Their agent properly replied to that edict, "Many of these Indians are intelligent, only using weapons when any well-disposed white person would have done so; and if one class is disarmed, all must be." The Commissioner replied that they could keep certain hunting weapons, but would have to leave them with their agent when visiting other towns or agencies. A forcible statement was made that any man that went unarmed in Kansas was a fool.

The Indian Commissioner reported in 1866 that, "The State of Kansas is fast being filled by an energetic population who appreciate good land; and as the Indian reservations were selected as being the best in the state, but one result could be expected to follow." That July a treaty was made that moved all the Delawares to the Indian Territory, except those who wished to become citizens of Kansas. Thus the way was clear for the Government to make a quick sale of their lands to more white settlers.

With twenty thousand dollars worth of stock and twenty-eight thousand dollars worth of timber having been stolen in two years from the little village of farmers, it was no wonder that they were said to be "sufficiently prepared to move". The perpetual expectation of being made to move, had unsettled the whole community, and made them indifferent to further effort and improvement. The return of their young men from the Civil War also had a demoralizing effect. Drunken frays were common, in which deadly weapons were used, in spite of the Department's regulations disarming all Indians.

In July, 1867, the Delawares were said to be quite impatient to be gone from their reservation, in order to build houses that autumn for winter use, and to be fencing fields for the coming year. Annuities due them had not been paid, delaying their move. Many of their young men were still away, serving as scouts and guides in the Army. During that year and the next, they moved in detachments to the Indian Territory.

It was decreed in 1869 that they were to lose their nationality and become identified with the Cherokees. By 1870 nearly all the Delawares were in Indian Territory, but owing to a carelessly surveyed boundary, some three hundred of them had been settled outside the Cherokee Reservation, on lands which had been assigned to the Osages. The unfortunate three hundred were made to move again, this time to the land of the Peorias, where they asked for permission to settle.

Enlarging this problem was further Government bungling or indifference: As previous arrangements had been made with the Cherokees, all the Delaware funds, such as they were, were transferred to the Cherokee Nation. With no help from the Government, all parties were admonished to "reconcile there unsettled affairs to mutual advantage."

In official reports there are no further distinctive mention of the Delawares by name during the 1870s, except for a few who had for some time been living in the Indian Territory, and were not included in the treaty provisions at the time of their forced removal from Kansas. This little handful, some eighty-one in all, were all that remained to bear the name of that strong and friendly people to whom, a little more than a hundred years before, were promised that they would be brothers with the white man forever, and be entitled to representation in Congress.

On the Wichita Agency, in Indian Territory, that small band of Delawares was associated with six other dwindled remnants of tribes: The Caddos, Ionies, Wichitas, Towaconies, Wacos, Keechies, and Comanches. It was said of the Delawares in 1878 that they were unable to cultivate as much land as they had intended, "on account of loss of stock by horse-thieves". Thus ended the century of greatest dishonor to the Delawares,

THE CHEYENNES

The first treaty with the Cheyennes was made in 1825, at the mouth of the Teton River. It, like most first treaties with Indians, was merely a declaration of amity and friendship, and acknowledgment on the part of the Cheyennes of the "supremacy" of the United States.

Two years before, President Monroe reported the "Chayenes" to be, "a tribe of three thousand two hundred and fifty souls, dwelling and hunting on a river of the same name, a western tributary of the Missouri, a little above the Great Bend."

Ten Years later, George Catlin, the famous painter of Indians, met a "Shienne" chief and squaw among the Sioux and painted their portraits. He said, "The Shiennes are a small tribe of about three thousand in number, living neighbors to the Sioux on the west of them, between the Black Hills and the Rocky Mountains. There is no finer race of men than these in North America, and none superior in stature, except the Osages: scarcely a man in the tribe full grown who is less than six feet in height."

They are ," the richest in horses of any tribe on the continent; living where the greatest herds of wild horses are grazing on the prairies, which they catch in great numbers, and sell to the Sioux, Mandans, and other tribes, as well as to the fur-traders."

In 1842 a line running north and south, so as to cross the Missouri about the mouth of the Vermilion River, was proposed to designate the limits beyond which civilized men were never likely to settle. The Cheyennes were spoken of then as, "a wandering tribe on the Platte," and in the same year, D. D. Mitchell, Superintendent of Indian Affairs, wrote, " A beneficent Creator seems to have intended this dreary region as an asylum for Indians, when the force of circumstances shall have driven them from the last acre of the fertile soil which they once possessed. Here no inducements are offered to the ever-restless Saxon breed to erect their huts.

This "civilization line", ran just east of Dakota, through the extreme eastern portion Nebraska, a little to the east of the middle of Kansas through the middle of Indian Territory and Texas, to the Gulf of Mexico. Montana, Idaho, Colorado, and New Mexico all lie west of it.

Nevertheless, the Cheyennes and other Indians living on the Platte complained bitterly of the passage of increasing numbers of emigrants through their country. They felt that they ought to be paid for the right of way, and that the emigrants should be restricted by law and the presence of a military force from burning the grass, and from unnecessary destruction of game. The Indians were systematically plundered and demoralized by traders. Whiskey was plentiful; sugar and coffee sold at the outrageous price of a dollar a pound. Ten-cent calico went for a dollar a yard, and corn whiskey at seventy-five cents a gallon and higher, several-fold what it sold for to whites.

In 1848, estimated returns to traders amounted to some $400,000. Among the items were 25,000 buffalo tongues. Since the Indians were relatively prosperous, hostilities against whites lessened, but it was still perilous to cross the Plains, where some forty-six thousand Upper Missouri Indians lived.

It was forcibly brought to the attention of the United States Government in 1849 that a treaty was needed to open a safe highway across the continent. Even in this late, lopsided diplomacy with the Indians, it was still recognized that the tribes had a right to certain control as well as to occupancy of their homeland.

Treaty provisions promised good will and peace, which attracted the Indians more than and goods or monies offered. All the tribes were looking forward to it. The bill providing for the treaty was passed unanimously by the Senate, but "the unhappy difficulties existing on the subject of slavery" delayed it in the House until it was too late to be carried into effect.

By 1849 the buffalo herds were thinning and disappearing due to gross over-hunting by whites, who wanted only the hides for sale to a clamoring public back east. The buffalo had always furnished the Plains Indians with food, clothing, and shelter. With its disappearance, starvation stared at them, and they knew it. All the tribes of the region were anxious for friendly relations with the federal government, and wanted some arrangement for means of future subsistence, and some certainty of enough land to live on.

In the summer of 1851 this much desired treaty was made. Seven of the prairie and mountain tribes gathered in great force at Fort Laramie. By this treaty the Indians formally conceded to the United States the rights to establish roads, military or otherwise, throughout the Indian country, "so far as they claim or exercise ownership over it".

For all the damages which the Indians had suffered up to that time in consequence of the passing whites, they accepted the presents then received as payment in full. An annuity of $50,000 for fifty years was promised as the price of the "right of way".

"Fifty thousand dollars for a limited period of years is a small amount to be distributed among at least fifty thousand Indians, especially when we consider that we have taken away from them all means of support," said one of the makers of the treaty. A dollar a year, even assured to one for fifty years, seems hardly an adequate compensation for the surrender of all other "means of support."

The Secretary of the Interior, in his report for 1851, speaks with satisfaction of the treaties negotiated during the year, saying, "It cannot be denied that most of the depredations committed by the Indians on our frontiers are the offspring of dire necessity. ...All history admonishes us of the difficulty of civilizing a wandering race who live mainly upon game. To tame a savage you must tie him down to the soil."

The Cheyennes, therefore, pledged to peace and goodwill toward their Indian neighbors, and to the white emigrants pouring thorough their country. For this conceded right of way they were to have a dollar each, in "goods and animals", and it was supposed that they would be able to eke out that support by hunting buffalos, which were still not quite extinct.

Comment on the bad faith of this action on the part of Congress is a waste of words, but its impolicy is so glaring that astonishment can not be kept silent; its impolicy and also its incredible cheapness. A dollar apiece a year, "in goods, animals, et cetera", those Indians had been promised that they should have for fifty years.

It must have been obvious to the weakest intellect that this was little to pay each year to any man from whom was being taken "his means of support". However, unluckily for the Indians, there were fifty thousand of them. Some thrifty Congressman multiplied fifty thousand by fifty, and the total terrified everybody.

The sophistry is too transparent; it does not in the least gloss over the fact that within the first year after making a treaty of any moment with these tribes; while the whole fifty thousand of them kept faith with the Government, The United States broke faith with them in the meanest of ways; robbing them of more than two thirds of the piddling sum that had been promised. Congress voted to amend the treaty to offer the dollar a year for fifteen rather than fifty years, not bothering to tell the Indians, who eventually assented to the "minor change".

Some of the Indians began to raise corn, beans, pumpkins and so forth, but still depended chiefly on hunting. The agent sent distribute the yearly dollar per person, reported, " The Cheyennes and the Arapahoes, and many of the Sioux, are actually in a starving state." In spite of such suffering, these Indians committed no depredations, and showed increasing kindness to and confidence in the whites.

The agent concluded his report with, "the systems of removals, and congregating tribes in small parcels of territory, has eventuated injuriously on those who have been subject to it. It is the legalized murder of a whole nation."

In the summer of 1854 the Cheyennes began to show dissatisfaction and impertinence. At a gathering of the northern band at Fort Laramie, one of the chiefs demanded that the travel over the Platte Road be stopped. If the interpreter was to be relied on, which is doubtful, the chief also said that the Government must send them one thousand white women for wives.

Constantly observed by all friendly Indians, were the hostiles, who continually plundered and attacked emigrant wagon trains, making more profit from war than from peace. The friendly tribes kept their peace, but in the summer of 1856, the Cheyennes, by a disastrous accident, were forced into the position of hostiles.

A small war-band went out to attack the Pawnees. They were in camp near the North Platte Road, and as the mail-wagon was passing, to Cheyennes ran toward it to beg for tobacco. The terrified mail carrier fired on them, and the Indians fired back, wounding him. The chiefs rushed out, stopped the firing, explained the matter, and then severely flogged the Indians who had returned the mail-carriers fire. However, the mischief had been done.

The mail-carrier reported having been shot at by a Cheyenne Indian, and the next day, troops from Fort Kearney attacked the Indians, killing six of the war party. The thoroughly exasperated war-party attacked an emigrant train, killed two men and a child, and took one woman captive. The next day they killed her because she could not ride on horseback and keep up with them.

Shortly, two more small war-bands left the band, attacked wagon trains, and killed two men, two women, and a child. The chiefs were able to bring the raiders back under control and asked their agent what they should do. Through that winter the Cheyennes remained in the agency, and strictly observed the conditions of the agent.

In the following August, however, a military force under General Sumner was sent "to demand from the tribe the perpetrators of the outrages on the whites, and for ample security for their good conduct." General Sumner said the Cheyennes would not yield to his demands, and he therefor attacked them, burning their village and destroying their winter supplies, some fifteen to twenty thousand pounds of buffalo meat.

There is little record of how and where they survived the winter. The next year the Cheyennes were quite anxious for a new treaty, which would assign them to a country in which they could live safely. They knew that the prairies would soon be occupied by white villages. They wanted peace, and as the buffalo would soon disappear, they hoped for a home where they might be provided for and protected against the encroachments of the whites, at least until they had learned farming and other arts of civilized life.

One of the chiefs told the agent of the Upper Platte Agency that not many years before he had traveled to the Mississippi, then to the land of the Winnebagoes in Minnesota, and then to the Lake Michigan, and then to the tribes in the Dakotas. Almost nowhere did he see but a few white men. "Now our White Father tells us that the white man will never settle on our lands, and kill our game, but see!", he said, "The whites cover all those lands I have just described, and also the lands of the Poncas, Omahas, and Pawnees."

293

"On the South Platte the white people are finding gold, and the Cheyennes and Arapahos have no longer any hunting grounds. Our country has become very small, and before our children are grown up we shall have no game."

It was estimated that during the summer of 1859 over sixty thousand emigrants crossed these plains in their central belt. Valuable trains of wagons and cattle were frequent, and post lines and private expresses were in constant motion. A commissioner was sent in 1860 to hold a council and make a treaty with the Cheyennes and Arapahos at Bent's Fort on the upper Arkansas River. The Arapaho's were fully represented, but there were present only two prominent chiefs of the Cheyennes, Black Kettle and White Antelope, who was one of the chiefs brutally murdered five years later in the infamous Chivington massacre in Colorado.

Because the commissioner could not wait for the rest of the Cheyennes to make the long trip to Fort Bent, the two chiefs distinctly stated that they pledged only themselves and their own bands. The treaty was concluded in February, 1861, at Fort Wise. The chiefs of the Cheyennes and Arapahos there "ceded and relinquished" all the lands to which they had any claim, except a certain tract whose boundaries were defined. Relinquished were lands in Kansas and Nebraska, and all of that part of Colorado which is north of the Arkansas River, and east of the Rocky Mountains.

The desire of the Government to make farmers of these Indians was reiterated in this treaty, and evidenced by pledges of purchase of stock, agricultural implements, and so on. There was a clause that read, "their annuities may, at the discretion of the President of the United States, be discontinued entirely should said Indians fail to make reasonable and satisfactory efforts to improve and advance their condition; in which case such other provision shall be made for them as the President and Congress may judge to be suitable or proper." There could not have been a more complete signing away of all the benefits provided by the treaty.

The treaty also stipulated that the President, with the assent of Congress, would have the power to modify, "any of the provisions of former treaties, in such a manner and to whatever extent" he might best judge to be necessary and expedient for their best interests.

Could a community of people be delivered up more completely bound and at the mercy of the Government? Some of the unrepresented Cheyenne bands were extremely dissatisfied with the treaty, as they had great reason to be. As time went on, all the bands disapproved. Two years later, instead of being settled on their farms "in severalty", the land survey had just been completed, and that a contract, "would soon be made for the construction of a ditch for the purpose of irrigating their arable land."

Things grew rapidly worse in Colorado. Those "preparations for their subsistence by agriculture and grazing", which took so much room to describe in the treaty, had not been made. Many Cheyennes and Arapahos took pilfering reprisals from emigrant wagon trains, and in the resulting fights they murdered many whites. All the tribes on the plains were more or less engaged in these outrages, and it was evident, before midsummer of 1864, that the Government must interfere strongly to protect the emigrants and western settlers from the consequences of its own bad faith with the Indians.

The Governor of Colorado received military aid and authority to wage war on the Indians. In June he proclaimed that all friendly Indians come to designated places to be assured of safety and protection. several bands of peaceful Cheyennes and Arapahos came to Fort Lyon. There on the 29th of November, occurred one of the foulest massacres which the World had ever seen. This camp of friendly Indians was surprised at Daybreak, and men, women, and children were butchered. Most of those who escaped fled north, and joining other bands of the tribe, at once took fearful and natural revenge.

A terrible war followed. Some Cheyenne confederated with the Sioux, and waged relentless war on all the emigrant routes across the plains. The bitter hostilities were in proportion to the bitterness of resentment felt by the refugees of what is now known in the annals of treachery as the Sand Creek Massacre.

"It will be long before faith in the honor and humanity of the whites can be reestablished in the minds of these barbarians," says an official report, "and the last Indian who escaped the brutal scene at Sand Creek will probably have died before its effects will have disappeared".

In October of the next year some of the bands gathered to hold a council with the United States Commissioners on the Little Arkansas. Black Kettle, the Chief over whose lodge at Sand Creek the American Flag flew, with a white flag tied beneath it at the time of the wholesale slaughter, said, "I once thought that I was the only man that persevered to be the friend of the white man; but since they have come and cleaned out our lodges, horses, and everything else, it is hard for me to believe white men any more." Continuing with such calm and reason, he said, "That fool-band of soldiers cleared out our lodges, and killed our women and children. This is hard on us."

By the terms of the new treaty, a new reservation was to be set apart for the Cheyennes and Arapahos, and of course the hackneyed lie, "No whites shall be allowed on the reservation", was included. A large tract was to be relinquished by the Indians, but they were permitted to live on it and roam at pleasure through the unsettled portions. The Indians felt that at last they had a treaty they could trust. They hoped that in their new home they would have greater safety and peace.

The Cheyennes could not long remain at peace. In the summer the Senate amended the latest treaty to require that their new reservation be, "entirely outside the state of Kansas, and not within any Indian territory, except on consent of the tribes interested. As the recently designated reservation had been partly in Kansas, and partly on Cherokee land, they were left without any home whatever.

Young men of the tribe began to join with other hostile Indians in raids along the great mail-routes on the plains. Again they received summary vengeance by United States troops, and in the summer of 1867 a Cheyenne village of three hundred lodges was burned by soldiers under General Hancock.

A precarious peace was confirmed by yet another treaty, but was almost immediately broken by Government failure to comply with its provisions. In October of that year, Major Wynkoop, a faithful friend of the Cheyennes and Arapahos ever since the days of Sand Creek, published his last protest on their behalf, in a letter to the Commissioner of Indian Affairs. He said that the failure of the government to deliver promised supplies, and the refusal to allow the Indians promised arms and ammunition, left them without any means of securing game; hence the depredations.

All the Indians of the Upper Arkansas River joined the struggle. On October 27th, 1868, Black Kettle and his entire band were killed by General Custer's command at Antelope Hills, on the Wichita River.

In 1869 many Cheyennes and Arapahos made their way to Montana, and were living among the Gros Ventres. Most of those remaining in the south were quiet, but implored to be moved further north where they might hunt buffalo. Some consideration was shown the southern Cheyennes in 1870, and in 1872 both tribes were reported as allied to the Government in maintaining peace on the border. Raiding bands of Kiowas had made strong inducements to the Cheyennes to join them, but they remained loyal and peaceful.

Thirty Northern Cheyenne lodges rejoined the tribe in 1872, but many still roamed among the Northern Sioux. In 1874 there were said to be over three thousand Northern Cheyennes and Arapahos at the Red Cloud

Agency. The Government refused to let them stay, and after protests, the Cheyennes consented to go to Indian Territory. The move was delayed, however, due to fresh troubles among the Southern Cheyennes.

White horse-thieves on the reservation brought on a general war against whites in the region and during the next few months the Cheyennes, Kiowas, Osages, and Comanches raided and murdered many whites. Sixty lodges of Cheyennes took refuge under the troops at the agency, and the old problem arose, of how to punish the guilty without harming the innocent. After a vigorous campaign by General Miles' command, the main body of hostiles surrendered in the Spring of 1875.

The defeated Indian bands straggled in, half-starved, half-naked, without lodges and ponies. It was amazing that they had held out so long. Thirty-three of the most desperate hostiles were to be sent to prison in Saint Augustine, Florida, but before the selection could be made, the surrendered braves stampeded, and 400 escaped.

They held their ground from two P.M. until dark, against three cavalry companies and two Gatlin guns. They escaped during the stormy night that followed, leaving only three dead.

The friendly Cheyennes remained loyal, despite not having enough food, and being cut off from hunting. In 1875 their agent wrote, "On last year's flour contract not a single pound was received until the fourteenth day of First Month, 1875, when six months of cold weather and many privations had passed, notwithstanding the many protestations and urgent appeals from the agent."

The Northern Cheyennes on the Red Cloud Agency remained troublesome and restless. In 1877 they were moved to the Cheyenne and Arapaho Agency, in Indian Territory. Reports say they asked to be taken there. In Autumn, the reunited tribe went on a grand buffalo hunt, accompanied by a small detail of troops from Fort Reno.

Early that winter white horse-thieves stole Indian ponies valued at two thousand nine hundred dollars, repeating the act that had goaded the Indians into war in 1874. Somehow the natives resisted retaliation, and had two years of improved conditions, due to their determination to become self-sufficient.

The winter of 1877, and the summer of 1878, however, were terrible for the Cheyennes. Their fall hunt was unsuccessful, and they straggled home, destitute and hungry. The usual horse stealing by Whites became bolder. Their Government rations were cut to insufficiency, but these were only the beginnings of their troubles.

The summer was unusually hot. Extreme heat, chills and fever, aggravated by lack of food, brought on terrible waves of sickness. There was no malarial treatment for them, and at least two thousand were gravely ill on the reservation.

Early in the Autumn, a band of some three hundred Northern Cheyennes took the desperate step of running off and attempting to make their back to Dakota. They fought desperately when pursued, but finally overpowered, they surrendered on the condition that they be taken to Dakota. They said they would rather die by bullets than go back to Indian Territory and die of chills, fever, and starvation.

They were made prisoners of war at Fort Robinson, Nebraska. They were ordered back to the Indian Territory, and the local Commander tried to starve them into submission. He stopped feeding them, and cut off their fuel while the mercury froze at Fort Robinson. After two days he said that the women and children could come out he would feed them. Not a woman emerged.

On the fourth night, or some accounts say on the sixth, the starving, freezing Indians broke out, overpowered the guards, and fled into the winter night with their women and children. For several days they held pursuing troops at bay. They made their final stand in a frozen ravine, and all were killed.

Fifty Cheyenne women and children, and some seven men, who had been held in a different part of the fort, did not have the good fortune to share in the outbreak meet a quick death in the ravine. All were sent to prison at Fort Leavenworth, the men to be tried for the deaths of soldiers they had fought on their way north.

Red Cloud, the great Sioux Chief, came to Fort Robinson immediately after the massacre, and asked to be allowed to take the Cheyenne widows and orphans into his tribe. The Government, in its kindness, permitted twenty-two widows, and thirty-two children, many of whom were orphans, to join the Oglala Sioux.

To his great shame, The Commissioner of Indian Affairs, said in his report of 1879 that the Indians were not starving at the time of their flight. The attempt only rebounded to his disgrace, and he was found guilty of absolute dishonest in his estimates, and that the quantity of beef issued to his Cheyene Agency was greatly less than he had reported. It was proven that the Indians, exactly as they had said, were indeed starving.

fifty native children starved to death on that reservation in 1877 and 1878, along with many young men and women, as well as the elderly.

As the century of great dishonor ended for the Cheyennes, there was not even warm clothing for them, let alone enough to eat. In the melancholy record of suffering of American Indians, a more glaring instance of confused multiplication of injustices can not be found. The Cheyennes, in their desperation, were pursued and slain for daring to leave the deadly reservation, which apparently, was not their reservation at all, they having had removed their legal right to any place on Earth. There are no adequate words to characterize such treatment of a handful of helpless people by a powerful, rich nation.

THE NEZ PERCES

Oregon: wide, healthful, beautiful, abundant, and inviting; no wonder it was coveted and fought for. When Lewis and Clarke visited it at the beginning of the 1800s, they found many tribes of Indians, numbering at least twenty to thirty thousand. Of all these, the Nez Perces were the richest, noblest, and most gentle.

To the Cayuses, one of the most warlike tribes, Lewis and Clarke presented an American flag, telling them it was an emblem of peace. The beauty and bright coloring of the flag, allied to its significance, deeply impressed the poetic minds of these natives. They set the flag up in a beautiful valley called the Grande Ronde,a fertile basin some twenty-five miles wide, surrounded by high basaltic walls, watered by a branch of the Snake River.

Around this flag they met their old enemies, the Shoshones, and swore to keep perpetual peace with them. The spot became consecrated to an annual sort of fair, where the Cayuse, Nez Perce, and Walla Walla Indians came every summer and traded their roots, skins, elk and buffalo meats, for salmon and horses, with the Shoshones. It was a beautiful spot, nearly circular, luxuriantly covered with grass, the hill wall around it thick with evergreen trees, chiefly larch. The Indians called it *Karpkarp*, which translates to "Balm of Gilead".

The life of these Indians was peculiar. Most had several homes, and as they lived only a part of the year in each, were frequently spoken of by travellers as nomadic tribes, while in fact they were as wedded to their homes as any civilized people. Their wanderings were as systematic as the seasonal moving of wealthy city people from town homes to country places. Each season had its duty and appointed place for the Nez Perce, and year after year the same month found them in the same spot.

In 1833 a delegation from these Oregon Indians went to Saint Louis, and through the artist, George Catlin, made known their object, which was "to inquire for the truth of what some white men had told them, that the American's religion was better than theirs, and that they would all be lost without it."

Two members of this delegation were Nez Perces; *Hee-oh 'ks-te-kin* and *H'co-a-h'co-a-h'cotes-min*; or "rabbit-skin leggings", and "No horns on his Head". Their portraits are found in *Catlin's American Indians*. One of these died on the way back to Oregon, but the other told his tribe that the report which they had heard was true, and that good and religious men would soon come among them to teach this religion, so that they could all understand and benefit by it.

Two years later the Methodist Episcopal Society and the American Board both sent missionaries to Oregon. The efforts brought profound results among the natives. The Nez Perces became devout Christians.

The earliest mention of the Nez Perces in the official records of the Indian Bureau is in the year 1843. In that year an agent was sent to investigate the condition of the Oregon tribes, and he reported, "The only tribes from which much is to be hoped , or anything to be feared in this part of Oregon, are the Walla Wallas, Cayuses, and Nez Perces, inhabiting a district on the Columbia and its tributaries, commencing two hundred and forty miles from its mouth, and stretching four hundred and eighty miles in the interior."

The Nez Perces, living farther inland, "inhabit a beautiful grazing district, not surpassed by any I have seen for verdure, water privileges, climate, or health. This tribe forms an honorable exception to the general Indian character, being more noble, industrious, sensible, and better disposed toward the whites and their improvements in the arts and sciences; and though brave as Caesar (the Indians), the whites have nothing to dread at their hands in case of their dealing out to them what they conceive to be right and equitable."

When this agent arrived a the missionary station among the Nez Perces, he was met by a large body of Indians, with twenty-two of their chiefs. The missionaries received them, "with joyful countenances and glad hearts"; the Indians, "with civility, gravity, and dignified reserve."

He addressed them at length, explaining to them the kind intentions of the Government toward them. They listened with "gravity, fixed attention, and decorum". Finally an aged chief, ninety years of age, arose and said, "I speak today, Perhaps tomorrow I die. I am the oldest chief of the tribe. I was the high chief when your brothers, Lewis and Clarke, visited this country."

"They visited me, and honored me with their friendship and counsel. I showed them my numerous wounds, received in bloody battle with the Snakes. They told me it was not good; It was better to be at peace; and gave me a flag of truce. I held it up high. We met and talked, but never fought again. Clarke pointed to this day - to you and this occasion. ...I am glad to live to see you and this day."

At this council the Nez Perces elected a head chief named Ellis, and adopted a civil and just Code of Laws, except for the introduction, by the white agent, of punishment for certain crimes by whipping or flogging. The agent was written of by an historian of the period, as being, "a notorious blockhead". One cannot argue with his opinion, since the whipping-post was offered as a first installment of the United States' "kind intentions" towards these Indians.

A report by a Reverend Spauld, who had lived six years among the Nez Perces, says, "nearly all the principal men and chiefs are members of the school; that they are as industrious in their schools as on their farms. They cultivate their lands with much skill and to good advantage, and many more would do so if they had the means. About one hundred are printing their own books with the pen. This keeps up a deep interest, as they daily have new lessons to print; and what they print must be committed to memory as soon as possible."

"A good number are now so far advanced in reading and printing as to render much assistance in teaching. Their books are taken home at night, and every lodge becomes a schoolroom. Their lessons are Scripture lessons; no others (except the laws) seem to interest them."

The 1843 report of the Secretary of War reads, "The Nez Perce Tribe have adopted a simple code of laws that teach them self-restraint. ...It is remarkable that there should so soon be several well-attended, well-conducted schools in Oregon". It is not that remarkable, considering that the Congregationalists, the Methodist Episcopalians, and the Roman Catholics all had their missionaries at work there for eight years.

The Oregon Tribes, including the Nez Perces, disappeared in 1846 from the official records of the Indian Bureau. Congress decided to discontinue what had been a "temporary service" among the Oregon Indians. The missions were abandoned in 1847, after the Cayuse massacred the missionaries among them. Deprived of their teaching, The Nez Perces kept their faith and goodwill toward the whites.

301

A superintendent and three agents in 1851 were appointed for Indian service in Oregon. Treaties were negotiated, but not ratified and honored by the United States. "They have become distrustful of all promises made them by the United States", says the Oregon Superintendent. ...The settlement of the whites on the tracts which they regarded as secured to them by solemn treaty stipulations, ...augments bitter animosities and resentments."

Governor Stephens of Washington Territory wrote ,"These hitherto neglected tribes, whose progress from the wild wanderers of the plains to kind and hospitable neighbors, ...are entitled, by every consideration of justice and humanity, to the fatherly care of the Government." The Governor's opinion was ignored.

In 1855 there was a general outbreak of hostilities by the Oregon Indians. Tribe after tribe fell into the ranks of the hostiles. Terrified Oregon settlers, "were without discipline, without order, and similar to madmen", says one report.

"Every day they run off the horses and cattle of the friendly Indians. I will soon no longer be able to restrain them." It is difficult to do justice to the moral courage which is shown by those who remained friendly to whites under such conditions.

The hostiles then told the Nez Perces to join them against the whites or be wiped out. The Nez Percés had no ammunition, and the whites would give them none. The hostiles said, "we have plenty. Join us and save your lives." The defenseless Nez Perces were greatly alarmed, but were willing to make almost any sacrifice to obtain peace.

After sharp fighting, the outbreak ended with about equal losses on both sides. There was a sort of armistice, which left the Indians emboldened, confident that they could contend successfully against the whites. Failure to ratify previous treaties, and continued extension of white settlers, without consideration or compensation, was a constant source of hostile feelings among the natives.

An agent's report reflected truthfully, "Such a proceeding is not only contrary to our policy hitherto, but is repugnant alike to the dictates of humanity and the principles of natural justice." As expected, the armistice failed, and in 1848 the Oregon and Washington territories had another Indian war. The Nez Perces. along with the Flatheads, and Pend d'Oreilles, fought with the United States against the hostiles. One detachment of federal troops was saved by taking refuge with them.

When asked what they wanted, the Nez Perce said, "Peace, Plows, and Schools". In 1859 the Indians were considered conquered. The treaties of

1855 were ratified, and tranquility returned to the territories. Congress was implored quickly to grant the money stipulated in the treaties, to prevent another war. The Superintendents did not point out to Congress that had they lived up to the treaties, there most likely would have been no war.

The reservation granted to the Nez Perces was a fine tract, one hundred miles long and sixty wide, well-timbered, watered, and with great natural resources. The Indians immediately began cultivating and irrigating their fields, and developed large herds of horses.

In less than two years the peace of the Nez Perces was invaded by a deadly foe, the greed for gold. "To attempt to restrain miners would be like attempting to restrain the whirlwind," wrote the Washington Territory Superintendent.

For the next few years the Nez Perces were dismayed at the steady stream of settlers pouring into their country. That they did not resist by force can only be explained in the power of their religious spirit. In 1865 there land became part of the new Idaho Territory.

A powerful party arose among the Nez Perces, urging the formation of a league with the Crows and Blackfeet against the whites. The non-arrival of promised supplies and money, and the unchecked influx of miners on the reservation, put strong weapons into the hands of the disaffected. Adding to the fervor was that the warriors who had fought so well for the United States in 1856 had still not been paid.

How many white communities would remain peaceable, loyal, and friendly under such a strain?

Also in 1866, The Governor of Idaho wrote to the Department of the Interior, "Could this loyal tribe have been kept aloof from the contaminating vices of white men, and had it been in the power of the Government promptly to comply with the stipulations of the treaty of 1865, there can be no doubt that their condition at this time would have been a most prosperous one."

The patience of the Nez Perces began to wear thin in 1867. The Idaho Governor again warns the federal Government, "...Serious trouble is imminent. It could all be settled by prompt payment by the Government of their just dues; but if delayed to long I greatly fear open hostilities. ...If neglected, war may be reasonably expected. If the Nez Perces strike a blow, all over our Territory and around our boundaries will blaze the signal-fires and gleam the tomahawks of the savages -- Kootenays, Pen d'Oreilles, Coeur d'Alenes, Blackfeet, Flat-heads, Spokanes, Pelouses, Bannocks, and Shoshones will be involved."

In spite of increasing disaffection, the Nez Perces remained industrious and prosperous. In 1869 their reservation was still unsurveyed, and when the Indians again claimed that whites were settling inside the lines, there was no way of proving it. In 1870, seven years after being promised, the reservation was surveyed, but the manner in which it was done proved to be a scandalous fraud.

The fence posts were not well set, much of the board lumber was deficient in width and length, and they were joined and nailed haphazardly, so that the entire structure soon fell down.

A commission was sent to hold council in 1873 with the Nez Perces in the Wallowa Valley, in Oregon, "with a view to their removal to the Nez Perce Reservation in Idaho." The relocation was reported as impractical, and the Wallowa Valley was removed from sale to settlers and set apart for the Nez Perces, by Executive Order.

The Commission's report quoted Chief Joseph's reason for not wanting schools and churches on his Wallowa Valley reservation. He said, "We do not want schools. We do not want churches. They will teach us to quarrel about God, as the Catholics and Protestants do. ...We do not want to learn that. We may quarrel with men sometimes about things on this earth, but we never quarrel about God."

White settlers greatly resented The Wallowa Valley being ceded to the Nez Perces, and in 1875 the Commissioner of Indian Affairs warned of great trouble if Chief Joseph could not be persuaded to join others of his tribe in Idaho. Only two years after officially setting apart the valley for them, the Department was planning on "compelling" them to leave.

The Indian Bureau recommended revoking the Executive Order, and President Ulysses Grant promptly did so, assuring that the Nez Perce would be subjected "merely to the same just and equal laws by which the President and all his people are ruled". Chief Joseph replied to the President that he asked nothing of him; that he could take care of himself; and that he no longer wanted the Wallowa Valley because it would subject his band to the will and laws of others. He wanted to move peaceably.

Government officials knew well the enormity of their lie about "equal and just laws", and that the instant Joseph and his band moved onto the Idaho reservation that they became subject to restrictive, totally different laws than those by which whites were bound. The Indians, as on all reservations, would be mere convicts in a prison without walls. For the sake of their own honor and integrity, it is amazing that four Government officials would sign their names to such a scurrilous document.

Of course, the Government had not fulfilled its treaty obligations to those already on the Idaho reservation. The Agent pointed out to the Government that continued failure to fulfill the treaty would add to the Indian's distrust in the faith of the Government. He was not heeded.

Facing the inevitable, Chief Joseph finally consented to move to the Lapwai Reservation. The chief's own words are recorded of the council, as were General Howard's, who negotiated for the Government. The General said he listened to the "oft-repeated dreamer nonsense of the chief, 'Too-hool-hool-suit' (An old chief under Joseph)," and finally said to him, "Twenty times over I hear that the Earth is your mother, and about the chieftaincy of the Earth. I want to hear it no more."

Joseph said, "General Howard lost his temper, and said, 'Shut up! I don't want to hear any more of such talk'".

Too-hool-hool-suit answered, said the General, "Who are you, that you ask us to talk, and then tell me I shan't talk? Are you the Great Spirit? Did you make the World?"

Joseph said, "General Howard replied, 'You are an impudent fellow, and I will put you in the guardhouse,' and then ordered a soldier to arrest him. Too-hool-hool-suit made no resistance. He asked General Howard, 'Is that your order? I don't care. I have expressed my heart to you. I have nothing to take back. I have spoken for my country. You can arrest me, but you cannot change me, or make me take back what I have said.' ...Too-hool-hool-suit was prisoner for five days..."

Chief Joseph, as always, spoke with common sense as well as natural feeling, in saying, "I turned to my people and said, 'The arrest of Too-hool-hool-suit was wrong, but we will not resent the insult. We were invited to this council to express our hearts, and we have done so."

Consenting to move, Joseph said, "I said in my heart, that rather than have war, I would give up my country. I would give up my father's grave. I would give up everything rather than have the blood of white men upon the hands of my people." The young men wanted to fight, and Joseph had to ride among them brandishing a pistol and threatening to shoot the first of his warriors that resisted the Government.

Finally, they gathered all the stock they could find, and began the move. A storm raised the river so high that some of the cattle could not be taken across and were left behind with Indian guards. White men attacked the guards and took the cattle.

Joseph could no longer restrain his men, and two months of war followed, masterfully campaigned by the Indians. They were pursued by

General Howard, they had General Crook on their right, and General Miles in front, yet not once were they hemmed in.

When they at last surrendered at Bear Paw Mountain, in the Montana Hills, it was not because they were beaten, but because as Joseph said, "I could no longer bear to see my wounded men and women suffer any longer. We had lost enough already. We could have escaped if we left our wounded, old women and children behind. We were unwilling to do this. We had never heard of a wounded Indian recovering while in the hands of white men."

On the fifth day, after having been promised by General Miles that they would be returned to Lapwai Reservation, Joseph said, "I went to General Miles and gave up my gun, and said, 'From where the sun now stands, I will fight no more.' My people needed rest; we wanted peace."

The terms of the surrender, as was routine, were shamefully violated. Joseph and his band were taken first to Fort Leavenworth and then to Indian Territory. While at Leavenworth they were placed in the river bottom, with only dirty river water to drink.

"Many of my people sickened and died, and we buried them in this strange land," said Joseph. "I cannot tell how much my heart suffered for my people while at Leavenworth. The Great Spirit Chief who rules above seemed to looking some other way, and did not see what was being done to my people."

Within a few months after arriving in Indian Territory, the sickness contracted while at Leavenworth killed at least a quarter of Joseph's followers. There the remainder languished till the end of the 1870s. Of the remainder of the Nez Perces, those on the Lapwai Reservation, the report of the Indian Bureau for 1879 said that they "support themselves entirely without subsistence from the Government."

As the Century of Dishonor ended for the Nez Perces, there was already a cloud on the horizon. The Lapwai Reservation was being lusted after by whites.

THE PONCAS

In 1803 Captain Lewis and Lieutenant Clarke, of the First United States Infantry, were commissioned by Congress to explore the Missouri River from its mouth to its source, to "seek the best water communication from thence to the Pacific Ocean," and to confer with all the Indian tribes on their route, with a view to the establishment of commerce with them.

They reported the "Poncars" as, "the remnant of a nation once respectable in numbers; they formerly resided on a branch of the Red River of Lake Winnepeg; being oppressed by Sioux, they removed to the west side of the Missouri, on Poncar River, where they built and fortified a village, and remained some years; but, being pursued by their ancient enemies, the Sioux, and reduced by continual wars, they have joined and now live with the Mahas (Omahas), whose language they speak."

They were numbered at about two hundred by Lewis and Clarke, but the count was probably low because most of the tribe was away on a buffalo hunt. In an 1829 census, they were listed at six hundred. The artist Catlin visited them a few years later and counted them a little less.

While painting the portrait of Chief Shoo-de-ga-cha (Smoke), Catlin wrote, " He related to me with great coolness and frankness the poverty and distress of his nation--and with the method of a philosopher predicted the certain and rapid extinction of his tribe, which he had not the power to avert."

"He told me he had 'once been powerful and happy; that the buffaloes which the Great Spirit had given them for food, and which formerly spread all over their green prairies, had all been driven out by the approach of white men, who wanted their skins; that their country was now entirely destitute of game, and even of roots for food, as it was one continuous prairie; that his people had foolishly become fond of firewater, and had given away everything in their country for it.'"

"He further said that it had destroyed many of his warriors, and would soon destroy the rest; that his tribe was too small and his warriors too few to go to war with the tribes around them; and that he was still more alarmed from the constant advance of the pale faces--their enemies from the east--with whiskey, and smallpox, which had already destroyed four-fifths of his tribe, and would soon impoverish and at last destroy the remainder of them."

The United State's first treaty with this handful of gentle and peaceable Indians was made it 1817, and was the usual "peace and friendship: prelude. In 1825 another was made, in which the Poncas admit that "they reside within the territorial limits of the United States, acknowledge their supremacy, and claim their protection." They also admit, "the right of the United States to regulate all trade and intercourse with them." The United States, on their part, "agree to receive the Poncar tribe of Indians into their friendship and under their protection."

For the next thirty years there was little mention of the Poncas in official Government records. The peaceable Poncas were left to shift for themselves because other tribes in the Upper Missouri region were so troublesome and aggressive. In 1846 the agent of the Upper Platte mentions incidentally that their lands were being fast intruded upon by squatters.

The Commissioner for Indian Affairs writes in 1858, "Treaties were entered into in March and April last with the Poncas and Yankton Sioux, who reside west of Iowa, for the purpose of extinguishing their title to all the lands occupied and claimed by them, except small portions on which to colonize and domesticate them. This proceeding was deemed necessary in order to obtain such control over these Indians as to prevent their interference with our settlements, which are rapidly extending in that direction."

In good faith, the Poncas abandoned their settlements and hunting grounds and were moved to their new home. Having been unsuccessful in their summer hunt, and having no crop to rely on, they were desperate and destitute. Since nothing had been done for them under the treaty, they conclude it was void and threatened to return to their ancestral home, ehich in the meantime had been filled with white settler.

Because of Government delay, the Untied States had to "incur a heavy expense, to give enough food to keep the Poncas from starving. In 1859, under this pressure, the Senate finally ratified the treaty. The Poncas had lost all but a small tract between the Ponca and Niobrara Rivers. The treaty stipulated $20,000 in aid the first year (very little of which was actually received), plus diminishing annuities for thirty years.

The Agent had no money to feed them, so he induced the Ponca to go on a hunt. They straggled back in less than a month, begging for food for their women and children, whom they had left half-starved on the Plains. They had found no game, and only a few wild turnips. They had to trade away most of their blankets and other goods.

The reports are more pitiful for 1863. After the first hoeing of their corn, they went on a mostly unsuccessful buffalo hunt. Their crops withered before their return. The plains had been burned over and they could find no roots, berries, or anything else to eat. Through all these troubles the Poncas remained loyal and peaceable, and were "unwavering in their fidelity to their treaty" said the Indian Commissioner.

In December of the same year, a marauding group of soldiers at first taunted a small traveling group of Ponca women and boys. Then they destroyed their belongings and killed their ponies. As the Indians fled in terror, most were killed and mutilated by the men of Company B of the Seventh Iowa Cavalry. There was some correspondence between military authorities, but nothing was done.

The Poncas' reservation was extended down the Niobrara to the Missouri River in 1865, and the Government agreed to pay them $15,000 for their loss in the recent outrage and in others. Of course it took two more years to ratify this provision, and that, plus other promised money and goods fell far short, or didn't arrive at all.

In 1870, $5,000 was appropriated to resume the Poncas' school that had been discontinued due to non-receipt of promised funds. The Poncas were encouraged at this, and built many substantial homes despite being half-starved by lack of government-promised rations. The always peaceful, always loyal Poncas were digging wild roots to stay alive , and still did not complain when the saw wagons of food and herds of cattle being driven across their lands to feed the lately hostile Sioux, who continued to raid and drive off the little remaining stock of the Poncas.

They worked industriously for two years under these terrible conditions, but in 1873 the Missouri overflowed and entirely destroyed the Ponca village. The tribe worked around the clock for weeks to salvage what they could and move it further from the river. A year later they had recovered marvelously, having built new homes and put three hundred acres of land under cultivation.

The Poncas could not get through the year without more disaster. First came a drought; then three visitations of locusts, leaving nothing in the fields but straw. All newly planted trees withered and died.

The locusts came again in 1875, and destroyed all but the wheat crop. Much of the wheat was lost anyway, because there was only one reaping machine on the agency, and it could not do all the work. The Indians cut what could with knives, but much of it dried up and perished before it could be harvested.

1875 was also marked by a flagrant injustice of the helplessness of Indians in the courts. Two Poncas were waylaid by a party of Santees; one of the Poncas was murdered, the other seriously wounded. The courts dismissed the case, saying they had no jurisdiction over crimes committed between Indians.

The next year, in an absurd bit of reasoning, it was assumed that the Poncas would not mind being sent to Indian Territory in Oklahomas, since they had agreed to their earlier move. After much protest, the tribe at last gave what the United States Government called their "consent" to be moved.

The influences, deceits, and coercions brought to bear on these unfortunate creatures before this was brought about, is one of the most harrowing records of dealings with the Indians. A party of chiefs was induced to go

309

with a United States Inspector to see that the new area would suit them. They were distinctly promised that if it did not suit them, they could go to Washington to consult with the President as to a suitable plan.

Chief Standing Bear, one of those who made the trip said they were suddenly approached by the Inspector who told them to pack up and move to Indian Territory immediately. They were told that the President would sell their land and give them the money after the move.

The Chief told him they didn't want to go, saying, "When a man owns anything, he does not let it go till he has received payment for it." The Inspector said that he would show them the land and if they didn't like they could see the President and tell him so.

He took ten chiefs to Oklahoma and showed them three poor tracts. He told them they had to choose one, and that they would not be paid for the land they left. When the chiefs told him he had lied, he angered, and told them that if they did not do as they were told he would leave them there, a thousand miles from home, without money or an interpreter. He did exactly that.

It was winter. They started for home on foot, sleeping in haystacks at night, barely keeping from freezing. Their moccasins wore out and they were barefoot in the snow, eating dried corn they found in harvested fields. Fifty days on the road, they were almost dead when they reached the Otoe Agency, leaving bloody footprints on the floor of the Agent's office when they told their story.

The agent had received a telegram from the cruel, deceitful inspector, saying the chiefs were runaways, and not to help them in any way. He was dismayed and sympathetic when her heard their plight. There they were fed and rested for ten days. The Otoes gave each a pony, and in seven days ride they reached the Omaha Reservation. They sent a telegram to the President, asking if he had authorized their treatment. There was no answer.

Four more days on the road and they reached their home, only to find the Inspector there. When the Poncas were alarmed at his arrival without their chiefs, he told them, "Tomorrow you must be ready to move. If you are not, you will be shot. Then the soldiers came to the doors with bayonets, and ten families were frightened. The soldiers brought wagons; they put their things in and were carried away", said Standing Bear. The rest of the tribe would not move.

"When we got there, we asked the inspector why he had done this thing, and he got very angry," said Standing Bear. "Then we said to him, 'We did not think we would see your face again, after what has passed. ...But

310

here you are. This land is ours. Let us alone. Go away from us. You may take all the money that is to be paid to us for twelve years, if you will go and leave us our lands."

The Inspector called for more troops, but Standing Bear and his brother refused to go. Their families were driven across the river and the two men were jailed at a nearby fort. When the Commanding Officer heard their story, he said that they had done no wrong, but he was a soldier and had to obey orders.

The officer did send a telegram to the President about the affair. The President answered that he knew nothing about it. After ten days in jail, the chiefs, with their families and remaining tribal members were forced to begin the trip. Many died on the road, and most of their horses died after they reached the new land. The bad water killed all their cattle.

Standing Bear stayed until a hundred and fifty of his people died. He then he ran away with thirty men, women and children. Three months on the road, they were weak, sick and starved when they reached the Omaha Reservation. The Omahas gave them a piece of land and they were anxious to plow and put in wheat.

Soldiers arrived and arrested them, determined to return them to the Oklahoma. However, news of their arrest and the Government's intentions roused excitement in Omaha. An editor and two lawyers tested whether the Government had a legal right to do such a thing.

A Judge Dundy, whose name should stand with that of Lincoln in the matter of emancipation acts, considered the case several days and gave a decision that struck at the root of the whole matter, a decision which, when finally enforced throughout the Nation, took the ground from under the feet of the horde of unscrupulous thieves that robbed, oppressed, and maddened the Indians for so long.

When Standing Bear found that by the decision of Judge Dundy he was a free man, and could go where he pleased, he made a speech which should never be forgotten or left out of the history of the dealings of the United States Government with the Indians.

After he touchingly thanked his attorneys, he said, " Hitherto, when we have been wronged, we went to war to assert our rights and avenge our wrongs. We took the tomahawk. We had no law to punish those who did wrong, so we took our tomahawks and went to kill. If they had guns and could kill us first, it was the fate of war. But you have found a better way. You have gone into court for us, and I find that our wrongs can be righted there. Now I have no more use for the tomahawk. I want to lay it down forever."

Eloquently expressive, the old Indian stooped and placed his tomahawk at his feet. Then, standing erect, he folded his arms with native dignity and continued, "I lay it down. I have no more use for it. I have found a better way."

Stooping again, and taking up the weapon, he placed it in the hands of one of his attorneys, a Mr. Webster, and said, "I present it to you as a token of my gratitude. I want you to keep it in remembrance of this great victory which you have gained. I have no further use for it. I can now seek the ways of peace."

The first thing Standing Bear did with his freedom was to try to gain the freedom of his tribe, and to establish their legal right to their old home in Dakota. Accompanied by a young and well-educated Omaha girl and her brother as interpreters, and by Mr. Tibbles, the champion and friend to whom he owed his freedom, he went East, telling the story of the sufferings and wrongs of his tribe to large audiences in many of the larger cities.

Money was generously subscribed everywhere to bring suits to test the question of the Poncas' legal right to the lands which the United States had by treaty ceded to them in specified "townships," thus giving to them the same sort of title which would be given to any corporation or individual.

This movement of Standing Bear and his companions soon produced a strong effect on the community. This attracted the authorities in Washington, and letters were published contradicting Standing Bear's assertions. statements were circulated injurious to all members of the party. For some mysterious reason, the Department of the Interior was unwilling that the Poncas should be reinstated on their lands.

Discussions grew heated. The cruel Inspector involved with their forced move, published long letters attacking Standing Bear's veracity. The chief's pithy answers proved the falsity of many of the inspectors statements. What soon became clear to observers was that either the Secretary of the Interior or the inspector, or both, were liars.

Interest in the cas brought about a committee being appointed to represent the case in Washington, and to secure legislation on it. Standing Bear made a powerful impression on Congress. Once started on the subject, Congressional committees called for evidence regarding several other striking instances of injustices to Indians.

A bill was introduced in Congress to restore to the Poncas their old reservation in Dakota, and putting their houses, farms,and so on, in the same good condition they were at the time of their removal from them.

Damning to the Department of the Interior was the report of the agent who had superintended the forced move. Strangely, the Department made it part of its official record of the management of Indian affairs for 1877. It graphically documented the misery, horror, and wretched conditions the Poncas endured. Despite the official evidence in their own files, the Department of the Interior still contended that the Indians were not moved by force.

There was never any accusation brought against the military for brutality in this case. However, the very presence of the troopers was brutal and coercive. There was no doubt about the orders the "military force" would have carried out had the Poncas not finally submitted to the move.

"It is a matter of astonishment to me," said the Agent in charge in his report, "that the government should have ordered the removal of the Ponca Indians from Dakota to the Indian Territory without having first made some provision for their settlement and comfort."

"Before their removal was carried into effect an appropriation should have been made by Congress sufficient to have located them in their new home, by building a comfortable home for the occupancy of every family of the tribe. As the case now is, no appropriation has been made by Congress except a sum little more that sufficient to remove them, and the result is that these people have been placed on an uncultivated reservation, to live in their tents as best they may, and await further legislative action."

The Agent's journal is the best record that can ever be written of the sufferings of the Poncas in being taken from their homes. It cannot be discredited. It is an"official record", authorized and endorsed by being published in the Annual Report of the Secretary of the Interior.

In 1880, at the end of the hundred most shameful years in United States history, the remainder of the tribe was still in Indian Territory, anxiously awaiting the results of the efforts to restore them their old homes, and to establish their indisputable legal right to them.

THE WINNEBAGOES

The Winnebagoes belonged to the Dakota (Sioux) family, but were known as a naturally peace-loving people, and had no sympathy with their more warlike relatives. The Algonquins gave them the name of Winnebagoes, or "people of the saltwater", and as the Algonquin word for saltwater and stinking-water was the name, the French called them "les Puants," or "Stinkards." The Sioux gave them a more melodious and pleasing name, "O-ton-kah," which meant "The large, strong people."

313

Bancroft, in his account of the North American tribes, says, "One little community of the Dakota (Sioux) family had penetrated the territories of the Algonquins, The Winnebagoes, dwelling between Green Bay and the lake that bears their name, and preferred to be environed by Algonquins than to stay in the dangerous vicinity of their own kindred."

The earliest mention of this tribe in the diplomatic history of the United States, is in the council reports of July, 1815, at "Portage des Sioux", in Missouri, after the Treaty of Ghent. The Winnebagoes refused to send delegates, which was considered important. The Americans thought that British influence kept the Winnebagoes away, but it is more likely that they already had a general distrust of all white men. When visited later, one official observed, "There is no other tribe which seems to possess so much jealousy of the whites, and such reluctance to have intercourse with them..."

In spite of this reluctance, in 1816 they made a treaty "of peace and friendship with the United States," agreeing "to remain distinct and separate from the rest of their nation or tribe, giving them no assistance whatever until peace shall be concluded between the United States and their tribe or nation."

In 1825 the United States Government, unable to endure the spectacle of Indians warring among themselves, and massacring each other, appears in the Northwestern country as an unselfish pacificator, and compels the Sacs, Foxes, Chippewas, and Sioux, including the Winnebagoes, to make a treaty of peace and friendship with each other and with the United States.

Treaty terms were precarious, especially as it was understood by all parties that "no tribe shall hunt within the actual limits of any other without their consent." The lands of the Winnebagoes at that time lay between the Rock and Wisconsin Rivers, along the shore of Winnebagoe Lake, and the six hundred member tribe claimed the whole lake.

The Winnebagoes signed a third treaty in 1827, along with the Chippewas, and Menomonies, with the United States. This treaty completed the systems of boundaries of their lands, which had been only partially defined by the two previous treaties. Schoolcraft said, "these three conferences embody a new course and policy for keeping the tribes in peace, and are founded on the most enlarged consideration of the aboriginal right of fee-simple to the soil,... and contain no cession of territory (to the United States)."

314

They were the last such treaties, as by 1828, the people of Northern Illinois began to covet and trespass on Indian areas. Commissioners were sent to persuade the Indians to surrender their lands. The Indians refused, and the treaty was deferred. The United States then agreed to pay the four tribes $20,000, "in full compensation for all injuries and damages sustained by them in consequence of the occupation any party of the mining country."

In 1829 a benevolent scheme for the rescue of these hard-pressed tribes of the Northwest Territory was proposed that suggested the forming of a colony of them in the Lake Superior Region, stating, "The Indian is in every view entitled to sympathy. They are a political nonentity,... with no vote to give. The whole Indian race is not worth one white man's vote."

Congressional appropriations were sadly behind. Promises made to Indians were unfulfilled simply because there was no money. Nonetheless, the all-engrossing topic of Congress in 1830 was "the removal of the Indians."

Meanwhile, the Indians were warring among themselves, and retaliating on white squatters on their lands. The inevitable conquest began in earnest, and in September of 1832 the Winnebagoes were compelled to make their first great cession of territory to the United States. In exchange for it they accepted a tract west of the Mississippi, and before June, 1833, most of those living on the ceded lands had crossed the river to their new homes.

Their title to this new area was not as good as supposed, for the treaty expressly stated that it was granted to them "to be held as other Indian lands are Held." In other words, they could again be evicted and moved at Government whim. With the recent cession, the United States had promised $10,000 annually for 27 years, plus buildings, teachers, and various allowances for stock implements, and so on, plus a doctor.

Five years later the Winnebagoes found the treaty scrapped, as they were forced to cede all their remaining lands east of the Mississippi, plus the right to occupy, "except for hunting," a portion of that which they "owned" on the west side. For this they were to receive $200,000, with a part of this sum to pay debts, part to pay for their removal from relinquished lands, and the rest "to be invested by the United States Government for their benefit."

This deceitful phrase, often appearing in one version or another in later treaties, merely meant that Indians received nothing.

The Winnebagoes were forced into another treaty in 1846, by which they ceded and "sold" to the United States "all right, title, interest, claim, and privilege to all lands heretofore occupied by them;" and accepted as their home, a tract of 800,000 acres north of Saint Peter's and west of the Mississippi River,with again the nullifying phrase, "to be held as other Indian lands are held".

For this third forced move they were to to be paid $190,000, $150,000 for the land they gave up, and $40,000 for relinquishing hunting rights on adjacent lands. As usual , part of this was to be spent in moving the Indians, with the remainder "left in trust" with the Government at five per cent interest. This of course translated to the Indians getting little or nothing.

The new reservation was totally unsuitable, and the tribe grew restless and discontented. Large numbers roamed back to their old homes in Iowa and Wisconsin. In 1855 another treaty was made, and they ceded all the land they had received in the 1846 treaty, in exchange for eighteen square miles on the Blue Earth River in Minnesota.

The improved lands they had been living on, including mills and buildings, were to be sold, and the amount received to pay for there forced move, some subsistence, and supposedly to help make them comfortable in their next home, which was to be "permanent". Since that false promised had not been used in prior treaties, it is presumed that the Winnebagoes took heart. Again, they went to work immediately, "Plowing, planting, and building."

Minnesota citizens did not like their new neighbors. Indignation meetings were held, and the move started to oust the Winnebagoes from their dearly-purchased land. All this tended to discourage the Indians from hoping to remain in their "permanent home." Nevertheless, they worked on, improving their area, and keeping good faith with the whites and their Government. However, they showed bad effects of repeated forced removals, and several hundred began roaming in Wisconsin.

They worked hard at farming, but were hampered by lack of promised horses and plows. Soon many asked to have their farms granted to them individually. The Government took advantage of this desire and devised the Treaty of 1859, that allotted lands to individuals, "in severalty," and the rest of the tribal holdings were to be sold, with the proceeds to be partly expended in farm improvements, and the rest held for them by the Government. This threw open hundreds of thousands of acres to white exploitation, and the greedy belt of civilization drew tighter around the natives.

To the Winnebagoes, however, prospects apparently brightened. With their farms supposedly given to them for their own, and with a promised sufficient sum of land sale money to help them improve their holdings, it looked like prosperity and comfort lay ahead for them.

In 1860 the Commissioner of Indian Affairs writes, "The Winnebagoes continue steadily on the march of improvement... The Indians were promised that new and comfortable houses would be built for them. The treaty not yet being ratified, I have no funds in my hands that could be made applicable to this purpose."

The next year he wrote that the funds the Indians were depending on, had still not been paid. "The Indians who have had their allotments made are clamoring for their certificates."

Drunkenness became a serious vice of the tribe. They were surrounded on all sides by whites that sold whiskey, and who were anxious to degrade the natives as much as possible, hoping to push them off their land. By 1863 the Winnebagoes were in trouble. The Sioux had massacred some white squatters, and Minnesota citizens demanded the expulsion of all Indians from the state. The Winnebagoes had refused to join the Sioux in their attack, and were threatened with death by the Sioux as well as by whites.

The Winnebagoe could not leave their reservation without fear of being shot. They never received their allotted farm implements. Game on their lands was exhausted, and their arms had been taken from them. They were starving. Somehow the tribe remained loyal.

The people of Minnesota triumphed in February, 1863, when Congress authorized the "peaceful and quiet removal of the Winnebagoe Indians from the State of Minnesota, and settling them on a new reserve, on the Missouri River, somewhere within a hundred miles of Fort Randall."

All their remaining weapons were taken, and the hostile Sioux were to be relocated to a reservation adjoining the new Winnebagoe location. Many Winnebagoe abandoned the Indian life, refused to go, and more or less "qualified for civilized life." Many enlisted in the military, and all tried to keep the homes allotted to them by treaty. The Government immediately sold the tribal lands and kept the money.

The bulk of the tribe was rounded up, uncomfortably transported at their own expense, and dumped on a sandy, inhospitable beach on the west bank of the Missouri River, at the Crow Creek Agency in Dakota Territory, at their own expense. The weather was harsh, the soil was sterile, and rather than face certain starvation, the tribe abandoned that barren spot. After a miserable trek, with several hundred starving or freezing on the way, they arrived at the Omaha Agency in a condition that aroused sympathy from most who learned of the wrong they had suffered.

In May 1863, the Winnebagoes were gathered at Fort Snelling to journey to yet another "suitable home". The tribe of about two thousand arrived at a wilderness along the Missouri River that was almost barren, with dry, hard, unplowable soil. A drought had parched the grass. There was no suitable timber, and the channel of the Missouri was so changeable,and the banks so low, that it was dangerous to get too near. They had to settle a half-mile from the river, and were understatedly reported as, "not pleased with their location."

They began making canoes to join the Omahas or others down the river. They were warned not to attempt to leave or they would be shot by troops stationed down-river. In spite of the threat, the dread of withering at the new location spurred the Indians to continue making boats and escaping in small groups, arriving at the Omaha Agency, begging for food.

By the autumn of 1863, over 1,200 of the 2000 destitute Winnebagoes had escaped and made their way to the Nebraska Omaha Reservation. The Government, in a moment of largesse, agreed to feed them until Spring.

Their stay in the totally unsuitable wilderness had left terrible effects on the tribe. They were spiritless and desperate from their sufferings, and were demoralized by again being forced into contact with their deadly, sworn enemy, the Sioux. They fought off attacks, and relapsed so far into the barbaric life that at one dance they roasted and ate the heart of a Sioux prisoner. Yet in less than a year, their hopes were rekindled for a "permanent home."

The long-suffering tribe made a new treaty with the Government in 1865, which by giving up all rights in the Dakota Reserve, they were to receive a tract of 128,000 acres in Nebraska, as the "future home of the Winnebagoe Indians forever". The promised land was a part of the Omaha Reservation that the Omahas agreed to sell.

The United States of course agreed to also erect mills, break land, furnish seeds, tools, guns, horses, oxen and wagons, and to feed the tribe for one year, "as some small reparation for the terrible losses and sufferings they had experienced." The Winnebagoes possibly took courage from the word "forever."

Showing much industry, The tribe was noted in 1866 to be improving, despite poor health resulting from their recently being hunted, herded and starved. Almost five hundred had died from being pushed out of Minnesota. It was totally unjust that the Indians themselves should have to pay for all they had been forced to endure. It was clearly a debt of the covetous people of Minnesota who were so vehement in forcing them out.

The stray Winnebagoes left behind in Wisconsin tried to claim their "allotted" lands and were to receive some Government allocations as they merged into local communities, becoming useful and productive citizens. Yet by 1872 the whites complained of them, and Congress approved their being gathered and shunted west of the Mississippi. They were not wanted anywhere. The Agent of the new Winnebagoe Reservation protested their being sent there, since "Nebraska does like Indians any better than Wisconsin or Minnesota..."

The tribal members in Nebraska began to fear anew that they would not get patents to their new lands, despite having lived on and improved them greatly for three years. In the winter of 1874, the discontented Wisconsin "strays" were herded and shipped to the Nebraska Reservation. In less than a year about half of them had wandered back to Wisconsin. The Government did little to recapture them, yet with a small weak tribe like the Poncas, whose thirty or so starving members ran for their lives from Indian Territory in Oklahoma, were hunted, arrested, and treated like thieves escaping with stolen property.

Only two hundred Wisconsin Winnebagoes were left in Nebraska in 1875. Meanwhile, the Nebraska portion of the tribe were praised as "being nearly civilized," with hundreds of new homes built and much of their land under cultivation. In 1876 they were "fast emerging from a condition of dependence upon their annual appropriations. The Winnebagoes once more were quietly established in comfortable, yet somewhat primitive homes.

How did the Government welcome this heroic triumph of a patient people over disheartening obstacles and suffering? It decided that all Indians should be concentrated upon a few reservations, "the fewer the better." In the federal wisdom, all Indians should be given 75 acres in the Indian Territory of Oklahoma. The true purpose of such a plan was that "most of the land now occupied as reserves reverting to the Government, would be open to entry and sale."

The Winnebagoes had been fleeing from this necessity to open Indian lands "to entry and sale" for thirty-eight years, 1815 to 1863. They were no safer in the 1870's. The Commissioner of Indian Affairs reliably stated, "with a fair degree of persistence, the removal can be secured," and no doubt it could. A barrage of such high-sounding, hypocritical phrases from the Government effectually hid from the American people the iron hand of injustice and cruelty which had grasped the Indians for a hundred years.

319

As part of the great injustice, in 1876 the Government cut funds drastically for Indian Agency operations, closing fine buildings, schools, and vital services. As usual, the Indians themselves received nothing for having all they owned taken from them.

In 1877 the Secretary of the Interior persistently recommended that the Indians be "gradually gathered together on smaller reservations," to the end that "greater facilities be afforded for civilization.

Since in 1878 "There is a vast area of land in the Indian Territory not yet occupied," writes the Commissioner of Indian Affairs, a bill was drawn "providing for the removal and consolidation of certain Indians in the States of Oregon, Colorado, Iowa, Kansas, Nebraska, Wisconsin, and Minnesota, and the Territories of Washington and Dakota... A reduction of twenty-five reservations and eleven agencies will thus be effected... There will be restored to the public domain 17,642,455 acres of land... Further consolidations of like character are not only possible, but expedient and advisable."

With the same ludicrous, complacent logic as before, he proceeded to give the reason for uprooting all these Indians from the home where they were beginning to thrive and take root, and moving them again, for the third, fourth, fifth, sixth, or seventh time. He forcibly argued, with great appeal to Congress, that the cost of uprooting and relocation would be met from the sale of vacated lands.

In continuing pompous, illogical reasoning, it was admitted that "the lands belong to the Indians", yet they would be compelled to restore over seventeen and half million acres of them "to the public domain." This statement perhaps is a high-water mark of the sophistry and dishonesty of the Department's position. The slyness continued: the Indians were "clearly entitled to receive the full value of the same when sold," but they would be compelled to expend that "full value" in moving them to a place they did not want to go.

The Commissioner concluded, "Every means that human ingenuity can devise, legal or illegal, has been resorted to for the purpose of obtaining possession of Indian lands." When news of such schemes reached the reservations, the Indians were greatly alarmed.

At the end of the most infamous hundred years of Government injustice to Indians, the Winnebagoes were anxious and desperate, facing the wicked inevitable. Citizenship was clamored for, in hopes of protecting what little they had.

THE CHEROKEES

The Cherokees were the original Eastern Mountaineers of America. Their country stretched along the Tennessee River, and into the highlands of Georgia, Carolina, and Alabama, the loveliest region east of the Mississippi River. Beautiful and grand, with lofty mountains and rich valleys fragrant with flower, and forests of magnolia and pine filled with singing birds and melodious streams, rich in fruits and nuts and wild grains, it was a country worth loving, worth fighting for, worth dying for, as thousands of its lovers have fought and died, white men as well as Indians, from 1780 to 1880.

When Oglethorpe came with this cargo of Madeira wine and respectable paupers from England in 1733, and lived in tents in midwinter on the shores of the Savannah River, one of the first conditions of safety for his colossal almshouse, in the shape of a new colony, was that all the Indians in the region should become its friends and allies.

The reputation of his goodness and benevolence soon penetrated to the fastnesses of their homes, and tribe after tribe sent chiefs and headmen to greet him with gifts and welcome. When the Cherokee chief appeared, Oglethorpe said to him, "Fear nothing. Speak freely." "I always speak freely," answered the mountaineer. "Why should I fear? I am now among friends: I never feared, even among my enemies."

The principal purposes of the Georgia English colony was to make a home for Englishmen who were "in decayed circumstances," and to "civilize the savages." In 1734 Oglethorpe took eight Indian chiefs to England. Nothing was neglected, we are told, "that was likely to awaken their curiosity or impress them with a sense of the power and grandeur of the nation." The tribes at home were gratified and impressed by the attentions paid to their chiefs.

When Wesleyian missionaries arrived in Georgia in 1736, they were met by some of the chiefs, bearing gifts of milk and honey, and one of them told Mister Wesley, "...we would not be made Christians as the Spaniards make Christians; we would be taught before we are baptized."

Wesley was enthusiastic, but intolerant and injudicious. He was unsuccessful with both Indians and whites. The same chief, when urged to become a Christian, said, "Christians get drunk! Christians beat men! Christians tell lies! Me no Christian!"

For twenty years Oglethorpe's colony struggled on . There were wars with France and Spain; tiresome squabbles with and among Methodist missionaries. At last the trustees of the Georgia Colony lost patience. Very bitterly they had learned that paupers, however worthy, are not good stuff to build new enterprises of. In June, 1752, the Georgia trustees resigned their charter and washed their hands of the colony.

The province was formed into a royal government, and soon had frightful Indian wars. Their old friend Oglethorpe was gone, and the new authorities neither understood nor kept faith with the Indians. The same scenes of treachery and massacre which took place up North, began to be repeated with heart-sickening similarity. Indians fought Indians, being allies with the French, and then with the English. Treaties made were broken immediately, and there was no peace or safety in Georgia.

At last a treaty was concluded in 1763 with the chiefs and headmen of five tribes, which promised better things. The Creeks and Cherokees granted the King of England a large tract of land, clearing their "debts to England" with the sum paid for it. Peace was destroyed several years later with the revolt of the American Colonies against Great Britain.

The British availed themselves of the Cherokees allegiance to the Crown. Atrocities were committed by all involved, disproving that innate cruelty is an exclusive Indian trait. The Cherokees had the worst of the fighting on the British side, as the British had no compunctions in throwing them on the front lines.

The first diplomatic relations of the United States Government with the Cherokees were in the making of the treaty of Hopewell, 1n 1785. The United States commissioners said to the Cherokees, "Congress is now the sovereign of all our country which we now point out to you on the map. They want none of your lands, nor anything else that belongs to you."

The chiefs complained bitterly of the encroachments of white settlers upon lands which had been by old treaties distinctly reserved to the Cherokees. They demanded that some of these settlers be removed. When the commissioners said that there were too many settlers for the Government to remove, one of the chiefs satirically asked, "Are Congress, who conquered the King of Great Britain, unable to remove those people?"

Finally, the chiefs agreed to accept payment for the lands that had been taken. New boundaries were established, and a general feeling of goodwill and confidence was created. In four years, the Cherokees had lost some 650 of their estimated 2650 people, mostly due to wars with frontier people. It was a deplorable situation for the tribe, and was an admitted "indispensable obligation of the United States to vindicate their faith, justice, and national dignity."

The Indians were charged with atrocities while evicting squatters for their lands, lands the Government had solemnly guaranteed that the

Cherokees might "punish him or not as they please." Even the Secretary of the Interior reported that as a result of the bad faith of the Government, "The Indian tribes can have no faith in such imbecile promises, and the lawless whites will ridicule a government which shall on paper only make Indian treaties and regulate Indian boundaries."

The Treaty of Holston was made with the Cherokees in July 1791, establishing new boundaries and promising $1000 a year for the lands relinquished. The treaty reiterated the old, always broken promise that if anyone other than a Cherokee tried to settle on their land, they could punish him as they pleased.

The next year the Cherokees asked for an additional $500 a year. As a chief said, the $1000 a year, "would not buy a breech-clout for each of my nation". They got the $500, but not the promised plows, hoes, cattle, and so on, badly needed since "Game is going fast from among us."

White settlers continued to go where they pleased. Cherokees murdered them, as they were permitted to do. Whites retaliated by attacking friendly Indians, and the Indians retaliated again. Equally unjust to all parties, these miserable affairs continued for years.

At last the Government offered another treaty, but the Cherokees refused to cede any more lands, or let roads be built through their territory. After four more years of misery, the Indians acquiesced, giving up several large tracts and right of ways for several roads. In 1805 the United States took more land, and in 1816 they took all Cherokee lands in South Carolina.

In 1817, the Government promised six hundred and forty acres to each Indian that would become a citizen, and took even more lands from the tribe. So, in less than twenty years, the Cherokee Nation was found piteously pleading to be allowed to remain undisturbed on even a small portion of what had been theirs.

In the whole history of Government dealings with the Indian tribes, there is probably no record as black as its perfidy to the Cherokees. It would later seem almost incredible.

From the beginning of the 19th century they had been steadily advancing in civilization. There is no instance in all history of a race of people passing in so short a time from the barbarous stage to the agricultural and civilized. Yet, on December 19, 1829, the State of Georgia, by one highhanded outrage, made outlaws of the Cherokees.

They passed a law "to annul all laws and ordinances made by the Cherokee nation of Indians;" declaring "all laws, ordinances, orders, and regulations of any kind whatever, made, passed, or enacted by the Cherokee Indians, either in general council or in any other way whatever, or by any authority whatever, null and void, and of no effect, as if the same had never existed; also, that no Indian, or descendant of any Indian residing within the Creek or Cherokee nations of Indians;, shall be deemed a competent witness in any court of this State to which a white man may be a party."

The doom of the Cherokees had been sealed on the day they declared, once and for all, that they would not give up another foot of land. Georgia demanded that the Indians should be made to vacate their lands, peaceably or otherwise.

The dignified and pathetic remonstrances of the Cherokee chiefs, and their firm reiterations of their resolve not to part with their lands, were called by the Georgia Governor, "tricks of vulgar cunning,... insults from the polluted lips of outcasts and vagabonds." He openly threatened the President that Georgians would make war if the Indians did not leave.

Earlier, President Jefferson had assured the Cherokees that they had a right to their lands and would be protected by the United States. General George Washington had told them that in the future they would not be defrauded of their lands. Yet thirty years later, they saw the United States uphold the State of Georgia.

Federal agents attempted all sorts of seductions of native leaders, but never did mountaineers cling more desperately to their homes than did the Cherokees. Year by year high-handed oppressions continued and multiplied. Military law reigned everywhere. The federal Government continued to say they couldn't protect the Indians, and kept offering them money for their country.

Nevertheless, they clung to their land. When the bill for their removal was before Congress, which to its credit must be noted that the bill passed the Senate by only one vote. Remonstrances poured into Congress from around the nation, all imploring the Government to keep its faith with the Cherokees.

As a last resort the Indians carried their case before the Supreme Court. The learned justices got out of it by declaring that the Cherokee Tribe was not a nation and could not bring the suit, although the court was manifestly sympathetic. This did not help the Cherokees.

Many were ready to remain and suffer death rather than give up. Wiser counsels prevailed, and in the last days of 1835 a treaty was made that relinquished all the lands claimed by them east of the Mississippi River. The United States did "guarantee to the Cherokee nation a perpetual outlet west, and a free and unmolested use of all the country west of the western boundary,... as far west as the sovereignty of the United States and their rights of soil extend."

A great part of the Indian Nation refused to sanction the treaty, saying it did not represent their wish, and hundreds refused money or supplies from the Government, lest they be considered thereby to have committed themselves to the treaty. For two years, with many near starvation, to the last moment allowed by the treaty, they clung to their homes, and at last were removed by military force. The Cherokee leaders had made no further protest against going, but simply asked to undertake the whole charge of the removal themselves.

The military commander quibbled with them about their estimated costs being too high, feeling for example, that sixteen cents a day for individual rations was too high. Since the costs were to be paid from tribal funds controlled by the Government, they were nobly liberal in finally agreeing to the small amounts requested.

To dwell here on the picture of the removal, the infamous "Trail of Tears", is not possible, and is dealt with better elsewhere. Hundreds and hundreds died on the midwinter trek over thirteen hundred miles west to the Indian Territory. No imagination so dull, no heart so hard as not to see and to feel, at the bare mention of such a forced emigration, what horrors and what anguish it must have involved.

For some years after this removal, fierce dissent rent the Cherokee Nation. Several of the signers of the treaty, influential members of the tribe, were murdered. The progress of the Cherokees in the following ten years, however, was almost beyond belief.

In 1860, agitation over slavery began, with stormy scenes also near the Kansas line. For several years white settlers had persisted in taking up farms there, and the Cherokees had in vain implored the Government to drive them away. An officer in charge finally forced a few out, burning their cabins over them.

In the first year of the Civil War a large number of Cherokees took up arms on the rebel side. The opportunity of fighting against Georgians could not but have been welcome to the soul of a Cherokee, but their defection to the Southerners was no doubt largely due to terror.

All United States troops had been withdrawn from their country. They were without any protection from the Government, and to leave them without any incentive to loyalty, the United States suspended the payment of their meager annuities.

The Confederate Government artfully promised to pay what the Northerners refused. Amazingly, thousands of Indians did remain loyal, and

325

fled for their lives. Almost half of the Creek Nation, many Seminoles, Chickasaws, Quapaws, Cherokees, and half a dozen other tribes, over six thousand in all, fled to Kansas. Their suffering there in the winter of 1862 was heart-rending.

The party feeling between the loyal and disloyal Cherokees ran as high as it did between the loyal and disloyal whites. It appeared impossible that opposing Cherokees could agree to live side by side, as it would to make discharged soldiers from Georgia and Maine settle in one village together.

However, after long and troublesome negotiations a treaty was concluded in 1866, by which all necessary points seemed to be established of a general amnesty and peace. The Indians were of course at great disadvantage in making these treaties. Government superintendents admitted that the rebel Cherokees had no choice in their loyalties, but were nevertheless, "at our mercy" and their treaty rights had been abrogated.

With a recuperative power far in advance of that shown by any small white Southern communities, The Cherokees at once began to rebuild their homes and reconstruct their national life. Thus a second time they recovered themselves, after what would seem to be well nigh their destruction as a people. Yet, the Indian's fate of perpetual insecurity, alarm, and unrest did not abandon them.

In 1870 they were said to be "extremely uneasy about the security of the possession of the lands they occupied. When asked why they had not reestablished schools, and the like, the reply came, "we expect to have our lands taken away. What is the use of all that when our doom as a nation is sealed?"

When their delegates had gone to Washington in 1866 to make the new treaty, they were naturally alarmed to be told that the Cherokees, as a nation had forfeited its rights for having side with the Confederacy. It mattered not to the United States that only one third of the Cherokees had in any way aided the rebels, or that two Cherokee regiments had fought in the Union Army.

They could not refuse any conditions imposed upon them, and were intimidated into selling a large tract in Southeastern Kansas to white speculators at a dollar an acre. This fell into the hands of a railroad corporation. The Cherokees, also against their wishes, granted right of way for two railroad lines through their lands.

The rapacity of the railroad companies was as insatiable as their methods were unscrupulous. "Extinguishing Indian land titles" came to be associated with the prevailing attitude that extinction was the ultimate and inevitable fate of the Indian.

This is the only explanation of the unconscious inhumanity of many good men's modes of thinking and speaking in regard to the Indians being driven from home after home, and robbed of tract after tract of their lands.

Even though the Cherokees had been solemnly pledged seven million acres of land, and were entitled to them by the supreme law of the land, the Report of the Indian Bureau for 1876 stated, "By treaty the Government has ceded to the so-called civilized tribes--the Cherokees, Creeks, Choctaws, Chickasaws, and Seminoles--a section of country altogether disproportionate in amount to their needs."

The Department of the Interior in 1876 said the affairs in the Indian Territory are "complicated and embarrassing, and the question is directly raised whether an extensive section of country is to be allowed to remain for an indefinite period practically an uncultivated waste, or whether the Government shall determine to reduce the size of the reservation."

The phrase "whether the Government shall determine to reduce the size of the Reservation" sounded much better than "whether the Government shall rob the Indians of a few million acres of land." The latter phrase is truth, and the other is the spirit of lying.

The commissioner opined that "public policy will soon require the disposal of a large portion of these lands to the Government for the occupancy either of other tribes of Indians or of white people. There is a very general and growing opinion that observance of the strict letter of treaties with Indians is in many cases at variance with their own best interests and with sound public policy."

He then made the preposterously contradictory sentence, that it must not be understood from this recommendation that it was "the policy or purpose of this office to in any way encourage the spirit of rapacity which demands the throwing open of the Indian Territory to white settlement."

So it went for the Cherokees during Century of Dishonor. It is doubtful if their rapid progress to that of civilization and enlightenment has any parallel in the history of the World. What required five hundred years for the Britons to accomplish in this direction, the Cherokees accomplished in a hundred years.

THE SIOUX

The word Sioux is a contraction from the old French word "Nadouessioux," or "Enemies," the name given by French traders to this most powerful and warlike of all the Northwestern tribes. They called themselves "Dakota," or "many in one," because so many bands under different names were joined. At the time of Captain Carver's travels among the North American Indians, there were twelve known bands of the "Nadou-wessies."

Nothing in the history of the earliest relations between the friendly tribes of North American Indians and the arriving Europeans is more pathetic than the accounts of their simple hospitality, their unstinted invitations, and their innocent desire to learn more of white men's ways.

Diplomatic relations between the United States Government and the Sioux began in 1815. In that year and the next, the Government made sixteen treaties of peace and friendship with different tribes, treaties demanding no cessions beyond the original grants made to these tribes by the French, English and Spanish Governments. "Perpetual peace" was promised, and "every injury or act of hostility committed by one or the other... shall be mutually forgiven and forgot."

Three of these treaties were made with bands of the Sioux: "Sioux of the Leaf, Sioux of the Broad Leaf, and Sioux who shoot in the Pine-tops." In 1825 four more treaties were made with separate Sioux bands. One of these treaties, that of Prairie de Chien, defined boundaries between the Chippewas and the Sioux, in hopes that their incessant feuds might end. The long-standing conflict had slowly driven the Sioux south and west.

A treaty couldn't keep peace between such ancient enemies, and fighting continued. White traders suffered almost more than the Indians. The Government couldn't stop the war, and merely hoped that the eventual loser would be lost as a separate power.

The next treaty, also at Prairie du Chien, in 1830, began boundary disputes that caused great misunderstanding and outbreaks by The Sioux for decades, compounded by unfairness on the side of the whites, and unwillingness on the part of the Indians.

All the early Government treaty-makers congratulated themselves on getting valuable land by the millions of acres for almost nothing, and as years went on, openly lamented that "Indians were beginning to find out what lands were worth."

Meanwhile the Indians, anxious, alarmed, hostile at heart, seeing themselves hard-pressed on all sides, driven "to provide other sources for supplying their wants besides those of hunting, which must soon fail them," yielded mile after mile with increasing sense of loss. They were powerless to prevent it, or the resentment it was unwise to show.

Soon after these treaties the artist George Catlin made his famous journeys among the Indians. He spent several weeks among the Sioux, and said of them, "There is no tribe on the continent of finer looking men, and few tribes who are better and more comfortably clad and supplied with the necessities of life.

Had the provisions of these first treaties been fairly and promptly carried out, there would have been living in Minnesota in the late 1800s, thousands of Sioux families, good and prosperous farmers and mechanics.

The Sioux were cheated out of their annuities by the Government. In 1836 Congress appropriated the puny sum of $2000 "for the purpose of extinguishing the Indian title between the State of Missouri and the Missouri River." This was the very land granted to the Sioux under the Treaty of Prairie du Chien, but the good people of Missouri wanted it. The Indians soon saw that they could not prevail and gave up the huge tract.

In 1837 The Government took a number of chiefs to Washington, D.C. to threaten them with the strength of the nation should the Indians "venture to attack our borders." Duly impressed with the show of might, the Sioux delegates, of the Medawakanton Band, reluctantly ceded to the United States "all their land east of the Mississippi River, and all their islands in the same." As usual, the Indians only got a fraction of what was promised.

For the next ten years affairs went badly with the Sioux; they were continually attacked by the Chippewas, Ottawas, and others, and continually retaliated. This was all fine with white authorities, as it seemed the best way to keep the whites safe. Whiskey traders and fur traders found it more profitable to deal with drunken Indians, and the Sioux rapidly grew demoralized.

Their government annuities were always in arrears, and in 1842 several bands were half-starved due to crop failure and Congressional failure to ratify a treaty they had made with the Sioux in 1841. The remaining buffalo had long since been driven far away, and most Indians were too poor to own a horse on which to hunt. The Government did see fit to keep most of them alive during the following winter, but in 1849, the "needs" of the white settlers on the east side of the Mississippi made it imperative that the Sioux should again be forced off their lands.

The commissioners were sent with absurd instructions: "Though the proposed purchase is estimated to contain some twenty millions of acres, and some of it no doubt of excellent quality, there are sound reasons why it is comparatively valueless to the Indians, and a large price should not be paid for it." Apparently it was "desirable, and absolutely necessary for white settlers," yet worthless to Indians.

"On full consideration,...it is the opinion of this office (The Department of the Interior) that from two to two and a half cents an acre would be an ample amount for it." Those same instructions rationalized that by giving the Indians practically nothing for their lands, The Government was doing the natives a favor since "it was a well-ascertained fact that no greater curse can be inflicted on a tribe so little civilized as the Sioux than to have large sums of money coming to them as annuities."

Apparently along those same "humanitarian" lines, the annual annuity to the Sioux was withheld from 1837 to 1850.

In plain English, the Government had in 1830 promised to let a band of men take out tracts of land, and settle down like other men on their homesteads. For ten years the men had begged to do so, and were refused. Then, thinking there was no hope of anything better, they sold the land back to the Government.

The United States did not pay, and nine years later congratulated itself, that since all these agreements had not been fulfilled, "the land was still held only in same manner as other Indian titles are held." In other words, it was not "held" at all, only used on sufferance of the Government, and could be taken back at the Government's pleasure.

The Government than took back another 143,000 acres apparently "of much less value than valueless," as the Indians got nothing from the deal but another eviction.

Meanwhile, the bands of the Medewakanton Sioux were occupying a large tract on the west shore of the Mississippi, while the Yanktons, Santees, and other bands lived high up the Saint Peter's River. All these bands were almost always hungry. The Government supplied them little food, and none of the badly needed farm implements that they had promised.

Why did the United States Government keep on its obstinate way, feeding the Indian in gross and reckless improvidence with one hand, plundering him with the other, and holding him steadily down at the level of barbarism? No, forcing him below it by the newly added vices of gambling and drunkenness, and yet all the while boasting of its desire to enlighten, instruct, and civilize him. It was as inexplicable as it was infamous; a phenomenon in the history of the world.

In the summer of 1851 the desired treaties were made. The Indians could see they had no choice, but held out for eight to nine cents per acre for their thirty five Million acres. Through usual Government chicanery,

Governor Ramsey was able to boast that the total of $3,075,000 to be paid actually came down to just $575,000 that might eventually make it to the tribes. Mills, schools, and farms were to erected for them, "as soon as practicable."

As expected, the Government view was that, "to the Indians themselves the broad regions which have been ceded are of inconsiderable value." Again we have a juxtaposition of thinking that defies logic, for the same writer also said that for the eight thousand people who, "have outlived in a great degree the means of subsistence of the hunter state," and must soon "resort to the pursuits of agriculture," nothing could have been more fortunate than to have owned and occupied thirty-five million fertile, well-watered acres such as those just taken from them.

Two years after relieving the Sioux of their worthless land, and having shoved the tribes into a supposedly worthless western fragment, the Government now wanted that land, also. The Indians were "induced" to agree, and part of the wording stipulated that the President could further relocate them, "if deemed expedient."

Whites poured into the ceded territories and on into the more or less temporary reservation. The reserve was poorly suited to sustain the Sioux anyway, and many agreed to be sent to the Indian Territory, but most desparately wanted the reservation confirmed to them. Added to this, the monies for removal of that portion that would abandon the area, "had been expended, their provision eaten up."

Here was a picture of a helpless people. Forced to give up what the Governor had said was "the garden spot of the State," and accept in its stead an "insignificant tract, on the greater part of which there is not wood, or timber, or coal sufficient for civilization;" and then, before the ink of that treaty had dried, told that even from this insignificant tract they must promise to move in five years.

What words could characterize such a transaction between a man and a man? There is not a country, a people, a community in which it would even be attempted. It was more the base, being between a strong government and a feeble race. Public outcry prevented the United States from this infamy, and the President decreed that the Indians remain "permanently" on their "insignificant tract."

While this went on, the Upper Missouri Sioux were still suffering and destitute. Among those peaceable and friendly bands a few half-starved groups started to raid whites. The Government in its maddening way, declared that all these Sioux had not "improved their condition", when they had nothing to improve it with.

The summer of 1857 was long remembered by Minnesotans. It opened with terrible massacres, the work of a wandering band of no more than fifteen Sioux outcasts. It started innocently enough, but the natives with pent-up fury lashed back at offending settlers, killing an entire small settlement.

The overwhelming majority of the Sioux, entirely innocent, were attacked by the Army. A group of loyal Sioux even pursued, fought, killed and captured some of the offenders. The hostilities came to an end, but the Sioux were not reassured, since the overwhelming sentiment among whites was to kill the entire Indian race.

The promised annuities were still greatly in arrears. More innocent tribesmen were killed by whites. Any further provocation by whites could suddenly throw the Indians into antagonism and hostility grossly disproportionate to the apparent cause. This was the condition of the Minnesota Sioux in the summer of 1862.

Starving Indians broke into a government warehouse. The Army retaliated, and the record of the resultant massacres of that summer is scarcely equaled in the history of Indian wars. Hostile Indians forced peaceable bands to join them, but many fled for their lives from their own tribesmen.

For three days the hostile bands, continually reinforced, went from settlement to settlement, killing and plundering. A belt of country some two hundred miles by fifty miles was abandoned by whites, who flocked in panic to towns and forts. Nearly a thousand of them were killed, and millions of dollars in property was destroyed.

The military quickly snuffed the outbreak, and a large number of Indians were captured. Three hundred of them were to be hanged, but all but 39 were reprieved. They endured sufferings worse than death for three years in a barren desert in Dakota Territory. The rest escaped to the Upper Missouri region or to Canada.

Minnesota, at a terrible cost to herself and to the United States, was at last free from of Indians, who were her enemies only because they had been treated with injustice and bad faith. Those that escaped to the North, joined the more or less hostile bands of Sioux in the Upper Missouri region.

In 1865, the Government having spent some forty million dollars on the campaigns, sent out a commission to treat with them, knowing well that the 14,000 Indians there had always wanted peace. The Government knew well, also, that unless the tribes were reassured, there would be another formidable Indian war.

Nine treaties with nine tribes had the Indians pledging not to fight each other or the whites, in return for fifteen dollars per person each year, with twenty five dollars going to those who would become farmers. They kept faith during a bad winter, suffering from cold and hunger.

Still further treaties were made the next summer, seeing all Sioux pledged to peace. There was a bureaucratically bungled attempt to show some mercy to the thousand friendly old men, women, and children who were orphaned and widowed by Army actions.

Efforts were made to get reparations for friendly Indian farmers who had given all they had to help support and quarter Army troops during the conflicts. In 1866, in spite of strong protests of Nebraskans, these Sioux were settled on reservations of marginal land on the Niobrara River, in Northern Nebraska. In the Fall they were moved from that unsuitable area to the mouth of Bazile Creek, where they managed to stay alive during the winter.

They were cheered at having a delegation being taken to the Nation's capitol the next Spring, but all they got were promises of a commission to visit them the next year. They were told to move to Breckenridge, on the west bank of the Missouri River and plant crops there. If they liked it, they should have it "secured to them as a permanent home."

Before the new crops were harvested, the commission arrived and told them to move farther up the Missouri, where If they would farm like whites, they could keep the land and be assisted by the Government. The Indians gladly agreed to this treaty, but in 1868 the treaty had still not been ratified, and the appropriation was cut in half.

They were shuttled, abused, tricked, cheated on all sides, and starving half the time. There was never a tribe of all the persecuted tribes that endured a more piteous record than the Sioux. Nevertheless, by 1870 the Sioux somehow advanced in civilization. All were anxious to farm, as agreed to, but the promised equipment, seed, and assistance never came.

Chief Red Cloud led a delegation of chiefs to Washington in 1869, to plead their cause, receiving Government promises of good intentions. Red Cloud became an ardent and determined advocate of peace and loyalty.

Another important event in Sioux history occurred in 1870, when part of the Santee band withdrew from the tribe to take up farms under the Homestead Act, becoming independent citizens. These Indians, in taking up their homesteads, were required to renounce, on oath, all claims on the United States for annuities. Without doubt, citizenship, and protection of United States Law, is worth a great sum, but was it right to require natives

333

of this country to purchase, at a price of several thousands of dollars, that which was given free to every immigrant from Asia, Europe, or Africa, who asked for it?

The requirement of the Sioux to buy citizenship was appealed by friendly whites, who also argued for help for all the Sioux in establishing farms. In 1873 the Government yielded and sent out oxen, wagons, plows, and the like, enough to stock a whole thirty farms. The few who benefited were grateful, and apparently gave up hope of ever getting the money due them for the lands taken from them in Minnesota.

Also in 1873, a commission was sent to treat with some of the wilder bands of Sioux, for relinquishment of their right to hunt over a large part of their "unneeded" territory in Kansas and Nebraska. The Indians were coerced into yet another cession. By 1875 there were still about a thousand hostile Sioux roaming under their famous chief Sitting Bull, living by the chase when they could, and by depredations when they had to. Occasionally they appeared at Indian agencies, drawing rations among the other Indians unsuspected. The remainder of the bands were working their way toward civilization.

In the Spring of 1876, owing to failure of appropriations, the Indian Bureau had been unable to send supplies, and the Indians, being in "almost a starving condition", went north in large numbers to join the hostile camps of Sitting Bull. In Summer the same thing happened, and even more Indians left to join the hostiles.

Companies of Army troops had to be stationed at reservations to prevent outbreaks among those who remained. Grasshoppers devoured the crops of many. Martial law was imposed. The natives faced starvation, and were constantly urged by friends and relatives to join in fighting the treacherous Government that had kept faith with nobody.

United States troops burned villages of friends and foes alike, including some encampments containing only women and children. Bands of friendly Indians living peacefully under Government protection at Sand Creek, in Colorado, were butchered in a surprise attack. Blood from The Sand Creek massacre will never be washed from the honor of Colorado and the United States Government.

It was at this time that Sitting Bull made his famous reply to Officials who wanted to treat with him, "Tell them at Washington if they have one man who speaks the truth to send him to me, and I will listen to what he has to say."

The record of the military campaign against the Sioux in 1876 and 1877 is treated elsewhere, but another history, which can never be read, was written in the hearts of the widowed women in the Sioux Nation, and in the nation of the United States.

Before midsummer, the Sioux War was over. The indomitable Sitting Bull had escaped to Canada, the refuge of Indians and slaves. In the Fall a commission entreated him and his followers to return and be assigned to agencies, and to be treated "in as friendly a spirit as other Indians had been who had surrendered."

This was a strange invitation from a Government that knew that those who fled to Sitting Bull had been starving on the reservation. Secure on British soil, the Indians for once had freedom of speech, and replied with scathing sarcasm.

The commissioners returned from their fruitless effort, and the Interior Department simply recorded that "Sitting Bull and his adherents are no longer considered wards of the Government." The United States then went to work taking land from the Sioux that remained in the country, assigning them to the Indian Territory. Red Cloud and Spotted Tail were ordered with their bands to new agencies on the Missouri River.

The site chosen was the old Ponca Reserve that the Government had kicked that tribe out of earlier. The Commissioner said, " The removal of fourteen thousand Sioux Indian at this season of the year, a distance of three hundred miles from their old agencies in Nebraska to their new quarters near the Missouri River, is not a pleasant matter to contemplate."

The usual ill fortune attended the moving of these Indians. They were placed on more barren land, where there was no possibility of farming, no hope of becoming self-sufficient, and where they were kept as hopeless paupers. In hopes of placing them on arable land, they were hastily moved back to the Missouri River. The supplies for the coming winter had been delivered to the wrong agency, and owing to the lateness of the season, it was impossible to move them to where the needy Indians were. Accordingly, the Indians were compelled to travel in the midst of snows and storms, which had already set in.

This idiotic management of Indian affairs was enough by itself to call for an entirely new system. So many and such hasty, ill-considered, uninformed, capricious, and cruel decisions of arbitrary power could hardly be found in a seven year's record of any tyrant; and there is no tyrant whose throne would not have been rocked, if not upset, by the revolutions which would have followed such oppressions.

There is a sequel to the removal of the Red Cloud and Spotted Tail bands, who had consented to go the old Ponca Reservation only after being told that all their supplies had been sent to a certain point on the Missouri River, and it was to late to move all this freight northward again, and that they would starve if they stayed where they were.

Having a written pledge from General Crook that the Government would allow them to go back in the Spring, they most reluctantly consented to go the Ponca Reservation for the winter. In Spring, no orders came. March and April passed without orders. The chiefs sent word to their friend General Crook, who begged them not to break away.

Finally in May, the Commissioner of Indian Affairs went to them himself. When he rose to speak, Chief Spotted Tail sprang up, walked toward him, waving the paper containing the Government promise to return them to White Clay Creek, and exclaimed, "All the men who come from Washington are liars, and the bald-headed ones are worst of all!"

"I don't want to hear one word from you--you are a bald-headed old liar! You have but one thing to do here, and that is to give an order for us to return to White Clay Creek. Here are your written words; and if you don't give this order, and everything here is not on wheels inside of ten days, I'll order my young men to tear down and burn everything in this part of the country!"

"I don't want to hear anything more from you, and I have nothing more to say to you." He turned his back on the Commissioner and walked away. Such language would not be taken from unarmed and helpless Indians, but when it came from a chief with four thousand armed warriors at his back, it was another affair altogether.

The order was written. In less than ten days everything was "on wheels," and the whole body of these Sioux on the move to the country they had indicated. The Secretary of the Interior, in his report for 1878, naively said, "The Indians were found to be quite determined to move westward, and the promise of the Government in that respect was faithfully kept."

For the remaining two years of the Century of Dishonor, The Sioux showed rapid and encouraging improvement, despite for example, that the Ogallala Band had been moved eight times since 1863. It was a wonder that any Indians had any hope for the future. That all this should be true of these wild, warlike Sioux, after so many hardships and forced wanderings and removals, was incontrovertible proof that there was in them a strength of character, power of endurance, and indomitable courage.

WHITE MASSACRES OF INDIANS

When the English first entered Pennsylvania, Conestoga Indian messengers welcomed them with gifts of corn, venison, and skins. The entire tribe entered into a treaty of friendship with William Penn, which was to last "as long as the sun should shine, or the waters run into the rivers."

Pennsylvania historical records frequently mention this tribe in the early 1700s. The Governor, in 1705, sent a delegation to the Conestogas to meet for "purposes of mutual understanding and confidence." In the same year a party of Quakers were likewise welcomed by the tribe. The Governor himself visited the Conestogas the next year. Two nations were represented in the Conestoga band, the Senecas and the Shawanese.

Still preserved in records, this was said to him by an old chief, "Father, we love quiet; we suffer the mouse to play; when the woods are rustled by the wind we fear not; when the leaves are disturbed in ambush, we are uneasy; but when the rays appear, they give great heat to the body and joy to the heart. Treachery darkens the chain of friendship, but truth makes it brighter than ever. This is the peace we desire."

In the Spring of 1722, a Conestoga was killed by two white brothers. The Governments of New York and Pennsylvania conferred with the tribal chief as to what punish should be given. Surprisingly, the Indian king said, "One life, on this occasion, is enough to be lost There should not two die."

There were only twenty Conestoga left in 1763: seven men, five women, and eight children. They were miserably poor, living in their village on Shawanee Creek, and were wholly peaceful and unoffending. They had even named their children after kind whites, and strove in every way to show their goodwill.

At daybreak on December 14, a band of white "Presbyterians" from Paxton, attacked the little village, finding only six Indians at home; three men, two women, and a boy. The rest were away, working for whites or selling homemade wares. All six were shot, stabbed, or hatcheted to death. They were scalped and horribly mangled, and their huts burned.

When Lancaster magistrates heard the shocking news, they brought the remaining Indians into town for protection, harboring them in the town jail. The Governor ordered all lawmen to seek out the killers. The "Paxton Boys", fifty strong, broke into the jail and killed every Indian there with hatchets and bullets. With victory shouts, thee murderers rode off unmolested, after more horrible mutilations of the bodies.

The Governor offered a reward of $600 for the capture of any three of the ringleaders. The Paxton killers were like beasts that had tasted blood, and threatened to kill Quakers or anyone else befriending Indians. They openly mocked the Governor and announced that they would kill all the Moravian Indians who had been placed in protective custody in Philadelphia.

Along their route they acted like maniacs, terrorizing all they met. It is almost beyond belief that many people justified their acts. An Episcopalian clergyman in Lancaster vindicated them, "bringing scripture to prove that it was right to destroy the heathen." "The Presbyterians think they have a better justification—nothing less than the Word of God," said one of the writers on the massacre.

Horrid perversion of Scriptures to father the worst of crimes was nothing new. The wickedness was repeated often against Indians for the next century, the century of greatest dishonor in American History. What Pennsylvania pioneers did in 1763 to helpless and peaceful Conestoga Indians, was done in 1864 by Colorado pioneers to helpless and peaceful Cheyennes at Sand Creek, for but one example.

Soon after the Conestoga massacre, the earliest "removal" of Indians on record took place, one whose cruelty and cost to suffering natives well entitle it to a place in the gory narrative of genocidal exterminations. Everywhere in the Northern Provinces, fanatics renewed the old cry that the Indians were the Canaanites whom God had commanded Joshua to destroy; and that these wars were a token of God's displeasure with the Europeans for permitting "heathen" to live.

It was dangerous for the devoted Moravian Indians to be seen in public. There was a furious outcry all over the country at continued massacres of innocent Indians, which even included Christian Indians in its unreasoning hatred. The Moravian missionaries went along with the Governor's order that all baptized Indians from Nain and Wechquetank should be "brought to Philadelphia, and be protected in that city, having first delivered up their arms."

The aged, sick and little children were carried in wagons. The rest went on foot down roads heavy with November rains. The weary and heartbroken plodders were jeered, cursed, and abused on all sides. A threatening mob in Germantown taunted them with threats of tortures, burning, and hanging. A heavy storm reportedly prevented them such pleasure.

The four days of misery on the road was not over when they reached Philadelphia. Despite the Governor's order, the military commander refused to let them enter the barracks. They stood at the gates for hours as a riotous mob thickened. The brave accompanying missionaries tried in vain to protect the Indians, but drew the same threats and insults.

After five hours of this, the Governor, unable to compel the garrison to open the barracks, ordered the Indians be taken to Province Island, in the Delaware River, joined to the mainland by a dam. Six miles more, at increasing risk and terror, they passed again through the city.

They were settled in some comfortless unused buildings where they were confined for their own safety . Before they had been there a month, some of the villages they had left were burned, and the Paxton mob announced its intention of marching on Province Island to kill every Indian there. Public sentiment was so inflamed that the Government was practically powerless.

When the murderous mob moved toward the island, the Governor sent two sloops to take the Moravians to New York, to be placed under the protection of the English Army. Barely escaping the rioters, they made it to the ships, docked at Amboy, waiting to ferry them to safety. However, the Governor of New York had sent an angry order that not an Indian should set foot in that territory.

Greatly perplexed, the Moravian Indians were placed in the Amboy barracks, where they held daily religious meetings. The Governor of Pennsylvania had no choice, and ordered them back again to Province Island in the severest part of the Winter. Although the Indians set out with cheerfulness and trust in The Lord, the journey was hard. Elders had weakened from the repeated hardships, and the little children suffered pitifully. In crossing some of the frozen rivers, the feeble had to crawl on hands and knees.

Amidst molesting and threatening mobs, they reached Philadelphia on January 24. The Governor had eight heavy cannon installed and a rampart thrown up in front of the barracks. Good citizens were called to arms, and even Quakers took guns and hurried to defend the Indians. The Governor visited them with reassurances and promises of protection.

On February 4, rioters in large force approached Philadelphia. The whole city was roused in defense. Four more cannon were mounted, and the bullies wisely halted. The excitement subsided, and all through the Spring and Summer the Indians remained prisoners in the barracks. Confinement, unwholesome diet, and depression made their situation grave. To add to their misery, smallpox broke out among them, killing fifty-six over the summer.

At last, after a year of such imprisonment and suffering, on December 4, news of peace reached Philadelphia. A Government proclamation declared the "war" ended and hostilities should cease. The imprisoned Indians were joyous, but it was still unsafe to return to their old homes, which were thickly surrounded by white settlers who mere no less hostile at heart than they had been before.

It was decided, therefore, that they should make a new settlement in the Indian country on the Susquehanna River. After a touching farewell to those who had protected them for sixteen months, they set out on April 3 for their new home in the wilderness. For the third time their aged, sick, and very young were crowded into overloaded wagons, for a far harder and longer journey than any they had yet taken.

The inhospitable wilderness was worse than the curses and threats of riotous mobs. They struggled through snow storms, and camped in icy swamps, shivering around smouldering fires of wet wood. To avoid hostile whites they had to take great circuits through unbroken forests, cutting each foot of the path through the trees.

The men waded streams and made rafts for the women and children. Sometimes they had to camp while making canoes for deeper streams. Food gave out. They ate only bitter wild potatoes. They gave the sweet-juiced inner bark of chestnut trees to hungry, crying children. Their only water was often from shallow, muddy puddles. Once they were surrounded by blazing woods. Several died and were buried by the way.

On May 9 they arrived at Machwihilusing, forgot their pain, and "with renewed courage" started to build homes. They called their settlement "Friedenshutten" (Tents of Peace).

These natives had suffered all this persecution simply because they were Indians, and all would have been killed, were it not for the Government that kept the frontiersmen of Pennsylvania from driving them out or killing them. This would all be played out again in a hundred years, when the frontiersmen of Colorado and Nebraska would try to do the same to the helpless, hunted creatures that dared stand in their way.

Sixteen years after the Conestoga Massacre came the blackest crime on the long list, whose equal for treachery and cruelty cannot be pointed out in the record of massacres of whites by Indians.

The Gnadenhutten Massacre

In 1779 the congregations of Moravian Indians at Gnadenhutten, Salem, and Schonbrun, on the Muskingum River, were forced by hostile Indians to go north to the Sandusky River. The English instigated the move, convinced that Moravian missionaries were on the side of the colonies. These Indians had no part in the war, but The English found it easy to stir up hostile tribes to do their deeds.

The hostiles who escorted the forced march were commanded by English officers. "The savages drove them forward like cattle," said an old narrative. For a month these unfortunates were driven through the wilds, and then dumped on the banks of the Sandusky in the middle of October without game, provisions, utensils, weapons, or tools. They built huts of logs and bark, but had no blankets or beds.

The missionaries finally convinced the English that neither they nor their Indian congregations had aided the American colonists. They were told they could return home without attacks by the English-controlled hostile tribes. They faced a deadly, more insidious enemy, death by cold and starvation, while waiting to be able to return home in the Spring.

Some began to die of starvation, and they had almost no food left, so a group started to trek the 125 miles back to where their crop of corn, though withering in the fields and weatherbeaten, would still be a priceless store for them. On the way they were advised to go back openly in their deserted towns, assured that the the Americans were friendly to them now.

This they did, and spent several weeks gathering, husking, and storing corn to pack back to their families on the Sandusky. On the very day they were to have set off, some two hundred whites showed up, saying they were glad to see them and would take them to Pennsylvania where they would not be persecuted by hostile Indians or the English.

The Christian Indians believed them, and were advised to stop their work and go with the whites to Pittsburg, where they would be given all that they needed. The trusting Indians even showed them where they had been hiding their corn in the woods. The Americans helped them load everything up and even helped empty their beehives.

The whites also attracted the Salem Indians to join their "protective" caravan, all the while discussing spiritual matters with the Christian natives. In the meantime the defenseless Indians at Gnadenhutten were suddenly attacked, driven together, and bound with ropes. As soon as the Salem Indians arrived, they met the same fate.

By a vote, it was decided to kill all the Indians the next day. To the credit of humanity, a group of whites protested, declaring the Indians innocent and harmless, and should be set free. The majority were unmoved, and only disagreed on how to kill their victims.

Some preferred burning them alive. Others thought tomahawking and scalping would be best. The latter was agreed upon, and they told the Indians that since they were Christians, they should prepare themselves for death the next day.

The terrified Indians soon collected themselves and allowed the men to be separated from their families. Some whites wanted to start the killings immediately, but the natives begged a short delay to prepare themselves. As they prayed and sang to God, the impatient killers interrupted to ask if they were ready yet to die.

One of the killers picked up a cooper's mallet and killed fourteen with blows to their heads. He said his arm was tired and handed the mallet to a fellow murderer, saying, "I think I have done pretty well." In the women's house, an aged, pious old woman was first to be slain in front of the others.

Ninety-six patient Christians were slaughtered that day. Miraculously, two boys about fourteen years of age, managed to escape. One was scalped and left for dead, and the other had hidden in a cellar. At night he crept into the woods and met the other. The two, after incredible hardships, made their way back to Sanduskey.

A false account of the massacre was printed in the Pennsylvania Gazette, April 17, 1782: "The people greatly alarmed, and having received intelligence that the Indian town on the Muskingum had not moved, as reported, a number of men, properly provided, collected and rendezvoused on the Ohio, opposite the Mingo Bottom, with a desire to surprise the above towns."

"One hundred men swam the river, and proceeded to the towns of Muskingum, where the Indians had collected a large quantity of provisions to supply their war-parties. They arrived at the town in the night, undiscovered, attacked the Indians in their cabins, and so completely surprised them that they killed and scalped upward of ninety--but a few making their escape--about forty of whom were warriors, the rest old women and children."

"About eighty horses fell into their hands, which they loaded with plunder, the greatest part furs and skins, and returned to the Ohio without the loss of a man."

Massacres of Apaches

In less than a hundred years from the Gnadenhutten massacre, a United States Army officer, stationed at Camp Grant, in Arizona Territory, wrote to his commanding officer that he had allowed a some 525 destitute Apaches to make camp near the post, and had given the starving group rations after never receiving a reply from higher authority on what to do with them.

The young officer related how he had grown to admire the Indians and had done all he could to help them, including getting work on nearby ranches for them. The Apache were hopeful and anxious to hear from the distant General that they might stay there and build homes.

On April 30, 1871, the officer learned that a large party of Tucson citizens was enroute to kill all the Indians at his post. He sent a messenger to their camp to tell them to come immediately to the post for protection. The messengers found a burning village, strewn with dead and mutilated women and children. The soldiers formed a burial party, and later sent interpreters into the mountains to assure any surviving Apaches that the Army had nothing to do with the sacking of their village.

In two days, some 128 survivors and escapees straggled in, weary and gaunt from hunger. They kept faith with the Officer, but could not understand, since they were at peace and had no wrong intent, why they should be murdered. They asked for help in getting back their captured women and children, and that they be allowed to live here in their old homes, where nature supplied nearly all their needs.

This was not the only cruel outrage committed by white men on the Apaches. In the Report of the Board of Indians Commissioners for 1871, a letter was included from an Arizona pioneer who had spent 1840 and 1841 among the Apaches, a time when they were friendly to all Americans going among them.

Many American trappers were taking beaver on the headwaters of the Gila River at that time. The valleys were full of Apaches, whose closest enemies were the Mexicans, who feared them greatly and could not fight them man to man.

One of the trappers, a man named Johnson, went on a spree in Sonora. The Governor of Sonora offered him an ounce of gold for every Apache scalp brought to him. The trapper secured a small howitzer, and returned to his camp with supplies for his party. On approaching the valley he was welcomed back by the Indians who began preparing a feast.

While they were gathered in a laughing, chatting group near the fire, the trapper told some of his associates of the Mexican offer, easily overcoming the small supply of scruples among them. Since they were always armed with rifles and pistols, they needed no preparation.

The howitzer, which the Indians might have supposed was merely a small keg of whiskey, was placed on the ground and pointed at the group of warriors, squaws, and children around the fire, watching the roasting meal. Johnson gave the signal and fired the howitzer. All who were not killed by the blast were shot with rifles.

A very few escaped and fled to others of their tribe. The Apaches showed that they could imitate their civilized white brothers. A band immediately fell upon a group of trappers, killing almost all of them. The story then spread, of course, that the Apaches were cruel and treacherous, with no mention of what had first been done to them.

These are but four massacres out of scores, whose history, when fully known, proved that the Indian had not always been the aggressor, and that treachery and cruelty were by no means exclusively Indian traits.

CONCLUSION

There were about 300,000 Indians in the United States in the late 1870's, by best estimates, made up of nearly three hundred tribes and bands. There were, "In Minnesota and States east of the Mississippi, about 32,500; In Nebraska, Kansas, and the Indian Territory (present Oklahoma), 70,650; In the territories of Dakota, Montana, Wyoming, and Idaho, 65,000; In Nevada and the Territories of Colorado, New Mexico, Utah, and Arizona, 84,000; On the Pacific slope, 48,000."

Almost half were self-supporting on their own reservations, "receiving nothing from the Government except interest on their own moneys, or annuities granted them in consideration of the cession of their lands to the United States. Of the remainder, 84,000 were partially supported by Government monies due them, and by their annuities provided by treaties, being inadequate to their subsistence on the reservations where they are confined.

In many cases, those Indians furnished up to two-thirds of their support "by fishing and root-digging". Those facts should have disposed of the persistent accusation that Indians would not work. There were about 55,000 who never visited an agency, over whom the Government did not pretend to have either control or care. They lived, "by fishing, hunting, on roots, nuts, berries, and the like, and by begging and stealing." Some 31,000 were entirely supported by the Government.

All of the three hundred tribes or bands had suffered at the hands of the Government or of white settlers. The poorer, the smaller the group, the more helpless the band, the more certain the cruelty and outrage they endured.

This was especially true of the Indians of the Pacific Slope who were caught up in the tidal wave of gold-seekers. There was no time for Government treaties to be made, or even community laws. The tales of the wrongs to Pacific Slope Indians from 1850 to 1880 fills many volumes, and is too monstrous to at first be believed.

Wherever the record of Indian history is opened, every page and every year has a dark stain. The story of one tribe is the story of all, time and place making no difference in the facts. Colorado was as greedy and unjust in 1880 as was Georgia in 1830, and Ohio in 1795. The United States broke promises deftly throughout the period, with added ingenuity from long practice.

There are hundreds of pages of unimpeachable testimony on the side of the Indian, but they all went for nothing, tossed aside and forgotten. Presidential commission after commission contained eloquent statements of wrongs done by the Government, with recommendations to Tell the truth, keep promises, make fair bargains, ad deal justly in all ways and all things.

These reports were bound up in annual reports, and that was the end of them. Probably not one American citizen in 10,000 ever saw them or knew that they existed. The swamp of Indian affairs needed clearing, with the goal of making the Indians full citizens, with all rights and responsibilities. It was to be long in coming.

Cheating, robbing, and breaking promises were the main things the United States Government needed to stop doing.

INDIAN TREATIES OF NEW HAMPSHIRE AND THE EASTERN WOODLANDS

HOW TO SUPPRESS INDIANS

In 1995, the Native American Rights Fund, A Colorado-based advocacy group distributed a treatise titled *A Brief U.S. Government guide to the Use of Laws to Suppress Indians*. They indicated that such a guide was never actually published, but based on the Government's two hundred years of experience with Indians, it certainly could have been, and it would have read something like this:

To suppress Indian cultures and absorb Indian people into white society in a manner according to law, it is vital to create a body of law that supports this intention.   Therefore, the government must move quickly on these five fronts to pass laws and carry out policies that:

1. Destroy Native Economies.
The best way to control Indians, better even than a well-armed cavalry, is to destroy the economies on which their lives depend. Act immiediately to impose an economic monopoly on Indians. Pass laws that prohibit tribes from selling their land to any party escept the government.   Enforce restrictions that require Indians to engage in commerce exclusively with government agents.   By excluding Indians from free market competition, they will by necessity become dependent on the government for their survival.

2. Take Away Indian Land.
At the same time, take away lands that are the base of both tribal economies and cultures. Many of these lands may be obtained wih ease by the signing of treaties between presidents and tribal chiefs, who are naively trusting and consistently uphold their agreements.

Should future disputes arise over the rightful ownership of land, these treaties can be easily ignored, as Indians possess no knowledge of our laws, only their own primitive customs. If tribes refuse to vacate lands that are desirable for the nation's growth and progress, pass laws to force their removal, creating "reservations" for Indians on western lands that are undesirable for civilized society.

This new reservation system will provide the double advantage of further undermining Indian economies while making Indians easier for for government agents to control.

3. Dismantle Indian Families and Cultures.

Education is the most powerful tool for dismantling Indian cultures and assimilating Indians in to civilized society. However, because adult Indians are generally resistant to civilizing influences, government programs must focus on the children.

Create federal policy that authorizes and funds a system of government boarding schools where Indian children can be isolated from their families. Require uninterrupted attendance for four to eight years. Use the harshest discipline to stamp out Indian languages and culture, whipping or depriving food to recalcitrant chilldren who continue to speak their Indian language.

As resistance to this systematic breakup of the family may be strong, and parents may try to withhold their children from boarding schools, authorize the United States Cavalry to enter reservations each Fall and round up the children.

4. Stamp Out Indian Religions.

Because religion is the foundation that holds Indian communities and cultures together, the suppression of Indian religions is vital to domination. Pass laws that prohibit on reservations the practice of religions, dances, and other cultural events of tribal importance. At Indian boarding schools, severely punish children who attempt to continue to attend Indian religious ceremonies. Accompany these actions with passive support of the prevalent belief among white citizens that Indians are culturally and spiritually inferior.

Make no move to protect Indian "worship" sites, which are usually nothing more that forests, waterfalls, and other such natural sites, from development and destruction. Offer no protection to the remains of Indian dead. Rather, encourage anthropologists and treasure hunters to dig up Indian graves and to sell remains and burial items to private collectors and museums.

Constant devaluation of native religions and desecration of sacred sites will cause Indians, in the words of President Andreww Jackson, "to cast off their savage habits and become and in interesting, civilized, and Christian community."

5,   Eradicate Powers of Tribal Self-Government and Self-Determination.

The notion that each tribe is a sovereign, self-governing nation is dangerous, but unfortunately confirmed in the earliest federal law of the Americannation. Rather than try to overturn the law, ignore it. Tacitly allow states to pass their own laws that illegally extend their rule over tribes. Make no move to stop the states from destroying tribal and personal rights, from subjecting Indians to endless harassment and invasion of their lands by white settlers, or from taxing tribes for their resources.

Ignore the authority of tribal courts to settle disputes on reservations and force Indians to travel hundreds of mile to bring their grievances to white courts where their ignorance of the system and lack of facility with the English language will put them at a serious disadvantage.

By using laws in these five crucial areas to undermine Indian culture and economy, it can be expected that within a relatively short time, Indians living on this land will be assimilated into white society or sufficiently suppressed as to pose no serious threat to the advancement and development of the United States of America.

The presentation of the following treaties with Plains and western Indians gives vivid testimony to these views with the words and names of the participants. The first with a tribe is of course a pledge of friendship, and later treaties become instruments of dominance.

The Publisher

TREATY WITH THE WYANDOT, ETC.
1785, Jan. 21

Articles of a treaty concluded at Fort Mc'Intosh, the twenty-first day of January, one thousand seven hundred and eighty-five, between the Commissioners Plenipotentiary of the United States of America, of the one Part, and the Sachems and Warriors of the Wiandot, ware, Chippawa and Ottawa Nations of the other.

The Commissioners Plenipotentiary of the United States in Congress assembled, give peace to the Wiandot, Delaware, Chippewa, and Ottawa nations of Indians, on the following conditions:

ARTICLE 1. Three chiefs, one from among the Wiandot, and two from among the Delaware nations, shall be delivered up to the Commissioners of the United States, to be by the retained till all the prisoners, white and black, taken by the said nations, or any of them, shall be restored.

ARTICLE 2. The said Indian nations do acknowledge themselves and all their tribes to be under the protection of the United States and of no other sovereign whatsoever.

ARTICLE 3. The boundary line between the United States and the Wiandot and Delaware nations, shall begin at the mouth of the river Cayahoga, and run thence up the said river to the portage between that and the Tus-carawas branch of Meskingum; then down the said branch to the forks at the crossing place above Fort Lawrence; then westerly to the portage of the Big Miami, which runs into the Ohio, at the mouth of which branch the fort stood which was taken by the French in one thousand seven hundred and fifty-two; then along the said portage to the Great Miami or Ome river, and down the south-east side of the same to its mouth; thence along the south shore of lake Erie, to the mouth of Cayahoga where it began.

ARTICLE 4. The United States allot all the lands contained within the said lines to the Wiandot and Delaware nations, to live and to hunt on, and to such of the Ottawa nation as now live thereon; saving and reserving for the establishment of trading posts, six miles square at the reserving for the establishment of trading posts, six miles square at the mouth of Miami or Ome river, and the same at the portage on that branch of the Big Miami which runs into the Ohio, and the same on the lake of Sanduske where the fort formerly stood, and also two miles square on each side of the lower rapids of Sanduske river, which posts and the lands annexed to them, shall be to the use and under the government of the United States.

ARTICLE 5. If any citizen of the United States, or other person not being an Indian, shall attempt to settle on any of the lands allotted to the Wiandot and Delaware nations in this treaty, except on the lands reserved to the United States in the preceding article, such person shall forfeit the protection of the United States, and the Indians may punish him as they please.

ARTICLE 6. The Indians who sign this treaty, as well in behalf of all their tribes as of themselves, do acknowledge the lands east, south and west of the lines described in the third article, so far as the said Indians formerly claimed the same, to belong to the United States; and none of their tribes shall presume to settle upon the same, or any part of it.

ARTICLE 7. The post of Detroit, with a district beginning at the mouth of the river Rosine, on the west end of lake Erie, and running west six miles up the southern bank of the said river, thence northerly and always six miles west of the strait, till it strikes the lake St. Clair, shall be also reserved to the sole use of the United States.

ARTICLE 8. In the same manner the post of Michillimachenac with its dependencies, and twelve miles square about the same, shall be reserved to the use of the United States.

ARTICLE 9. If any Indian or Indians shall commit a robbery or murder on any citizen of the United States, the tribe to which such offenders may belong, shall be bound to deliver them up at the nearest post, to be punished according to the ordinances of the United States.

ARTICLE 10. The Commissioners of the United States, in pursuance of the humane and liberal views of Congress, upon this treaty's being signed, will direct goods to be distributed among the different tribes for their use and comfort.

SEPARATE ARTICLE. It is agreed that the Delaware chiefs, Kelelamand or lieutenant-colonel Henry, Hengue Pushees or the Big Cat, Wicocalind or Captain White Eyes, who took up the hatchet for the United States, and their families, shall be received into the Delaware nation, in the same situation and rank as before the war, and enjoy their due portions of the lands given to the Wiandot and Delaware nations in this treaty, as fully as if they had not taken part with America, or as any other person or persons in the said nations.

TREATY WITH THE WYANDOT, ETC.
1789, Jan. 9
Proclamation, Sept. 27, 1789.

Articles of a Treaty Made at Fort Harmar, between Arthur St. Clair, Governor of the Territory of the United States North-West of the River Ohio, and Commissioner Plenipotentiary of the United States of America, for removing all Causes of Controversy, regulating trade, and settling Boundaries, with the Indian Nations in the Northern Department, of the one Part; and the Sachems and Warriors of the Wiandot, Delaware, Ottawa, Chippewa, Pattawatima and Sac Nations, on the other Part.

ARTICLE 1. WHEREAS the United States in Congress assembled, did, by their Commissioners George Rogers Clark, Richard Butler, and Arthur Lee, Esquires, duly appointed for that purpose, at a treaty holder with the Wyandot, Delaware, Ottawa, and Chippewa nations, at Fort M'Intosh on the twenty-first day of January, in the year of our Lord one thousand seven hundred and eighty-five, conclude a peace with the Wyandots, Delawares, Ottawas and Chippewas, and take them into their friendship and protection: And whereas at the said treaty it was stipulated that all prisoners that had been made by those nations, or either of them, should be delivered up to the United States. And whereas the said nations have now agreed to and with the aforesaid Arthur St. Clair, to renew and confirm all the engagements they had made with the United States of America, at the before mentioned treaty, except so far as are altered by these presents. And there are now in the possession of some individuals of these nations, certain prisoners, who have been taken by others not in peace with the said United States, or in violation of the treaties subsisting between the United States and them; the said nations agree to deliver up all the prisoners now in their hands (by what means soever they may have come into their possession) to the said Governor St. Clair, at Fort Harmar, or in his absence, to the officer commanding there, as soon as conveniently may be; and for the true performance of this agreement, they do now agree to deliver into his hands, two persons of the Wyandot Nation, to be retained in the hands of the United States as hostages, until the said prisoners are restored; after which they shall be sent back to their nation.

ARTICLE 2. And whereas at the before mentioned treaty it was agreed between the United States and said nations, that a boundary line should be fixed between the lands of those nations and the territory of the United States; which boundary is as follows, viz:Beginning at the mouth of Cayahoga river, and running thence up the said river to the portage between that and the Tuscarawa branch of Muskingum, then down the said branch to the forks at the crossing-place above fort Lawrence, thence westerly to the portage on that branch of the Big Miami river which runs into the Ohio, at the mouth of which branch the fort stood which was taken by the French in the year of our Lord one thousand seven hundred and fifty-two, then along the said portage to the Great Miami or Omie river, and down the south-east side of the same to its mouth; thence along the southern shore of Lake Erie to the mouth of Cayahoga, where it began.

And the said Wyandot, Delaware, Ottawa and Chippewa Nations, for and in consideration of the peace then granted to them by the said United States, and the presents they then received, as well as of a quantity of goods to the value of six thousand dollars, now delivered to them by the said Arthur St. Clair, the receipt whereof they do hereby acknowledge, do by these presents renew and confirm the said boundary line; to the end that the same may remain as a division line between the lands of the United States of America, and the lands of said nations, forever.

And the undersigned Indians do hereby in their own names, and the names of their respective nations and tribes, their heirs and descendants, for the consideration above-mentioned, release, quit claim, relinquish and cede to the said United States, all the land east, south and west of the lines above described, so far as the said Indians formerly claimed the same; for them the said United States to have and to hold the same in true and absolute propriety forever.

ARTICLE 3. The United States of America do by these presents relinquish and quit claim to the said nations respectively, all the lands lying between the limits above described, for them the said Indians to live and hunt upon, and otherwise to occupy as they shall see fit:. But the said nations, or either of them, shall not be at liberty to sell or dispose of the same, or any part thereof, to any sovereign power, except the United States; nor to the subjects or citizens of any other sovereign power, nor to the subjects or citizens of the United States.

ARTICLE 4. It is agreed between the said United States and the said nations, that the individuals of said nations shah be at liberty to hunt within the territory ceded to the United States, without hindrance or molestation, so long as they demean themselves peaceably, and offer no injury or annoyance to any of the subjects or citizens of the said United States.

ARTICLE 5. It is agreed that if any Indian or Indians of the nations before mentioned, shall commit a murder or robbery on any of the citizens of the United States, the nation or tribe to which the offender belongs, on complaint being made, shall deliver up the person or persons complained of, at the nearest post of the United States; to the end that he or they may be tried, and if found guilty, punished according to the laws established in the territory of the United States north-west of the river Ohio, for the punishment of such offences, if the same shall have been committed within the said territory; or according to the laws of the State where the offence may have been committed, if the same has happened in any of the United States. In like manner, if any subject or citizen of the United States shall commit murder or robbery on any Indian or Indians of the said nations, upon complaint being made thereof, he or they shall be arrested, tried and punished agreeable to the laws of the state or of the territory wherein the offence was committed; that nothing may interrupt the peace and harmony now established between the United States and said nations.

ARTICLE 6. And whereas the practice of stealing horses has prevailed very much, to the great disquiet of the citizens of the United States, and if persisted in, cannot fail to involve both the United States of America and the Indians in endless animosity, it is agreed that it shall be put an entire stop to on both sides; nevertheless, should some individuals, in defiance of this agreement, and of the laws provided against such offences, continue to make depredations of that nature, the person convicted thereof shall be punished with the utmost severity the laws of the respective states, or territory of the United States north-west of the Ohio, where the offence may have been committed, will admit of: And all horses so stolen, either by the Indians from the citizens or subjects of the United States, or by the citizens or subjects of the United States from any of the Indian nations, may be reclaimed, into whose possession soever they may have passed, and, upon due proof, shall be restored; any sales in market overt, notwithstanding. And the civil magistrates in the United States respectively, and in the territory of the United States north-west of the Ohio, shall give all necessary aid and protection to Indians claiming such stolen horses.

ARTICLE 7. Trade shall be opened with the said nations, and they do hereby respectively engage to afford protection to the persons and property of such as may be duly licensed to reside among them for the purposes of trade, and to their agents, factors and servants; but no person shall be permitted to reside at their towns, or at their hunting camps, as a trader, who is not furnished with a license for that purpose, under the hand and seal of the Governor of the territory of the United States north-west of the Ohio, for the time being, or tinder the hand and seal of one of his deputies for the management of Indian affairs; to the end that they may not be imposed upon in their traffic. And if any person or persons shall intrude themselves without such licence, they promise to apprehend him or them, and to bring them to the said Governor, or one of his deputies, for the purpose before mentioned, to be dealt with according to law: And that they may be defended against persons who might attempt to forage such licenses, they further engage to give information to the said Governor, or one of his deputies, of the names of all traders residing among them from time to time, and at least once in every year.

ARTICLE 8. Should any nation of Indians meditate a war against the United States, or either of them, and the same shall come to the knowledge of the before mentioned nations, or either of them, they do hereby engage to give immediate notice thereof to the Governor, or in his absence to the officer commanding the troops of the United States at the nearest post. And should any nation with hostile intentions against the United States, or either of them, attempt to pass through their country, they will endeavor to prevent the same, and in like manner give information of such attempt to the said Governor or commanding officer, as soon as possible, that all causes of mistrust and suspicion may be avoided between them and the United States: In like manner the United States shall give notice to the said Indian nations, of any harm that may be meditated against them, or either of them, that shall come to their knowledge; and do all in their power to hinder and prevent the same, that the friendship between them may be uninterrupted.

ARTICLE 9. If any person or persons, citizens or subjects of the United States, or any other person not being an Indian, shall presume to settle upon the lands confirmed to the said nations, he and they shall be out of the protection of the United States; and the said nations may punish him or them in such manner as they see fit.

ARTICLE 10. The United States renew the reservations heretofore made in the before mentioned treaty at Fort M'Intosh, for the establishment of trading posts, in manner and form following; that is to say: Six miles square at the mouth of the Miami or Omie river; six miles square at the portage upon that branch of the Miami which runs into the Ohio; six miles square upon the lake Sandusky where the fort formerly stood; and two miles square upon each side the Lower Rapids on Sandusky river, which posts, and the lands annexed to them, shall be for the use and under the government of the United States.

ARTICLE 11. The post at Detroit, with a district of land beginning at the mouth of the river Rosine, at the west end of lake Erie, and running up the southern bank of said river six miles; thence northerly, and always six miles west of the strait, until it strikes the lake St. Clair, shall be reserved for the use of the United States.

ARTICLE 12. In like manner the post at Michilimackinac, with its dependencies, and twelve miles square about the same, shall be reserved to the sole use of the United States.

ARTICLE 13. The United States of America do hereby renew and confirm the peace and friendship entered into with the said nations, at the treaty before mentioned, held at Fort M'Intosh; and the said nations again acknowledge themselves, and all their tribes, to be under the protection of the said United States, and no other power whatever.

ARTICLE 14. The United States of America do also receive into their friendship and protection, the nations of the Pattiwatimas and Sacs; and do hereby establish a league of peace and amity between them respectively; and all the articles of this treaty, so far as they apply to these nations, are to be considered as made and concluded in all, and every part, expressly with them and each of them.

ARTICLE 15. And whereas in describing the boundary before mentioned, the words, if strictly constructed, would carry it from the portage on that branch of the Miami, which runs into the Ohio, over to the river Au Glaize; which was neither the intention of the Indians, nor of the Commissioners; it is hereby declared, that the line shall run from the said portage directly to the first fork of the Miami river, which is to the southward and eastward of the Miami village, thence down the main branch of the Miami river to the said village, and thence down that river to Lake Erie, and along the margin of the lake to the place of beginning.

Done at Fort Harmar, on the Muskingum, this ninth day of January, in the year of Our Lord one thousand seven hundred and eighty-nine.

Be it remembered, That the Wyandots have laid claim to the lands that were granted to the Shawanese, at the treaty held at the Miami, and have declared, that as the Shawanese have been so restless, and caused so much trouble, both to them and to the United States, if they will not now be at peace, they will dispossess them, and take the country into their own hands; for that the country is theirs of right, and the Shawanese are only living upon it by their permission. They further lay claim to all the country west of the Miami boundary, from the village to the lake Erie, and declare that it is now under their management and direction.

SEPARATE ARTICLE.

Whereas the Wyandots have represented, that within the reservation from the river Rosine along the Strait, they have two villages from which they cannot with any convenience remove; it is agreed, that they shall remain in possession of the same, and shall not be in any manner disturbed therein.

SEPARATE ARTICLE.

Should a robbery or murder be committed by an Indian or Indians of the said nations upon the citizens or subjects of the United States or any of them, or by the citizens or subjects of the United States or any of them, upon any Indian or Indians of the said nations, the parties accused of the same shall be tried, and, if found guilty, be punished according to the laws of the state, or of the territory of the United States, as the case may be, where the same was committed; and should any horses be stolen, either by the Indians of the said nations from the citizens or subjects of the United States or any of them, or by any of the said citizens and subjects from any of the said Indians, they may be reclaimed, into whose possession soever they may have come; and, upon due proof, shall be restored, any sales in open market notwithstanding. And the parties convicted shall be punished with the utmost severity the laws will admit; and the said nations engage to deliver the parties that may be accused of their nations of either of the before-mentioned crimes, at the nearest post of the United States, if the crime was committed within the territory of the United States, or to the civil authority of the States, if it shall have happened within any of the United States.

TREATY WITH THE SIX NATIONS
1789, Jan. 9

Articles of a treaty made at Fort Harmar, the ninth day of January, in the year of our Lord one thousand seven hundred and eighty-nine, between Arthur St. Clair, esquire, governor of the territory of the United States of America, north-west of the river Ohio, and commissioner plenipotentiary of the said United States, for removing all causes of controversy, regulating trade, and settling boundaries, between the Indian nations in the northern department and the said United States, of the one part, and the sachems and warriors of the Six Nations, of the other part:

ARTICLE 1. WHEREAS the United States, in congress assembled, did, by their commissioners, Oliver Wolcott, Richard Butler, and Arthur Lee, esquires, duly appointed for that purpose, at a treaty held with the said Six Nations, viz: with the Mohawks, Oneidas, Onondagas, Tus-caroras, Cayugas, and Senekas, at fort Stanwix, on the twenty-second day of October, one thousand seven hundred and eighty-four, give peace to the said nations, and receive them into their friendship and protection: And whereas the said nations have now agreed to and with the said Arthur St. Clair, to renew and confirm all the engagements and stipulations entered into at the beforementioned treaty at fort Stanwix: and whereas it was then and there agreed, between the United States of America and the said Six Nations, that a boundary line should be fixed between the lands of the said Six Nations and the territory of the said United States, which boundary line is as follows, viz: Beginning at the mouth of a creek, about four miles east of Niagara, called Ononwayea, or Johnston's Landing Place, upon the lake named by the Indians Cawego, and by us Ontario; from thence southerly, in a direction always four miles east of the carrying place, between lake Erie and lake Ontario, to the mouth of Tehoseroton, or Buffalo creek, upon lake Erie; thence south, to the northern boundary of the state of Pennsylvania; thence west, to the end of the said north boundary; thence south, along the west boundary of the said state to the river Ohio.

The said line, from the mouth of Ononwayea to the Ohio, shall be the western boundary of the lands of the Six Nations, so that the Six Nations shall and do yield to the United States, all claim to the country west of the said boundary; and then they shall be secured in the possession of the lands they inhabit east, north, and south of the same, reserving only six miles square, round the fort of Oswego, for the support of the same. The said Six Nations, except the Mohawks, none of whom have attended at this time, for and in consideration of the peace then granted to them, the presents they then received, as well as in consideration of a quantity of goods, to the value of three thousand dollars, now delivered to them by the said Arthur St. Clair, the receipt whereof they do hereby acknowledge, do hereby renew and confirm the said boundary line in the words before mentioned, to the end that it may be and remain as a division line between the lands of the said Six Nations and the territory of the United States, forever.

And the undersigned Indians, as well in their own names as in the name of their respective tribes and nations, their heirs and descendants, for the considerations beforementioned, do release, quit claim, relinquish, and cede, to the United States of America, all the lands west of the said boundary or division line, and between the said line and the strait, from the mouth of Ononwayea and Buffalo Creek, for them, the said United States of America, to have and to hold the same, in true and absolute propriety, forever.

ARTICLE 2. The United States of America confirm to the Six Nations, all the lands which they inhabit, lying east and north of the beforementioned boundary line, and relinquish and quit claim to the same and every part thereof, excepting only six miles square round the fort of Oswego, which six miles square round said fort is again reserved to the United States by these presents.

ARTICLE 3. The Oneida and Tuscarora nations, are also again secured and confirmed in the possession of their respective lands.

ARTICLE 4. The United States of America renew and confirm the peace and friendship entered into with the Six Nations, (except the Mohawks), at the treaty beforementioned, held at fort Stanwix, declaring the same to be perpetual. And if the Mohawks shall, within six months, declare their assent to the same, they shall be considered as included.

Done at Fort Harmar, on the Muskingum, the day and year first above written.

SEPARATE ARTICLE. Should a robbery or murder be committed by an Indian or Indians of the Six Nations, upon the citizens or subjects of the United States, or by the citizens or subjects of the United States, or any of them, upon any of the Indians of the said nations, the parties accused of the same shall be tried, and if found guilty, be punished according to the laws of the state, or of the territory of the United States, as the case may be, where the same was committed. And should any horses be stolen, either by the Indians of the said nations, from the citizens or subjects of the United States, or any of them, or by any of the said citizens or subjects from any of the said Indians, they may be reclaimed into whose possession soever they may have come; and, upon due proof, shall be restored, any sale in open market notwithstanding; and the persons convicted shall be punished with the utmost severity the laws will admit. And the said nations engage to deliver the persons that may be accused, of their nations, of either of the beforementioned crimes, at the nearest post of the United States, if the crime was committed within the territory of the United States; or to the civil authority of the state, if it shall have happened within any of the United States.

TREATY WITH THE SEVEN NATIONS
OF CANADA
1796, May 31
Proclamation, Jan. 1, 1797.

At a treaty held at the city of New York, with the Nations or Tribes of Indians, denominating themselves the Seven Nations of Canada; Abraham Ogaen, Commissioner, appointed under the authority of the United States, to hold the Treaty; Ohaweio, alias Goodstream, Teharaywanege, alias Thomas Williams, two Chiefs of the Caghnawayas; Atiatoharongwan, alias Colonel Lewis Cook, a Chief the St. Regis Indians, and William Gray, Deputies, authorized to represent these Seven Nations or Tribes of Indians at the Treaty, and Mr. Gray, serving also as Interpreter; Egbert Benson, Richard Vrick and James Watson, Agents for the State of New York; William Constable and Daniel M'Cormick, purchasers under Alexander Macomb:

THE agents for the state, having, in the presence, and with the approbation of the commissioner, proposed to the deputies for the Indians, the compensation hereinafter mentioned, for the extinguishment of their claim to all lands within the state, and the said deputies being willing to accept the same, it is thereupon granted, agreed and concluded between the said deputies and the said agents,-as follows: The said deputies do, for and in the name of the said Seven Nations or tribes of Indians, cede, release and quit claim to the people of the state of New-York forever, all the claim, right, or title of them, the said Seven Nations or tribes of Indians, to lands within the said state: Provided nevertheless, That the tract equal to six miles square, reserved in the sale made by the commissioners of the land-office of the said state, to Alexander Macomb, to be applied to the use of the Indians of the village of St. Regis, shall still remain so reserved.

The said agents do, for, and in the name of the people of the state of New-York, grant to the said Seven Nations or tribes of Indians, that the people of the state of New-York shall pay to them, at the mouth of the river Chazy, on Lake Champlain, on the third Monday in August next, the sum of one thousand two hundred and thirty-three pounds, six shillings and eight-pence, and the further sum of two hundred and thirteen pounds six shillings and eight-pence, lawful money of the said state, and on the third Monday in August, yearly, forever thereafter, the like sum of two hundred and thirteen pounds six shillings and eight-pence: Provided nevertheless, That the people of the state of New-York shall not be held to pay the said sums, unless in respect to the two sums to be paid on the third Monday in August next, at least twenty, and in respect to the said yearly sum to be paid thereafter, at least five of the principal men of the said Seven Nations or tribes of Indians, shall attend as deputies to receive and to give receipts for the same.

The said deputies having suggested, that the Indians of the village of St. Regis have built a mill on Salmon river, and another on Grass river, and that the meadows on Grass river are necessary to them for hay.

In order, therefore, to secure to the Indians of the said village, the use of the said mills and meadows, in case they should hereafter appear not to be included within the above tract so to remain reserved; it is, therefore, also agreed and concluded between the said deputies, the said agents, and the said William Constable and Daniel M'Cormick, for themselves and their associates, purchasers under the said Alexander Macomb, of the adjacent lands, that there shall be reserved, to be applied to the use of the Indians of the said village of St. Regis, in like manner as the said tract is to remain reserved, a tract of one mile square, at each of the said mills, and the meadows on both sides of the said Grass river from the said mill thereon, to its confluence with the river St. Lawrence.

AGREEMENT WITH THE SENECA
1797, Sept. 15

Contract entered into, under the sanction of the United States of America, between Robert Morris and the Seneca nation of Indians.

This indenture, made the fifteenth day of September, in the year of our Lord one thousand seven hundred and ninety-seven, between the sachems, chiefs, and warriors of the Seneca nation of Indians, of the first part, and Robert Morris, of the city of Philadelphia, Esquire, of the second part:

Whereas the Commonwealth of Massachusetts have granted, bargained, and sold unto the said Robert Morris, his heirs and assigns forever, the pre-emptive right, and all other the right, title and interest which the said Commonwealth had to all the tract of land hereinafter particularly mentioned, being part of a tract of land lying within the State of New York, the right of pre-emption of the soil whereof, from the native Indians, was ceded and granted by the said State of New York, to the said Commonwealth: and whereas, at a treaty held under the authority of the United States, with the said Seneca nation of Indians, at Genesee, in the county of Ontario, and State of New York, on the day of the date of these presents, and on sundry days immediately prior thereto, by the Honorable Jeremiah Wadsworth, Esquire, a commissioner appointed by the President of the United States, to hold the same in pursuance of the constitution, and of the act of the Congress of the United States, in such case made and provided, it was agreed, in the presence and with the approbation of the said commissioner, by the sachems, chiefs and warriors of the said nations of Indians, for themselves and in behalf of their nation, to sell to the said Robert Morris, and to his heirs and assigns forever, all their right to all that tract of land above recited, and hereinafter particularly specified, for the sum of one hundred thousand dollars, to be by the said Robert Morris vested in the stock of the bank of the United States, and held in the name of the President of the United States, for the use and behoof of the said nation of Indians, the said agreement and sale being also made in the presence, and with the approbation of the honorable William Shepard, Esquire, the superintendent appointed for such purpose, in pursuance of a resolve of the General Court of the Commonwealth of Massachusetts, passed the eleventh day of March, in the year of our Lord one thousand seven hundred and ninety-one; now this indenture witnesseth, that the said parties, of the first part, for and in consideration of the premises above recited, and for divers other good and valuable considerations them thereunto moving, have granted, bargained, sold, aliened, released, enfeoffed, and confirmed; and by these presents do grant, bargain, sell, alien, release, enfeoff, and confirm, unto the said party of the second part, his heirs and assigns forever, all that certain tract of land, except as is hereinafter excepted, lying within the county of Ontario and State of New York, being part of a tract of land, the right of pre-emption whereof was ceded by the state of New York to the Commonwealth of Massachusetts, by deed of cession executed at Hartford, on the sixteenth day of December, in the year of our Lord one thousand seven hundred and eighty-six, being all such part thereof as is not included in the Indian purchase made by Oliver Phelps and Nathaniel Gorham, and bounded as follows, to wit: easterly, by the land confirmed to Oliver Phelps and Nathaniel Gorham by the legislature of the Commonwealth of Massachusetts, by and act passed the twenty-first day of November, in the year of our Lord one thousand seven hundred and eighty-eight.

From there southerly, by the north boundary line of the State of Pennsylvania; westerly, partly by a tract of land, part of the land ceded by the State of Massachusetts to the United States, and by them sold to Pennsylvania, being a right angled triangle, whose hypothenuse is in or along the shore of Lake Erie; partly by Lake Erie, from the northern point of that triangle to the Southern bounds of a tract of land a mile in width, lying on and along the east side of the strait of Niagara, and partly by the said tract to lake Ontario; and on the north, by the boundary line between the United States and the King of Great Britain; excepting, nevertheless, and reserving always out of this grant and conveyance, all such pieces or parcels of the aforesaid tract, and such privileges thereunto belonging as are next hereinafter mentioned, which said pieces or parcels of land so excepted are, by the parties to these presents, clearly and fully understood to remain the property of the said parties of the first part, in as full and ample manner as if these presents had not been executed; that is to say, excepting and reserving to them, the said parties of the first part, and their nation, one piece or parcel of the aforesaid tract, at Canawaugas, of two square miles, to be laid out in such manner as to include the village extending in breadth one mile along the river; one other piece or parcel at Big Tree, of two square miles, to be laid out in such manner as to include the village, extending in breadth along the river one mile,

One other piece or parcel of two square miles at Little Beard's town, extending one mile along the river, to be laid off in such manner as to include the village; one other tract of two square miles at Squawky Hill, to be laid off as follows, to wit: one square mile to be laid off along the river, in such manner as to include the village, the other directly west thereof and contiguo's thereto; one other piece or parcel at Gar-dean, beginning at the mouth of Steep Hill creek, thence due east until it strikes the old path, thence south until a due west line will intersect with certain steep rocks on the west side of Genesee river, then extending due west, due north and due east, until it strikes the first mentiones bound, enclosing as much land on the west side as on the east side of the river. One other piece or parcel at Kaounadeau extending in length eight miles along the river and two miles in breadth. One other piece or parcel at Cataraugos, beginning at the mouth of the Eighteen mile or Koghquaugu creek, thence a line or line to be drawn parallel to lake Erie, at the distance of one mile from there, to the mouth of Cataraugos creek, thence a line or lines extending 12 miles up the north side of said creek at the distance of one mile therefrom, thence a direct line to the said creek, thence down the said creek to lake Erie, thence along the lake to the first mentioned creek, and thence to the place of beginning. Also one other piece at Cataraugos, beginning at the shore of lake Erie, on the south side of Cataraugos creek, at the distance of one mile from the mouth thereof, thence running one mile from the lake, thence on a line parallel thereto, to a point within one mile from the Connondau-weyea creek, thence up the said creek one mile, on a line parallel thereto, thence on a direct line to the said creek, thence down the same to lake Erie, thence along the lake to the place of beginning.

Also one other piece or parcel of forty-two square miles, at or near the Allegenny river. Also, two hundred square miles, to be laid off partly at the Buffalo and partly at the Tonnawanta creeks. Also, excepting and reserving to them, the said parties of the first part and their heirs, the privilege of fishing and hunting on the said tract of land hereby intended to be conveyed. And it is hereby understood by and between the parties to these presents, that all such pieces or parcels of land as are hereby reserved and are not particularly described as to the manner in which the same are to be laid off, shall be laid off in such manner as shall be determined by the sachems, chiefs, residing at or near the respective villages where such reservations are made, a particular note whereof to be indorsed on the back of this deed, and recorded therewith, together with all and singular the rights, privileges, hereditaments, and appurtenances thereunto belonging, or in anywise appertaining. And all the estate, right, title, and interest, whatsoever, of them the said parties of the first part and their nation, of, in, and to the said tract of land above described, except as is above excepted, to gave and to hold all and singular the said granted premises, with the appurtenances to the said party of the second part, his heirs and assigns, to his and their proper use, benefit and behoof forever.

In witness whereof, the parties to these presents have hereunto interchangeably set their hands and seals, the day and year first above written.
Pursuant to a resolution of the legislature of the Commonwealth of Massachusetts, passed the eleventh day of March, in the year of our Lord one thousand seven hundred and ninety-one, I have attended a full and general treaty of the Seneka nation of Indians, at Genesee, in the county of Ontario, when the within instrument was duty executed in my presence by the sachems, chiefs, and warriors of the said nation, being fairly and properly understood and transacted by all the parties of Indians concerned, and declared to be done to their universal satisfaction: I therefore certify and approve of the same.

TREATY WITH THE MOHAWK
1797, Mar. 29
Proclamation, Apr. 27, 1798.

Relinquishment to New York, by the Mohawk nation of Indians, under the sanction of the United States of America, of all claim to lands in that state.

At a treaty held under the authority of the United States, with the Mohawk nation of Indians, residing in the province of Upper Canada, within the dominions of the king of Great Britain, present, the honorable Isaac Smith, commissioner appointed by the United States to hold this treaty; Abraham Ten Broeck, Egbert Benson, and Ezra L'Hommedieu, agents for the state of New York; captain Joseph Brandt, and captain John Deserontyon, two of the said Indians and deputies, to represent the said nation at this treaty.

The said agents having, in the presence, and with the approbation of the said commissioner, proposed to and adjusted with the said deputies, the compensation as hereinafter mentioned to be made to the said nation, for their claim, to be extinguished by this treaty, to all lands within the said state: it is thereupon finally agreed and done, between the said agents, and the said deputies, as follows, that is to say: the said agents do agree to pay to the said deputies, the sum of one thousand dollars, for the use of the said nation, to be by the said deputies paid over to, and distributed among, the persons and families of the said nation, according to their usages.

The sum of five hundred dollars, for the expenses of the said deputies, during the time they have attended this treaty: and the sum of one hundred dollars, for their expenses in returning, and for conveying the said sum of one thousand dollars, to where the said nation resides. And the said agents do accordingly, for and in the name of the people of the state of New York, pay the said three several sums to the said deputies, in the presence of the said commissioner. And the said deputies do agree to cede and release, and these presents witness, that they accordingly do, for and in the name of the said nation, in consideration of the said compensation, cede and release to the people of the state of New York, forever, all the right or title of the said nation to lands within the said state: and the claim of the said nation to lands within the said state, is hereby wholly and finally extinguished.

In testimony whereof, the said commissioner, the said agents, and the said deputies, have hereunto, and to two other acts of the same tenor and date, one to remain with the United States, one to remain with the said State, and one delivered to the said deputies, to remain with the said nation, set their hands and seals, at the city of Albany, in the said State, the twenty-ninth day of March, in the year one thousand seven hundred and ninety-seven.

TREATY WITH THE SENECA
1802, June 30
Ratified Jan. 12,1803:
Proclaimed Jan.12 1803.

This Indenture, made the thirtieth day of June, in the year of our Lord one thousand eight hundred and two, between the Sachems, Chief, and Warriors of the Seneca nation of indians, of the first part, and Wi/hem Wi//ink, Pieter Van Eeghen, Hendrik Vol/enhoven, W Wi//ink the younger, I Wi/link the younger (son of Jan) Jan Gabriel Van Staphorst, Roe/of Van Staphorst, the younger, Come/is Vollen-hoven, and Hendrik Seye, a/I of the city ofAmsterdam, and repubik ofBatavia, by Joseph El/icott, esquire, their agent and attorney, of the second part

WHEREAS at a treaty held under the authority of the United States with the said Seneca nation of Indians, at Buffalo creek, in the county of Ontario, and state of New-York, on the day of the date of these presents, by the honorable John Taylor, esquire, a commissioner appointed by the President of the United States to hold the same, in pursuance of the constitution, and of the act of the Congress of the United States, in such case made and provided, a convention was entered into in the presence and with the approbation of the said commissioner, between the said Seneca nation of Indians and the said Wilhelm Willink, Pieter Van Eeghen, Hendrik Vollenhoven, W. Willink the younger, I. Willink the younger (son of Jan) Jan Gabriel Van Staphorst, Roelof Van Staphorst the younger, Cornelis Vollenhoven, and Hendrik Seye, by the said Joseph Ellicott, their agent and attorney, lawifilly constituted and appointed for that purpose.

NOW THIS INDENTURE WITNESSETH, That the said parties of the first part, for and in consideration of the lands hereinafter described, do hereby exchange, cede, and forever quit claim to the said parties of the second part, their heirs and assigns, ALL those lands situate, lying and being in the county of Ontario and state ofNew-York, being part of the lands described and reserved by the said parties of the first part, in a treaty or convention held by the honoraNe Jeremiah Wadsworth, esquire, under the authority of the United States on the Genesee river the 15th day of September, one thousand seven hundred and ninety-seven, in words following, viz:

"BEGINNING at the mouth of the eighteen mile or Kogh-quaw-gu creek, thence a line or lines to be drawn parallel to lake Erie, at the distance of one mile from the lake, to the mouth of Cataraugos creek, thence a line or lines extending twelve miles up the north side of said creek, at the distance of one mile therefrom, thence a direct line to the said creek, thence down the said creek to lake Erie, thence along the lake, to the first mentioned creek, and thence to the place of beginmng. Also one other piece at Cataraugos, beginning at the shore of lake Erie, on the south side of Cataraugos creek, at the distance of one mile from the mouth thereof; thence running one mile from the lake, thence on a line parallel thereto, to a point within one mile from the Con-non-dau-we-gea creek, thence up the said creek one mile on a line parallel thereto, thence on a direct line to the said creek, thence down the same to lake Erie, thence along the.lake to the place of beginning;" reference being thereunto had will fully appear. TOGETHER with all and singular the rights, privileges, hereditaments and appurtenances thereunto belonging, or in any wise appertaining. AND all the estate, right, title, and interest whatsoever, of them, the said parties of the first part, and their nation, of; in and to the said tracts of land, above described, TO HAVE AND TO HOLD all and singular the said granted premises, with the appurtenances, to the said parties of the second part, their heirs and assigns, to their only proper use, benefit and behoof forever.

AND in consideration of the said lands described and ceded as aforesaid, the said parties of the second part, by Joseph Ellicott, their agent and attorney as aforesaid, do hereby exchange, cede, release, and quit claim to the said parties of the first part, and their nation (the said parties of the second part, reserving to themselves the right of preemption) all that certain tract or parcel of land situate as aforesaid. BEGINNING at a post marked No.0. standing on the bank of lake Erie, at the mouth of Cataraugos creek, and on the north bank thereof; thence along the shore of said lake N. 110 E. 21 chains; N. thirteen degrees east 45 chains; N. 9O E. 14 chains 65 links to a post; thence east 119 chains to a post; thence south 4 chains 27 links to a post; thence east 640 chains to a post standing in the meridian between the 8th and 9th ranges; thence along said meridian south 617 chains 75 links, to a post standing on the south bank of Cataraugos creek; thence west 160 chains to a post; thence north 290 chains 25 links to a post; thence west 482 chains 31 links to a post; thence north 219 chains 50 links to a post standing on the north bank of Cataraugos creek; thence down the same and along the several meanders thereof; to the place of beginning. To HOLD to the said parties of the first part in the same manner and by the same tenure as the lands reserved by the said parties of the first part in and by the said treaty or convention entered into on Genesee river, the 15th day of September, one thousand seven hundred and ninety-seven, as aforesaid, were intended to be held.

TREATY WITH THE SENECA
1802, June 30
Ratified Feb. 7,1803.
Proclaimed, Feb. 7,1803.

At a treaty he/d under the authority of the United States, at Buffa/o Creek in the county of Ontario, and state ofNew- York between the Sachems, Chief and Warriors of the Seneca Nation of Indians, on behaTfofsaid nation, and Oliver Pheips, Esq. of the county of Ontario, Isaac Bronson, Esq. of the city ofNew- York and Horatio Jones, of the said county of On tano, in the presence of John Tay/er, President of the United States Esq. Commissioner appointed by the for ho/ding said treaty.

KNOW ALL MEN by these presents, that the said Sachems, Chiefs and Warriors, for and in consideration of the sum of twelve hundred dollars, lawful money of the United States, unto them in hand paid by the said Oliver Phelps, Isaac Bronson and Horatio Jones, at or immediately before the sealing and delivery hereof; the receipt whereof is hereby acknowledged, HAVE and by those presents DO grant, remise, release and forever quit claim and confirm unto the said Oliver Isaac Bronson and Horatio Jones, and to their heirs and assigns, ALL that tract of land commonly called and known by the name of Little Beard's Reservation, situate, lying and being in the said county of Ontario, BOUNDED on the East by the Genesee river and Little Beard's Creek, on the south and west by other lands of the said parties of the second part, and on the north by Big Tree Reservationcontaining two square miles, or twelve hundred and eighty acres, together with all and singular, the hereditaments and appurtenances whatsoever thereunto belonging, or in any wise appertaining, to hold to them the said Oliver Phelps, Isaac Bronson and Horatio Jones, their heirs and assigns, to the only proper use and behoof of them the said Oliver Phelps, Isaac Bronson and Horatio Jones their heirs and assigns forever In terimony, the and commissioner have hereunto, and to two other instruments of the same tenor and date, one to remain with the United States, one to remain with the Seneka nation of Indians, and one to remain with the said Oliver Pheips, Isaac Bronson, and Horatio Jones, interchangeably set their hands and seals. Dated the 30th day of June, in the year of our Lord one thousand eight hundred and two.

TREATY WITH THE OTTAWA, ETC.
1807, Nov. 17
Proclamation, Jan. 27, 1808.

Articles of a treaty made at Detroit, this seventeenth day of November, in the year of our Lord, one thousand eight hundred and seven, by William Hull, governor of the territory of Michigan, and superintendent of Indian affairs, and sole commissioner of the United States, to conclude and sign a treaty or treaties, with the several nations of Indians, North west of the river Ohio, on the one part, and the sachems, chiefs, and warriors of the Ottoway, Chippeway, Wyandotte, and Pottawatamie nations of Indians, on the other part. To confirm and perpetuate the friendship, which happily subsists between the United States and the nations aforesaid to manifest the sincerity of that friendship, and to settle arrangements mutually beneficial to the parties; after a full explanation and perfect understanding, the following articles are agreed to, which, when ratified by the President, by and with the advice and consent of the Senate of the United States, shall be binding on them, and the respective nations of Indians.

ARTICLE 1. The sachems, chiefs, and warriors of the nations aforesaid, in consideration of money and goods, to be paid to the said nations, by the government of the United States as hereafter stipulated; do hereby agree to cede and forever quit claim, and do in behalf of their nations hereby cede, relinquish, and forever quit claim, unto the said United States, all right, title, and interest, which the said nations now have, or claim, or ever had, or claimed, in, or unto, the lands comprehended within the following described lines and boundaries: Beginning at the mouth of the Miami river of the lakes, and running thence up the middle thereof, to the mouth of the great Au Glaize river, thence running due north, until it intersects a parallel of latitude, to be drawn from the outlet of lake Huron, which forms the river Sinclair; thence running north east the course, that may be found, will lead in a direct line, to White Rock, in lake Huron, thence due east, until it intersects the boundary line between the United States and Upper Canada, in said lake, thence southwardly, following the said boundary line, down said lake, through river Sinclair, lake St. Clair, and the river Detroit, into lake Erie, to a point due east of the aforesaid Miami river, thence west to the place of beginning.

ARTICLE 2. It is hereby stipulated and agreed on the part of the United States, as a consideration for the lands, ceded by the nations aforesaid, in the preceding article, that there shall be paid to the said nations, at Detroit, ten thousand dollars, in money, goods, implements of husbandry, or domestic animals, (at the option of the said nations, season-ably signified, through the superintendent of Indian affairs, residing with the said nations, to the department of war) as soon as practicable, after the ratification of the treaty, by the President, with the advice and consent of the Senate of the United States.

Of this sum, three thousand three hundred and thirty three dollars thirty three cents and four mills, shall be paid to the Ottoway nation, three thousand three hundred and thirty three dollars thirty three cents and four mills, to the Chippeway nation, one thousand six hundred sixty six dollars sixty six cents and six mills, to the Wyandotte nation, one thousand six hundred sixty six dollars sixty six cents and six mills, to the Pottawatamie nation, and likewise an annuity forever, of two thousand four hundred dollars, to be paid at Detroit, in manner as aforesaid: the first payment to be made on the first day of September next, and to be paid to the different nations, in the following proportions: eight hundred dollars to the Ottoways, eight hundred dollars to the Chippeways, four hundred dollars to the Wyandottes, and four hundred dollars to such of the Pottawatamies, as now reside on the river Huron of lake Erie, the river Raisin, and in the vicinity of the said rivers.

ARTICLE 3. It is further stipulated and agreed, if at any time hereafter, the said nations should be of the opinion, that it would be more for their interest, that the annuity aforesaid should be paid by instalments, the United States will agree to a reasonable commutation for the annuity, and pay it accordingly.

ARTICLE 4. The United States, to manifest their liberality, and disposition to encourage the said Indians, in agriculture, further stipulate, to furnish the said Indians with two blacksmiths, one to reside with the Chippeways, at Saguina, and the other to reside with the

Ottaways, at the Miami, during the term of ten years; said blacksmiths are to do such work for the said nations as shall be most useful to them.

ARTICLE 5. It is further agreed and stipulated, that the said Indian nations shall enjoy the privilege of hunting and fishing on the lands ceded as aforesaid, as long as they remain the property of the United States.

ARTICLE 6. It is distinctly to be understood, for the accommodation of the said Indians, that the following tracts of land within the cession aforesaid, shall be, and hereby are reserved to the said Indian nations, one tract of land six miles square, on the Miami of lake Erie, above Roche dè Boeuf, to include the village, where Tondaganie, (or the Dog) now lives. Also, three miles square on the said river, (above the twelve miles square ceded to the United States by the treaty of Greenville) including what is called Presque Isle; also four miles square on the Miami bay, including the villages where Meshkemau and Wau-gau now live. Also, three miles square on the river Raisin, at a place called Macon, and where the river Macon falls into the river Raizin, which place is about fourteen miles from the mouth of said river Raizin; also, two sections of one mile square each, on the river Rouge, at Seginsiwin's village; also two sections of one mile square each, at Tonquish's village, near the river Rouge; also three miles square on lake St. Clair, above the river Huron, to include Machonce's village.

Also, six sections, each section containing one mile square, within the cession aforesaid, in such situations as the said Indians shall elect, subject, however, to the approbation of the President of the United States, as to the places of location. It is further understood and agreed, that whenever the reservations cannot conveniently be laid out in squares, they shall be laid out in paralelograms, or other figures, as found most practicable and convenient, so as to contain the area specified in miles, and in all cases they are to be located in such manner, and in such situations, as not to interfere with any improvements of the French or other white people, or any former cessions.

ARTICLE 7. The said nations of Indians acknowledge themselves to be under the protection of the United States, and no other power, and will prove by their conduct that that are worthy of so great a blessing.

In testimony whereof, the said William Hull, and the sachems and war chiefs representing the said nations, have hereunto set their hands and seals.

TREATY WITH THE WYANDOT, ETC.
1814, July 22
Ratified, Dec. 13, 1814.
Proclaimed Dec. 21 1814.

At treaty of Peace and friendship between the United States of America, and the tribes of Indians called thee Wyandots, Delawares, Shawanoese, Senecas, and Miamies.

THE said United States of America, by William Henry Harrison, late a major general in the army of the United States, and Lewis Cass, governor of the Michigan territory, duly authorized and appointed commissioners for the purpose, and the said tribes, by their head men, chiefs, and warriors, assembled at Greenville, in the state of Ohio, have agreed to the following articles, which, when ratified by the president of the United States, by and with the advice and consent of the Senate thereof, shall be binding upon them and the said tribes.

ARTICLE 1. The United States and the Wyandots, Delaware's, Shawanoese, and Senecas, give peace to the Miamie nation of Indians, formerly designated as the Miamie Eel River and Weea tribes; they extend this indulgence also to the bands of the Putawatimies, which adhere to the Grand Sachem Tobinipee, and to the chief Onoxa, to the Ottawas of Blanchard's creek, who have attached themselves to the Shawanoese tribe, and to such of the said tribe as adhere to the chief called the Wing, in the neighborhood of Detroit, and to the Kickapoos, under the direction of their chiefs who sign this treaty.

ARTICLE 2. The tribes and bands abovementioned, engage to give their aid to the United States in prosecuting the war against Great-Britain, and such of the Indian tribes as still continue hostile; and to make no peace with either without the consent of the United States. The assistance herein stipulated for, is to consist of such a number of their warriors from each tribe, as the president of the United States, or any officer having his authority therefor, may require.

ARTICLE 3. The Wyandot tribe, and the Senecas of Sandusky and Stony Creek, the Delaware and Shawanoes tribes, who have preserved their fidelity to the United States throughout the war, again acknowledge themselves under the protection of the said states, and of no other power whatever; and agree to aid the United States, in the manner stipulated for in the former article, and to make no peace but with the consent of the said states.

ARTICLE 4. In the event of a faithful performance of the conditions of this treaty, the United States will confirm and establish all the boundaries between their lands and those of the Wyandots, Delawares, Shawanoese and Miamies, as they existed previously to the commencement of the war.

TREATY WITH THE WYANDOT, ETC.
1815, Sept. 8
Ratified Dec. 26, 1815.

A Treaty between the United States of America and the Wyandot, Delaware, Seneca, Shawanoe, Miami, Chippewa, Ottawa, and Potawatimie, Tribes of Indians, residing within the limits of the State of Ohio, and the Territories of Indiana and Michigan.

WHEREAS the Chippewa, Ottawa, and Potawatimie, tribes of Indians, together with certain bands of the Wyandot, Delaware, Seneca, Shawanoe, and Miami tribes, were associated with Great Britain in the late war between the United States and that power, and have manifested a disposition to be restored to the relations of peace and amity with the said States; and the President of the United States having appointed William Henry Harrison, late a Major General in the service of the United States, Duncan M'Arthur, late a Brigadier in the service of the United States, and John Graham, Esquire, as Commissioners to treat with the said tribes; the said Commissioners and the Sachems, Headmen, and Warriors, of said tribes having met in Council at the Spring Wells, near the city of Detroit, have agreed to the following Articles, which, when ratified by the President, by and with the advice and consent of the Senate of the United States, shall be binding on them and the said tribes:

ARTICLE 1. The United States give peace to the Chippewa, Ottawa, and Potawatimie, tribes.

ARTICLE 2. They also agree to restore to the said Chippewa, Ottawa, and Potawatimie tribes all the possessions, rights, and privileges, which they enjoyed, or were entitled to, in the year one thousand eight hundred and eleven, prior to the commencement of the late war with Great Britain; and the said tribes, upon their part, agree again to place themselves under the protection of the United States, and of no other power whatsoever.

ARTICLE 3. In consideration of the fidelity to the United States which has been manifested by the Wyandot, Delaware, Seneca, and Shawanoe, tribes, throughout the late war, and of the repentance of the Miami tribe, as manifested by placing themselves under the protection of the United States, by the treaty of Greenville, in eighteen hundred and fourteen, the said States agree to pardon such of the chiefs and warriors of said tribes as may have continued hostilities against them until the close of the war with Great Britain, and to permit the chiefs of their respective tribes to restore them to the stations and property which they held previously to the war.

ARTICLE 4. The United States and the beforementioned tribes or nations of Indians, that is to say, the Wyandot, Delaware, Seneca, Shawanoe, Miami, Chippewa, Ottawa, and Potawatimies, agree to renew and confirm the treaty of Greenville, made in the year one thousand seven hundred and ninety-five, and all subsequent treaties to which they were, respectively, parties, and the same are hereby again ratified and confirmed in as full a manner as if they were inserted in this treaty.

TREATY WITH THE OTTAWA, ETC.
1816, Aug. 24
Proclamation, Dec. 30, 1816.

A treaty of Peace, Friendship, and Limits, made and concluded between Ninian Edwards, William Clark, and Auguste Chouteau, commissioners plenipotentiary of the United States of America, on the part and behalf of said states, of the one part, and the chiefs and warriors of the united tribes of Ottawas, Chippewas, and Pottowotomees, residing on the Illinois and Melwakee rivers, and their waters, and on the southwestern parts Lake Michigan, of the other part.

WHEREAS a serious dispute has for some time past existed between the contracting parties relative to the right to a part of the lands ceded to the United States by the tribes of Sacs and Foxes, on the third day of November, one thousand eight hundred and four, and both parties being desirous of preserving a harmonious and friendly intercourse, and of establishing permanent peace and friendship, have, for the purpose of removing all difficulties, agreed to the following terms:

ARTICLE 1. The said chiefs and warriors, for themselves and the tribes they represent, agree to relinquish, and hereby do relinquish, to the United States, all their right, claim, and title, to all the land contained in the before-mentioned cession of the Sacs and Foxes, which lies south of a due west line from the southern extremity of Lake Michigan to the Mississippi river, And they moreover cede to the United States all the land contained within the following bounds, to wit: beginning on the left bank of the Fox river of Illinois, ten miles above the mouth of said Fox river; thence running so as to cross Sandy creek, ten miles above its mouth; thence, in a direct line, to a point ten miles north of the west end of the Portage, between Chicago creek, which empties into Lake Michigan, and the river Depleines, a fork of the Illinois; thence, in a direct line, to a point on Lake Michigan, ten miles northward of the mouth of Chicago creek; thence, along the lake, to a point ten miles southward of the mouth of the said Chicago creek; thence, in a direct line, to a point on the Kankakee, ten miles above its mouth; thence, with the said Kankakee and the Illinois river, to the mouth of Fox river, and thence to the beginning: Provided, nevertheless, That the said tribes shall be permitted to hunt and fish within the limits of the land hereby relinquished and ceded, so long as it may continue to be the property of the United States.

ARTICLE 2. In consideration of the aforesaid relinquishment and cession, the United States have this day delivered to said tribes a considerable quantity of merchandise, and do agree to pay them, annually, for the term of twelve years, goods to the value of one thousand dollars, reckoning that value at the first cost of the goods in the city or place in which they shall be purchased, without any charge for transportation; which said goods shall be delivered to the said tribes at some place on the Illinois river, not lower down than Peoria. And the said United States do moreover agree to relinquish to the said tribes all the land contained in the aforesaid cession of the Sacs and Foxes, which lies north of a due west line, from the southern extremity of Lake Michigan to the Mississippi river, except three leagues square at the mouth of the Ouisconsing river, including both banks, and such other tracts, on or near to the Ouisconsing and Mississippi rivers, as the president of the United States may think proper to reserve:-Provided, That such other tracts shall not in the whole exceed the quantity that would be contained in five leagues square.

ARTICLE 3. The contracting parties, that peace and friendship may be permanent, promise that in all things whatever, they will act with justice and correctness towards each other, and that they will, with perfect good faith, fulfill all the obligations imposed upon them by former treaties.

TREATY WITH THE WYANDOT, ETC.
1818, Sept. 17
Proclamation, Jan. 4, 1819.

Articles of a treaty made and concluded, at St. Mary's, in the state of Ohio, between Lewis Cass and Duncan McArthur, commissioners of the United States, with full power and authority to hold conferences, and conclude and sign a treaty or treaties, with all or any of the tribes or nations of Indians within the boundaries of the state of Ohio, of and concerning all matters interesting to the United States and the said nations of Indians, and the sachems, chiefs, and warriors, of the Wyandot, Seneca, Shawnese, and Ottawas, tribes of Indians; being supplementary to the treaty made and concluded with the said tribes, and the Delaware, Potawatamie, and Chippewa, tribes of Indians, at the foot of the Rapids of the Miami of Lake Erie, on the twenty-ninth day of September, in the year of our Lord one thousand eight hundred and seventeen.

ARTICLE 1. It is agreed, between the United States and the parties hereunto, that the several tracts of land, described in the treaty to which this is supplementary, and agreed thereby to be granted by the United

States to the chiefs of the respective tribes named therein, for the use of the individuals of the said tribes, and also the tract described in the twentieth article of the said treaty, shall not be thus granted, but shall be excepted from the cession made by the said tribes to the United States, reserved for the use of the said Indians, and held by them in the same manner as Indian reservations have been heretofore held. But (it) is further agreed, that the tracts thus reserved shall be reserved for the use of the Indians named in the schedule to the said treaty, and held by them and their heirs forever, unless ceded to the United States.

ARTICLE 2. It is also agreed that there shall be reserved for the use of the Wyandots, in addition to the reservations before made, fifty-five thousand six hundred and eighty acres of land, to be laid off in two tracts, the first to adjoin the south line of the section of six hundred and forty acres of land heretofore reserved for the Wyandot chief, the Cherokee Boy, and to extend south to the north line of the reserve of twelve miles square, at Upper Sandusky, and the other to adjoin the east line of the reserve of twelve miles square, at Upper Sandusky, and to extend east for quantity.

There shall also be reserved, for the use of the Wyandots residing at Solomon's town, and on Blanchard's fork, in addition to the reservations before made, sixteen thousand acres of land, to be laid off in a square form, on the head of Blanchard's fork, the centre of which shall be at the Big Spring, on the trace leading from Upper Sandusky to fort Findlay; and one hundred and sixty acres of land, for the use of the Wyandots, on the west side of the Sandusky river, adjoining the said rivet', and the lower line of two sections of land, agreed, by the treaty to which this is supplementary, to be granted to Elizabeth Whitaker.

There shall also be reserved, for the use of the Shawnese, in addition to the reservations before made, twelve thousand eight hundred acres of land, to be laid off adjoining the east line of their reserve of ten miles square, at Wapaughkonetta; and for the use of the Shawnese and Senecas, eight thousand nine hundred and sixty acres of land, to be laid off adjoining the west line of the reserve of forty-eight square miles at Lewistown. And the last reserve hereby made, and the former reserve at the same place, shall be equally divided by an east and west line, to be drawn through the same. And the north half of the said tract shall be reserved for the use of the Senecas who reside there, and the south half for the use of the Shawnese who reside there.

There shall also be reserved for the use of the Senecas, in addition to the reservations before made, ten thousand acres of land, to be laid off on the east side of the Sandusky river, adjoining the south line of their reservation of thirty thousand acres of land, which begins on the Sandusky river, at the lower corner of William Spicer's section, and excluding therefrom the said William Spicer's section.

ARTICLE 3. It is hereby agreed that the tracts of land, which, by the eighth article of the treaty to which this is supplementary, are to be granted by the United States to the persons therein mentioned, shall never be conveyed, by them or their heirs, without the permission of the President of the United States.

ARTICLE 4. The United States agree to pay to the Wyandots an additional annuity of five hundred dollars, forever; to the Shawnese, and to the Senecas of Lewistown, an additional annuity of one thousand dollars, forever; and to the Senecas an additional annuity of five hundred dollars, forever; and to the Ottawas an additional annuity of one thousand five hundred dollars, forever. And these annuities shall be paid at the places, and in the manner, prescribed by the treaty to which this is supplementary.

ARTICLE 5. This treaty shall take effect, and be obligatory on the contracting parties, as soon as the same shall be ratified by the President of the United States, by and with the advice and consent of the Senate thereof.

TREATY WITH THE OTTAWA AND CHIPPEWA
1820, July 6
Proclamation, Mar. 8, 1821.

Articles of a treaty, made and concluded at L'Arbre Croche and Michilimackinac, in the territory of Michigan, between the United States of America, by their Commissioner Lewis Cass, and the Ottawa and Chippewa nation of Indians.

ARTICLE 1. The Ottawa and Chippewa nations of Indians cede to the United States the Saint Martin Islands in Lake Huron, containing plaster of Paris, and to be located under the direction of the United States.

ARTICLE 2. The Ottawa and Chippewa nations of Indians acknowledge to have this day received a quantity of goods in full satisfaction of the above cession.

ARTICLE 3. This treaty shall be obligatory on the contracting parties after the same shall be ratified by the President of the United States, by and with the advice and consent of the Senate thereof.

In testimony whereof, the said Lewis Cass, commissioner as aforesaid, and the chiefs and warriors of the Ottawa and Chippewa nations of Indians, have hereunto set their hands, at Michilimackinac and L'Arbre Croche, in the territory of Michigan, this 6th day of July, in the year of our Lord one thousand eight hundred and twenty.

TREATY WITH THE OTTAWA, ETC.
1821, Aug. 29
Proclamation, Mar. 25, 1822.

Articles of a treaty made and concluded at Chicago, in the State of Illinois, between Lewis Cass and Solomon Sibley, Commissioners of the United States, and the Ottawa, Chippewa, and Pottawatamie, Nations of Indians.

ARTICLE 1. The Ottawa, Chippewa, and Pottawatamie, Nations of Indians cede to the United States all the Land comprehended within the following boundaries: Beginning at a point on the south bank of the river St. Joseph of Lake Michigan, near the Parc aux Vaches, due north from Rum's Village, and running thence south to a line drawn due east from the southern extreme of Lake Michigan, thence with the said line east to the Tract ceded by the Pottawatamies to the United States by the Treaty of Fort Meigs in 1817, if the said line should strike the said Tract, but if the said line should pass north of the said Tract, then such line shall be continued until it strikes the western boundary of the Tract ceded to the United States by the Treaty of Detroit in 1807, and from the termination of the said line, following the boundaries of former cessions, to the main branch of the Grand River of Lake Michigan, should any of the said lines cross the said River, but if none of the said lines should cross the said River, then to a point due east of the source of the said main branch of the said river, and from such point due west to the source of the said principal branch, and from the crossing of the said River, or from the source thereof, as the case may be, down the said River, on the north bank thereof to the mouth; thence following the shore of Lake Michigan to the south bank of the said river St. Joseph, at the mouth thereof, and thence with the said south bank to the place of beginning.

ARTICLE 2. From the cession aforesaid, there shall be reserved, for the use of the Indians, the following Tracts:
One tract at Mang-ach-qua Village, on the river Peble, of six miles square.
One tract at Mick-ke-saw-be, of six miles square.
One tract at the village of Na-to-wa-se-pe, of four miles square. One tract at the village of Prairie Ronde, of three miles square.
One tract at the village of Match-e-be narh-she-wish, at the head of the Kekalamazoo river.

ARTICLE 3. There shall be granted by the United States to each of the following persons, being all Indians by descent, and to their heirs, the following Tracts of Land:

To John Burnet, two sections of land.
To James Burnet, Abraham Burnet, Rebecca Burnet, and Nancy Burner, each one section of land; which said John, James, Abraham, Rebecca, and Nancy, are children of Kaw-kee-me, sister of Top-ni-be, principal chief of the Potwatamie nation.
The land granted to the persons immediately preceding, shall begin on the north bank of the river St. Joseph, about two miles from the mouth, and shall extend up and back from the said river for quantity.
To John B. La Lime, son of Noke-no-qua, one-half of a section of land, adjoining the tract before granted, and on the upper side thereof.
To Jean B. Chandonai son of Chip-pe-wa-qua, two sections of land, on the river St. Joseph, above and adjoining the tract granted to J. B. La Lime.

To Joseph Dazé, son of Chip-pe-wa-qua, one section of land above and adjoining the tract granted to Jean B. Chandonai.

To Monguago, one-half of a section of land, at Mish-she-wa-ko-kink.

To Pierre Moran or Peeresh, a Potawatamie Chief, one section of land, and to his children two sections of land, at the mouth of the Elkheart river.

To Pierre Le Clerc, son of Moi-qua, one section of land on the Elkheart river, above and adjoining the tract granted to Moran and his children.

The section of land granted by the Treaty of St. Mary's, in 1818, to Peercab or Perig, shall be granted to Jean B. Cicot, son of Pe-say-quot, sister of the said Peeresh, it having been so intended at the execution of the said Treaty.

To O-she-ak-ke-be or Benac, one-half of a section of land on the north side of the Elk-heart river, where the road from Chicago to Fort Wayne first crosses the said river.

To Me-naw-che, a Potawatamie woman, one-half of a section of land on the eastern bank of the St. Joseph, where the road from Detroit to Chicago first crosses the said river.

To Theresa Chandler or To-e-ak-qui, a Potawatamie woman, and to her daughter Betsey Fisher, one section of land on the south side of the Grand River, opposite to the Spruce Swamp.

To Charles Beaubien and Medart Beaubien, sons of Man-na-ben-a-each one-half of a section of land near the village of Ke-wi-go-eem, on the Washtenaw river.

To Antoine Roland, son of I-gat-pat-a-wat-a-mie-qua, one-half of a section of land adjoining and below the tract granted to Pierre Moran.

To William Knaggs or Was-es-kuk-son, son of Ches-qua, one-half of a section of land adjoining and below the tract granted to Antoine Roland.

To Madeline Bertrand, wife of Joseph Bertrand, a Potawatamie woman, one section of land at the Parc aux Vaches, on the north side of the river St. Joseph.

To Joseph Bertrand, junior, Benjamin Bertrand, Laurent Bertrand. Theresa Bertrand, and Amable Bertrand, children of the said Made-line Bertrand, each one half of a section of land at the portage of the Kankakee river.

To John Riley, son of Me-naw-cum-a-go-quoi, one section of land, at the mouth of the river Au Foin, on the Grand River, and extending up the said River.

To Peter Riley, the son of Me-naw-cum-e-go-qua, one section of land, at the mouth of the river Au Foin, on the Grand River, and extending down the said river.

To Jean B. Le Clerc, son of Moi-qua, one half of a section of land, above and adjoining the tract granted to Pierre Le Clerc.

To Joseph La Framboise, son of Shaw-we-no-qua, one section of land upon the south side of the river St. Joseph, and adjoining on the upper side the land ceded to the United States, which said section is also ceded to the United States.

The Tracts of Land herein stipulated to be granted, shall never be leased or conveyed by the grantees or their heirs to any persons whatever, without the permission of the President of the-United States. And such tracts shall be located after the said cession is surveyed, and in conformity with such surveys as near as may be, and in such manner as the President may direct.

ARTICLE 4. In consideration of the cession aforesaid, the United States engage to pay to the Ottawa nation, one thousand dollars in specie annually forever, and also to appropriate annually, for the term of ten years, the sum of fifteen hundred dollars, to be expended as the President may direct, in the support of a Blacksmith, of a Teacher, and of a person to instruct the Ottawas in agriculture and in the purchase of cattle and farming utensils. And the United States also engage to pay to the Potawatamie nation five thousand dollars in specie, annually, for the term of twenty years, and also to appropriate annually, for the term of fifteen years, the sum of one thousand dollars, to be expended as the President may direct, in the support of a Blacksmith and a Teacher. And one mile square shall be selected, under the direction of the President, on the north side of the Grand River, and one mile square on the south side of the St. Joseph, and within the Indian lands not ceded, upon which the blacksmiths and teachers employed for the said tribes, respectively, shall reside.

ARTICLE 5. The stipulation contained in the treaty of Greenville, relative to the right of the Indians to hunt upon the land ceded while it continues the property of the United States, shall apply to this treaty.

ARTICLE 6. The United States shall have the privilege of making and using a road through the Indian country, from Detroit and Fort Wayne, respectively, to Chicago.

ARTICLE 7. This Treaty shall take effect and be obligatory on the contracting parties, so soon as the same shall be ratified by the President of the United States, by and with the advice and consent of the Senate thereof.

AGREEMENT WITH THE SENECA
1823, Sept. 3
Unratified.

At a treaty held under the authority of the United States at Moscow, in the county of Livingston, in the State of New York, between the sachems, chiefs, and warriors of the Seneka nation of Indians in behalf of said nation, and John Greig and Henery B. Gibson of Canandaigua in the county of Ontario, in the presence of Charles Carroll, esquire, commissioner appointed by the United States for holding said treaty, and of Nathaniel Gorham, esquire, superintendent, in behalf of the State of Massachusetts.

Know all men by these presents, that the said sachems, chiefs, and warriors, for and in consideration of the sum of four thousand two hundred and eighty-six dollars, lawful money of the United States, to them in hand paid by the said John Greig and Henry B. Gibson, at or immediately before the ensealing and delivery of these presents, the receipt whereof is hereby acknowledged, have granted, bargained, sold, aliened, released, quit claimed and confirmed unto the said John Greig and Henry B. Gibson, and by these presents do grant, bargain, sell, alien, release, quit claim, and confirm, unto the said John Greig and Henry B. Gibson, their heirs and assigns, forever, all that tract, piece or parcel of land commonly called and known by the name of the Gordeau reservation, situate, lying and being in the counties of Livingston and Genesee, in the State of New York, bounded as follows, that is to say: Beginning at the mouth of Steep Hill creek, thence due east, until it strikes the Old Path, thence south until a due west line will intersect with certain steep rocks on the west side of Genesee river, thence extending due west, due north, and due east, until it strikes the first mentioned bound, enclosing as much land on the west side as on the east side of the river, and containing according to the survey and measurement made of the same by Augustus Porter, surveyor, seventeen thousand nine hundred and twenty-seven 137-160 acres, be the same more or less: excepting nevertheless, and always reserving out of this grant and conveyance, twelve hundred and eighty acres of land, bounded as follows.

That is to say; on the east by Genesee river, on the south by a line running due west from the centre of the Big Slide so called, on the north by a line parallel to the south line and two miles distant therefrom, and on the west by a line running due north and south, and at such a distance from the river as to include the said quantity of twelve hundred and eighty acres and no more; which said twelve hundred and eighty acres are fully and clearly understood, to remain the property of the said parties of the first part, and their nation, in as full and ample a manner, as if these presents had not been executed: together with all and singular the rights, privileges, hereditaments, and appurtenances, to the said hereby granted premises belonging or in anywise appertaining, and all the estate, right, title, and interest, whatsoever, of them the said parties of the first part, and of their nation, of, in, and to, the said tract of land above described, except as is above excepted. To have and to hold all and singular the above granted premises with the appurtenances, unto the said John Greig and Henry B. Gibson, their heirs and assigns, to the sole and only proper use, benefit, and behoof, of the said John Greig and Henry B. Gibson, their heirs and assigns forever.

TREATY WITH THE SENECA
1831, Feb. 28
Proclamation, Mar 24, 1831.

Articles of agreement and conventions, made and concluded at the City of Washington, on the twenty-eighth day of February, in the year of our Lord, one thousand eight hundred and thirty-one, by and between James B. Gardiner, specially appointed Commissioner on the part of the United States, of the one part, and the undersigned, principal Chiefs and Warriors of the Seneca tribe of Indians, residing on the Sandusky river in the State of Ohio, on the part of said tribe, of the other part; for the cession the lands now owned and occupied by the said tribe of

Indians, lying on the waters of the Sandusky river, and situate within the territorial limits of the organized counties of Seneca and Sandusky, in said State of Ohio.

WHEREAS the tribe of Seneca Indians, residing on Sandusky River, in the State of Ohio, have earnestly solicited the President of the United States to negotiate with them, for an exchange of the lands, now owned and occupied by them, for lands of the United States, west of the river Mississippi, and for the removal and permanent settlement of said tribe: Therefore, in order to carry into effect the aforesaid objects, the following articles have been agreed upon:

ARTICLE 1. The Seneca tribe of Indians, in consideration of the stipulations herein made on the part of the United States, do forever cede., release and quit claim to the United States, the lands granted to them, by patent, in fee simple, by the sixth section of the Treaty, made at the foot of the Rapids of the Miami River of Lake Erie, on the twenty-ninth day of September, in the year 1817, containing thirty thousand acres, and described as follows: "beginning on the Sandusky river at the lower corner of the section granted to William Spicer; thence down the river on the east side, with the meanders thereof at high water mark, to a point east of the mouth of Wolf Creek; thence, and from the beginning, east, so far that a north line will include the quantity of thirty thousand acres."

And said tribe also cede, as aforesaid, one other tract of land, reserved for the use of the said Senecas, by the second article of the treaty, made at St. Mary's, in the State of Ohio, on the seventeenth day of September, in the year 1818, which tract is described in said treaty as follows: "Ten thousand acres of land, to be laid off on the east side of the Sandusky river, adjoining the south side of their reservation of thirty thousand acres, which begins on the Sandusky river, at the lower corner of William Spicer's section, and excluding therefrom the said William Spicer's section:" making, in the whole of this cession, forty thousand acres.

ARTICLE 2. In consideration of the cessions stipulated in the foregoing article; the United States agree to cause the said tribe of Senecas, consisting of about four hundred souls, to be removed in a convenient and suitable manner, to the western side of the Mississippi river; and will grant them, by patent, in fee simple, as long as they shall exist as a nation and remain on the same, a tract of land, situate on, and adjacent to the northern boundary of the lands heretofore granted to the Cherokee nation of Indians, and adjoining the boundary of the State of Missouri; which tract shall extend fifteen miles from east to west, and seven miles from north to south, containing about sixty-seven thousand acres, be the same more or less; for which the President of the United States shall cause letters patent to be issued, in due form of law, agreeably to the Act of the last session of Congress.

ARTICLE 3. The United States will defray the expenses of the removal of the said Senecas, and will moreover supply them with a sufficiency of wholesome provisions, to support them for one year, after their arrival at their new residence.

ARTICLE 4. Out of the first sales, to be made of the lands herein ceded by the Senecas, the United States will cause a grist mill, a saw mill, and a blacksmith shop to be erected on the lands herein granted to the Senecas, with all necessary tools, to be supported and kept in operation, at the expense of the United States, for the sole benefit of the said Senecas; and for these purposes, the United States will employ a miller and a blacksmith, for such term as the President of the United States, in his discretion, may think proper.

ARTICLE 5. As the Seneca Indians, on their removal, will stand in need of funds to make farms and erect houses; it is agreed that the United States will advance them six thousand dollars, in lieu of the improvements which they have made on the lands herein ceded to the United States; which sum shall be reimbursed from the sales of the lands ceded. An equitable distribution of this sum shall be made by the Chiefs, with the consent of the tribe, in general council assembled, to such individuals of the tribe, as, having left improvements, may be properly entitled to receive the same.

ARTICLE 6. The live stock, farming utensils, and other chattel property which the Senecas now own, and may not be able to take with them, shall be sold by some agent, to be appointed by the President; and the proceeds paid to the owners of such property, respectively.

ARTICLE 7. The expenses of the Chiefs, in coming to and remaining at Washington, and returning to Ohio, as well as the expenses and per diem pay of the native Interpreter accompanying them, shall be paid by the United States.

ARTICLE 8. The United States will expose to public sale, to the highest bidders, at such time and in such manner as the President may direct, the tracts of land herein ceded by the Seneca Indians: And, after deducting from the proceeds of such sale, the minimum price of the public lands; the cost of building the saw and grist mills and blacksmith shop for the Senecas; the cost of surveying the lands; and the sum of six thousand dollars, to be advanced in lieu of their present improvements: it is agreed that any balance which may remain, of the avails of the lands after sale as aforesaid, shall constitute a fund for the future exigencies of the tribe, on which the Government of the United States consent and agree to pay to the Chiefs of the nation, for the use and general benefit of the nation, annually, five per cent on said balance, as an annuity: And if, at any time hereafter, the Seneca Chiefs, by and with the advice and consent of their tribe in General Council assembled, shall make known to the President, their desire that the fund, thus to be created, should be dissolved and given to the tribe; the President shall cause the same to be paid over to them, in such manner as he may direct; provided he shall become satisfied of the propriety of so doing.

ARTICLE 9. It is agreed that any annuity, accruing to the Senecas, by former treaties, shall be paid to them at their intended residence, west of the Mississippi, under the direction of the President.

ARTICLE 10. The United States hereby agree to give to the Senecas, as presents, one hundred rifles, as soon as practicable, and four hundred blankets, for the use of the tribe, to be delivered to them at such time and place as may be directed by the Secretary of War. Also fifty ploughs, fifty hoes and fifty axes, will be given to the tribe, as aforesaid, to assist them in commencing farming.

ARTICLE 11. The Chiefs of the Senecas, being impressed with gratitude towards Henry C. Brish, their sub-agent, for his private advances of money and provisions, and numerous other acts of kindness towards them, as well as his extra services in coming with them to Washington; and having expressed a wish that a quarter section of a hundred and sixty acres of the lands ceded by them, should be granted to him in consideration thereof: the same is hereby granted to him and his heirs to be located under the direction of the President the United States.

ARTICLE 12. The lands granted by this Agreement and Convention to the Seneca tribe of Indians shall not be sold or ceded by them, except to the United States.

ARTICLE 13. It is communicated by the Chiefs here, that, in Council, before they left home, it was agreed by the tribe, that, for their services in coming to the City of Washington, each should receive one hundred dollars, to be paid by said tribe: At the request of said Chiefs, it is agreed that the United States will advance the amount, to wit: five hundred dollars, to be hereafter reimbursed from the sale of their lands in Ohio.

TREATY WITH THE SENECA, ETC.
1831, July 20
Proclamation, Apr. 6, 1832.

Articles of agreement and convention, made and concluded at Lewistown, in the county of Logan, and State of Ohio, on the twentieth day of July, in the year of our Lord one thousand eight hundred and thirty-one, by and between James B. Gardiner, specially appointed commissioner on the part of the United States, and John McElvain, Indian agent for the Wyandots, Senecas and Shawnees, on the one part, and the undersigned principal chiefs and warriors of the mixed band of Senecas and Shawnee Indians residing at and around the said Lewistown, of the other part, for the cession of the lands now owned and occupied by said band, lying on the waters of the Great Miami river, and within the territorial limits of the organized county of Logan, in said State of Ohio.

WHEREAS the President of the United States, under the authority of the Act of Congress, approved May 28th, 1830, has appointed a special commissioner to confer with the different Indian tribes residing within the constitutional limits of the State of Ohio, and to offer for their acceptance the provisions contained in the before recited act. And whereas the mixed band or tribes of Seneca and Shawnee Indians residing at and around Lewistown in said State have expressed their perfect assent to the conditions of said act, and their willingness and anxiety to remove west of the Mississippi river, in order to obtain a more permanent and advantageous home for themselves and their posterity: Therefore, in order to carry into effect the aforesaid objects, the following articles have been agreed upon by the aforesaid contracting parties; which, when approved by the President and ratified by the Senate of the United States, shall be mutually binding upon the United States and the said Seneca and Shawnee Indians.

ARTICLE 1. The Seneca and Shawnee Indians, residing at and around Lewistown in the State of Ohio, in consideration of the stipulations herein made on the part of the United States, do for ever cede, release and quit claim to the United States, the lands granted to them by patent in fee simple by the sixth article of the treaty made at the foot of the rapids of the Miami river of Lake Erie, on the twenty-ninth day of September, in the year 1817, containing forty-eight square miles, and described in said treaty as follows:" Beginning at the intersection of the line run by Charles Roberts in the year one thousand eight hundred and twelve, from the source of the Little Miami river, to the source of the Scioto river, in pursuance of instructions from the commissioners appointed on the part of the United States, to establish the western boundary of the Virginia military reservation, with the Indian boundary line established by the treaty of Greenville in one thousand seven hundred and ninety-five from the crossings above Fort Lawrence to Loramie's store, and to run from such intersection, northerly, with the first mentioned line, so as to include the quantity as nearly in a square form as practicable, after excluding the section of land granted to Nancy Stewart."

And the said Senecas and Shawnees also cede to the United States, in manner aforesaid, one other tract of land, reserved for them by the second article of the treaty made at St. Mary's, in Ohio, on the seventeenth of September, in the year 1818, which tract is described in said treaty as follows: "Eight thousand nine hundred and sixty acres, to be laid off adjoining the west line of the reserve of forty-eight square miles at Lewistown."

ARTICLE 2. In consideration of the cessions stipulated in the foregoing article, the United States agree to cause the said band of Senecas and Shawnees, consisting of about three hundred souls, to be removed in a convenient and suitable manner to the western side of the Mississippi river, and will grant by patent, in fee simple to them and their heirs forever, as long as they shall exist as a nation and remain on the same, a tract of land to contain sixty thousand acres, to be located under the direction of the President of the United States, contiguous to the lands granted to the Senecas of Sandusky by the treaty made with them at the City of Washington, on the 28th of February 1831, and the Cherokee settlementsthe east line of said tract shall be within two miles of the west line of the lands granted to the Senecas of Sandusky, and the south line shall be within two miles of the north line of the lands held by the Cherokees and said two miles between the aforesaid lines, shall serve as a common passway between the before mentioned tribes to prevent them from intruding upon the lands of each other.

ARTICLE 3. The United States will defray the expense of the removal of the said Senecas and Shawnees, and will moreover supply them with a sufficiency of good and wholesome provisions to support them for one year after their arrival at their new residence.

ARTICLE 4. Out of the first sales to be made of the lands herein ceded by the said Senecas and Shawnees, the United States will cause a saw-mill and a blacksmith shop to be erected on the lands granted to the said Indians west of the Mississippi, with all necessary machinery and tools, to be supported and kept in operation at the expense of the United States, for the mutual and sole benefit of the said Senecas and Shawnees, and the United States will employ a blacksmith to execute the necessary work for the said Indians for such time as the President of the United States, in his discretion may think proper.

ARTICLE 5. In lieu of the improvements which have been made on the lands herein ceded; it is agreed that the United States shall advance to the said Senecas and Shawnees the sum of six thousand dollars, to be reimbursed from the sales of the lands herein ceded by them to the United States. A fair and equitable distribution of this sum shall be made by the Chiefs of the said Senecas and Shawnees, with the consent of their tribes in general council assembled, to such individuals of the tribes as, having left improvements, may be properly entitled to the same.

ARTICLE 6. The live stock, farming utensils, and other chattel property, which the said Senecas and Shawnees now own, and may not be able to carry with them, shall be sold under the superintendence of some suitable person appointed by the Secretary of War, and the proceeds paid over to owners of such property respectively.

ARTICLE 7. The said Senecas and Shawnees shall be removed to their new residence under the care and protection of some competent and proper person, friendly to them and acquainted with their habits, manners and customs; and the chiefs of the said tribes shall have the privilege of nominating such person to the President, who, if approved of by him, shall have charge of their conveyance.

ARTICLE 8. The United States will expose to public sale to the highest bidders, in the manner of selling the public lands, the tracts of land herein ceded by the Senecas and Shawnees; and after deducting from the proceeds of such sale the sum of seventy cents per acre, exclusive of the cost of surveying the lands, the cost of the saw mill and blacksmith shop, and the sum of six thousand dollars to be advanced in lieu of the improvements on the ceded lands; it is agreed that any balance which may remain of the lands after sale as aforesaid, shall constitute a fund for the future necessities of said tribes, on which the Government of the United States agree and consent to pay to the chiefs for the use and general benefit of the said tribes annually, five per cent. on the amount of the said balance as an annuity. Said fund to be continued during the pleasure of Congress, unless the chiefs of the said tribes, by and with the consent of the whole of their people in general council assembled, should desire that the fund thus to be created, should be dissolved and paid over to them, in which case the President shall cause the same to be paid over, if in his discretion he shall think the happiness and prosperity of said tribes would be promoted thereby.

ARTICLE 9. It is agreed that any annuities accruing to the said Senecas and Shawnees by former treaties shall be paid to them at their intended residence west of the Mississippi under the direction of the President.

ARTICLE 10. In consideration of the former good conduct and friendly disposition of the aforesaid band of Senecas and Shawnees towards the American Government, and as an earnest of the kind feelings, and good wishes of their great father for the future welfare and happiness of themselves and their posterity, it is agreed that the United States will give them as presents, the following articles, to wit: one hundred blankets, twenty ploughs, one hundred hoes, fifty axes, ten rifles, twenty sets of horse gears, and Russia sheeting sufficient to make forty tents; the whole to be delivered to them as soon as practicable after their arrival at their new residence, except the blankets and the Russia sheeting for the tents, which shall be given at the time of their setting out on their journey; all of said articles to be distributed by the chiefs according to the just claims and necessities of their people.

ARTICLE 11. The lands granted by this agreement and convention to the said band of Senecas and Shawnees, shall not be sold or ceded by them except to the United States. And the United States guarantee that said lands shall never be within the bounds of any State or Territory, nor subject to the laws thereof; and further that the President of the United States will cause said tribe to be protected at their new residence against all interruption or disturbance from any other tribe or nation of Indians, or from any other person or persons whatever; and he shall have the same care and superintendence over them in the country to which they design to remove, that he has heretofore had over them at their present place of residence.

ARTICLE 12. At the request of the chiefs of the Senecas and Shawnees, there is granted to James McPherson, one half section of land to contain three hundred and twenty acres, to be laid off in such part of the lands here ceded as he may select, so that the said half section shall adjoin the land heretofore donated to him near the southeast corner of that part of the lands herein ceded which was assigned to the Shawnees by the second article of the treaty made at St. Mary's, on the 17th of September, 1818. And this grant is made in consideration of the sincere attachment of the said chiefs and their people for the said James McPherson, who has lived among them and near them for forty years, and from whom they have received numerous and valuable services and benefits; and also in consideration of the able and candid manner in which he has explained to the Indians the policy of the United States in regard to the future welfare and permanent settlement of the Indian tribes.

ARTICLE 13. At the request of the aforesaid chiefs, there is hereby granted to Henry H. McPherson, an adopted son of their nation, a half section of land, to contain three hundred and twenty acres, to be added to a half section of land granted to him by the said chiefs on the 20th day of March 1821, and approved by the President of the United States, which is to be so laid off as to enlarge the last mentioned grant to a square section.

ARTICLE 14. At the special request of the aforesaid chiefs, one quarter section of land, to contain one hundred and sixty acres, is hereby granted to Martin Lane their interpreter, who married a quarter blood Indian woman, and has lived a long time among the Senecas. The said quarter section is to be located under the direction of the President of the United States.

ARTICLE 15. It is understood and agreed by the present contracting parties that the words, "the lands heretofore donated to him" in the twelfth article of this treaty, have direct and sole reference to a verbal donation heretofore made by the said Senecas and Shawnees to the said McPherson, and that the intention is that this treaty should confirm the former as well as the latter grant, so that the said McPherson is entitled to one whole section to be located in the southeast corner of the Shawnee part of the lands herein ceded as aforesaid.

TREATY WITH THE OTTAWA
1831, Aug. 30
Proclamation, April 6, 1832.

Articles of agreement and convention made and concluded this thirtieth day of August, in the year of our Lord one thousand eight hundred and thirty-one, by and between James B. Gardiner, specially appointed commissioner on the part of the United States, on the one part, and the chiefs, head men and warriors of the band of Ottoway Indians residing within the State of Ohio on the other part, for a cession of the several tracts of land now held and occupied by said Indians within said State, by reservations made under the treaty concluded at Detroit on the 17th day of November, 1807, and the treaty made at the foot of the rapids of the Miami river of Lake Erie, on the 29th of September, 1817.

WHEREAS the President of the United States, under the authority of the act of Congress, approved May 28, 1830, has appointed a special commissioner to confer with the different Indian tribes residing within the constitutional limits of the State of Ohio, and to offer for their acceptance the provisions of the before mentioned act: And whereas the band of Ottoways residing on Blanchard's fork of the Great Auglaize river, and on the Little Auglaize river at Oquanoxie's village, have expressed their consent to the conditions of said act, and their willingness to remove west of the Mississippi, in order to obtain a more permanent and advantageous home for themselves and their posterity:

Therefore, in order to carry into effect the aforesaid objects, the following articles of convention have been agreed upon, by the aforesaid contracting parties, which, when ratified by the President of the United States, by and with the consent of the Senate thereof, shall be mutually binding upon the United States and the aforesaid band of Ottoway Indians.

ARTICLE 1. The band of Ottoway Indians, residing on Blanchard's fork of the great Auglaize river, and at Oquanoxa's village on the Little Auglaize river, in consideration of the stipulations herein made on the part of the United States, do forever cede, release and quit claim to the United States, the lands reserved to them by the last clause of the sixth article of the treaty made at the foot of the Rapids of the Miami of the Lake on the 29th of September, 1817; which clause is in the following words: "There shall be reserved for the use of the Ottoway Indians, but not granted to them, a tract of land on Blanchard's fork of the Great Auglaize river, to contain five miles square, the center of which tract is to be where the old trace crosses the said fork; and one other tract, to contain three miles square on the Little Auglaize river, to include Oquanoxa's village," making in said cession twenty-one thousand seven hundred and sixty acres.

ARTICLE 2. The chiefs, head men and warriors of the band of Ottoway Indians, residing at and near the places called Roche de Boeuf and Wolf rapids, on the Miami river of Lake Erie, and within the State of Ohio, wishing to become parties to this convention, and not being willing, at this time, to stipulate for their removal west of the Mississippi; do hereby agree, in consideration of the stipulations herein made for them on the part of the United States, to cede, release and forever quit claim to the United States the following tracts of land, reserved to them by the treaty made at Detroit on the 17th day of November, 1807, to wit, the tract of six miles square above Roche de Boeuf, to include the village where Tondagonie (or Dog) formerly lived; and also three miles square at the Wolf rapids aforesaid, which was substituted for the three miles square granted by the said treaty of Detroit to the said Ottoways to include Presque Isle," but which could not be granted as stipulated in said treaty of Detroit, in consequence of its collision with the grant of twelve miles square to the United States by the treaty of Greenville; making in the whole cession made by this article twenty-eight thousand one hundred and fifty-seven acres, which is exclusive of a grant made to Yellow Hair (or Peter Minor) by the 8th article of the treaty at the foot of the Rapids of Miami, on the 29th of September, 1817, and for which said Minor holds a patent from the General Land Office for 643 acres.

ARTICLE 3. In consideration of the cessions made in the first article of this convention, the United States agree to cause the band of Ottoways residing on Blanchard's fork, and at Oquanoxa's village, as aforesaid, consisting of about two hundred souls., to be removed, in a convenient and suitable manner, to the western side of the Mississippi river; and will grant, by patent in fee simple, to then, and their heirs for ever, as long as they shall exist as a nation, and remain upon the same, a tract of land to contain thirty-four thousand acres, to be located adjoining the south or west line of the reservation equal to fifty miles square, granted to the Shawnees of Missouri and Ohio on the Kanzas river and its branches, by the treaty made at St. Louis, November 7th, 1825.

ARTICLE 4. The United States will defray the expense of the removal of the said band of Ottoways, and will moreover supply them with a sufficiency of good and wholesome provisions to support them for one year after their arrival at their new residence.

ARTICLE 5. In lieu of the improvements which have been made on the lands ceded by the first article of this convention, it is agreed that the United States shall advance to the Ottoways of Blanchard's fork and Oquanoxa's village, the sum of two thousand dollars, to be reimbursed from the sales of the lands ceded by the said first article. And it is expressly understood that this sun, is not to be paid until the said Ottoways arrive at their new residence, and that it is for the purpose of enabling them to erect houses and open farms for their accommodation and subsistence in their new country. A fair and equitable distribution of this sum shall be made by the chiefs of the said Ottoways, with the consent of their people, in general council assembled, to such individuals of their band as may have made improvements on the lands ceded by the first article of this convention, and may be properly entitled to the same.

ARTICLE 6. The farming utensils, live stock and other chattel property, which the said Ottoways of Blanchard's fork and Oquanoxa's village now own, shall be sold, under the superintendence of some suitable person appointed by the Secretary of War; and the proceeds paid to the owners of such property respectively.

ARTICLE 7. The United States will expose to sale to the highest bidder, in the manner of selling the public lands, the tracts ceded by the first article of this convention, and after deducting from the proceeds of such sales the sum of seventy cents per acre, exclusive of the cost of surveying, and the sum of two thousand dollars advanced in lieu of improvements; it is agreed that the balance, or so much thereof as may be necessary, shall be hereby guaranteed for the payment of the debts, which the said Ottoways of Blanchard's fork, and Oquanoxa's village may owe in the State of Ohio and the Territory of Michigan, and agree to be due by them, as provided in the sixteenth article of this convention; and any surplus of the proceeds of said lands, which may still remain, shall be vested by the President in Government stock, and five per cent. thereon shall be paid to the said Ottoways of Blanchard's fork and Oquanoxa's village, as an annuity during the pleasure of Congress.

ARTICLE 8. It is agreed that the said band of Ottoways of Blanchard's fork and Oquanoxa's village, shall receive, at their new residence, a fair proportion of the annuities due to their nation by former treaties, which shall be apportioned under the direction of the Secretary of War, according to their actual numbers.

ARTICLE 9. The lands granted by this agreement and convention to the said band of Ottoways residing at Blanchard's fork and Oquanoxa's village shall not be sold nor ceded by them, except to the United States. And the United States guarantee that said lands shall never be within the bounds of any State or territory, nor subject to the laws thereof, and further, that the President of the United States will cause said band to be protected at their new residence, against all interruption or disturbance from any other tribe or nation of Indians and from any other person or persons whatever: and he shall have the same care and superintendence over them in the country to which they design to remove, that he now has at their present residence.

ARTICLE 10. As an evidence of the good will and kind feeling of the people of the United States towards the said band of Ottoways of Blanchard's fork and Oquanoxa's village; it is agreed that the following articles shall be given them, as presents, to wit: eighty blankets, twenty-five rifle guns, thirty-five axes, twelve ploughs, twenty sets of horse gears, and Russian sheeting sufficient for tents for their whole band; the whole to be delivered according to the discretion of the Secretary of War.

ARTICLE 11. In consideration of the cessions made in the second article of this convention by the chiefs, head men and warriors of the band of Ottoways residing at Roche de Boeuf and Wolf rapids, it is agreed that the United States will grant to said band by patent in fee simple, forty thousand acres of land, west of the Mississippi, adjoining the lands assigned to the Ottoways of Blanchard's fork and Oquanoxa's village, or in such other situation as they may select, on the unappropriated lands in the district of country designed for the emigrating Indians of the United States. And whenever the said band may think proper to accept of the above grant, and remove west of the Mississippi, the United States agree that they shall be removed and subsisted by the Government in the same manner as is provided in this convention for their brethren of Blanchard's fork and Oquanoxa's village, and they shall receive like presents, in proportion to their actual numbers, under the direction of the Secretary of War.
It is also understood and agreed that the said band, when they shall agree to remove west of the Mississippi, shall receive their proportion of the annuities due their nation by former treaties, and be entitled in every respect to the same privileges, advantages and protection, which

are herein extended to their brethren and the other emigrating Indians of the State of Ohio.

ARTICLE 12. The lands ceded by the second article of this convention shall be sold by the United States to the highest bidder, in the manner of selling the public lands, and after deducting from the avails thereof seventy cents per acre, exclusive of the cost of surveying, the balance is hereby guaranteed to discharge such debts of the Ottoways residing on the river and bay of the Miami of Lake Erie, as they may herein acknowledge to be due, and wish to be paid. And whatever overplus may remain of the avails of said lands, after discharging their debts as aforesaid, shall be paid to them in money, provided they shall refuse to remove west of the Mississippi, and wish to seek some other home among their brethren in the Territory of Michigan. But should the said band agree to remove west of the Mississippi, then any over-plus which may remain to them, after paying their debts, shall be invested by the President, and five per centum paid to them as an annuity, as is provided for their brethren by this convention.

ARTICLE 13. At the request of the chiefs residing at Roche Boeuf and Wolf rapids, it is agreed that there shall be reserved for the use of Watt be ga kake (one of the chiefs) for three years only, from the signing of this convention, a section of land below and adjoining the section granted to and occupied by Yellow Hair or Peter Minor; and also there is reserved in like manner and for the term of three years, and no longer, for the use of Muck-qui-on-a, or Bearskin, one section and a half, below Wolf rapids, and to include his present residence and improvements. And it is also agreed that the said Bearskin shall have the occupancy of a certain small island in the Maumee river, opposite his residence, where he now raises corn, which island belongs to the United States, and is now unsold; but the term of this occupancy is not guaranteed for three years; but only so long as the President shall think proper to reserve the same from sale. And it is further understood, that any of the temporary reservations made by this article, may be surveyed and sold by the United States, subject to the occupancy of three years, hereby granted to the aforesaid Indians.

ARTICLE 14. At the request of the chiefs of Roche de Boeuf and Wolf rapids, there is hereby granted to Hiram Thebeault (a half blooded Ottoway) a quarter section of land, to contain one hundred and sixty acres and to include his present improvements at the Bear rapids of the Miami of the Lake. Also, one quarter section of land, to contain like quantity, to William McNabb, (a half blooded Ottoway) to adjoin the quarter section granted to Hiram Thebeault. In surveying the above reservations no greater front is to be given on the river, than would properly belong to said quarter sections, in the common manner of surveying the public lands.

ARTICLE 15. At the request of the chiefs of Roche de Boeuf and Wolf rapids, there is granted to the children of Yellow Hair, (or Peter Minor) one half section of land, to contain three hundred and twenty acres, to adjoin the north line of the section of land now held by said Peter. Minor, under patent from the President of the United States, bearing date the 24th of November, 1827, and the lines are not to approach nearer than one mile to the Miami river of the Lake.

ARTICLE 16. It is agreed by the chiefs of Blanchard's fork and Oquanoxa's village, and the chiefs of Roche de Boeuf and Wolf rapids, jointly, that they are to pay out of the surplus proceeds of the several tracts herein ceded by them, equal proportions of the claims against them by John E. Hunt, John Hollister, Robert A. Forsythe, Payne C. Parker, Peter Minor, Theodore E. Phelps, Collister Haskins and S. and P. Carlan. The chiefs aforesaid acknowledge the claim of John E. Hunt to the amount of five thousand six hundred dollars; the claim of John Hollister to the amount of five thousand six hundred dollars; the claim of Robert A. Forsythe to the amount of seven thousand five hundred and twenty-roar dollars, in which is included the claims assigned to said Forsythe by Isaac Hull, Samuel Vance, A. Peltier, Oscar White and Antoine Lepoint.
They also allow the claim of Payne C. Parker to the amount of five hundred dollars; the claim of Peter Minor to the amount of one thousand dollars; the claim of Theodore E. Phelps to the amount of three hundred dollars; the claim of Collister Haskins to the amount of fifty dollars, but the said Haskins claims fifty dollars more as his proper demand: and the claim of S. and P. Carlan to the amount of three hundred and ninety-eight dollars and twenty-five cents. The aforesaid chiefs also allow the claim of Joseph Laronger to the amount of two hundred dollars, and the claim of Daniel Lakin to the amount of seventy dollars. Notwithstanding the above acknowledgments and allowances, it is expressly understood and agreed by the respective

parties to this compact, that the several claims in this article, and the items which compose the same, shall be submitted to the strictest scrutiny and examination of the Secretary of War, and the accounting officers of the Treasury Department, and such amount only shall be allowed as may be found just and true.

ARTICLE 17. On the ratification of this convention, the privileges of every description, granted to the Ottoway nation within the State of Ohio, by the treaties under which they hold the reservations of land herein ceded, shall forever cease and determine.

ARTICLE 18. Whenever the deficiency of five hundred and eighty dollars, which accrued in the annuities of the Ottoways for 1830, shall be paid, the parties to this convention, residing on Blanchard's fork and Oquanoxa's village, shall receive their fair and equitable portion of the same, either at their present or intended residence.

ARTICLE 19. The chiefs signing this convention, also agree, in addition to the claims allowed in the sixteenth article thereof, that they owe John Anderson two hundred dollars; and Francis Lavoy two hundred dollars.

ARTICLE 20. It is agreed that there shall be allowed to Nau-on-quai-quc-zhick, one hundred dollars, out of the surplus fund accruing from the sales of the lands herein ceded, in consequence of his not owing any debts, and having his land sold, to pay the debts of his brethren.

TREATY WITH THE WYANDOT
1832, Jan. 19
Proclamation, Apr. 6, 1832.

Articles of agreement and convention made and concluded at McCutcheonsville, Crawford county, Ohio, on the nineteenth day of January, 1832, by and between James B. Gardiner, specially appointed commissioner on the part of the United States, and the Chiefs Headmen and Warriors of the band of Wyandots, residing at the Big Spring in said county of Crawford, and owning a reservation of 16,000 acres at that place.

WHEREAS the said band of Wyandots have become fully convinced that, whilst they remain in their present situation in the State of Ohio, in the vicinity of a white population, which is continually increasing and crowding around them, they cannot prosper and be happy, and the morals of many of their people will be daily becoming more and more vitiatedAnd understanding that the Government of the United States is willing to purchase the reservation of land on which they reside, and-for that purpose have deputed the said James B. Gardiner as special commissioner to treat for a cession for the same.

Therefore, to effect the aforesaid objects, the said Chiefs, Headmen and Warriors, and the said James B. Gardiner, have this day entered into and agreed upon the following articles of convention.

ARTICLE 1.   The band of Wyandots residing at the Big Spring in the county of Crawford, and State of Ohio, do hereby forever cede and relinquish to the United States the reservation of sixteen thousand acres of land, granted to them by the second article of the treaty made at St. Mary's, on the seventeenth day of September, eighteen hundred and eighteen, which grant is in the following words, to wit: "There shall be reserved for the use of the Wyandots residing at Solomon's town and on Blanchard's fork sixteen thousand acres of land, to be laid off in a square form, on the head of Blanchard's fork, the centre of which shall he at the Big spring, on the road leading from Upper Sandusky to Fort Findlay."

ARTICLE 2.   The United States stipulate with the said band of Wyandots that, as soon as practicable after the ratification of this treaty, the aforesaid tract of sixteen thousand acres shall be surveyed into sections and put into market and sold in the ordinary manner of selling the public lands of the United States; and when the same shall be sold, or as soon as any part thereof shall be disposed of, (be the price received therefore more or less) there shall be paid to the chiefs, headmen and warriors, signing this treaty, for the benefit of all the said band of Wyandots, the sum of one dollar and twenty-five cents per acre for each and every acre so sold or for sale. The said price shall be paid in silver, and in the current coin of the United States.

ARTICLE 3. For the improvements now made upon said reservation the United States agree to pay a fair valuation in money, according to the appraisement of Joseph McCutcheon, Esq. (or such person as the Secretary of War may depute for that purpose) and an appraiser to be chosen by the said band of Wyandots. And in case the said appraisers shall not be able to agree upon any of their valuations, they shall call to their assistance some competent citizen of the county of Crawford.

ARTICLE 4. There shall (be) reserved for Roe-nu-nas, one of the oldest chiefs of said band, one half section, to contain three hundred and twenty acres, and to include the improvements where he now lives.

ARTICLE 5. It is expressly understood between the present contracting parties, that the said band of Wyandots may, as they think proper, remove to Canada, or to the river Huron in Michigan, where they own a reservation of land, or to any place they may obtain a right or privilege from others Indians to go.

ARTICLE 6. (Rejected.)

ARTICLE 7. Inasmuch as the band of Wyandots, herein treating, have separated themselves from the Wyandots at Upper Sandusky and on the Sandusky plains, they ask of the General Government that there may be a special sub-agent and protector appointed for them whilst they remain in the State of Ohio, and they respectfully recommend Joseph McCutcheon, Esq. of the county of Crawford, as a fit and proper person to act in such capacity; and that he may have the power to employ such interpreter as he may think proper in his intercourse with said band.

The aforesaid articles of agreement shall be mutually binding upon the present contracting parties, when ratified by the President of the United States, by and with the consent of the Senate thereof.

EXPLANATION. In the first draft of this treaty, provision was made for the removal of the band west of the Mississippi, but they refused to accept of a grant of land, or to remove there, and the articles having relation thereto were accordingly omitted. It was therefore necessary to omit the 6th article; and circumstances did not admit of time to remodel and copy the whole treaty.

TREATY WITH THE SENECA AND SHAWNEE
1832, Dec. 29

Proclamation, Mar. 22,1833.

Articles of agreement, made, and concluded at the Seneca agency, on the head waters of the Cowskin river, this 29th day of December, in the year of our Lord one thousand eight hundred and thirty-two, by and between Henry L. Ellsworth and John F. Schermerhorn, Commissioners, on behalf of the United States, and the Chiefs and Headmen of the "United Nation" of the Senecas and Shawnee Indians, on behalf of said Tribe or Nation.

WHEREAS certain articles of agreement and convention were concluded at Lewistown, Ohio, on the 20th day of July, A. D. 1831, by and between the United States and the Chiefs and Warriors of the mixed band of the Senecas and Shawnee Indians, residing at or near Lewistown, in the State of Ohio: And whereas, by the and article of said agreement, the United States stipulated and agreed, with said Tribe, in the words following, to wit: "to grant by patent, in fee simple, to them, and their heirs forever, as long as they shall exist as a nation and remain on the same, a tract of land, to contain sixty thousand acres, to be located trader the direction of the President of the United States, contiguous to the lands granted to the Senecas of Sandusky, by the treaty made with them at the City of Washington, on the 28th of February 1831, and the Cherokee settlementsthe east line of said tract shall be within two miles of the west line of the lands granted to the Senecas of Sandusky.

The south line shall be within two miles of the north line of the lands held by the Cherokeesand said two miles between the aforesaid lines, shall serve as a common passway between the before-mentioned Tribes, to prevent them from intruding upon the lands of each other." And the treaty aforesaid was ratified and confirmed by the President and Senate of the United States, on the 6th day of April, A. D. 1832. And whereas, the said mixed Band of Senecas and Shawnees removed from their homes in Ohio to settle upon the lands assigned them west of the Mississippi, in pursuance of the provisions and stipulations of the treaty aforesaid: And whereas, the said Senecas from Sandusky, and the mixed Band of Senecas and Shawnees, have lately formed a confederacy, and have expressed their anxiety to unite as one Tribe or Nation, to be called the "United Nation of Senecas and Shawnees," to occupy their land as tenants in common and have the whole of the country provided for them by the United States located on the east side of Ne-o-sho or Grand river, which runs through and now divides the same: For the purpose of affording a more convenient and satisfactory location to said United Nation, the parties aforesaid do, therefore, hereby stipulate and agree its follows:

ARTICLE 1. The United Tribe of Senecas and Shawnee Indians do hereby cede, relinquish and forever quit claim to the United States, all the land granted to them on the west side of Ne-o-sho or Grand river, by treaties made respectively with the Senecas of Sandusky and the mixed Band of Senecas and Shawnees of Lewistown, Ohio, on the 20th day of July, 1831, and on the 28th day of February, 1831.

ARTICLE 2. In consideration of said lands, described and ceded as aforesaid, the United States will grant, by letters patent, to the Tribe or Nation of Indians aforesaid, in manner as hereinafter mentioned, the following tract of land lying on the east side of Ne-o-sho or Grand river, viz: bounded on the east by the west line of the State of Missouri; south by the present established line of the Cherokee Indians; west by Ne-o-sho or Grand river; and north by a line running parallel with said south line, and extending so far from the present north line of the Seneca Indians from Sandusky, as to contain sixty thousand acres, exclusive of the land now owned by said Seneca Indians, which said boundaries include, however, all the land heretofore granted said Senecas of Sandusky, on the east side of Grand river.

And the United States will grant said tract of land, by two letters patent; the north half, in quantity, to be granted to the mixed band of the Senecas and Shawnees of Ohio, and the south half to the Senecas from Sandusky, aforesaid: the whole to be occupied in common, so long as the said Tribes or Bands shall desire the same. The said patents shall be granted in fee simple; but the lands shall not be sold or ceded without the consent of the United States.

ARTICLE 3. The United States, at the request of said "United Nation," agree to erect immediately a grist mill, a saw mill and a blacksmith shop, and furnish the necessary tools and machinery in anticipation of a re-imbursement from sales of land, ceded to the United rates, by the treaties aforesaid, of 28th of February, 1831, and July 20th, 1831, and so far in fulfillment of the same.

ARTICLE 4. The United Nation of Seneca and Shawnees having presented a claim for money advanced by them for forage while removing to their new homes in the west, and for horses and other property lost on the journey, the United States, in order to a final settlement of such claim, agree to pay one thousand dollars, as follows, viz:six hundred dollars to the Seneca tribe of Indians from Sandusky; and the sum of four hundred dollars to the Senecas and Shawnees from Lewistown, Ohio, to be distributed by their respective tribes among the claimants, as they may deem just and equitable; and to be received by them in full payment and satisfaction of all the claims aforesaid.

ARTICLE 5. Nothing in these articles of agreement shall be construed to affect the respective rights of the Seneca tribe of Indians from Sandusky, and the Senecas and Shawnees from Lewistown, Ohio, as secured by existing treaties, except so far as said treaties are inconsistent with the provisions of the articles aforesaid.

ARTICLE 6. This agreement or treaty shall be binding and obligatory upon the contracting parties from and after its ratification by the President and Senate of the United States.

TREATY WITH THE OTTAWA
1833, Feb. 18
Proclamation, Mar. 22, 1833.

Articles of a treaty made at Maumee in the State of Ohio, on the eighteenth day of February in the year of our Lord one thousand eight hundred and thirty-three, between George B. Porter, Commissioner on the part of the United States, of the one part; and the undersigned Chiefs and Head men of the Band of Ottawa Indians, residing on the Indian Reserves, on the Miami of Lake Erie, and in the vicinity thereof, representing the whole of said band, of the other part:

WHEREAS, by the twentieth article of the treaty concluded at the foot of the Rapids of the Miami of Lake Erie, on the twenty-ninth day of September A. D. 1817, it is provided as follows: "The United States also agree to grant, by patent, to the Chiefs of the Ottawa tribe of Indians for the use of the said tribe, a tract of land, to contain thirty-four square miles, to be laid out as nearly in a square form as practicable, not interfering with the lines of the tracts reserved by the treaty of Greenville, on the south side of the Miami River of Lake Erie, and to include Tush-que-gan, or McCarty's village; which tracts, thus granted, shall be held by the said tribe, upon the usual conditions of Indian reservations, as though no patent were issued."

And whereas by the sixth article of the treaty concluded at Detroit, on the seventeenth day of November A. D. 1807, it is provided, for the accommodation of the Indians named in the treaty, that certain tracts of land, within the cession then made, should be reserved to the said Indian nations, among which is a reservation described as follows: "Four miles square on the Miami Bay, including the villages where Meskeman and Waugan now live," which reservation was expressly made for the Ottawa tribe.

By virtue of which stipulations and reservations the said Band of Ottawas are now in the occupancy and enjoyment of the two tracts of land therein described;and for the consideration hereinafter stated, have agreed to cede the same to the United States; and bind themselves to each and all of the articles, and conditions which follow:

ARTICLE 1. The said Ottawa Band cede to the United States all their land on each or either side of the Miami River of Lake Erie, or on the Miami Bay, being all the lands mentioned or intended to be included in the two reservations aforesaid, or to which they have any claim. No claims to be made for improvements.

ARTICLE 2. It is agreed that out of the lands hereby ceded, the following reservations shall be made: and that patents for each tract shall be granted by the United States to the individuals respectively and their heirs for the quantity hereby assigned to each, that is to say :A tract of fifteen hundred and twenty acres shall be laid off at the mouth of the River, on the south side thereof, and to be so surveyed as to accommodate the following persons, for whose use respectively, each tract hereinafter described is reserved, viz: three hundred and twenty acres for Au-to-kee, a Chief, at the mouth of the river, to include Presque Isle :eight hundred acres for Jacques, Robert, Peter, Antoine, Francis and Alexis Navarre, to include their present Improvements:one hundred and sixty acres for Way-say-on, the son of Tush-qua-guan, to include his father's old cabin :the remaining two hundred and forty acres to be set off in the rear of these two sections:eighty acres hereof for Pe-tau, and if practicable to include her cabin and field: eighty acres more thereof for Che-no, a Chief, above, or higher up the little creek, and the other eighty acres thereof, for Joseph Le Cavalier Ranjard, in trust for himself, and the legal representatives of Albert Ranjard, deceased. Also, the following tracts on the north side of said river:one hundred and sixty acres for Wau-sa-on-o-quet, a Chief, to include the improvement where he now lives on Pike creek, and to front on the Bay :eighty acres for Leon Guoin and his children, adjoining the last and on the south side thereof :one hundred and sixty acres for Aush-cush and Ke-tuck-kee, Chiefs, to be laid off on the north side of Ottawa creek, fronting on the same, and above the place where the said Aush-cush now lives.

One hundred and sixty acres for Robert A. Forsyth of Maumee, to be laid off on each side of the turnpike road where half-way creek crosses the same: and one hundred and sixty acres, fronting on the Maumee River, to include the place where Ke-ne-wau-ba formerly resided:-one hundred and sixty acres for John E. Hunt, fronting on the said river, immediately above and adjoining the last; and also one hundred and sixty acres, to adjoin the former tract, on the turnpike road. The said tracts to be surveyed and set off, under the direction of the President of the United States.

The said Au-to-kee, Wa-say-on, Pe-tau-che-no, Wau-sa-on-o-quet, Aush-cush, and Ke-tuck-kee, being Indians, the lands hereby reserved for them, are not to be alienated without the approbation of the President of the United States.

The said Leon Guoin has resided, for a long time among these Indians ;has subsisted them when they would otherwise have suffered, and they are greatly attached to him. They request that the grant be to him and his present wife, during their joint lives, and the life of the survivor, and to their children in fee.

The said Jacques, Robert, Peter, Antoine, Francis and Alexis Navarre have long resided among these Indiansintermarried with them, and been valuable friends.

The said Albert Ranjard, deceased, had purchased land of them previous to the late war, upon which, before he died, he had paid them three hundred dollars, for which his family have never received any equivalent.

The reservations to the said Robert A. Forsyth and John E. Hant, being at the especial request of the said band, in consideration of their long residence among them, and the many acts of kindness they have extended to them.

ARTICLE 3. In consideration of which it is agreed that the United States shall pay to the said band of Indians the sum of twenty-nine thousand four hundred and forty dollars, to be, by direction of the said band, applied in extinguishment of their debts, in manner following: that is to say, to John Hollister and Company, seven thousand three hundred and sixty-five dollars, which includes other claims, directed by the said Indians to be by him paid, amounting to thirteen hundred and nine-five dollars, as per schedule A. herewith:To John E. Hunt, nine thousand nine hundred and twenty-nine dollars, which includes other claims, directed by the said Indians to be by him paid, amounting to two thousand six hundred and seventy-five dollars, and sixty-three cents, as per schedule B. herewith :To Robert A. Forsyth of Maumee, ten thousand eight hundred and ninety dollars, which includes other claims directed by the said Indians to be by him paid, amounting to four thousand four hundred and ten dollars, as per schedule C. herewith.To Louis Beaufit seven hundred dollars. To Pierre Menard four hundred dollars. To John King, one hundred dollars. To Louis King fifty-six dollars. (These schedules are not on file at Washington.)

Within six months after payment by the United States, of the said consideration money the said Indians agree to remove from all the lands herein ceded. And it is expressly understood that in the meantime no interruption shall be offered to the survey of the same by the United States.

And whereas the said Band have represented to the said Commissioner that under the treaty, as interpreted to them, entered into with John B. Gardiner, Commissioner on the part of the United States, on the 30th day of August, 1831, for the cession of a part of their lands, there is due to them, jointly with that portion of the tribe that has emigrated, eighteen thousand dollars, and for which they have made claim: whenever this deficiency shall be paid, it is agreed that out of said fund there shall be paid to Joseph Leronger in full satisfaction of all his claim, four hundred dollars; and to Pierre Menard in like satisfaction, sixteen hundred dollars; to Gabriel Godfroy, junior, in like satisfaction, two hundred dollars, to Waubee's daughter Nau-quesh-kum-o-qua, fifty dollars; to Charles Leway or Nau-way-nes, fifty dollars; to Dr. Horatio Conant, two hundred dollars in full satisfaction of all his claim; to Joseph F. Marsac, fifty dollars.

This treaty, after the same shall have been ratified by the President and Senate of the United States, shall be binding on the contracting parties. In testimony whereof, the said George B. Porter, and the undersigned chiefs and head men of the said band, have hereunto set their hands, at Maumee, the said day and year.

TREATY WITH THE OTTAWA, ETC.
1836, Mar. 28
Proclamation, May 27, 1836.

Articles of a treaty made and concluded at the city of Washington in the District of Columbia, between Henry R. Schoolcraft, commissioner on the part of the United States, and the Ottawa and Chippewa nations of Indians, by their chiefs and delegates.

ARTICLE 1. The Ottawa and Chippewa nations of Indians cede to the United States all the tract of country within the following boundaries: Beginning at the mouth of Grand river of Lake Michigan on the north bank thereof, and following up the same to the line called for, in the first article of the treaty of Chicago of the 29th of August 1821, thence, in a direct line, to the head of Thunder-bay river, thence with the line established by the treaty of Saganaw of the 24th of September 1819, to the mouth of said river, thence northeast to the boundary line in Lake Huron between the United States and the British province of Upper Canada, thence northwestwardly, following the said line, as established by the commissioners acting under the treaty of Ghent, through the straits, and river St. Mary's, to a point in Lake Superior north of the mouth of Gitchy Seebing, or Chocolate river, thence south to the mouth of said river and up its channel to the source thereof, thence, in a direct line to the head of the Skonawba river of Green bay, thence down the south bank of said river to its mouth, thence, in a direct line, through the ship channel into Green bay, to the outer part thereof, thence south

411

to a point in Lake Michigan west of the north cape, or entrance of Grand river, and thence east to the place of beginning, at the cape aforesaid, comprehending all the lands and islands, within these limits, not hereinafter reserved.

ARTICLE 2. From the cession aforesaid the tribes reserve for their own use, to be held in common the following tracts for the term of five years from the date of the ratification of this treaty; and no longer; unless the United States shall grant them permission to remain on said lands for a longer period, namely: One tract of fifty thousand acres to be located on Little Traverse bay: one tract of twenty thousand acres to be located on the north shore of Grand Traverse bay, one tract of seventy thousand acres to be located on, or, north of the Pierre Marquetta river, one tract of one thousand acres to be located by Chingassanoo,or the Big Sail, on the Cheboigan. One tract of one thousand acres, to be located by Mujeekewis, on Thunder-bay river.

ARTICLE 3. There shall also be reserved for the use of the Chippewas living north of the straits of Michilimackinac, the following tracts for the term of five years from the date of the ratification of this treaty, and no longer, unless the United States shall grant them permission to remain on said lands for a longer period, that is to say: Two tracts of three miles square each, on the north shores of the said straits, between Point-au-Barbe and Mille Coquin river, including the fishing grounds in front of such reservations, to be located by a council of the chiefs. The Beaver islands of Lake Michigan for the use of the Beaver-island Indians. Round island, opposite Michilimackinac, as a place of encampment for the Indians, to be under the charge of the Indian department.

The islands of the Chenos, with a part of the adjacent north coast of Lake Huron, corresponding in length, and one mile in depth. Sugar island, with its islets, in the river of St. Mary's. Six hundred and forty acres, at the mission of the Little Rapids. A tract commencing at the mouth of the Pississowinig river, south of Point Iroquois, thence running up said stream to its forks, thence westward, in a direct line to the Red water lakes, thence across the portage to the Tacquimenon river, and down the same to its mouth, including the small islands and fishing grounds, in front of this reservation. Six hundred and forty acres, on Grand island, and two thousand acres, on the main land south of it.

Two sections, on the northern extremity of Green bay, to be located by a council of the chiefs. All the locations, left indefinite by this, and the preceding articles, shall be made by the proper chiefs, under the direction of the President. It is understood that the reservation for a place of fishing and encampment, made under the treaty of St. Mary's of the 16th of June 1820, remains unaffected by this treaty.

ARTICLE 4. In consideration of the foregoing cessions, the United States engage to pay to the Ottawa and Chippewa nations, the following sums, namely.

First. An annuity of thirty thousand dollars per annum, in specie, for twenty years; eighteen thousand dollars, to be paid to the Indians between Grand River and the Cheboigun; three thousand six hundred dollars, to the Indians on the Huron shore, between the Cheboigan and Thunder-bay river; and seven thousand four hundred dollars, to the Chippewas north of the straits, as far as the cession extends; the remaining one thousand dollars, to be invested in stock by the Treasury Department and to remain incapable of being sold, without the consent of the President and Senate, which may, however, be given, after the expiration of twenty-one years.

Second. Five thousand dollars per annum, for the purpose of education, teach-era, school-houses, and books in their own language, to be continued twenty years, and as long thereafter as Congress may appropriate for the object.

Third. Three thousand dollars for missions, subject to the conditions mentioned in the second clause of this article.

Fourth. Ten thousand dollars for agricultural implements, cattle, mechanics' tools, and such other objects as the President may deem proper.

Fifth. Three hundred dollars per annum for vaccine matter, medicines, and the services of physicians, to be continued while the Indians remain on their reservations.

Sixth. Provisions to the amount of two thousand dollars; six thousand five hundred pounds of tobacco; one hundred barrels of salt, and five hundred fish barrels, annually, for twenty years.

Seventh. One hundred and fifty thousand dollars, in goods and provisions, on the ratification of this treaty, to be delivered at Michilimackinac, and also the sum of two hundred thousand dollars, in consideration of changing the permanent reservations in article two and three to reservations for five years only, to be paid whenever their reservations shall be surrendered, and until that time the interest on said two hundred thousand dollars shall be annually paid to the said Indians.

ARTICLE 5. The sum of three hundred thousand dollars shall be paid to said Indians to enable them, with the aid and assistance of their agent, to adjust and pay such debts as they may justly owe, and the overplus, if any, to apply to such other use as they may think proper.

ARTICLE 6. The said Indians being desirous of making provision for their half-breed relatives, and the President having determined, that individual reservations shall not be granted, it is agreed, hat in lieu thereof, the sum of one hundred and fifty thousand dollars shall be set apart as a fund for said half-breeds. No person shall be entitled to any part of said fund, unless he is of Indian descent and actually resident within the boundaries described in the first article of this treaty, nor shall any thing be allowed to any such person, who may have received any allowance at any previous Indian treaty. The following principles, shall regulate the distribution. A census shall be taken of all the men, women, and children, coming within this article. As the Indians hold in higher consideration, some of their half-breeds than others, and as there is much difference in their capacity to use and take care of property, and, consequently, in their power to aid their Indian connexions, which furnishes a strong ground for this claim

It is, therefore, agreed, that at the council to be held upon this subject, the commissioner shall call upon the Indian chiefs to designate, if they require it, three classes of these claimants, the first of which, shall receive one-half more than the second, and the second, double the third. Each man woman and child shall be enumerated, and an equal share, in the respective classes, shall be allowed to each. If the father is living with the family, he shall receive the shares of himself, his wife and children. If the father is dead, or separated from the family, and the mother is living with the family, she shall have her own share, and that of the children. If the father and mother are neither living with the family, or if the children are orphans, their share shall be retained till they are twenty-one years of age; provided, that such portions of it as may be necessary may, under the direction of the President, be from time to time applied for their support. All other persons at the age of twenty-one years, shall receive their shares agreeably to the proper class. Out of the said fund of one hundred and fifty thousand dollars, the sum of five thousand dollars shall be reserved to be applied, under the direction of the President, to the support of such of the poor half breeds, as may require assistance, to be expended in annual instalments for the term of ten years, commencing with the second year. Such of the half-breeds, as may be judged incapable of making a proper use of the money, allowed them by the commissioner, shall receive the same in instalments, as the President may direct.

ARTICLE 7. In consideration of the cessions above made, and as a further earnest of the disposition felt to do full justice to the Indians, and to further their well being, the United States engage to keep two additional blacksmith-shops, one of which, shall be located on the reservation north of Grand river, and the other at the Sault Ste. Marie. A permanent interpreter will be provided at each of these locations. It is stipulated to renew the present dilapidated shop at Michilimackinac, and to maintain a gunsmith, in addition to the present smith's establishment, and to build a dormitory for the Indians visiting the post, and appoint a person to keep it, and supply it with fire-wood. It is also agreed, to support two farmers and assistants, and two mechanics, as the President may designate, to teach and aid the Indians, in agriculture, and in the mechanic arts. The farmers and mechanics, and the dormitory, will be continued for ten years, and as long thereafter, as the President may deem this arrangement useful and necessary; but the benefits of the other stipulations of this article, shall be continued beyond the expiration of the annuities, and it is understood that the whole of this article shall stand in force, and inure to the benefit of the Indians, as long after the expiration of the twenty years as Congress may appropriate for the objects.

ARTICLE 8. It is agreed, that as soon as the said Indians desire it, a deputation shall be sent to the southwest of the Missouri River, there to select a suitable place for the final settlement of said Indians, which country, so selected and of reasonable extent, the United States will forever guaranty and secure to said Indians. Such improvements as add value to the land, hereby ceded, shall be appraised, and the amount paid to the proper Indian. But such payment shall, in no case, be assigned to, or paid to, a white man. If the church on the Cheboigan, should fall within this cession, the value shall be paid to the band owning it. The net proceeds of the sale of the one hundred and sixty acres of land, upon the Grand River upon which the missionary society have erected their buildings, shall be paid to the said society, in lieu of the value of their said improvements. When the Indians wish it, the United States will remove them, at their expence, provide them a year's subsistence in the country to which they go, and furnish the same articles and equipments to each person as are stipulated to be given to the Pottowatomies in the final treaty of cession concluded at Chicago.

ARTICLE 9. Whereas the Ottawas and Chippewas, feeling a strong consideration for aid rendered by certain of their half-breeds on Grand river, and other parts of the country ceded, and wishing to testify their gratitude on the present occasion, have assigned such individuals certain locations of land, and united in a strong appeal for the allowance of the same in this treaty; and whereas no such reservations can be permitted in carrying out the special directions of the President on this subject, it is agreed, that, in addition to the general fund set apart for half-breed claims, in the sixth article, the sum of forty-eight thousand one hundred and forty-eight dollars shall be paid for the extinguishment of this class of claims, to be divided in the following manner: To Rix Robinson, in lieu of a section of land, granted to his Indian family, on the Grand river rapids, (estimated by good judges to be worth half a million) at the rate of thirty-six dollars an acre: To Leonard Slater, in trust for Chiminonoquat, for a section of land above said rapids, at the rate of ten dollars an acre: To John A. Drew, for a tract of one section and three quarters, to his Indian family, at Cheboigan rapids, at the rate of four dollars; to Edward Biddle, for one section to his Indian family at the fishing grounds, at the rate of three dollars.

To John Holiday, for five sections of land to five persons of his Indian family, at the rate of one dollar and twenty-five cents; to Eliza Cook, Sophia Biddie, and Mary Holiday, one section of land each, at two dollars and fifty cents: To Augustin Hamo-lin junr, being of Indian descent, two sections, at one dollar and twenty-five cents; to William Lasley, Joseph Daily, Joseph Trotier, Henry A. Levake, for two sections each, for their Indian families, at one dollar and twenty-five cents: To Luther Rice, Joseph Lafrombois, Charles Butterfield, being of Indian descent, and to George Moran, Louis Moran, G.D. Williams, for half-breed children under their care, and to Daniel Marsac, for his Indian child, one section each, at one dollar and twenty-five cents.

ARTICLE 10. The sum of thirty thousand dollars shall be paid to the chiefs, on the ratification of this treaty, to be divided agreeably to a schedule hereunto annexed.

ARTICLE 11. The Ottawas having consideration for one of their aged chiefs, who is reduced to poverty, and it being known that he was a firm friend of the American Government, in that quarter, during the late war, and suffered much in consequence of his sentiments, it is agreed, that an annuity of one hundred dollars per annum shall be paid to Ningweegon or the Wing, during his natural life, in money or goods, as he may choose. Another of the chiefs of said nation, who attended the treaty of Greenville in 1793, and is now, at a very advanced age, reduced to extreme want, together with his wife, and the Government being apprized that he has pleaded a promise of Gen. Wayne, in his behalf, it is agreed that Chusco of Michilimackinac shall receive an annuity of fifty dollars per annum during his natural life.

ARTICLE 12. All expenses attending the journeys of the Indians from, and to their homes, and their visit at the seat of Government, together with the expenses of the treaty, including a proper quantity of clothing to be given them, will be paid by the United States.

ARTICLE 13. The Indians stipulate for the right of hunting on the lands ceded, with the other usual privileges of occupancy, until the land is required for settlement.

In testimony whereof, the said Henry R. Schoolcraft, commissioner on the part of the United States, and the chiefs and delegates of the Ottawa and Chippewa nation of Indians, have hereunto set their hands, at Washington the seat of Government, this twenty-eighth day of March, in the year one thousand eight hundred and thirty-six.

Schedule referred to, in the tenth article.
1. The following chiefs constitute the first class, and are entitled to receive five hundred dollars each, namely: On Grand river, Muccutay Osha, Namatippy, Nawequa Geezhig or Noon Day, Nabun Egeezhig son of Kewayguabowequa, Wabi Windego or the White Giant, Cawpemossay or the Walker, Mukutay Oquot or Black Cloud, Megis Ininee or Wampum-man, Winnimissagee: on the Maskigo, Osawya, and Owun Aishcum; at L'Arbre Croche, Apawkozigun, or Smoking Weed, Nisowakeout, Keminechawgun; at Grand Travers, Aishquagonabee, or the Feather of Honor, Chabwossun, Mikenok: on the Cheboigan, Chingassamo, or the Big Sail; at Thunder-bay; Mujeekiwiss; on the Maniatic North, Mukons Ewyan; at Oak Point on the straits, Ains: at the Chenos, Chabowaywa: at Sault Ste. Marie, Iawba Wadick and Kewayzi Shawano; at Tac quimenon, Kawgayosh; at Grand Island, Oshawun Epenaysee, or the South Bird.

2. The following chiefs constitute the second class, and are entitled to receive two hundred dollars each, namely: On Grand river, Keeshaowash, Nugogikaybee, Kewaytowaby, Wapoos or the Rabbit, Wabitouguaysay, Kewatondo, Zhaquinaw, Nawiqua Geezhig of Flat river, Kenaytinunk, Weenonga, Pabawboco, Windecowiss, Muccutay Penay or Black Patridge, Kaynotin Aishcum, Boynashing, Shagwabeno son of White Giant, Tushetowun, Keway Gooshcum the former head chief, Pamossayga; at L'Arbre Croche, Sagitondowa, Ogiman Wininee, Megisawba, Mukuday Benais; at the Cross, Nishcajininee, Nawamushcota, Pabamitabi, Kimmewun, Gitchy Mocoman; at Grand Traverse, Akosa, Nebauquaum, Kabibonocca; at Little Traverse, Miscomamaingwa or Red Butterfly, Keezhigo Benais, Pamanikinong, Paimossega; on the Cheboigan, Chonees, or Little John, Shaweenossegay; on Thunder bay, Suganikwato; on Maskigo, Wassangazo; on Ossigomico or Platte river, Kaigwaidosay; at Maniatee, Keway Gooshcum: on river Pierre Markette, Saugima: at Saulte Ste. Marie, Neegaubayun, Mukudaywacquot, Cheegud; at Carp river west of Grand island, Kaug Wya-nais: at Mille Cocquin on the straits, Aubunway: at Michilimackinac, Missutigo, Saganoah, Akkukogeesh, Chebyawboas.

3. The following persons constitute the third class, and are entitled to one hundred dollars each, namely: Kayshewa, Penasee or Gun lake, Kenisoway, Keenable of Grand river: Wasso, Mosaniko, Unwatin

Oashcum, Nayogirna, Itawachkochi, Nanaw Ogomoo, Gitchy, Peen-
dowan or Scabbard, Mukons, Kinochimaig, Tekamosimo,
Pewaywitum, Mudji Keguabi, Kewayaum, Paushkizigun or Big Gun,
Onaausino, Ashquabaywiss, Negaunigabowi, Petossegay, of L'Arbre
Croche: Poiees or Dwarf and Pamossay of Cheboigan: Gitchv
Ganocquot and Pamossegay of Thunder Bay: Tabusshy Geeshick and
Mikenok, of Carp river south of Grand Traverse; Wapooso, Kaubinau,
and Mudjeekee of river Pierre Markuette: Pubokway, Manitowaba, and
Mis-hewatig, of White river: Shawun Epenaysee and Agausgce of
Grand Traverse: Micqumisut, Chusco of Mackinac; Keeshkidjiwum,
Waub Ojeeg, Aukudo, Winikis, Jaubeens, Maidosagee, Autya, Ishquag-
unaby, Shaniwaygwunabi son of Kakakee, Nittum Egabowi, Magisan-
ikway, Ketekewegauboway, of Sault Ste. Marie: Chegauzehe and
Waubudo of Grand island: Ashegons, Kinuwais, Misquaonaby and
Mongons of Carp and Chocolate rivers; Gitchy Penaisson of Grosse
Tete, and Waubissaig of Bay de Nocquet: Kainwaybekis and Pazhik-
waywitum of Beaver islands: Neczhick Epenais of the Ance: Ahda-
nima of Maniatic: Mukwyon, Wahzahkoon, Oshawun, Oneshannocquot
of the north shore of Lake Michigan: Nagauniby and Keway Goosh-
kum of the Chenos.

SUPPLEMENTAL ARTICLE. To guard against misconstruction in
some of the foregoing provisions, and to secure, by further limitations,
the just rights of the Indians, it is hereby agreed: that no claims under
the fifth article shall be allowed for any debts contracted previous to the
late war with Great Britain, or for goods supplied by foreigners to said
Indians, or by citizens, who did not withdraw from the country, during
its temporary occupancy by foreign troops, for any trade carried on by
such persons during the said period. And it is also agreed: that no
person receiving any commutation for a reservation, or any portion of
the fund provided by the sixth article of this treaty, shall be entitled to
the benefit of any part of the annuities herein stipulated. Nor shall any
of the half-breeds, or blood relatives of the said tribes, commuted with,
under the provisions of the ninth article, have any further claim on the
general commutation fund, set apart to satisfy reservation claims, in the
said sixth article. It is also understood, that the personal annuities,
stipulated in the eleventh article, shall be paid in specie, in the same
manner that other annuities are paid. Any excess of the funds set apart
in the fifth and sixth articles, shall, in lieu of being paid to the Indians,

be retained and vested by the Government in stock under the conditions mentioned in the fourth article of this treaty.

TREATY WITH THE WYANDOT
1836, Apr. 23
Proclamation, May 16, 1836.

Articles of a treaty made and concluded between John A. Bryan, commissioner on the part of the United States, and William Walker,

John Barnett, and Peacock, chiefs and principal men of the Wyandot tribe of Indians in Ohio, acting for and on behalf of the said tribe.

ARTICLE 1. The Wyandot tribe of Indians in Ohio cede to the United States a strip of land five miles in extent, on the east end of their reservation in Crawford county in said Statealso, one section of land lying in Cranberry Swamp, on Broken Sword creek, being the one mile square specified and set forth in the treaty made with the said tribe on the twenty-ninth day of September in the year of our Lord one thousand eight hundred and seventeenalso, one hundred and sixty acres of land which is to be received in the place and stead of an equal quantity set apart in a supplemental treaty made with the said Indians on the seventeenth day of September in the following year, all situate and being in the said county of Crawford.

ARTICLE 2. The said five mile tract, as also the additional quantities herein set forth, are each to be surveyed as other public lands are surveyed by the Surveyor General, and to be sold at such time and place, allowing sixty days' notice of the sale, as the President may direct.

ARTICLE 3. A Register and Receiver shall be appointed by the President and Senate, in accordance with the wishes of the delegation of chiefs, whose duties shall be similar to those of other Registers and Receivers.

They shall receive such compensation for services rendered, not exceeding five dollars per day for every day necessarily employed in the discharge of their duties, as the President may determine.

ARTICLE 4. All expenses incurred in the execution of this treaty, and in the sale of the lands included in it, shall be defrayed out of the funds raised therefrom, including such expenses and disbursements as may have been incurred by the delegation to Washingtonand such allowance to individuals who have assisted in the negotiation, as the chiefs in council, after a full and fair investigation, may adjudge to be reasonable and just, shall in all cases be made.

ARTICLE 5. Such portion of the monies not exceeding twenty thousand dollars, arising from the sales as the chiefs may deem necessary for the rebuilding of mills, repair and improvement of roads, establishing schools, and other laudable public objects for the improvement of their condition, shall be properly applied under their direction, and the remainder to be distributed among the individuals of said tribe as annuities are distributed.

ARTICLE 6. The monies raised by the sales of the lands for all the above mentioned objects, except the last, shall be paid by the receiver on the order of the chiefs;and such order, together with the receipt of the persons to whom payment shall be made, shall be the proper voucher for the final settlement of the accounts of the Receiver;but the funds for the tribe shall be distributed by the Register and Receiver to each person entitled thereto.

ARTICLE 7. By the 21st article of the treaty concluded at the foot of the rapids of the Miami of Lake Erie, dated the twenty-ninth day of September in the year one thousand eight hundred and seventeen, and the schedule thereunto attached, there was granted to Daonquot, or half King, Rontondee, or Warpole, Tayarrontoyea, or Between the Logs, Danwawtout, or John Hicks, Mononcue, or Thomas, Tayondot-tauseh, or George Punch, Hondaua-waugh, or Matthews, chiefs of the Wyandot nation, two sections of land each, within the Wyandot res-ervation-The aforesaid chiefs, their heirs or legal representatives, are entitled to, and allowed one section of land each, in the above designated tract of five miles, to be selected by them previous to sale, and the same shall be sold as the other lands are sold, and they allowed to receive the respective sums arising from said sale.

ARTICLE 8. If during the progress of the sale, the Indians are not satisfied with the prices at which the lands sell, the Register and Receiver shall, on the written application of the chiefs, close the sale, and report the proceedings to the War Departmentand the President may appoint such other time for the sale as he may deem proper.

ARTICLE 9. The President shall give such directions he may judge necessary for the execution of this treaty, through the proper Departments of the Government.

Signed this twenty-third day of April, in the year of our Lord one thousand eight hundred and thirty-six.

TREATY WITH THE NEW YORK INDIANS
1838, Jan. 15
Proclamation, Apr. 4, 1840.

Articles of a treaty made and concluded at Buffalo Creek in the State of New York, the fifteenth day of January in the year of our Lord one thousand eight hundred and thirty-eight, by Ransom H. Gillet, a commissioner on the part of the United States, and the chiefs, head men and warriors of the several tribes of New York Indians assembled in council witnesseth:

WHEREAS, the six nations of New York Indians not long after the close of the war of the Revolution, became convinced from the rapid increase of the white settlements around, that the time was not far distant when their true interest must lead them to seek a new home among their red brethren in the West: And whereas this subject was agitated in a general council of the Six nations as early as 1810, and resulted in sending a memorial to the President of the United States, inquiring whether the Government would consent to their leaving their habitations and their removing into the neighborhood of their western brethren, and if they could procure a home there, by gift or purchase, whether the Government would acknowledge their title to the lands so obtained in the same manner it had acknowledged it in those from whom they might receive it; and further, whether the existing treaties would, in such a case remain in full force, and their annuities be paid as heretofore.

And whereas, with-the approbation of the President of the United States, purchases were made by the New York Indians from the Menomonie and Winnebago Indians of certain lands at Green Bay in the Territory of Wisconsin, which after much difficulty and contention with those Indians concerning the extent of that purchase, the whole subject was finally settled by a treaty between the United States and the Menomonie Indians, concluded in February, 1831, to which the New York Indians gave their assent on the seventeenth day of October 1832. And whereas, by the provisions of that treaty, five hundred thousand

acres of land are secured to the New York Indians of the Six Nations and the St. Regis tribe, as a future home, on condition that they all remove to the same, within three years, or such reasonable time as the President should prescribe,

And whereas, the President is satisfied that various considerations have prevented those still residing in New York from removing to Green Bay, and among other reasons, that many who were in favour of emigration, preferred to remove at once to the Indian territory, which they were fully persuaded was the only permanent and peaceful home for all the Indians.

And they therefore applied to the President to take their Green Bay lands, and provide them a new home among their brethren in the Indian territory. And whereas, the President being anxious to promote the peace, prosperity and happiness of his red children, and being determined to carry out the humane policy of the Government in removing the Indians from the east to the west of the Mississippi, within the Indian territory, by bringing them to see and feel, by his justice and liberality, that it is their true policy and for their interest to do so without delay.

Therefore, taking into consideration the foregoing premises, the following articles of a treaty are entered into between the United States of America and the several tribes of the New York Indians, the names of whose chiefs, head men and warriors are hereto subscribed, and those who may hereafter give their assent to this treaty in writing, within such time as the President shall appoint.

GENERAL PROVISIONS.

ARTICLE 1. The several tribes of `New York Indians, the names of whose chiefs, head men, warriors and representatives are hereunto annexed, in consideration of the premises above recited, and the covenants hereinafter contained, to be performed on the part of the United States, hereby cede and relinquish to the United States all their right, title and interest to the lands secured to them at Green Bay by the

Menomonie treaty of 1831, excepting the following tract, on which a part of the New York Indians now reside: beginning at the southwesterly corner of the French grants at Green Bay, and running thence southwardly to a point on a line to be run from the Little Cocaclin, parallel to a line of the French grants and six miles from Fox River; from thence on said parallel line, northwardly six miles; from thence eastwardly to a point on the northeast line of the Indian lands, and being at right angles to the same.

ARTICLE 2. In consideration of the above cession and relinquishment, on the part of the tribes of the New York Indians, and in order to manifest the deep interest of the United States in the future peace and prosperity of the New York Indians, the United States agree to set apart the following tract of country, situated directly west of the State of Missouri, as a permanent home for all the New York Indians, now residing in the State of New York, or in Wisconsin, or elsewhere in the United States, who have no permanent homes,

Said country is described as follows, to wit: Beginning on the west line of the State of Missouri, at the northeast corner of the Cherokee tract, and running thence north along the west line of the State of Missouri twenty-seven miles to the southerly line of the Miami lands; thence west so far as shall be necessary, by running a line at right angles, and parallel to the west line aforesaid, to the Osage lands, and thence easterly along the Osage and Cherokee lands to the place of beginning to include one million eight hundred and twenty-four thousand acres of land, being three hundred and twenty acres for each soul of said Indians as their numbers are at present computed.

To have and to hold the same in fee simple to the said tribes or nations of Indians, by patent from the President of the United States, issued in conformity with the provisions of the third section of the act, entitled "An act to provide for an exchange of lands, with the Indians residing in any of the States or Territories, and for their removal west of the Mississippi," approved on the 28th day of May, 1830, with full power and authority in the said Indians to divide said lands among the different tribes, nations, or bands, in severalty.

They have the right to sell and convey to and from each other, under such laws and regulations as may be adopted by the respective tribes, acting by themselves, or by a general council of the said New York Indians, acting for all the tribes collectively. It is understood and agreed that the above described country is intended as a future home for the following tribes, to wit: The Senecas, Onondagas, Cayugas, Tuscaroras, Oneidas, St. Regis, Stockbridges, Munsees, and Brothertowns residing in the State of New York, and the same is to be divided equally among them, according to their respective numbers, as mentioned in a schedule hereunto annexed.

ARTICLE 3. It is further agreed that such of the tribes of the New York Indians as do not accept and agree to remove to the country set apart for their new homes within five years, or such other time as the President may, from time to time, appoint, shall forfeit all interest in the lands so set apart, to the United States.

ARTICLE 4. Perpetual peace and friendship shall exist between the United States and the New York Indians; and the United States hereby guaranty to protect and defend them in the peaceable possession and enjoyment of their new homes, and hereby secure to them, in said country, the right to establish their own form of government, appoint their own officers, and administer their own laws; subject, however, to the legislation of the Congress of the United States, regulating trade and intercourse with the Indians.

The lands secured to them by patent under this treaty shall never be included in any State or Territory of this Union. The said Indians shall also be entitled, in all respects, to the same political and civil rights and privileges, that are granted and secured by the United States to any of the several tribes of emigrant Indians settled in the Indian Territory.

ARTICLE 5. The Oneidas are to have their lands in the Indian Territory, in the tract set apart for the New York Indians, adjoining the Osage tract, and that hereinafter set apart for the Senecas; and the same shall be so laid off as to secure them a sufficient quantity of timber for their use. Those tribes, whose lands are not specially designated in this treaty, are to have such as shall be set apart by the President.

ARTICLE 6. It is further agreed that the United States will pay to those who remove west, at their new homes, all such annuities, as shall properly belong to them. The schedules hereunto annexed shall be deemed and taken as a part of this treaty.

ARTICLE 7. It is expressly understood and agreed, that this treaty must be approved by the President and ratified and confirmed by the Senate of the United States before it shall be binding upon the parties to it. It is further expressly understood and agreed that the rejection, by the President and Senate, of the provisions thereof, applicable to one tribe, or distinct branch of a tribe, shall not be construed to invalidate as to others, but as to them it shall be binding, and remain in full force and effect.

ARTICLE 8. It is stipulated and agreed that the accounts of the Commissioner, and expenses incurred by him in holding a council with the New York Indians, and concluding treaties at Green Bay and Duck Creek, in Wisconsin, and in the State of New York, in 1836, and those for the exploring party of the New York Indians, in 1837, and also the expenses of the present treaty, shall be allowed and settled according to former precedents.

SPECIAL PROVISIONS FOR THE ST. REGIS.

ARTICLE 9. It is agreed with the American party of the St. Regis Indians, that the United States will pay to the said tribe, on their removal west, or at such time as the President shall appoint, the sum of five thousand dollars, as a remuneration for monies laid out by the said tribe, and for services rendered by their chiefs and agents in securing the title to the Green Bay lands, and in removal to the same, the same to be aportioned out to the several claimants by the chiefs of the said party and a United States' Commissioner, as may be deemed by them equitable and just. It is further agreed, that the following reservation of land shall be made to the Rev. Eleazor Williams, of said tribe, which he claims in his own right, and in that of his wife, which he is to hold in fee simple, by patent from the President, with full power and authority to sell and dispose of the same, to wit: beginning at a point in the west bank of Fox River thirteen chains above the old milldam at the rapids of the Little Kockalin; thence north fifty-two degrees and thirty minutes west, two hundred and forty chains; thence north thirty-seven degrees and thirty minutes east, two hundred chains, thence south fifty-two degrees and thirty minutes east, two hundred and forty chains to the bank of Fox river; thence up along the bank of Fox river to the place of beginning.

SPECIAL PROVISIONS FOR THE SENECAS.

ARTICLE 10. It is agreed with the Senecas that they shall have for themselves and their friends, the Cayugas and Onondagas, residing among them, the easterly part of the tract set apart for the New York Indians, and to extend so far west, as to include one half-section (three hundred and twenty acres) of land for each soul of the Senecas, Cayugas and Onandagas, residing among them; and if, on removing west, they find there is not sufficient timber on this tract for their use, then the President shall add thereto timber land sufficient for their accommodation, and they agree to remove; to remove from the State of New York to their new homes within five years, and to continue to reside there.

And whereas at the making of this treaty, Thomas L. Ogden and Joseph Fellows the assignees of the State of Massachusetts, have purchased of the Seneca nation of Indians, in the presence and with the approbation of the United States Commissioner, appointed by the United States to hold said treaty, or convention, all the right, title, interest, and claim of the said Seneca nation, to certain lands, by a deed of conveyance a duplicate of which is hereunto annexed; and whereas the consideration money mentioned in said deed, amounting to two hundred and two thousand dollars, belongs to the Seneca nation, and the said nation agrees that the said sum of money shall be paid to the United States.
The United States agree to receive the same, to be disposed of as follows: the sum of one hundred thousand dollars is to be invested by the President of the United States in safe stocks, for their use, the

income of which is to be paid to them at their new homes, annually, and the balance, being the sum of one hundred and two thousand dollars, is to be paid to the owners of the improvements on the lands so deeded, according to an appraisement of said improvements and a distribution and award of said sum of money among the owners of said improvements, to be made by appraisers, hereafter to be appointed by the Seneca nation, in the presence of a United States Commissioner, hereafter to be appointed, to be paid by the United States to the

individuals who are entitled to the same, according to said apprisal and award, on their severally relinquishing their respective possessions to the said Ogden and Fellows.

SPECIAL PROVISIONS FOR THE CAYUGAS.
ARTICLE 11. The United States will set apart for the Cayugas, on their removing to their new homes at the west, two thousand dollars, and will invest the same in some safe stocks, the income of which shall be paid them annually, at their new homes. The United States further agree to pay to the said nation, on their removal west, two thousand five hundred dollars, to be disposed as the chiefs shall deem just and equitable.

SPECIAL PROVISIONS FOR THE ONONDAGAS RESIDING ON THE SENECA RESERVATIONS.
ARTICLE 12. The United States agree to set apart for the Onondagas, residing on the Seneca reservations, two thousand five hundred dollars, on their removing west, and to invest the same in safe stocks, the income of which shall be paid to them annually at their new homes. And the United States further agree to pay to the said Onondagas, on their removal to their new homes in the west, two thousand dollars, to be disposed of as the chiefs shall deem equitable and just.

SPECIAL PROVISIONS FOR THE ONEIDAS RESIDING IN THE STATE OF NEW YORK.
ARTICLE 13. The United States will pay the sum of four thousand dollars, to be paid to Baptista Powlis, and the chiefs of the first Christian party residing at Oneida, and the sum of two thousand dollars shall be paid to William Day, and the chiefs of the Orchard party residing there, for expenses incurred and services rendered in securing the Green Bay country, and the settlement of a portion thereof; and they

hereby agree to remove to their new homes in the Indian territory, as soon as they can make satisfactory arrangements with the Governor of the State of New York for the purchase of their lands at Oneida.

SPECIAL PROVISIONS FOR THE TUSCARORAS.

ARTICLE 14. The Tuscarora nation agree to accept the country set apart for them in the Indian territory, and to remove there within five years, and continue to reside there. It is further agreed that the Tuscaroras shall nave their lands in the Indian country, at the forks of the Neasha river, which shall be so laid off as to secure a sufficient quantity of timber for the accommodation of the nation. But if on examination they are not satisfied with this location, they are to have their lands at such place as the President of the United States shall designate.

The United States will pay to the Tuscarora nation, on their settling at the West, three thousand dollars, to be disposed of as the chiefs shah deem most equitable and just. Whereas the said nation owns, in fee simple, five thousand acres of land, lying in Niagara county, in the State of New York which was conveyed to the said nation by Henry Dearborn and they wish to sell and convey the same before they remove West.

Now therefore, in order to have the same done in a legal and proper way, they hereby convey the same to the United States and to be held in trust for them, and they authorize the President to sell and convey the same, and the money which shall be received for the said lands, exclusive of the improvements, the President shall invest in safe stocks for their benefit, the income from which shall be paid to the nation, at their new homes, annually.

The money which shall be received for improvements on said lands shall be paid to the owners of the improvements When the lands are sold. The President shall cause the said lands to be surveyed, and the improvements shall be appraised by such persons as the nation shall appoint; and said lands shall also be appraised, and shall not be sold at a less price than the appraisal, without the consent of James Cusick, William Mountpleasant and William Chew, or the survivor, or survivors of them; and the expenses incurred by the United States in relation to this trust are to be deducted from the moneys received before investment.

And whereas, at the making of this treaty, Thomas L. Ogden and Joseph Fellows, the assignees of the State of Massachusetts, have purchased of the Tuscarora nation of Indians, in the presence and with the approbation of the commissioner appointed on the part of the United States to hold said treaty or convention, all the right, title, interest, and claim of the Tuscarora nation to certain lands, by a deed of conveyance, a duplicate of which is hereunto annexed: And whereas, the consideration money for said lands has been secured to the said nation to their satisfaction, by Thomas L. Ogden and Joseph Fellows; therefore the United States hereby assent to the said sale and conveyance and sanction the same.

ARTICLE 15. The United States hereby agree that they will appropriate the sum of four hundred thousand dollars, to be applied from time to time, under the direction of the President of the United States, in such proportions, as may be most for the interest of the said Indians, parties to this treaty, for the following purposes, to wit: To aid them in removing to their homes, and supporting themselves the first year after their removal; to encourage and assist them in education, and in being taught to cultivate their lands; in erecting mills and other necessary houses; in purchasing domestic animals, and farming utensils and acquiring a knowledge of the mechanic arts.

SCHEDULE A.
CENSUS OF THE NEW YORK INDIANS AS TAKEN IN 1837.
Number Residing on the Seneca reservations.

Senecas 2, 309		
Onondagas	194	
Cayugas	130	
	2, 633	
Onondagas, at Onondaga	300	
Tuscaroras	273	
St. Regis, in New York	350	
Oneidas, at Green Bay	600	
Oneidas, in New York	620	
Stockbridges	217	

Munsees   132
Brothertowns 360

The above was made before the execution of the treaty.

SCHEDULE B.

The following is the disposition agreed to be made of the sum of three thousand dollars provided in this treaty for the Tuscaroras, by the chiefs, and assented to by the commissioner, and is to form a part of the treaty:

To Jonathan Printess, ninety-three dollars.

To William Chew, one hundred and fifteen dollars. To John Patterson, forty-six dollars.

To William Mountpleasant, one hundred and seventy-one dollars. To James Cusick, one hundred and twenty-five dollars. To David Peter, fifty dollars.

The rest and residue thereof is to be paid to the nation. The above was agreed to before the execution of the treaty.

SCHEDULE C.

Schedule applicable to the Onondagas and Cayugas residing on the Seneca reservations. It is agreed that the following disposition shall be made of the amount set apart to be divided by the chiefs of those nations, in the preceding parts of this treaty, any thing therein to the contrary notwithstanding.

To William King, one thousand five hundred dollars. Joseph Isaacs, seven hundred dollars. Jack Wheelbarrow, three hundred dollars. Silversmith, one thousand dollars. William Jacket, five hundred dollars. Buton George, five hundred dollars.

The above was agreed to before the treaty was finally executed.

At a treaty held under the authority of the United States of America, at Buffalo Creek in the county of Erie, and State of New York, between the chiefs and head men of the Seneca nation of Indians, duly assembled in council, and representing and acting for the said nation, on the one part, and Thomas Ludlow Ogden of the city of New York and Joseph Fellows of Geneva, in the county of Ontario, on the other part, concerning the purchase of the right and claim of the said Indians m and to the lands within the State of New York remaining in their occupation: Ransom H. Gillet, Esquire, a commissioner appointed by the President of the United States to attend and hold the said treaty, and also Josiah Trowbridge, Esquire, the superintendent on behalf of the Commonwealth of Massachusetts, being severally present at the said treaty, the said chiefs and head men, on behalf of the Seneca nation did agree to sell and release to the said Thomas Ludlow Ogden and Joseph Fellows, and they the said Thomas Ludlow Ogden and Joseph Fellows did agree to purchase all the right, title and claim of the said Seneca nation of, in and to the several tracts, pieces, or parcels of land mentioned, and described in the instrument of writing next hereinafter set forth, and at the price or sum therein specified, as the consideration, or purchase money for such sale and release; which instrument being read and explained to the said parties and mutually agreed to, was signed and sealed by the said contracting parties, and is in the words following:

This indenture, made this fifteenth day of January in the year of our Lord one thousand eight hundred and thirty-eight, between the chiefs and head men of the Seneca nation of Indians, duly assembled in council, and acting for and on behalf of the said Seneca nation, of the first part, and Thomas Ludlow Ogden, of the city of New York, and Joseph Fellows of Geneva, in the county of Ontario, of the second part witnesseth: That the said chiefs and head men of the Seneca nation of Indians, in consideration of the sum of two hundred and two thousand dollars to them in hand paid by the said Thomas Ludlow Ogden and Joseph Fellows, the receipt whereof is hereby acknowledged, have granted, bargained, sold, released and confirmed, and by these presents do grant, bargain, sell, release and confirm unto the said Thomas Ludlow Ogden and Joseph Fellows, and to their heirs and assigns, all that certain tract, or parcel of land situate, lying and being in the county of Erie and State of New York Commonly called and known by the name of Buffalo Creek reservation, containing, by estimation forty-nine thousand nine hundred and twenty acres be the contents thereof more or less.

Also, all that certain other tract, or parcel of land, situate, lying and being in the counties of Erie, Chatauque, and Cattaraugus in said State commonly called and known by the name of Cattaraugus reservation, containing by estimation twenty-one thousand six hundred and eighty acres, be the contents thereof more or less. Also, all that certain other tract, or parcel of land, situate, lying and being in the said county of Cattaraugus, in said State, commonly called and known by the name of the Allegany reservation, containing by estimation thirty thousand four hundred and sixty-nine acres, be the contents more or less. And also, all that certain other tract or parcel of land, situate, lying and being partly in said county of Erie and partly in the county of Genesee, in said State, commonly called and known by the name of the Tonawando reservation, and containing by estimation twelve thousand, eight hundred acres, be the same more or less; as the said several tracts of land have been heretofore reserved and are held and occupied by the said Seneca nation of Indians, or by individuals thereof, together with all and singular the rights, privileges, hereditaments and appurtenances to each and every of the said tracts or parcels of land belonging or appertaining; and all the estate, right, title, interest, claim, and demand of the said party of the first part, and of the said Seneca nation of Indians, of, in, and to the same, and to each and every part and parcel thereof: to have and to hold all and singular the above described and released premises unto the said Thomas Ludlow Ogden and Joseph Fellows, their heirs and assigns, to their proper use and behoof for ever, as joint tenants, and not as tenants in common.

In witness whereof, the parties to these presents have hereunto and to three other instruments of the same tenor and date one to remain with the United States, one to remain with the State of Massachusetts, one to remain with the Seneca nation of Indians, and one to remain with the said Thomas Ludlow Ogden and Joseph Fellows, interchangeably set their hands and seals the day and year first above written.

At a treaty held under and by the authority of the United States of America, at Buffalo Creek, in the county of Erie, and State of New York, between the sachems, chiefs and warriors of the Tuscarora nation of Indians, duly assembled in council and representing and acting for the said nation, on the one part and Thomas Ludlow Ogden of the city of New York and Joseph Fellows of Geneva in the county of Ontario, on the other part, concerning the purchase of the right and claim of the said nation of Indians in and to the lands within the State of New York, remaining in their occupation: Ransom H. Gillet, Esquire, a commissioner appointed by the President of the United States to attend and hold the said treaty, and also Josiah Trowbridge, Esquire, the superintendent on behalf of the Commonwealth of Massachusetts, being severally present at the said treaty, the said sachems, chiefs and warriors, on behalf of the said Tuscarora nation, did agree to sell and release to the said Thomas Ludlow Ogden and Joseph Fellows, and they, the said Thomas Ludlow Ogden and Joseph Fellows did agree to purchase all the right, title and claim of the said Tuscarora nation of, in and to the tract, piece, or parcel of land mentioned and described in the instrument of writing next hereinafter set forth, and at the price, or sum therein specified, as the consideration or purchase money for such sale and release; which instrument being read and explained to the said parties, and mutually agreed to, was signed and sealed by the said contracting parties, and is in the words following:

This indenture, made this fifteenth day of January in the year of our Lord one thousand eight hundred and thirty-eight, between the sachems, chiefs, and warriors of the Tuscarora nation of Indians, duty assembled in council, and acting for and on behalf of the said Tuscarora nation of the first part, and Thomas Ludlow Ogden of the city of New York, and Joseph Fellows of Geneva, in the county of Ontario, of the second part witnesseth: That the said sachems, chiefs and warriors of the Tuscarora nation,, in consideration of the sum of nine thousand six hundred dollars, to them in hand paid by the said Thomas Ludlow Ogden and Joseph Fellows, the receipt whereof is hereby acknowledged, have granted, bargained, sold released, and confmned, and by these presents do grant, bargain, sell, release and confirm to the said Thomas Ludlow Ogden and Joseph Fellows, and to their heirs and assigns, all that tract or parcel of land situate, lying and being in the county of Niagara and State of New York, commonly called and known by the name of the Tuscarora reservation or Seneca grant, containing nineteen hundred and twenty acres, be the same more, or less, being the lands in their occupancy, and not included in the land conveyed to them by Henry Dearborn, together with all and singular, the rights, privileges, heraditaments, and appurtenances to the said tract or parcel of land belonging, or appertaining, and all the estate, right, title, interest,, claim and demand of the said party of the first part, and of the said Tuscarora nation of Indians of, in and to the same, and to every part and parcel thereof. To have and to hold all and singular the above described and released premises unto the said Thomas Ludlow Ogden and Joseph Fellows, and their heirs and assigns, to their proper use and behoof for ever, as joint tenants and not as tenants in common.

Supplemental article to the treaty concluded at Buffalo Creek in the State of New York, dated January 15 1838.

The undersigned chiefs and head men of the St. Regis Indians residing in the State of New York having heard a copy of said treaty read by Ransom H. Gillet, the commissioner who concluded that treaty on the part of the United States, and he having fully and publicly explained the same, and believing the provisions of the said treaty to be very liberal on the part of the United States and calculated to be highly beneficial to the New York Indians, including the St. Regis, who are embraced in its provisions do hereby assent to every part of the said treaty and approve the same. And it is finther agreed, that any of the St. Regis Indians who wish to do so, shall be at liberty to remove to the said country at any time hereafter within the time specified in this treaty, but under it the Government shall not Compel them to remove. The United States will, within one year after the ratification of this treaty, pay over to the American party of said Indians one thousand dollars, part of the sum of five thousand dollars mentioned in the special provisions for the St. Regis Indians, any thing in the article contained to the contrary notwithstanding.

We the undersigned chiefs of the Seneca tribe of New York Indians, residing in the State of New York, do hereby give our free and voluntary assent to the foregoing treaty as amended by the resolution of the Senate of the United States on the eleventh day of June 1838, and to our contract therewith, the swne having been submitted to us by Ransom H. Gillet, a Commissioner on the part of the United States, and fully and fairly explained by him, to our said tribe, in council assembled.

TREATY WITH THE WYANDOT
1842, Mar. 1
Proclamation Oct. 5, 1842.

John Tyler, President of the United States of America, by John Johnston, formerly agent for Indian affairs, now a citizen of the State of Ohio, commissioner duly authorized and appointed to treat with the Wyandott Nation of Indians for a cession of all their lands lying and being in the States of Ohio and Michigan; and the duly constituted chiefs, counsellors, and head-men, of the said Wyandott Nation, in full council assembled, on the other part, have entered into the following articles and conditions, viz:

ARTICLE 1. The Wyandott Nation of Indians do hereby cede to the United States all that tract of land situate, lying, and being in the county of Crawford and State of Ohio, commonly known as the residue of the large reserve, being all of their remaining lands within the State of Ohio, and containing one hundred and nine thousand one hundred and forty-four acres, more or less.

The said nation also hereby cedes to the United States all their right and title to the Wyandotte Reserve, on both sides of the river Huron, in the State of Michigan, containing four thousand nine hundred and ninety-six acres, be the same more or less, being all the remaining lands claimed or set apart for the use of the Wyandotts within the State of Michigan; and the United States hereby promises to pay the sum of five hundred dollars towards the expenses of removing the Indians of the river Huron to Upper Sandusky, but before the latter clause of this article is binding on the contracting parties, the consent of the head-men of the river Huron Wyandotts is to be had in writing.

ARTICLE 5. In consideration of the foregoing cession, the United States hereby grant to the aforesaid Wyandott Nation a tract of land west of the Mississippi River, to contain one hundred and forty-eight thousand acres, and to be located upon any lands owned by the United States, now set apart, or may in future be set apart for Indian use, and not already assigned to any other tribe or nation.

ARTICLE 3. The United States agree to pay the Wyandott Nation a perpetual annuity of seventeen thousand five hundred dollars in specie, the first payment to be made within the present year, 1842, to enable the nation the more speedily to remove to their new home in the West; this includes all former annuities.

ARTICLE 4. The United States agree to make a permanent provision of five hundred dollars per annum, for the support of a school, to be under the direction of the chiefs, and for no other purpose whatever, the first payment to be made three years hence, and afterwards at the payment of the annuity in each succeeding year.

ARTICLE 5. The United States agree to pay the Wyandotts the full value of their improvements in the country hereby ceded by them in

Ohio and Michigan, which valuation shall be made by two persons to be appointed by the President of the United States, who shall be sworn faithfully to do justice to the parties, the amount of such valuation to be paid at any time after the 1st day of April, 1843, as shall be acceptable to the Wyandott chiefs, to meet their arrangements for emigrating.

ARTICLE 6. The United States hereby agree to pay the debts due by members of the Wyandott Nation to citizens of the United States, amounting to twenty-three thousand eight hundred and sixty dollars, in conformity to a schedule hereto annexed.

ARTICLE 7. The Wyandotts shall be allowed the use and occupancy of their improvements until the 1st of April, 1844, on the condition that they nor any persons claiming or occupying under them by lease or otherwise shall not commit waste or damage on the premises hereby ceded, but this is not to prevent the United States from surveying and selling the land at any time previous to the said 1st day of April, 1844.

ARTICLE 8. The United States engage to provide and support a blacksmith and an assistant blacksmith for the Wyandott Nation, and to furnish annually a sufficient quantity of iron, steel, coal, files, tools, and all other things necessary and proper in such on establishment, and to erect a suitable shop and house or houses for the residence of the blacksmith and his assistant.

ARTICLE 9. The United States engage to maintain and support a sub-agent and interpreter to reside among the Wyandotts to aid them in the protection of their persons and property, and to manage their intercourse with the Government and citizens of the United States.

ARTICLE 10. The buildings and farm occupied by the mission of the Methodist Episcopal Church shall remain in possession of the present incumbents until the 1st day of April, 1844, and permission is hereby given to harvest and remove the crop of fall-grain which may be then sown.

ARTICLE 11. All persons identified as members of the Wyandott Nation, and their heirs, and who may emigrate to the west, shall participate equally in the benefits of the annuity, and all other national privileges, and it is expressly understood that those who do not emigrate, and any that may hereafter cease to remain with the nation, will not be entitled to the benefits and privileges aforesaid,

ARTICLE 12. Whereas by the 8th article of the treaty of Miami Rapids of September 29th, 1817, (proclaimed January 4, 1819) there was granted unto Horonu, or Cherokee Boy, a Wyandott chief, one section of land, to contain six hundred and forty acres; and whereas the said Horonu did during his life-time sell and convey to James Whitaker one quarter-section of said land, containing 160 acres, which sale was confirmed by the President of the United States. The said Horonu died in the month of March, 1826, having by his last will bequeathed the remaining three quarter-sections, containing 480 acres, to Squeendehtee and Sooharress, or Isaac Williams, they being the nearest of kin to the deceased, now to the intent that the purposes of the testator may be fully complied with, it is hereby agreed the 480 acres of land, as aforesaid, shall be immediately sold under the directions of the President of the United States, and the net proceeds, after deducting all expenses, be paid over to the heirs aforesaid.

ARTICLE 13. The chiefs of the Wyandott Nation hereby agree to remove their whole people to the west of the Mississippi River with out any other cost to the United States than the sum of ten thousand dollars; five thousand dollars of which is to be paid the said chiefs when the first detachment of their people sets out on their journey to the west, and the remaining five thousand dollars on the arrival of the whole nation at the place of their destination in the west.

ARTICLE 14. The United States agree to grant by patent in fee-simple to each of the following-named persons, and their heirs all of whom are Wyandotts by blood or adoption, one section of land of six hundred and forty acres each, out of any lands west of the Missouri River set apart for Indian use, not already claimed or occupied by any person or tribe, viz: Silas Armstrong, John M. Armstrong, Matthew R. Walker, William Walker, Joel Walker, Charles B. Garrett, George Garrett, George J. Clark, Irwin P. Long, Ethan A. Long, Joseph L. Tennery, Robert Robertaile, Jared S. Dawson, Joseph Newell, John T. Walker, Peter D. Clark, James Rankin, Samuel McCulloch, Elliot, McCulloch, Isaiah Walker, William M. Tennery, Henry Clay Walker, Ebenezer Z. Reed, and Joel Walker Garrett, and to the following chiefs and councillors one section each: Francis A. Hicks, James Washington,

Squeendehtee, Henry Jaques, Tauroonce, Doctor Grey Eyes, George Armstrong, Warpole, John Hicks, Peacock, and George Punch. The lands hereby granted to be selected by the grantees, surveyed and patented at the expense of the United States, but never to be conveyed by them or their heirs without the permission of the President of the United States.

ARTICLE 15. The United States agree to pay to William Walker and Joel Walker, each, the sum of two hundred and fifty dollars, and to John M. Armstrong the sum of one hundred and fifty dollars, for services rendered as interpreters in the progress of the negotiation; and to Warpole, a former chief of the Wyandott Nation, one hundred and fifty dollars, money expended by him as one of the party who accompanied Joseph McCutchen, a former commissioner of the United States, to the city of Washington in September, 1839.

ARTICLE 16. In the year 1812 the houses, barns, stables, fences, horses, cattle, and hogs, with farming utensils and household furniture, to a large amount, the property of the late William Walker, of Brownstown, in the Territory of Michigan, was destroyed by the enemy while in the occupancy of the United States forces; and by reason of his attachment to the cause of his country, being a native citizen, taken prisoner in early life by the Wyandott Indians, intermarried, and ever afterward living among them, the evidence of all which is ample and conclusive. There is therefore granted unto Catharine Walker, widow of the said William Walker, and to his heirs, the sum of three thousand dollars, in full satisfaction of their claim, to be paid by the United States to her or them after the ratification of this treaty.

ARTICLE 17. There shall be reserved from sale, and forever devoted to public use, two acres of ground as near as can be in a square form, to include the stone meeting-house and burying-ground near to and north of Upper Sandusky, one acre to include the burying-ground on the bank near the council-house at Upper Sandusky, and one-half acre to include the burying-ground on the farm of Silas Armstrong, which several lots of ground shall forever remain open and free to all persons for the purpose of interment and houses of worship, and for no other purposes whatever.

ARTICLE 18. This treaty shall take effect and be obligatory on the contracting parties as soon as the same shall be ratified by the President of the United States, by and with the advice and consent of the Senate thereof.

We, the undersigned, chiefs and counsellors of the Wyandott nation of Indians, residing in the State of Ohio, and representing also the Wyandotts of the River Huron, in Michigan, do hereby give our free and voluntary assent to the amendments made by the Senate of the United States on the 17th day of August; one thousand eight hundred and forty-two, to the treaty concluded by us with the United States on the 17th day of March, 1842, the same having been submitted and fully explained to us by John Johnston, commissioner on the part of the United States for that purpose, in full council assembled.

TREATY WITH THE SENECA
1842, May 20
Proclamation, Aug. 26, 1842.

Articles of a treaty made and concluded at Buffalo Creek, in the State of New York, on the twentieth day of May in the year one thousand eight hundred and forty-two, between the United States of America, acting herein by Ambrose Spencer their Commissioner, thereto duly authorized, on the one part, and the chiefs, headmen and warriors of the Seneca nation of Indians, duly assembled in council, on the other part.

WHEREAS a treaty was heretofore concluded, and made between the said United States, and the chiefs, headmen, and warriors of the several tribes of New York Indians, dated the fifteenth day of January in the year one thousand eight hundred and thirty-eight, which treaty having been afterwards amended, was proclaimed by the President of the United States, on the fourth of April one thousand eight hundred and forty, to have been duly ratified.

And whereas on the day of making this treaty, and bearing even date herewith, a certain indenture was made executed and concluded by and between the said Seneca nation of Indians and Thomas L. Ogden, and Joseph Fellows, assignees under the State of Massachusetts, in the presence, and with the approbation of a Commissioner appointed by the United States, and in the presence and with the approbation of Samuel

Hoare, a superintendent on the part of the commonwealth of Massachusetts, which indenture is in the words and figures following to wit:

"THIS INDENTURE made and concluded between Thomas Ludlow Ogden of the city of New York, and Joseph Fellows of Geneva, in the county of Ontario of the one part, and the chiefs and headmen of the Seneca nation of Indians, on the other part at a council duly assembled and held at Buffalo Creek in the State of New York on the twentieth day of May in the year one thousand eight hundred and forty-two in the presence of Samuel Hoare, the superintendent thereto authorized and appointed by and on the part of the commonwealth of Massachusets, an of Ambrose Spencer a Commissioner thereto duly appointed and authorized on the part of the United States.

"Whereas at a council held at Buffalo Creek on the fifteenth day of January in the year one thousand eight hundred and thirty eight, an indenture of that date was made and executed by and between the parties to this agreement, whereby the chiefs and headmen of the Seneca nation of Indians for the consideration of two hundred and two thousand dollars did grant, bargain, release and confirm unto the said Thomas Ludlow Ogden and Joseph Fellows, all those four several tracts of land, situate within the State of New York, then and yet occupied by the said nation, or the people thereof, severally described in the said indenture, as the Buffalo Creek Reservation, containing by estimation forty-nine thousand nine hundred and twenty acres of land, the Cattaraugus Reservation containing by estimation twenty-one thousand six hundred and eighty acres of land, the Allegany Reservation, containing by estimation thirty thousand four hundred and sixty-nine acres of land, and the Tonnewanda Reservation containing by estimation twelve thousand eight hundred acres of land; a duplicate of which indenture was annexed to a treaty of the same date made between the United States of America and the chiefs, headmen, and warriors of the several tribes of New York Indians assembled in council; which treaty was amended and proclaimed by the President of the United States on the fourth of April one thousand eight hundred and forty, as having been duly ratified; as by the said indenture, treaty and proclamation more fully appear.

"And whereas divers questions and differences having arisen between the chiefs and headmen of the Seneca nation of Indians or some of them, and the said Thomas Ludlow Ogden and Joseph Fellows in relation to the said indenture, and the rights of the parties thereto, and the provisions contained in the said indenture being still unexecuted, the said parties have mutually agreed to settle, compromise and finally terminate all such questions and differences on the terms and conditions hereinafter specified.

"Now therefore it is hereby mutually declared, and agreed, by and between the said parties as follows.

"ARTICLE 1. The said Thomas Ludlow Ogden, and Joseph Fellows in consideration of the release and agreements hereinafter contained, on the part of the said Seneca nation do on their part consent, covenant and agree that they the said nation (the said indenture notwithstanding) shall and may continue in the occupation and enjoyment of the whole of the said two several tracts of land, called the Cattaraugus Reservation, and the Allegany Reservation with the same right and title in all things, as they had and possessed therein immediately before the date of the said indenture, saving and reserving to the said Thomas Ludlow Ogden, and Joseph Fellows the right of pre-emption, and all other the right and title which they then had or held in or to the said tracts of land.

"ARTICLE 2. The chiefs and headmen of the Seneca nation of Indians in consideration of the foregoing, and of the agreement next hereinafter contained, do on their part grant, release and confirm unto the said Thomas Ludlow Ogden, and Joseph Fellows, and to their heirs and assigns, in joint tenancy, the whole of the said two tracts of land severally called the Buffalo Creek Reservation, and the Tonnewanda Reservation, and all the right and interest therein of the said nation.

"ARTICLE 3. It is mutually agreed, between the parties hereto that in lieu of the sum expressed in the said indenture, as the consideration of the sale, and release of the said four tracts of land, there shall be paid to the said nation a just consideration sum, for the release of the two tracts, hereby confirmed to the said Ogden and Fellows, to be estimated and ascertained as follows.

"The present value of the Indian title to the whole of the said four tracts of land including the improvements thereon, shall for all the purposes of this present compact, be deemed and taken to be two hundred and two thousand dollars, of which sum one hundred thousand dollars shall be deemed to be the value of such title in and to all the lands within the said four tracts exclusive of the improvements thereon, and one hundred and two thousand dollars to be the value of all the improvements within the said four tracts, and of the said sum of one hundred thousand dollars the said Ogden and Fellows shall pay to the Seneca nation such proportion as the value of all the lands within the said two tracts called the Buffalo Creek, and Tonnewanda Reservations shall bear to the value of all the lands within all the said four tractsand of the said sum of one hundred and two thousand dollars, the said Ogden and Fellows shall pay such proportion as the value of the improvements on the same two tracts, shall bear to the value of the improvements on all the said four tracts.

"ARTICLE 4. The amount of the consideration monies to be paid in pursuance of the last preceding article, shall be determined by the judgment and award of arbitrators, one of whom shall be named by the Secretary of the War Department of the United States, and one by the said Ogden and Fellows, which arbitrators in order to such judgment and award, and to the performance of the other duties hereby imposed on them, may employ suitable surveyors to explore examine and report on the value of the said lands and improvements, and also to ascertain the contents of each of the said four tracts, which contents shall govern the arbitrators as to quantity in determining the amount of the said consideration money.

"The same arbitrators shall also award and determine the amount to be paid to each individual Indian out of the sum which on the principles above stated, they shall ascertain and award to be the proportion.-ate value of the improvements on the said two tracts called the Buffalo Creek Reservation and the Tonnewanda Reservation, and in case the said arbitrators shall disagree as to any of the matters hereby submitted to them, they may choose an umpire whose decision thereon shall be final and conclusive, and the said arbitrators shall make a report in writing of their proceedings in duplicate, such reports to be acknowledged or proved according to the laws of the State of New York, in order to their being recorded, one of such reports to be filed in the office of the Secretary of the Department of War, and the other thereof to be delivered to the said Thomas L. Ogden and Joseph Fellows.

"ARTICLE 5. It is agreed, that the possession of the two parts hereby confirmed, to the said Ogden and Fellows, shall be surrendered and delivered up to them, as follows, viz: The forest or unimproved lands on the said tracts, within one month after the report of the said arbitrators shall be filed, in the office of the Department of War, and the improved lands within two years after the said report shall have been so filed; Provided always that the amount to be so ascertained and awarded, as the proportionate value of the said improvements, shall on the surrender thereof be paid to the President of the United States, to be distributed among the owners of the said improvements, according to the determination and award of the said arbitrators, in this behalf, and provided further that the consideration for the release and conveyance of the said lands shall at the time of the surrender thereof be paid or secured to the satisfaction of the said Secretary of the War Department, the income of which is to be paid to the said Seneca Indians annually.

But any Indian having improvements may surrender the same, and the land occupied by him and his family at any time prior to the expiration of the said two years, upon the amount awarded to him for such improvements being paid to the President of the United States, or any agent designated by him for that purpose by the said Ogden and Fellows, which amount shall be paid over to the Indian entitled to the same, under the direction of the War Department.

ARTICLE 6. It is hereby agreed and declared to be the understanding and intent of the parties hereto, that such of the said Seneca nation, as shall remove from the State of New York, under the provisions of any treaty, made or to be made, between the United States and the said Indians, shall be entitled in proportion to their relative numbers to the funds of the Seneca nation, and that the interest and income of such their share and proportion of the said funds, including the consideration money to be paid to the said nation in pursuance of this Indenture, and of all annuities belonging to the said Nation shall be paid to the said Indians so removing at their new homes, and whenever the said tracts called the Allegheny and the Cattaraugus Reservations, or any part thereof shall be sold and conveyed by the Indians remaining in the

State of New York, the Indians so removing shall be entitled to share in the proceeds of said sales in the like proportion.

And it is further agreed and declared, that such Indians owning improvements in the Cattaraugus and Alleghany tracts as may so remove from the State of New York, shall be entitled on such removal, and on surrendering their improvements to the Seneca nation, for the benefit of the nation to receive the like compensation for the same, according to their relative values, as in the third and fourth articles of this treaty are stipulated to be paid, to the owners of improvements in the Buffalo Creek and Tonnewanda Tracts, on surrendering their improvements; which compensations may be advanced by the President of the United States, out of any funds in the hands of the Government of the United States, belonging to the Seneca nation, and the value of these improvements shall be ascertained and reported by the Arbitrators, to be appointed in pursuance of the fourth article.

ARTICLE 7. This Indenture is to be deemed to be in lieu of, and as a substitute for the above recited Indenture made and dated the fifteenth day of January, one thousand eight hundred and thirty eight, so far as the provisions of the two instruments may be inconsistent, or contradictory, and the said Indenture so far as the same may be inconsistent with the provisions of this compact, is to be regarded and is hereby declared to be rescinded and released.

ARTICLE 8. All the expenses attending the execution of this Indenture and compact including those of the arbitration and surveys hereinbefore referred to and also those of holding the treaty now in negotiation between the United States and the said Seneca Nation, except so far as may be provided for by the United States, shall be advanced and paid by the said Ogden and Yellows.

ARTICLE 9. The parties to this compact mutually agree to solicit the influence of the Government of the United States to protect such of the lands of the Seneca Indians, within the State of New York, as may from time to time remain in their possession from all taxes, and assessments for roads, highways, or any other purpose until such lands shall be sold and conveyed by the said Indians, and the possession thereof shall have been relinquished by them.

In witness whereof, the parties to these presents have hereunto, and to three other instruments of the same tenor and date, one to remain with the United States, one to remain with the State of Massachusetts, one to remain with the Seneca Nation of Indians, and one to remain with the said Thomas Ludlow Ogden and Joseph Yellows, interchangeably set their hands and seals the day and year first above written."

THEREFORE taking into consideration the premises it is agreed and stipulated by and between the United States of America and the Seneca nation of Indians, as follows, to wit:

First, The United States of America consent to the several articles and stipulations contained in the last recited Indenture between the said nation, and the said Thomas Ludlow Ogden and Joseph Fellows, above set forth.
Second, The United States further consent and agree that any number of the said nation, who shall remove from the State of New York, under the provisions of the above mentioned Treaty proclaimed as aforesaid, on the fourth day of April one thousand eight hundred and forty, shall be entitled in proportion to their relative numbers to all the benefits of the said Treaty.

Third, The United States of America further consent and agree, that the tenth article of said Treaty proclaimed as aforesaid on the fourth day of April one thousand eight hundred and forty, be deemed, and considered as modified, in conformity with the provisions of the Indenture hereinabove set forth, so far as that the United States will receive and pay the sum stipulated to be paid as the consideration money of the improvements therein specified, and will receive hold and apply the sum to be paid, or the securities to be given for the lands therein mentioned, as provided for in such Indenture.

AGREEMENT WITH THE DELAWARES AND WYANDOT
1843, Dec. 14

Ratified July 25,. 1848, with the proviso: "That the Wyandot Indian Nation shall take no better right or interest in and to said lands than is now vested in the Delaware Nation of Indians.

Agreement between the Delaware and Wyandot nations of Indians, concluded on the 14th day of December, 1843.

Whereas from a long and intimate acquaintance, and the ardent friendship which has for a great many years existed between the Delawares and Wyandots and from a mutual desire that the same feeling shall continue and be more strengthened by becoming near neighbors to each other; therefore the said parties, the Delawares on one side, and the Wyandots on the other, in full council assembled, have agreed, and do agree, to the following stipulations, to Wit:-

ARTICLE 1. The Delaware nation of Indians, residing between the Missouri and Kansas rivers, being very anxious to have their uncles, the Wyandots, to settle and reside near them, do hereby donate, grant and quitclaim forever, to the Wyandot nation, three sections of land, containing six hundred and forty acres each, lying and being situated at the point of the junction of the Missouri and Kansas Rivers.

ARTICLE 2. The Delaware chiefs, for themselves, and by the unanimous consent of their people; do hereby cede, grant, quitclaim to the Wyandot nation and their heirs forever, thirty-six sections of land, each containing six hundred and forty acres, situated between the aforesaid Missouri and Kansas rivers, and adjoining on the west the aforesaid three donated sections, making in all thirty-nine sections of land, bounded as follows, viz:: Commencing at the point at the junction of the aforesaid Missouri and Kansas rivers, running west along the Kansas river sufficiently far to include the aforesaid thirty-nine sections: thence running north to the Missouri river; thence down the said river with its meanders to the place of beginning; to be surveyed in as near a square form as the rivers and territory ceded will admit of.

ARTICLE 3. In consideration of the foregoing donation and cession of land, the Wyandot chiefs bind themselves, successors in office, and their people to pay to the Delaware nation of Indians, forty-six thousand and eighty dollars, as follows, viz: six thousand and eighty dollars to be paid the year eighteen hundred and forty-four, and four thousand dollars annually thereafter for ten years.

ARTICLE 4. It is hereby distinctly understood, between the contracting parties, that the aforesaid agreement shall not be binding or

obligatory until the President of the United States shall have approved
the same and caused it to be recorded in the War Department.

TREATY WITH THE WYANDOT
1850, Apr. 1
Ratified Sept. 24, 1850.
Proclaimed Sept. 30, 1850.

Articles of a convention concluded in the city of Washington, this first
day of April, one thousand eight hundred and fifty, by and between
Ardavan S. Loughery, commissioner especially appointed by the
President of the United States, and the undersigned head chief and
deputies of the Wyandot tribe of Indians, duly authorized and
empowered to act for their tribe.

WHEREAS, By the treaty of March 17, 1842, between the United
States and the Wyandot nation of Indians, then chiefly residing within
the limits of the State of Ohio, the said nation of Indians agreed to sell
and transfer, and did thereby sell and transfer, to the United States their
reservations of land, one hundred and nine thousand acres of which was
in the State of Ohio, and Six thousand acres were in the State of
Michigan, and to remove to the west of the Mississippi River: And
whereas, among other stipulations it was agreed that the United States
should convey to said Indians a tract of country for their permanent
settlement in the Indian territory west of the Mississippi River, to
contain one hundred an (and) forty-eight thousand acres of land: And
whereas, The said Indians never did receive the said one hundred and
forty-eight thousand acres of land from the United States, but were
forced to purchase lands from the Delaware nation of Indians, which
purchase was agreed to and ratified by the United States: Now, in order
to settle the claim of the Wyandot tribe of Indians to said land, the
United States having appointed A. S. Loughery a commissioner on
their part, who, with the undersigned delegates from the Wyandot
nation, have agreed to the following treaty:

ARTICLE 1. The United States, in consideration that the Wyandot
nation of Indians shall and do hereby release, relinquish, and give up all
claim to the said one hundred and forty-eight thousand acres of land
agreed to be assigned and given to them by the treaty of March 17,
1842, hereby stipulate and agree to pay to the said Wyandot tribe of

Indians the sum of one hundred and eighty-five thousand dollars, being at and after the rate of one dollar and twenty-five cents per acre, in the manner and form following, to wit: One hundred thousand dollars to be invested in United States Stocks, bearing five per cent interest per annum, which interest shall be paid to them at the time and in the manner in which their present annuities are paidand for the purpose of enabling the Wyandot Indians to pay and extinguish all their just debts, as well what is now due to the Delawares for the purchase of their lands as to others, the balance of said sum, being the sum of eighty-five thousand dollars, shall be paid to the Wyandot nation, or on their drafts, specifically describing for what the drafts are given.

ARTICLE 2. All the reasonable expenses attending the negotiation of this treaty, including a reasonable allowance for the expenses of the delegation, signers hereto, in coming to Washington, whilst here on the business connected herewith, and m returning to their nation, shall be defrayed by the United States.

In testimony whereof, the said commissioners on the part of the United States, and the said head chief and deputies, delegates on the part of the Wyandot tribe or nation of Indians, have hereunto set their hands, at the city of Washington, D.C., this first day of April, in the year of our Lord eighteen hundred and fifty.

TREATY WITH THE OTTAWA AND CHIPPEWA
1855, July 31
Ratified April 15, 1856.
Proclaimed Sept. 10, 1856.

Articles of agreement and convention made and concluded at the city of Detroit, in the State of Michigan, this the thirty-first day of July, one thousand eight hundred and fifty-five, between George W. Many-penny and Henry C. Gilbert, commissioners on the part of the United States, and the Ottawa and Chippewa Indians of Michigan, parties to the treaty of March 28, 1836.

In view of the existing condition of the Ottowas and Chippewas, and of their legal and equitable claims against the United States, it is agreed between the contracting parties as follows:

ARTICLE 1. The United States will withdraw from sale for the benefit of said Indians as hereinafter provided, all the unsold public lands within the State of Michigan embraced in the following descriptions, to wit:

First. For the use of the six bands residing at and near Saulte Ste. Marie, sections 13, 14, 23, 24, 25, 26, 27, and 28, in township 47 north, range 5 west; sections 18, 19, and 30, in township 47 north, range 4 west; sections 11, 12, 13, 14, 15, 22, 23, 25, and 26, in township 47 north, range 3 west, and section 29 in township 47 north, range 2 west; sections 2, 3, 4, 11, 14, and 15 in township 47 north, range 2 east, and section 34 in township 48 north, range 2 east; sections 6, 7, 18, 19, 20, 28, 29, and 33 in township 45 north, range 2 east; sections 1, 12, and 13, in township 45 north, range 1 east, and section 4 in township 44 north, range 2 east.

Second. For the use of the bands who wish to reside north of the Straits of Macinac townships 42 north, ranges 1 and 2 west; township 43 north, range 1 west, and township 44 north, range 12 west.

Third. For the Beaver Island BandHigh Island, and Garden Island, in Lake Michigan, being fractional townships 38 and 39 north, range 11 west40 north, range 10 west, and in part 39 north, range 9 and 10 west.

Fourth. For the Cross Village, Middle Village, L'Arbrechroehe and Bear Creek bands, and of such Bay du Noc and Beaver Island Indians as may prefer to live with them, townships 34 to 39, inclusive, north, range 5 westtownships 34 to 38, inclusive, north, range 6 westtownships 34, 36, and 37 north, range 7 west, and all that part of township 34 north, range 8 west, lying north of Pine River.

Fifth. For the bands who usually assemble for payment at Grand Traverse, townships 29, 30, and 31 north, range 11 west, and townships 29, 30, and 31 north, range 12 west, and the east half of township 29 north, range 9 west.

Sixth. For the Grand River bands, township 12 north, range 15 west, and townships 15, 16, 17 and 18 north, range 16 west.

Seventh. For the Cheboygan band, townships 35 and 36 north, range 3 west.

Eighth. For the Thunder Bay band, section 25 and 36 in township 30 north, range 7 east, and section 22 in township 30 north, range 8 east.

Should either of the bands residing near Sault Ste. Marie determine to locate near the lands owned by the missionary society of the Methodist Episcopal Church at Iroquois Point, in addition to those who now reside there, it is agreed that the United States will purchase as much of said lands for the use of the Indians as the society may be willing to sell at the usual Government price.

The United States will give to each Ottawa and Chippewa Indian being the head of a family, 80 acres of land, and to each single person over twenty-one years of age, 40 acres of land, and to each family of orphan children under twenty-one years of age containing two or more persons, 80 acres of land, and to each single orphan child under twenty-one years of age, 40 acres of land to be selected and located within the several tracts of land hereinbefore described, under the following rules and regulations:

Each Indian entitled to land under this article may make his own selection of any land within the tract reserved herein for the band to which he may belongProvided, That in case of two or more Indians claiming the same lot or tract of land, the matter shall be referred to the Indian agent, who shall examine the case and decide between the parties.

For the purpose of determining who may be entitled to land under the provisions of this article, lists shall be prepared by the Indian agent, which lists shall contain the names of all persons entitled, designating them in four classes. Class 1st, shall contain the names of heads of families; class 2d, the names of single persons over twenty-one years of age; class 3d, the names of orphan children under twenty-one years of age, comprising families of two or more persons, and class 4th, the names of single orphan children under twenty-one years of age, and no person shall be entered in more than one class. Such lists shall be made and closed by the first day of July, 1856, and thereafter no applications for the benefits of this article will be allowed.

At any time within five years after the completion of the lists, selections of lands may be made by the persons entitled thereto, and a notice thereof, with a description of the land selected, filed in the office of the Indian agent in Detroit, to be by him transmitted to the Office of Indian Affairs at Washington City.

All sections of land under this article must be made according to the usual subdivisions; and fractional lots, if containing less than 60 acres, may be regarded as forty-acre lots, if over sixty and less than one hundred and twenty acres, as eighty-acre lots. Selections for orphan children may be made by themselves or their friends, subject to the approval of the agent.

After selections are made, as herein provided, the persons entitled to the land may take immediate possession thereof, and the United States will thenceforth and until the issuing of patents as hereinafter provided, hold the same in trust for such persons, and certificates shall be issued, in a suitable form, guaranteeing and securing to the holders their possession and an ultimate title to the land. But such certificates shall not be assignable and shall contain a clause expressly prohibiting the sale or transfer by the holder of the land described therein.

After the expiration of ten years, such restriction on the power of sale shall be withdrawn, and a patent shall be issued in the usual form to each original holder of a certificate for the land described therein, Provided That such restriction shall cease only upon the actual issuing of the patent; And provided further That the President may in his discretion at any time in individual cases on the recommendation of the Indian agent when it shall appear prudent and for the welfare of any holder of a certificate, direct a patent to be issued. And provided also, That after the expiration of ten years, if individual cases shall be reported to the President by the Indian agent, of persons who may then be incapable of managing their own affairs from any reason whatever, he may direct the patents in such cases to be withheld, and the restrictions provided by the certificate, continued so long as he may deem necessary and proper.

Should any of the heads of families die before the issuing of the certificates or patents herein provided for, the same shall issue to the heirs of such deceased persons.

The benefits of this article will be extended only to those Indians who are at this time actual residents of the State of Michigan, and entitled to participate in the annuities provided by the treaty of March 28, 1836; but this provision shall not be construed to exclude any Indian now belonging to the Garden River band of Sault Ste. Marie.

All the land embraced within the tracts hereinbefore described, that shall not have been appropriated or selected within five years shall remain the property of the United States, and the same shall thereafter, for the further term of five years, be subject to entry in the usual manner and at the same rate per acre, as other adjacent public lands are then held, by Indians only; and all lands, so purchased by Indians, shall be sold without restriction, and certificates and patents shall be issued for the same in the usual form as in ordinary cases; and all lands remaining unappropriated by or unsold to the Indians after the expiration of the last-mentioned term, may be sold or disposed of by the United States as in the case of all other public lands.

Nothing contained herein shall be so construed as to prevent the appropriation, by sale, gift, or otherwise, by the United States, of any tract or tracts of land within the aforesaid reservations for the location of churches, school-houses, or for other educational purposes, and for such purposes purchases of land may likewise be made from the Indians, the consent of the President of the United States, having, in every instance, first been obtained therefor.

It is also agreed that any lands within the aforesaid tracts now occupied by actual settlers, or by persons entitled to pre-emption thereon, shall be exempt from the provisions of this article; provided, that such pre-emption claims shall be proved, as prescribed by law, before the 1st day of October next.

Any Indian who may have heretofore purchased land for actual settlement, under the act of Congress known as the Graduation Act, may sell and dispose of the same; and, in such case, no actual occupancy or residence by such Indians on lands so purchased shall be necessary to enable him to secure a title thereto.

In consideration of the benefits derived to the Indians on Grand Traverse Bay by the school and mission established in 1838, and still continued by the Board of Foreign Missions of the Presbyterian Church, it is agreed that the title to three separate pieces of land, being parts of tracts Nos. 3 and 4, of the west fractional half of section 35, township 30 north, range 10 west, on which are the mission and school buildings and improvements, not exceeding in all sixty-three acres, one hundred and twenty-four perches, shall be vested in the said board on payment of $1.25 per acre; and the President of the United States shall issue a patent for the same to such person as the said board shall appoint.

The United States will also pay the further sum of forty thousand dollars, or so much thereof as may be necessary, to be applied in liquidation of the present just indebtedness of the said Ottawa and Chippewa Indians; provided, that all claims presented shall be investigated under the direction of the Secretary of the Interior, who shall prescribe such rules and regulations for conducting such investigation, and for testing the validity and justness of the claims, as he shall deem suitable and proper; and no claim shall be paid except upon the certificate of the said Secretary that, in his opinion, the same is justly and equitably due; and all claimants, who shall not present their claims within such time as may be limited by said Secretary within six months from the ratification of the treaty, or whose claims, having been presented, shall be disallowed by him, shall be forever precluded from collecting the same, or maintaining an action thereon in any court whatever; and provided, also, that no portion of the money due said Indians for annuities, as herein provided, shall ever be appropriated to pay their debts under any pretence whatever; provided, that the balance of the amount herein allowed, as a just increase of the amount due for the cessions and relinquishments aforesaid, after satisfaction of the awards of the Secretary of the Interior, shall be paid to the said Chippewas or expended for their benefit, in such manner as the Secretary shall prescribe, in aid of any of the objects specified in the second article of this treaty.

ARTICLE 2. The United States will also pay to the said Indians the sum of five hundred and thirty-eight thousand and four hundred dollars, in manner following, to wit:

First. Eighty thousand dollars for educational purposes to be paid in ten equal annual instalments of eight thousand dollars each, which sum shall be expended under the direction of the President of the United States; and in the expenditure of the same, and the appointment of teachers and management of schools, the Indians shall be consulted, and their views and wishes adopted so far as they may be just and reasonable.

Second. Seventy-five thousand dollars to be paid in five equal annual instalments of fifteen thousand dollars each in agricultural implements and carpenters' tools, household furniture and building materials, cattle, labor, and all such articles as may be necessary and useful for them in removing to the homes herein provided and getting permanently settled thereon.

Third. Forty-two thousand and four hundred dollars for the support of four blacksmith-shops for ten years.

Fourth. The sum of three hundred and six thousand dollars in coin, as follows: ten thousand dollars of the principal, and the interest on the whole of said last-mentioned sum remaining unpaid at the rate of five per cent annually for ten years, to be distributed per capita in the usual manner for paying annuities. And the sum of two hundred and six thousand dollars remaining unpaid at the expiration of ten years, shall be then due and payable, and if the Indians then require the payment of said sum in coin the same shall be distributed per capita in the same manner as annuities are paid, and in not less than four equal annual instalments.

Fifth. The sum of thirty-five thousand dollars in ten annual instalments of three thousand and five hundred dollars each, to be paid only to the Grand River Ottawas, which is in lieu of all permanent annuities to which they may be entitled by former treaty stipulations, and which sum shall be distributed in the usual manner per capita.

ARTICLE 3. The Ottawa and Chippewa Indians hereby release and discharge the United States from all liability on account of former treaty stipulations, it being distinctly understood and agreed that the grants and payments hereinbefore provided for are in lieu and satisfaction of all claims, legal and equitable on the part of said Indians jointly and severally against the United States, for land, money or other thing guaranteed to said tribes or either of them by the stipulations of any former treaty or treaties; excepting, however, the right of fishing and encampment secured to the Chippewas of Sault Ste. Marie by the treaty of June 16, 1820.

ARTICLE 4. The interpreters at Sault Ste. Marie, Mackinac, and for the Grand River Indians, shall be continued, and another provided at Grand Traverse, for the term of five years, and as much longer as the President may deem necessary.

ARTICLE 5. The tribal organization of said Ottawa and Chippewa Indians, except so far as may be necessary for the purpose of carrying into effect the provisions of this agreement, is hereby dissolved; and if at any time hereafter, further negotiations with the United States, in reference to any matters contained herein, should become necessary, no general convention of the Indians shall be called; but such as reside in the vicinity of any usual place of payment, or those only who are immediately interested in the questions involved, may arrange all matters between themselves and the United States, without the concurrence of other portions of their people, and as fully and conclusively, and with the same effect in every respect, as if all were represented.

ARTICLE 6. This agreement shall be obligatory and binding on the contracting parties as soon as the same shall be ratified by the President and Senate of the United States.

TREATY WITH THE OTTAWA OF BLANCHARD'S FORK AND ROCHE DE BOEUF
1862, June 24
Ratified July 16, 1862.
Proclaimed July 28, 1862.

Articles of agreement and convention, made and concluded at Washington City, on the twenty-fourth day of June, eighteen hundred and sixty-two, by and between William P. Dole, commissioner, on the part of the United States, and the following-named chief and councilmen of the Ottawa Indians of the united bands of Blanchard's Fork and of Roche de Boeuf, now in Franklin County, Kansas, viz: Pem-ach-wung, chief; John T. Jones William Hurr, and James Wind, councilmen, they being thereto duly authorized by said tribe.

ARTICLE 1. The Ottawa Indians of the united bands of Blanchard's Fork and of Roche de Boeuf, having become sufficiently advanced in civilization, and being desirous of becoming citizens of the United States, it is hereby agreed and stipulated that their organization, and their relations with the United States as an Indian tribe, shall be dissolved and terminated at the expiration of five years from the ratification of this treaty; and from and after that time the said Ottawas, and each and every one of them, shall be deemed and declared to be citizens of the United States, to all intents and purposes, and shall be entitled to all the rights, privileges, and immunities of such citizens, and shall, in all respects, be subject to the laws of the United States, and of the State or States thereof in which they may reside.

ARTICLE 2. It is hereby made the duty of the Secretary of the Interior to cause a survey of the reservation of the said Ottawas to be made as soon as practicable after the ratification of this treaty, dividing it into eighty-acre tracts, with marked stones set at each corner; and said Ottawas having already caused their reservation to be surveyed, and quarter-section stones set, it is hereby stipulated that such survey shall be adopted, in so far as it shall be found correct.

ARTICLE 3. It being the wish of said tribe of Ottawas to remunerate several of the chiefs, councilmen, and head-men of the tribe, for their services to them many years without pay, it is hereby stipulated that five sections of land is (are) reserved and set apart for that purpose, to be apportioned among the said chiefs, councilmen, and head-men as the members of the tribes shall in full council determine; and it shall be the duty of the Secretary of the Interior to issue patents, in fee-simple, of said lands, when located and apportioned, to said Indians. In addition thereto, said last-named persons, and each and every head of a family in said tribe, shall receive 160 acres of land, which shall include his or her house and all improvements, so far as practicable; and all other members of the tribe shall receive 80 acres of land each, and all the locations for the heads of families, made in accordance with this treaty, shall be made adjoining, and in as regular and compact form as possible, and with due regard to the rights of each individual and of the whole tribe.

ARTICLE 4. To enable said tribe to establish themselves more fully in agriculture, and gradually to increase their preparations for assuming the responsibilities and duties of citizenship, it is stipulated that, subject to the limitations hereinafter mentioned, the sum of eighteen thousand ($18,000) dollars shall be paid to said tribe in the manner of annuities, out of their-moneys now in the hands of the United States, in September, 1862, and subject to the limitations of this treaty. There shall be paid to them in four equal annual payments thereafter, as near as may be, all the moneys which the United States hold, or may hold, in any wise for them, with accruing interest on all moneys remaining with the United States.

ARTICLE 5. It being the desire of the tribe to pay all lawful and just debts against them contracted since they were removed to Kansas, it is agreed that such demands as the council of the tribe and the agent shall approve, when confirmed by the Secretary of the Interior, may be received in payment for the lands hereinafter provided to be sold, or otherwise such debts shall be paid out of the funds of said Ottawas, but in no case shall more than $15,000 be allowed and paid for such debts.

ARTICLE 6. The Ottawas deeming this a favorable opportunity to provide for the education of their posterity, and feeling that they are able to do so by the co-operation of the United States, now, in pursuance of this desire of the Ottawas, after the selections and allotments herein provided have been made, there shall be set apart, under the direction of the Secretary of the Interior, twenty thousand acres of average lands for the purpose of endowing a school for the benefit of said Ottawas; also one section of land, upon which said school shall be located, which section of land shall be inalienable, and upon which, and all the appurtenances and property for school purposes thereon, no tax shall ever be laid by any authority whatever.

Five thousand acres of said land may be sold by the trustees hereinafter named, the proceeds of which may be devoted to the erection of proper buildings and improvements upon said section for reception of the pupils; and the residue of the school-lands may, in like manner, be sold from time to time, as full prices can be obtained for the same. The money received therefor shall be loaned upon good real estate security, to be improved farms in the county of the reservation, the same not to be a security for more than half the appraised value of the land as returned by the county assessor, and no land to be taken as security for such loan or loans which shall be encumbered in any man-her, or the title to which shall have been derived from or held by any judicial, administrator, or executor's sale, or by the sale of any person acting in a fiduciary capacity. The security shall never be avoided on account of any rate of interest reserved, and the interest only shall be applied to the support of the school, so that the principal sum shall never be diminished.

And to the end that the Ottawas may derive the greatest advantage from said school, the pupils shall be instructed and practiced in industrial pursuits suitable to their age and sex, as well as in such branches of learning as the means of the institution and the capacity of the pupils will permit.

The lands hereby set apart shall not be subject to taxation until they are sold. They may be sold upon such credit as the trustees may think most for the interest of the enterprise. Security for the payment shall be taken with interest, the interest to be paid annually, but no title shall be made until the purchase money is all paid.

John T. Jones, James Wind, William Hurt, Joseph King, who are Ottawas, and John G. Pratt, and two other citizens of Kansas, who shall be elected by the said Ottawa Indians, are, by the parties agreed, to be trustees to manage the funds and property by this article set apart. They and their successors shall have the control and management of the school, and the funds arising from the sales of lands set apart therefor, and also the reserved section whereon the school is situated. Upon the death, resignation, or refusal to act, by either of them, the vacancy shall be filled by the survivors, provided that the board of trustees shall always have three white citizens members of said board.

A majority of the trustees shall form a quorum to transact business, but there shall be two of the white trustees present at the transaction of business. All acts of the trustees shall be recorded in a book or books to be by them kept for that purpose, and the proceedings of each meeting shall be signed by the president, to be by them elected out of their number. They shall also elect a treasurer and secretary from their number. All contracts of the trustees shall be in the name of their treasurer, who shall be competent to sue and be sued in all matters affecting the trust; he shall give bond conditioned for the faithful discharge of his duty, and the proper accounting for all money or property of the trust coming to his hands, with at least two good freehold sureties, in the penalty of ten thousand dollars, to be approved by a judge of a court of record in Kansas.

And the secretary and treasurer may be allowed, from time to time, such sum, from the proceeds of the trust, as the trustees in their judgment shall think just. Upon a sale of any of the lands by the trustees, upon their request, the same shall be conveyed by the United States, by patent, to the purchaser.

And it is hereby expressly provided and agreed that the children of the Ottawas and their descendants, no matter where they may emigrate, shall have the right to enter said school and enjoy all the privileges thereof, the same as though they had remained upon the lands by this treaty allotted.

ARTICLE 7. There shall be set apart ten acres of land for the benefit of the Ottawa Baptist church, and said land shall include the church buildings, mission-house, and graveyard, and the title to said property shall be vested in a board of five trustees, to be appointed by said church, in accordance with the laws of the State of Kansas.

And in respect for the memory of Rev. J. Meeker, deceased, who labored with unselfish zeal for nearly twenty years among said Ottawas, greatly to their spiritual and temporal welfare, it is stipulated that 80 acres of good land shall be, and hereby is, given, in fee-simple, to each of the two children of said Meeker, viz, Emmeline and Eliza; their lands to be selected and located as the other allotments herein provided are to be selected and located, which lands shall be inalienable to the same as the lands allotted to the Ottawas.

And all the above-mentioned selections of lands shall be made by the agent of the tribe, under the direction of the Secretary of the Interior. And plats and records of all the selections and locations shall be made, and upon their completion and approval proper patents by the United States shall be issued to each individual member of the tribe and person entitled for the lands selected and allotted to them, in which it shall be stipulated that no Indian, except as herein provided, to whom the same may be issued, shall alienate or encumber the land allotted to him or her in any manner, until they shall, by the terms of this treaty, become a citizen of the United States; and any conveyance or encumbrance of said lands, done or suffered, except as aforesaid, by any Ottawa Indian, of the lands allotted to him or her, made before they shall become a citizen, shall be null and void.

And forty acres, including the houses and improvements of the allottee, shall be inalienable during the natural lifetime of the party receiving the title: Provided, That such of said Indians as are not under legal disabilities by the local laws may sell to each other such portions of their lands as are subject to sale, with the consent of the Secretary of the Interior, at any time.

ARTICLE 8. That upon the ratification of this treaty a census of all the Ottawas entitled to land or money under the treaty shall be taken under the direction of the Secretary of the Interior. The principal to be paid to the minors shall be paid to their parents, unless the council of the tribe shall object because of the incompetency of the parent, growing out of ignorance, profligacy, or any other good cause; the council may also object to the payment of the money to any such incompetent which may be coming to himself or herself; and in all such cases the principal sum shall be withheld, and only the annuity paid, until such minor comes of age, or the disability is removed by the action of the council: Provided further, That the money of minors may, in all cases, be paid to guardians appointed by the local laws.

ARTICLE 9. It being the desire of the said Ottawas, in making this treaty, to insure, as far as possible, the settlement of their reservation by industrious whites, whose example shall be of benefit to the tribe at large, it is stipulated that after all the above-mentioned locations, assignments, and sales are made, the remainder of the land shall be sold to actual settlers at not less than $1.25 per acre, in the following manner: Any white person desiring to obtain any unsold, unlocated tract of the land, may file his proposition, in writing, with the agent of the Ottawas, for the purchase of the tract, stating the price which he proposes to pay for said tract, not less than $1.25 per acre, a copy of which proposition, as well as all others herein contemplated, shall be posted for thirty days, dating from the first posting at the agency, in some conspicuous place; and if no person will propose a better price therefor within thirty days next after the first posting, in which further proposition the first person may join, he, or such other person as shall have offered the best price, shall upon the payment of one-quarter of the price offered, be taken and deemed the purchaser of said tract, and shall be entitled to a patent therefor from the United States at the end of one year, if he shall pay the remainder of the price offered, have occupied the land, and placed lasting and valuable improvements upon said tract to the extent and value of two hundred dollars to each quarter section entered: Provided, That if said Ottawas, by their council, shall, at any time before any person shall become the purchaser of any tract of land, file their protest in writing against such purchaser, he shall not be permitted to enter upon said lands or become the purchaser thereof, and white persons not purchasers shall not be permitted to settle upon said lands, it being the duty of the agent to prevent such settlement, or their occupancy by the whites who are not purchasers, and only to the extent of their purchase.

And provided, further, That if any purchaser shall fail to pay for the land by him purchased under this treaty at the time stipulated, it shall be the duty of the agent to dispossess him as an intruder upon the lands, and his advances, payments, and all his improvements, shall enure to the benefit of the Ottawas, and the land shall be sold for their benefit, as herein provided. But no person under this article shall be entitled to enter more than 320 acres. And all the lands which are not thus entered with the agent within two years from the ratification of this treaty may, upon the request of the council, be offered for sale at not less than $1.25 per acre, upon a credit of one year, under the direction of the Secretary of the Interior; and if any lands thereafter remain unsold, they may be sold upon such terms as the council of said tribe and the Secretary of the Interior shall mutually agree upon. And all the moneys derived from the sales of the above-described lands shall be paid at the time and place where the Secretary of the Interior may direct.

ARTICLE 10. And it is stipulated that the United States shall pay to the said Ottawas the claims for stolen ponies, cattle, and timber, already reported and approved by the Secretary of the Interior, amounting to $13,005 95/100. And also other claims for damages within two years, or since the taking of testimony for the above-mentioned damages, upon the presentation of sufficient proof: Provided, Such last-mentioned claims shall not exceed $3,500.

ARTICLE 11. It is hereby made the duty of the Indian Department to appoint an interpreter for said tribe, in the customary manner, to be continued during the pleasure of the Secretary of the Interior. And it is expressly understood that all expenses incurred by the stipulations of this treaty shall be paid out of the funds of the aforementioned tribe of Ottawas, and their annuities shall be paid semi-annually.

TREATY WITH THE SENECA, MIXED SENECA AND SHAWNEE, QUAPAW, ETC.
1867, Feb. 23
Ratified June 18, 1868.
Proclaimed Oct. 14, 1868.

Articles of agreement, concluded at Washington, D.C., the twenty-third day of February, one thousand eight hundred and sixty-seven, between the United States, represented by Lewis E Bogy, Commissioner of Indian Affairs, W. H. Watson, special commissioner, Thomas Murphy, superintendent of Indian Affairs, George C. Snow, and G. A. Colton, U. S. Indian agents, duly authorized, and the Senecas, represented by George Spicer and John Mush; the Mixed Senecas and Shawnees, by John Whitetree, John Young, and Lewis Davis; the Quapaws, by S. G. Vallier and Ka-zhe-cah; the Confederated Peorias, Kaskaskias, Weas, and Piankeshaws, by Baptiste Peoria, John Mitchell, and Edward Black; the Miamies, by Thomas Metosenyah and Thomas Richardville, and the Ottawas of Blanchard's Fork and Roche de Boeuf, by John White and J. T. Jones, and including certain Wyandott(e)s, represented by Tauromee, or John Hat, and John Karaho.

Whereas it is desirable that arrangements should be made by which portions of certain tribes, parties hereto, now residing in Kansas, should be enabled to remove to other lands in the Indian country south of that State, while other portions of said tribes desire to dissolve their tribal relations, and become citizens; and whereas it is necessary to provide certain tribes, parties hereto, now residing in the Indian country, with means of rebuilding their houses, re-opening their farms, and supporting their families, they having been driven from their reservations early in the late war, and suffered greatly for several years, and being willing to sell a portion of their lands to procure such relief; and whereas a portion of the Wyandottes, parties to the treaty of one thousand eight hundred and fifty-five, although taking lands in severalty, have sold said lands, and are still poor, and have not been compelled to become citizens, but have remained without clearly recognized organization, while others who did become citizens are unfitted for the responsibilities of citizenship; and whereas the Wyandottes, treated with in eighteen hundred and fifty-five, have just claims against the Government, which will enable the portion of their people herein referred to begin anew a tribal existence: Therefore it is agreed:

ARTICLE 1. The Senecas cede to the United States a strip of land on the north side of their present reservation in the Indian country; the land so ceded to be bounded on the east by the State of Missouri, on the north by the north line of the reservation, on the west by the Neosho River, and running south for the necessary distance, to contain twenty thousand acres; for which the Government is to pay twenty thousand dollars upon the ratification of this treaty; the south line of said tract to be ascertained by survey, at the cost of the United States.

ARTICLE 2. The Senecas now confederated with the Shawnees, and owning an undivided half of a reservation in the Indian country immediately north of the Seneca reservation mentioned in the preceding article, cede to the United States one-half of said Seneca and Shawnee reserve, which it is mutually agreed shall be the north half, bounded on the east by the State of Missouri, north by the Quapaw reserve, west by the Neosho River, and south by an east and west line bisecting the present Seneca and Shawnee reserve into equal parts, the said line to be determined by survey, at the expense of the United States; for which tract of land, estimated to contain about thirty thousand acres, the United States will pay the sum of twenty-four thousand dollars.

ARTICLE 3. The Shawnees, heretofore confederated with the Senecas, cede to the United States that portion of their remaining lands, bounded as follows, beginning at a point where Spring River crosses the south line of the tract in the second article ceded to the United States, thence down said river to the south line of the Shawnee reserve, thence west to the Neosho River, thence up said river to the south line of the tract ceded in the second article, and thence east to the place of beginning; supposed to contain about twelve thousand acres, the area to be ascertained by survey, at the expense of the United States; the United

States to pay for the same at the rate of one dollar per acre, as soon as the area shall be ascertained.

ARTICLE 4. The Quapaws cede to the United States that portion of their land lying in the State of Kansas, being a strip of land on the north line of their reservation, about one half mile in width, and containing about twelve sections in all, excepting therefrom one half section to be patented to Samuel G. Vallier, including his improvements. Also the further tract within their present reserve, bounded as follows: Beginning at a point in the Neosho River where the south line of the Quapaw reserve strikes that stream, thence east three miles, thence north to the Kansas boundary-line, thence west on said line to the Neosho River, thence down said river to the place of beginning; and the United States will pay to the Quapaws for the half-mile strip lying in Kansas at the rate of one dollar and twenty-five cents per acre, whenever the area of the same shall be ascertained; and for the other tract described in this article at the rate of one dollar and fifteen cents per acre, whenever the area of the same shall be ascertained by survey, said survey to be made at the cost of the tribe to which said tract is herein provided to be sold under the pre-emption laws of the United States; but all such pre-emption shah be paid in the money of the United States, at the proper land-office, within one year from the date of entry and settlement.

PROVISIONS RELATING TO THE SENECAS.

ARTICLE 5. The Senecas now confederated with the Shawnees, the said Shawnees thereto consenting, agree to dissolve their connection with the said Shawnees, and to unite with the Senecas, parties to the treaty of February twenty-eighth, one thousand eight hundred and thirty-one, upon their reservation described in article second of said treaty; and the several bands of Senecas will unite their funds into one common fund for the benefit of the whole tribe; and an equitable division shall be made of all funds or annuities now held in common by the Senecas and Shawnees.

ARTICLE 6. Of the sum of twenty-four thousand dollars to be paid to the Senecas, as provided in the second article, the stun of four thousand dollars shall be paid to them immediately after the ratification of this treaty, to enable them to re-establish their homes and provide themselves with agricultural implements, seed, and provisions for themselves and their families; and the balance of the said first-mentioned sum, being twenty thousand dollars, shall be consolidated with the twenty thousand dollars in the first article provided to be paid, and invested for the tribe of Senecas, as constituted by this treaty, at five per cent. interest, to be paid per capita semi-annually; and their

annuity of five hundred dollars in specie, provided by article four of the treaty of September twenty-ninth, one thousand eight hundred and seventeen, shall likewise become the property of the tribe.

ARTICLE 7. The amount annually due the Senecas under the provisions of article four of the treaty of February twenty-eight, one thousand eight hundred and thirty-one, for blacksmith, after their separation from the Shawnees, shall be annually paid to them as a national fund, to enable them to purchase such articles for their wants and improvements in agriculture as the chiefs, with the consent of their agent, may designate; and this provision shall apply also to the fund for support of a miller belonging to the Senecas heretofore occupying the southernmost reserve referred to in this treaty; and there shall be added to the said fund whatever amount belonging to either band of the Senecas shah be found due and unpaid upon an examination of their accounts with the Government, and particularly the amount of bonds and stocks invested in their name; and the interest thereon shall be annually paid to the said Senecas for the purposes mentioned in this article.

PROVISIONS RELATING TO THE SHAWNEES.

ARTICLE 8. Of the amount in the third article provided to be paid to the Shawnees by the United States for the lands therein ceded, the sum of two thousand dollars shall be advanced to them to be used in establishing their homes, and the balance of the said amount shall be invested for the said tribe, under the name of Eastern Shawnees, and five per cent be paid semi-annually thereon; and the amount due and unpaid upon the bonds or stocks invested in their name shall be paid to them, as well as the interest thereon hereafter to become due.

It is to be used under the direction of the chiefs, with the consent of the agent, for the purchase of agricultural implements or other articles necessary for the general welfare of the people; and the one-half of the blacksmith fund remaining after the division to be made with the Senecas provided for in article five shall remain devoted to the same purpose, and the Government will add thereto the sum of five hundred dollars annually for five years.

PROVISIONS RELATING TO THE QUAPAWS.
ARTICLE 9. Of the amount to be paid to the Quapaws for the lands ceded by them in the fourth article of this treaty, the sum of five thousand dollars shall be paid to them upon the ratification of this treaty, to assist them in re-establishing themselves at their homes upon their remaining reservation; and the balance of said amount shall be invested as a permanent fund at five per cent. interest, payable per capita, semi-annually.

ARTICLE 10. If the Osage mission school should be closed, so that the school fund of the Quapaws cannot be used for them to advantage at that institution, the said fund shall remain in the Treasury of the United States until such time as it can, under the direction of the Secretary of the Interior, with the consent of the chiefs, be used to advantage in establishing a school upon their reservation.

ARTICLE 11. The amount now due and unpaid for a farmer, under the provisions of the third article of their treaty of May thirteen one thousand eight hundred and thirty-eight (three), may be used by the chiefs and council for the purchase of provisions, farming-implements, seed, and otherwise for the purpose of assisting the people in agriculture; and their annual income now paid for farmer shall hereafter be set apart for the purposes of assistance and improvement in agriculture.

CLAIMS FOR LOSSES BY THE WAR.
ARTICLE 12. Whereas the aforesaid Senecas, Mixed Senecas and Shawnees, and Quapaws were driven from their homes during the late war, and their property destroyed, it is agreed that a commission of not to exceed two persons shall be appointed by the Secretary of the Interior, who shall proceed to their country and make careful investigation of their claims for losses, and make full report of the same to the Department; and the Secretary of the Interior shall report the same to Congress.

PROVISIONS IN RELATION TO THE WYANDOTTES.

ARTICLE 13. The United States will set apart for the Wyandottes for their future home the land ceded by the Senecas in the first article hereof, and described in said article, to be owned by the said Wyandottes in common; and the Secretary of the Interior is hereby authorized and required to appoint three persons whose duty it shall be to ascertain and report to the Department the amount of money, if any, due by the United States to the Wyandott(e) Indians under existing treaty stipulations, and the items mentioned in Schedule A, appended to this treaty, and the report of the persons so appointed, with the evidence taken, shall be submitted to Congress for action at its next session. A register of the whole people, resident in Kansas and elsewhere, shall be taken by the agent of the Delawares, under the direction of the Secretary of the Interior, on or before the first of July, one thousand eight hundred and sixty-seven, which shall show the names of all who declare their desire to be and remain Indians, and in a tribal condition, together with incompetents and orphans, as described in the treaty of one thousand eight hundred and fifty-five; and all such persons, and those only, shall hereafter constitute the tribe: Provided, That no one who has heretofore consented to become a citizen, nor the wife or children of any such person, shall be allowed to become members of the tribe, except by the free consent of the tribe after its new organization, and unless the agent shall certify that such party is, through poverty or incapacity, unfit to continue in the exercise of the responsibilities of citizenship of the United States, and likely to become a public charge.

ARTICLE 14. Whenever the register in the next preceding article shall have been completed and returned to the Commissioner of Indian Affairs, the amount of money in said article acknowledged to be due to the Wyandott(e)s shall be divided, and that portion equitably due to the citizens of said people shall be paid to them or their heirs, under the direction of the Secretary of the Interior; and the balance, after deducting the cost of the land purchased from the Senecas by the first article hereof, and the sum of five thousand dollars to enable the Wyandott(e)s to establish themselves in their new homes, shall be paid to the Wyandott(e) tribe per capita.

ARTICLE 15. All restrictions upon the sale of lands assigned and patented to "incompetent" Wyandott(e)s under the fourth article of the treaty of one thousand eight hundred and fifty-five, shall be removed after the ratification of this treaty, but no sale of lands heretofore assigned to orphans or incompetents shall be made, under decree of any court, or otherwise, for or on account of any claim, judgment, execution, or order, or for taxes, until voluntarily sold by the patentee or his or her heirs, with the approval of the Secretary of the Interior; and whereas many sales of land belonging to this class have heretofore been made, contrary to the spirit and intent of the treaty of one thousand eight hundred and fifty-five, it is agreed that a thorough examination and report shall be made, under direction of the Secretary of the Interior, in order to ascertain the facts relating to all such cases, and, upon a full examination of such report, and hearings of the parties interested, the said Secretary may confirm the said sales, or require an additional amount to be paid, or declare such sales entirely void, as the very right of the several cases may require.

PROVISIONS RELATING TO THE OTTAWAS.

ARTICLE 16. The west part of the Shawnee reservation, ceded to the United States by the third article, is hereby sold to the Ottawas, at one dollar per acre; and for the purpose of paying for said reservation the United States shall take the necessary amount, whenever the area of such land shall be found by actual survey, front the funds in the hands of the Government arising from the sale of the Ottawa trust-lands, as provided in the ninth article of the treaty of one thousand eight hundred and sixty-two, and the balance of said fund, after the payment of accounts provided for in article five of the treaty of one thousand eight hundred and sixty-two, shall be paid to the tribe per capita.

ARTICLE 17. The provisions of the Ottawa treaty of one thousand eight hundred and sixty-two, under which all the tribe were to become citizens upon the sixteenth of July, one thousand eight hundred and sixty-seven, are hereby extended for two years, or until July sixteenth, one thousand eight hundred and sixty-nine; but any time previous to that date any member of the tribe may appear before the United States district court for Kansas, and declare His intention to become a citizen, when he shall receive a certificate of citizenship, which shall include his family, and thereafter be disconnected with the tribe, and shall be entitled to his proportion of the tribal fund; and all who shall not have made such declaration previous to the last-mentioned date shall still be considered members of the tribe. In order to enable the tribe to dispose of their property in Kansas, and remove to their new homes and establish themselves thereon, patents in fee-simple shall be given to the heads of families and to all who have come of age among the allottees under the treaties of one thousand eight hundred and sixty-two, so that they may sell their lands without restriction; but the said lands shall remain exempt from taxation so long as they may be retained by members of the tribe down to the said sixteenth of July, one thousand eight hundred and sixty-nine; and the chiefs and council of the said tribe shall decide in the case of disputed heirship to real estate, taking as a rule the laws of inheritance of the State of Kansas.

ARTICLE 18. The United States agree to pay the claim of J. T. Jones, for which a bill of appropriation has passed one of the branches of Congress, but which has been withdrawn from before Congress, being for destruction by tire of his dwelling and other property by whites in one thousand eight hundred and fifty-six, shall be allowed and paid to him, amounting to six thousand seven hundred dollars.

ARTICLE 19. The sixth article of the treaty of one thousand eight hundred and sixty-two shall remain unchanged, except as provided in this article. The children of the tribe between the ages of six and eighteen (6 and 18) shall be entitled to be received at said institution, and to be subsisted, clothed, educated, and attended in sickness, where the sickness is of such a nature that the patient promises a return to study within a reasonable period; the children to be taught and practised in industrial pursuits, suitable to their age and sex, and both sexes in such branches of learning, and to receive such advantages as the means of the institution will permit; these rights and privileges to continue so long as any children of the tribe shall present themselves for their exercise. And the Secretary of the Interior and the senior corresponding secretary of the American Baptist Home Mission Society shall be members ex officio of the board of trustees, with power to vote in person or by proxy, it being the special intention of this provision to furnish additional supervision of the institution, so that the provisions of this article may be carried into effect in their full spirit and intent.

ARTICLE 20. it is further agreed that the remaining unsold portion of trust-lands of the Ottawas, amounting to seven thousand two hundred and twenty-one and twenty one-hundredths acres, shall be sold to the trustees of Ottawa University, to be disposed of for the benefit of said institution at the appraised value thereof, and that the said trustees shall have until July sixteenth, one thousand eight hundred and sixty-nine, to dispose of the same and pay to the Government the value of said lands: Provided, That the said trustees shall furnish, within thirty days after the ratification of this treaty, to the Secretary of the Interior, a satisfactory bond for the fulfilment of their obligations.